The political economy of underdevelopment

International Library of Sociology

Founded by Karl Mannheim

Editor: John Rex, University of Warwick

Arbor Scientiae
Arbor Vitae

A catalogue of books available in the **International Library of Sociology**
and other series of Social Science books published by Routledge & Kegan Paul
will be found at the end of this volume.

The political economy of underdevelopment

S. B. D. de Silva

Deputy Director,
Agrarian Research and Training Institute,
Colombo, Sri Lanka

Routledge & Kegan Paul

London, Boston and Henley

in association with the

Institute of Southeast Asian Studies, Singapore

First published in 1982
by Routledge & Kegan Paul Ltd
39 Store Street,
London WC1E 7DD
9 Park Street,
Boston, Mass. 02108, USA and
Broadway House,
Newtown Road,
Henley-on-Thames,
Oxon RG9 1EN
Printed in Great Britain by
Thomson Litho Ltd, East Kilbride, Scotland
© S. B. D. de Silva 1982

Library of Congress Cataloging in Publication Data

De Silva, S. B. D., 1926—
    The political economy of underdevelopment.
(International library of sociology)
Includes bibliographical references and index.
1. Underdeveloped areas. 2. Plantations.
3. Underdeveloped areas—Labour supply.
I. Title. II. Series.
HC59.7.D35   330.9172'4   81–13957

ISBN 0–7100–0469–9   AACR2

Contents

Preface

Research in the social sciences in underdeveloped countries has, of late, metamorphosed into a variety of big
business. Institutes and research agencies flourish in
rich profusion, with virtually a business interest in
staging seminars, symposia and workshops and in sponsoring
publications. In contrast, concerned activity committed
to exposing the real roots of social disarray is, remarkably, absent. Work and leisure are sharply demarcated,
with work being restricted to the conventional workplace
with its prescribed regimen of working hours. In a landscape that is intellectually sparse and monotonous, any
contribution to, or contact with scientific effort becomes
magnified. In such a wasteland collaboration including
scrutiny and comments on work in progress is hard to get,
especially when not directly related to one's professional
commitments. However, the advancement of knowledge is not
generally possible without some degree of collaboration -
preferably of an interdisciplinary nature - and this means
working together, not just good fellowship. One carries
out research as well as participates in it, whether in
formulating problems, in administering questionnaires and
obtaining data, or in subjecting to criticism what one
writes before publication.

There are several reasons why social scientists would
want to publish their works. One of them is that knowledge has to be tested and developed through a process of
confrontation. This need first found public expression in
the scientific journal and the device of the learned
paper. 'It is astonishing', said Keynes, 'what foolish
things one can temporarily believe in if one thinks too
long alone.' Another reason for publication is that the
development of science is a process of interchange, and
an individual's work must be adjusted to already existing
work and also pave the way for others. In the end there

is inevitably a personal element - not just a 'narcissis-
tic instinct' to see one's ideas in print but the expression of one's social involvement. As Erich Fromm explained, every human being has a natural urge to become
related to society through ideas and moral values. The
social scientist cannot endure loneliness; for him com-
munion is life.

This book is not the product of alienated labour.
There was throughout a psychological dimension, involving
a voluntariness and spontaneity of effort - unrelated to
considerations of professional survival or advancement.
Free to apply myself unremittingly, I could explore a wide
range of ideas and facts, restraining myself long enough
from adding to that 'superabundance of literature' which
some think has become one of the petty ailments of
science. The nature and intensity of the effort that
underlay the writing of this book also arose from a conscious desire to join in the social conflicts of our time.
This effort was inspired not by scholars and academics who
apply themselves in the isolation of the study or the
lecture room but by those who themselves engage in the
transformation of society. They are not content to be a
cork in the gushing waters of their time but would ride
the crest of the wave and attempt to direct its course,
giving it greater thrust by whipping up the social forces
which constitute the underlying current.

I must here express my gratitude to Professor John Rex
who at an early stage commented on the substance and
organization of the manuscript with a view to publication.
In Sri Lanka, L.N.T.Mendis read extensive portions of the
work and improved my capacity to resolve, to my satisfaction at least, many of the issues I have raised. One or
a few chapters in the final stages were commented on by
Sunila Abeysekera, Neil Kuruppu, Manel Tampse, Lalitha
Gunawardena, John Farrington, M.I.Kuruwila, Kumar
Rupesinghe and G.V.S. de Silva. Most of all I have to
thank Charles Abeysekera with whom I discussed the final
draft. I had the benefit of his ability to scan a lengthy
argument, and look critically at its form and structure.
He also helped me to sort out innumerable points of concept and exposition. The bibliographical and termino-
logical detail dogging the preparation of the typescript
for the press was clarified with the special aid of H.A.I.
Goonetileke. Marie Pinto Jayawardena helped me appreciably with her stylistic skills in effecting changes in the
successive versions of the text in this regard I owe her
a debt which can never be repaid but can only be recorded.

Introduction

This book began as a university thesis that was written several years ago and accepted for publication. Though growing out of that work the book has no affinity with it. The earlier MS tried to analyse the backwardness of Sri Lanka's peasant sector in terms of its failure to absorb growth impulses that were thought to emanate from the plantation sector. As I stretched the boundaries of the problem in attempting a pre-publication revision, I found that the plantations themselves were merely another backward sector with no impulses to spread. The traditionally accepted contrasts with the peasant sector were superficial. The present work 'The Political Economy of Underdevelopment' is the final outcome of my attempt to place in the world context what was essentially a country-based study, entitled 'Investment and Economic Growth in Ceylon', and to examine the problem of underdevelopment in terms of more generalized analytical categories.

This involved an extensive search in an area where knowledge is not a straightforward accretion. There was also a need for dismantling accepted concepts and approaches. Problems raised gave rise to others in succession, causing the horizon to recede with each advance. In this process there was no clear demarcation of stages in which one first gathers data and then proceeds to write them up. The comprehension of the problems and issues involved and the recourse to data were themselves linked with attempts at achieving increasing clarity in the analysis.

The rejection of the concept of dualism, which regards the export sector as modern, progressive and advanced, underlies several aspects of the present work. First, I consider underdevelopment holistically, as a phenomenon not confined to the peasant sector alone. Second, underdevelopment is the product of a definite politico-histori-

cal process, and not an original condition which can be
overcome as the modernizing influences of a metropolis
permeate the entire economy. Third, a study of underdevelopment must be made outside the framework of orthodox
economics and development theory, taking in diverse disciplines - politics, economics, history and sociology.
Lastly, the study of underdevelopment requires a return to
the concepts and categories of classical Marxism, based on
modes of production and the factors governing the transition from one mode of production to another. This means a
rejection of both neo-classical economics and the professed radical approach of the 'liberal developmentalists-
cum-pluralists' who, though moved away from neo-classical
economics, yet do not differ in fundamentals from it.

In the classical approach to the social sciences,
economics and what are now regarded as its border disciplines - especially politics, sociology and history - were
entwined. The first to incorporate political economy in
their writings were the eighteenth-century Scottish moral-
ists, including Joseph Hume, who were concerned with the
effects of the development of commerce and wealth on political power as well as on human happiness. (1) Adam
Smith's designation at the University of Glasgow was significantly enough Professor of Political Economy and Moral
Philosophy. At the time he wrote 'The Wealth of Nations'
he had a reputation from an earlier work on 'The Theory of
Moral Sentiments'. In the same way, J.S.Mill called his
major work 'Principles of Economy with Some of Their Applications to Social Philosophy'. 'For practical purposes, Political Economy', explained Mill, 'is inseparably
intertwined with many other branches of social philosophy.
Except on matters of mere detail, there are perhaps no
practical questions, even those which approach nearest to
the character of purely economical questions, which admit
of being decided on economical premises alone.' (2) 'In
so far as the economical condition of nations ... are dependent on *institutions and social relations* ... their
investigation belongs not to physical but to moral and
social science, and is the object of what is called political Economy.' (3) Smith recognized that a community
comprised a series of 'different orders and societies' and
that the development of trade and manufactures affected
the political power of the landed class. Marx conceived
of human society as an interrelated nexus of both economic
and non-economic elements. (4)

The classical economists themselves could not see, or
were unwilling to admit, the historical specificity of
capitalism - the mode of production which asserted its
supremacy in their time. Yet, they criticized the feudal

order for constraining the development of productive
forces by limiting the mobility of labour and by the
profligacy of the feudal aristocracy, compared with the
accumulative propensities of the bourgeoisie. They were
thus concerned with questions of unproductive output/con-
sumption, though they did not express this concept very
precisely - as Marx later did by his distinction between
productive and unproductive labour. When the proletariat
became a class to contend with, capitalism produced what
Marx called a 'herd of vulgar economic apologists' who
abandoned the basic concern of classical economics with
problems of production and growth for a formal but distorted analysis of the economy at the level of the market.
The relation between men was replaced by a relation between things - the commodity fetishism about which Marx
spoke. At the level of the market, the different classes
are 'partners in exchange'; 'a very Eden of the innate
rights of man'. (5)

The creation and disposal of surplus value were now
viewed in terms of productive factors abstracted from the
social and political relations of production. These productive factors, as well as markets, were treated as exogenous to the growth process. A pre-existing savings
fund is thus thought necessary to initiate an investment
process just as the capitalist entrepreneur is assigned
the role of a creator rather than the creature of the process. 'The root cause [of economic stagnation] is factor
scarcity. ... In underdeveloped economies ... entrepreneurs are an extremely small tribe and this is one important reason why development is so slow.' (6) When applied to the underdeveloped countries the mechanism of development then becomes the transfer of capital, enterprise
and technology from the already developed countries, instead of an appropriate class structure, and a corresponding set of production relations, within which accumulation
takes place.

Whereas until about 1830 the theoreticians of the bourgeoisie had been relatively objective in their assessment
of alternative social systems, this objectivity was no
longer possible in later years. Bohm-Bawerk, having
referred to Adam Smith's 'complete neutrality' in the exposition of interest as a category of income, explained
that in Smith's time 'the relations of theory and practice
still permitted such a neutrality, but it was not long allowed to his followers'. (7) The degeneration of economics to which Marx referred was evident at the onset of the
'great depression' of 1873-86 when economists were unprepared even to recognize the crisis-ridden nature of capitalism. Ignoring the declining profit rates, they quoted

income tax figures to show that Britain's national wealth
was increasing. In 1885 Professor Cunningham was thus led
to remark: 'The science of Political Economy speaks with
far less authority and receives less respectful attention
than it did some years ago.' (8)

Economics also excluded from its purview the non-
economic components of a social problem, even while these
components were having an increasing impact on the economy. (9) 'The borderlands of economics', wrote Lionel
Robbins, 'are the happy hunting-ground of minds averse to
the effort of exact thought.' (10) The accent on econom-
ism resulted in an irrational or religious conception of
the economy - as though the economist is in possession of
a kind of revealed knowledge about the working of the
economy. Furthermore, economics was regarded as a positive science. 'It is a method rather than a doctrine, an
apparatus of the mind, a technique of thinking which helps
its possessor to draw correct conclusions.' (11) The
economist's role became to 'explore and explain', not to
'uphold or condemn'. Devoid of prescriptive and policy
implications and evaluative norms, economics served to
legitimize the political rule of the bourgeoisie. It
became a divine right theory of existing society. The
capitalist mode of production was vested with an automaticity in its working, a harmony of interests and a permanence which it did not intrinsically possess. The specific was apotheosized into the universal. In keeping
with these changes there was an abandonment of political
economy - the term used by the classical economists for
what is now called economics.

With pretensions to objectivity and scientific preci-
sion, economists have resorted to considerable word-play
by which they have tried to conjure away some of the more
seamy aspects of the existing economic and social order.
They now speak of 'market economies' and the 'centrally
planned economies' instead of capitalist and socialist
economies - unconcerned with alternative socio-economic
systems, having different class structures and different
patterns of property rights and income. Professor Rostow
tried to substitute the word 'take-off' for industrial
revolution. For reasons best known to them economists
have now dropped the term underdevelopment in favour of
'developing' economies. The term originated in what may
have been a political gesture by the international aid
agencies. It was readily adopted by economists, heedless
of the fact that it served to mask the hard reality that
these economies were not 'developing' but underdeveloping.

With the formalization of economics and the abandonment
of the framework of classical political economy, economics

was also seized by an anti-theoretic tendency; it began
to lean heavily on statistics (observable and quantifiable
facts). Thus a great many studies in underdevelopment,
despite their title, belong to the field of applied economics, and are in the nature of investigative reports
devoid of intuition, 'reason', 'thinking' or 'theory'.
They have suffered from a heavy empiricism based on
questionnaires and social surveys. In the beginning was
the question, said Lewis S.Feuer rather irreverently. (12)
There is a laborious compilation of facts and statistical
material, whose analysis becomes limited to their algebra-
ic relations, or to descriptive summaries of the data arranged under merely commonsense captions. Such was the
practice of the Narodnik economists of pre-revolutionary
Russia to whom Lenin referred: 'They make a study like
amateurs, of endless columns and rows of figures, just as
though they have set out to astonish the world by their
arithmetical zeal.' (13) Though having an air of formal
objectivity, these purely empirical studies make little
addition to knowledge beyond what the statistics themselves make apparent.
     The variables in a social phenomenon are so numerous
and their interrelations so complex that there are no
mechanistic or invariant relations between them, and observable data are often limited. Unlike in the natural
sciences, phenomena cannot be observed in their most typical form, nor can controlled experiments be carried out so
as to untangle specific elements of a phenomenon. For instance, one cannot re-enact the battle of Waterloo to find
out why Wellington won and Napoleon lost, nor can one
carry out a statistical survey of the Middle Ages. A
socio-economic process is an indissoluble whole, composed
of a complicated network of human relations and responses,
whose general character may be disturbed by 'accidental'
elements that cannot be isolated. 'In the analysis of
economic forms', Marx stated, 'neither microscopes nor
chemical reagents are of use.'
     If in the social sciences incontrovertible truths
cannot always be gathered from observable data, it does
not mean that what cannot be directly observed or experienced cannot be analysed. In the absence of experiments,
analysis in the social sciences must rely largely on de-
ductive reasoning, and therefore becomes a process of dis-
tilling, in one's mind, the numerous properties of a phenomenon, so as to capture the 'essential' or the general.
Through such a process, the historically specific elements
are isolated from the general. Marx referred to the different ways in which hunger is satisfied in different
cultures: 'Hunger is hunger; but the hunger that is

satisfied by cooked meat eaten with knife and fork differs
from hunger that devours raw meat with the help of hands,
nails and teeth.' (14)   Abstract concepts embodying the
unalterable features of a phenomenon enable us to general-
ize and to see a unity in diversity. Generalization is
the prerequisite of science, not the uniqueness of the
unique.

The development of a theoretical framework requires a
process of abstraction and distillation, based on the comparative knowledge of a phenomenon in a wide range of
settings, both now and in the past. The procedure of
analysis is like examining several photographic slides of
a landscape from various angles, each with a different
focus, so as to get a generalized outline. A comparable
device is the 'identikit' used by Scotland Yard, whereby
the 'true' face of a wanted man is constructed with the
aid of numerous rough sketches each of which resembles him
better, or more sharply, in some respects than in others.
A taxonomic approach requires the study of a social phenomenon in several historical periods and in several
regions, taking account of its peculiarities over time and
space. Its different attributes may be highlighted more
sharply in some situations than in others. The relation
between the general and the particular was explained by
Marx: (15)

Events strikingly analogous but taking place in different historic surroundings [have] led to totally different results. By studying each of these forms of evolution separately and then comparing them one can easily
find the clue to this phenomenon, but one will never
arrive there by the universal passport of a general
historico-philosophical theory, the supreme virtue of
which consists in being super-historical.

While Marx's exposition of social problems was primarily theoretical, he was opposed to a 'mere a priori construction' and the 'self sufficiency speculation' of
Hegel. (16) For example, his conclusions on the working
conditions and living standards of the English proletariat
were supported by a knowledge of the reality as given by
factory inspectors, medical reporters, and governmental
commissions into food and housing. Marx studied the detailed and first-hand reports of these officials for whom
he had a good word. They were 'competent men, free from
partisanship and respect of persons'. He used England to
illustrate his theoretical ideas not only because of the
fuller development of capitalism in England at that time
but also because of the richer and more reliable statistical material that was available, compared with the
'wretchedly compiled' social statistics of Germany and the

rest of Continental Western Europe. (17)   Likewise, in
order to assess Russia's economic development, he 'learnt
Russian and then for many years studied the official publications and others bearing on the subject'. (18)   In
regard to the empirical component of Marx's methodology a
contemporary reviewer of 'Capital' stated that in a critical social inquiry 'the confrontation and the comparison
of a fact ... [is] not with ideas but with another fact'.
(19)
    An application of this method is seen in 'Pre-Capital-
ist Economic Formations', (20) where Marx, concerned with
how man interacts with nature, analysed society at a high
level of abstraction.   The theory of social and economic
evolution which he derived enabled him to periodize history in terms of analytical categories.   His specific objective was an analysis of capitalism.   In analysing a
social phenomenon he tried to discover its strategic variables - those which amidst an 'endless host of accidents'
are 'finally decisive'.   This involved questions regarding
the primacy and priority of different elements of a phenomenon, such as production and exchange, and base and
superstructure.   Marx's methodology was one of detecting
the general in the particular and the particular in the
general.
    In comparison with the methodology elaborated and
adopted by Marx, much of the research and writings on the
underdeveloped countries veer between the excessively
theoretical and the excessively empirical.   Western
scholars whose theoretical insights are sharply developed
are constrained in their analysis by limitation in the
range of data to which they have access;   without sufficient facts at hand, they suffer the disadvantages of a
man who is reviewing a play without actually having seen
it.   On the other hand, scholars in underdeveloped countries tend to burden themselves with a load of data to the
neglect of a theoretical framework.   Yet, as John Dewey
has said, it is 'when ideas, hypotheses, begin to play
upon the facts' that 'light dawns'. (21)
    The changes in the framework, focus and methodology of
economics have had a parallel in sociology where a neo-
positivist school sought to discard normative elements and
to renounce the sociologist's possible role as an agent of
social change.   He was to be neutral, and not to touch on
phenomena which when analysed may disturb the ruling
interests;   for instance, imperialism, capitalism, class
conflict, consumerism and notions about productive and unproductive labour.   Thus George A.Lundberg viewed 'real
social scientists' as those who like physicists and physicians 'would be as indispensable to Fascists or Communists

and Democrats'. (22) In spite of this it is curious that
sociology - a late developer among the social sciences -
has not been pervaded by the same ahistorical, apolitical
and amoral approach as economics. Along with history and
politics, sociology has been reaching out with far less
inhibition to areas of knowledge which require value
judgments, investigations into property rights and power
relations in society, and exercise of the 'sociological
imagination'. Problems of development and underdevelopment, previously regarded as purely economic problems,
have been brought within its purview.

   In recent years economists, on and off, have referred
to 'an air of unreality' in their analyses. But this is
usually attributed to the unsuitability of 'Western concepts'; for example, for analysing the unemployment problem in underdeveloped economies, this being a structural
problem and one of underemployment. Two such critics,
(23) while accepting 'the general validity of economic
theory as developed in the West', have pointed to the
theoretical rigidities preventing the adaptation of
existing models and even to a difficulty in communicating
to students in underdeveloped countries 'fundamental (and
often) simple principles or truths'. Such a criticism obscures the limitations of neo-classical economics to which
I have referred, preventing the 'Western economists' from
properly explaining even the economic problems of their
own society. On the other hand, a belated recognition of
the suffocating exclusivism of economics has led social
science departments of universities to introduce 'inter-
disciplinary'/'multidisciplinary' studies. But a refusal
to see the fragmentation of knowledge as one aspect of the
methodology of vulgar political economy, which substituted
the study of market 'appearances' for the 'real relations
of production', has nullified the effect of these curri-
cular reforms. The various disciplines are merely juxta-
posed, and studied in isolation, instead of being interwoven in their application. The disciplines are related
to each other like the members of an espionage network,
each one not knowing the other!

   Economists nowadays, trying to overcome the limitations
of neo-classical theory, include institutional factors in
their analysis, such as human attitudes, motivations and
values, and the level of probity and efficiency of government. To take an example, according to some writers, the
ethics of Theravada Buddhism militated against capital accumulation and development; it lacked a predestination
morality glorifying economic success, and was concerned
with distribution rather than production. On a more
general plane, underdevelopment is viewed as arising from

the behavioural traits of various indigenous groups. This
attempt to see problems in a social and even cultural
context, while suggestive of a return to the methods of
classical political economy, has, however, suffered in its
results by the non-economic factors ('values and attitudes') being treated as independent of their prevailing
social milieu. There is also in this a psychological
underpinning which regards social or commercial contact
with the Westerner, per se, to be civilizing and modernizing process; the African slaves were considered to have
benefited from their capture and transportation to America. A similar presumption pervades the dualistic model of
underdevelopment which differentiates, economically and
sociologically, between an export sector based on foreign
capital and enterprise and an indigenous peasant sector.
The former was advanced and modern; the latter backward
and traditional.

An adjunct of this tradition/modernity dichotomy is the
standard portrayal of precolonial societies as turbulent,
decadent and tyrannical. The author of a widely used book
on Southeast Asia says in a 'summarizing' sentence on
Burma that its political history was 'a never-ending
struggle between ... indigenous groups'. (24) Colonial
rule, 1826-1948, 'established law and order', 'thrust
Burma from the backwater into the mainstream of world
events', and made 'efforts to prepare the people for self-
rule'. Self-rule was what the Burmese had till the British conquered them! As shown by John F.Cady, (25) the
removal of indigenous authority led to periodic civil
strife, lawlessness and criminal activity. In a very recent work, Michael Adas (26) views with dismay the refusal
of the Burmese monarchs to 'co-operate' with the early
foreign investors, and with the 'political designs of the
East India Company officials'. Thus Burma is said to have
been deprived until its annexation of technological and
organizational skills. The British administration is depicted 'as one of the most beneficent of European colonial
regimes'. The imperial establishment was 'development-
oriented' and under its aegis there was 'sustained economic growth'. The encouragement of rice growing was 'influenced by a sincere desire to insure that the mass of
the Burmese obtained real benefits from participation in
Lower Burma's development'.

In these models, underdevelopment is a primordial condition, like original sin - to be overcome by contact with
the culture and organization of the already dominant economies, regardless of the terms on which such contact takes
place. The transformative process that occurred in the
developed economies through changes in modes of production

is totally ignored. A logical stage in this train of
thought is the justification it lends to colonial rule,
notwithstanding the effect of colonial rule on the
strengthening of precapitalist structures dominated by
merchants, usurers and landlords. In the post-independence phase, a continuation or revival of foreign contact,
under the aegis of the multinational corporations (MNCs)
and of international lending agencies, is supposed to
result in technology transfers and growth.

The critique of neo-classical methodology which has
been sketched here, all too briefly, is intended merely
to demonstrate the inappropriateness of neo-classicism,
even despite recent attempts to bring non-economic elements and 'interdisciplinary' studies into development
economics. These inadequacies essentially spring from the
social location of the bourgeois social scientists, im-
pelling them to be apologists of a social order which is
no longer rational. An objective or critical analysis of
a society at a given stage of development is possible only
if one is free in real life to proceed to the next stage
of social development. In reaction to this neo-classical
approach, there emerged a profusion of radical writings on
the problems of underdevelopment. The rapidity with which
they gained acceptance was due both to the sterility of
bourgeois social science and to the uncomplicated picture
of exploitative relations on a world scale which they portrayed. In attempting to place the study of underdevelopment within the Marxist paradigm, we must embark upon a
careful examination of these writings which during the
past decade and a half have attempted a critique of the
'vulgar economics' which Marx decried.

These writings have released development economics from
the narrow confines of bourgeois doctrine and methodology.
They have taken the international economy as the unit of
analysis, and sought to examine it through a politico-
historical lens. Yet, by connecting underdevelopment
merely with a centre-periphery dichotomy, the emphasis in
these writings has been on the inequalities encountered in
the world market, and the reverse transfer of resources to
the developed countries. The analysis of inter-nation relations has not been rooted in the conditions of production. The attempt in these writings to explain world relations in terms of market structures is shared by the
reformers of the United Nations Committee for Trade and
Development and is akin both in analytical method and in
its political effects to the 'commodity fetishism' of the
neo-classical economists. Very specifically, there is an
omission in this model of the social relations of production based on the character of the dominant capital and of
the dominant classes.

It is the production relations that determine the type
of exploitation, and the specific interaction, under different historical conditions, between 'centre and periphery', 'metropole and satellite', or 'dominance and dependency'. The primacy of production was basic to Marx's
methodology. 'Over certain epochs people live by plunder', he wrote as though foreseeing the false premise of
the present day 'dependency' theorists. 'But in order to
be able to plunder, there must be something to be plundered, and this implies production. Moreover, the manner of
plunder depends itself on the manner of production, e.g.
a stock-jobbing nation cannot be robbed in the same way as
a nation of cowherds.' (27) The involvement of underdeveloped countries in the world economy was not significant
in itself but only for the impact it had on the internal
class structure of these countries, locking into position
certain classes which stood in the way of a capitalist
transformation. These classes were representatives of
merchant capital, landlord capital and usurer capital.
The production relations, which, as James Petras noted,
condition the scope for the reproduction of capital, (28)
may conceivably have developed independently of their external articulation. These relations must be examined together with the way in which the state as the final em-
bodiment of political power mediates between them.
    If a theory of colonialism is to explain underdevelop-
ment, it should be grounded on Marx's basic concept of
production modes, examining the effects of colonialism on
class structures. As observed by Utsa Patnaik, a perceptive participant in the Indian debate on the mode of production, colonialism led to a strengthening of 'trading
capital, moneylending capital, [and] land purchasing capital'. She distinguished capital in the sphere of exchange
from capital in the sphere of production; there was an
'inordinate development' of the former and, in peasant
agriculture at any rate, a 'conspicuous absence' of the
latter. Having argued against categorizing the peasant
economy of India as capitalist, Utsa Patnaik stated
parenthetically that 'only the plantations represented
capitalist production; but they formed a tiny foreign
owned and export oriented enclave'. My discussion of the
colonial mode of production with reference to the plantation sector will show that this exclusion was unnecessary.
Here I shall merely say that underdevelopment signifies a
set of production relations which have become a barrier to
the development of the productive forces. It is in this
sense a condition which could affect even the capitalist
societies at a certain stage of their development. The
problems of underdevelopment are not the contradictions of

capitalism arising from the accumulation process but the
absence of accumulation - there was no class whose existence was bound up with the continued reproduction of capital. Without such a class the question is: if the surplus was domestically held, would it have been capitalized?

While the current writings on underdevelopment have not
failed to refer to the mode of production in the periphery, it has generally been presented as some variant of
capitalism - e.g. 'backward' capitalism, 'deformed' capitalism, 'dependent' capitalism or 'peripheral' capitalism.
The proliferation of terms itself suggests a lack of
clarity about the substantive character of this mode of
production. To differentiate it from what is presumably
capitalism proper, it is also said that in the periphery
capitalism was not a natural or organic growth but an implantation or superimposition on the pre-existing mode.
This notion of a capitalist mode of production which did
not emerge from the womb of the feudal order, propelled by
a crisis in the latter as in Western Europe, would apply
equally to capitalism in the white settler regions. As
Trotsky explained, the highest achievements of European
civilization 'inserted themselves' into the existing society, with a 'skipping' of a 'whole series of intermediate stages'; 'the European colonists in America did not
begin history all over again from the beginning'. (29)
Yet, in these regions capitalism, though very much of an
implantation or superimposition, differed radically in its
character and results from the prevailing mode of production in the periphery, to which the term capitalism is
also applied with some epithet or other. It may be
thought that the use of the epithets, or the fact of
superimposition, is designed to show the specificity of
capitalism in the periphery. But while the question at
issue is whether this mode of production can properly be
described as capitalism, such qualifications hardly serve
to identify the specificity of the mode of production -
if it could at all be regarded as capitalist.

The idea of capitalism as a transformative agency on a
world scale has recently become almost an article of faith
among Marxists. They have not sufficiently examined the
forces underlying the development of capitalism outside
the specific historical experience which Marx took account
of. Marx explained that his analysis of primitive accumulation, whereby society became divided between wage
workers and capitalists, 'does not pretend to do more than
trace the path by which, in Western Europe, the capitalist
order emerged'. (30) His study related directly to England, where the development of capitalism was 'radically

accomplished', and he pointed to a similar prospect in
'all countries of Western Europe'. In answering a
Narodnik critic, he warned against 'metamorphosing' 'my
historical sketch of the genesis of capitalism in Western
Europe into a historico-philosophic theory of the marche
generale [general path - editor of Marx and Engels,
'Selected Correspondence'] imposed by fate upon every
people whatever the historic circumstances in which it
finds itself'. (31) Marx gave as an example the condition
of slavery to which, in ancient Rome, the plebeians, after
becoming dispossessed, were reduced, instead of becoming a
wage proletariat. Likewise Engels emphasized that a
social phenomenon has specific properties arising from the
historical circumstances in which it occurs; but for
these differences 'the application of ... theory to any
period of history one chose would be easier than the solution of a simple equation of the first degree'. (32)

The conclusions reached by those who overlook Marx's
warning about generalizations only serve to validate both
his methodology and the meticulous care that he applied to
the analysis of social phenomena. 'It happens only too
often', wrote Engels, (33)

> that people think they have fully understood a theory
> and can apply it without much ado from the moment they
> have mastered its main principles, and those even not
> always correctly. And I cannot exempt many of the more
> recent 'Marxists' from this reproach, for the most
> wonderful rubbish has been produced from this quarter
> too.

The subtleties shown by Marx and Engels in their intellectual inquiries were more than their propagandists could
grasp.

A theory of colonialism, which dominates most radical
writings of recent years, does not by itself explain the
non-development of capitalism. In the capitalist countries themselves the transition from merchant capital to
industrial capital was not historically inevitable or
necessary but was the product of a combination of events,
some of them fortuitous. Capitalism did not automatically
unfold itself over time nor was there a certainty that it
would have done so in the periphery in the absence of
colonialism. After the unification of Italy and its emancipation from Austrian domination, the Italian bourgeoisie
(34)

> would not and could not complete its victory. It
> neither destroyed the remains of feudalism nor trans-
> formed national production according to the modern
> capitalist pattern.... Here too one can say with Marx:
> 'like all the rest of Continental Western Europe we are

tortured not only by the development of capitalist production, but by the lack of its development. Side by
side with modern distress ... ancient and antiquated
methods of production ... continue to vegetate.
'Dependency' does not also explain the historically uneven
development of capitalism at the centre and in the periphery itself. Such unevenness is seen in the different
patterns of growth in the settler colonies compared with
the nonsettler colonies and, in the present day, in a few
countries such as Taiwan, South Korea, Hong Kong and
Singapore compared with the rest of the periphery. The
capitalist development of these countries occurred without
their disengagement from the centre.

As the book arrives at an understanding of the process
of underdevelopment, it is my hope that the recent profusion of writings will be seen, even though employing
Marxist concepts, not as an application but as a reifica-
tion of Marx's thought. The concepts they propound, such
as 'Third World' and 'Dependency', have served to cloud
the class dynamics of different societies. These writings
have been so pervasive in their appeal that they have also
brought into common usage expressions like 'centre-periphery'. I myself have adopted this expression as a convenient descriptive term while questioning the appropriateness and applicability of the basic tenets associated
with such terms. The use of 'centre-periphery' seemed
justified owing to a formal change in the old metropolis-
colony relations. But while exploitative relations on a
world scale, at one level, take the form of the subjugation of a whole society and culture by another, at another
level this subjugation occurs in the context of specific
class alignments both in the centre and in the periphery.
The significance of this aspect will be seen in my discussion of the plantation economy, where the effect of
imperialism was to strengthen merchant capital, both
foreign and local, in the periphery at the expense of production capital. There was even a conflict of interests
between merchant capital from the centre and production
capital in the centre, constituting the absentee investors
in the plantations. On the other hand, a harmony of
interests may exist, rather than conflict between certain
classes in the centre and in the periphery.

The problems with which this book is concerned span an
area almost too vast to be dealt with in a single study
and too complex for final answers. As Landes said about
the economic breakthrough in Europe, such problems 'involve numerous factors or variable weights in changing
combinations. This sort of thing is hard to deal with
even if one has precise data that lend themselves to re-

fined techniques of analysis'. (35)   The case of underdevelopment is even more complicated and definitive answers
are far more limited.   For although underdevelopment is a
positive phenomenon as much as development, and there is
an interdependence between them, a study of underdevelopment unlike that of development is also beset by comparisons of 'what is' and 'what might have been'.

The intermeshed and the polemical aspects of our problem require a framework which is both comparative and historical, straddling geographical or political units and
conventional time zones.   If the determinants of underdevelopment are to be understood, it must be done within the
international framework to which underdevelopment as a
phenomenon belongs;   such a framework inevitably includes
the process of colonial expansion and imperialism.   The
appropriate unit of study must therefore be the world
economy.   A broadness of sweep does not exclude studies
in depth;   they are not mutually exclusive.   A social
scientist, wrote Marc Bloch, must be (36)

> like an explorer making a rapid survey of the horizon
> before plunging into the thickets from which the wider
> view is no longer possible.... Unless we cast our eye
> over France as a whole, we cannot expect to grasp what
> is singular in the development of the various regions.
> And what was happening in France can only be properly
> appreciated when seen in the context of Europe.

The extended scope of the discussion, evident from the
size of this book, also arises from the need for a questioning of received doctrine.   To adopt an expression of
Myrdal, the burden of proof is on those who say that
things are not what they seem to be.   If the discussion
would seem at certain points to cross its legitimate
boundaries, involving at times a complete shift of scene,
this is because the issues raised are of a kind on which
a short statement is of no value.   Considerations of perspective and scale are liable to be strained when the
questions being examined are ramified or complex.   The
reader has to be conducted over a broad hinterland by a
guide who hopes not to have become a part of the underdeveloped landscape.

An important aspect of my treatment of the problem of
underdevelopment is also its historical orientation.   As
J.A.Schumpeter stated, (37)

> Nobody can hope to understand the economic phenomena of
> any, including the present, epoch who has not an ade-
> quate command of historical *facts* and an adequate
> amount of historical sense or of what may be described
> as *historical experience*. *[*The historical report*]* af-
> fords the best method for understanding how economic

and non-economic facts are related to one another and
how the various social sciences *should* be related to
one another.... Most of the fundamental errors
currently committed in economic analysis are due to
lack of historical experience more than to any other
shortcoming of the economist's equipment.

The historical approach to social phenomena needs more
than a mere knowledge of facts and events in their chrono-
logical order. As Colin Leys aptly said, history is not
the same thing as a time dimension. Facts must be applied
to establish the historical specificity of a social phenomenon in terms of its constituent elements and of the
relations between these elements, which determine the
structure of the phenomenon and give it coherence. The
assembling of relevant historical facts would involve
movement up and down the time scale and over a wide social
expanse. The rudiments of more advanced forms of a social
phenomenon that are present in the less advanced forms,
explained Marx, can be understood only by studying the
more advanced forms. 'If one knows rent, it is possible
to understand tribute, tithe, etc., but they do not have
to be treated as identical.' (38) 'The anatomy of man is
a key to the anatomy of the ape.' (39) The development of
man as it were telescopes the development of the ape; the
embryonic outlines of man are not discernible in the ape.
The recourse to history is common enough, and much historical work is rich in empirical detail but faulty in its
key concepts of social change. The historical material
used in this book does not aim at making it an economic
history. Rather, selected themes and issues will be pursued. The distinctive problems of underdevelopment are
cast in history and we must go wherever these problems
lead.

1 Economic underdevelopment: a politico-historical perspective

The underdeveloped countries before coming into contact
with Western society were not technologically static.
Their progress is apparent from the interest which was
shown in Asia by the early Europeans who came as merchants, not as explorers or settlers. The Chinese had
begun using gunpowder in the tenth century, a knowledge
of which spread to Korea, Japan and Java. They had also
invented the printing process. Artillery as good as that
in the West was made in Asia long before the arrival of
the Portuguese. In the Mogul empire, engineering works
were found by Francis Bernier to be of astonishing size
by the standards of the time, (1) as were the stone and
metal structures of the Mauryan period to which Professor
Basham has referred. The Iron Pillar of Mecharauli, near
Delhi, 'could not have been produced by the best European
iron founders until one hundred years ago'. (2)   In Sri
Lanka, (3)

> remarkable levels of development in the arts, religion,
> technology and civil organisation [were] first achieved
> more than a thousand years ago.... This ancient cul-
> ture was built on rice production which flourished in
> the unfriendly environment of the Dry Zone by means of
> complex, ingenious and extensive irrigation works.

In the manufacture of consumer articles, especially
cotton and silk textiles, some of the non-European countries until comparatively recently held a technological
lead. The nearness of Italy to the Orient enabled 'skills
for the development of the silk industry [to] spread to
Italy long before they came to other parts of Europe'. (4)
The textile industry in England, which led the industrial
revolution, was adversely affected by imports from Asia.
To safeguard the English woollen and silk industries, an
Act of Parliament in 1700 prohibited the import of 'dyed,
printed or stained' cloths and silks. Similar measures
were taken by France and Spain. From the sixteenth to the

eighteenth centuries the chief obstacle to Europe's trade
with the East was the lack of European goods which could
have been offered in exchange; and throughout the seventeenth century Britain's trade balance with India was
generally unfavourable. Attempts were made to export
paintings and objets d'art. The Amsterdam Company tried
to sell engravings of Madonnas to the Chinese and then,
equally unsuccessfully, prints with an erotic appeal and
'less decent pictures'. (5)

But from the eleventh to the fifteenth centuries the
European countries forged ahead in the manufacture of
firearms and in the art of metallurgy. The inter-European
wars of this period led to further progress. In Holland
an industry sprang up for the manufacture of cannon, and
in the early seventeenth century Sweden vastly upgraded
its armaments industry. Thus by the fifteenth century,
the European countries had enhanced their overall technological lead, and this was evident both in the manufacture
of cannon and in the technology of naval warfare, navigation and shipping. In the first half of the sixteenth
century the Portuguese demonstrated the pre-eminence of
Europe when they asserted their supremacy in the Indian
Ocean and later annihilated the Turkish fleet at Lepanto
in 1571. While generally the state of technology and
economic organization in the Western societies even at
this time was superior to that in the non-Western countries, as is seen from the success of the Western world in
subjugating them, the productivity gap had not assumed an
explosive potential.

The technological disparity between what later became
the developed and the underdeveloped countries is very
hard to explain, as are also the broad economic changes
associated with technological advance. Europe's superiority at this stage represented an unbalanced technological
maturation in certain specific areas, essentially in
weapons, which later had its impact on other areas of the
economy. The interrelations between war and industry are
too complex to admit of easy generalization. J.U.Nef
regarded warfare not as an independent or primary factor
in economic growth but as the product of a great number of
other factors, 'making it easy for some states and difficult for others to wage war or to abstain from waging it'.
(6) In England during the sixteenth and early seventeenth centuries, there were several industries whose development had no relation to military needs - e.g. salt
and alum, coal mining, printing, glass and paper making,
soap boiling, brewing and sugar refining. While one
should be hesitant to regard warfare as a unique source
of technological and social change, there were specific

situations in which advances in military technology had an
economic and social impact.   For instance, the introduction of the stirrup in the eighth century - a simple
technical innovation - touched off a change both in the
conduct of war and in the organization of society.   (7)
The technological disparity between the European and the
non-European societies prior to the Industrial Revolution
had, however, a great deal to do with the socio-political
structures in the European and the non-European societies.
The technological advances in European societies were
predicated on the disruption of feudal institutions and
the emergence of a class structure that was favourable to
capital accumulation and investment.   (8)

> By 1900 European affairs were coming more and more
> under the control of new social groups that had a flair
> for organisation rather than splendour, for efficiency
> rather than gallantry.   And such groups could count on
> an increasingly numerous class of craftsmen with a
> taste for mechanics and metallurgy.

The changes in the socio-political structure provided an
appropriate framework for technical progress and were
themselves influenced by the latter.   Changes of an analogous nature did not occur in the non-European societies
for reasons which need examination.

Nevertheless, a society that may have lagged behind
during a period contains within itself the possibility of
a surge forward later;   belatedness and unevenness of development are an inevitable element in the progress of
different societies.   Adequate historical evidence exists
of such belated development - e.g. Russia during the time
of Peter the Great, and post-Meiji Japan.   This is to say,
there are times when the pace of history is quickened.   It
was this telescoping of development which was the basis of
the law of combined development which Trotsky sought to
incorporate in his theory of history.   But the impact of
colonialism was that it completely forestalled such a possibility, and instead conserved and ossified in the metropolitan interests social institutions, structures and
classes which were hostile to progressive change.

The overseas economic expansion of Europe forced the
underdeveloped countries out of their comparative isolation, linking them to the world economy of the nineteenth
century.   A system of production was developed in mines
and on plantations, which in some respects differed from
traditional forms of activity.   It involved the use of
wage labour and production for distant markets.   The
financial and management practices of the new enterprises
were highly rationalized and subjected to more searching
accounting devices.   A large export-import sector required

the development of railways, docks and warehouses. Along
with this infrastructure were introduced the organization,
habits and practices of a modern commercial society, including new legal concepts to regulate the property relations appertaining to such a society.

The 'opening up' of these countries led to a relatively
spectacular increase in output and income. 'For at least
two or three decades, but frequently for longer periods
... the rate of expansion in their export production was
far in excess of any possible natural population growth.'
(9) The proportion of capital investment to national
income, which is usually accorded a central place in the
formal mechanism of growth, would have been high over
several years. In the conditions of their time, the scale
of investments bore the character of a 'big push'. In
Assam an estimated Rs 10 million was invested annually for
the last two decades of the nineteenth century, or about
15-20 per cent of the national income in this period. (10)
The rate of return on these investments was also high,
though not wholly reflected in the profits of the plantation and mining companies. A portion of the wealth generated was dispersed among numerous commercial enterprises
and intermediaries. In the chapter on plantation agency
houses I shall point to these ramifications.

A correlative to the terms of admission of the underdeveloped countries into the world economy was the division
of activities between them and the advanced countries.
Referring to India, Vera Anstey wrote: the economic
changes under British rule 'brought about a peculiar
interdependence between India and the West whereby India
tended to produce and export in the main raw materials and
foodstuffs, and to import iron and steel goods, machinery
and miscellaneous manufactures of the most varied description'. (11) The underdeveloped countries were a hinterland to the industrialized nations of the West - in J.S.
Mill's oft-quoted dictum, places 'where England finds it
convenient to carry on the production of sugar, coffee and
a few other tropical commodities'. (12) They were drawn
into the world economy as appendages of the metropolitan
countries rather than as partners. An improvement occurred in aggregate output and income in these countries
alongside a relative deterioration on a world scale.
Also, the overwhelming mass of the people, even those employed in plantations and mines (the 'advanced' sector of
the economy), were at a bare subsistence level.

In distinguishing between 'underdeveloped' natural resources and 'backward' people, Myint considered the latter
as essentially a problem of distribution of economic activity and incomes. While acknowledging the existence of

resource underdevelopment, he considered economic backwardness as the central problem. 'The natural resources
have ... been as fully and rapidly developed as market
conditions permitted while the inhabitants have been left
out, being either unable or unwilling or both to participate fully in the process.' He thus advocated 'a clean
break with the "underdevelopment" approach [and a need]
to recognise the problem of "backwardness" as a major
problem in its own right which may occur even when there
is no important underdevelopment of resources'. (13) This
hypothesis has considerable merit in the case of the
settler colonies which I will discuss in later chapters.
These colonies tended to develop along the lines of the
metropolitan societies, from whose control the settler investors became increasingly detached. The settler investors developed as a bourgeoisie in its own right; free
from the control of merchant capital, it tended to repli-
cate the investment patterns of the metropolis, developing
secondary production for domestic and regional markets.
All the same, while the resources of these territories
became relatively developed, a monopoly of political power
by the settlers led to a total repression of the indigenous people. Their condition of poverty was thus essentially the result of the 'disequalizing forces' to which
Myint referred. On the other hand, in the nonsettler
colonies, where the European nationals lived as expatriates, investing only in trade and primary production for
export markets, productivity and per capita incomes were
low even in the predominantly European sector of the
economy. Investment and production activities were metropolitan oriented. Merchant capital dominated, mediating
between the production structures of the metropolis and
the colony. The development of the forces of production
was feeble.
  Such a pattern of development had its origin in the
opening up process of these countries. This process,
unlike the classical vision of countries with different
factor endowments trading with one another under conditions of competition, was brought about by the metropolitan powers through physical force and monopolistic
privileges. The case of China was referred to by Harold
Isaacs: (14)

> Treaties were exacted by foreigners at the cannon's
> mouth ... coastal and river ports [were] opened to
> trade, ... the Chinese tariff [was limited] to a nomi-
> nal 5 per cent ... territorial footholds and conces-
> sions [were granted] whence later came the different
> 'spheres of influence', and ... the system of extra
> territoriality which exempted foreigners from the
> jurisdiction of Chinese taxes.

In other underdeveloped countries, India, Sri Lanka, Malaysia, for example, where subjugation preceded foreign enterprise (trade followed the flag), the basis of absorption into the world economy and its results were no different.   In virtually every colonial territory a certain number had to be killed before the survivors would accept the new prospects.   This might even be said to introduce a new concept into the study of political economy - the indispensable minimum of murder. (15)   The opening up process also led, especially in the nonsettler colonies, to the compartmentalization of investment and trade flows according to the respective metropolitan nodes to which the various countries of Asia, Africa and Latin America were attached.   The division of labour, based on an agriculture-industry dichotomy, while being optimal from the . standpoint of each metropolitan country was sub-optimal from that of its constituent but subordinate units.

The role of the colonial state in the opening up process was unique both in its scope and its character.   In the developed countries, the supremacy of new classes, and the replacement of old forms of production by the new were achieved basically within a framework of market competition whereby the survival of the productive system became contingent on its renewed vitality, at a higher plane of technique and productivity.   The superiority of capitalism over the precapitalist forms of production enabled it to secure the latter's productive resources.   In this way the factory triumphed over the small artisan just as a system of capitalized agriculture superseded peasant farming. There was at the time a disintegration of the feudal mode of production, brought about by a stagnation in productivity and later by the desertion of the manors as the lords' exactions on the peasantry increased.   Feudalism as a system of production was thus ceasing to be viable and had entered a stage of internal crisis when the forces of capitalism were beginning to overwhelm it.   The decline of the precapitalist forms of production furnished a growing labour supply to the capitalist sectors.   Furthermore, though the capitalist state resorted to extra-economic pressures to exclude competitors and secure markets and raw material sources, and never wholly renounced its support of private business, by the mid-nineteenth century such intervention had become greatly reduced in scope. Technological processes from this time onwards conferred on the already developed countries a self-reinforcing advantage.   The strength of external economies, the lumpiness of capital investment and relations of direct (non-market) interdependence ruled out, in the case of the late developers, a gradual progression from simple techniques

and small workshops to complex technology. The economic
hegemony of the metropolitan powers and the structuring of
world markets in their favour imbued existing production
and trading patterns with an automaticity which was devoid
of any conscious element.

Though, as Marx pointed out, in the metropolitan countries themselves the use of state power underlay 'the
transformation of the feudal mode of production into the
capitalist mode', shortening the transition of one mode to
the other, to see such intervention in its perspective it
must be contrasted with that in the colonial economies.
State intervention in the colonies was immeasurably greater in scale and more blatant in character, and it was predominantly on behalf of the metropolitan investors. An
informal relationship often existed between investors and
the Colonial Office in London; the votaries of free
enterprise, sometimes directly and at other times through
their organizations, made use of the machinery of government to influence economic trends in the colonies. In
taxation and trade a double standard prevailed at home and
in the colonies. The revenue measures in Sri Lanka, said
Sir John Elphinstone in 1865, were maintained, 'in the
face of an Imperial policy of an entirely opposite character'. 'A large proportion of the Revenue of Ceylon is
drawn from sources condemned and disused by the Home
Government.' (16) In chapter 13 I shall discuss the
framework and mechanisms of metropolitan intervention
and control.

In colonial situations where the government was the
direct agency for the diversion of resources - labour and
land - from traditional activities, this function was due
partly to the character of the new forms of production -
which did not grow out of or replace the old, inheriting
by virtue of a technological superiority the productive
forces of the latter. In a detailed discussion of this in
chapters 11 and 12, I shall show the backward nature of
the plantations in terms of their technology as well as
their social relations of production; and in chapter 10
it will be explained that the plantations had no inherent
superiority over smallholdings. Governmental intervention
was also aimed at checking the growth of forms of production that would compete with the parent economy.

State intervention in colonial societies was basically
due to the comparative stability of their precapitalist
economy which enabled it to withstand market pressures for
the release of its productive resources - principally
labour. As Rosa Luxemburg explained, the 'social and
economic ties of the natives' had to be 'relentlessly'
severed. (17)

Accumulation, with its spasmodic expansion, can no more
wait for, and be content with a natural internal disintegration of non-capitalist formations and their
transition to commodity economy, than it can wait for,
and be content with, the natural increase of the working population.

In Africa, the obstacle to investment was an abundance of
land. By administrative means labour had therefore to be
prised out of peasant farming. Land was sequestered and
the Africans were relegated to areas which were the least
fertile and remote from transport and marketing facilities. The migrant labour system, wrote Jack Woddis, like
'a giant grab, constantly dips, scoops and denudes whole
villages of their manpower'. (18) The weakening of the
tribal economy due to an initial loss of manpower created
secondary and tertiary outflows, leaving behind mostly
women and children. The exodus of labour was stimulated
by taxation and discriminatory prices for peasant produce.

The necessity and the scope of state intervention have
differed in the settler and the nonsettler colonies. The
degree of intervention required in the settler colonies to
divert resources into the hands of the settler investors
was far greater than in the nonsettler colonies; this was
on account of the need to break down the precapitalist
forms of social organization (which in sub-Saharan Africa
were of a tribal nature) and of the greater involvement of
the settlers in production as opposed to trade. On the
other hand, in the nonsettler colonies the disruption of
the traditional economy did not entail an extensive expropriation of the peasants, as for instance occurred both in
the Maghreb and in other parts of Africa. This was because of the availability of migrants from the great
labour pools of India and China. In the nonsettler colonies state intervention was aimed far more at obtaining
captive markets for the metropolitan economy by developing
a division of labour in which these colonies were relegated to the position of primary product suppliers.

In assessing the impulses to development of underdeveloped countries in the past, emphasis is usually laid on
the social overhead investments which the export economy
produced. But the infrastructure facilities resulting
from such investments were severely limited in scope and
were discriminatory in the interests which they served.
Being highly specific to the export-import economy, they
were tantamount to hidden subsidies to metropolitan interests. While reinforcing the role of the underdeveloped
countries as appendages of the metropolis, the infrastructure facilities inhibited a broader and sustaining process
of development beyond the immediate investment activities

they served. The stultifying effects of the colonial
infrastructure on the development of internally oriented
forms of production and trade are easily seen from a few
instances to which I shall now refer.

In Africa, infrastructure facilities had crippling effects on both the internal and the regional economy.
'Natural' frontiers were violated, demographic groupings
broken up and potential market areas upset. The railway
network consisting generally of a 'series of short, dis-
connected' lines made interstate communications circuitous
and prohibitively costly. The roads linking Rhodesia and
Zambia were not suited for goods traffic. Though the road
journey between Salisbury and Ndola is 500 miles, goods
had to be carried 1,000 miles via Bulawayo and Livingstone. (19) Local producers could not compete with
European imports in neighbouring states. Until recently,
textiles produced in the Uganda mill at Jinga could not be
taken to the Dar-es-Salaam market owing to the lack of a
rail link with Tanzania. The siting of the capital
cities, delinked from the rest of the country including
other urban areas, brought these countries closer to their
respective metropolises. 'Illogical gaps, detours and
discontinuities' in transport and communication systems
intensified this result. 'The external trade which is
such an important aspect of the life of these cities, also
continues to follow metropolitan channels to an extraordinary degree, with most of the Francophone countries
in particular being incapable of cutting this umbilical
cord.' (20) Johan Galtung appropriately drew the analogy
between serfs and their manor lord. 'Just as serfs were
restricted to interactions with one manor lord, so too are
periphery nations constrained to one center nation.' 'Just
as horizontal interaction among serfs was structurally
discouraged by feudal society, so too is horizontal interaction among nations in the periphery kept to a minimum.'
(21) In many of these countries the centrifugal forces
were evident even after independence. (22)

In railway building, in certain cases, the dominant
aims were political and military. The government of
India's financial involvement in the Calcutta-Delhi railway was due to the prospective saving in military expenses. 'From a political point of view [the railway]',
Hardinge, the Governor-General, explained, (23)

   would give the Government great additional powers, approaching almost to ubiquity.... From a military point
   of view ... the value of moving troops and stores with
   great rapidity would be equal to the services of four
   regiments of infantry. The reduction of the military
   establishment would be a saving of £50,000 a year, on

the lowest ... *[the railway would also provide]* the
facility of a prevention of an insurrection, the speedy
termination of a war, or the safety of an empire.

Steam navigation on the Ganges and the Brahmaputra river
owed its impetus to the Sepoy rebellion in the 1850s. (24)
Even when such investments served economic interests, they
'had very little impact on the bulk of the domestic agrarian economy'. (25)

In India, the infrastructure contributed to 'deindustrialization'. Along with such measures as tariff policy,
the railways uprooted indigenous manufactures, exposing
them to foreign competition. The iron industry was virtually stamped out except in very remote places. However,
the coal industry of Bengal had no market outside the
province; railway freights were so high that outside
Bengal it was cheaper to buy imported coal in Calcutta at
four or five times its price. (26) Railway rates discriminated against indigenous commercial interests. The
rate on goods traffic to and from the ports was lowered so
as to benefit foreign trade at the expense of production
for the home market. (Likewise, in Burma when in the
1890s small rice mills were started in the rice-growing
districts, the system of railway tariffs was changed to
favour the carriage of paddy rather than rice. (27) This
benefited the European-owned mills in Rangoon.) In India,
after the Railways Act of 1890 introduced uniform rates,
there was discrimination in the acceptance of cargo.
Furthermore, the railways developed at the expense of
existing modes of transport. The predatory way in which
they were built resulted in the disuse of river transport.

In Sri Lanka, while the importation of rice from Burma
and its transport to the plantation districts was an
elaborate enterprise, involving European millers, shipping
agencies and insurance firms, and the railway, in the vicinity of the plantations there were no cart roads to provide an outlet for any surplus of locally grown paddy.
(28) The 'villages are entirely cut off from each other',
wrote an Assistant Agent in 1895. The banks of the
Kotmale Kira (29)

have no bridges except where ... *[the river]* passes
through planting districts. In wet weather the river
cannot be crossed in boats, and the villages ... have
no cart roads and no bridges. The Sinhalese villages
lie below the banks of the river and they have no road.

In one instance 'a trace that had been made for a road
outlet for the Kurundu Oya valley estates, through an 8
mile stretch of dense forest *[was]* for the purposes of
benefiting one estate only'. (30)

The infrastructure facilities, geared overwhelmingly to

the needs of the export sector, not merely failed to benefit village interests but involved a repudiation of these
interests. In the allocation of expenditure on the construction and maintenance of roads, village roads were
discriminated against. On the other hand, the road tax
was paid almost entirely by the villagers, plantation
labour being exempt. The repair and maintenance of existing irrigation works were neglected. Like many of the
more significant issues in the political economy of
development, the effects on the peasant economy of the diversion of resources to support export agriculture are not
easily quantifiable. I shall, however, furnish some specific evidence, relating to Sri Lanka, based on official
reports of the period.

The planters' interests in road building were 'quite
opposite' to those of the villagers - as the Government
Agent for Uva explained in 1907. (31) The villagers
wanted footpaths cleared of jungle, and footbridges and
cart roads, and the planters wanted bridle paths which
were more expensive. Yet, the expenditure on village
roads, even in terms of these modest requirements, was
meagre. According to one Government Agent, 'Large sums of
public money have been spent to give a few estates an improved outlet to the railway. A small sum might well be
added to extend that outlet to a populous and thriving
native community.' (32) 'The people who benefit by the
roads are purely the land-owners and the richer they are
and the more extensive and valuable their lands the
greater their need for good roads.' (33) Financial provision for Nuwara Eliya in 1898, the Assistant Agent
wrote, was 'a perfectly absurd sum compared to the wants
of the district', and the bulk of the available funds was
spent on estate roads. 'As it is the planters get a great
deal more than their share', wrote the Assistant Agent in
1904. (34)

Road policy was dictated by the planters. The District
Road Committee, responsible for financial allocations, was
composed mainly of planters - the officials who represented indigenous interests 'would attend /meetings/ and
vote as the Chairman wished'. (35) In 1907 the Assistant
Agent for the Uva province stated: 'I consider that
planters have too much influence.... The upcountry roads
get an /undue/ proportion of money, and there is not
enough left in the construction and upkeep of roads in the
parts of the Province where there are no estates.' (36)
Though road expenditure predominantly benefited the
estates, it was financed by a tax levied mainly on the
villagers. 'The prevailing /District Road Committee/
system', an Assistant Agent had stated in 1886, 'required

the poverty stricken villager of Walapane who scarcely
sees money from one year to another ... to pay exactly the
same as the European Civil Servant, Planter or Merchant.'
(37) As a result while the plantation acreage expanded
total collections remained unchanged and the planters made
a first claim on the funds. To rectify this, in 1907 the
Government Agent of Uva proposed the creation of Estate
Road Boards and of District Road Boards; the former to be
financed by estates and the latter to use the tax contributions of the villagers on inter-village lines of roads,
without interference by planters. (38) This proposal went
unheeded, and in 1916 the Government Agent of the North
Western Province noted: 'The D.R.C. roads are starved and
stationary.... New estates are springing up and using our
roads ... which are maintained by a road tax on villagers.' (39)

The cutting of plantation roads caused considerable
damage to irrigation channels and paddy fields. The Wadu
Ela (an irrigation channel in the Nuwara Eliya district),
the Assistant Agent wrote in 1887, 'had been blocked up
and destroyed' by a road extension that was made under the
direction of the Provincial Road Committee. (40) Cultivation was suspended. 'The villagers have lost two harvests, and unless the ela [irrigation channel] is in
working order within the next six weeks they will lose ...
a third.' (41) A year later the Assistant Agent wrote:
'It is strange that no notice has been taken at the time
of the injury to the village interests that the cutting of
the road has caused.' The Colonial Secretary minuted, 'So
it is to me. How accounted for? [Sgd] A.H.G.' (42) The
construction of this road damaged another channel, the
Warella Ela. 'It runs above the extension and the cutting
of the road has seriously weakened the lower bank of the
channel and it is in immediate danger of collapsing altogether.'

As in tariff policy, railway freights, and transportation facilities, in irrigation matters, too, there was a
general repudiation of indigenous interests by the planters and the colonial bureaucracy. In 1897 the Assistant
Government Agent for Nuwara Eliya wrote:

No notice whatever appears to have been taken of my
irrigation proposals ... made last July. We go from
bad to worse, and what money had hitherto been spent
in the district is being rendered pointless for want
of repairs, and you too can get tired after a time of
making proposals when you can't get an answer even in
the negative.

The 'district [is one] which with a little encouragement
could pour a large supply of rice into the estates'. (43)

A proposed irrigation channel for the Bolagandawela lands,
the Assistant Agent wrote in 1889, (44)

> has been 'interrupted' since ... 1872, and has been
> recommended by every A.G.A. ... since 1876 ... and I
> myself [did so] in 1881.... We are agreed that it is a
> most desirable work and that it could confer a great
> benefit if taken up, but somehow or other it has always
> been shelved.

This project had 'been solemnly inspected ... at regular
intervals during the last half century', but by 1901 no
progress was made. (45)

> We have impoverished the villagers by the sale of their
> paddy lands. We are still further doing so by re-
> stricting their chena cultivation. We keep on promis-
> ing them assistance if they will drop chenas and take
> to paddy growing and yet it is the most difficult thing
> in the world to get irrigation works actually carried
> out.

He wrote, 'A walk over the Ela is much more interesting
than a wade through the file.... It ought to make one
weep to see the fine masonry work all along this Ela going
to rack and ruin.' The channels of the Bodi Ela irrigation scheme, breached by earthslips, lay unattended for
more than ten years. The Assistant Agent wrote in 1904,
'The Bodi Ela scheme forces itself on one's attention
everytime one comes this way ... it cannot escape notice,
hence the frequent reference to it in my diary.' (46)
Three years previously he had written: 'There is no
question that the Ela is badly wanted and that there is
more [cultivable] land under it than it will irrigate. I
do not anticipate difficulty about getting the people benefited to pay water rates'; (47) and he had added: 'If
these slips had occurred to the channel taking water to a
tea factory the damage would without doubt have been made
good within a few months.' (48)

The upkeep of existing irrigation facilities which the
paddy economy required, at the very least, was neglected.
The provincial administration was grossly understaffed,
and too engrossed in revenue collection and court work.
'To know and understand what is going on and the real
state of the district,' wrote an Assistant Agent in 1850,
(49)

> I should be acquainted with everything connected with
> it, as regards people, the revenue and the lands....
> I should institute inquiries which is now done at Kandy
> and at such distance from Matale.... Independent of
> this there are many matters which for want of an es-
> tablishment devolve on me personally such as receiving
> money and all matters connected with money.

Almost half a century later the neglect of peasant affairs
for the same reason was noted: 'It is ridiculous to suppose that this department and provincial Kachcheries can
do without a land clerk, the most important in the Department and with ... all the irrigation work of this province
the Native department cannot do justice to Government
interests.' (50)

I have thus far illustrated the process of incorporation of the underdeveloped countries into the world economy under the aegis of the colonial powers and the function
of the colonial state in assisting foreign investors to
gain access to the resources of these countries by extra-
economic means. The production activities which foreign
investment engendered were, in their economic and technological basis, not necessarily superior to those already
carried out in the traditional economy of these countries.
As will be shown in later sections of this book, the plantation system involved merely a 'restructuring' of existing methods of production rather than a transformation.
The allocation of labour and land to foreign investors was
thus contingent upon intervention by the colonial government in a more blatant manner and on a far bigger scale
than that of the nation states in Europe on behalf of the
rising bourgeoisie during the transition to capitalism.

The production activities which foreign investment engendered are commonly supposed to have made a positive
contribution to the expansion of the underdeveloped economies; Myint spoke of 'net additions [to output] made possible by the utilization of new resources'. Historical
research has not really examined the nature and the effects of these investments on the indigenous sector.
Though the negative and the positive factors are difficult
to balance or to compare, some of them being quantitative
and others of a qualitative nature, the negative effects
of foreign investment on the indigenous sector and its un-
actualized potential may well have outstripped the positive effects which usually claim attention. These repercussions are not comprehensively dealt with in this book
though I shall refer to them from time to time. The adverse effects of the growth of the export sector on the
peasant economy have already been discussed in the case
of Sri Lanka. To further illustrate these effects I shall
refer briefly to the impact of tin mining on the paddy
economy in Malaysia and also to the effect of foreign investment in tin on the indigenous mining interests both in
Nigeria and in Malaysia.

In Malaysia, mining operations caused damage to agricultural land, due to a deposit of silt and other debris
in irrigation channels and paddy fields. The situation

worsened as mining activity spread to districts where
paddy was extensively grown. According to an administrative officer quoted by Lim Teck Ghee, (51) 'Tin mining and
rice-growing will not prosper side by side; the latter
must inevitably go to the wall.' At the same time, the
mining interests used their economic and administrative
influence to forestall any measures to relieve the paddy
cultivators if these measures were detrimental to mining
activity. The opposition of the mining interests, and the
futility of official intervention, were referred to by the
Tailings Commission of 1904, and again by the commission
of 1914. The hesitancy of the government to control the
effects of tin mining on peasant agriculture was noted by
the Chamber of Mines in 1918: 'Much of the damage was
done in the past before any restriction of tailings were
[sic] imposed.' (52)

In Nigeria, European mining activity completely dislodged African enterprise. The Africans usually got no
compensation for the loss of ownership of mineral-bearing
land, though the lessees were required by law to pay the
owner an annual rent and the value of the damage to
buildings and crops. The indigenous tin smelting industry
became virtually extinct in the Lurei district - a 'most
regrettable occurrence', said the British Resident of the
Bauchi province. (53) Nigeria had at the outset resisted
the intrusion of foreign mining companies - personnel of
the Royal Niger Company were killed and mining equipment
was destroyed. The government then gave protection to the
companies. The eclipse of African enterprise, in both
mining and smelting, was not wholly due to a technological
inadequacy but also to the use of state power in various
forms. The Tin Restriction Scheme, under which output
quotas had to be purchased, kept out Africans for want of
capital. Second, the foreign companies acquired large
tracts of mining land with the connivance of the local
chiefs - and later the government regulated mining concessions in favour of the companies. Third, in 1914 the
government, under pressure from the companies, revoked a
100 acres' lease of tin-bearing land which it had already
given to Nigerian smelters who had lost their own tin-
bearing land. (54) Finally, to safeguard the companies
against thefts of ore the government ordered the closure
of four out of seven Nigerian smelting furnaces.

In Malaysia, the colonial administration reserved the
best rubber land for the British planters; British land
policy 'consciously aimed at giving European enterprise
undue advantage over Asians wishing to enter the industry'. (55) State intervention also helped the Europeans
to gain control over the tin-mining industry. In Perak

(the chief mining state) land policy from 1906 was exceptionally favourable to the foreign companies. Land
held by the Chinese and Malays was turned over to the companies at nominal rates and after 1912 land grants in all
the tin-bearing states were made only to those who had
large sums of capital. The control over the labour market
by the Chinese mining enterprises was also undermined,
apart from by the suppression of the secret societies, by
a change in the procedure for recruiting migrant labour.
The abolition in 1894 and 1895 of the credit ticket system
of recruitment made labour free to move to the European
enterprises; and the consequent rise in wages affected
the labour intensive Chinese mines. (56) From about the
1890s, when British capital was acquiring mining interests
in Malaysia, the administration as a matter of policy
sided with the British interests. Their determination to
profit from Britain's political control of Malaysia was
made quite explicit by the 'Mining Journal' in 1896. 'We
did not undertake the task of keeping order in this Peninsula from purely philanthropic motives. We went there
as becomes a "nation of shopkeepers" because there was
something to be made by it - and that something is dependent on the mineral wealth of the country.' (57)
     Economic underdevelopment, as suggested earlier, is not
a distributional problem of income, employment and economic activities, nor can it be thought of as a kind of
partial development, which stopped short of some critical
point which turns an underdeveloped economy into a developed one (perhaps like Rostow's 'take-off' point). In
these formulations, the economic changes are presumed to
have led the underdeveloped economies along the road to
development; a journey whose completion requires some
residual investment or the grafting on of an industrial
sector (which is acknowledgedly lacking) within the existing framework of institutional structures and relationships. The opening up process is presumed to have involved a transmission of 'growth' to the underdeveloped
countries (Myrdal), and the economic and social changes
under colonial rule are regarded as positive accomplish-
ments, representing important advances towards creating
the conditions for general economic development. (58)
'In most cases, the colonies probably developed further
than if they had been left alone.' (59)
     Colonial rule cannot be seen in isolation from the
total result. The conceptual method of Paul Baran is applicable here. What finally matters is not a comparison
of 'what is' and 'what was', that is to say, the condition
of society or economy before and after its subjugation,
but the (admittedly difficult) comparison between 'what

is' and 'what might have been' had these countries been
free to develop as independent entities under the patronage of a national government. The former comparison is
between the condition of the economy frozen at the time of
their subjugation and its condition today. The latter involves the possibility that the expansion which occurred
shunted the economy on to a track along which it could not
proceed very far. 'Development' then becomes prejudicial
in the long run. As Phyllis Deane explained in the case
of Egypt, (60)

> The economy began to grow ... on the strength of its
> exports. But it was advancing into a blind alley....
> When export markets collapsed and terms of trade turned
> against primary producers in the twentieth century
> Egyptian incomes lost ground almost as rapidly as they
> had gained it.

There was not simply a retardation of the economy, which
manifested itself when the growth of the export sector
petered out, but its deformation as an organic entity.
Very aptly Ruth C.Young stated: 'Economists ... have
oversimplified the nature of the problem by talking only
of levels of development, and ignoring the fact that some
nations not only lack development but are locked into a
stagnant state where development is impossible.' (61)
This condition of stagnation should not be taken to mean
an investment pattern which by hindsight is found to be
lacking in growth propensities, implying that a different
choice would have had other results. The export oriented
investment pattern which is now acknowledged to have led
into a blind alley cannot be abstracted from the nature of
the dominant class whose interests the export economy
served.

The underdeveloped nature of the export economies is
presumed to lie in their lack of diversification and the
overwhelming export bias. 'Nearly all the British colonies', wrote H.A. de S.Gunasekera, were characterized by
'the investment of British capital in a narrow range of
plantation crops'. (62) Likewise Snodgrass: 'productive
activity' in them 'is heavily oriented towards supplying
a few primary commodities to the world market and consumption is largely made up of imported goods'. (63) The
externally derived instability, due to this narrow export
base, was apparently the basis of the early formulations
of the dependency concept. 'The colonies are "dependent
economies" in the sense that their money national incomes
are determined primarily by external events.... [Booms
and slumps] are forced on them from abroad and are not,
to any significant extent, the result of changes in local
investment decisions.' (64) In the perception of Myint,

while the developed economies generate their own trade cycle, the underdeveloped ones receive the fluctuations transmitted from abroad. Some others have regarded export orientation as a reflection of a country's colonial status. 'For the greater part of our period Ceylon was a British Colony.... A corollary of her colonial status was the dependence of her economic life on the world markets for her exports.' (65) 'For most of the period studied here [by Snodgrass] Ceylon was both an export economy and a colony.' (66)

'Lopsidedness' and 'imbalance', as also the extrovertness of the export economy, are of little explanatory significance. They are neither sufficient nor necessary conditions for underdevelopment. For example, lopsidedness and imbalance are not found in India and China but are at the same time a feature of developed economies such as New Zealand and Australia. With capitalism as a world system the susceptibility to fluctuations abroad (somewhat like the propagation effect of bank failures) is a feature of the developed economies as well. The source of their instability may even be vagaries in the supply and prices of the primary products of underdeveloped countries. Violent price swings originating abroad do not make the developed economies 'dependent' in any meaningful sense, any more than the sharp and uncontrolled escalation of oil prices in 1973 made them dependent economies of the Arab states.

A departure from the view of underdevelopment expressed in terms of its commercial attributes was attempted by Snodgrass. In Sri Lanka, a typical plantation economy, the growth problems were seen by him to be due to the static nature of its production technology rather than the predominance of the export sector and its susceptibility to exogenous influence. (67)

The particular nature of the product specialization, however, is not the critical characteristic of Ceylon's economy.... Rather what is fundamental is the basic nature of the plantation system which underwent relatively little modification as it shifted its attentions from one crop to another.

The emphasis is apparently on low productivity. But the discussion of this question (in a chapter called The Structure and Dynamics of the Classical Economy) deviates from his promising beginning. For what he seeks to demonstrate is the lack of linkages ('intersectoral flows') between the plantations and the rest of the economy rather than the nature of the plantations as a system of production. 'The estates depended on the village neither for productive inputs nor for end products', and the plantation surpluses were not available for investment 'in other

parts of Ceylon's economy'. More explicitly, 'The peasant
sector ... received little direct stimulus from the growth
of the modern sector. Its traditional patterns of resource allocation, technology, and commercial structure
were relatively little altered by the rise of the estates.' (68) Snodgrass then concludes, 'This is the fatal
flaw of economic growth within the classical export economy model: the "spread effects" of modern sector growth to
the traditional sector are very slight'. (69) The notion
of dualism, according to which the plantations are a developed sector, presumably has in it also elements of the
surplus leakage model which we shall discuss later.
    Pursuing this line Snodgrass refers to the enclave
nature of the export economy, with 'important consequences
for its working and capacity for growth', foreign ownership and management - including financing by British banks
and agency houses, control of the import-export trade by
the British, a dependence on imported inputs and on
foreign, especially British markets. (70) This interpretation, while factually correct, fails to locate underdevelopment in the 'basic nature of the plantation system'.
The weakness of the plantations as a system of production
is readily seen in the fact that indigenous ownership per
se would not have improved its growth potential, if the
indigenous owners had related themselves to the productive
process in the same way as the British investors. A case
in point is the economy of Peru in the nineteenth century,
based overwhelmingly on guano production - an extractive
form of activity but the source of enormous profits.
Migrant Chinese labour was employed at the lowest possible
wages and subjected to harrowing cruelties. Though largely in Peruvian hands from 1851, the profits generated had
no impact on the economy. (71) On the other hand, British
capital whose enclave character Snodgrass emphasizes was
in certain situations not lacking in growth propensities.
In Britain it carried out an industrial revolution and in
the regions of new settlement (and to a lesser degree in
the settler colonies) it was an 'engine of growth'. The
growth impact of the infrastructure which arose from the
export economy also varied in different situations. It
was in the nonsettler colonies that such capital had a
negative dynamic and generated underdevelopment. To com-
prehend these differences, one needs to base the analysis
on the character of the dominant class and the organic
nature of the capital which it represented or controlled
- merchant capital or productive capital. Snodgrass, as
in standard presentations of underdevelopment, abstracts
from the specific types of capital.
    As the product of European capital, enterprise and

management, the plantations are assumed to have been not
merely a modern sector but also one embodying the capitalist form of production. Such a categorization pre-empts
an inquiry into the nature of the plantation system and
leads one to search for the causes of underdevelopment in
the peasant sector. The next step in this conventional
model is to pose the problem of underdevelopment in terms
of the failure of the plantation system to spread its supposed dynamism to the peasant sector. In following this
line of thought Snodgrass runs into a difficulty. He
notes that plantation production is 'relatively labour
intensive' (as in the peasant sector) (72) and attempts
to reconcile this obvious fact with the hypothesis about
the modernity of the plantations by asserting that they
were 'specialised [and] capital-using'. To avoid the implication of a high labour productivity, he then refers
ambivalently to 'large-scale factory-style operations of
the estates using massive forces of Indian labour specially imported for the purpose'. He finally speaks of an
'estate revolution ... typical of the profound economic
transformations wrought ... by the rapid expansion of
international trade during the 19th century'. There is
both ambivalence and confusion. This revolution created
'on a substantial scale the chief characteristics of a
modern economy ... with a capitalized and technologically
advanced but highly labour-and-land intensive system'.
(73) 'The effect of the coffee revolution on the economy
was electric.' (74) I.H. van den Driesen is the historian
of Sri Lanka's coffee era, on whom Snodgrass relies: 'new
modes of economic behaviour [were brought in] and a host
of concepts foreign to the prevalent economic system';
with the establishment of the coffee plantations, 'capitalism had arrived'. (75) When one studies only a single
phase or aspect of a historical process, shutting out an
extended view both in space and in time, the novel elements in that one phase are likely to be magnified far
beyond their true proportions; in fact not merely magnified but distorted.

    The notion that the plantations were a modern/de-
veloped/capitalist sector (whose dynamism failed to
spread) implies, among other things, that underdevelopment
is an original condition anterior and unrelated to the
structure of metropolis-colony relations. This is to say,
the foreign investors (and therefore colonialism as the
framework in which they operated) brought about a partial
development of the economy - limited to one segment of it.
A counter-hypothesis which I shall explore relates to the
possibility that the production process in the 'modern'
sector, i.e., the plantations, had no dynamism. If the

relevant attribute of dynamism is taken to be the degree
of capital intensity, and therefore the level of technology and of labour productivity, rather than the rate of
dividends, or foreign exchange earnings (i.e. looking at
the conditions of production and not the conditions of
exchange), the plantation-based export sector (excepting
for sugar cane) was little different from the rest of the
underdeveloped economy, and it differed profoundly from
the production process in the developed economies whether
in industry or in agriculture. The export economy expanded on the basis of a static technology, through an enlarged commitment of resources - essentially land and
labour. The division of labour and the improvement in
skills were minimal. The 'specialization' of the plantation system meant virtually monoculture, or the absence of
diversification - the production of one or a few crops
instead of many.

These issues are mentioned only as a preview of a
fuller discussion later on the technology of plantation
production, its structure of labour relations and its
surplus generating potential. More generally, I shall
locate underdevelopment in the character and interests of
the dominant classes and the wider framework of imperialist relations, within which investment and entrepreneurial
decisions were made. It may be briefly noted here that
the control of the plantation economy by merchant capital
was linked to the growth of absentee ownership. In the
coffee-tea transition in Sri Lanka, with the displacement
of the proprietary planters and partnerships by corporate
enterprises, financed by capital markets abroad, the
interests of merchant capital and productive capital
become sharply differentiated. While serving as the agent
of productive capital, merchant capital appropriated large
sums as trading profits and commissions - a price which
productive capital paid for operating on an absentee
basis. The enhanced role of merchant capital, whose substantive interest was trade and not production, gave a
distinctive character to the plantations and to the economy as a whole. Merchant capital, though not having a proprietary involvement in plantations, exercised the dominant role in the colonial export economy, conditioning the
pattern of investment and surplus utilization.

The notion of 'dualism' which underlies Snodgrass's exposition of underdevelopment is also implicit in Myrdal's
'weak spread effects'; the export sector absorbed growth
impulses originating in the metropolis but failed to dif-
fuse these impulses to the rest of the economy. The expansionary momentum of international trade and shipping
does not usually spread beyond the 'immediate surroundings

of a port'. (76) The productive facilities of the underdeveloped countries, 'which were so largely a result of
foreign investment', wrote H.W.Singer, 'never became a
part of ... *[the]* internal economic structure ... except
in the purely geographical and physical sense'. (77)
These facilities were protrusions from the metropolitan
economy. For example, the American owned sugar mills in
Cuba, explained V.P.Timoshenko and B.C.Swerling, are
'located frequently near the coast, served by their own
sub-ports, operating self-contained transportation systems, importing directly most of their supply needs (sometimes even the labour supply) and distributing dividends
to non-resident stockholders'. (78) In this view the
problem is a lack of linkages, resulting in a failure of
the non-plantation sector to 'upgrade its production
organisation and technology to conform with that of the
plantations'. A spatially, or sectorally, limited development of the economy which the model implies is contrasted by another writer with the extent of the changes
that occurred in the regions of white settlement, e.g.
Australia and New Zealand, where 'the indigenous economy
did not survive the introduction of the capitalist economy'. (79)

The lack of 'spread effects', though appealing in its
simplicity, like the clichéd trickle-down effect which
refuses to trickle, explains nothing. There is no reason
why 'intersectoral flows' or 'linkages', even if they
exist, should have a transformative effect on the rest of
the underdeveloped economy. The slave-supplying states of
West Africa were linked with the cotton plantations of the
southern USA, and the plantation South was linked with the
industrial North, just as were the plantation economies of
Asia with the industrialized West (in fact, the periphery
and the centre). The development impact of the linkages
was, however, a one-way street. It was felt beneficially
in the cotton region of the southern USA rather than in
West Africa, in the industrial North rather than in the
cotton South, and in the centre rather than in the periphery. Instead of a levelling up process, there emerged a
hierarchy of production modes with a progressively widening gulf.

From the explanation of underdevelopment in terms of
'weak spread effects' which Myrdal shares with some
others, he proceeds to the more positive concept of the
'backwash effects', which involves a 'strengthening *[of]*
all the forces in the markets which anyhow were working
towards internal and international inequalities'. (80) A
possibility of this kind was recognized by H.J.Habbakkuk:
'In principle, the rapid growth of one area is capable of

inhibiting as well as stimulating growth in less developed regions.' (81) The impoverishment of the weak, whenever contact occurs with the outside world, is presented as a kind of general law. Historical situations seem to confirm this view. In India partial isolation from world trade during the first and second world wars was a fillip to industrial growth, but with the resumption of metropolitan links the forces of underdevelopment revived. The ebb and flow in the fortunes of the Indian capitalist class were an expression of this tendency. During the Great Depression, 1929-34, it had again greater access to the domestic market, and several industries developed including sugar, cement, metals and iron and steel. (82) The Depression was also a stimulus to Asia's regional trade in a wide range of low-priced goods - textiles from Japan, India and Hong Kong and intermediate and capital goods such as cement and galvanized iron. As G.C.Allen and A.G.Donnithorne wrote, 'The Western entrepreneur for the first time was thrown on the defensive.' (83) In Southeast Asia European import agencies and commercial firms tended to be displaced by Chinese and Indian traders.

A conscious policy of isolation from world trade is feasible only in the absence of a politically powerful class whose fortunes are linked with commerce or by the existence of a state capable of subordinating purely trading interests to those of production capital. In Japan, isolation as part of its development strategy occurred within a specific political context. After the commercial treaties of 1856 and 1866 had opened the country freely to foreign trade, the competition of imports dealt a crippling blow to domestic manufactures. A price inflation, resulting from a chronic trade deficit and a drain of bullion, eroded the incomes of the Samurai and made them rebel against the government. A spate of peasant uprising also endangered the political prospects of the Meiji rulers. To check the opposition that was building up, the Meiji rulers saw their only option in the creation of a viable industrial structure. (84) However, their policy at this stage, of controlled withdrawal from world trade, operated mainly through its impact on the trading class. The trading patterns and structures that developed retarded the growth of the trading class while giving it a purely domestic orientation.

Trade and capital flows have not invariably led to backwash effects in countries at relatively low levels of development. The export of capital in the nineteenth century, with an expanding network of multilateral trade, was an 'engine of growth' in some areas of the world. The

dynamic effects of specialization and trade were felt in
the USA, and the white dominions, especially Australia,
New Zealand and Canada. British capital in their case was
the basis of an industrial revolution, giving international investment its 'brilliant record and general reputation'. (85) Productivity and income levels caught up with
and, in some instances, surpassed those in the countries
from which their capital was initially derived. As W.K.
Hancock said, by borrowing from Holland in the eighteenth
century, England did not make herself a dependency, nor
did the USA in the nineteenth century. 'But in the
history of China or Persia or Turkey, foreign investment
makes a very different picture and a gloomy one.' (86)
In a later chapter I shall refer to the contrasting cases
of Zambia and Rhodesia during the Second World War; cut
off from world trade, the latter (a settler colony) experienced an appreciable spurt of industrial growth whereas the former stagnated.
    The missing element in Myrdal's hypothesis is the
framework of political relations within which trade and
investment are conducted. Myint wrote that metropolitan
investment in underdeveloped countries 'frequently took
place ... under conditions which diverged from the ideal
competitive norm due to monopolistic concessions, zoning
of spheres of influence ... institutional rigidities and
monopsonistic elements in the labour market'. (87) It was
the political domination of these countries by their
metropolitan trading partner which restrained them from
taking countervailing measures. The political forces
underlying economic underdevelopment, omitted by Myrdal in
his exposition of the backwash effect, were alluded to in
an earlier work (published in 1956): 'Colonial governments directed from a metropolitan centre implied that
these people had no home government of their own interest.' (88) In the 'Asian Drama' (published more recently)
Myrdal is even less categorical about political forces.
'Between economies on such different levels there is a
natural mechanism tending toward greater inequality. But
the mechanism was continually supported by policy measures.' (89) These 'policy measures' were indeed the nub
of the problem, and I shall discuss them in later chapters.
    An analogous view to that of Myrdal, that interaction
of underdeveloped countries with the world economy necessarily begets a relation of inequality, is that the investment of foreign capital produces a satellitic condition. Through foreign head offices and boards of directors resident abroad, the locus of decisive entrepreneurship was externally situated. As outposts of the metro-

politan economy, the underdeveloped countries drew their
dynamism from that economy and fertilized it with the surpluses generated from the investments. The coffee plantations of Sri Lanka in the nineteenth century, John
Ferguson wrote, used to a 'a sort of incubator to which
the capitalists sent their eggs to be hatched and whence
a good many of them received from time to time an abundant
brood, leaving sometimes but their shells for our local
portion'. (90) The remission of the surplus to the
centres of financial control was not solely as dividends,
profits, trade commissions, etc. The financial reserves
of expatriate companies were held abroad. (91) Likewise
the foreign exchange assets of colonial governments were
invested mostly in government or municipal securities in
the metropolis. The expatriate nature of the dominant investors and their political control over the client territory disallowed production that was competitive with the
parent economy. Capital and enterprise under such a
framework entered a colony as the servant of the metropolitan economy rather than of the colony. The latter,
subjected to external restraints and distortions imposed
from outside, ceased to obey its own impulses to development but was made to respond to the requirements of the
metropolitan region. To express this lack of autonomy,
Jenks used the term 'semi-economies'. 'There is no
Egyptian, Argentinian, almost no Indian, certainly no
Cuban or Peruvian economic system. They form organic
portions of the British or American economic system.' (92)
     It is this lack of autonomy of the underdeveloped eco-
nomies which has given rise to the concept of a dependent
bourgeoisie and to the related expression 'dependent capitalism'. However, when applied to a class, 'dependency'
is a more complex situation than the term implies. Capitalism as an international phenomenon involves the interdependence of nations and also of classes on a world
scale. An asymmetry in this interdependence creates
dominant-dependent relations, based on a monopoly of resources by an expatriate commercial or industrial class;
the resources are principally markets and technology.
These dependent relations are neither wholly antagonistic
nor complementary. There is an interaction of opposites,
embodying both antagonistic and complementary relations.
The predominance of the former gives rise to a 'national
bourgeoisie' and of the latter to a 'compradore bourgeoisie'. The limited options open to the 'compradore bourgeoisie' and the benefit it derives from the dependent relation make it unable or unwilling to attempt to overcome
its dependency. It acquiesces in its dependent relation,
regardless of the fact that such a relation hampers the

transition to capitalism and the growth of productive
forces.

The effects of the asymmetry in the interdependence of
nations and of classes on a world scale are incorporated
in the so-called surplus leakage model, which emphasizes
the barriers to development imposed by metropolitan trade
and investment. Surplus transfers as the expression of
colonial exploitation had an earlier ancestry in the
'drain theory', vigorously expounded by Romesh Dutt, which
attributed India's impoverishment to regular financial
transfers to Britain, as 'home charges', profits and dividend payments, and interest on its external debt. The
recent models of surplus transfer based on 'unequal exchange' set out the resource loss more sharply by focusing
on commodity prices and the terms of trade. The policy
implication of this model is the need for a 'resource
transfer' to underdeveloped countries through an expansion
in foreign aid and loans, to enhance their bargaining
power in the world market. Various panaceas, such as the
Common Fund, and indexation of the prices of raw material
exports to the prices of industrial goods, have been proposed for a redivision of financial benefits from external
trade and investment.

Projecting the image of the robber baron, the model implies a constant diminution in productive capacity, making
the growth of productive forces on a world scale a zero-
sum game. It fails to see surplus transfers as part of a
process of surplus generation through an expansion in production in the territory whose surplus is transferred.
The outflow of surpluses was contingent upon an inflow of
capital (or a plough-back of current profits) to finance
an expansion in productive capacity - for example in the
case of the plantations in Sri Lanka there was a 4-5 year
period before dividends were declared. What a theory of
underdevelopment must perforce explain is why the surplus
generated from the initial investments was not recycled
often or long enough to increase the total volume of surplus generated: whether by revolutionizing production
techniques ('deepening' the existing investment) or by a
continued 'widening' of capital - ultimately incorporating
new branches of production. As Norman Girvan asked, (93)

> If the object of imperial capital is to extract a sur-
> plus from the country as such, and assuming that other
> possible investment opportunities exist ... why is the
> surplus not invested in these other sectors after
> having made a killing in the mineral [or plantation-
> cum-mining] sector?

Underdeveloped countries in the past have amassed large
surpluses, not all of which were transferred abroad.   A

portion of them was disbursed internally without the prospect of an economic breakthrough. The indigenous bourgeoisie of these countries failed to capitalize the surplus which accrued to itself nor was it concerned about
the surpluses that went out. The disposition of this
class was reflected in the minor role it played in the
struggles against imperialism; the Indian bourgeoisie
which was developing an industrial base was a possible
exception. A notable attempt to impound the surplus was
that of the settler bourgeoisie of Rhodesia, led by Sir
Roy Welensky, which took measures to terminate the payment
of royalties on the Rhodesian copper mines to the British
South Africa Company whose shareholders were abroad. As
Myrdal once said, were it not for exchange controls far
more of the current surplus of underdeveloped countries
would be spent abroad by its indigenous owners. The
greater part of the revenue of OPEC is recycled in the industrialized countries, directly or else as payment for
imports. The surplus transfer, causing what the model regards as a lack of capital, is no more the determining
element in the stagnation of productive forces than is the
appropriation of the surplus by feudal lords the reason
for the non-emergence of capitalism. To presume that had
the surplus been retained the final outcome would have
been different is to analytically separate surplus transfers from the mode of production which generates the surplus.

Surplus transfers in their various forms express the
problem of underdevelopment at the level of the market;
they explain what happens to a commodity once it is produced and brought to the market, not the conditions of
production. The surplus transfer models, while directing
attention exclusively to the external dimension of centre-
periphery relations, also fail to express the changing
nature of the centre's involvement in the periphery and,
correspondingly, of the surplus extraction process in its
various forms: booty or tribute, outright commercial
profits and rentier incomes, and surpluses arising from
production capital of varying organic composition. Like
the drain theory, the surplus transfer model is trapped in
a framework of financial and commercial relations, obscuring the forces which underlie the respective modes of
production in the centre and the periphery. The conditions of production, inclusive of the structure of internal class relations which support the world division of
labour, are left in splendid inviolability; and likewise
the in-built and systemic obstacles to a qualitatively
different utilization of economic surpluses. By excluding
from purview the prevailing class structure and the fac-

tors both external and internal influencing the transformation of that structure, the surplus transfer models have
suffered from the lack of a broad theory of history to explain the crucial changes that occurred in the already developed economies or in those in which a forward movement
is tending to occur. Surplus transfer models, and cognate
concepts such as dependency, have naturally appealed to
liberal developmentalists who are concerned with de-empha-
sizing the importance of class relations as a transformative factor.

More fundamentally the surplus transfer models give a
distorted view of the rise of capitalism, by the significance they attach to a pre-existing saving fund. In
England, the transition to capitalism was accomplished
long before the colonial export economies of Asia and
Africa had created a reverse flow of surpluses. What was
achieved thereafter was the expansion of capitalism's productive forces amidst a growing rivalry for raw materials
and markets. In Germany, the USA and other white dominions, and to some extent in Japan, the rise of capitalism
did not require extensive interaction with a periphery.
The German colonial empire was of no significance as
sources of raw materials or as markets for German manufactured goods. Her colonial trade in 1913 represented only
½ per cent of Germany's total trade; furthermore, Germany
did not monopolize the trade of her colonies. (94) Some
underdeveloped countries, including Taiwan, South Korea
and Singapore, have very recently come close to transforming their economies, while transferring surpluses to
various metropolitan centres. Spain, Portugal and the
Netherlands were among the earliest colonial powers but
only belatedly developed the capitalist mode of production.

A 'previous accumulation of capital' was a notion advanced by Adam Smith, but later reformulated by Marx to
rid it of its circular reasoning. The development of
capitalism does not depend upon an original 'stockpiling
of capital'. 'The so-called primitive accumulation ... is
nothing else than the historical process of divorcing the
producer from the means of production.' (95) The transformation of wealth (money or commodities) into capital
requires a capital-wage labour relation which continually
extends and reproduces itself. Capitalism had an internal
dynamic which was far more important to its functioning
than the plunder of the periphery. As Robert Brenner observed, the source of its contradiction was this in-built
mechanism of surplus generation. (96)

Capitalism differs from all pre-capitalist modes of
production in its *systematic* tendency to unprecedented,

though neither continuous nor unlimited economic development - in particular through the expansion of what
might be called (after Marx's terminology) relative as
opposed to absolute surplus labour.

Underdevelopment, then, is not a question of degree or
scale, as is suggested by the evolutionary model to which
I earlier referred, nor could it be explained solely in
terms of the external articulation of a country, giving
rise to dominant-dependent relations. The problem of
underdevelopment relates fundamentally to the barriers to
the growth of productive forces which the prevailing production relations constitute. The external articulation
of an underdeveloped economy, or its dependency, is significant not in itself but in its effects on the internal
class structure. Internal class structures through which
the external influences mediate are far more difficult to
characterize and explain than the external influences
themselves. All the same, these analytical difficulties
must be overcome because the problem of underdevelopment
has to be subsumed under the general question of the
failure of countries to effect the transition to the capitalist mode of production; specifically, what has to be
probed is the continued dominance of merchant capital and
of usurer and landlord capital over extensive segments of
their economy. One of my concerns in this book is to explain the role of merchant capital in the plantation economies; the peasant sector is not dealt with, though the
same concepts and categories of analysis are also applicable to its failure to develop along capitalist lines.

Underdevelopment was also a total phenomenon. It was
not confined to peasant agriculture in contrast to the
plantations nor confined to the realm of economic activities alone. As Adam Curle observed, an underdeveloped
society is not merely an underdeveloped economy but is
literally an underdeveloped society, and its study should
include the non-economic components - social, political
and administrative. (97) When it was advantageous to do
so, metropolitan interests allied themselves with elements
in the indigenous society that were 'archaic, conservative
and backward'. Sometimes privileged classes were created
who 'were, by and large, primarily interested in preserving the social and economic status quo under which
they were privileged'. (98) Under the moulding pressure
of metropolitan influences there grew up a bureaucracy and
a class who were known for their loyalty and conformity to
metropolitan values and interests. A 'popular type of
native was the educated emulator of his rulers, the adept
pupil who learned well from his masters in the civil
service and became "whiter than the whites"'. (99) This

Anglomania, as Amaury de Reincourt said of colonial society in India, produced generations of people who 'found
themselves rootless, out of touch with their own country
and its enduring culture, yet unable to compete with the
British in their own language and their own techniques'.
(100) Thus an aspect of the underdevelopment of these
societies was the entrenchment of retrogade social structures and ideologies. Various colonial regimes offer excellent examples of this situation.

The efforts of local officials to emulate the white
rulers produced results which even the white rulers found
ridiculous. In Sri Lanka, a Government Agent in 1884
noted with dismay in his official diary the efforts of
some Sinhala officials to conform to a Western style of
dress. (101)

> The Korales of Kadawat and Meda Korales met me in this
> village [Bambarabotuwa] in black coats and black hats.
> ... Both these young men have been educated at the
> Academy and cannot bring themselves to wear costume
> which suits them so much better and would I think bring
> them nearer to the people over whom they are placed.

The Governor minuted in the AGA's diary: 'They should be
ridiculed and scolded.' On another occasion when the
Agent visited a rural hamlet, the Aracci (the village
headman) came to meet him in a black frock coat and a
Kandyan hat. 'The coat he was immensely proud of for he
had put it over the usual Kandyan dress.' (102) The
Governor minuted, 'I hope you ridiculed his absurdity.'
(103) An Assistant Agent in Sri Lanka wrote in 1895 how
'agitated' the chiefs are 'over the Ball to be given in
honour of the departing Governor. They are all anxious
to do what they can to show their respect to H.E. [His
Excellency] ... though they don't dance.... Besides,
their full dress is out of place at Colombo'. (104) A not
insignificant fraction of the Kandyan aristocracy rolled
down a Gadarene slope of degeneracy and became insensi-
tized to the interests of the mass of the indigenous society. (105)

In Vietnam, French rule promoted feudalism through a
new class of large landowners who 'functioned on several
levels as an instrument of French rule'. (106) They advanced financially by landlordism and usury and by the
sale of rice to the French exporters in Saigon. They were
lured by the prospect of French citizenship, jobs in the
administration and membership of the Colonial Council,
whose functions included the approval of land grants exceeding 25 hectares. Very few Vietnamese were eventually
made French citizens, but they 'came to depend on the
French presence as a guarantor of their wealth and securi-

ty'. (107) In the Portuguese colonies in Africa, the prospect of Portuguese citizenship was held out to those who
became assimilados by adopting the Portuguese language,
religion, habits and culture.
  In China, when the Taipings failed to overthrow the
Manchu dynasty (which represented the whole system of
privilege and corruption in Chinese society) the foreign
powers after exacting concessions from the prostrated
Manchu regime became its protectors. In Taiwan, the
Japanese made far-reaching improvements in agriculture
with a view to making the country a granary of Japan -
even overcoming by force the conservatism of the peasants.
Yet, they showed a 'strong reluctance to interfere more
than necessary in village affairs'. (108) They retained
the traditional social structure, whose dominant element
was the ta-tsu, a class of hereditary landowners. In
Malaysia, the pax Britannica which ended the feuds among
Malay chiefs safeguarded their political authority and
their revenues. They were awarded regular incomes and accorded a 'protective social umbrella' which enhanced their
position in the feudal hierarchy. The court life of the
Malay aristocracy 'became in some ways more splendid than
... before'. (109) The aristocracy at the same time profited from the economic expansion of the country, investing
its wealth in the rubber and the tin-mining companies.
'The more effective sanctions now open to British-support-
ed sultans produced an authoritarian form of religious administration much beyond anything known to the [Malay]
peninsula'. (110)
    The sultans, royalty, and the traditional elite would
    have nothing of democracy and equal rights. ... They
    took their monthly pensions and said: 'Ordinary Malays
    mustn't meddle in politics, because the politics of the
    state and its people are in the hands of the sultan and
    the traditional elite, who must be given complete
    loyalty. No Malay can betray his Raja.' (111)
The submissiveness of the Malays towards the aristocracy,
whose moral and social authority was strengthened, extended to their acceptance of the colonial power structure
in toto. In northern Nigeria, where the administration
was based on 'indirect' rule as in Malaysia, the traditional social structure was strengthened, with the feudal
class as its apex. The British took refuge in the sanctity of this class. The Fulani rulers remained 'remarkably
loyal' to the British; when the Satiru uprising was
quelled, the Emirs themselves took reprisals against their
dissident colleagues. (112)
  As a general rule the rulers did not, in the colonial
territories, wholly succeed in detaching the dominant in-

digenous class from the stream of national interests. A
faction of this class became critical of colonial domination; influenced partly by the rationalistic spirit of
European culture and its democratic conceptions and
values, it organized political reform movements and provided an ideological basis to popular agitation. This
progressive faction was ahead of its time, developing and
asserting itself in a preindustrial economy - it was not
typical of the colonial intelligentsia. When, however,
the pressures of 'reactive nationalism' were removed by
the transfer of political power, they relaxed their anti-
colonial fervour and showed a disinclination for radical
changes affecting the foreign interests. In some of the
underdeveloped countries in their post-independence phase,
economic circumstances compelled the ruling class to dismantle strictly overt colonial relationships: for example
in Sri Lanka, the take-over of American oil distributing
firms, the nationalization of insurance, the restrictions
placed on foreign banks, and the development of trade relations with countries outside the traditional Western
bloc. But these measures do not indicate a real repudiation of metropolitan links. In this stage of late capitalism, production capital flows to the periphery, without
the mediation of merchant firms, under the aegis of the
multinationals. There is now a revival of the symbiotic
relation (economic rather than political in form) between
the former colonial interests and the dominant indigenous
class effectively installed in power.

Part one

Investment patterns in the settler and nonsettler situations

2   Economic underdevelopment and the settler/nonsettler dichotomy

The diverse results of foreign capital and enterprise, as reflected in the scale and character of the economic expansion that took place, can be studied in terms of (1) the territories dominated by expatriate investors (mostly the plantation or the plantation-cum-mining economies), (2) the regions of 'new settlement' which were inhabited overwhelmingly by European settlers (e.g. Canada, the USA and Australia), and (3) the settler colonies, which a European minority came to regard as their permanent home (e.g. South Africa, Kenya, Rhodesia, and the lands of the Maghreb). In the regions of new settlement which became developed economies, and to a lesser extent in the settler colonies, the progressive effects of foreign enterprise seem to be connected with the fact that such enterprise involved the migration of the capitalist and often the transfer of his national allegiance. Successive streams of settlers became assimilated with the earlier immigrants to form a local community.

The Englishman who went to America, or to Australia, was soon absorbed, and he or his family ceased to be foreign [just as] the Dutchman or Frenchman who came to reside in Tudor England became Englishmen in due course - their children grew up in English schools (such as there were), inter-married, and lost their foreign allegiance. (1)

The reorientation of the immigrants' economic interests and, to some extent, of even their cultural identity, was also significant politically. The countries of new settlement freed themselves relatively early from the metropolis or they became dominions with rights equal to those of the metropolitan country. Regulations or restraints by the metropolitan country were not compatible with the settler status of its European communities. In colonial America the frustrations of the trading and planter capitalists arising from this incompatibility erupted in the War of Independence, but there always existed in varying degrees tensions and conflicts between the settler communities and the metropolitan country - as in South Africa, Kenya, Rhodesia and Algeria.   These metropolis-colony differences were more acrimonious in countries where the settlers included a European working class;   in the expatriate colonies - e.g. India, Sri Lanka and Malaysia - such a class was totally absent except as 'transient seamen and soldiers'.   The consider-able degree of political authority which a European settler class generally acquired - either by violent or by constitutional means - paved the way for more viable eco-nomic structures than in the nonsettler colonies;   this was especially reflected in the growth of manufacturing industry.

The expatriate dominated or nonsettler economies, on the other hand, were characterized by the limited entre-preneurial interests of the foreign investors, who virtu-ally confined themselves to trade, plantation crops and minerals.   There was a lack of dynamism in their staples base, which failed to transform itself along lines famil-iar in the settler colonies and a fortiori in the regions of white settlement.   Activities which were competitive with those in the metropolitan centres, including produc-tion for the domestic market, were as a rule excluded. Apart from the decade before the First World War when British investment created jute mills and engineering works in India, the expatriate investors had practically no hand in colonial industries.   For example, in 1915 the relative positions of British and non-British enterprises in India's large-scale manufacturing industries were such that cotton spinning and weaving, printing presses, rice mills and oil mills were entirely or overwhelmingly Indian;   and engineering workshops and iron and brass foundries, sugar, woollen mills and carpet manufacturing enterprises were British and Indian in more or less even proportions. (2)

As predominantly producers of raw materials and of certain foods and beverages, the nonsettler colonies es-tablished a strong complementarity with the metropolitan economy, becoming constituent but subordinate parts of that economy.   The development of export production, while causing a reorientation of their economy away from the domestic market, failed to bring about a structural change.   Export production did not of itself signify a higher stage of development nor did it, in the absence of a diversified production pattern, create vertical and horizontal linkages within the domestic economy, with a

'reciprocal generation of expanding industries'. An
export surplus, in whatever way it is derived, enables an
economy to import capital goods and technical and professional skills, so that in this sense the export sector was
the equivalent of a capital goods sector and therefore the
basis for the growth of secondary industries. But in
these countries, the development potential of the original
staples base lay completely unrealized.

1   THE SETTLER/NONSETTLER TYPOLOGY

In underdeveloped countries, with the partial exception of
the settler colonies, foreign investment was carried out
by Westerners who were not colonizers in the real sense.
The 'Colonies proper', wrote Engels, 'are those [like
Canada, the Cape, Australia] which were occupied by a
European population, as distinguished from those inhabited
by a native population [India, Algeria, the Dutch, Portuguese and Spanish possessions]'. (3) The term 'colony',
observed L.B.Clarence, does not apply to territories dominated by nonsettler investors. '"Colony" is a term which
sometimes grates on the ear, as applied to a tropical dependency in which ... the European immigrants [are no]
more than a drop in the bucket compared with the sons of
the soil.' (4) These countries, said J.S.Furnivall, were
colonized by capital rather than with men. (5) The
Europeans here were merely sojourners; their numbers were
relatively small and 'they seldom set their roots in the
area'. (6) 'A large section of British capitalists ...
did not even live in India. The majority of the British
investors in India ... lived in Britain.' (7)
    The British merchants and planters in Sri Lanka be-
longed to this category. As stated in a contemporary account, they were 'men for the most part who hoped to get
rich quickly, and to return to England with a fortune'.
(8) The transient interest of individual Britishers was
also noted by J.Ferguson. (9)

    In Ceylon a generation among European colonists has
    usually been considered not to exceed 10 years - not at
    all on account of mortality, for [the] hills of Ceylon
    have the perfection of a healthy climate, but from the
    constant changes in the element of the European com-
    munity - the coming and going of which in the past has
    made such a distinct change in the broad elements of
    society every 10 or certainly every 15 years.
A Sri Lanka writer makes it clearer: (10)
    The Englishman lived here for twenty or thirty years -
    as an administrator, or to plant his tea, or to carry

on his trade. But he always remained an Englishman,
and England was always his home. He went home on
leave, his children went home to school [and] when he
retired he went home to die.

The Europeans, that is to say, did not transfer their
allegiance to these lands or acquire a personal stake in
them. Their business interests were mainly an extension
of those of the metropolitan country, and limited both in
their range and time horizon. They confined themselves to
the administration, to plantations and to business, where
they held the top positions. Their stay, necessarily
short, was connected with the prospect of day-to-day gain.
This short-lived sojourn - tantamount to a posting abroad
- conditioned the social attitudes and the internal structure of the European community in the nonsettler colonies.
Demarcated by their incomes and by the colour of their
skin, they lived in small encapsulated groups. The sense
of exile and alienation was tempered by bodily comforts,
such as 'the indulgence available through the existence of
low-paid domestic service', and the satisfaction gained
from 'membership of the top status group in ... [a] multi-
racial society'. (11) Pomp and formality marked their
public behaviour and their private social life, imitative
of the aristocracy in England. They entertained in their
spacious homes or in exclusive clubs. 'Tennis, bridge and
billiards were played, whiskey was drunk, and gossip and a
certain amount of quiet business took place. These clubs
were uncompromisingly British in habits and atmosphere,
once again seeking to create an illusion of home.' (12)
Though their small numbers may have encouraged social cohesiveness, the transient nature of their interests was a
destabilizing element. (13) Only a few Europeans grew up
in these colonies; there was a preponderance of males, a
shortage of unmarried women and the virtual absence of
children of school-going age.

Whereas the nonsettler colonies were predominantly
primary-product based export economies (or, as in India,
had an export sector dominated by foreign capital), the
settler colonies had more varied and complex socio-economic structures. These colonies differed from one another
in regard to the size and composition of the settler population; for example, in Central and East Africa, European
working-class elements were excluded, but they appeared in
South Africa and the French colonies of the Maghreb. The
settler colonies were themselves underdeveloped, yet they
exhibited a different pattern of investment and their economic structures were far more viable than those in the
nonsettler colonies. Demographically and socially, too,
the Europeans in the settler colonies (and a fortiori

those in the regions of new settlement) were different
from those in the nonsettler colonies. They were relatively numerous and established a permanent stake in their
country of residence. This commitment of settler investors to the host country had economic and political implications which I shall discuss in later chapters. The
settlers sought to develop an economy that was independent
of the metropolis and in competition with it while entirely repudiating the indigenous interests.

There are, however, three territories which do not
closely fit this settler/nonsettler typology: viz. the
Belgian Congo, Indonesia and Indochina. The pattern of
economic development in the Belgian Congo and Indochina
did not conform with their largely nonsettler status;
their economic structures somewhat resembled those of the
settler colonies. On the other hand, Indonesia was demographically and socially more like a settler colony than
the Belgian Congo and Indochina, but its pattern of economic development was very much nonsettler in its orientation. In the case of the Belgian Congo the scale and
character of economic development was unusual for a largely nonsettler colony. Likewise Indochina which, though
demographically and socially even more of a nonsettler
colony than the Belgian Congo, exhibited an economic
pattern which in some respects resembled that of a settler
colony. These deviant cases will be discussed in some
detail in a later chapter. Here I shall examine the con-
flicting elements in the demographic and social character
of the white population in both Indonesia and Indochina
which make their position on the settler/nonsettler scale
difficult to locate.

Indonesia held a complex position in the settler/non-
settler typology. The Dutch settlers, inclusive of
Eurasians, were few compared with the Indonesians but were
greater in number than the Europeans in a typical nonsettler colony. The ratio of Europeans to the total population in 1920 was three and a half per 1,000; in India
at about this period the corresponding ratio of Europeans
(and Anglo Indians) was only seven-eighths per 1,000. In
Indonesia the 'relative numerical strength' of the Europeans was thus four times that in India, and twice that in
Indochina. Though the ratio of Europeans to the total
population had increased by 1930 to nearly four per 1,000,
the 'indigenization' of the Dutch was checked with the
influx after 1900 of a new type of migrant - the trekkers
or temporary sojourners. The cultural and social life of
the earlier Dutch settlers (blijvers) was swamped by the
newcomers whose life-style set the pace for the established Dutch community. The latter now developed a rigid

Dutch identity, withdrawing into a close community as the
British did from the outset in the nonsettler colonies.
The trekkers migrated to the Indies, usually with Dutch
wives, for a specific period, and went home on leave or
on retirement. 'Thus, they differed markedly from the
older, smaller group of Dutch blijvers (stayers), who
thought of the Indies as their home.' (14)

Despite this change in social outlook, which made the
Dutch community more clearly identified with the mother
country, a high proportion of the Dutch in Indonesia were
settlers. In 1930 nearly 70 per cent of them were born
locally. (15) They were employed at most levels of the
administration and engaged in a large range of economic
activities. These included the lower ranks of the public
service - the railway, tramways, and posts and telegraphs
- and junior supervisory jobs on the plantations. They
even worked as unskilled labour and as shop assistants.
(16) In contrast with the settler colonies, in Indonesia
there was a class of poor whites. Indonesia was even
looked on as an outlet for Holland's surplus population;
and the social and economic heterogeneity of the Dutch in
Indonesia was reflected in their political activity which
followed the lines of division in the Netherlands. There
was both a Social Democratic Party and a Liberal Party.
The presence of working-class Dutchmen encouraged political radicalism, and even fraternization with Indonesian
labour. The first trade union in Indonesia formed in 1908
by railway workers was composed of Europeans, Indo-Europe-
ans and Indonesians. A seminal figure in the Indies
Social Democratic Association, which later became the
Indonesian Communist Party, was a Dutchman employed in
Indonesia, and the ISDA's first meeting in 1914 was attended mostly by Dutch. (17) A situation such as this was
impossible in the nonsettler colonies. However, though
the Dutch in Indonesia, as indicated earlier, had some of
the features of a settler community, they made little
impact on the economy, unlike the European settlers in
other colonies. The Indonesian economy closely resembled
that of a nonsettler colony - e.g. India, Malaysia, Sri
Lanka; it was based on primary production for export to
the metropolitan countries and on a backward peasant
sector, and there was an almost complete lack of manufacturing industry.

Indochina occupies much more of a border position on
the settler/nonsettler scale than Indonesia. In 1937
there were about 42,000 Europeans out of a total population of 23 million, or a ratio of 0.18 per 1,000. They
included some non-whites having the status of Europeans,
and the real whites numbered only about 30,000. The

French residents in Indochina were mostly retired government officers, discharged military personnel, and missionaries. In the early 1940s over 10,000, or 20 per cent, of
those gainfully employed were army or navy personnel and
3,900, or 9 per cent, were 'functionaries'. The expatriate nature of the European community was also shown in its
demographic composition: there was a preponderance of
males; few Europeans were in the age group of 10-20
years, and about 70 per cent had been in the country for
less than sixteen years. There was, however, a skeleton
European settlement of about 11,000. Many of them had
completely adapted themselves to the country, having lived
there fifteen years or more, while some had even married
Indochinese women. There was also a sprinkling of career
women and students at Hanoi university. (18)

From the 1890s France encouraged settlement in Indochina but met with little response. Though there was a
distinct settler element, their small numbers cannot be
satisfactorily explained by geopolitical reasons, such as
the absence of population pressure in France or the
remoteness of Indochina. Perhaps the real reason was the
presence of the Chinese who were an 'exceedingly powerful
racial minority'. At the time of the French occupation,
they were more or less established in Indochina, and monopolized foreign trade. Later they owned about 80 per cent
of the rice mills and controlled the entire rice trade and
about half of the semi-wholesale trade in commodities such
as corn and salt. Shortly before the Second World War
there were about a million Chinese, a virtual 'state
within a state'. (19)

If we leave out these deviant cases which do not readily fit a settler/nonsettler model, the economic structures
that emerged in the underdeveloped countries seem to be
connected with the type of colony which they represented.
The relative economic viability of the settler colonies,
and the politico-economic impulses to their development,
will be explained in the succeeding three chapters. As a
prelude to that discussion I shall here refer to the perceptions of a few earlier writers and indicate in the
barest outline the developmental significance of the
settler/nonsettler distinction.

Countries with many settlers, both Europeans and alien
Asians, were regarded by J. Van Gelderen as being more
'intensely colonized' than those where expatriates predominated. (20) On this basis he distinguished colonialism in Indonesia from that in India. C.F.Remer made a
similar distinction between 'entrepreneurial' or 'direct'
investments and 'rentier' and portfolio investments or
government borrowings. Entrepreneurial investment, he

explained, 'almost always does bring the foreigner himself', whose residence in the country of investment enables him to play an 'active part' in his enterprise,
unlike the rentier, and to get a hold over the host economy and society. Remer therefore regarded entrepreneurial
investments and the physical presence of the foreigner, as
the 'mark of colonial status'. (21) In distinguishing between resident and nonresident capital, or between entrepreneur and rentier investments (which in our terminology
correspond to settler and nonsettler investments), both
Van Gelderen and Remer also emphasized the political implications of the two types of investment. Resident or
entrepreneurial investments result in foreign domination
and control.

Professor Heinz Arndt expressed the different implications for economic development of absentee and resident
capital, respectively, in terms of 'exploitative colonial
investment' and 'nation-building investment'. The former
- e.g. in colonial Africa, the Middle East, India and
Southeast Asia - was 'unaccompanied by any permanent emigration [of the investors]' and such investment 'concentrated on the exploitation of raw materials, and sometimes
[always!] cheap labour, for export to the mature lending
countries'. The latter 'nation-building investment' involved the migration of the investor as well - as in 'the
U.S., the white British Dominions and possibly parts of
Latin America'. (22) W.H.B.Court also mentioned 'colonies
of exploitation of the African type' and 'colonies of
settlement, Australia, New Zealand, Canada and South
Africa'; or 'colonisation d'exploitation' and 'colonisation de peuplement'. (23) Though these two groups of
countries can be distinguished by their different economic
structures and their politico-economic relations with the
metropolitan countries, there has been little or no recognition of their divergent patterns of entrepreneurship.
In one case, the locus of investment and decision making
was the country of investment, and in the other the metropolitan centre. To bring out fully the development implications of these two types of investment it is, however,
necessary to go beyond the polar opposites of the expatriate colonies and the regions of new settlement, and to
consider the settler colonies as well. These colonies
were of a hybrid character. They differed from the USA,
Canada, Australia, etc., which were composed wholly or
almost wholly of settlers, as well as from the nonsettler
colonies where expatriate investors predominated. The
white dominions outgrew their colonial status quite early
and became developed economies. The other imperial possessions continued as colonies until after the Second

World War, with persistently underdeveloped economies. Their centre-periphery relations were fundamentally different.

Among these imperial possessions the settler colonies had a pattern of economic development which differed in several respects from that of the nonsettler colonies. I can now elaborate on what I said earlier. First, the settler colonies underwent greater industrial and/or urban growth and established a diversified system of agriculture (including grain, livestock and fruit farming) like the advanced economies. Second, development was internally oriented with a corresponding reinvestment of profits which extended beyond the original lines of investment; a large volume of production was for local or regional markets. Third, settler communities replicated to some extent the socio-political structure of the metropolitan country. These communities had a far greater social heterogeneity than the expatriate communities and they usually included a class of workmen, artisans, small farmers and petty traders. Political activity, in many instances, was patterned on class lines, and labour unions were formed by the white workers. In Southern Rhodesia, European labour soon after the First World War resorted to strikes. Though white workers organized themselves on strictly racial lines, preventing competition from poorly paid Africans, their militancy in defence of their interests contrasted with the class solidarity of Europeans in the nonsettler colonies. (24) Fourth, the settlers exercised considerable political and administrative control over the disposition of local resources. The expropriation of peasant cultivators to secure their labour had no parallel in the nonsettler colonies. Finally, the settlers developed a sense of economic and cultural identity different from that of the parent societies, tending thereby to transform themselves into proto-nationalities.

The relative autonomy of the settlers and their greater involvement in the local economy and society were reflected in their often sharp conflicts with the mother country. The French colonies in the Maghreb, though closely integrated with France, were not without such conflicts. At the same time, the broad-based nature of the settlers' economic interests and their complete domination of the local society resulted in extensive repression of the indigenous community - by means of discriminatory land policies, racist attitudes and a gross neglect of indigenous welfare inclusive of health and education. A fundamental expression of these policies was the absence of an indigenous bourgeoisie in the settler colonies.

The significance for economic development of the set-

tler/nonsettler dichotomy will be elaborated in the next
chapter, where the contrasting developmental impact of
export staples will be explained. The discussion will
show the nonsettler colonies and the regions of new settlement to be polar opposites. The three succeeding chapters will discuss more specifically the economic, social
and political differences between the settler and the nonsettler colonies. But before embarking on this extensive
discussion, the question why the Europeans settled in some
countries and not in others needs to be dealt with.

2   FACTORS CONDITIONING EUROPEAN SETTLEMENT

The reluctance of Europeans to become domiciled in some
countries and not in others has been attributed to physical and cultural factors. Climatic considerations, said
L.B.Clarence, determined white settlement overseas. (25)
Arthur Lewis thought an inhibiting factor was the 'differences in race, religion, and in ways of living from the
[indigenous] people'. (26) Similar barriers to acculturation were emphasized by Louis Firth: 'Ethnic, linguistic, and religious differences will continue to divide
people, and the prejudices that go with them cannot
suddenly be wiped out by fiat.' (27) Health hazards were
also taken to be a deterrent to European settlement in the
tropics, and manual labour was thought to be too exhausting in this climate. A British administrator in Zambia
believed that 'Europeans were not able to retain their
vigour in the tropics'. (28) The International Congress
of Geographers in 1938 held that a tropical climate affected the special qualities of the Europeans - their
initiative, physical energy and moral standards. (29)   In
the American South where Negro slaves replaced 'white
servants' in agriculture, the saying was: 'Only black men
and mules can face the sun in July.'
    The white races, nevertheless, seem hardy and adaptable
enough, considering the numerous white settlements overseas. Though certain parts of the tropical world were
clearly unsuited for European settlement - e.g. French
Equatorial Africa, where debilitating diseases were rampant - this was not a universal impediment. While the
'regions of new settlement' generally had a climate similar to that of countries from which the Europeans migrated, climate was not crucial in their decision to
settle. European settlement took place in several tropical and subtropical areas - e.g. Rhodesia, Algeria, Indonesia and the Northern Territory of Australia.
    In Surinam, on the northern coast of South America,

there were European settlers from the first half of the
nineteenth century. (30) A Dutch physician, Dr Hostmaan,
who had practised there, wrote to the magazine 'De
Kolonist' in 1839 advocating state aided migration. The
prospects for white settlers in Surinam were also acknowledged by a Dutch Royal Commission in 1857. The early
settlers failed not because of the climate but because of
the wrong choice of land and their lack of agricultural
experience. The settlers were illiterate and of incon-
tinent habits. At the end of the nineteenth century migration was resumed, but by then the freed Negro slaves
and Indian settlers, some of whom were former indentured
labourers, were an economic force to reckon with. They
competed with the Dutch peasants as market gardeners and
dairymen. From 1940 when produce prices rose the prospects for the Dutch peasants improved; and they established themselves as a stable though marginal element
in Surinam's population - the children moved out of agriculture into professions or trade. Marriages increased in
this period between Europeans and well-educated coloureds
of white and Negro, or Chinese and Negro parents.
    This second phase of colonization was a complete suc-
cess. On the outskirts of Paramaribo 'the peasants had
found a satisfactory existence and they were healthy and
fit for labour in the warm climate.' (31) E.F.Verkade-
Cartier van Dissel, in an account of the settlements of
white peasants and farmers in a number of tropical countries, concluded that the climate and health conditions
were no longer an obstacle to the performance of heavy
work by the whites and that the success of colonization
depended on economic conditions. The countries referred
to included Surinam (which she visited), the Dutch island
of Saba in the West Indies, and Rhodesia and Queensland.
Likewise in Barbados the whites had worked for more than
a hundred years, and in Georgia they had been employed in
rice cultivation.
    In the tropical belt of Northern Australia black labour
was sought not because it was suitable but because it was
cheap. A lucrative traffic in kidnapped Polynesians was
carried out by merchants in Sydney to supply the sugar and
cotton planters in Queensland. Captain George Palmer, RN,
FRGS, in the anti-slavery tradition publicized the 'gross
abuse' of labour employed on the estates. He doubted the
necessity for black labour and thought the whites were
capable of work on the plantations. (32) The Australian
press exposed 'the pretence that these people [the blacks]
are alone suited to the climate of the extreme north'. It
explained, (33)
    the very same persons who advocate their introduction

and assist in it, are those who used every assertion to
get a station for European prisoners established at
Rockingham Bay, Cape York, or the Gulf of Carpentaria
... all far away north, and all intended as depots to
supply the labour market. Cheap work is the desideratum at the bottom of all.

Later sugar cultivation was based wholly on white labour;
and, as Dr Williams remarked, this did not lead to the
physical degeneration of the Australian worker but merely
to an increase in the cost of producing sugar - a cost
which Australia bore to remain a white man's country. (34)

The countries where the Europeans remained temporary
residents were not always less congenial climatically than
those where they settled. John Ferguson, commenting in
1903 on 'The Present Prospects for Capitalists in Ceylon',
wrote: 'the Ceylon plantations [are] far more congenial
than the Australian bush', and the hills of Sri Lanka have
'the perfection of a healthy climate'. (35) Much earlier
Lord Grey mentioned the 'salubrious climate' as a factor
in Sri Lanka's general condition and prosperity. (36)
Even when physical or cultural factors were unfavourable,
as on the west coast of Africa, they do not sufficiently
explain settler/nonsettler decisions. A.O.Dike observed
how in the nineteenth century 'climate and physical impediments did not prevent the appearance of European
enterprises [in these territories] when Europeans had
overcome African opposition'. (37) In the case of middle-
and working-class Europeans a more serious obstacle to
settlement was the presence of migrant Asian communities -
the Indians in East Africa or the Chinese in Malaya.
Their economic prospects were hampered more by the competition offered by these communities than by the indigenous
population.

Furthermore, in some countries Europeans tended to
settle in the earlier period of colonization but not in
the later periods - a difference in attitude which was un-
connected with physical or cultural factors. In Penang
during the time of the East India Company there developed
an 'independent, land-owning European community'. Though
regulations forbade the immigration of Europeans into
India and the Straits Settlements, the directors of the
company became amenable to 'responsible Europeans' settling in two of the company's territories - Penang and
Singapore. (38) The Europeans in this period established
permanent interests in the 'Settlement'; out of seventy-
four residents in Singapore 'not one of them could be
called an "adventurer"', commented the British Resident in
1824. (39) This generation of Europeans had settler
characteristics. 'Their returns to their homeland were

infrequent and their connexions more tenuous. Many began
to invest capital and sought a local investment, preferably one that they could supervise personally.' (40)
    There was similarly a tendency for European settlement
in Sri Lanka until the introduction of tea in the 1880s,
as also in Malaysia until the early years of this century, when rubber superseded numerous other crops, viz.
coffee, pepper, sugar cane and gambier. In these countries, during the first phase of European enterprise, the
proprietor planter or trader was dominant - he at least
lived in the colony for much longer than the expatriate
businessmen and executives who came later. The eclipse of
the resident investor and the growth of absentee capital
are connected with the growth of corporate ventures financed by the capital market in Britain. Absentee ownership in the colonies, which underlay the company form of
organization, began after 1880 when metropolitan capital
became increasingly mobile. (41) Absentee investments
abroad were also made possible by the development of telegraphic communication and by improvements in the machinery
of the British capital market. A whole range of financial
institutions were developed which superseded the small
promoter as a channel for investitive funds.
    According to Professor Preston E.James, 'the tropics'
are themselves a matter of definition; they contain many
different climates, none of which 'is as hot as some found
in the middle latitudes. There is no climatic reason why,
with proper clothing, proper diet, and proper housing,
people may not live and work energetically in the low
latitudes.' (42) The constraining factor in European
settlement was, therefore, not that the white man was
physiologically incapable of manual labour in the tropical
colonies. 'White men can do it if they try', felt Richard
Pares, referring to the experience of sugar planters in
Queensland. (43) In other instances they were exempted
from trying because of a moral rather than a physical constraint, inhibited as they were by the special type of
inter-human relationships in colonial societies. It was
not manual labour as such to which they were averse but to
any kind of work which was exclusively associated with
subject people. As E.T.Thompson explained, the climatic
theory 'is part of an ideology which rationalizes and
naturalizes an existing social and economic order, and
this everywhere seems to be an order in which there is a
race problem'. (44) The availability and cheapness of
coloured labour reinforced this attitude, as seen in the
replacement of white indentured servants by Africans not
only on the plantations of the West Indies and the American South, with a tropical or subtropical climate, but
also in Virginia and Carolina.

The small planter in the American colonies and the
Caribbean islands in the seventeenth century had utilized
indentured European labour. They were taken from the
British Isles and Germany, from among the mass of people
ejected from traditional occupations during the disloca-
tion and turmoil which marked the birth of capitalism in
Europe. There was also some involuntary labour which had
been kidnapped. Shipowners and contractors made a business out of transporting these white migrants, in vessels
called 'white Guinea-men'. (45) Though 'freedom dues'
were payable to them upon release, the regular cost of
employing white servants was only their subsistence, and
their condition at this time was probably no better than
that of the African slaves on which the plantations came
later to depend. According to some contemporaries, the
'European servant was in a less favoured position than the
Negro slaves'. (46)

These indentured 'white servants' formed more than half
of all European immigrants to the American colonies south
of New England. Yet, their number was never sufficient.
(47) The situation gradually worsened when the white
servants moved out to settle on their own after serving
their time. Towards the end of the seventeenth century,
while land was becoming less plentiful in Pennsylvania and
New York, there were attractive opportunities for those
who had a freedom of choice. This led to the fleeing of
white servants before the end of their contract period;
in Georgia rewards were offered by the white masters and
by the trustees of the colony for the capture of runaway
servants. (48) The white skin of these indentured servants did not allow for their easy and complete differentiation from free workers. Servants from Virginia and
South Carolina found refuge in the up-country of North
Carolina.

White servants, apart from their scarcity, proved un-
satisfactory for several reasons. They were difficult to
control and manage. An abundance of them, said a Reverend
Hugh Jones, 'do great mischief, commit robbery and murder
and spoilt servants, that were before very good'. (49)
First, the heterogeneity of white labour, who were voluntary bond servants, kidnapped persons, debtors or even
criminals, precluded a uniform standard of treatment.
Second, the whites, it seemed, were not equal to the
Negroes in performing the arduous field labour on the
plantations; and the illness of a white servant 'cost his
master as much as would have maintained a Negro for four
years'. (50) Third, the upkeep of Negroes was much less,
there being a 'great disproportion between the maintenance
and clothing of white servants and negroes'. (51) Most

importantly, the labour of a Negro slave and children was
available for life. Female slaves who provided offspring
were a source of capital gain to planters, whereas white
women could not even be employed as field hands. Thus the
more fertile areas of a plantation specialized in agricultural staples, while the unproductive land was used for
breeding slaves, any surplus being sold to the labour-
short regions of the Cotton South. (52)

The lack of white labour was as unexpected as it was
historically significant. It ended the hopes both of the
authorities in Virginia and of the Board of Trade in
Britain of creating in the American colonies a yeomanry
after the English pattern. More fundamentally, it conditioned the institutional basis of the plantation economy
in the islands of the West Indies, giving rise to absentee
interests and slave labour. While the success of plantations in the New World continued to hinge on the possession of a cheap labour supply, the ethnic composition of
the labour force now changed; and the Negro gradually replaced the white indentured servant. The use of European
labour declined abruptly towards the end of the seventeenth century - by 1720 they were scarcely employed,
except as skilled workmen; and slaves became the indispensable basis of the plantation system. The racial
origins of the workforce even influenced employment and
agricultural patterns and the choice between plantations
and small farms. In Cuba, where both forms existed, this
correlation was particularly apparent. Tobacco was produced by free labour on small farms that were intensively
cultivated, but sugar on large plantations that were extensively cultivated using black labour. In Virginia the
presence of black labour for tobacco cultivation led to a
change from small units to large plantations. While the
change-over to black labour was broadly due to the difficult manpower situation in Europe after the ravages of the
Thirty Years' War, and a growing demand for labour in England, there were some specific reasons underlying this
preference, to some of which I have referred earlier.

Just as topography or climate or the problem of physical toil were no barrier to white immigration, such immigration has also not been deterred by socio-cultural factors, including religion and ethnicity. Both in the
tropical countries and in the West, different races have
lived side by side permanently although differing from
each other in language, religion, and even in political
organization. A sociological study of Greek migrants in
Toronto (53) suggests a dualistic model of acculturation:
isolationism of the migrants and particularistic values in
their private social life but universalistic standards in

the 'public domain'. The interaction of the migrants with
the host society was determined by their employment patterns and their economic roles.   In New Zealand some of
the early Europeans lived as members of Maori tribes -
they were known as the Pakeha Maoris. (54) In Thailand
the Chinese migrants were continually absorbed into the
local society. The offspring of mixed marriages retained
some elements of the Chinese culture but 'soon became indistinguishable from the Siamese'. (55) Chinese also
settled in Malaysia and Indonesia despite profound differences with the indigenous people in language, religion and
food. Likewise the Puerto Ricans and the African Negroes
in America.

In Trengganu (Malaysia), the Chinese who came from
Fukien province in the late eighteenth century were assimilated culturally and through intermarriage. They
spread to the rural districts and finally settled in the
central Trengganu River Valley. The Trengganu Babas,
while retaining their own community structure and the
basically Chinese aspects of their life cycle, were barely
distinguishable from the Malays - in appearance, manners,
social life and in their mode of agriculture. They inter-
married, wore Malay dress, adopted Malay cuisine, ate with
their fingers (not with chopsticks), and spoke perfect
Trengganu Malay. (56) In Malacca and the Straits Settlement the Chinese became 'for all practical purposes ...
the natives of the Malayan States, having lost touch with
China in every respect'. (57) They spoke little Chinese,
and communicated in an idiom known as Baba Malay which was
closer to Malay than to Chinese. Their magico-religious
beliefs were strongly influenced by Malay culture. The
imposition of British rule, however, checked the acculturation of the Straits Chinese, when greater benefits were
held out to those who identified with the British instead
of the Malays. (58)

While ecological and cultural obstacles to the settlement of people in foreign lands are more apparent than
real, a major factor which determined the choice of settlements in the nineteenth century was the sparseness of
the indigenous population. In the East African Protectorate the settlement of Europeans was encouraged by a belief
that the indigenous people were even fewer than their
actual numbers. Only when the northern areas inhabited
by the Kikuyu and allied tribes were fully explored was a
realistic estimate available. Until then the settlers
hoped to make East Africa another New Zealand, 'a white
man's country in which the native questions present but
little interest'. (59) The sparseness of indigenous
people did not represent, however, a question of the

availability of land, of living space, or of the need for
cultural homogeneity; its significance lay in the 'absence of opposition from the natives'.

People, rather than physical impediments, as a conditioning factor in European settlement was mentioned by
Adam Smith. In this connection Smith contrasted the various West African territories, which were not conducive to
settlement, with the Cape of Good Hope. Whereas West
Africa had relatively dense populations and established
civilizations and political structures, the Cape region
'was inhabited by a race of people (the Hottentots) almost
as barbarous and quite as incapable of defending themselves as the natives of America'. (60) In the Kenya
highlands, which attracted European settlers, the Africans
were 'from the relevant points of view conspicuously
inept', unlike those in other parts of East Africa. 'None
of the Kenya tribes had rulers comparable with the forward-looking aristocracies of Buganda, which was able in
some degree to communicate European ideals and aspirations
to the mass of the people; most of them, indeed, had no
rulers or aristocracies at all.' (61) On the other hand,
those who were capable of mounting any resistance were
treated warily. In Kenya, while the Africans were generally denuded of rights to land (as were the American
Indians, the Hottentots of South Africa, and the Australian aborigines), a more liberal policy was adopted towards the 'supposedly formidable Masai' (as towards the
Maoris of New Zealand). The Masai, reputed for their
ferocity and warlike qualities, were given new lands 'at
a safe distance from the settlers in the railway zone'.
(62)

In all instances where the Europeans had forcibly occupied foreign territory, the problem of security was a
paramount concern. The victims of the despoliation were
a potential threat. In Rhodesia the Ndebele, though defeated in 1893, continued their armed conflicts with the
Europeans for many years. The Shona, another of the
tribes, vanquished in 1896-7, rose in rebellion intermittently until 1903. (63) In Surinam in the eighteenth
century Europeans had to establish armed villages to
defend the plantations from the Bush Negroes of Marrons
(the descendants of fugitive slaves) who waged a protracted guerrilla war. (64) In Algeria, the colons (French
Algerians) for several decades lived in fear of the Arabs.
Those on isolated farms were massacred during the insurrection of 1839, after which village centres were established where French families were given land free or on
concessional terms to induce them to reside. (65) Until
around 1900, fear of the Arabs made the colons reluctant
to employ them as farm labourers. (66)

Smith's insight into the security problem is borne out
by the division between expatriate and settler colonies in
Africa. It is easy to see why settlers did not consider
West Africa to be congenial territory. The penetration of
West Africa was not 'remarkably easy and peaceful' as had
been thought. According to some recent studies, the
Europeans encountered 'bitter and often skillful' resistance. (67) After the 1860s the Europeans had a definite
superiority in armaments supported by an efficient system
of drill and field manoeuvres; they yet failed to match
the guerrilla tactics of their African opponents. In some
cases an appeal to militant Islam intensified the resistance to the European invader. In Ghana the British were
thus careful not to interfere with indigenous land ownership or mineral rights, being 'fully aware of the stiff
native political resistance towards any attempt [to do
so]'. (68) In Nigeria, as mentioned in an earlier chapter, when the Europeans were given exclusive concessions
to mining land, the government had to protect European
mining enterprises against attack by the Africans. Some
of the staff of the Royal Niger Company were massacred and
its mining equipment was destroyed. In Germany's African
colonies 'the hostility of many of the native tribes' was
one of the 'factors which discouraged settlement'; and as
a result the overwhelming number of over a million Germans
who emigrated between 1887 and 1906 went to the USA. In
South-West Africa, consequent on the losses sustained by
the South-West Africa companies by the Herero rebellion of
1904-7 compensation was sought in a sum of £550,000 from
the German Government. In Germany's African colonies,
equally serious were the Majimaji revolt in East Africa in
1905-6 and the Hottentot rebellion which, like the Herero
rebellion, broke out in 1904-7. (69)
The obstacle to European settlement arising from the
presence of a large indigenous population had also an economic aspect. The heterogeneity of settler communities,
which in some cases included a European working class,
obliged them to seek means of livelihood lower down the
occupational scale - at levels to which the indigenous
(and immigrant Asian) groups also aspired. As I shall
demonstrate in a later chapter, settler communities for
this reason were far less tolerant of the economic rights
of the indigenous people than were expatriate investors.
The rivalry was greater in countries with a large indigenous population who had also reached a relatively advanced
stage of development. The Europeans in such situations
were unable to compete with 'natives' as artisans and
petty traders and in certain forms of agriculture where
European technology was irrelevant. In Uganda, Tanganyika

and West Africa indigenous peasant farms based on family
labour precluded the Europeans from carrying out agriculture even for export.

In Kenya, where the Africans were economically too weak
to stand in the way of European interests, the Indians
were a factor to reckon with. They had migrated from the
early days of British influence and had taken up employment suited to the lower-ranking Europeans. The presence
of Indian artisans, petty traders and clerks caused the
Europeans to abandon a scheme for the mass colonization of
East Africa. The territory, explained Wrigley, 'was
really no place for the small European trader or artisan,
for in these fields white men were in direct competition
with the Indians, who provided similar services at a much
lower cost'. (69)   In Surinam, the Dutch peasants who settled around the mid-nineteenth century had a similar difficulty. They had to compete with Indian plantation
labourers who at the expiry of their contracts started
farming on land ceded by government. As a result emancipated Indians competed fiercely with the Dutch settlers in
supplying the urban market; the produce included fresh
milk. By the 1920s and 1930s the settlers were virtually
ousted from farming. With this decline the children of
the Dutch settlers left the land for other occupations and
became teachers, clerks and constables. (70)

Even when incomes of the whites were below their accustomed level, race consciousness prevented them from
engaging in work that was considered beneath their status.
The white man after all was not expected to hire his own
labour. It was too bad - a preserve of 'natives' only.
In Kenya, as Wrigley shrewdly put it, 'with black labour
in the neighbourhood it was economically difficult and
socially shocking [for a white man] to work with his hands
for hire. On the contrary, he was to be, from the start,
an employer of native labour'. (71)   The structure of race
relations in the colonial situation made manual labour degrading. 'Planting and hoeing in the manner of a native
woman' was the lot of one European who had no Africans to
work on his farm. The influence of racial attitudes on
the choice of work by Europeans was pointed out by
Robequain. In Indochina (73)

The European cannot engage in the same kind of agricultural tasks as the Indo-chinese, without being degraded to the status of the 'poor white' struggling
vainly against the competition of the coloured man....
[Thus] the European colonist rarely plays the role of
peasant.... He does not engage in actual farm work,
but instead manages and superintends the cultivation of
a relatively large holding.

The consciousness of racial superiority was also reflected in the high salaries required by Europeans in the
colonial situation in order to maintain a style of living
in keeping with their role as a ruling race. (74)   'To
spend like a white man' was a popular aphorism which conformed to the image of the Europeans as God's most expensive creatures.   Eugene Genovese explained that in the
analogous case of slave society a propensity for extravagance, however wasteful and irrational it might seem,
provided the ruling class with the façade necessary to
assert its dominance. (75)   A corollary of this was the
aloofness of these expatriates whose lives seem to have
been 'highly unnatural', with exclusive shopping areas,
racial clubs and segregated schools. (76)   For instance,
selected Asians may have been admitted to English clubs in
England but they were not allowed in such places in the
colonies. (77)   The Europeans formed a solid upper class
whose functions were solely in 'ruling, owning and managing'.   Any other form of occupation or life style would
be degrading and damaging to their prestige.   Thus a proposal in 1881 to employ Britishers as police constables in
Singapore was turned down partly for fear of undermining
white superiority.   'The whole idea of Britons working as
common constables was considered "impolitic", embarrassing
and highly damaging to the prestige of the white man by
the *Tuan Besars*, whose sentiments could not be lightly
ignored.' (78)

In his study of Kenya Brett offers an alternative explanation of the settlers' attitude to work.   First, there
was an African population who 'could not simply be swept
into a corner, but had to be made to work for [the set-
tlers]' and, second, white men were unwilling 'to work
much harder than they were accustomed to do in other parts
of Africa equally open to settlement'. (79)   The fact is,
as stated earlier, white men would not work at all in the
presence of those whom they dominated.   For instance, in
Algeria a French author observed in 1856:   'They [the set-
tlers] never departed from the sentiment of hierarchy;
they dominate and must dominate, for if the master loses
face, the servant despises him and cuts him down.' (80)
A third reason given by Brett for the work habits of the
European is somewhat obscure;   the settler (81)

> came out as a fully developed capitalist man;   he did
> not expect to build his own house and furniture, grow
> his own food, and make a large portion of his own
> clothing.   He expected to produce for the market on a
> level which would enable him to purchase these neces-
> sities in a sufficiency which matched the expectations
> that he brought with him.

If this implies that the settlers were market oriented, it still does not explain why they refrained from manual labour only in the colonial situation, and not in their parent society or abroad in countries where they belonged to an all-white community.

The territories chosen for European settlement contained a vacuum in which the settlers could live and pursue their interests untrammelled by any rival claims; these territories had a sparse population and their indigenous economy and society were at an elementary stage of development. Sir Charles Eliot, a leading figure in the Protectorate of East Africa in the first years of European settlement declared: 'We are not destroying any old or existing system but introducing order into blank, uninteresting, brutal barbarism.' (82) Again, 'We have in East Africa the rare experience of dealing with a tabula rasa, an almost untouched and sparsely inhabited country, where we can do as we will, and open or close the door as we deem best.' (83) In some of these territories the coloured population was so small that it almost ceased to exist not long after the establishment of European rule. In others it was too large to be wiped out, yet small enough to be confined in reserves away from the settlers. The separation of the settler occupied lands from those cultivated or inhabited by Africans, according to L.H. Gann, was connected with the improved farming practices of the settlers. These could not be adopted in an area of inefficient farming, and thus the settler outlook resembled that of the 'enclosing landlords' of eighteenth-century England. (84) This analogy overlooks the comprehensive repression of the Africans as a racial group, of which their expulsion outside the horizon of the settler farms was merely one facet. The policy of exclusiveness pursued by the settlers, to an almost paranoid extent, had more to it than the claims of scientific agriculture.

In all of these territories the refusal of Europeans to become assimilated with the indigenous society was complex in its causation and results. Racial segregation was linked with a whole institutional mechanism, involving legislative sanctions and psychological devices, whereby the white races maintained and rationalized their domination. The socio-cultural gulf which they created for this purpose, with a depersonalizing of contacts across the colour line, sought to legitimize the distribution of political power, the allocation of economic resources, and the differential access to occupational opportunities and privileges between the settlers and the subjugated communities. At the same time, the vast technological and cultural gap between the settlers and the indigenous popu-

lation caused the economic aims of settlement to be compounded with humanistic claims such as underlay the 'dual
mandate' in Africa - a civilizing mission, a moral force,
pax Britannica, and trusteeship.   In regions where the repression of the indigenous people was greatest, such ideas
gave stability and a sense of permanence to British rule.

3 Export staples and their contrasting impact on development — the settler and the nonsettler regions

Three phases in the development of the regions of new settlement can be broadly distinguished. In the first phase, the investment pattern was inwardly orientated. To meet their immediate wants, the settlers began producing food and other consumer goods as well as their own implements and equipment. In America until the first decades of the nineteenth century, farming enterprises had a high degree of self-sufficiency based on a union of agriculture and manufactures. With an assortment of tools every farmer (1)

> made wooden implements, as forks and rakes, handles for his hoes and ploughs, spokes for his wagon, and various other implements.... [He] produced flax and hemp and wool and cotton ... [which] were spun into yarn, woven into cloth, made into garments, and worn at home.

Manufacturing developed woollen mills, factories for making brooms, rope and wooden ware, pork-packing establishments, and canning and fruit-preserving houses. (2) These enterprises later moved from the farms to the cities, and their scale of production increased. For instance, the wagon-maker's shop and the shoemaker's shop in the neighbourhood gave way to the large establishment in the city where most of the work was done by machines. In Canada, the French-Canadian industrial bourgeoisie grew up with the 'small-scale consumer-goods enterprises emerging in the towns and villages'. (3)

The next stage in the development of these regions bore some resemblance historically to the underdeveloped countries. From being self-sufficient at an elementary level, the economy was based on a handful of export staples. In the Pacific Northwest of Canada, cod fish, fox furs, minerals, and grain and lumber were produced; in America, tobacco, rice, indigo and naval stores - the only secondary activity was shipbuilding; in Australia, wool and, later, wheat and minerals. Except in mining, production techniques were land extensive; they required simple technology, and the linkages with the domestic economy were slight. Domestic markets were limited by the sparseness of population. Production was overwhelmingly export oriented, except for the purely service trades, which were tied to the point of consumption, and industries which had a natural protection. These regions depended heavily on the parent economies for capital, markets and manufactured goods.

Within a relatively short period this satellite relationship was disturbed. At first the staples base became enlarged; there was an expansion in output, due to the introduction of new staples, but more critically to improved production techniques. The innovations during this stage, as in plantation agriculture, raised output per acre rather than per man - they were agronomic rather than mechanical. Later, machinery was used in farming operations; in plantation agriculture, by contrast, the improvements continued to be agronomic and modern technology was confined to the 'distance inputs' which are of a once-for-all type confined to the opening-up phase. A crucial element in the development of the settler regions was the change in the production function in the export staples themselves. Such a change, which also occurred in the settler colonies, cannot be attributed to the presence or absence of a cheap labour supply, but to the entrepreneurial options of the class which invested in or controlled export production. As will be shown in a later chapter, in Algeria, Kenya and Rhodesia relatively capitalized forms of agriculture were developed by the settler investors despite the presence of cheap African labour.

During the period of export-led growth, industries sprang up that were based on local processing: in the USA and Canada, for example, sugar refining, distilleries, flour mills, wood processing and the refining of minerals (some of which, like aluminium ore, required considerable electricity generating capacity). Related to these were wood products, the manufacture of tin plate, bottling plants, and the food-processing industry - cereal products, fish canning, preserved fruit, and flavouring materials and essences. Likewise cattle and hog rearing led to animal feed industries, meat and dairy production, and the manufacture of leather and footwear. Some other industries serviced, or were secondary to, the production of export staples, such as specialized agricultural implements and logging and lumbering equipment. Grain production and shipbuilding led to flour and lumber milling industries. (4) In America, after a time, merchants began

substituting flour in barrels for the shipment of grain
in the raw state. Following its earlier expansion, the
staples base declined relatively with the growth of
secondary production. As economic expansion transcended
the staples base, it also acquired a domestic orientation,
feeding upon itself. Development nodes proliferated that
were independent of any external stimuli. Rapid urbanization and high wages overcame the small market base with
which the settler investors started. There was now an
internalization of the growth process and, as N.G.Butlin
said about Australia, the path of the satellite became
independent. (5)
  The derivative industries of the staples base, con-
tributing to a diversification of output and production
processes, gave the economy a new quality. This occurred
even before significant changes in the production functions. The growth process became detached from its original moorings and acquired a non-agricultural focus. Paradoxically, in the Australian economy where this change was
starkly evident, rural investment generated urban growth.
Centralized transport systems fanned out from the capital
cities. The mobile building construction and railway
workers and, obviously, new migrants, showed a preference
for the cities. In New South Wales two thirds of the increase in the total population between 1861 and 1891 was
urban based. (6) Urbanization created a huge demand for
social overheads: housing and communal amenities, including sewerage, water supply, street lighting, tramways
and telecommunications. The building materials industry
benefited directly, but the ripples spread beyond to types
of manufacturing which enjoyed a natural protection.
Though the expansion was based on machinery and equipment
brought in from outside, rising maintenance commitments
required the development of engineering shops and repair
services internally.
  From the First World War manufacturing began to dominate the investment pattern. The armed forces provided an
assured demand for textiles and footwear. As a settler
territory Australia could avail itself of the growth possibilities offered by such exogenous impulses, often
fortuitous; nevertheless, it was the process of urbanization which provided the main stimulus to industrial
growth. A steel-manufacturing plant which had been set up
in Newcastle in 1912 played an 'initiatory role' in developing a wide range of manufactures. There was also an
investment of capital in depth with an increase in the
value of plant and machinery per worker, based on new
techniques. Sustained urban growth consolidated this
trend. When the building boom abated from the beginning

of this century, and the urban labour market began to
ease, manufacturers were already locating themselves in
the cities. (7)

Though these changes in the different settler regions
cannot be sharply demarcated or clearly explained, there
was a certain distinctiveness in their development pattern, compared with that in the underdeveloped economies
where the staples base retained its dominance, and compared also with the much older and densely populated countries of Europe. The so-called staples theory of growth
as applied to the settler regions rests on the changing
behaviour of the staples base over time. (8)   A disturbance of the staples base was seen by D.C.North (9) in
terms of shifts in the demand/supply curves. On the
demand side, these shifts were brought about by changes in
income or tastes or in the nature of the raw materials
used in manufacture; and on the supply side, by changes
in costs or in the physical availability of primary products. We shall, however, explain the growth propensity
of the staples base on somewhat different lines to those
of North. Since our interest is fundamentally with underdevelopment, which was characteristic of the nonsettler
colonies, the discussion of the dynamism of the staples
base in the regions of new settlement will be interlaced
with frequent references to the contrasting case of the
underdeveloped countries.

The dynamism of the staples base was due first, and
fundamentally, to the locus of capital ownership. The
permanent domicile of the investors in the host country
caused capital inflows to acquire a local base and an
autonomous potential. In colonial America there was thus
an 'accumulation of large capitals in American hands,
[and] decreasing dependence on British investors'. (10)
As Arghiri Emmanuel said, there was an 'actual immigration
of capitals and of their decision-making centres'. (11)
Their detachment from the parent economy and their eventu-
al autonomy enabled the settler investors to propagate development impulses. They were free to respond to opportunities which the local resource endowment offered, and
to invest in lines of production which were competitive
with those abroad. The different entrepreneurial foci of
settler and nonsettler investors are crucial in the generation of development and of underdevelopment. In later
chapters a fuller discussion will be made of the growth
impulses of this nature in the context of the settler
colonies as distinguished from the regions of new settlement. In the later part of this chapter, I shall demonstrate the obverse phenomenon - how underdevelopment in
the nonsettler colonies was basically linked with extra-

territoriality of the investors.   In passing I refer here
to the eighteenth-century English planters in the West
Indies who, as agents of absentee landlords, resident in
England, practised a 'single-crop exploitative agriculture' on a plantation basis, while Spanish, Dutch and
Danish farmers in central America, as owner-operators,
'cultivated directly their smallholdings and diversified
their crops'. (12)   In the North American colonies, as
Richard Pares commented, the settler communities were 'un-
hampered by remote control from investors 3,000 miles
away.   In general, the colonies which throve best were
those with residential proprietors'. (13)

Second, the dynamism of the staples base of the regions
of new settlement was due to the competition from the produce of developed regions;   in the settler colonies, such
as Kenya and Rhodesia, the technical and scientific improvements in their agricultural system occurred in the
face of cheap imports available from the USA and Canada.
The settler investors went in for the growing of these
crops in the context of a regime of world competition;
this was not entirely the result of ecological factors,
and therefore accidental, but stemmed from the relative
autonomy of the settler investors which enabled them to
develop economic structures which were parallel rather
than complementary to those in the already developed countries.   On the other hand, the technical progress in the
growing of plantation crops has been essentially of an
agronomic kind - raising yields per acre with little
change in labour productivity and in the cost per unit of
output.   The single exception to this was sugar cane, and
I will demonstrate in a later chapter the effects of competition in forcing down its production costs.   The low
levels of mechanization of plantation crops, and their
extremely limited processing in the countries of origin,
caused production to be largely of an extractive nature -
the heavy labour costs required in harvesting constituted
a large proportion of production costs.   It was thus possible for these crops to be grown on a plantation basis or
by peasants, or entirely by peasants.   In the case of palm
oil, though modern technology in the final stages of production improves quality and reduces costs, West African
peasants using traditional methods continued to produce
for the world market.   Technological change in plantation
crops, both in its character and its extent, was circumscribed by the dominance of merchant capital whose interests lay in maximizing the volume of output and of the
gross proceeds of sale rather than net profits.   In a
later chapter I shall explain in these terms the absence
of cost-reducing technology in plantation production.

Third, given a framework of capital investment which
was inwardly oriented and had an essentially indigenous
base, the export staples of the regions of new settlement
favoured the growth of secondary industries. These
staples required considerable processing in order to be
made into an exportable form. They gave rise to butter
and cheese canneries, meat-packing and refrigeration
plants, flour mills, vineries, and wood-working complexes
in the vicinity of the primary resources. British ship-
builders found it more economical to build their vessels
in the American colonies, importing certain materials,
than in England. (14) Most plantation products needed
only simple processing to be made exportable, such as the
transforming of rubber latex into crepe or smoked sheet,
oil seeds or palm kernels into oil, or green tea leaf into
'made' tea. Cocoa could be dispatched before or after
fermentation, and coffee before or after drying and husk-
ing. In Zambia copper ore merely goes through a preliminary sifting to be made into blister copper for export
and the secondary processing is still carried out in the
industrialized countries.

Another reason for the choice to export the primary
products of the underdeveloped countries in a more or less
unprocessed form was that it was not more expensive to
transport them to their destination in this form. For example, the saving in cost of transporting coconut oil
(packed in drums) rather than copra was minimal until the
bulk shipping of oil in tankers became possible after the
Second World War. Yet the use of this facility had certain limitations. Variations in the specific gravity and
the fatty acid content of oil preclude the loading of oil
into tankers bringing oil from other sources or for other
consignees. In the case of sugar, though the processing
of the raw material is a complex and highly capitalized
process, sugar refining causes very little weight loss.
Unrefined sugar is also easier to transport and handle
than refined sugar, and its transport costs are lower. In
such instances where bulk- or weight-reducing considerations were not significant, despite the long distance over
which primary products were transported, there was little
impetus to the development of materials-oriented industries. The metropolitan interests had, therefore, a wide
option in locating their industrial plants. Like the
multinations of the present day, they could 'use the world
economy' in a way that benefited the profits centre
abroad, with a skewed distribution of gains among the
various segments.

Some other products of the settler regions, catering to
final consumption - e.g. meat and dairy produce, and fruit

and fruit juice - had a demand that was susceptible to
even minor variations in quality, including appearance,
flavour, culinary properties and standards of packing.
Improvements were needed to ensure that these standards
reached back to the preliminary stages of production, such
as crop cultivation and stock rearing. There are examples
of such changes in the primary products of the underdeveloped countries too: improvements sponsored by the
shipping and trading firms in Nigeria in the quality of
pineapples, oranges, fruit juices, and ginger, and on the
tobacco plantations in Deli in Sumatra, where scientific
research led to a product of distinctive quality and
having a special demand. But, in general, in the primary
products of the tropical and subtropical lands, quality
variations do not critically affect demand or else they
depend primarily on natural factors, as in the case of tea
and coffee.

   In the settler regions the high level of wages and
interest rates and the general level of prices induced
technological improvements; in Australia they even encouraged non-export industries. (15) The expansion of the
staples base per se induced technological change, due to a
competition for land. In the Australian wool industry,
the rising cost of land by the late 1840s caused profitability to decline as output expanded. To arrest this
tendency, from the 1850s investments were made in fencing,
water conservation, and improvements in pasture and breeding, leading to a reduction in cost which made the expansion of the industry viable. In fox fur production in
Canada and in America, a dramatic change was that from a
purely hunting technology that was land extensive to sed-
entary farming, which shortened the lines of traffic and
reduced expenditure on 'scouting and the maintenance of
trading stations'.

   An underlying factor in the development of the settler
regions, not specifically connected with the staples base,
was the role of the state. Generally, state intervention
was of an altogether different order from that in the nonsettler colonies, and it served broader and longer-term
interests than those of expatriate investors concerned
with trade or export production. This intervention was
not confined to the provision of facilities to produce for
an existing export market through land transfers, the
organizing of a labour supply, and the provision of social
overhead capital which was more or less specific to the
export sector. The role of the state in Australia and in
the USA, as also in the settler colonies (Rhodesia and
Kenya, for example), was 'positive and non-minimal', not
passive or 'negative'. (16) Though in the USA this role

was less pronounced, in line with the accepted ethos, in
Australia the government was an initiator and 'risk-
taker'. There was an attempt at managing the economy as
a separate and distinct entity from the metropolitan country.

Thus tariffs introduced, despite considerably higher
domestic prices, tended to create economic structures competitive with those in the metropolitan centres. Tariff
protection had also welfare goals, as in Victoria at the
end of the 1850s when the manufacturing sector was encouraged to provide work for unemployed miners, and 'depression works' and labour villages were financed by
government. After 1871 such protectionist policies spread
throughout Australia. The state also played a role as an
investor and in creating or organizing demand. Government
expenditure, because of its sheer magnitude, had a greater
and more direct expansionary impact than the tariff. From
1884 such expenditure 'became a riot, limited only in its
violence by the amount of accommodation available in
London'. (17) Government expenditure led to a massive
demand for labour and a rise in wages. High wages, though
hampering the economy in times of recession, encouraged
cost-reducing innovations; e.g. in the pastoral industry
by the introduction of spout washing, fencing and water
conservation.

In analysing economic development in the settler regions the intervention by the state should not be viewed
as a fortuitous or independent factor. It was an organic
element in a set of circumstances in which the settlers,
by virtue of their detachment from the metropolitan
centre, sought to create a viable economy and society.
In contrast, the aim of state policy in nonsettler colonies was to hold down wages - by means of cheap migrant
labour as well as unregulated imports - and to stifle attempts at indigenous production which might have competed
with such imports.

In the nonsettler countries the failure of the staples
base to transform itself on the lines familiar in the regions of new settlement, stemmed from a variety of factors. Some of the factors pertaining to the production
and marketing of the staples concerned have emerged out of
my explanation of the reasons for the dynamism of the
staples base in the regions of new settlement. The failure of the staples base in the underdeveloped countries or
the periphery to generate growth resolves itself into the
more specific question of the non-emergence of an industrial sector. However, before I deal with this question
it is necessary to indicate certain perceptions which attribute the non-industrialization of these countries to

market limitations. This view is sometimes merely asserted and at other times explained by the impoverishment of
the periphery as a result of colonial relations. Thus
Nurkse stated: 'Since the domestic market is small, ...
[foreign] investment tends inevitably ... to concentrate
on extractive industries ... producing raw materials for
export mainly to advanced countries'. (18) 'The big
markets in the past were in the industrial countries.
Foreign capital in the underdeveloped areas found it
profitable to work for these markets, rather than for the
domestic consumers whose purchasing power in real terms
was miserably low.' (19) Michael Barratt Brown and Harry
Magdoff, while accepting the reality of centre-periphery
relations, regarded market limitations arising from the
impoverishment of the periphery as a limiting factor on industrial investment. Barratt Brown spoke of the 'obvious
contradiction in the idea that capital would flow to impoverished colonies, except to enclaves of direct raw
material extraction', and Harry Magdoff referred to
'profitable investment opportunities in such countries
[being] limited by the very conditions imposed by the
operations of imperialism'. (20) A corollary of this view
which attaches significance to market limitations is that
the pattern of 'specialization' with an over-expanded
primary goods sector precluded industrialization as an
alternative. 'Restricted market demand and industrial
backwardness are products of the lopsided economic and
social structures associated with the transformation of
these countries into suppliers of raw materials and food
for the metropolitan countries.' (21) The argument, cast
in terms of comparative costs, presumes full employment of
resources. Its unreality is too obvious for comment.
    In different portions of this book I shall endeavour to
show that the barrier to industrialization was neither the
existing size of markets nor a particular pattern of specialization as such. It will also be pointed out that
while it was the capital goods sector in the metropolis
which benefited most from colonial investment connected
with the infrastructure needs of the export economy, the
colonial market for such goods being independent of the
level of domestic purchasing power, the market for consumer goods, especially for articles of mass consumption, was
far from insignificant. Regional markets were, of course,
even larger, and in East Africa investors availed themselves of such markets in the settler colonies. Many
underdeveloped countries, apart from a geographical pro-
pinquity, had a common political framework which should
have facilitated a regional division of labour instead of
the symbiotic relation which each of them developed with

the metropolitan country. The problem is that even in the
presence of large markets foreign capital avoided industrial investments and confined itself to primary production and public utilities whereas, as is seen in the case
of India, it was indigenous capital that sought out opportunities for industrial investment. The manufacture of
both cotton textiles and iron and steel failed to attract
foreign capital, though local markets and the level of
profits were very promising. In fact, (22)

> the growth of the [cotton textile] industry led to con-
> siderable alarm and anxiety to Lancashire, which was
> then the dominant overseas supplier in India. The same
> is true of the development of the steel industry ...
> [which] in India was never plagued by a lack of demand
> particularly after railway building was started.

In India itself, as pointed out in a later chapter, an attempt to set up an iron and steel industry in the 1880s
was stifled by the metropolitan interests. Similar obstacles were placed in the way of industrialization in
Uganda and Tanganyika whereas the settler dominated economy of Kenya was hospitable to industrialization. The
theoretical validity of the view which regards the existing size of markets as a constraint on industrialization
also needs to be questioned.

While the size of the market determines the industrial
equipment which can profitably be installed, flexibility
in the size of capital equipment enables industries to
produce efficiently for markets of varying size. As Celso
Furtado said, 'A market is small only in relation to something.... The market of underdeveloped countries is small
in relation to the type of equipment used by developed
countries.' (23) The large industrial plant in the metropolitan countries corresponded to the large overseas
market which they came to acquire. However, the cost-
reducing effects of such large-scale production and of
equipment embodying the highest capital intensity are less
than might be supposed. In a study of the differences in
productivity between the USA and Britain, L.Rostas found
that 'there is some interrelationship between output and
productivity in certain cases; but not a close one'. (24)
A comparison of productivity and market size in Britain
with those in Sweden and Holland showed that 'relative
productivity is in no way related to the size of the
market [and that] the optimum plant [or firm] and specialisation can be achieved within the limits of a smaller
market'. E.Rothbarth was of the same view. America's
technical superiority, dating back to about 1870, preceded
the expansion of the market. In Australia, Canada, New
Zealand and Argentina industries showed 'high efficiency

without having access to particularly large markets'. (25)
Those who regard the size of markets to be a barrier to
industrial growth may do well to ponder on the extremely
small market in these countries with which the settler/
investors started.

The economies of scale which suggest a need for large
markets do not also apply uniformly to all products or all
components of a product;   e.g. the heels of shoes are more
amenable to mass-production techniques than the uppers.
The variation in the extent of scale economies in the different components of a product has made it possible for
many underdeveloped countries of the present day to produce for a small home market, using some imported components. (26) Furthermore, economies of scale do not relate
merely to the production process but also to packing,
transportation and marketing. The economies to be derived
from a large scale of output for an international market,
which requires high standards of packaging to withstand
the rigours of long-distance transport and marketing, are
irrelevant when producing for a smaller home market. For
example, Belgian sheet glass, which had traditionally been
sold in Europe, requires relatively low standards of
safety in packing, while the British glass industry, whose
market is mainly overseas, and where the risk of damage in
transit is higher, underwent greater specialization in
packing; a prerequisite of this development was bulk
orders and a large scale of output.

Moreover, the market for what is broadly the same
manufactured good is in many cases heterogeneous. This
means that the actual scale of production of each specific
good within a related group is smaller than is suggested
by the value of output of the group. In such instances
the potential economies of scale are more apparent than
real. For example, the demand for cotton piece goods and
footwear in the Afro-Asian countries had a certain degree
of specificity imposed by income levels and the tropical
climate, thinner fabrics and open footwear being in vogue.
It was the prevalence of such a differentiation between
products, and between markets, which enabled Calcutta and
Dundee to coexist as centres of the world's jute industry,
both based on British capital - one specializing in the
coarser grades of hessian for the Indian and Burmese
markets, and the other in finer grades. (27)

A variation of this view which attributes non-industrialization to market limitations is concerned with the
specificity of entrepreneurial abilities. Differential
entrepreneurial capabilities of those who control capital
are said to account for a 'structural immobility' of capital between trade and primary production, on the one hand,
and manufacturing industry, on the other. If (28)

the people who run a Company ... decide to invest they
will use their capital to start plantations or some
allied industry. The limitations of knowledge and
entrepreneurial capacity of earners of capital make
liquid capital - to most intents and purposes - il-
liquid. The heterogeneous capacity [capabilities?] of
owners of capital make liquid capital heterogeneous
within these limits.

In an analogous way Wheelwright spoke of 'non-competing'
groups among investors. (29) According to the Puthucheary-
Wheelwright argument, specialization in trade and plantation production 'limits ... [the] capacity [of entrepre-
neurs] to expand into industrial enterprise', with a
'temptation to stick to the fields in which they have
specialised knowledge'. There is also the presumption
that the distribution of profits to shareholders abroad
encourages reinvestment in the metropolitan country which
can offer both 'good profits and security'. I shall comment on each of these in turn.

An extensive spread of the business activities of the
agency houses which managed and controlled the plantations
shows that their specialization was not of as highly
specific a kind as to preclude an extension of the same
managerial abilities to industrial enterprise. In Malaysia one agency house had proprietary or management interests in plantations, transport, shipping, brickworks,
motor-car importing and servicing, plywood, and cane manufactures. Another agency house was concerned with mag-
netic ore dressing, lumber, soft drinks, steamships,
trading, collieries and cement. A third had interests in
plantations, rice milling, real estate, metal box manufacture, cold stores, engineering and brickworks. In Singapore, Guthrie & Co., had a similar spread; it invested in
tin and gold mines, tobacco and tapioca plantations, and
was the agent for rubber estates, insurance companies,
banks, the Singapore Electric Tramway Company, and for
Rudge motor bicycles and several makes of motor cars. (30)
In India, agency houses were usually 'heterogeneous collections of businesses', comprising indigo and tea plantations, coal mines, iron and steel works, and jute mills.
(31) One of them had interests in 'tea plantations, flour
mills, ships, etc.'. The second jute mill that was started in India was owned by the Borneo Company, whose primary
interest shifted from trade to jute manufacture. The non-
specificity of entrepreneurial and managerial skills is
clearly shown in Sri Lanka after the recent nationalization of the plantations; agency houses, which had been
concerned solely with investments in plantations and
closely related activities when they were in control of

the plantation economy, began speedily and efficiently to embark on an assortment of new ventures - hotels, tourism, travel services, and even the management of manufacturing industries.

The second basis of the 'heterogeneity' argument - viz. that the remission of plantation profits to foreign shareholders induced such profits to be retained abroad rather than invested locally - is unrealistic. It does not explain why these foreign shareholders invested originally in the plantations, instead of in the metropolitan country. Decisive control over the companies and over the disposition of funds was exercised by their managing agents, some of whom were domiciled in the colonies. 'Secretarial firms', wrote James Puthucheary himself, have 'very great influence on the voting decisions of independent and non-specialist investors. Consequently they exercise far greater control of the companies than would seem possible by looking at their financial interests.' (32) The financial policy of the plantation companies in their early phase dictated the retention of current profits for expanding the assets of these companies; as mentioned later in this chapter, the shareholders for several years acquiesced in a self-denying policy.

While entrepreneurial interests had a certain flexibility, with a corresponding mobility of capital, they did not extend to industrial investment. This limitation is not to be explained in terms of entrepreneurial capabilities or of a 'structural immobility' of funds as an inherent feature of capital. Such an explanation is ahistorical - it overlooks the manufacturing interests acquired by those who had been exclusively merchants, as in Western Europe during the seventeenth and eighteenth centuries and in Russia in the nineteenth. The merchant turning into an industrialist was one of two ways in which the transition to capitalism was made. Even in the underdeveloped countries expatriate investors extended their interests from trade and primary production to industries, but only to those which enjoyed a natural protection; e.g. iceworks, brickworks, rice mills, tramways, printing establishments, and the repair and servicing of tea and rubber machinery. Such a pattern of investment, which was not competitive with the metropolitan economy and was basic to the whole problem of underdevelopment, has to be located in the prevailing class structure of the underdeveloped countries, influenced as it was by the centre-periphery relationship in which it was involved; to say merely that plantations-cum-trade and manufacturing industry were two different spheres does nothing to aid our understanding of the matter. I shall attempt in later

parts of this chapter to discuss some aspects of this relationship, although its ramifications will cause the discussion to spill over into other chapters.

The real impediment to the growth of industry in the
nonsettler regions was not market limitations but the
extra-territoriality of the investors, together with the
restrictions imposed by the commercial and fiscal policies
of the metropolitan interests. Lacking a permanent involvement in the country of investment, the investors who
constituted merely a segment of the metropolitan bourgeoisie confined their activities essentially to trade and
primary production for export. However, before I discuss
the effects of extra-territoriality, we should look at the
historical context - the fact that industrial technology
and production capacity had developed in Europe before·
large-scale exports of raw materials from the underdeveloped countries became possible. By this time the
centre was assuming an embryonic form whose fuller development required the expansion of its incipient industrial
capacity on the basis of cheap supplies of raw materials
from countries that were later to constitute the periphery. In this phase Europe's colonial expansion dovetailed
with the needs of its emerging industrial potential. A
technological disparity had already arisen, which the
periphery could not overcome - short of a 'Tokugawa solution'. For instance, a rubber industry had existed in
Europe, based on supplies of wild rubber, before plantation rubber was developed. The first factory in England
utilizing scrap rubber was started in 1820, and another in
Scotland three years later. From about 1844, when the
vulcanization process became known, rubber manufacturing
expanded both in Britain and America. The technological
advances, including Dunlop's invention of the pneumatic
tyre in 1889, and the progress made in the chemistry of
rubber manufacture in 1906-7, were paralleled by the development of London as the leading Para rubber market -
with special facilities for weighing, sampling, warehousing and transhipment as well as brokering. (33) A
seed-crushing industry existed in Europe before oil seed
from underdeveloped countries entered the world market.
The manufacture of margarine, until about 1918, was based
chiefly on animal fats, and the use of palm oil was relatively recent. In the manufacture of cocoa, improved
technology was devised in France in the eighteenth century. Holland became a leading producer of cocoa powder and
cocoa butter after Van Houten's invention in 1828 for extracting the oil from the cocoa bean. The invention of
milk chocolate in 1862 placed the Swiss chocolate industry
on a firm basis. (34) The tin-plate industry had made

considerable progress in Britain by 1875, using tin ore
from the Cornish mines; in 1841-50, 86 per cent of tin
consumed in Britain was based on Cornish ore. It was only
when the demand for tin in Europe outran the supplies from
Cornwall that attention shifted to the East. America had
a flourishing tin-plate industry even before 1860, stimulated by the military needs of the Civil War.

    In fact, it was the technological developments in the
metropolitan countries which created the demand for primary products to feed already established industries, or
broadened the uses of raw material, as, for example, the
vulcanization process in rubber. In palm oil technological changes caused a shift from non-edible to edible
uses; soap, candles and compound lard began to be manufactured from cheaper substitutes, and palm oil was used increasingly to produce edible oils and fats. The technological developments occurring in the metropolitan countries also reduced the costs of final goods. In motor
vehicles the assembly line technique introduced in 1913,
by reducing construction time, led to a phenomenal increase in vehicle output and therefore in the demand for
rubber. A further encouragement to the world division of
labour, in which technological improvements were concentrated at the manufacturing end, was the small percentage
which most raw materials represent in the cost of final
goods. For example, in the rubber industry, the products
requiring high technology, like motor vehicles and most
machine parts, use very little rubber, whereas simple
finished goods like rubber clothing and footwear use much
more.

    Shipping policy and the structure of freight rates
strengthened this pattern of industrial location. Freight
rates are not merely a function of distance, and therefore
of the costs actually incurred by the carrier; they are
determined partly by 'elements of monopoly or collusion,
navigation laws, the relationship between inward and outward cargoes on a route', etc. (35) There occurred during
the nineteenth century a greater decline in freight than
in prices of commodities, and the freight on long hauls
declined more than that on short hauls. The cost of
carrying manufactured goods from the raw material producing countries to regional markets thus increased relatively to the carriage of goods over long distances, as
from either Europe or Japan to Southeast Asia. For instance, the freight on rubber shoes from Singapore to
Europe was as high as that from Japan to Europe. (36)
Furthermore, a change from about 1870 in the pattern of
Europe's outward and inward cargoes led to a surplus of
shipping space on the homeward voyage. The consequent

lowering of the freight on primary products 'tended to
prevent the development of some kinds of locally oriented
industry and made the region remain largely dependent on
imports'. (37)   Before 1897, when the Straits Homeward
Conference secured a virtual monopoly of cargo consigned
from the Straits Settlements, 'tin was sometimes carried
[to Europe] free in place of ballast'. (38)   On the other
hand, cement and other heavy commodities, which served as
bottom cargo on the outward voyage, were also charged
extraordinarily low rates, giving manufacturers in Europe
a competitive advantage. These changes benefited the exporters of industrial goods in Europe and Japan.

Finally, the metropolitan countries by means of restrictive commercial practices discouraged the entry of
processed or finished goods while giving fiscal inducements to the entry of unprocessed primary products. These
practices were adopted at the time when many colonial raw
materials came into general use in the industrialized
countries. For example, the development of the seed-
crushing industry in the USA and in Australia was based
on protective tariffs. (39) The economic doctrine underlying this policy that 'no manufacturing industries should
be developed in the colonies, has undoubtedly continued to
influence [the world] division of labour' even after the
colonies became independent. (40) While tariffs and
quotas are imposed on manufactured or processed products
imported into the industrialized countries, raw materials
are allowed free entry. The import tariffs are made to
escalate with successively higher stages of manufacture.
Processed products are discriminated against compared with
raw materials and the more processed products compared
with the less processed. The differential tariffs not
only protect the processing industries in the raw material
importing countries but also militate against the development of these industries in the raw material exporting
countries. (41)

As a prelude to explaining the lack of dynamism of the
staples base in the nonsettler colonies I have critically
examined the notion that market limitations played a significant role. Among the impediments to the growth of
processing industries I also drew attention to the prior
development of such industries in Europe as well as to the
fiscal and commercial policy of the metropolitan countries. At the outset of this chapter I sought to explain
the dynamism of the staples base in the settler regions in
terms of the autonomy of foreign capital in the host country, where it became permanently committed. The resulting
autonomy of the investors led them to create economic
structures competitive with those of the parent society -

an outcome which was partly determined by the mediation of the state on behalf of the settler investors who had by this time come to constitute a national bourgeoisie. In resuming my discussion on the failure of the staples base in the nonsettler colonies to generate comparable changes, I shall now explain this failure in terms of the extra-territoriality of the investors; such an explanation will parallel my argument that the locus of capital ownership was a fundamental factor in the development of the settler regions.

Extra-territoriality of the investors in nonsettler colonies generally militated against industrial invest-ment. This is to be explained by two sets of reasons. One is the impracticality of operating industrial enter-prises on an absentee basis, which I shall elaborate presently. The other set of reasons relates to the metro-politan investors as a whole wanting to safeguard the capital value of already existing production facilities in the home country against the possible development of com-peting facilities elsewhere. As mentioned earlier, the technological superiority of Europe which had arisen by this time was the basis on which dominant-dependent rela-tions on a world scale were to develop subsequently.

At a stage in the development of the world economy when communications, technology and management systems were re-latively undeveloped, manufacturing industries were not easy to operate and control from abroad. Though the con-sistency and calculability of machine operations make an industrial activity amenable to accounting procedures and thus easier to superintend, industrial activity requires a certain autonomy and flexibility of management, including co-ordination of production inputs, quality control measures, and adjustments to market situations, which cannot easily be routinized. The delegation of only very limited authority to overseas branch managers, which was characteristic of extra-territorial investments, was, in the case of industrial enterprises, not conducive to ef-ficiency. The complexities of metropolitan control were greater when production was for the local market. Ab-sentee ownership and control cause problems in agriculture as well. Efficiency norms or stable ratios between ex-penditure and output cannot easily be imposed. Mere ac-counting procedures would not reveal, for example, whether manure and labour shown as items of cost have, in fact, been used. Mismanagement or fraud will not be apparent until much later, when yields decline; and the possibili-ty of natural hazards may not make it easy to place re-sponsibility for the loss.

In the plantations, however, absentee ownership and

control acquired a degree of compatibility due basically
to a framework of organization, which expressed itself in
the form of locally domiciled merchants' firms which
served as managing agents. The agency system, under which
the management of several estates and plantation companies
was grouped together, created career incentives to estate
superintendents, dissuading them from making small gains
by improper means. The prospect of promotion from a
smaller to a larger estate, or of appointment as a part-
time visiting agent and eventually as a board member of a
plantation company, encouraged long service and loyalty.
The integrity of a few senior executives and superintend-
ing staff was also ensured by the payment of high salaries, which was possible on a plantation because of its
very small ratio of salaries to wages; a slight underpay-
ment of the large labour force could finance the generous
emoluments of the managerial staff. Absentee ownership
and control of a plantation were made possible, secondly,
by specific management practices which were highly system-
atized and routinized. Visiting agents regularly inspect
the estates, and the monthly reports of the superintendents show at a glance the performance of an estate both in
the field and in the factory. (42) The agency house
intervenes only if significant deviations from the average
or base figures cannot be explained by the superintendent's remarks. The uniformity of plantation organization
and practices (unlike the heterogeneity of industrial
enterprises) lends itself with ease to this model of
management and supervision. Third, the historical circumstances in which the agency system developed caused the
investors to abdicate entrepreneurial control and responsibility to their agents. The investors were numerous
scattered shareholders, many having inherited small parcels of shares; essentially rentiers, they were content
with receiving their dividend warrants. In a later chapter the control exercised over the plantations by the
agency firms will be fully explored.

Trading enterprises themselves could not be conducted
on an absentee basis, owing to the nature of their entrepreneurial responsibility and also the high risk of fraud
due to the large liquid funds which they held; decision
making was of a short-term or even of a day-to-day nature.
But there were other circumstances that were conducive to
the investment of trading capital in the colonies. The
limited value of the fixed assets of trading enterprises,
and their easily realizable nature, drastically reduced
the need for equity capital. Trading capital especially
appealed to expatriate investors because of the flexibility it imparted to their investments, and for other reasons

to which I shall presently refer. A preference for trading activities, due to the small value of their fixed
assets, was shown, for example, in the choice of investments by James Finlay & Co. in India. As a biography of
the firm states, 'with the instincts of general merchants,
always ready to shift the basis of their trading activities to a variable demand, they were reluctant to commit
large sums of capital in [tea] estates from which it could
not be withdrawn'. (43)

    The small value of equity capital also enabled the
ownership and management of trading enterprises to be confined to a few partners or principal shareholders who frequently resided in the colonies. Trading capital, though
not necessarily small in the aggregate, is mostly working
capital with a rapid annual turnover - easily qualifying
for bank loans; and the joint stock company, which was a
device par excellence for the drawing in of outside capital, was unnecessary. The poor infrastructure of underdeveloped countries, no doubt, required investment in fixed
assets such as warehouses, office buildings and motor
vehicles. These investments, lucrative per se, were relatively limited. They were also of a nonspecific kind,
having alternative uses, and therefore readily mortgage-
able or disposable. In brief, these assets were easily
shed without loss. A comparison with industrial capital
brings these characteristics of trading capital into sharp
focus. Industrial enterprises required fixed assets of a
much higher value (both absolutely and as a ratio of the
working capital); being in the form of specialized plant
or machinery, they are far less flexible in their use and
cannot easily be retrieved. A high degree of specificity
also reduces their value as collateral. Industrial assets
consequently have to be financed out of the paid-up capital rather than from short-term borrowing. While industrial enterprises, for these reasons, have to be organized
as joint stock companies, the difficulty of managing and
controlling such enterprises from abroad discourages absentee investment.

    Trading firms, however, were typically partnerships or
sole-proprietor concerns whose owners usually resided in
the country of investment. In Sri Lanka after the Second
World War most of the expatriate trading firms were made
private limited liability companies, but without any real
broadening of capital ownership and management. Incorporation enabled the original proprietors, when retiring
from the colony, to withdraw a portion of their assets or
even to sort out and separate some of their private funds
which had become merged in the business. Outside capital
participation in the new companies was minimal, and the

shares were not freely transferable. The original proprietors became governing directors for life, retaining
control of the business. (44)   Management shares gave them
'the right to all the profits or other monies of the company available for dividends', and a claim on its surplus
assets. The proprietary directors had absolute discretion
over share transfers; they had the first right to purchase at par any shares of an intending transferor and
could select the person to whom shares could be sold.

While in the nonsettler colonies production capital was
invested on an absentee basis, constraining the scope of
its activities, the character of trading capital enabled
trading enterprises to be operated on the basis of the
local domicile of the principal investors. Nevertheless,
such enterprises were limited in their entrepreneurial
reach. They confined themselves to activities which were
relatively risk-free, in which the prospect or the existence of monopoly profits was the basic inducement. The
actual extent of monopoly is greater than is suggested by
the number of trading firms, some of which are only nominally independent. Long-established firms, having goodwill and trading connections, are seldom dissolved even
when they cease to be viable and are acquired by other
firms; they are allowed to exist nominally with their
original name and style. Some other firms for various
reasons serve as a façade or cover from the outset. (45)
Whereas the monopolistic nature of the colonial export
trade is generally acknowledged, in the import trade the
presence of a greater number of firms and of products has
induced a notion that competition prevailed. According to
Kathleen Stahl, the relations between the British importing firms in Sri Lanka were 'keenly competitive'. (46)
Likewise another writer has asserted: 'In contrast to the
monopolistic organisation of the export trade, the import
business was handled by a large number of firms and individuals.' (47) But in fact there were greater barriers to
the entry of indigenous merchants into the import trade
than into the export trade; in Malaysia, for example, a
substantial volume of export produce, such as smallholders' rubber, was collected, processed and exported by
non-European traders. The growth of local produce markets
(for rubber in Singapore and Colombo, and for tea in
Colombo) also enabled indigenous trading to engage in the
export trade. Concentration of trade in the hands of a
few was as prevalent in exports as in imports. Though
corporate giants are better known on the export side, the
ramifications of the importing firms are no less real.
(48)

Several factors underlay the monopolistic structure of

foreign trade in the colonies. First, a handful of traders who were first on the scene when the plantations were
founded gained a historical ascendancy in the economy. At
a time when land was plentiful and cheap, they were able
to pre-empt the best location for their business. For example, in Colombo, the premises of James Finlay & Co. had
as their most valuable aspect proximity to transport.
Purchased around 1900, this property comprised 'two blocks
of land, one bordering the Colombo Lake with its access
to the Harbour and the other with warehouses on the land-
ward side of the road'. (49) The possession of water-
front stores considerably reduced the costs of loading,
transporting and unloading produce. In other instances
roads, railways or wharfs tended to gravitate towards the
area where these firms were situated. For example, in
Singapore the Tanjong Pagar docks were built in the 1860s
on land belonging to Guthrie & Co., from which later a
railway line led to the main business area in the town.
(50) The large British agency houses - such as Guthrie,
Boustead, Sime Darby, the Borneo Company, Harrisons &
Crosfield, MacAlister, Mansfield - had 'the Peninsular
railway terminating in their own backyard, so to speak'.
(51)
     Second, the monopoly position of these firms was due
to their financial resources. Though trade has a quicker
financial turnover and a lower ratio of fixed to working
capital than plantations and manufacturing industry, the
critical minimum funds were more than most firms in the
colonies could afford. For instance, in the export of
coconut oil there are considerable cost economies in investment in storage tanks, weigh bridges, oil drums and
motor vehicles. (52) The warehouses of trading and managing agency firms in Colombo, used for storing export produce, fertilizers and other materials, were a rich source
of profit. In recent years inadequate storage capacity on
the estates led to increased investment in warehouses by
agency firms, shippers and exporters. Fixed investments
by individual firms were an oligopolistic device to impede
the entry of new firms. These firms were also able to
finance the indigenous retail traders who had no access to
the banks.
     Third, the hegemony of the European firms derived from
the large share of imports which they had engrossed,
partly in their role as managing agencies of plantations.
A stable portion of their business was thus the importation of plantation materials, e.g. fertilizers, tea chests
and tea-packing accessories, agricultural tools, building
materials for factories and estate housing, and tea and
rubber machinery. These firms had also a monopoly over

the sale or distribution of branded goods, for which they
were the sole agents. For instance, in Sri Lanka Delmege
Forsyth was the distributor of Cadbury's chocolates and
Clarke's sewing thread and also controlled the trade in
petroleum products. Through area agreements with manufacturers abroad the trade in such goods was fenced into
separate preserves. Rarely were goods imported independently of the agent, but whatever the channel of purchase
he as the area overlord clipped his commission. While the
entry of new firms into a business was blocked, secretive-
ness regarding commissions and suppliers' prices abroad
permitted a degree of local price manoeuvring by the indenting agents.

Whether as estate agencies or as trading enterprises,
the European firms plucked all of the shipping and insurance business. One of them, James Finlay & Co., had a
proprietary interest in the Clan Line steamships, which
from 1878 carried the expanding exports of tea and jute
from India, and it later acted for several other shipping
lines as full agent or as discharging agent. (53) Shipping and insurance companies almost always had as the
local agent an established merchant house through which
they obtained business at less expense than by setting up
a branch with separate staff and premises. (54) As with
foreign-owned plantations, in shipping and insurance the
agency function arose from the absentee nature of colonial
investments. A major responsibility was the collection
and safe custody of funds which, pending their remittance
abroad, were banked or invested locally on a pattern decided by the principals. The agent also attended to local
tax matters, supplied office space and supervised the
staff. The principals met half the salaries of the staff
and the entire cost of developing new business. The agent
received a commission on the premiums and a agency fee.

Insurance and shipping were lucrative and riskless
adjuncts to the trading activities of European firms. As
stated in a house history of George Steuart & Co., 'With
the growth of the Estate Agency it was realised that the
firm should be in a position to insure the various buildings that were being constructed.' (55) In Sri Lanka,
during the early years of the plantation economy the insurance taken was mostly on account of loss by fire of
coffee stores and estate bungalows. Later the volume of
insurance grew and came to include 'consequential loss of
profits' as well as marine, motor and accident insurance.
Tea factories accounted for a large proportion of the
value of the policies written - in 1892 for 'not less than
£50,000' - and 'enormous profits [were] being made out of
Ceylon insurance'. (56) The tea factories were isolated

buildings, less prone to fire than produce stores in
London which were close together and in a drier climate.
Yet, the insurance rate in the 1890s was nearly twice that
on comparable stores in London (20s. and 11s. 9d. a year,
respectively). (57) Estate owners felt that it should not
have been more than half of what was charged. According
to the Ceylon Chamber of Commerce, the agents were 'levying arbitrary rates, in the belief that insurers cannot
help themselves'. (58) The insurance business generated
by the plantations was largely monopolized by the managing
agents. According to Sri Lanka exchange control data (un-
published), during 1948-62 ten estate agencies collected
two thirds of the total premiums on non-life insurance and
a like proportion of the commissions. The commissions
averaged 23 per cent of the premiums paid, and the agencies were reimbursed with at least half of the expenses
incurred in collection.

Shipping agencies, apart from being an extra source of
income, contributed to the commercial dominance of the
European firms. As agents for shipping lines, they had a
first claim on the available freight. The need to carry
stock pending shipment was thus reduced, and the period of
capital turnover shortened. In the initial decades of the
plantation economy, when there was a serious scarcity of
freight, the control over shipping was of fundamental importance. 'It would be very easy for us to send you
plenty of ships if we had the means of giving outward
freight', Kirkham Finlay in Glasgow wrote to his son
Alexander Struthers Finlay, a partner of Ritchie, Steuart
& Co., Bombay, in 1836. 'But ... how is it possible for
us to find freight?' (59) Even in later years the direct
access to shipping facilities was a prerequisite for
large-scale trading. The first big rivals to the Europeans in the rice trade in Sri Lanka were the Memon merchants, who were connected with the Scindia Steam Navigation Co., Bombay. The monopoly power of European trading
enterprise was thus based on the pre-emption of markets
and supply sources, economies of scale, access to funds,
and the lateral integration with insurance and shipping
business.

Another aspect of the limited entrepreneurial reach of
the foreign trading enterprises, even when they were
locally domiciled, arose from the relation between the
rulers and the ruled. It was the enclave existence of the
expatriate European community which created the need for a
compradore merchant as a broker or intermediary between
the European houses and the indigenous producers or consumers. Isolated socially, the Europeans lacked direct
knowledge of the market, nor could they adopt trading pro-

cedures suited to local conditions. Thus the imports of
the European firms were standardized goods - e.g. fertilizer, tea chests, agricultural tools, cement and building
materials - which had an assured or predictable market,
free from rapid or erratic fluctuations. They also imported general merchandise such as rice, flour, sugar,
textiles, stationery and sundry goods, but their involvement in this trade was limited; they usually booked
orders in return for a commission based on the value of
indents. The import orders were undertaken on the advice
of an indigenous 'guarantee broker' - a man of wealth who
was held liable for unsettled claims. Unlike early commercial enterprise, where merchant firms traded on their
own account, venturing substantial sums and carrying
stocks, the indenting system was virtually riskless.

While business that was relatively safe was a prerogative of the European firms, trading risks were taken by
the indigenous and other Asian traders. Their imports
were of a heterogeneous range, involving a differentiation
in prices, grades and quality. In rice, potatoes, onions,
chillies, dried fish and pulses, there was also a high
degree of market instability, due to the vagaries of production, the irregularity of shipments, and the generally
perishable nature of the goods. Prompt unloading and
clearing from the wharf was required, as well as speedy
disposal. The trading organization and procedures were
complicated. Unfettered initiative by the staff and a
high degree of personal responsibility were required as
well as irregular working hours and recourse to unorthodox
methods of circumventing customs and port delays. An intricate system of market intelligence prevailed (including
anticipation of the plans of rival importers) to achieve
an even spread of imports if steep price fluctuations were
to be avoided. At the same time, the optimal level of
stocks was small because of the perishableness of the
goods and the relative nearness of supply sources - mainly
India, Burma and Java. The monopoly advantages which
underlay British commercial dominance in the colonies were
of little relevance in this trade. In Sri Lanka it was in
these circumstances that European enterprise was ousted
from the trade in rice, flour, sugar and textiles. The
Memon merchants dominated this trade from about 1908 onwards and later indigenous traders gained a share in it.
(60)

The decline of British merchant houses in Asia in the
1930s shows the disabilities of expatriate businessmen,
living in enclaves and socially distant from the indigenous community. In Indonesia, amidst a general decline in
European trade, the British firms lost more than the Dutch

firms; the latter's proprietors and staff were locally resident. In Sri Lanka, an increase in the imports of Japanese cotton piece goods during 1932 threatened the trade with the UK and India with 'complete extinction'. While the European firms generally did not engage in retail trade, the astonishing success of Japanese import firms in this period was due to their first-hand knowledge of market requirements and popular taste. Furnivall wrote of how, in the retail shops, 'small lads were doing a thriving business for their Japanese employers ... [while along] the "Bond Street" of Bandung, one passed shop after shop with an impressive display of European luxuries, but empty except for the European assistants'. (61) The Japanese, having used the existing distributive channels, later exercised direct control over the bazaar trade. Free from any social barriers, they set up their own dis-tributive agencies which reached down to the local con-sumer. As both importers and retail distributors, the Japanese held all the links between the consumer and the manufacturer abroad. (62) The trade in Japanese goods was also on an 'open market' basis allowing for price cutting by rival importers, in contrast to the exclusive trade channels of the European firms, based on a system of agents and sub-agents.

The 'ostensibly "super-normal" profits in the expatri-ate trading sector', which P.J.Drake recognized, (63) were thus due to its monopoly position, and are not to be ex-plained, as he tried to do, as rewards to scarce factors such as capital, entrepreneurship and knowledge, or to high commercial risks and as a compensation for dangers to life in the tropics. Risks were high only in the initial decades of foreign enterprise, and were due chiefly to agricultural hazards, shipping delays and fluctuating ex-change rates. When large-scale financing of colonial export agriculture began from the 1880s, it no longer had a reputation for riskiness. Equally questionable is Drake's explanation of super-normal profits in terms of the access of European enterprises 'to short-term credit in the commercial centres of the advanced countries'. The expatriate trading enterprises did not resort to foreign borrowing even at the outset. They were, in fact, a source of liquid funds for the plantations - a circum-stance which led some of them to develop into managing agency houses. The colonial economy had a surplus of liquid funds alongside the scarcity of credit in the indi-genous sector. (64)

As for export production, though it was based initially on funds from abroad, it later became self-financing to a very large extent. An interesting corollary manifested

itself when in Sri Lanka, from 1948, the plantation companies became subject to an exchange control regulation
which restricted dividends payable abroad to the current
profits (including income from investments abroad). The
companies then began distributing as dividends the entire
disposable profits (including income from investments
abroad), thereby ending the accumulation of reserve funds.
While the regular working expenditure of the companies had
increased in these years, owing to rising export duties,
taxation and production costs, these companies then became
under-capitalized. The sterling companies now began to
meet their requirements by overdrafts taken directly from
the local banks. The credit which they obtained in Sri
Lanka was both cheap and convenient. Generally no security was required to cover their overdrafts, though occasionally they were based on a lien on stocks or a deposit of title deeds carrying only an 'undertaking to
mortgage' if called upon to do so. Many of the overdrafts, though intended as short-term, extended for much
longer periods. The local commercial banks, having excess
liquidity, were very willing to lend at 'favoured rates'
to expatriate interests.

The narrow range of interests of European capital in
nonsettler colonies was of necessity due to the extra-
territoriality of the investors. The investments they
made were in projects which did not need expensive machinery and other fixed assets and which therefore could be
liquidated without loss. The lack of a permanent involvement in the host economy limited them to established or
proven ventures or to those that subserved the profits
centre in the metropolis. In the Straits Settlements,
even export agriculture was pioneered by the Chinese and
by British planters who had made their home in the Settlements. 'British capitalists', wrote Sir Frank Swettenham,
'declined to risk even small sums in the Malay states till
years after the enterprise and industry of the Chinese had
developed the [tin] mines and the government had in their
experimental plantations proved the capabilities of the
soil.' (65) In tin mining also the Chinese dominated,
even when the British had asserted their political power
and made liberal mining concessions to British investors.
(66) Rubber planting on a commercial scale was begun by a
Chinese in 1895, and three years later a syndicate of
Chinese set up the Malacca Rubber and Tapioca Company.
The Resident Councillor of Malacca noted the absence of
comparable European enterprises at the time. (67) The
Europeans were preoccupied with trade, and even the planters preferred crops with relatively quick returns. 'There
is the absence here of the planting interest ... the

[British] people don't care about rubber or peppers or
cultural products', wrote Ridley, the Director of the
Singapore Botanical Gardens from 1888.   'At present everything is commerce.' (68)
   The plantations as the major sphere in which production
capital was invested were only an apparent exception to
the general immobility of capital on an absentee basis.
Plantation investment had a specific history and a set of
circumstances which made it eligible for such investment.
It required only a small value of fixed assets.   Land was
had free by the early planters or else for a nominal sum.
In Sri Lanka, between 1823 and 1832 a total of 12,928
acres was given away to prospective planters, and in 1841,
78,658 acres were sold at 5 shillings an acre.   Later, the
Colonial Office, wanting to realize the true value of the
land, introduced a system of public auctions, but the
planters refrained from bidding against each other and
only the 'upset price' was paid (usually 5 shillings).
(69)   In Malaysia, from 1847, extensive tracts were alienated at 10 cents an acre during the first ten years of a
Crown lease, and later at 50 cents an acre. (70)   Capital
markets abroad required to be tapped only in later decades, when the price of land and other fixed assets of
plantations increased.
   While the improved functioning of the British capital
market in this phase was more conducive to capital exports, the increased investment in plantations was associated with a low degree of risk.   In the first place, such
capital was used for the purchase of estates that were already developed and 'had proved themselves to be profitable', (71) or else whose purchase price was payable in
cash instead of in shares to the vendors.   Drabble observed that the investors in London 'were particularly
anxious to acquire land already planted with rubber, for
this reduced the initial investment and ensured quicker
returns'. (72)   Having taken over estates already in production, these companies were able to pay dividends in the
first year or soon after their incorporation - a reas-
suring prospect to absentee investors.   Second, in India,
Sri Lanka and Malaysia a significant portion of the capital of plantation companies consisted of preference shares
and debentures.   Like government stock, this capital
earned a fixed return and was redeemable for cash after a
specified period.   Furthermore, the leading investors were
those who were well acquainted with the prospects for
colonial export products.   They were the insiders - a
narrow circle of planters, merchants and produce brokers
who were 'linked by a common interest in finance, commerce
or through personal connections with the East'. (73)

This is to say, direct financing by the British capital
market took place after the profitability of export production had become assured. Absentee investors overcame
their hesitance only when resident investors had blazed a
trail. For a decade prior to the rubber boom of 1905-6,
rubber growing in Malaysia was financed by resident planters and government officials or by similar groups in Sri
Lanka who were already acquainted with the prospects. (74)
The pioneering work had been done during the pre-company
phase, by individual planters venturing their own funds,
and absentee capital led merely to an expansion of existing lines of production. In Sri Lanka, tea growing, which
eventually became a corporate enterprise dominated by
absentee capital, was pioneered by individual planters who
were quasi-settlers. (75) This was also a feature of the
regions of new settlement where nonresident capital was
invested typically in 'existing export industry rather
than in new, untried enterprises'. (76) The conservative
bias of the overseas investor was also reflected in a discontinuity in foreign capital inflows, according to the
changing prospects of the staples base. Economic growth
in these regions has consequently been uneven and erratic.
    While a considerable amount of the initial capital of
plantation companies was loan capital, having a comparatively low degree of risk, the locally incorporated companies were financed by the resident European community -
planters, merchants, administrators and professional men -
out of earnings in the colony. In Sri Lanka most of
the rubber companies, which were on a joint stock basis
from the outset of rubber planting, needed little capital
at the time of incorporation. The purchase value of their
assets was small - the assets were often tracts of undeveloped land or else estates whose vendors accepted payment in shares or mortgages and debentures. The issued
capital was usually called up in instalments over a five-
to-six-year period between land clearing and the first
harvest. These companies not merely kept down the issued
capital to a bare minimum but also financed themselves out
of current profits. As explained by a company chairman
whom I quoted earlier, the shareholders acquiesced in a
'self-denying policy', whereby 'the profits earned year
by year [were] steadily returned to meet the cost of capital expenditure'. (77) The Kelani Valley Rubber Co. of
Ceylon Ltd stated likewise in its report for 1907: 'The
same conditions prevail today as in the previous year,
during which essential expenditure exceeded the estimate,
making it advisable that the profit should be carried forward as working capital instead of being distributed as
dividends.' The development of these companies was con-

tinually thwarted by an inadequacy of funds. Sometimes
they were unable to cultivate the whole acreage which they
possessed and were obliged to lease or sub-lease unopened
land.

The nonsettler colonies attracted altogether little
production capital and the bulk of it was in the infrastructure investments. Nurkse even tended to regard these
'distance inputs' - roads, railways, docks, telegraphs,
etc. - as the typical form of colonial investment. (78)
All of this capital was riskless, being borrowed directly
by colonial governments on the basis of guaranteed interest and sinking fund charges on the revenue of the colonies. The investors received their return, even when, as
in India, the railways for more than a generation did not
pay their way. As the Rt Hon. W.N.Massey testified in
1872 in regard to these railway investments, 'the money
came from the English capitalist, and so long as he was
guaranteed 5 per cent on the revenues of India, it was im-
material to him whether the funds that he lent were thrown
into the Hooghly or converted into brick and mortar'. (79)
The 'struggle for the 5% guarantee' was led by the Manchester cotton manufacturers in defiance of laissez faire
precepts. (80) Despite the clamour by the commercial and
industrial interests in Britain for the construction of
railways in India, risk capital was not forthcoming.

In the nonsettler colonies, the constricted channels of
investment of foreign capital (trade and plantations and
not industrial ventures) must be seen against the impediments imposed by extra-territoriality on the mobility of
capital on a world scale. In the period we are concerned
with, rapid telecommunication and transportation facilities did not exist, such as the telex and jet aircraft,
which promote the management and control of investments
from abroad. The mobility of capital on a world scale was
also constrained by the division of the world into colonial empires. The internationalization process was one of
markets rather than of capital, as I shall explain fully
in a later chapter. Internationalization requires both
the mobility of capital across national boundaries - i.e.
a transnational flow - and multinational ownership.
Whereas the transnationalization of capital had existed
for several centuries, the scope of this process was
itself limited owing to the reasons to which I have referred. Multinational investments which are the final expression of the internationalization of capital had not
yet begun to occur. The circuits of capital, within each
colonial empire, were themselves affected by the division
between the settler and the nonsettler colonies. The
movement of capital was mainly to the settler territories

(with the migration of both capital and the capitalist),
and it also took the form of cross-investment among the
capitalist countries.

4   Economic development in the settler and the nonsettler colonies: differences in scope and orientation

A permanent locus of European settlers in the country of
investment had significant implications for development -
as is evident from the experience of South Africa, and to
a lesser extent that of Rhodesia after the Second World
War, Kenya and the countries of the Maghreb - i.e. Algeria, Morocco and Tunisia. The economic activity of the
settlers was generally inwardly oriented; they tended to
produce for the local market, displacing imports. (1)   In
Zambia, while the expatriate investors were solely concerned with copper mining, the few settlers grew maize for
sale in Katanga. (2)   In Rhodesia, the maize growers regarded 'the provision of local consumption requirements as
their first task'. (3)   The settlers also developed export
agriculture but only as an outgrowth of production for the
local market which had been built up under tariff protection; e.g. in Kenya and Rhodesia - grain, livestock, and
meat products. Alternatively, export production was a
response to a change in the relative profitability of
different crops. Thus in Rhodesia, from the late 1940s
the switch from maize to tobacco as the principal crop
was prompted by a spectacular rise in the export price
of tobacco. Nonsettler investors, on the other hand, were
throughout concerned with export production to the exclusion of everything else. Furthermore, the exports of the
settler colonies to a significant degree entered regional
markets and not the metropolitan ones. Basically, the
economic results of export production differed from those
in the nonsettler colonies. Dividends were not transferred out but reinvested, after a time spilling over into
different lines beyond the original investment.
    These divergent interests can be seen clearly in coun-
tries where there were both settlers and expatriates. In
South Africa, the expatriate investors were confined
mainly to mining and foreign trade; but the shift to

agriculture and manufacturing which was to transform the
economy was brought about by the settlers. The mining
companies and the metropolitan based commercial bourgeoisie were wholly export oriented and concerned with already
existing markets, whereas the settlers relied on the home
market. They produced many of the requirements of the
mines - such as clothing and food for the mine workers,
and explosives and similar necessities. The mining companies later invested in manufacturing enterprises that were
ancillary to their main activity but they did not initiate
industrialization. The stimulus to industrialization came
largely from the settlers. (4) While the availability of
mineral resources was a general factor conditioning
Africa's industrial growth, it was in the preponderantly
settler colonies of South Africa, Southern Rhodesia and
North West Africa that industrialization proceeded farthest. (5) 'Where there were no European settlers, in
West Africa for example, there was before the war no development.' (6) Though in the absence of settlers an
indigenous bourgeoisie tended to develop in these nonsettler colonies, with the exception of the Congo manufacturing industry was minimal - confined to the processing of minerals for export, such as diamonds in Tanzania,
iron ores in Sierra Leone, and copper in Zambia.

In Kenya, where ecological factors permitted both plantations and a homestead type of agriculture with multicropping and animal husbandry, the plantations attracted
'the type of investor known collectively as "the City"'.
These, the expatriate investors, opened up tea plantations
in the early 1920s; before that they organized cotton
cultivation both in Kenya and Uganda. The metropolitan
interests, which these predominantly export crops served,
were blatantly evident in the activities of the British
East Africa Corporation (later far more important in
Uganda). The corporation, financed mainly by the British
Cotton Growing Association, sought to reduce Lancashire's
dependence on American supplies just as the British East
India Company, much earlier, had sponsored tea growing in
Assam when supplies from China became uncertain. The
settlers, too, engaged in cotton cultivation but they did
so as proprietary farmers, unlike the 'great London finan-
ciers'.

While the expatriate interests in Kenya responded exclusively to metropolitan needs, the settlers were concerned with the domestic market and produced for export
only when the prospects were too good to pass by. They
grew maize to meet the demand from African workers on the
coffee plantations, and undertook wheat and dairy production. 'The growth of the maize industry', wrote G.C.

Wrigley, 'was a by-product of the general growth of the
economy, especially of the plantation industries, for it
was the feeding of African labour that provided the maize
growers with the most lucrative market.' (7)   The settlers
were slow to take advantage of the prospects for coffee,
for which the East African highlands were eminently suited
and for which an export market existed.   Their interest in
coffee, which later became one of Kenya's foremost products, developed only after the First World War.   'The
connotations of coffee-growing did not accord with ...
[Lord Delamere's] own tastes or his ideal of a British
colony of settlement.' (8)

The difference in entrepreneurial interests between
settler and nonsettler investors was reflected fundamentally in the production structures to which their activities gave rise.   The settlers' production activities
paralleled rather than complemented those in the metropolitan and other developed economies.   They replicated
the production pattern of these economies, tending thereby
to make the colony competitive with them.   Compared with
expatriate interests, the settlers constituted themselves
into a 'national' bourgeoisie detached from the metropolitan economy and society.   They pre-empted the domestic and
regional markets, through protective tariffs and financial
subsidies and by seizing control over indigenous land and
labour.   They did not passively respond to existing market
opportunities, or conform to a metropolitan based division
of labour, but carried out what was tantamount to a resource reallocation - transforming social relations and
production technology.   The relatively developed urban-
cum-industrial sector reduced the role of the settler
colonies as sources of primary produce and as markets for
metropolitan industry.   Even when mineral production retained its central importance, the settlers thus exhibited
certain progressive qualities both in their production
structures and in their external economic relations. (9)

In Africa south of the Sahara, if one excludes the
Union of South Africa which stands out as a developed
country (where settler influence was paramount, somewhat
like the regions of new settlement), a distinction may be
drawn between a group of less underdeveloped countries and
the overwhelmingly underdeveloped.   The distinction corresponds broadly with the political and economic influence
of the settler bourgeoisie vis-à-vis international capitalism represented by expatriate enterprise.   The pattern
and extent of development in the settler colonies can be
discerned in relation to several factors: the extent of
industrialization and the relative weight of secondary
production, the commodity composition and destination of

exports - i.e. the importance of national and/or regional
as opposed to metropolitan markets, the degree of diversification of their economies, the scope of state intervention on behalf of activities that were competitive
with metropolitan interests, and the extent of urbanization and wage employment.

Industrialization appears to have made headway only in
the Federation of Rhodesia and Nyasaland, in Kenya and the
Congo. After the Second World War their manufacturing
output as a proportion of gross national product (GNP)
ranged from 10 to 12 per cent whereas in Ghana, Nigeria,
Ethiopia and Guinea it was well below 5 per cent. (10) In
energy consumption, the leading countries were Zambia and
Rhodesia, Nyasaland and the Congo. The statistics of industrialization for Zambia, Nyasaland and the Congo, however, are somewhat illusory. Those for Zambia and the
Congo include metal working and power generation (adjuncts
of mineral production) and for Nyasaland tea processing -
which are not strictly industrial. Among the countries
mentioned only Rhodesia and the Congo achieved notable
progress in industry, as seen from the extent of industrial employment, the volume and composition of manufacturing
output, and from the pattern of imports. In Rhodesia, in
the early 1950s, 18 per cent of the African workforce was
in the manufacturing sector excluding mining; in Kenya
the proportion was 16 per cent; but only 12 per cent for
twelve other countries. (11) In both Rhodesia and the
Congo, industrial production comprised a high proportion
of intermediate and capital goods, and imports were mainly
of raw materials and equipment - with a limited share of
light consumer goods. (12)

By contrast, the nonsettler economies of Zambia,
Uganda, Tanzania and Nyasaland exhibited the classical
pattern of an underdeveloped export economy based on
absentee capital. This pattern of production and foreign
trade involved a tight complementarity with the metropolis. In 1963, of the total value of exports of Nyasaland
and Zambia, 63 per cent and 61 per cent, respectively,
were taken by Britain. (For Rhodesia the corresponding
figure was 46 per cent, (13) and 20 per cent of its total
exports by value was absorbed by South Africa - a regional
market.) In Nyasaland, Zambia and, to a much lesser
extent, the Congo, export production as the dominant economic activity was limited in range and wholly extractive
in nature. In both Zambia and the Congo the domestic processing of copper ore generated a high level of national
income, though the associated urban development was of an
enclave nature; in Northern Zambia it was confined virtually to the mining compounds. The developmental impact of

copper mining, however, differed markedly in the Congo
compared with Zambia. As mentioned before, the Congo,
although a nonsettler colony, reached a high level of economic advancement. I shall attempt to answer this riddle
at a later stage.

In Rhodesia, several secondary industries sprang up,
some of which were agro-based: food processing (bacon
factories and creameries), cigarettes and tobacco, wood
products, textiles, oil and oil seed crushing, soap and
sugar. Another group of industries were based on imported
raw materials, and comprised flour mills, breweries and
garment factories. Third, there was the building materials industry - including cement, iron and steel - which
arose mainly from the demand for housing by European migrants and from the construction needs of farms. Industrial growth was constrained at the outset by a dependence
on imported inputs, but later when the flow of imports was
interrupted, as during the Second World War, development
surged ahead. Between 1938 and 1945 the number of industrial employees more than doubled, and between 1938 and
1949 manufacturing output increased sixfold in value from
£5.1 million to £31.1 million. (14)

This wartime expansion was sustained. Between 1945 and
1952 the industrial workforce again doubled and the number
of enterprises increased by 90 per cent. (15) Many of
these outgrew the small manufactory stage, and acquired
large accumulations of capital. Alongside an appreciable
growth in national income, the share of manufacturing rose
from 'about 15% in the early 1950s to over 18% in the
early 1960s' while that of mining declined from about 10
per cent to 5 per cent. (16) The postwar growth was based
mainly on textiles and clothing and on the metal and
building materials industry, including iron and steel.
The clothing industry consisted of six enterprises by
1951, and a fully integrated textile industry created 'the
prospect of meeting all the lower quality textile requirements and particularly the demands of the Africans in
Central Africa'. (17) The iron and steel industry changed
from imported scrap iron to local ore. The output of
finished steel more than doubled between 1948 and 1953,
(18) and the metal industry was diversified with engineering works, foundries, steel window factories, aluminium
and enamel works, tin smelting and manufacturing, a steel
pipe-drawing plant, a nail factory, a wire-drawing plant
and a plough factory. (19) An insufficient domestic
demand for manufactures was partly overcome by the regional market in Central and South Africa, with exports comprising cigarettes, processed fish, meat, clothing, sugar,
wheat flour and meal, tung oil and steel and engineering
products. (20)

The economic transformation of Southern Rhodesia after
the Second World War was influenced by a large influx of
settlers. The number of migrants, exclusive of certain
employment categories, rose from 4,041 in 1946 to an
annual average of 6,157 for 1947-51; (21)   net immigration
during 1946-56 averaged more than 7,000 a year compared
with less than 800 a year in the preceding two and a half
decades. Immigration on this scale produced a large capital inflow, which was augmented by nonsettler capital following the accession to power of a white settler government in 1948. The confidence of international capitalism
in the new regime led to the direct channelling of funds
into the country 'instead of being routed via Johannes-
burg'. (22) The migratory wave also triggered off a boom
in housing and related amenities. The ratio of investment
to national income was unprecedented, increasing from 13
per cent in 1946 to 30 per cent during 1949-51, with a
peak figure of 50 per cent in 1952.

This transformation was brought about by the pattern of
investment rather than the number of settler migrants per
se or by the mere volume of investment. The investments
had a decidedly industrial complexion, as is seen from the
data on occupational distribution. While 12.8 per cent of
the migrants entered agriculture and mining during 1947-51
(compared with 19.6 per cent in 1946), the proportion in
building and manufactures was 33.2 per cent (compared with
24.4 per cent in 1946). The employment pattern of Africans showed a similar change. Those in manufacturing and
construction (excluding railway workshops) increased over
the same period from 13.5 per cent to 20.0 per cent. (23)
The shift towards industrial-cum-urban investments was
linked to the dominance of the settler bourgeoisie, under
whose aegis even expatriate capital entered into a relatively wide range of investments.

The entrepreneurial orientation of settler investors in
Rhodesia has so far been referred to in terms of their
ability to respond to growth opportunities such as those
which arose during wartime, their wide range of investments - with an emphasis on secondary production - and
their concern with domestic or regional markets. Two
other characteristics were manifest. First, cultivation
remained on a small scale, on the homestead pattern, and
involved large numbers of producers instead of corporate
enterprise owned and financed abroad. From the 1940s,
when tobacco replaced maize as the leading crop, Rhodesian
agriculture became export based; yet cultivation remained
on a small scale, the number of tobacco farms increasing
from about 1,000 to 2,699 between 1945 and 1958. (24)   In
gold mining small- and medium-scale enterprises were also

the rule. The geological structure facilitated small
workings by those who had been employed as skilled labour
in other types of mining. (25) Second, along with the
small-scale nature of their investments, the internal
locus of the settler investors and their permanent interests in the host economy caused a shift of attention to
different lines of investment as entrepreneurial prospects
changed. This meant fairly competitive market structures,
with an 'intersectoral mobility of capital'. The response
of the Rhodesian farmers to the slump in grain and cattle
prices during 1921-3, to which Arrighi has referred, (26)
was typical. They turned to other lines of production
some of which used the depressed staples as inputs; e.g.
dairying, pig rearing, tobacco cultivation and gold
mining. The settlers also improved their future prospects
by investing in capital assets - farm buildings and other
fixed structures such as sheds, dipping tanks, stockyards,
roads, dams, canals, silos, fences and wells. The capacity to finance these expenditures was partly due to the
retention of export proceeds within the country.

The character of settler entrepreneurs becomes even
clearer when contrasted with the limited commitment of
expatriates in the host economy. The latter's interests
were transitory, narrow and inflexible; and their investments were owned and controlled abroad. They confined
themselves to the production of one or a few commodities
and wound up when these investments failed; for example,
the European coffee planters of Sri Lanka migrated to
Malaya in the 1880s after the destructive blight, and
recently tea planters from Sri Lanka have been moving to
Kenya when faced with higher taxation and the threat of
nationalization. These differences between the settler
and nonsettler investors were not mere attitudinal traits
but resulted from the nature and strength of their respective metropolitan links. Their entrepreneurial behaviour determined the varying economic structures which
took root in the underdeveloped world. These structures,
when viewed in abstraction from the interests of the
dominant entrepreneur class and, ultimately, from the
framework of metropolis-colony relations, are so often
mistaken for types of specialization dictated by local resource endowments.

The developmental impact of the settlers in Rhodesia is
highlighted by the backwardness of its sister colony
Zambia, where expatriate capital was dominant. Zambia is
far richer in natural resources and, with roughly the same
population, had a higher income per head. This income,
however, was based on copper mining. Manufacturing output
was minimal; its value, inclusive of ore smelting and re-

fining, was only one third of that for the Federation of
Rhodesia and Nyasaland. (27) Manufacturing proper was
almost confined to products which enjoy a natural protection, with a large bulk or weight per unit value - like
building materials, furniture and veneer, and bottled
drinks. The output of consumer goods was negligible -
mainly soap, clothing and blankets. The Second World War
did not change this pattern; mining continued to expand
along with the production of small components for explosives made in the mine and railway workshops. The natural
wealth of Zambia remained largely unexplored - especially
coal, timber and limestone. In Nyasaland, also a nonsettler colony - with only 5,000 Europeans in 1933 (0.2 per
cent of the population), manufacturing industry was even
more limited; and was confined to the processing of
export crops, mainly tobacco.

The economic backwardness of Zambia, despite a valuable
mineral resource, must be related to the dominance of expatriate interests. Here settlers were insignificant;
their ratio to the total population was in 1950 less than
one third of that in Rhodesia. The pronounced dispersal
of population, which made infrastructure and urban facilities more costly, was only a minor factor. Mining was
controlled by four companies which were concerned with
only a single commodity - copper - without the shifts in
interest which in Rhodesia characterized the growth of
mineral production and of the economy in general. Zambia,
since the time it was opened up to foreign capital, has
thus depended on copper, with little industrial development and with scarcely any urbanization outside the mining
enclaves. Furthermore, the mineral rights of the large
companies yielded vast profits over which the protectorate
had no control. Remittances of interest, dividends and
profits after the Second World War were usually more than
half of total export earnings.

In Africa generally urbanization and the growth of a
proletariat was till very recently limited or to some
extent illusory. Wage labour even in mines and factories
was not truly urbanized. Africans employed by these
enterprises had a dual existence - shuttling to and fro
between village and town. Their share of the produce of
the subsistence economy encouraged the payment of a 'bach-
elor wage', and low wages in turn inhibited a total break
from the subsistence economy. The administration also
controlled the presence of Africans in the towns. The
deformed nature of their urbanization, (28) besides
benefiting urban employers, sustained the power relations
between the settlers and the Africans. An urban African
proletariat 'in the view of the Administration, would have

disrupted the whole existing social and political order
[of the whites]'. (29) With these limitations, urbanization and the growth of a proletariat in Africa were confined to the settler colonies, which alone underwent some
degree of industrialization. African wage earners were
relatively numerous only in the settler territories of
South Africa, Rhodesia and Kenya and, north of the Sahara,
in the Maghreb. The single exception to this was the
Belgian Congo - which I shall discuss later. In South
Africa and in Rhodesia in the early 1950s, as mentioned
earlier, 21 per cent and 18 per cent, respectively, were
industrial employees. In Rhodesia the number of African
wage earners doubled between 1941 and 1956, from 303,000
to 610,000. (30) Of the three Central African territories, in 1956 out of a total of nearly 1 million African
wage earners, nearly 59 per cent were in Rhodesia (as
against 25 per cent and 16 per cent, respectively, in
Zambia and Nyasaland). (31)

Agriculture in the settler colonies, both in its institutional and agronomic aspects, represented a sharper
break with traditional agricultural systems than did plantations or the peasant-based export crops of West Africa,
Burma and Thailand. The novel features of settler agriculture are worth recapitulating. It was broad-based and
land intensive. A wide range of crops was grown, combining tillage with animal husbandry - in the Maghreb soft
wheats, vines, olives, tobacco, etc. There was specialization in the true sense conforming to variations in soil
and climate, as opposed to the virtual monoculture of the
plantations or the peasant-based export economies. The
land intensiveness of settler agriculture was evident in
the Maghreb, where vineyards, fruit farms and spring
vegetable gardens supported from four to six times as much
labour per hectare as cereal farming. Entirely new crops
and strains of cattle were acclimatized after prolonged
experimentation and research - unlike plantation crops
which were well suited to the ecology of the countries
where they came to be grown. In both Rhodesia and Kenya
rust-resistant varieties of wheat were evolved, merino
ewes and cattle imported, and local pastures upgraded by
the admixture of imported grass. (32) Likewise, farm
machinery was adapted to local conditions. The use of
capital and technology improved the quality of agricultural produce and lowered costs.

A significant aspect of settler agriculture was also
the secondary activities to which it gave rise in the producing areas - such as wine production, sugar refining,
textile manufacture, oil extraction, fish canning, the
manufacture of meat and dairy products, and food process-

ing and preserving. Such secondary production did not
entail, ab initio, complex technology, large accumulations
of capital and extensive markets. The technology required
was relatively simple - unlike the primary products of the
nonsettler colonies which were grown specifically to
supply the manufacturing plants in the metropolitan countries, protected as they were by a wide technological gap
between them and the suppliers of primary produce. The
barriers to what is now known as the transfer of technology were thus far less formidable than in the nonsettler colonies. The settlers not merely brought the requisite technology with them but - and this is the crucial
factor - they were also in a position to apply this technology in competition with metropolitan producers. The
domestic market which they appropriated by means of a
tariff also gave them a ready-made launching pad.

    Dualism - whose applicability to the plantation econo-
mies will be questioned in the concluding part of this
book - was a feature of the settler colonies, in which
productivity levels and rates of capital accumulation were
decidedly higher in the settler dominated sector of the
economy. (The efficiency of settler agricultural practices in the Maghreb, as reflected in a high productivity
per hectare - even allowing for the appropriation of the
best land by the settlers - will be set forth in detail
later in this chapter.) Initially settler agriculture
developed through the use of state power. The competitiveness of peasant producers was undermined by the despoliation of their land, and by discrimination in taxes,
marketing policies and in the location of social overhead
facilities, etc. Yet after a time settler agriculture
became self-generating and independent of those political
mechanisms; its viability was based on increased productivity and lower costs. As Arrighi explained in the
case of Rhodesia, thenceforth the productivity gap between
the two sectors was a response to market forces, which
'deepened the dualism of the economy'. (33)

    The production structures which emerged in the settler
colonies had elements of a development policy. As latecomers, these colonies had serious difficulties to contend
with. Whereas the primary producers in the USA, Canada,
Australia, New Zealand and the Baltic countries could rely
on the British market when, after the Corn Laws repeal in
1846, the centre of gravity of the British economy shifted
irrevocably from agriculture to industry, Rhodesia and
Kenya, for instance, had to compete with already established primary producers. In Rhodesia, the output of
wheat and dairy produce was expanded in the face of cheap
imports available from the United States and Canada. The

competitiveness of its agricultural produce on the East
African market was hampered by several factors. Fertilizer, agricultural machinery and repair services were
more expensive than those available to farmers in North
America 'working within the framework of a highly developed and integrated economy'. Agricultural research was
needed, and the railway built for the mining industry was
not always helpful. (34) The policy of protection to
which the settlers resorted, while raising the structure
of internal costs, resulted in a somewhat broad-based and
viable economy - internally focused and having a dynamism
independent of the metropolitan system. As a result productive capital tended to gain precedence over merchant
capital. In the nonsettler colonies, by contrast, unregulated imports were desired by the trading interests which
dominated the economy and also as a means of holding down
wages in the export sector which produced agricultural raw
materials and minerals. This in the context of Malaysia
was the 'rubber and tin mentality' to which Wheelwright
referred.

The settlers also attempted to manage the economy as a
separate entity distinct from the metropolitan centre.
For this purpose settler activities required a formidable
backing from the state. Though it must be mentioned that
state intervention in nonsettler colonies was certainly
not lacking - e.g. in labour migration and in setting up
an infrastructure for the export economy - such intervention in the settler colonies was more extensive and of
an altogether different order. Its object was to create
investment opportunities for the white bourgeoisie as well
as employment for the white workers. Official concern for
development was greatest in colonies where there was a
white working class. Unemployment and poverty, besides
causing unrest, would have been too bad for white superiority - the psychological prop to the domination which the
settlers exercised. The building of a viable economy was
thus in the interests of both the settlers and the colonial state. In both South Africa and Rhodesia protective
tariffs were levied, state industrial monopolies were established, and subsidized employment was provided for the
settlers. In South Africa the state-owned enterprises
(e.g. in electricity, iron and steel, armaments, oil
synthesis) contributed substantially to both employment
and capital formation. (35)

In Rhodesia, where settler agriculture had to compete
with both imports and peasant production, the state
favoured the settlers - e.g. by a favourable siting of
railways and the fixing of rates, by providing regulated
credit and guaranteed prices and, above all, by proletari-

anizing the peasants. Extensive evictions were possible
with the active enforcement of the Land Apportionment Act
amidst declining peasant productivity. The domestic
labour supply was easily supplemented by an influx from
Zambia and Nyasaland, where employment opportunities were
limited. The government began controlling the operations
of the large expatriate enterprises such as the British
South Africa Company and the United Tobacco Company; the
former administered the railways and the latter almost
monopolized the purchase of tobacco from settler farmers.
This domination of the United Tobacco Company was curbed
by the Tobacco Marketing Act of 1936. Furthermore, domestic producers were assisted by tariffs and regional
trading arrangements. From 1955 there was greater tariff
autonomy, though even before that trading arrangements
were made with the Union of South Africa to help Rhodesian
manufacturers. Industrial enterprises were also sponsored
and given protection. The two largest - a cotton-spinning
mill and an iron and steel works - were due to government
initiative. The Rhodesia Iron and Steel Commission was
set up by an Act of Parliament in 1942. Finally, direct
financial aid was given to selected industries, to agricultural enterprises, and for small-scale mining.

In Rhodesia and Kenya the customs tariff was used to
promote domestic production rather than as a source of
public revenue. At first in Rhodesia protectionism was
not necessary. The bigger internal market required by
the agrarian bourgeoisie, and the employment needs of
white workers, seemed to be met by the expansion of overhead capital and housing. Agriculture benefited from the
overhead capital (mainly roads) as well as from public
utilities and from state sponsored industrial enterprises.
Furthermore, the construction materials industry - with
its cluster of secondary production activities - enjoyed
a natural protection. Manufacturing in this phase was
largely confined to low-quality goods for Africans. But
from the early 1920s the tariff was of direct benefit to
manufacturing industry. Protective duties were levied on
imports of finished products, while capital equipment and
industrial inputs were eligible for low duties or for duty
rebates. Even before the Second World War when the
government was careful to give protection to manufacturing
industry in general, (36) several state enterprises were
fully protected - e.g. iron foundries, cotton mills, and
raw material processing plants including sugar mills.

In Kenya, from 1920, when the tariff limitations imposed by the Treaty of Berlin were removed, the settlers
wanted protection for their nascent industries. In 1924
import duties of more than 10 per cent were levied on

several locally produced commodities; three years later
imported wheat was taxed at 30 per cent, after which wheat
production increased appreciably. (37) Protection was
later extended to sugar, lumber and butter. In the mid-
1920s the Customs Tariff Committee and the Economic and
Finance Committee affirmed the use of tariffs as an instrument of development. Tariffs were maintained despite
increased domestic prices for grain, meat, dairy produce
and sugar and higher building costs. Though agriculture
as the key sector in the economy benefited most, processing and manufacturing industries were also given protection. Industrialization was seen as a means of expanding the market for agricultural products. The protectionist measures of this period led to the development
of flour-milling, meat-canning and sugar-refining industries as well as those producing beer, cigarettes and
sisal bags. The British expatriates became interested in
secondary production, based on low-cost labour, only towards the end of the 1930s, when they had virtually lost
the East African market in imported cotton piece goods to
the Japanese.
    The encouragement of industries in Kenya contrasted
with the policy in Tanzania and Uganda, where tariff protection was disallowed. In Tanzania, mostly a trading
colony, the government's attitude was that imports were
a good thing: first, as a source of revenue and, second,
because any reduction in imports would have to be met by
domestic production which it was said would force Africans
into wage labour. All this was excellent for the industrial interests in Britain. It 'destroyed two potentially
significant enterprises' - a match factory catering for
domestic demand and the manufacture of sisal twine for
export. (38) An excise duty was levied on locally produced matches to offset the loss of customs revenue from
imports. (In Kenya a similar excise duty on beer and
cigarettes was linked to a higher import tariff so as to
ensure a margin of protection.) Britain intervened more
directly to strangle the Tanganyika Cordage Company which
had begun exporting binder twine. The Secretary of State
for the Colonies wanted the company to reach an agreement
with the Rope, Twine and Networkers' Federation in Britain
on the sale price of its products, or to face 'a protective duty on binder twine imported to Britain from the
Colonial Dependencies'. It wound up in 1938, having
failed to obtain favourable terms from the federation.
The different policies in Kenya and in Tanganyika and
Uganda were also evident at the Governor's Conference in
1935 which refused to give any concessions for a proposed
blanket factory in Uganda. Whereas the Acting Governor of

Kenya favoured the project, it was opposed by the Governors of Uganda and Tanzania; the latter held the view
that 'it was undesirable to accelerate the industrialization of East Africa which must, for many years to come,
remain a country of primary produce'.

In nonsettler colonies as a rule the tariffs were not
merely very modest, being essentially revenue raising, but
they were a means of preventing industrial growth.   In
Nigeria, they were devised 'not to keep foreign goods out
or to raise their price to such a level as to enable domestic produce to compete with them'. (39)   Manufacturing
was officially discouraged. The United Africa Company in
the 1930s failed to get government's approval for a spinning and weaving mill and a garment factory. (40)   In the
early 1950s, numerous textile projects, the World Bank
Mission found, had 'a cool over-cautious reception' by
the government instead of the 'active consideration' they
warranted. (41) The UK Trade Commissioner in Lagos
stressed the importance of the Nigerian market for British
textiles even after a large modern mill was opened in
1957: 'Not the least satisfactory aspect of the venture',
he pointed out, 'is that the output of the mill will not
adversely affect British textile exports, as imports into
Nigeria of the type of cloth to be manufactured are practically all from India, Hong Kong and Japan.' (42)   The
opposition to industrialization is also seen in the differential export duties levied on Nigerian palm oil and
palm kernel at £2 and 10s. 6d., respectively, stifling the
development of local oil milling. It was the same in the
Federation of Malaya, where 'the tariff was clearly designed to allow most imports from British Commonwealth
countries open access to the Federation market'. Imports
from outside the British Commonwealth were taxed at the
average rate of 10 per cent to 25 per cent. 'Under such
circumstances, the Federation's internal market was originally virtually a preserve for Commonwealth imports -
especially British manufactures.' (43)

The settler colonies, besides fostering forms of production which competed with those of the metropolitan
countries, had a regional bias in their commercial relations. In sub-Saharan Africa this led to the development
of South Africa as a regional node (a peripheral-centre),
followed by Rhodesia and Kenya. They became a common
sphere of influence for the movement of capital, and of
goods, white migrants and African labour. The ties between South Africa and Rhodesia were especially close.
South Africa during 1950-2 supplied 31 per cent of Rhodesia's imports and took 15 per cent of its exports; (44)
of the whites who settled in Rhodesia during 1947-53 about
half were of South African birth. (45)

Rhodesia and South Africa adopted uniform duties and
gave preferential treatment to each other - and a complete
removal of tariffs and other trade barriers was envisaged
by the Customs (Interim) Agreement of 1949. Though Rhodesia's industries were now exposed to competition from its
more powerful neighbour, its textile and woven apparel
industry expanded rapidly within the framework of these
special relations. However, Rhodesia from 1953 fared best
from the federation with Zambia and Nyasaland, where its
high-cost goods found a privileged market. Kenya's relationship with Uganda and Tanzania was analogous to that
between Rhodesia and South Africa. Under a customs and
currency union formed in 1922, the processed agricultural
goods, cement and light consumer articles of Kenya were
sold in Uganda and Tanzania. Kenya gained almost unilat-
erally from the union - perhaps at the expense of Uganda.
There was a net transfer of capital from Uganda to Kenya
(and elsewhere) - estimated at £6 million for 1957, equivalent to 5 per cent or more of Uganda's domestic money
incomes. (46)
     The economic structures and patterns in the settler
colonies south of the Sahara were in many ways duplicated
in the Maghreb. Demographically and socially, the Maghreb
was settler oriented. Algeria had more than a million
Europeans - 11 per cent of the total population; Morocco
600,000 Europeans; and Tunisia nearly a quarter of a million. In Algeria the settlers were socially heterogeneous
- farmers, administrators, professional men and traders,
and a working class both in the countryside and in the
cities; 3 per cent of the Europeans were domestic servants. (47) Maghrebin agriculture generated both a European bourgeoisie and a proletariat. In the 1870s the Algerian settlers were mostly peasant, but from the beginning of this century businessmen and rich farmers from
France purchased extensive blocks of land to be worked by
wage labour. Viticulture and the dry farming of cereals
promoted large capital outlays - in the case of viticulture, for wine-processing cellars, vats and other equipment, and for the transport of wine. In Tunisia and
Morocco the social stratification of the settlers was very
similar to that in Algeria.
     As settlers, the Europeans set their roots in the
Maghreb. From 1896, the Europeans born in Algeria began
to outnumber the migrants. At the time of the Maghreb's
independence most of the Europeans had been born there;
the figure was over 90 per cent in Algeria. In Morocco,
by the end of the 1860s the Europeans were no longer migrants; they invested in real estate in the towns, (48)
they were building houses, marrying local women, them-

selves mostly of Spanish origin, and moving from trade to
sheep and cattle rearing. (49) By the beginning of this
century, the Maghrebin settlers were almost alienated from
their compatriots in Europe yet completely aloof from the
Arabs. Despite class differences, the privileges they
shared gave them a political solidarity. Incomes and
social conditions between the Europeans and the indigenous
people differed immensely. The middle and lower income
settlers, less well off than similar groups in France,
showed a fanatical resolve to better their lot at the expense of the totally impoverished Arabs. The Algerians
were treated as an amorphous mass, distinguished from the
settlers only by their religion (skin colour or social
habits not being clear dividing lines). The term
'Muslim', used for indigenous people as the counterpart
of 'colon' or 'French Algerian', signified 'backwardness,
underprivileged political status and generally being economically dispossessed'. (50)

The similarity of the Maghrebin economies to those of
other settler colonies was in the agricultural pattern and
in the growth of an urban-cum-industrial sector along with
a large wage proletariat. In the Maghreb, just as in
Rhodesia and Kenya, settler agriculture, in its institutional and technical basis, differed from peasant farming
and the plantation system. First, there was a preponderance of owner-operated farms 10 to 30 acres in size though
large holdings also existed - some of more than 1,250
acres owned by corporations. The large holdings were
usually devoted to monoculture of cereals or vines, while
the medium and small holdings were mixed farming. Second,
the crops introduced by the settlers - vine, citrus fruit,
soft wheat, potato and the olive - were not a mere extension of traditional farming patterns but required new
techniques. The growing of cereals was modernized; and
dry farming made it possible to cultivate the semi-arid
regions of the south, just as viticulture profited from
the technique of refrigerating unfermented wine. Irrigated agriculture was expanded, by utilizing both surface
and ground water resources. Third, settler agriculture
was land intensive, with high inputs of both labour and
capital. In the plains of Sebou in Morocco, in the Oran,
the Mitidja and Bone in Algeria and in the Medjerda in
Tunisia the cropping pattern, based on viticulture and the
growing of vegetables and citrus fruit, required a phenomenal input of labour per hectare. On the larger farms
mechanization was widespread; 20,000 tractors were used
in Algeria in the 1950s.

Though data on yields per hectare are lacking, the productivity of settler agriculture in the Maghreb is evident

from the proportion of agricultural output of the settlers
and of the arable land they held. In Algeria the settlers
farmed 40 per cent of the land and accounted for 58 per
cent of total agricultural output; in Tunisia 30 per cent
and 80 per cent respectively. For Morocco the two proportions were the same owing to the relative importance
of cereals; the large mechanized cereal farms had a lower
productivity per hectare than those engaged in grape and
fruit farming. While the settlers had the better quality
land and optimal sized holdings, their high productivity
was essentially due to their farming practices. The
'dualism' between the European and the indigenous production sectors in Algeria was reflected in a ratio of 1:7
in the value of output per head between the countryside
and the towns; the disparity within the countryside or in
agriculture was even greater. As Samir Amin has commented, 'The agrarian colonization which engulfed Algeria and
then Tunisia, and finally Morocco in successive intervals
of 30 years or so certainly revolutionised agricultural
methods.' (51)

Urbanization and the growth of a proletariat, as
mentioned earlier, were characteristic of the Maghrebin
economies. Urban growth since the end of the First World
War has been phenomenal. In Morocco the ratio of urban to
total population rose from 16 per cent in 1936 to 29.3 per
cent in 1960. (52) In Algeria in the early 1960s a third
of the population, and in Tunisia and Morocco a quarter,
lived in cities of more than 20,000 inhabitants. Another
feature of this urban growth was its extensive area
spread. With the probable exception of Tunis, which is
more than ten times the size of the next largest town in
Tunisia, a 'system of cities' sprang up in a way which did
not occur in most nonsettler colonies. Algiers closely
shared its urban status with Oran and Constantine, followed by numerous cities of lesser size. These cities
everywhere led to a spread of urban influence and to an
interdependence between economic sectors. Though the
creation of national markets in the Maghreb was by no
means complete, an appreciable degree of unification had
taken place. In Algeria this integrated process of urbanization and economic development was seen in the layout of
its transportation grid. From a transversal railway and
road axis paralleling the coast, numerous routes penetra-
ted the interior towards the south. In the Maghreb as a
whole the road mileage and the traffic were greater than
anywhere in the continent except South Africa.

In the 'portuary perimeter' where urbanization and settlement were greatest, the port towns tended to specialize. For instance, Algiers and Oran mostly handled gener-

al cargo, Bone iron ore and phosphate, and Bougie exported
crude oil; Arzew exported alfalfa and salt and was the
marine terminal of a natural gas pipeline; Mostaganem was
the outlet for agricultural exports and mineral clays.
(53) The type of export or import cargo even varied
during the year - according to the fruit season, the wine
harvest time, etc. The differentiation in port facilities
and services led to the use of specialized equipment for
the handling and storage of minerals (petroleum, coal,
etc.), of grain elevators, wine banks connected by pipe-
lines to the ships, and food-packaging and food-freezing
plants. Far more industrial activity sprang up around
these ports than in the port towns of the plantation or
plantation-cum-mining economies. The latter were mostly
depots for the storage and transfer of goods and administrative, commercial and financial centres; they were not
nodes of production.

Urbanization in the Maghreb was not merely a demographic phenomenon. To some extent there was a flight of
peasants from conditions of rural poverty (and, in the
case of Oujda in Morocco, of refugees from the Algerian
revolution), adding to the hunger and squalor of the
bidonvilles. But the major factors in urban growth were
the agricultural pattern and the relative dynamism of the
town and its peripheral areas. The land intensive nature
of agriculture, with a preponderance of small and medium-
sized holdings, fostered close settlement. The processing
of the various agricultural products before export or
final consumption was the basis of light industries. For
instance, Mekines in Morocco, as the centre of a settler
agricultural tract, developed oil pressing, fruit and
vegetable canning, and wine manufacture.

Urbanization itself stimulated industrial growth, with
its demand for building materials and electric power,
mostly for domestic and public lighting. In Algeria the
supply of electricity increased by 7 per cent per annum
between 1930 and 1939, and by 10 per cent per annum between 1948 and 1954. In Tunisia it increased by 9 per
cent per annum between 1945 and 1955. Morocco, where the
electricity supply was negligible before 1925, caught up
with Algeria in 1939, and the rate of expansion from 1945
to 1955 was 17 per cent per annum. (54) The building
industry in Tangier at the end of the Second World War
employed 'thousands of workers ... [with] an investment of
millions of pounds'. (55) Besides housing and community
facilities, the towns created a demand for consumer items
and served as magnets for the development of secondary
production. The expanding urban market for food and other
agricultural products stretched the boundaries of the town

economy into small farms started by the settlers. The
size of the urban market (more significant for manufacturing industry) was due both to the scale of urbanization
and to the concentration of settlers in the towns.   In
Algeria in an urban population of around 2.7 millions in
1955 there were 800,000 settlers. (56)

A primary impetus to the growth of markets on a national scale was, however, the commercialization of agriculture. The colonization of the Maghreb gave rise to a
large rural proletariat. In Algeria, 50 per cent of the
peasantry was proletarianized, and in Tunisia 37 per cent.
(57) The land expropriations started this process, and it
was carried through by the capitalist development of agriculture. The dominance of commercial crops and large
capital outlays exposed the producers fully to the property inequalities of the market. There was also a mechanization of both agriculture and industry and even of traditional trades, e.g. hand-made garments, tents, bed-
spreads and carpets. (58) The virtual destruction of the
Maghrebin peasantry and the displacement of labour intensive production, while impoverishing the mass of the
people, expanded the home market; for, as wage earners
they were 'consuming less but buying more' (in Lenin's
famous expression apropos the growth of capitalism in
Russian agriculture). The spread of capitalist social
relations and the impact of wage labour on the growth of
the home market were significant when contrasted with the
nonsettler colonies. The large peasant sector in these
colonies was based on family labour, and rent and interest
payments were in kind, while in their plantation and
mining sectors there was a non-cash component in wages and
the migrant labourers repatriated some of their incomes.
The effect of employment on market demand was thus limited.

The 'profound transformation' of the Maghrebin economies was not brought about only by agriculture and by
urbanization with its demand for social overhead activities. Manufacturing industry was another source of
dynamism, whose rate of growth for a long period outstripped that of agriculture. In Algeria the share of agriculture and mining in the GNP during the period of colonization declined from 46 per cent to 31 per cent, in Tunisia
from 43 per cent to 34 per cent, and in Morocco from 47
per cent to 38 per cent. (59) In Algeria, the share of
industry in the GNP, excluding services, rose from about
18 per cent in 1880 to 45 per cent in 1955. (60) In both
Algeria and Morocco the foundations of light industry were
laid, with relatively large investments, during 1948-53.
The industrial expansion comprised a fairly large range of

manufactures: in Algeria, for example, modern oil-pressing factories, flour mills, pasta and biscuit factories, tuna and sardine canneries, and the manufacture of footwear, textiles, cork and paper. In Morocco, the 'industrial boom' of 1949-53 had a similar spread - flour mills, sugar refineries, vegetable oil factories, breweries, the manufacture of food preserves, and textiles. There were also some embryonic basic industries - paper, cement, sulphuric acid and superphosphate. These and the agro-based light industries, which transformed primary materials into finished goods, had a bigger developmental impact than the industrial efforts of many underdeveloped countries - with a high import content and the assembly of finished or semi-finished components.

My generalization on the differences in the development processes and patterns in the settler and the nonsettler colonies, as stated earlier, has two apparent exceptions, viz. the Belgian Congo and Indochina. Their settler/nonsettler status cannot easily be categorized. Though not specifically settler colonies they became more industrially advanced than could normally be expected. If the development implications of the settler/nonsettler dichotomy are to hold, the complex situation of the Congo and Indochina must be examined, in terms of their colonial forms and the unusual nature of the development that occurred in them.

In the Congo the settlers were relatively few, and the influence of Belgian corporate capital was overwhelming. After an abortive scheme to settle Belgian farmers in Katanga in 1911 and 1912, peasant cultivation was encouraged. All the same, Belgian companies obtained large land concessions for mining and plantation agriculture. By the end of the 1950s, there were about 100,000 Europeans - less than 1 per cent of the population. (61) The entry of Europeans into the Congo was officially regulated. Those allowed in were generally professional men with assured employment, including an unusual number of Belgian civil servants - at the time of independence there were 10,000 of them in the Congo. (62) These professional groups merely wanted a career in the colony. Every few years they took a vacation in Belgium and on retirement they returned there permanently. (63) In 1956, only about one fifth of the Europeans were settlers.

The expatriate nature of the Europeans in the Congo had two marked exceptions in the landowners of Kivu and the Katanga settlers. The latter were mainly Flemish, and had a high degree of social and cultural homogeneity - tending even to become parochial. Their group consciousness, sense of independence, and attachment to the province was

also due to the Comité Spécial du Katanga, under whose
auspices the first migrants arrived and which exercised
administrative control until 1910. The Katanga settlers
nurtured separatist sentiments. They tried to achieve
relative autonomy for their province, and resented Belgian
control. As settlers they also had an antipathy towards
the Congolese, whom they wanted to set apart in a system
of reserves on the lines of South Africa.

The Congo achieved an impressive level of economic advance. Manufacturing output in the 1950s was about 10 per
cent of the total GDP, as in Rhodesia and Kenya; the
ratio for nine other African countries included by
Ligthart and Abbai in their comparative study was 'well
below 5%'. (64) Manufacturing production was mainly of
intermediate goods and industrial materials; chemicals
constituted 46 per cent. There was also an all-round development of the economy, comprising mining, manufacturing
industry and agriculture. While palm oil was produced on
plantations, cotton as well as foodstuffs for the mining
and industrial labour force were grown by peasants. Imports were mostly capital goods, which in 1954-7 represented over a third of the total value of imports, (65)
and light consumer goods only 14 per cent.

This economic advance was based on extraordinary mineral wealth. In 1959, the Congo produced 9 per cent of the
world's copper, 49 per cent of cobalt, 69 per cent of industrial diamonds, and nearly 7 per cent of tin. (66) It
was the sixth largest producer of zinc, one of the largest
producers of uranium and the only producer of radium. (67)
Its industrial-diamond mines are the world's largest. The
copper ores of Upper Katanga are the richest in the world.
(68) Katanga alone produces 7 per cent of the world's
copper and two thirds of the Congo's cobalt. (69) Mineral
production doubled between 1930 and 1950, and increased
tenfold between 1950 and 1959.

The specific character of the mining operations in the
Congo gave the economy a dynamism of its own. First,
these operations, especially the reduction of copper ore
before smelting, are far more complex than those for many
other metals, including iron and steel, and they released
a long line of products which were the basis of separate
industries - e.g. explosives, sulphuric acid, ferrous and
ferric sulphates, soda and pyrestrol, industrial glycer-
ine, insecticides, paints and varnishes, glass, pharmaceuticals and perfumery. (70) The impurities from copper refining include valuable metals - cobalt, zinc, lead,
cadmium and germanium; the treatment of cobalt leaves
behind a slag used in the manufacture of metallurgical
cement; sulphurous gases from the electrolyzing of zinc

are convertible into sulphuric acid. Second, the mineral
enterprise sustained a high degree of technological progress. In the mines of the Union Minière du Haut-Katanga,
labour productivity increased phenomenally; for instance,
during 1920 to 1925, there was a fourfold expansion in
output with only a 16 per cent increase in the workforce.
(71) For the Katanga as a whole between 1950 and 1959
copper output rose by about 60 per cent with practically
no change in the workforce. (72) Third, the continuing
need for capital to finance these improvements encouraged
savings and reinvestment. For several years running, the
mining companies ploughed back up to 40 or 50 per cent of
annual profits. (73) Gross capital formation for the economy as a whole exceeded 25 per cent of national expenditure, compared with less than 15 per cent in other African
countries (except Rhodesia). (74) Lastly, the mining
enterprise promoted an advanced infrastructure, including
engineering facilities and hydroelectric projects, with
obvious spillover effects. Abundant and inexpensive
electric power after the Second World War, and especially
from the mid-1960s when the Inga dam was completed, made
the local processing of copper ore very profitable. Electricity consumption, in 194 kilowatt hours per head, was
nearly twice that of Algeria and Morocco, three times that
of Ghana and almost four times Kenya's. (75)

The mineral-based industries thus constituted the main
component of manufacturing activity in the Congo. The
close nexus between mining and industrial development was
reflected in the predominance of the metal industries and
in particular chemicals. While mining was the core around
which manufacturing activity developed, agriculture provided a secondary basis of such activity. The agro-based
industries comprised the processing of oleaginous sub-
stances (palm kernels, peanuts, cotton seed and castor
seed); the manufacture of soap and margarine, textiles,
and cigarettes; and sugar refining. Soaps and detergents
were manufactured by about sixty enterprises, mostly
small-scale. The textile industry consisted of cotton
gins, clothing factories, fibre-cleaning establishments
and hosiery, rope, sacking and bag factories. A third
component of manufacturing production, besides the mineral-
based industries and the agro-based industries, was the
building materials industry. This included three cement
factories, a fibre-cement works, and numerous enterprises
producing concrete or cement fittings such as pipes,
cranks and traps, as well as ceramics.

The Congo underwent heavy urbanization. Its devasta-
tion and depopulation during King Leopold's rule led to a
serious labour scarcity when large-scale mining operations

began in the early 1920s, followed a few years later by
the opening of plantations. After an initial recourse to
forced labour, recruitment and employment patterns were
adopted so as to ensure a stable workforce. In the absence of sufficient Europeans, the Congolese were trained
and employed as technicians. They were still subjected to
penal sanctions for absenteeism or breaches of the labour
contract, yet in Katanga wage inducements and welfare
benefits were introduced - subsidized housing, education
and medical care. There was a permanent relocation of
Africans outside the tribal areas; they were recruited
on a family basis and housed in the mining towns. (76)
Though large numbers of urban Africans lived in small
regional centres having their links with the countryside,
(77) urbanization and the growth of wage labour in the
Congo had no parallel in Africa outside the settler colonies. After World War II, urbanization was especially
rapid, increasing from nearly 15 per cent in 1946 to 21
per cent in 1954. In 1954 urban Africans constituted
nearly one third of the adult males, and by 1949 two
fifths. Wage employment increased along with urbanization
and the growth of plantations and other forms of commercial farming. In 1934 some 253,000 Africans were in wage
employment, distributed almost equally between industry
and agriculture. (78)

Urbanization and wage labour fostered domestic trade
and markets. Regional specialization in both food and
manufactured goods developed far more than in other colonial export economies. Barring a small subsistence
sector, the economy became a fairly composite entity whose
different segments interacted rather than constituted an
assemblage of disarticulate parts converging on a metropolitan economy abroad. While mineral production was
export oriented, the major industrial regions catered for
a domestic demand, in exchange for food and raw materials
from the other provinces. Katanga supplied manufactured
goods such as cigarettes, confectionery, biscuits, beer,
textiles, metal and wood products. Its purchases included
maize, groundnuts and tobacco from Kasai; manioc and rice
from Kasai and Kivu; palm oil from Kasai, Oriental and
Leopoldville; sugar from Kivu; wood from Kasai and Kivu;
and coffee and cotton from the northern provinces. (79)

The growth of the domestic market was due both to the
extensive involvement of Africans in the wage economy and
to a relatively high level of consumption per head. From
1921 African labour in most European enterprises were
given food rations and after 1932 a cash equivalent was
paid. Labour productivity and wages in the large mining
or industrial enterprises were much higher than in most

African countries. After the Second World War real wages
in mining rose steadily - in 1957 by 8 per cent, in 1958
by 3 per cent, and again in the first half of 1959 by
3 per cent. (80) The employment of Congolese technicians
also led to the diffusion of purchasing power. Furthermore, consumption levels were supported by 'welfarism' as
a deliberate strategy. Thus, despite enormous disparities
between the average earnings of the Europeans and of the
Congolese, the share of national income accruing to the
latter tended to increase. Between 1950 and 1952, when
national income expanded by 28 per cent in real terms, the
share of the Congolese rose from 52 per cent to nearly
56 per cent. (81)

It will be evident that the Congo's economic expansion
reflects to some extent the unusual growth potential inherent in the exploitation of mineral resources of the
kind mentioned - copper, cobalt, industrial diamonds,
uranium and zinc. These products not merely had a strong
world demand but also promoted an advanced infrastructure.
The fact that the level of economic development in the
Congo was manifestly higher than in Zambia (in both of
which copper mining was predominant) is, however, not easy
to explicate in terms of our settler/nonsettler model,
since the Congo as a whole was not a settler colony. Yet
some reasons for this discrepancy which leave the model
substantially intact may be proffered.

Much of the Congo's industrial activity, based on
mining production, was concentrated in Katanga. Katanga
was the 'hinge on which the Congo's economy revolved'; it
contributed about a third of the value of domestic output,
more than two fifths of foreign trade, and a similar share
of public revenue. (82) In 1957 mining and metal extraction and related manufactures accounted for 51 per cent of
the total value of secondary production; and a significant component of this was chemicals - a by-product of the
mining enterprise. Manufacturing output that was independent of mining was 21 per cent of the value of industrial output. (83) While the Congo occupied an intermediate position in the settler/nonsettler model - not wholly
a settler colony but closer to one than Zambia - Katanga
province, where most of the mineral wealth and industrial
development was concentrated, was almost a separate unit,
despite a certain measure of commercial integration of the
Congo which I earlier noted. It was also in Katanga that
settler influence was greatest. The immense wealth and
high technological activity attracted the Europeans and
kept them there. Whereas Belgian corporate capital was
powerfully entrenched, the local staff of the companies
had interests and an outlook similar to those of the set-

tlers. The political manifestation of this settler orientation was found in Tshombe's rebellion. That is to say,
in Katanga settler influence was relatively strong and
urban-cum-industrial investment as well as political power
was concentrated. If Katanga had not been a constituent
unit, the Congo would be no different from Zambia.

I have so far explained the economic developments of
the Congo in terms of four main factors. First, the exceptionally rich natural resource base; second, the
strong settler influence in Katanga; third, the spread
of purchasing power due to extensive urbanization and wage
employment among the Congolese and to their relatively
high wages; and, fourth, the expansion of internal trade
and markets. There were three other factors which also
contributed to the high level of development. One of
these was the effects of an early start in mining. The
exceptional development impact of the production of heavy
minerals in the Congo compared with Zambia was thus historically determined. Copper mining was begun in the
Congo in 1910 - two decades earlier than in Zambia - and
the industrializing side-effects of mining were felt substantially in the Congo, from where they later spilled
over into Zambia. (84) Furthermore, in the absence of
preferential treatment for Belgian goods in the colonial
markets, Belgian manufacturers set up branches in the
Congo of industries such as textiles, sugar, beer, soap
and cement. Finally, official encouragement was given to
peasant agriculture - especially the production of foodstuffs, including rice, manioc and coffee. (85) This
policy was due to both economic and political considerations: the high cost of food imports and its effect on
wages, and a desire to reduce dependence on imports from
South Africa and Rhodesia. Thus the production of food
and other consumer articles for the domestic market became
complementary to the export sector, whereas in the classical plantation or mining economies they were in conflict.
In addition to the economic bases, the social composition
of the settlers in Katanga strengthened the local identity
of the settlers as opposed to the purely expatriate interests.

Though somewhat remarkable for its scale and tempo, the
process of economic development in the Congo had nevertheless fundamental limits. The dominance of the expatriate
groups, subordinated economically and politically to
Belgium, thwarted a fuller realization of the growth potential of the Congo. The plantation and mining concessions required each company 'to purchase more than half
of its materials from Belgium and to employ Belgians to the
extent of 60% of its European personnel'. (86) The Charte

Colonial of 1908 brought the Congo under the direct control of the Belgian government. Legislation was mostly
in the form of royal decrees. Major decisions - e.g. on
land or mining concessions and finance, and the Congolese
budget - required the assent of the Belgian Parliament.
In Brussels a Conseil Colonial safeguarded metropolitan
interests. The settlers for all their intolerance and repression of the Congolese were not a powerful group - the
political rights they demanded were not granted by
Belgium. (87) The settlers' economic interests complemented those of the large metropolitan corporations, and
both were politically represented in the Conkat (Confédé-
ration d'Associations Tribalese du Katanga), formed in
1958.

The domination by Belgian corporate capital resulted
per se from the large size of the investments in mining
and plantations. The size of these investments was economically justified only in mining. Land was virtually
given away so long as a percentage of the earnings was
turned in to the government's coffers. But most of the
grantees, while profiting from the general increase in
land values, neither provided adequate social services as
stipulated in the grants nor developed their properties.
(88) A 'multiplicity of vested interests' (89) 'battened
on their state guarantees', pre-empting others from mineral prospecting and development. Non-Belgian capital was
excluded, though the concessions were too large to be
worked effectively by Belgian investors. (90)

> Year after year the Colonial Commission of the
> /Belgian/ Senate had ascribed the lack of greater
> mining development in the Congo to the relative inac-
> tivity of the large concessionaire whose rights block
> the way to those who would be willing to engage in
> prospecting or development.

The ownership of the corporations and therefore almost all
financial power in the Congo was held by a few entrepreneurial groups in Belgium. The colonial officials looked
after the interests of the corporations. Some of them
after a career in government found employment in the corporations or held part-time executive positions in them;
yet others, with no obvious links with the corporations,
were remunerated 'for services rendered'. Despite a high
level of reinvestment in the mining industry, there was
an enormous outflow of profits and of payments for banking, transportation and insurance services, which turned
the Congo's favourable trade balances into recurrent payments deficits. (91)

The 'solid Belgian presence' in the Congo blocked any
advancement of indigenous interests. Congolese were em-

ployed in the mining and manufacturing enterprises as
technicians, foremen and skilled workers and in the lower
ranks of the administration. At the time of Independence
(1960), out of 11,428 officers in the administrative
service 86 per cent were Europeans; (92) likewise the
doctors in the country, the pharmacists, dentists, biolo-
gists, nurses, midwives and public health officers. As a
matter of policy, primary education was liberally given
but secondary education withheld. Congolese were not allowed to own land except for a 'handful of rural plots' in
Katanga ceded by the end of the Second World War. They
were denied the right of association, discouraged from
travelling from one province to another or from going
abroad, (93) and in the towns they were residentially
segregated. 'The most ferocious Anglo-Saxon colour-bar
had never produced so many measures of so rigid a segregation as our Belgian tutelage', wrote A.Rubbens. (94)

   A Congolese bourgeoisie never existed. Internal trade,
which in most colonies, including West Africa, was a
stamping ground for small-scale indigenous enterprise, was
dominated by Portuguese and Greeks. The closed trading
networks of these alien minorities were a barrier to all
but a handful of Congolese petty traders in Leopoldville.
More generally, commercial enterprise by the Congolese was
inhibited by the legalized restrictions on land ownership
and credit. As an economically retarded mass, they were
stratified on the basis of prestige or social status
rather than of income. A small distinguished group were
the évolués'. Taught to emulate the Belgians in their
life-style, they were a buffer between the colonial power
and the masses but without the full status of Europeans.
It was this lack of any group with a stake in colonial
rule which suddenly mobilized large sections of Congolese
and brought them to the verge of overthrowing Belgian
rule. The prospect of abolishing social disabilities and
economic discrimination mobilized an embryonic Congolese
'politico-administrative' elite against colonial rule.
Parliamentarians, soldiers, teachers, clerks and medical
assistants all looked for better opportunities from decolonization. (95) After Independence the first act of
the groups which inherited power was to help themselves
to privileges and higher incomes. (The parliamentarians
voted a fivefold increase in their salaries, from 100,000
to 500,000 francs a year.)

   The second exception to the developmental implications
of our settler/nonsettler dichotomy is Indochina, which,
like the Congo, cannot easily be categorized. Though
almost totally dominated by metropolitan capital, Indochina also exhibited a pattern of development markedly

different from that in nonsettler colonies; its industrialization was unusual for a colony. Before explaining the
exceptional nature of this development, Indochina's set-
tler/nonsettler status must be indicated as clearly as
possible. European settlers in Indochina were few and
their economic influence was limited. Most of them as
government officers, discharged military personnel and
missionaries had little capital or business experience.
They bought rice lands to be let out to share croppers,
combining landlordism with usury, and later invested in
rubber in the populated areas near Saigon. But from the
1920s expatriate interests began to dominate the economy.
Improved rubber prices after the Stevenson restriction
scheme led to the opening up of the more fertile lands far
from Saigon - in Cochin China and Cambodia. The large
capital requirements at this stage were financed by corporate enterprises in France.

The industrial development that occurred in Indochina
before the Second World War is apparent both from the
numbers employed and from the range of industries. (96)
The workers in modern industry, excluding mines, were estimated for 1929 at 89,000. Around the Haiphong coal
mines, there developed a cluster of fuel-using industries
- cement, ceramics and glass. The cement industry was
founded by a French firm in 1899. The extra-rapid hardening qualities of Indochinese cement gave it a premium in
the world market, and in 1937 more than half the output
was exported. The first modern textile mill, built in
1844, was also financed by French capital; in 1913 this
and two other mills started in the intervening period were
amalgamated. The new company in 1933 employed about 5,000
workers, and in 1938 probably some 10,000 workers irregularly. Its products comprised sewing thread, blankets,
towels and miscellaneous cotton fabrics. There was a
variety of other industries: the manufacture of metal
products, paper, cigarettes, vegetable oils, soap, paints
and varnish; distilleries and breweries; sugar refineries; electrical works; and shipyards. An export trade
in manufactured goods was developed. (97)

Some of these enterprises were large integrated units,
highly mechanized. For instance, the cement works in
Haiphong also manufactured wooden barrels, and had its own
power plant, and machinery for automatic bagging. An associated company at Hue produced cement along with glazed
and burnt bricks, and lime. Firms in the vicinity made
bricks, tiles, pipes and tanks and other earthenware. The
cotton mills in Nam Dinh combined spinning, weaving,
bleaching and dyeing; they, too, had their own power
plants (using about 40 tons of coal a day), a foundry, a

landing stage on the canal and a fleet of launches and barges.

Industrialization on this scale carried out by expatriate investors was the result of adventitious factors. In the first place, the distance of Indochina from the mother country and the irregularity of freight (compared with that between Britain and ports such as Colombo, Singapore and Rangoon) handicapped exports from France. The competitive disadvantage of French goods, due to the distance from France, was compounded by Indochina's proximity to alternative suppliers, viz. Japan and China. Excessively prohibitive duties to keep out non-French supplies encouraged contraband trade. As a pre-emptive measure, French industrialists therefore set up branch plants in Indochina. For example, a spinning mill was established at Hanoi in 1904 to provide yarn to an existing textile industry based on yarn imports from India. Incorporated in the Société Cotonnière de l'Indochine, the mill extended its activities to weaving, without seriously competing with cotton fabrics from France. For fear of losing the entire Indochinese market, French capital was also invested in the silk industry despite its prejudicial effects on silk manufacturers in France. Later the metropolitan industrialists looked beyond Indochina's internal market. Indochina was seen as a 'relay point', a 'balcony on the Far East', for the pursuit of French economic and political ambitions in the Far East. Metropolitan firms with branches in Indochina found the South China market a tantalizing prospect. (98)

In the second place, even ardent opponents of colonial industrialization recognized the potential of the fuel and raw materials found in Indochina. (99) With the fabulously rich anthracite ore in East Tonkin, the setting up of the fuel-based industries - e.g. cement, ceramics, glass and paper - could not easily be put off. Third, the limited industrial development of France relative to that of Britain and Germany allowed Indochina some leeway - in lines of production in which the industries of the mother country were neither entrenched nor interested. (100) Finally, a financial stimulus to industrial investment was the flight of funds to the piastre from 1924, after the depreciation of the French franc. Though these funds were partly speculative in nature, they augmented industrial capital in Indochina. One sixth of the total new issues of corporate capital during 1924-30 was in manufacturing enterprises. (101)

Development of this kind - unusual for a nonsettler colony - must, however, be kept in perspective, occurring as it does within the framework of colonial relations.

Metropolitan capital imposed a fundamental limitation on
the development process. A narrow bilateralism linked
Indochina with France, and the commercial ties were
strengthened from about 1933. In 1934, over half of Indochina's exports by value was taken by France, compared
with about one fifth in the 1920s; the proportion rose in
1936 to 61 per cent. Large purchases of Indochinese produce relieved France's balance of payments problems with
non-Empire countries. Furthermore, in the mid-1930s when
the market for Indochinese rice in both Japan and China
had seriously declined, sales to France helped to maintain
local purchasing power in the interests of French manufactured goods. On the other hand, rubber purchases, as part
of a policy of subsidies to the rubber growers, made
France independent of supplies from British sources.

The tie-up of Indochina's economy with France removed
it from the regional setting to which it belonged by
virtue of its geographical position and the nature of its
commodities. Rice, corn, coal and cement which were purchased by France (mainly to help its balance of payments)
were not complementary to the French economy; as bulky or
heavy commodities, they could more conveniently be exported to nearby countries. At the same time large French
imports affected Indochina's access to low-cost goods from
Japan and China; the volume of these imports was not
seriously reduced by the branch plants that were set up.
Indochina served the French economy less as a raw materials source than as an investment outlet and a market. It
was this prospect which had 'made the French Parliament
and industrialists willing to finance Ferry's conquest of
Tonkin'. (102) Thus Indochina in its relations with the
mother country differed from the classical export economies, where the plantation and mining interests were
averse to tariffs because of their effect on wage costs.
(103) The Saigon Chamber of Commerce in 1912 warned of
'The dangers of encouraging the Annamite to get used to
cheap, but inferior products'. (104) The fear of Japanese
competition was more real than the concern for the Annamite's quality of life.

France used three devices to pre-empt the Indochinese
market. First, drastic fiscal measures were imposed, also
benefiting French industrial capital invested in Indochina. As foreign competition increased, the tariffs were
raised to a level even higher than in France. The Tariff
Act of 1928, while purporting to allow Indochina some
fiscal autonomy, gave increased protection to French
interests. Second, where it was not practical to levy
tariffs without encouraging contraband trade, branch
plants were set up in Indochina without affecting French

interests. Third, to maintain purchasing power in Indochina in the interests of French industrialists, France
virtually underwrote the demand for Indochina's major
agricultural products when the world demand for them had
seriously shrunk. The patronage given to Indochina's
export produce was, however, regulated so as not to en-
danger the prospects for agriculture in France.

The French market on which colonial export produce was
forced to depend was a precarious one. The entry of
colonial produce was liable to be turned on and off according to the vagaries of domestic harvests and the mood
of the agricultural interests. (105)

It is easy to sell Indochina cereals in France if frost
has spoiled the feed cabbages in Poitou or if an early
winter sends cattle back to their stables in Britanny
and Normandy earlier than usual. On the other hand,
it is much harder to sell them after a good French
harvest of oats, barley, or even wheat.

The agricultural interests once campaigned against rice
and corn imports from Indochina. The entry of Indochina
pepper was regulated annually according to the stocks in
French warehouses. Colonial exports were also affected by
trade concessions given by France to other countries in
return for special benefits. For instance, in 1934 the
French market for Algerian wine and wheat was almost
closed as a result of trade agreements made with third
countries. (106) While Indochina's exports to France were
regulated French goods could enter Indochina freely. 'The
colony was wholly French when a purchaser, but half
French, when trying to sell - and in both cases the colony
was the loser.' (107) Furthermore, Indochina's export
trade with France was encumbered by heavy payments to
middlemen and other distributive agents (108) and by high
freight rates due to a monopoly by French vessels of the
shipping between France and the colonies.

Tariffs and financial subsidies encouraged the development of the production of minerals and agricultural raw
materials, compared with industrial investment. The colonies were not permitted to compete with France in any part
of the world market - in France, in the colonies, or outside the empire. If Madagascar purchased 'a few thousand
yards of Tonkinese cloth or a few tons of soap', it was
construed as a threat to France. (109) The glass industry
in Haiphong stopped producing sheet glass in 1933, in
deference to the glass manufacturers in France, and instead produced bottles. Shortly before the Second World
War, the Comité d'Etudes Minières pour la France d'Outre
Mer, representing the mineral and metallurgical industries, was inclined to leave the colonies free to indus-

trialize. (110)   But the French manufacturing interests
opposed any systematic efforts at industrialization.
Metropolitan capital in Indochina retained the first
option.   The exclusiveness of French interests was also
ensured by legislation shutting out investments by
'foreign powers'. (111)   Subject to the adventitious
factors which encouraged industrialization, the economy
of Indochina was thus heavily subordinated to France.

I have concentrated in this chapter on showing the development pattern in the settler colonies.   The inward
orientation of the settler bourgeoisie and its relative
political autonomy - the mainsprings of this pattern -
resulted in a structure of production which replicated
rather than complemented that in the metropolitan economy.
This bourgeoisie was able to use state power in the colony
to combat metropolitan interests while totally repressing
the indigenous inhabitants.   In this model of the investment patterns and stimuli in the settler colonies, the
Congo and Indochina were two apparent exceptions.   Though
predominantly nonsettler colonies, they experienced the
kind of industrialization which is characteristic of settler colonies.   As was explained at some length, their
lack of conformity with the settler/nonsettler dichotomy
was due to some very specific factors.   While their development was different from that of the nonsettler colonies generally, their basically colonial status precluded
the development process in them from acquiring the full
momentum displayed by a developed economy.   The specific
factors which underlay the development process in these
two countries would make their deviant nature in terms of
my model more apparent than real.   The partial autonomy of
the settler bourgeoisie, and its permanent and pervasive
involvement in the lands where it became domiciled, were
also reflected in political conflicts between the settler
colonies and the metropolitan governments and in its complete repudiation of the interests of the indigenous
people.   The next two chapters will provide a framework
for a discussion of these aspects.

5   Settler autonomy as a basis of growth impulses

The internal focusing of economic activities which was
shown to characterize the settler colonies was not solely
due to the richness of the domestic market as determined
by the numbers and high incomes of the settlers. Markets
were not lacking in the nonsettler colonies, India in particular, though they failed to attract foreign investment
into either manufacturing production or food crops. For
example, in Malaysia, Sri Lanka and India, European investors did not respond to the demand for rice caused by
an expansion of employment in the plantation and/or mining
sector, in sharp contrast to the thrust of settler agriculture in Kenya and Rhodesia which even produced maize
for consumption by African labour. The more significant
aspect of the settlers' economic activities, which will
concern us here, is the development of manufacturing production.

The development of manufacturing production by settler
investors is often explained in terms of their technical
skills and the urban-industrial milieu from which they
migrated. In Barratt Brown's view the settlers were
'proto-industrial capitalists ... [who] were mainly from
Britain, which was already on the way to industrialization
and with strong Protestant and rebellious tendencies'. (1)
Professor Heinz Arndt, in one of the early attempts to explain the contrasting results of international investment,
attributed the economic development of the regions of new
settlement to the presence of skilled European labour.
'The people who developed [them] ... had ... the skills,
the technical know-how of their time in agriculture, industry, commerce and professions, in administration, law,
banking, transport, medicine, and education.' (2) Likewise industrialization in Northern Ireland in the 1880s
has been ascribed, apart from the security of land tenure
which encouraged investment and capital accumulation, to

the 'presence of large numbers of "industrially oriented"
settlers'. (3)

European settlers, as also the expatriate investors,
admittedly came from an already industrialized society.
Most workers in Britain, especially from the 1840s, had a
technical background; they knew something about machines.
English agriculture at this time involved the use of
mechanical harvesters, and farm workers found seasonal
employment in rural industries such as straw plaiting,
paper making, nail manufacture and textiles. (4) Information on the nature of the skills possessed by those
who migrated is lacking, though it would seem that the migrants generally were not craftsmen or industrial workers.
The settlers in New Zealand in the 1840s, and in Australia
at about the same time, were 'overwhelmingly unskilled'.
According to A.H.Clark, this was to their advantage, as
they 'had little to unlearn. A dead weight of peasant
prejudice which might have blocked the rapid development
of new techniques was largely absent'. (5) In Rhodesia,
where an industrial sector developed, the settlers were a
miscellaneous lot: 'people from all walks of life, soldiers and policemen, civil servants with a taste for outdoor existence, cattle traders who decided to raise their
own beasts ...'. (6)

It will be argued in the present chapter that in the
conditioning of investment attitudes the fact that the
settlers came from an industrially advanced or advancing
society was not so important as their severance from
metropolitan ties. As an independent capitalist class
the settlers could engage in activities from which absentee capitalists or expatriate businessmen were precluded. Conversely, it has been argued in a previous
chapter that the factor inhibiting the development of
manufacturing industry in the nonsettler colonies was the
external locus, through principals and head offices
abroad, of the investors and of the apparatus of management and control. Before discussing the case of the settler colonies, differences in the social composition of
settler communities will be set out and their implications
for industrial development examined.

The composition of the settler communities in Kenya and
Zambia, for instance, was different from those in Rhodesia
and South Africa. In Rhodesia, and far more in South
Africa, the settlers included large numbers of artisans
and labourers. While these working-class elements enlarged the size of the settler community, their presence
was not merely of quantitative significance in the economic development of these colonies; the presence of a
white working class created pressures for employment op-

portunities - which for political and social reasons the
government was compelled to recognize; it could not coun-
tenance the existence of distress among unemployed white
settlers living amidst a 'native' population. In South
Africa at a time when its industrial development was still
inadequate to absorb all the white labour (whose wages
were too costly for private employers), the Hertzog
government arranged for subsidized employment in agriculture and in the railways and public works. 'One of the
first demands of the white working class was simply for
jobs.... The reduction of white unemployment was one of
the [Pact] government's self-declared priorities.' (7)
Apart from the notorious 'civilised labour' policy, designed to exclusively benefit white workers, there was a
conscious policy of industrial development through protective tariffs and state industrial monopolies. Even in
Australia, where such political exigencies arising from
white-black relationships did not exist, employment creation was an overriding concern of policy from the 1850s,
long before there was legislation to safeguard working
conditions and wages. Fiscal protection given to domestic
manufacturers had as its primary goal the promotion of
regular employment. (8) The industrial development of
these territories was thus as much a response to the
demand for employment by European labour as to the availability of such labour itself.

The presence of people with the skills, attitudes and
mores of an already advanced society helped the industrialization of the settler colonies, once the industrialization process got under way. The determining factor in
that process was, however, not the availability of skilled
labour but the presence of a settler bourgeoisie, who had
a permanent commitment to their new territory and were
free to invest and to develop its productive capacities
along autonomous lines. Arndt, while abstracting from the
larger framework of metropolis-periphery relations, which
in my view determined the nature of international investments in different regions, used a misleading analogy. He
regarded the white dominions as an extension of the metropolitan economy, implying that it was the nonsettler colonies that were independent of the metropolitan economy.
(9)

Development investment of the Australian nineteenth
century type ... was much more like domestic investment
than any international investment can be to-day. In
many respects, the development of Australia was no more
'foreign' investment than would have been the development by British people and capital of a miraculous extension of the British Isles by the emergence of an adjoining land area from the depths of the ocean.

In fact, the reverse was the case. (10)   Though the settler colonies were to a large extent cultural projections
of the metropolis, these colonies developed economically
as separate and autonomous entities.   It was the nonsettler colonies that were an appendage of the metropolitan
economy.   While this is a theme that is extensively discussed in this book, Arndt's presumption about the importance of skilled labour among the migrants as a determining factor in development requires comment here.

The importance of skilled labour in an industrialization process, like other elements of the factor-scarcity
model, has been overemphasized.   Such a view disregards
the role played by the colonial state in stifling the
overall propagation of skills, capabilities and industrial
habits.   While the colonial situation generally, as I
shall demonstrate, confined the acquisition and application of skills to the white minority, in the settler colonies, despite these constraints on the formation of
skills, there emerged forms of production that were competitive with those in the parent economy.   In territories
where a European settler minority wielded power, the diffusion of skills was obstructed by what Myint aptly called
a 'vertical' division of labour into 'non-competing'
racial groups.   The indigenous people were discriminated
against in every respect - economic, political and social.
These inequalities were tantamount to a caste system. (11)
The ability of the settlers 'to control the scarcity of
their own skills' was the basis of racially structured
employment and wage policies.   The presence of a European
working class had a most prejudicial effect.   For example,
in Rhodesia when the low wages of Africans discouraged the
employment of white labour, the Industrial Conciliation
Act in 1943, by introducing as a deliberate device a uniform wage irrespective of colour, induced employers to
engage only white labour. (12)   In Zambia in 1907 the settlers aggressively opposed the employment of Africans in
skilled crafts.   They censured the government for wanting
to employ African craftsmen to build a camp at Broken
Hill.   The 'Livingstone Mail' wrote on their behalf: 'In
defiance of the prejudices of the British race the world
over, the Administration is trying to create a class of
native artisans who are intended to perform the work elsewhere entrusted solely to white men.' (13)   The administration then assured the settlers that 'whilst Africans
would continue to be employed as telegraphists, typists
and compositors, no use would be made of them locally as
carpenters and bricklayers'.   In South Africa such discriminatory employment policies produced a wage differential between white and black labour which did not corre-

spond to their relative efficiencies. In the railways white labourers were paid twice as much as the Africans though the authorities found them to be 'perhaps 15% more efficient'; the Public Works Department allowed 10 per cent more on building contracts when whites were employed instead of Africans. (14)

Colonial rule was itself a barrier to the acquisition and diffusion of technical and management skills among the colonized people. Throughout the colonial world the technical posts and practically all the executive and professional ones in the administration, plantations, banks and other foreign-owned enterprises were monopolized by metropolitan nationals. The sharpest expression of this discrimination was in Africa. Europeans in the lower occupational groups were safeguarded by law against competition from Africans, who were even restricted from forming workers' associations. In the mining enterprises in Nigeria, Africans were denied elementary mechanical or other training that would fit them for any of the responsible posts. 'In fact, the law has been positively restrictive with regard to African participation in the industry.' (15) For example, lessees of mineral lands were required to have Europeans as agents, and Africans were debarred from being 'in charge of any plant, the indicated horsepower of which is over twelve'. Penelope Bower, who quoted this provision from Nigeria's legislative enactments, explained, 'If this legislation had not been intended to discriminate against Africans, it could have been phrased "unqualified persons" from performing the functions mentioned.' The proposed reason for such laws in instances where the discrimination was admitted was that Europeans and Africans were in different stages of social evolution; Wilbert Moore exploded this belief by suggesting that if a natural inequality existed 'biology would need no help from the politicians in keeping the African workers "in their place"'. (16)

Outside Africa racial discrimination was covertly practised, without the aid of legislative sanctions. In Sri Lanka non-Europeans were excluded from executive positions in British banks, as the Chairman of the Colombo Exchange Bankers' Association stated in his evidence before the Banking Commission in 1934: (17)

Q. Have you any Ceylonese officers in your Bank?
A. No, but our Shroff and head clerk and staff generally are Ceylonese.
Q. How is the work of the Ceylonese staff?
A. Quite excellent men, some of them are well educated.
Q. Do you think they can work as sub-accountants?

A. Yes.
Q. Can they independently carry on correspondence?
A. Yes.
Q. Why are Ceylonese not given chances to work as sub-accountants?
A. That is a question for our head office to decide and not for us. On matters of policy such as this we have no control.

The bias for British nationals at managerial level prevailed from the outset of plantation enterprise; in Sri Lanka those taken on as estate superintendents had no experience or agricultural knowledge of any kind. According to Sir James Emerson Tennent, writing in 1847, they were 'ex-soldiers, lads fresh from school ... and persons without any education or any other recommendation, than the accident of European birth'. (18) Likewise, in Malaysia the British estate managers and superintendents had no knowledge or experience of agriculture. A member of the Forestry Service, Gold Coast, who had visited the estates in Perak and Selangor, wrote that 'none of the European staff possessed any previous formal training in agriculture, resulting in a lack of attention to "all scientific questions"'. (19) 'The majority [of them] are absolutely ignorant of tropical agriculture', commented a 'Straits Times' report in the same year. They were 'competitive examination failures' - schoolmasters, sailors, soldiers, policemen, clerks and even journalists. (20)

The initiation of indigenous people into the technical aspects of Western culture and its scientific spirit would have undermined the monopoly of administrative, technological and scientific skills. A Surveyor-General of India wrote: 'In my own surveying parties I never permitted a native to touch a theodolite or make an original computation, on the principle that the triangulation or scientific work was the prerogative of the highly paid Europeans.' (21) Such a policy, which gave the Europeans an exclusive command over skills which had a much higher market value, was also politically motivated. The same Surveyor-General realized: 'It is suicidal for Europeans to admit that natives can do anything better than ourselves.' (22) Another British official contrasted the potential discontent of the 'educated natives' with the loyalty of the 'uneducated Indians'. (23) In Ghana, where the interest of Africans in education is 'as deep-rooted as it is widespread', (24) civil servants sought to play down the social value of education. With this in view, a chief Native Commissioner decided not to distinguish in any way between educated and uneducated Africans; any of them who came to his office were made to sit on the floor.

(25)   Institutional obstacles of this kind to the development and diffusion of skills did not exist in Australia
and the other white dominions, where for practical purposes all-white communities existed.

The education system in the colonies was generally
geared to make subject people fit into the colonial society and economy.   Educational facilities were mostly in
urban areas and succeeded in producing 'clerks and subordinate officers for the administration, the army and the
police'. (26)   In East Africa, 'the first great school at
Tanga, founded in 1893, and served as a model for others,
had three sections - one for children, one training
clerks, and one for the training of personal servants'.
(27)   In the nonsettler colonies, though educational opportunities were much better than in the settler colonies,
education was largely of a non-utilitarian nature, biased
in favour of literary and academic attainments.   The
general education given was useless from a vocational
standpoint and the majority who went through it were virtually unfit for anything.   As in the retort to Prospero
in Shakespeare's 'Tempest', the educated may well have
said: 'You taught me language, and all I know is how to
curse.'   There was hardly ever adequate provision for any
specific or specialized forms of education or training.
Those who gained it became the brahmins commanding prestige and high salaries which set them apart from the rest
of society.   A summing up of colonial educational policy
by a British writer appeared in the 'Year Book of Education' in 1938:   'The conception of the aim of education
was, that it should make useful citizens ... who would be
of use to us.   The conception was one of exploitation and
development for the benefit of the people of Great Britain
- it was to this purpose that such education was given and
directed.' (28)

The exaggerated significance attached to the industrial
skills which European migrants brought with them is seen
in the case of the Katanga copper mines.   The Congo,
before the development of mining and related manufacturing
industries, was, unlike some other parts of the underdeveloped world, not even urbanized;   and trade and secondary production were at an extremely low level.   Yet, the
demand for skilled labour by the new enterprises and the
dearth of European personnel caused Africans to be given
forms of employment from which elsewhere they were debarred on social grounds.   The moral of this exigency was
seen by Lord Hailey: 'African labour has shown itself
readily receptive of training and able to undertake work
demanding a sense of responsibility and considerable technical skill.' (29)   In Nigeria, where the railway admin-

istration found it necessary to organize the training of
Africans in manual skills, it produced even more skilled
labourers than the railway needed. (30) Where economic
reasons demanded the training of Africans in various
skills and crafts, such demands were able to override the
institutional barriers that were prevalent in colonial societies.

Such institutional barriers, though they had a political genesis, operated fundamentally in a situation where
'skills and technical know-how' were made irrelevant by the
particular role which colonies were expected to play in
the world economy - as primary producers and markets for
manufactured goods. The non-availability of technical and
administrative skills, by which Arndt sought to explain
underdevelopment, is not merely easily overcome, given the
demand for such skills, but a development process is not
always contingent upon an already existing supply of
skills. Whereas in the settler colonies a certain degree
of industrialization occurred despite the monopoly of
skills by the settlers, in the nonsettler colonies, where
such obstacles to the diffusion of skills did not operate
to the same extent, industrial development was hampered by
their subordination to the metropolitan interest.

The experience of the settler colonies, which I shall
presently set out and interpret, has wider implications
regarding the ability of capitalism to propagate itself
from an original base. There is in capitalism an immanent
tendency to stifle, suffocate and push back the full realization of the developmental potential of rival capitalisms. This propensity is characteristic of the nature of
capital itself which demands the ousting of rival businessmen - this is the very basis of the central contradiction in capitalism arising from the appropriation of
surplus value by fewer and fewer capitalists while the
production process is increasingly socialized.

The settler colonies, by virtue of their detachment
from the parent society, were able to combat or withstand
attempts by metropolitan capitalism to stifle their autonomous growth. The settlers won this freedom by their as-
sertiveness, through political conflicts with the metropolitan interests. Before discussing these conflicts, I
should mention that even in the settler colonies the relations of foreign investors with their home country were
not entirely harmonious. In Sri Lanka, for example, the
British coffee planters engaged themselves in the country's first constitutional struggles. They agitated for
a programme of public works - roads, bridges and railways
- and wanted a hand in the colonial budget. The planters
also opposed the imperial levy of £24,000 annually as

'Ceylon's contribution to the Queen's Chest', (31) and
tried to interfere with the imperial government's claim
on the revenues of the colony. The Secretary of State
warned the Governor in a dispatch in 1856: (32)

The colonists would be under a constant temptation to
dispute the claims of the mother country, and impede
the exaction by the latter of what was justly its due.
No extension of the Council should therefore take place
till some measure was taken to remove the chance of
collision on this particular subject.

Even in much later times there were disputes over issues
such as recourse to the Crown Agents in London, bypassing
the British firms resident in the colony. However, such
conflicts between the mother country and expatriate investors in the nonsettler colonies were not serious -
these investors had their permanent interests in the
metropolis and were a segment of the metropolitan bourgeoisie.

In the settler colonies, on the other hand, the mother
country's relationship with 'foreign' investors resembled
that between independent nations whose mutual antagonism
has been the source of commercial rivàlry, diplomatic conflicts and wars. 'The most difficult struggles of the
imperialist countries since the 18th century had ... been
with ... their own settlers.' (33) The Great Trek by the
Boers of South Africa - tantamount to a 'declaration of
independence' - foreshadowed in a different age and in a
different complex of circumstances the UDI of the Smith
regime in Rhodesia. The Boers objected to the emancipation of the Hottentots; they wanted greater protection
from the depredations of local cattle raisers; and they
disliked criticism by the missionaries. Piet Retief, one
of the best known Trekkers, complained in 1834 of prejudice and misunderstanding by the English. 'Unjustified
odium ... has been cast upon us by interested and discon-
tented persons under the name of religion, whose testimony
is believed in England to the exclusion of all evidence in
our favour.' (34) The Boers resented interference from
abroad and 'equality with the non-Europeans at home'.
White settlement demanded a greater commitment of the administration to settler interests than was automatically
forthcoming.

In their attempt to build autonomous economic structures, the clashes which the settlers had with the metropolitan interests were also represented in their relations
with the colonial administration. In Kenya, the settlers
clashed with the administration on at least four issues,
viz. land, stock thefts, railway policy and labour. (35)
Land titles were delayed owing to a lack of staff, in-

cluding surveyors. The settlers felt inadequately protected against stock thefts. Provision for the expansion of
the police force was limited compared with the scale of
military expenditure. The delay in establishing a pax
Britannica exposed the settlers to attacks by some of the
African tribes, e.g. the Masai and the Nandi. The Nandi
did not submit easily to British rule; they refused to
pay hut tax and fought the white man until the punitive
expedition of 1905. The settlers feared for their lives,
and could trust only the white police. (36) The working
of the railway also caused ill-feeling between the settlers and the administration. The financial grant by the
British Treasury caused the railway to run as a revenue-
earning department rather than a public utility for the
benefit of the settlers. Thus railway rates were kept
high and replacement expenditure rigidly controlled.
These conflicts cannot be attributed to the 'naturally
rebellious tendencies' of the settlers as Barratt Brown
thought. (37)

In the settler colonies labour was a constant problem.
The sparse population of these colonies, many of which
also had well-integrated economic structures, made it unnecessary for Africans to accept offers of work from the
Europeans. The settlers even considered using migrant
Indian labour as the sisal producers in Kenya attempted
in 1908 and 1909. (38) But the government disallowed
Indian immigration, in the larger interests of the settlers. The Indians brought in the 1890s to build the
Kenya and Uganda railway were by this time a 'distinct
threat' to the small white settlers, especially those in
the Kenya highlands. The situation demanded the dispossession of the Africans, in order to provide a labour
supply to the settlers, and also to remove competition
from Africans in the market for agricultural produce.
The settlers felt that the administration should be responsible for forcing the Africans out of their traditional economy.

There existed a more significant ground of conflict
than the impatience of the settlers with the administration at the delay in turning over to them the country's
resources at the expense of the indigenous people. Wanting financial and fiscal autonomy, the settlers, for all
intents and purposes, were 'economic nationalists' (39) -
unlike expatriate investors whose interests fitted closely
with those of the metropolitan economy, based on trade and
primary production for export. They pressed for 'policies
committed to building up internal rather than export
markets, and even for protection for industrialisation despite what they saw to be the opinion of British manufac-

turing interests'. (40)   In the relations of their territory with the metropolitan country, the settlers 'tend[ed]
always to incline the balance of authority away from the
centre to the periphery'. (41)   Where the settlers produced for export, as did the coffee and sisal growers in
Kenya, in matters of general policy they had 'a strong
antipathy towards direction from London commercial interests'. (42)   To strengthen the position of the coffee
growers and of local buyers or dealers vis-à-vis the commercial interests abroad, the Nairobi coffee market was
set up in 1935.   External intermediaries were reduced and
encouragement given to direct shipments of coffee, bypassing the auctions in London.   As a concomitant of this
struggle for financial and fiscal autonomy, the settlers
also demanded constitutional reforms.   After the transfer
of the East Africa Protectorate to the Colonial Office in
1905 they agitated through the Colonists' Association for
a legislative council and for appointed unofficial members
to represent them.   Though they had less influence over
imperial policy than the large expatriate investors resident in Britain, the settlers were an articulate body
which the Colonial Office could not easily ignore.

Having an entrepreneurial focus which was different
from that of expatriate investors, the settlers collided
with the vested interests in London.   In Kenya on two important issues in the 1920s the predominantly expatriate
interests consisting of the planters and the export-import
firms linked up with the administration against the railway contractors and shipping interests in Britain.   One of
the issues was the granting of contracts for railway construction.   The Uasin-Gishu line was built and partially
administered by a British firm (chosen by the Crown
Agents) at exorbitant cost, and the administration wanted
to transfer the work that yet remained on the Kenya-Uganda
railway to local firms directly under its control.   The
decision stirred up business circles and Tory politicians
in England - the managing director of the firm affected
most was a British Member of Parliament.   The Kenya
government was accused of repudiating private enterprise.
The trouble arose from a conflict between the monopoly
privileges of a British firm and the authority of the
railway administration in Kenya.   The Kenya government
eventually gained full responsibility for constructing and
administering the railway.   In the other instance the
government clashed with shipping companies over the unloading of cargo in Mombasa harbour.   Unloading was in the
hands of two lighterage companies that were interlocked
with British shipping interests.   Because of the high
charges made by the lighterage companies, the government

constructed a deep water berth in 1926, and made plans for
two others. The shipping interests in London opposed this
measure, fearing a loss of business due to greater control
by the Harbour Department over unloading facilities. The
Imperial Shipping Committee recommended that the lighterage companies should be allowed to operate without hindrance. But the Kenya government, backed by the producers
and exporters, again asserted itself, gaining full control
over the administration of the harbour. Brett, on whose
research my account of these two episodes is based, shows
clearly the changing balance of power between the contending interests. The railway contractors and shipping companies, 'despite their evident success in marshalling support in Britain', lost out to the local interests and 'in
all probability [to the benefit] of the local economy in
general'. (43)

In both South Africa and Rhodesia, similar conflicts
prevailed; the interests of the settlers differed sharply
from those of the foreign mining companies and their associated trading concerns. The settlers began providing
locally (instead of from imports) many of the demands of
the mines for stores, clothing, food, explosives, etc.
Above all they wanted, by means of taxation, to retain a
larger share of the mining profits within the colony. In
Zambia, mineral rights and taxes were serious grounds of
conflict between the settlers and the London interests.
The levies payable by the copper mines, the country's
principal asset, went largely to the British government
and the British South Africa Company. In 1938 about 60
per cent accrued abroad, and in the decade of the 1930s
taxes paid to the British government were about £24
million compared with only £136,000 received by the
colony. The British South Africa Company, under the terms
of its charter and with support from the British government, declined to retract its financial claims on the
copper mines. But the settlers, disregarding Britain's
'trusteeship doctrine', held out the threat of a royalties
tax which the Rhodesian legislature could sanction up to a
50 per cent limit. (44) Though a settlement was reached
in 1949, the Rhodesian Federation later tried to impound
even more of the profits of the Zambian mines for industrial investment in the South. (45)

Against this general background of a propensity for
conflict arising from the relative autonomy of the settler
bourgeoisie, its degree and intensity was conditioned by
the relative balance of forces between the settlers and
the metropolitan country, on the one hand, and between
them and the indigenous inhabitants, on the other. Where
the settler bourgeoisie was economically weak (for in-

stance, in the Maghreb compared with South Africa, Rhodesia or Kenya), it was more concerned about resisting any social and political concessions to the indigenous inhabitants than with wresting economic control from the metropolitan interests. In Algeria the settlers opposed the grant of French citizenship to Algerians. When the French government from about 1871 attempted a policy of assimilation, to 'de-arabize' the country and make the Algerians 'true Frenchmen' in the cultural sense, the colons resisted. Their differences with the metropolitan power arose from its professed attempts to act as the 'patron and protector' of all the people in the colony rather than exclusively of the settlers. In 1870, when the Second Empire fell, the colons 'threatened to secede from the parent country, as they were to do again in 1960-61'. (46) After expelling the officials of the empire they tried to govern through the Commune d'Algier. Napoleon III, disregarding the attitude of the settlers, had declared, 'The natives like the settlers have a right to my protection, and I am just as much Emperor of the French.... We must convince the Arabs that we are not here to despoil them, but to bring to them the benefits of civilisation.' (47) The settlers, to the very end, subverted attempts by France to grant political concessions to the Algerians or to make liberal reforms even if only to forestall an insurrection. (48) In Tunisia and Morocco, which were more directly under local administration 'obedient to the dictates of Paris', the settlers remained privileged and protected foreigners but could not interfere in the policies of the French Resident-General.

In the Netherlands East Indies, there was resentment between the settlers and the Dutch government over the latter's financial and fiscal control. The Governor-General had the last word in legislative matters, overriding the Volksraad, and the Dutch settlers wanted more 'elbow-room' against the heavy hand of the Netherlands government and of the States-General. (49) The 'economic collaboration' between Holland and the Indies, and especially the fiscal policy of Holland during the depression of the 1930s, displeased the 'vested European interests in Indonesia'. In this conflict of policies, the Dutch settlers naturally had also the support of Indonesian nationalists. They reacted against the 'heavy burdens' which were imposed on Indonesia, 'whereby not only ... half of the Dutch navy but even the subsidies to her shipping lines were financed in the form of high tariffs paid by her financially weak colony'. (50) Dutch products were freely admitted into the country while imports of Indonesian sugar and rubber into the Netherlands were regu-

lated. The demand of the Dutch in Indonesia for greater
political autonomy was, however, rejected by Holland.

The nature of metropolitan-settler conflicts depended
upon the relationship which the metropolitan governments
sought to achieve with their respective colonies. The
conflicts were greater in Britain's colonies, e.g. Rhodesia, South Africa and Kenya, than in the French colonies
in the Maghreb. The greater leeway enjoyed by settlers in
the British colonies, and the corresponding economic
structures which they were beginning to establish, made
them press for even greater autonomy. The relations between France and her settlers in these countries flared
up only after the decision to grant independence. In
Tunisia, Morocco and Algeria, unlike Rhodesia and Kenya,
the settlers were mostly small farmers, with a large body
of poor whites in the towns. France's close administrative control of her colonies left the settlers little
autonomy. The Belgian and the Portuguese colonies were
in a similar position: 'Neither the local whites nor the
blacks have been running the country, since ultimate power
has remained in the metropolitan country.' (51) The links
between Portugal and her colonies - 'direct, intense and
economically central' to the mother country - represented
an 'ultra-colonialism'. (52) In the Netherlands East
Indies administrative integration with the metropolitan
centre was only of a lesser degree than that of the Portuguese, Belgian and French colonies. That the Dutch
States-General could nullify any ordinance, decree, etc.,
passed by the Volksraad in Indonesia, and that the budget
required Holland's approval, show the extent of integration with the metropolitan centre.

The character and the speed of the decolonization process in the settler and the nonsettler colonies reflect
the divergent bases of economic and political power exercised by the Europeans. The cause-effect relation between
settler-nonsettler status and the extent of decolonization
that occurred is much too varied to enable any single
categorization of the different colonies. A broad generalization is nevertheless possible. The inward orientation of the settlers' interests meant that their power was
situated in the colony itself; while such a locus is less
easily dislodged than that of absentee investors in nonsettler colonies, yet once political power ceases to be
exercised by the colonial power the settler investments
are likely to suffer a root and branch extinction. However, a paradoxical development in the settler colonies
was the revival of foreign influence when the impact of
decolonization had spent itself, making the ultimate
result not so very different from that in the nonsettler

colonies. The reason for this probably lay in the character of the settler bourgeoisie; while exercising a greater measure of political and economic autonomy compared
with expatriate investors in the nonsettler colonies, it
occupied an ambivalent position in relation to the metropolitan country when compared to the bourgeoisie in the
white dominions.

In the Maghreb, where European influence was extensive,
the removal of settler interests was more complete and
faster in the areas where they had been most dominant - in
northern Algeria and Tunisia as compared with Morocco and
Libya. In Algeria within twelve months of its independence European landholdings began to be expropriated or
nationalized. With the massive departures of Frenchmen,
by the end of 1962 practically all the settler-owned land
was taken over and administered by the Algerians. In Morocco, with a settler population of 500,000 - half that in
Algeria, yet economically significant - decolonization was
far more gradual and less systematic than in Algeria and
Tunisia. (53) For three years after independence French
capital was still intact - in mining, agriculture, urban
real estate, public utilities, newspapers, manufacturing,
banking and commerce. In the administration, the judiciary and the army French personnel were retained. (54)
This exceptional prolongation of metropolitan influence
was the result of the collaboration of the Moroccan landed
aristocracy in the conquest of Morocco and the French
policy of shoring up the aristocracy as an ally to an unusual degree. Furthermore, the nationalist movement,
though expressing itself partly in sporadic mass action
and a militant underground network, became controlled by
the Istiqlal - a party whose dominant elements were merchants and landed proprietors. Their leading groups were,
respectively, the Moroccan Fassai and the olive growers of
Sfax, who had no real grievance with the settler economy.
(55)

The liquidation of colonial structures had, therefore,
to await a shift in power within the ranks of the Moroccan
ruling class. From 1960, in the face of an unfolding economic crisis, the state sector in the economy was expanded, partly by the nationalization of French assets -
farms, railways, electricity and water distribution. The
new mood was also inspired by the radical sweep of decolonization in Tunisia and Algeria. (Unlike in Tunisia
and Algeria, in Morocco the foreign owners were compen-
sated and allowed to repatriate half the payments received.) French small capital was also liquidated -
'farms, restaurants, bars, small hotels, and shops of all
kinds' - and transferred to Moroccans. (56) Almost

500,000 hectares of settler land were sold between 1956
and 1965 to big Moroccan landowners. (57)   During this
time the number of Europeans declined from 400,000 in 1960
to 260,000 in 1965 (and 100,000 in 1970);   during 1960-5
there was also an exodus of 100,000 of the local Jews.
(58)   Moroccans filled the vacant positions (200,000 in
the administration alone, including the military).   The
leading cities lost their European character and became
'arabized'.   In the early 1970s the Moroccanization programme was renewed, after a failure of the government's
economic policy and with demands by the middle class for
more opportunities.

The decisive breach in the relations of the settler
colonies with the former metropolitan powers, in contrast
to the neo-colonial outcome in the nonsettler colonies, is
attributable to two factors.   First, the economic and
social privileges of the settlers did not allow them a
half-way house which would accommodate local interests.   A
sharing of power would have drastically reduced their position in the colony, which had depended on a monopoly of
resources and a system of legalized discrimination against
indigenous interests.   The ending of the political dominance of the settlers was thus not a transition but a
traumatic break.   As Arghiri Emmanuel remarked, (59)

The White settler community could not come to terms
with anything; neither with the trusts nor with the
metropolitan country, far less with Africanisation or
independence.   It could be saved only by secession from
the metropolis and setting up an independent 'White
state'.

Second, the localized and small-scale nature of the settler enterprises, owner-operated for the most part, and
not backed by metropolitan financial and power groups,
facilitated their acquisition by national governments.
The physical eviction of the settlers - a process which
was no doubt prolonged and turbulent (as in Algeria, the
Congo, Biafra, Indonesia and Indochina) - led ipso facto
to a liquidation of their economic involvements.

The speed with which the settler interests were ex-
tinguished and the sweep of such action stemmed primarily
from the absence of an indigenous bourgeoisie.   The withdrawal of the Europeans, and the dismantling of the apparatus of coercion and political repression which had
upheld the white man's rule, left no force in the form of
a collaborationist class to control the process of the
transfer of power.   The metropolitan umbilical cord was
severed, though without the assurance of an independent
bourgeois development or of uninterrupted radical change.
By contrast, in the nonsettler colonies, where an indi-

genous bourgeoisie developed, to some extent the compradore role in which it mainly functioned gave it a vested
interest along with the semi-feudal landlords in preventing a total breakaway. It was the moderating influence of these compradore elements which had allowed the
colonial power to maintain its rule without too much repression. Thus the transfer of political power immediately brought about a neo-colonial nexus (invisible but pervasive) involving the survival and even the quiet expansion of foreign economic interests.

These reasons for the total breakaway of the settler
colonies from the mother country can be better understood
when contrasted with the decolonization process in the
nonsettler colonies. In the first place, in the nonsettler colonies the foreign interests, because of their expatriate basis, were capable of attuning themselves easily
to post-independence conditions. Operating impersonally
from abroad through large corporate enterprises, these
interests could accommodate themselves to the host society's aspirations, at least to the extent of changing their
public image, (60) compromising on such matters as the
indigenization of business management, the use of the
national language, and collaboration with the indigenous
ruling class. The growing intervention of governments in
the affairs of private business makes it entrepreneurially
helpful for the large, invariably expatriate firms to keep
the goodwill of politicians, and to take on to their staff
bureaucrats whose 'contacts established during their
service with the government' are invaluable to the firms,
in their dealings with government over foreign exchange
licences, raw material allocations, pricing, taxation, and
matters pertaining to foreign investments. Second, the
ownership and control of the foreign enterprises in the
nonsettler colonies were held by powerful corporations
abroad. Their sources of economic power lay outside the
country of investment and therefore out of reach of the
newly independent governments. The ramifications of such
external control extend over the whole of the colonial
export economy including the financing, marketing and sale
of plantation or mining products, and its roots are not
easy to unravel let alone exterminate.

This is to say that the remote control of the nonsettler economies from distant centres of financial and political power gave foreign capital an immunity from interference by national governments - an advantage which settler investors lack. There was also a strong complementarity between export economies, heavily dependent on metropolitan markets, and the metropolis which nothing short of
a bold political programme could remove. The difficulties

of taking over metropolitan investments, without action
that is revolutionary in its character and comprehensive
in scope, are seen in the backtracking of the Sri Lanka
government (1970-7) on its programme to nationalize
foreign banks, plantations and agency houses, for fear of
retaliation by the foreign interests. (61) The nationalization of the plantations which occurred only in 1975
became part of a land reform programme which the government was compelled to undertake to restore its image after
the insurrection of the Janatha Vimukthi Peramuna in April
1971. This nationalization also occurred with the leave
and licence, as it were, of the British government. By
this time the character of metropolitan capital exports
had changed; foreign merchant capital in the periphery
had declined in significance compared with MNC-based industrial capital, which was being invested directly without the mediation of the merchant firms which had managed
and controlled the plantation interests. Furthermore, in
the nonsettler colonies a considerable share of foreign
involvement is also in the service sector, comprising
banks, insurance and shipping companies and trading-cum-
managing agency firms. The liquid funds of these enterprises are substantially held or invested abroad, while
their tangible assets in the colony are minimal - mostly
office buildings and warehouses (not plant and machinery
as in the case of manufacturing industry); the prerequisite for their operations is merely the right to transact
business.

The independence of these colonies (say, India, Sri
Lanka, Malaysia) had led merely to a broadening of their
sources of foreign capital without a diminution in the
absolute volume of investments held by the former metropolitan power. While metropolitan capital acquired new
interests, it retained its traditional control over certain segments of the colonial export economy - plantations
(and mines), banking, insurance and shipping. The foreign
economic control of these countries is paralleled by the
strong colonial tradition in their education system,
social values and culture. (62) Metropolitan countries
when obliged to abandon imperial control have preferred,
for this reason, to bequeath political power not to their
own settlers but to 'responsible' indigenous groups who
would not seriously challenge metropolitan interests.

To the general tendency for a continuity of foreign
economic interests in the nonsettler colonies Burma is a
stark exception. In these colonies, whereas the existence
of an indigenous compradore bourgeoisie made a peaceful
transfer of power possible with a neo-colonial nexus, in
Burma political independence produced an intense reaction

against colonial vestiges.   Soon after its independence
Burma left the British Commonwealth. (63)   The assets of
foreigners were nationalized, and foreigners were virtually excluded from employment in Burma.   A currency demone-
tization in May 1964 depreciated cash hoards, which were
held mostly by foreigners.   In manufacturing, in motor
transport and in river and coastal traffic, foreign enterprises were brought under government control.   Repatriation of capital and of income was drastically curbed.   The
lands of dispossessed farmers, which were mostly foreign-
owned, were restored, and rural debts revoked.   The attack
on foreign interests by the Revolutionary Council after
March 1962, while reflecting a socialist ideology, was to
some extent merely nationalist in fervour. (64)   With the
transfer of political power, Burma thus made a thorough
and effective breakaway.   The Burmese experience requires
to be explained, like the case of the Congo and Indochina
in the preceding chapter.

A reaction of this nature, exceptional for a nonsettler
colony, was due to the repercussions of colonial rule on
all sections of society.   The indigenous political and
social structure was dismantled and the traditional elite
dislodged.   With the movement of peasants from the northern districts to the rice lands of the south, the ties of
the peasants with the king and hereditary chieftains were
broken.   After the third Anglo-Burmese war and the rebellion to which the chieftains lent their support, the
chieftains were removed, and the village headmen were
made salaried officials of the British but with no real
power or prestige.   'What we gave Burma', commented G.E.
Harvey, 'was not a government but an administration....
It was a curiously impersonal system.' (65)   There was no
indigenous class which gained from colonial rule.   Unlike
many Asian societies where a dominant class was strengthened and made use of by the colonial power, Burma underwent a social demolition.   The 'fabulous profits' of the
rice export trade almost completely bypassed the Burmese.

A disastrous aspect of colonial rule in Burma was the
enthronement of an alien Asian group.   Financially, and
commercially, Burma became a subordinate entity of India.
Like the remora which travels long distances by attaching
itself through its dorsal slicker to the body of a shark,
Indian capital went along with Britain's overseas expansion.   And in Burma, it found a very propitious field.
Indians controlled about two fifths of the value of
Burma's imports and about three fifths of the value of
exports.   Burma exported agricultural products and raw
materials to India, and imported mostly manufactured or
semi-manufactured goods.   Its foreign trade and shipping

were oriented to India, and one third of the tonnage was
carried by Indian ships. (66)   Large remittances were made
to head offices in India as interest, profits, taxes,
freight, insurance, etc. (67)   While Burma was 'doubly
colonial', in some ways its economic subordination to
India was greater than that to Britain.   Exports of rice
to Europe declined in volume from roughly more than half
in 1900 to less than 40 per cent in 1914 and to less than
20 per cent in 1918. (68)   European ownership of the milling industry had also declined considerably by 1936, (69)
and correspondingly the importance of European firms in
the financing, shipment and export marketing of rice.   It
was this non-metropolitan orientation of Burma's export
economy, and the relatively limited control by the metropolis over shipping, banking and insurance, that enabled
Burma to divest itself of foreign economic control without
fear of retaliation.

The Indians in Burma were ubiquitous.   Their interaction with the Burmese was at the level of the small production unit and the individual consumer, unlike the large
European companies which operated banks, insurance and
shipping agencies, rice mills, oil wells, etc., from head
offices located in the port towns and responsible in turn
to remote centres of financial power overseas.   The
Indians became the visible symbol of the whole system of
control and domination of Burma by foreigners.   As money
lenders and small traders they lubricated the colonial
economy;   they were the agents for the financing and collection of the rice crop as well as the landlords both in
the city and the countryside.   They were vested with the
responsibility for bringing practically all of the rice
crop (the sole agricultural export commodity) into the
hands of European rice millers and exporters.   They were
an essential part of Burma's metropolitan nexus.

Since the export staple by which the country was hauled
into the world economy was solely a peasant crop, the
impact of the export economy on the peasant producers in
Burma was more extended in scale and of greater intensity
than the disturbance that occurred in the peasant sector
of most other countries.   The resulting landlessness and
its depressive effect on wages was unique to Burma.   It
did not occur, for instance, in West Africa, where peasant
agriculture, as in Burma, was the basis of a large export
trade, nor in the peasant sector of the plantation economies.   In these economies the dispossession of the indigenous peasants was slower, owing to the virtual seclusion
of the 'subsistence' sector from the developments in
export agriculture.   In Burma indigenous tenant farmers
were evicted through the competition of Indians who were

willing to pay higher rents and were financially no better
off than wage labourers. The growth of landless wage
labour in Burma was partly due to technological unemployment caused by the loss of traditional occupations, mainly
salt boiling. Labour was also displaced from boating and
the hand-pounding of paddy, by the introduction of steam
ships and steam-driven rice mills respectively.

An unusual degree of rural indebtedness which also
underlay the problem of landlessness was due to the impositions of the landlord and usurer almost from the
outset. Capital was required for the clearing of forest
land and for constructing dykes, without which cultivation
in the deltaic swamps was not possible. This need was
fulfilled by the chettiyar money lenders. During the depression of the 1930s, there was a widespread transfer of
landownership to the chettiyars, and by 1936 they held approximately 25 per cent or 2.5 million acres of the rice
land in Lower Burma. (70) By 1941 they had engulfed a
much larger area, and their activities had become a 'potential cause of political trouble'. This 'continual
transfer of land from the agriculturist to the non-agri-
culturist', it was reported in 1937, 'is likely to result
in violent agitation for the ousting of foreign owners'.
(71) In the plantation economies the dispossession of the
indigenous peasantry was very limited in extent, and the
agent of dispossession was the indigenous landlord-cum-
trader, not an alien group consisting, as in Burma, of
the Indian chettiyars.

In Burma, the Indian presence was not limited to the
commercial-cum-money-lending class but included migrant
labour, who had a depressive effect on wages. (72)

Indian workers accustomed to extremely low living
standards were imported to perform the manual tasks;
thousands of Burmese were driven out from the unskilled
urban employments in which they had been engaged by
Indians who worked for what even to the Burmese were
'starvation wages'.

This was in contrast to Sri Lanka and Malaysia where the
export enclaves in the form of plantations limited the
interaction of migrant labour with the local society. In
Burma the widespread impoverishment resulting from proletarianization on so large a scale was reflected in low
rice consumption levels while exports expanded. In Lower
Burma consumption per head from the beginning of this
century remained constant and then declined during the
1930s. According to an estimate of V.D.Wickizer and M.K.
Bennett, consumption per head fell by 25 per cent. (73)
Furnivall, though critical of this figure, observed that
'the quantity of rice exported has grown at the expense of

that required for food'. (74)   The presence of an enormous
labour supply led to a considerable volume of seasonal employment.   In the rice districts, 'nearly half the land is
owned by foreigners, and a landless people can show little
for their labour but their debts, and for almost half the
year, most of them are unable to find work or wages'. (75)
Throughout Asia the loyalty and political passivity of
migrant groups had a stabilizing effect on colonial rule,
but in Burma the Indians fulfilled this role in an extraordinary way.   They were a 'hard-working and convenient
prop for a regime which could by no means always count on
Burmese cooperation'. (76)   The public service was staffed
overwhelmingly by Indians.   Indian soldiers and military
police were prominent in the suppression of rebellions and
in maintaining 'law and order'.   Burmese were generally
excluded from the armed forces until the eve of the Second
World War, ostensibly in 'the view that the Burman will
never be a soldier'. (77)   According to F.N.Trager, by
the beginning of the Second World War the employment of
Indians had become 'a studied British policy'. (78)   In
Moulmein by 1852 one third of the inhabitants were
Indians.   Rangoon, the new capital of Burma, developed as
'essentially a British Indian city' and the preponderance
of Indians made Hindustani the lingua franca. (79)   The
city's trade and its most valuable property were mostly
in the hands of Indians.   The Indians were not a national
minority, but were as much an enclave as the Europeans.
They remitted their savings, left frequently for India,
and altogether lacked a sense of belonging to the country
where they found gainful employment and, not a few of
them, the opportunity to amass wealth.   It seemed 'an
Indo-British occupation rather than a British occupation'.
(80)
It is these factors underlying the exceptional case of
Burma which highlight the politics of decolonization in
the settler and the nonsettler colonies, to which I have
already referred.   In the settler colonies, the achieve-
ment of independence was a violent and traumatic process,
and with the exodus of the settlers the vestiges of colonialism were speedily liquidated.   That metropolitan links
were later re-established even after such a traumatic experience is an irony of history.   The precise circumstances of their reincorporation and its bearing on the prevailing nature of underdevelopment will be dealt with in
the concluding chapter.
The internal locus of interests of foreign capital and
enterprise in the settler colonies made their development
a somewhat distinctive phenomenon.   These colonies were
manifestly underdeveloped in terms of the advanced indus-

trial economies. Yet, the development which took place in
them, both in its character and scale, was superior to
that in the nonsettler colonies - giving rise to what
Arrighi and Saul aptly termed the 'uneven development of
the periphery'. The complex pattern of development in the
settler colonies has even led to an ambivalence in the
interpretation of their development status. A general
tendency (influenced no doubt by the extreme poverty of
the indigenous inhabitants) has been to overlook the
structural changes in the economy which the settlers
brought about. (81) A realistic assessment of the economic changes requires a comparative perspective. Existing analyses seem limited by their undue concentration on
the settler colonies alone, or else by a tendency to take
the industrially advanced economies as a sole reference
point.

The development status of the settler colonies must
not, however, be seen as the half-way point on a Rostovian
continuum which leads to a complete transformation. Contradictory elements in their economy and social structure
gave them a hybrid nature. The settlers, as an investing
class, had certain 'national' characteristics. They exercised greater economic and political autonomy than did expatriate groups; their entrepreneurial horizon was broader and more inward oriented and concerned with production
rather than with export-import activities to which production was merely an accessory; they developed their
own socio-cultural traits which set them apart from the
parent society. These differences between settler and
metropolitan interests were reflected in the political
conflicts of the settlers with the colonial administration
as well as with the expatriate investors in the metropolis. Nevertheless, the autonomy of the settlers was
only partial, compared with that of the white dominions;
and they remained in varying degrees subject to metropolitan influence. In concluding this chapter I shall
assess the relative strength of the settler interests in
the different colonies and the limits to their autonomous
and unrestrained development.

In the French empire, the development potential of the
settlers was more limited than in the British colonies.
The French colonies were to an unusual degree tied to the
metropolis. They were represented in the French Parliament, and the colonial administration was responsible to
the appropriate ministry in France (like the relation between a large metropolitan firm and its overseas branch;
the several departments of the parent firm deal directly
with the corresponding departments of the overseas
branch). The senior officials were paid from Paris, and

budget deficits were met by grants from the French Treasury. The budget for Algeria until 1904 was a part of the national budget of France. In Morocco infrastructure projects (transport, power and irrigation), even when carried out by private firms, were largely financed with official French funds through the Protectorate budget or by loans guaranteed by both the French and Protectorate governments. (82) This financial relationship between the metropolis and the colonies was a two-way street. The colonies had to contribute to France's financial commitments; for instance, from 1929 Algeria paid 2.5 million francs annually towards the replacement of eight passenger ships plying between Algeria and France, which the French government had leased to private firms. (83) The political and administrative unification of the French colonies with the metropolis was very pronounced in the Maghreb, situated so close to France.

In the Maghreb the settlers were numerically large but economically weak. Algeria, the most developed of the Maghrebin economies which also had the largest number of settlers, was annexed at a time when capitalism in France was relatively backward. From the 1870s small farmers were encouraged; between 1871 and 1881 about 30,000 had settled (84) - mostly poor whites. The limited impact of French capitalism on Algeria and the total elimination of the Algerian landed aristocracy during the early years of the conquest were congenial conditions for the growth of an independent settler bourgeoisie, detached from the metropolis. The Algerian settler bourgeoisie was nevertheless weak compared with those in South Africa, Rhodesia or even Kenya. Like all French colonies, Algeria was firmly tied politically and commercially to France. Export production, as in other colonies, was closely geared to the French economy and allowed into France duty-free. The bulk of Algeria's exports of cereals and more than 75 per cent of its tobacco went to France. Half the fresh vegetables imported by France came from Algeria - supplies that left Algiers on a Wednesday reached Paris for sale on Saturday. The development of viticulture, which became an important agricultural activity in Algeria, was an attempt to relocate a branch of French agriculture after the phyloxera disease ravaged the French vineyards. Algerian wine production was at times adjusted in the interests of the French Midi.

From the beginning of the twentieth century the investment pattern in Algeria changed noticeably. Metropolitan capital became increasingly important, both in agriculture and in mining. The small farming units which typified settler agriculture began to be displaced, and numerous

settlers as well as rural Algerians moved to the towns.
Viticulture and the dry farming of cereals, because of
their large capital requirements, led to a concentration
of land ownership. More significant was the growing influence on the Algerian economy of expatriate firms partly
owned by banks and finance houses in France. They controlled the market in wine, esparto grass and cork - among
other products. The mining industry from this time was
overwhelmingly metropolitan owned. One financial group
controlled all iron workings, another the production of
phosphates, and a third lead and zinc mining. Finance
capital in France, a late developer, found a convenient
stamping ground in the Maghreb. (85)

In Morocco the economic influence of the settlers was
limited, first by their relatively small number - fewer
than in Algeria. Immigration was very rapid from 1926 to
1930 but almost ceased during the depression of the 1930s,
from which time land grants to settlers were suspended.
Though the Europeans had acquired the best land, the total
acreage they held was only about one twelfth of the land
cultivated by Moroccans. (86) This was partly due to the
density of the indigenous population and to the power of
the Moroccan feudal groups - the great caids of the Atlas.
Unlike such groups in other settler colonies, in Morocco
the caids were not vanquished. The French obtained their
collaboration in the conquest and final pacification of
Morocco in 1934, in return for which they were allowed to
retain extensive landholdings. (87) The settlers were
wedged between the indigenous feudal class and metropolitan mining and finance capital, owing to the relatively
late colonization of Morocco - which took place when
French industry and finance were well developed. Metropolitan capital became firmly entrenched from the start,
attracted by Morocco's extensive mineral wealth (cobalt,
phosphates, manganese, lead and molybdenum). 'The take-
over of the Moroccan economy by ... /big European firms/
was unparalleled in its thoroughness and rapidity.' (88)

The development of the settler colonies was affected
fundamentally by the fact that the settlers were not an
adequate substitute for an indigenous bourgeoisie. The
political framework in which their development occurred,
based on racial discrimination and inequalities, as Banton
observed, was economically dysfunctional. (89) The migrant labour system which excluded Africans from the settled workforce involved a wastage of their labour potential. It retarded the development of urban industrial
skills while affecting farming efficiency, owing to the
periodic absence of adult males from the village. (90)
The diffusion of skills among the largely indigenous work-

force was also checked by the employment patterns and the
restrictions on non-whites engaging in any but 'rough and
simple manual tasks'. The monopoly of skills by the settlers resulted in abnormally high wages for skilled
labour. In South Africa these wages, it was found in
1941, were 'many times higher' than in countries from
which manufactured goods were imported. (91) The classification of skilled workers to include the semi-skilled
further contributed to the relatively high proportion of
labour costs in manufacturing industry. The duplication
of social amenities resulting from segregationist policies
also led to higher overhead costs. (92) The survival of
local industries was thus contingent on a rigid import-
licensing policy and the patronage of the government and
municipal authorities. (93) In gold mining a succession
of favourable market circumstances obscured the effect of
these discriminatory wage practices on production costs,
but they merely postponed 'the final reckoning'. (94) The
politically structured wage rates for European and for
African labour, which were completely out of line with
market conditions or with the actual distribution of
skills, besides raising labour costs, have dampened work
efficiency.

The most serious impediment, however, to the viability
of the settler colonies, despite the level of advancement
already achieved, stemmed from the irrationalities and
contradictions of a system utilizing modern technology but
based on a quasi-Fascist ideology for maintaining the privileges, purity and status of a white minority. Societies
are never completely static and their foundations become
weakened by economic exigencies - for instance, as more
Africans become urbanized and politicized despite pre-
emptive measures. While the ludicrous results of such a
regime become progressively more evident and acute, the
inability of the privileged minority, which is both white
and settler, to renounce the culture of racism or else
emigrate en masse moves these societies ineluctably to the
point of explosion.

6   Settler growth and the repression of indigenous interests

The countries with a critical mass of white settlers (in terms of numbers and impact) displayed, as I have shown, a greater internal dynamism than the nonsettler colonies which remained producers of primary products for the metropolitan economy. As an investing class the settlers engaged in a more diverse range of activities, including manufacturing production. They generally catered for domestic or regional markets, often in competition with the metropolitan economy. A corollary of this entrepreneurial pattern was the dominance of production capital over merchant capital. Production capital in the settler colonies functioned in its own right, not in the service of a merchant class to whom production was of secondary interest and who were concerned with controlling markets rather than with improving production methods. The process of capital accumulation and investment thus acquired a national orientation, relatively free from external restraints and distortions.

The domicile of the Europeans in the settler colonies and their greater involvement in the local society, while promoting economic development, brought them into conflict not merely with their respective parent countries but also with the indigenous groups. As Arghiri Emmanuel said, the settlers struggled on two fronts. While the settlers were relatively free from metropolitan control, the position of the indigenous people, such as the Africans in Rhodesia or in the Union of South Africa, was the 'reverse of Independence' that most colonial countries achieved after the Second World War. The indigenous people, by far the larger component of the population, remained 'with no significant control or influence at any level - politically, socially or economically'. (1)   In South Africa and Rhodesia, what they are striving for is a reversal of the balance of political power within the country rather than

independence in the sense of freedom from outside control.
The size of the indigenous population in these colonies
was such that it prevented them from being decimated or
confined en masse to reserves as in the USA, Canada, Australia and New Zealand.   The Europeans existed as a powerful minority, wielding political authority and control
over labour and natural resources far more pervasively
than in nonsettler colonies.   The cohesiveness of the settlers as a racial group, even where there was a white
working class, made the relationship between the settlers
and the indigenous society decidedly more antagonistic
than that of nonsettler investors.   It was as though a
splinter-metropolis with a separate node of political and
economic authority had located itself within the territory.   This node, notwithstanding the admission as honor-
ary citizens of Japanese and people of other ethnic origins belonging to the select echelons of the international
business community, is none the less distinctly 'white' in
culture and concept.   The settler colonies, while exercising considerable though varying degrees of economic and
political autonomy vis-à-vis the metropolitan country, represented a form of internal colonialism from the standpoint of the indigenous people.

The development process, based on a monopoly of political power by an alien minority, was in a fundamental way
damaging to the indigenous people.   They were allowed only
in the basement of the settlers' economic edifice.   Their
social and economic position suffered a permanent disability.   The distinction between the settler and the nonsettler colonies which complicates the claim that the
former were more emancipated was perceptively stated by
Sir Harry Johnstone in 1897:   in 'tropical dependencies'
i.e. the nonsettler colonies, 'we merely impose our rule
to secure a fair field and no favour to all races and in-
ferentially for our trade, ... [and] the local government
must depend directly on London.'   In the settler territories, on the other hand, 'where climatic considerations
encourage true colonization, there undoubtedly the weakest
must go to the wall and the black must pay for the unpro-
gressive turn his ancestors took some thousands of years
ago.' (2)   This clash of ethnic interests was also noted
by Lord Lugard in 1922: (3)

The requirements of the settlers, to put it bluntly,
are incompatible with the interests and advancement of
the [African] agricultural tribes, nor could they be
otherwise than impatient of native development as rival
in the growing of coffee, flax and sisal.

The existence in certain countries of 'deliberate and
legalised political, economic and racial discrimination',

to which Hla Myint referred, is liable to lose its significance if one states, as he does, that similar disabilities were imposed in a veiled form in underdeveloped
countries generally. (4) The structure of race relations
was not the same in different colonial situations. As
Banton stated, 'it would be misleading to speak of the
existence of a colour line in ... [nonsettler] territories
if the same term is used for the position in colonies like
Rhodesia'. (5) The failure to distinguish between the two
situations obscures differences in the economic role and
status of the chief actors in the development process. In
fact, it was in terms of the 'distribution of economic
activity among the different groups and the different
roles they play in economic life' that Myint's interpretation of economic backwardness was based. (6) As he put
it, they were 'disequalising factors'. The distribution
of economic activity between the indigenous people and the
foreigners was linked to the prevailing patterns of race
relations, which Myint ignores.

At a very general level the economic role and status of
the indigenous people in the settler colonies was reflected in the virtual absence of an indigenous bourgeoisie.
The development of such a bourgeoisie was strangled in the
cradle or perhaps in the conception. The settler colonies, to be sure, were those where the traditional political and economic structures were less advanced than those
in the nonsettler colonies - a circumstance which favoured
and induced European settlement. At the same time, settler activities involved a complete repudiation of indigenous interests. These interests were nonexistent (from
non-recognition) and hardly conceivable in the cultural
mores of settler thinking. The settler colonies in this
respect differ radically from the nonsettler colonies
where as a rule an indigenous bourgeoisie developed to
some extent even though in a compradore's role. The
impact of the settlers' development process, in terms of
an indigenous bourgeoisie, is seen distinctly against the
contrasting situation in the nonsettler colonies. The
case of Nigeria and that of the Philippines - two such
colonies - will be briefly considered here.

In Nigeria, there developed a native bourgeoisie based
on export agriculture, commerce, transport and small-scale
urban industries. The Europeans from 1900 were administratively debarred from agricultural investment and were
limited to the export-import trade, mining, and timber extraction on a small scale. African farmers and traders
responded to the market prospects in groundnuts, cocoa and
palm oil, despite the government's encouragement of cotton
cultivation (for the British Cotton Growing Association in

Manchester).   'No infusion of Western business ethic was
needed to promote a new trade which significantly altered
cropping patterns, lines of commerce, and standards of
living.' (7) The internal marketing and transport requirements of the cocoa crop gave rise to a network of
African retailers and petty traders. Working for the exporting firms on a commission basis, these middlemen-cum-
financiers owned motor lorries, advanced cash to growers
on the mortgage of crops and amassed considerable property. (8) Nigerian firms had a large investment in saw
milling, rubber creping and palm oil extraction, motor
transport, and urban small-scale manufacturing (where a
total of about 100,000 were employed). (9)
     In the Philippines, as in Nigeria, a class of native
capitalists grew up under colonialism. Having set its
economic and political roots under Spanish rule with which
it ultimately came into conflict, this class expanded with
the growth of the export economy from the beginning of
this century. A determining factor in its expansion was
the scope of the American involvement in the economy of
the Philippines. American capital was invested mainly in
mining and public utilities - tramways, electric power and
lighting. In agriculture, American capital was confined
to the milling and marketing of the export crops, but cultivation (as in the peasant-based export economies of West
Africa) was in the hands of indigenous landowners. A
larger segment of the economy was thus left to the indigenous interests than in the plantation economies where
metropolitan capital dominated the cultivation of export
staples as well as their processing and marketing. (10)
     The fortunes of the Filipino capitalist class were
nourished by the traditional agrarian framework, involving
tenancy and debt bondage. It also had access to employment opportunities at most levels of the colonial administration. Wealthy families, some of whom represented a
fusion of merchant capital and the old landed interests,
came thereby to exercise a powerful influence on social
life and politics. Under the influence of this bourgeoisie the economy of the Philippines became far more internally oriented than other nonsettler economies. The bourgeoisie capitalized a portion of its revenue by investing
in manufacturing industries, trade and urban development.
Though primary production, comprising sugar, coconut,
tobacco and lumber, was the chief source of income and
employment, the Philippines became the most industrialized
country in Southeast Asia.
     It was in the settler colonies, on the other hand, that
the domination of the Europeans found its sharpest expression. Without exception there was a wholesale repudiation

of indigenous interests by means of an institutionalized
system of repression. In the case of Kenya the racialism
which underlay the structure of authority and privilege
was plainly stated by Sir Charles Eliot, Commissioner of
the East African Protectorate from 1901 to 1904: 'It is
mere hypocrisy not to admit that white interest must be
paramount and that the main object of our policy and
legislation should be to found a white colony.' (11)
Severe disabilities were imposed on the non-European
groups with regard to urban residence, ownership of farming land, and access to education, housing and medical
care. The best land was from the outset reserved for the
Europeans. Land ownership in the city of Nairobi reflected the inferior position of the Africans in relation to
the Indians, and of both Africans and Indians in relation
to the Europeans. One acre of European-owned land existed
for every seven Europeans, one acre of Asian-owned land
for every twenty-one Asians, and one acre of African land
for every 800 Africans. (12) Indians were prohibited from
trading outside the Central Business District, and had to
live in a separate quarter of the city. Though commercial
and residential segregation was legally ended in 1923, the
city was still zoned off on racial lines by means of
covenants inserted into land transactions and the transfer
of leases. Health hazards to Europeans from the ghettos
of the Indians caused new areas in the city to be assigned
to the Indians, where they were again segregated.
    In the settler colonies the mass of the people were in
a condition of absolute degradation. In Algeria, large
numbers were in a state of 'primary hunger' and in the
towns confined to ghettos. In the Casbah of Algiers
80,000 people inhabited one square kilometre, accounting
for 40 per cent of the country's TB cases, according to a
survey in 1961. (13) In South Africa, the living standards of the Africans were better than those elsewhere, yet
the Africans lacked basic amenities - water, drainage and
sewerage, roads, electricity and housing. The neglect of
their urban needs was linked to a policy of controlling
the presence of Africans in the towns. In East London
(South Africa), where the conditions of Africans is
'almost certainly typical' of that in many urban centres
of the Union, from 1928 to 1940 no municipal action was
taken in the main African urban location. In 1955, out
of nearly 43,000 Africans who were in this city, fewer
than 12,000 were municipally housed, and another 15,000
lived in their employers' premises. Large numbers were
shack-dwellers. In the wealthiest cities of the south
their deprivation was greatest. While the Europeans enjoy
one of the highest standards of living in the world, 'the

flotsam and jetsam of the African proletariat reaches a
depth of social and physical degradation unknown elsewhere'. (14)

   Colonial rule is commonly a barrier to educational advancement, but in the settler colonies there was a virtual
denial of education. In Algeria in 1957, only 12 per cent
of the children of school-going age were enrolled. Among
girls, in 1954, about one out of sixteen was in school.
(15) In Indonesia, where education was kept at the level
of 'extreme simplicity', in 1930 out of a total population
of 60 million 93 per cent were illiterate. At the secondary level (both academic and vocational) only 6,085 Indonesians were taught in Dutch; (16) those graduating from
the better high schools averaged 200 a year. (17) In Rhodesia in 1967 educational expenditure by government was
about £8 for every African child in school but £120 for
every European child. (18) Of the African children 0.04
per cent were attending school (and less than 2 per cent
of them had 8-9 years of schooling), (19) though more than
half of the European children received 10-11 years of
schooling and over a third of them had completed a pre-
university education.

   This educational policy in the settler colonies was em-
bedded in the system of unequal race relations. Where the
settlers included a European professional class, as in
Indonesia, the spread of higher education was restricted
by them with a view to maintaining the level of incomes of
the Europeans as a racial group. The lawyers wanted Indonesians excluded from a Law School set up in 1909, saying
that Indonesians could not judge impartially and so were
unsuited for a legal career. The Medical Association in
1913 opposed the establishment of a medical school which
would have enrolled Indonesians - the moral qualities of
a physician, it said, were by nature alien to Asians. (20)
In Rhodesia, many Europeans saw the educated African as a
danger to their privileged position and security. (21)
The uneducated African was 'the most honest, trustworthy
and useful' (22) - the last being perhaps his best qualification. The rigorous curtailment of Western education
was in contrast to the educational policy in nonsettler
colonies - e.g. India, Sri Lanka, Malaysia, and the West
Indies - where Westernization and Western education were
deliberately fostered. In these colonies not only did
large numbers of indigenous people find employment in the
administration and the professions but educational facilities ran ahead of employment opportunities. The conception of education as a political weapon which must not
get into indigenous hands, though prevalent throughout
Africa, found a more virulent expression in the settler
colonies.

The harsh racial discrimination in the settler colonies
was made possible by the cohesiveness and stability of
settler communities. Unlike expatriate communities, they
were large and integrated. The settlers were in a wide
range of occupations and professions - physicians, lawyers, teachers, clergymen, real estate agents, etc. The
male-female ratio was fair, and the birth rate high. In
the course of time, a good proportion of the settler community was locally born. (23) Despite class differences
the settlers as a whole had a uniform code of behaviour
towards the indigenous people. The central element in
this attitude was the taboo on sexual relations with the
blacks.

In the early period of European settlement, the scarcity of white women encouraged liaisons with black women -
as in the West Coast of Africa and in Brazil during the
period of Portuguese rule in the sixteenth and seventeenth
centuries. In Zambia the cohabiting of white men and
black women was informally condoned if it was done with
decorum and restraint. (24) In Indonesia planters cohabited with their housekeepers and military personnel
kept Indonesian women in the barracks. (25) In Burma,
during the early years marriages between British and
Burmese met with no official disapproval and were socially
not too embarrassing. (26) While sexual relations between
white men and coloured women did not imply racial equality
- as Philip Mason points out, they tended to ease racial
feelings. For instance, in Puerto Rico where concubinage
was practised by the hacienda-owners, the children of
slaves kept by white men advanced socially. They inherited property and were even given administrative posts in
the enterprises owned by the father. (27) With improved
communications and medical amenities came an influx of
women from the mother country, and racial attitudes hardened. Sex relations across the colour line were now defi-
nitely proscribed. (28)

The prejudices that developed at this stage against the
coloured races are ascribed partly to the jealousy of the
European women and their distorted image of the Africans
(or Asians, as the case may be). Influenced by their contact mostly with menials among the coloureds, 'the ad-
jective "African" came to symbolise lower material and
moral standards'. (29) The jealousy of the European women
arose mainly from the double standards which prevailed for
men and women in regard to interracial liaisons. White
men were not denied coloured women. This liberty, while
resulting in the humiliation of coloured males (per se a
vindication of white supremacy), was a source of anxiety
to the white women, constrained by the norms of propriety.

Their response to this was, on the one hand, to attribute
to Negro men primitive, uncontrolled emotions likely to
end in rape and murder and, on the other hand, to develop
a hostility towards coloured women. Such feelings among
white women, referred to by Banton in the colour-caste
system of the American South, (30) were vividly portrayed
in the case of South Africa and Rhodesia by Doris Lessing
in her novels. (31)

The solidarity of the settlers and their contempt for
the indigenous community bolstered their position as a
privileged racial minority. The ties of solidarity among
the settlers were tantamount to caste feeling - enabling
them to stand together against the indigenous people from
whom they were distinguishable on the basis of colour and
by the common benefits they enjoyed. In the rigid 'two-
category system' of authority and privilege, the most economically depressed whites had a status higher than that
of the highest native. Settlers therefore were not the
ones to espouse universal brotherhood, considering the
benefits they enjoyed without it.

There were various devices whereby white supremacy was
maintained. The status gap surrounding the settlers was
in itself too wide for deviant individuals to try to
bridge. There were informal controls and group sanctions
against any newcomer foolishly inclined to be a libertine.
Then again, persons unable to live up to a white skin were
discouraged from settling. For instance, in Zambia at
first settlement licences were refused to white traders
with insufficient capital (32) and Europeans whose living
standards were considered low were repatriated. In South
Africa, where there was a class of poor whites ('civilized
labourers'), steps were taken to ensure a minimum living
standard 'below which the European community was not willing to see nonskilled fellow whites fall'. (33) They were
given subsidized employment and nonskilled white labour
was preferred to skilled Africans.

Furthermore, the colonial peoples' conception of the
white man was controlled. Even social scientists were
required to carry their white status into the field. A
well-rounded comment worth repeating here was by the
'Central African Post' in 1953, referred to by Banton:
(34)

> In the name of science certain Englishmen enter this
> country ... [and] conduct themselves in such a way that
> they lose the deference traditionally accorded to White
> men by Africans.... They like to live closely to the
> African way of life as they can.... When Africans see
> European scientific men, who are considered by them to
> be a better type of European behaving as they were

Africans, then they lose their respect and deference
for all Europeans.
The moral probity of the white race was one of the many
justificatory myths which underlay its professed right to
govern and exploit. In keeping with this image a calculated social aloofness was maintained, screening the seamy
side of the white man's way of life.

The fear that the white man's image would be spoiled
and that the reverence with which the British were regarded might be lost was partly the basis of a law which in
1814 restricted Indian crews on vessels trading with
England to only 25 per cent. The preamble to it set out
in detail the objection to admitting large numbers of
Indian sailors into England. (35)

The native sailors of India ... on their arrival here
led into scenes which soon divest them of the respect
which they had entertained in India for the European
character. The contemptuous reports which they dis-
seminated on their return cannot fail to have a very
unfortunate influence upon the minds of our Asiatic
subjects, whose reverence for our character, which has
hitherto contributed to maintain our supremacy in the
east will be gradually changed for the most degrading
conceptions.

A greater threat came much later with the cinema. In
Africa, films viewed by the Africans were censored to exclude scenes suggestive of disreputable behaviour by Europeans. Westerns were harmful. (36) This controlled image
of the white man which the European settlers in Africa
were anxious to maintain was adopted throughout the colonies. For instance, in the 1920s there was a serious
concern about the effect of American films on Asian audi-
ences. An ex-governor of Mauritius, Sir Hesketh Bell,
after visiting Malaysia in 1926, wrote hysterically to
'The Times' about the exposure of subject peoples to the
'inner life of the European, and especially the side of it
which flourishes in centres of crime and infamy'. (36)

Pictures of amorous passages ... give a deplorable impression of the morality of the white man and, worse
still, of the white women.... To hear indeed, the
remarks and cat-calls which often proceed from the
cheap seats occupied by young coolies during these
'love passages' is sometimes enough to make one's blood
boil.

George V wished that the Secretary of State for the Colonies would do something to 'stop these horrible exhibi-
tions'. In 1930 the Secretary of State for the Colonies
directed colonial administrators not to allow Asians to
watch 'white men in a state of degradation' or scenes that

convey any antagonistic or strained relations between
white man and coloured people, 'especially with regard to
the question of sexual intercourse, moral or immoral, between individuals of different races'. (38)

Doris Lessing, in 'The Grass is Singing', shows the importance of this image to the white man. Slatter 'was
obeying the dictate of the first law of South Africa:
"Thou shalt not let your fellow white sink lower than a
certain point; because, if you do, the nigger will see
he is as good as you are"'. (39) White solidarity was
even evident in the Maghreb where there was considerable
ethnic diversity among the settlers; Spain, Corsica,
Malta, Sicily, Sardinia and Southern Italy were represented, apart from the large mass of Frenchmen. The
Maghrebin settlers were also stratified by wealth and
status - nearly 30 per cent of them were proletarian - but
in relation to the Algerians they were a homogeneous
group. They were largely urban-based (by 1950 more than
80 per cent were townsmen), they enjoyed common privileges
and higher living standards than the equivalent groups of
Algerians, they married inter-ethnically from the European
stock, and were welded, sociologically and as an ethnic
group, by the educational system and universal military
service. (40)

The settlers also developed a sense of local identity.
They acquired new loyalties and traditions, and even
socio-cultural traits, which tended to transform them into
'proto-nationalities'. (41) Their permanent domicile
abroad and, in most cases, a geographical isolation or
remoteness from the parent society (as in New Zealand,
America and in sub-Saharan Africa) produced fairly distinct cultures. (42) In Rhodesia this included a new kind
of speech, 'an accent of its own, a phonetic amalgam compounded by Africaans, Scottish and Cockney elements', just
as the Australians and Americans acquired characteristic
accents. The settlers, while retaining an outmoded loyalty to the empire, developed a sense of belonging to their
territory. This commitment was lacking among expatriate
groups who expected to return home at the end of their
working life, if not earlier when their contracts expired.
In the Maghreb, especially in Algeria, the settlers developed into a type of European different from that in
France. Abun-Nasr spoke of 'the appearance of a new
people'. (43) Samir Amin regarded them as a 'fossil society', closer to the France of the nineteenth century.
Most of them as pieds noirs were proud of their vigour and
looked down on their compatriots in France, branding them
patos (Spanish: 'ducks'). (44)

The permanent attachment of the settlers to their coun-

try of domicile was reflected also in an extensive ownership of urban land, which again is not typical of expatriates. In the city of Nairobi over 60 per cent of the
urban land was held by the two settler groups - Europeans
and Indians - the European area being composed mainly of
'large residential plots'. (45) The commitment of the
settlers, both individually and as a group, to the territories where they lived was the basis of Lord Stanley's
policy of granting freehold land to Europeans in Zambia.
They

> should be able to make in Rhodesia a permanent home for
> themselves and their children, and to become an inte-
> gral part of the local population, socially superior to
> the natives, politically dominant no doubt, but con-
> scious of a more than temporary association with the
> country and all its inhabitants.

Leasehold lands, on the other hand, would make the European nothing but an interloper and could actually encourage
him to exploit the soil as fast as he could before retiring for home. (46)

The extensiveness of their economic interests and the
social heterogeneity among the settlers caused them to
encroach on all but the lowest paid forms of employment;
their economic interests comprised agriculture for the
domestic market and small-scale industrial and commercial
enterprises as well as junior professional, technical and
administrative posts. In Algeria a good many of the
skilled and even the semi-skilled workers were settlers.
They also held 20,000-25,000 white-collar jobs, about two
fifths of these in the public services. (47) In Indonesia
and Indochina, which were permeated by European settler
influences, a similar situation prevailed. At the University of Hanoi the janitor was a Frenchman - and he was
paid more than a Vietnamese with a Ph.D. from Paris. (48)
Though the development process in the settler economies
led to a considerable growth of urban employment, the settlers blanketed and controlled these opportunities. Those
open to the indigenous people were severely restricted as
the size and heterogeneity of the settler community increased.

The racial privileges of the settlers were most helpful
to the small farmers, artisans and traders. They were the
groups who were to lose most by the economic advancement
of the non-Europeans. In Kenya, the Indians, engaged as
petty traders, market gardeners, butchers, clerks, carpenters and building workers, could effectively compete with
the Europeans whose overhead costs were high. The need to
protect the 'small white man' was thus the basis of the
anti-Indian policy in Kenya. The Indians 'fill all the

occupations and trades which would give employment to the poorer white colonists, especially those arriving now in the country', Delamere complained. 'That is what Indian immigration means in the early days of a new country in Africa. It means if open competition is allowed the small white colonist must go to the wall.' (49) While settler communities were more race conscious than expatriates (and long-established settlers more than those newly arrived), (50) the lowest-ranking settlers were the most virulent in their racism; for as a group they were economically and socially the most threatened. The colour line between the white settlers and the Indians thus transcended the class divisions in Kenyan society as a whole.

The interests and racial attitudes of Europeans which differed between the settler and the nonsettler colonies were reflected in the policies of the administration to- wards Indians in Kenya and in Uganda, briefly referred to earlier. In Kenya the settler status of the Europeans brought them to a head-on clash with the Indians who, as petty traders, artisans and clerks, formed 'a sort of im- pervious pan which prevented European enterprise from soaking into the subsoil of the country's economic life'. (51) The settlers denounced them in terms similar to those of the nationalist leaders of Burma in the 1930s or Idi Amin of Uganda; the Indians, they said, were sending money out of the country, and had come to 'exploit' the country, not to develop it! The settler politicians even argued that contact with Indians was detrimental to the Africans who had therefore to be protected. In point of fact, the presence of Indians was as injurious to the set- tlers, who found it hard to compete with them, as to the Africans. (52)

> It certainly sounds better to object to the nefarious
> exploitation of the Negro by the Indian than to say
> that the Indian is not wanted because he makes white
> people work harder to maintain their profits, and ren-
> ders their lives less pleasant than they would be if
> they did not have to compete with him.

The vulnerability of the settlers led to official discri- mination against Indians.

However, in Uganda Indians were well thought of and generally accepted by the Europeans as social equals. This 'comparative lack of prejudice' in Uganda was pointed out by R.C.Pratt. (53) Indians were admitted to the Uganda Development Commission of 1920 and to the Uganda Chamber of Commerce, whereas in Kenya they were debarred from such institutions. In Uganda the Local Government Committee which in 1930 recommended the establishment of a Kampala Municipal Council wanted its members to be elec-

ted by a common roll of property-owners. 'Nowhere else in
East Africa were the Europeans ready to accept at any
level of government a common roll on which at some future
date they might be outnumbered by either Asians or Africans.' (54) This liberal treatment of the Indians in
Uganda was due to the nonsettler character of the Europeans who 'never developed strong political ambitions as a
racial minority'. As expatriates, 'their political behaviour differed from that of European minorities who are
intent on turning a colonial territory into a white man's
country'. (55)

The extensive repression of the indigenous inhabitants
in the settler colonies was also due to the widespread
economic involvement of the settlers and to their monopoly
of political power. Through legislation, administrative
action and coercion of one form or another, 'serious imperfections' in the labour market were introduced in their
favour. (56) 'Political rather than economic forces were
... allowed to determine the structure of production.' In
these policies the settlers had the active support of the
colonial administration. In examining the political role
of the administration it would be helpful to refer briefly
to the contrasting case of the nonsettler colonies.

In the nonsettler colonies, the administration when de-
ciding upon the claims of foreign and indigenous interests
took a relatively neutral stance. As expatriates the
Europeans in these colonies were not significant either in
absolute numbers or relative to the indigenous population.
Their political and administrative power was also tempered
by a 'double division' - the division between the Europeans and the indigenous people and the division between the
Europeans and the officials in Whitehall. Furthermore,
the European officials, owing their primary allegiance to
the Crown, were less amenable to control by the investors.
These officials were recruited in England, and did not
stay very long in any one colony; (57) they were prohibited from purchasing land or subscribing to the capital
of any enterprise without the approval of the Colonial
Secretary. Consequently, administrative policies, as
Banton asserts, were 'more congenial to the interests of
the native peoples' than were those 'where European settlers were powerful'. (58) In Nigeria the officials even
took a paternalistic attitude towards the peasantry, and
the Land and Native Rights Ordinances reserved all agricultural activity to Nigerians.

In the settler colonies, on the other hand, Whitehall
was concerned mainly with the general stability of the
colony, and a large range of other matters was left solely
to the administration on the spot. The relative insigni-

ficance of metropolitan capital, and therefore of pressure groups in England, enabled the metropolitan government to take a larger or a longer view of problems without the rashness with which the settlers were inclined to pursue their aims. For instance, the Foreign Office dissuaded the British South Africa Company from over-taxing the Africans; in northwestern Rhodesia it wanted the company to get the acquiescence of the Barotse king in regard to the imposition of taxes; (59) and in East Africa it tried to forestall a clash between settlers and the Masai tribesmen over the large land concessions to Europeans which Charles Eliot was making in the Rift Valley. (60) Except for such rare cases, the settlers were free to encroach on the rights of the indigenous people without restraint. (61)

The administration was from the outset deeply committed to settler interests, since immigration was officially sponsored, if not actually subsidized as in Rhodesia, and the settlers were the sole source of revenue. Even where a colony was acquired for strategic reasons, its financial stability was a dominant concern of policy. (62) Though the French territories, with a greater unification of government budgets for the empire as a whole, were an apparent exception to this notion that colonies should be financially self-supporting, grants from the British Treasury were given only in crisis situations. In the West Indies after 1870 grants were confined to exceptional purposes such as hurricane relief. (63) The East African Protectorate had received grants-in-aid, but the Foreign Office, in order to curtail these grants, pressed for the development of the economy by bringing in Europeans and Indians. A well-endowed, self-sufficient type of European settler was sought after, 'who would contribute substantially to the country's development'. (64)

In the nonsettler colonies, by contrast, the government was not driven to intervene to the same extent in the process of development. These colonies from the outset generated a revenue for meeting administrative and military expenses. Their indigenous rulers had already been extracting a taxable surplus and in many cases an export trade either existed or was easily developed. (65) Where there was a ready basis of revenue the active sponsoring of European investors was not critically important to the administration. The problem of a labour supply was also less formidable, and official intervention was limited merely to facilitating labour migration. The creation of a proletariat, through the eviction of peasants from extensive areas or the undermining of the traditional economy, was not called for. In these colonies taxation had

revenue considerations in view, and was generally in the
form of indirect taxes (often an export duty); conversely, in the settler colonies direct taxes were levied (such
as the poll tax and the hut tax), whose purpose was to
divert labour to settler enterprises. (66)

In the settler colonies government officials shared a
vested interest with the investors in a power structure
which had a decidedly anti-'native' bias. Many of the
officials were themselves settlers, and were locally recruited and not transferable to other territories. They
had acquired property - houses and farms - and their political interests even overrode those of the metropolitan
government. (67)

> They had invested their capital in their farms, their
> enterprises and their homes; and without the power to
> defend their interests they could lose everything. Po-
> litical relations within the ruling minority therefore
> put local interests before imperial interests and
> minority interests before majority ones.

In any event the administration could not easily withstand the determination of the settlers to monopolize the
resources of the territory. The settlers recognized this
by their pronouncements and actions. For example, one of
them declared in the Kenya Legislative Council in 1930:
'We are British citizens in this country, and because we
accept the responsibilities and claim the privileges of
British citizens, *because we are on the spot, we mean
ultimately to control the destiny of Africa.'* (68) At
times the government modified its commitment to settler
interests. It tried to encourage production on land
farmed by the Africans and it upheld (along with liberal
opinion in Britain) that official intervention to secure
a labour supply for the settlers must be accompanied by
measures to regulate recruitment and working conditions.
But the settlers effectively fought back. In 1907 the
Colonists' Association of Kenya called any measures to
raise wages 'grossly unfair'. Later when a Chief Native
Commissioner, John Ainsworth, wanted to improve methods of
African farming, the settlers blamed him for the labour
shortage. A bill introduced in the Legislative Council in
1918 to promote African farming was withdrawn by government at the insistence of the settlers. (69) Fundamentally, the settlers could not promote their interests without
governmental intervention of a drastic kind - for reasons
to be given later. In this connection the development
process in the nonsettler colonies will be commented on as
a backdrop against which the economic problems in the settler colonies can be judged.

In the nonsettler colonies, the export sector, which

was a creation of foreign capital, took two different
lines of development. One (Sri Lanka, Malaysia and India)
was where it developed independently of and in isolation
from the surrounding peasant economy, without seriously
encroaching on the latter's land or labour. In this - the
plantation case - export production did not involve the
appropriation of peasant lands, and its labour requirements were met by organized migration from Southern India
and China. In the other line of development the export
sector was peasant-based, and in two types: (1) where the
export sector was the old peasant economy expanded far
beyond the limits of the domestic market (e.g. rice in
Burma - as also in Thailand, not a colony - and cotton,
groundnuts, palm oil and oil seeds in West Africa); (2)
where the export sector involved the growing of non-tradi-
tional crops by peasants using traditional production
techniques (e.g. coffee and cocoa in West Africa, and
sugar cane and coffee in Indonesia). (70) In both cases,
financing and export marketing, which required relatively
large capital resources as well as commercial contacts
abroad, were carried out by expatriate firms.

In neither of the two basic situations, i.e. plantations and peasant-based export crops, was there any
serious conflict between the peasant and the export sectors. In one, the growth of the export sector comprising
plantations and mines did not draw on the productive resources of the peasant economy but formed an enclave - a
circumstance from which the dual economy concept partially
derives. The peasant economy based on grain cultivation
had a considerable capacity for holding surplus labour -
the labour supply function being far more complex than the
theorists have assumed. While the non-mechanized technology used in rice cultivation caused the volume of
labour requirements (in terms of labour-time) to be quite
substantial, the system of atomized farming units magnified the aggregate labour demand, necessitating a dispro-
portionately large number of workers compared with the
actual labour input. The peasant economy, that is to say,
was unable to effectively utilize the available number of
labourers nor could it in the absence of organizational or
technological changes release labour to other sectors of
production. (71) The clash of interests between the
foreign investors and the traditional economy, based on
competition for resources, was of a relatively minor
order. In the second basic situation, as already explained, the export sector became the old peasant economy producing for export rather than domestic markets.

To be sure, the development process in the nonsettler
colonies was neither spontaneous nor a direct response to

market forces, but was induced by a political administration centralized in the hands of European civil servants. In some of the nonsettler colonies in Africa, the expansion of the peasant-based export economy was due to indirect compulsions. The peasants who before that time had grown export crops in conjunction with foodstuffs, balancing relative advantages, were forced primarily through taxation to concentrate on export crops. In French West Africa, they were made to grow cotton (for export to France) under the threat of imprisonment if the quality was indifferent or the quantity insufficient. (72)   In some other nonsettler colonies, the reorientation of the traditional economy from domestic to export markets was contingent upon positive measures taken by the government. For example, in Burma the phenomenal expansion in rice output was the result of tax exemptions on newly opened land, a waiving of the capitation tax for the first two years after the arrival of a Dry Zone peasant in the Delta, improvements in transport, the building of embankments to contain floods and promote drainage, the removal of the export ban on rice and the non-enforcement of the sumptuary laws. (73)   Furthermore, the economic changes under colonialism involved a disruption of the traditional society. The administrative structure of the village fell apart.   In Sri Lanka this structure had been based on the village council or gamsabhawa - a self-governing institution which settled disputes, exercised police functions and provided the managerial requirements of the rice economy. (74)   In Burma, a similar organization which had flourished under the Burmese kings was done away with. Finally, the growth of the export sector per se was detrimental to peasant agriculture.   In Sri Lanka, there was a loss of village pasture land, and a denudation of forests which caused soil erosion and the silting up of water courses and paddy fields. (75)

In the nonsettler colonies administrative intervention on behalf of European interests was, however, neither as comprehensive nor as penetrative as what occurred in the settler colonies.   The economic and social changes associated with the growth of the plantation sector did not destroy the equilibrium of the peasant economy, thus creating a supply of landless wage labour.   The changes merely loosened the bonds which held together the village economy, disorganized its corporate life and impoverished the cultivator.   They did not release labour or land to the export sector on a significant scale.   In Sri Lanka the process of disorganization was prolonged, and its effects were controlled by the efforts of governments to check the situation before it could reach the critical point of no

return. The government's interest in the repair of irrigation facilities for paddy arose partly from a need to
prevent the illicit felling of forests and the cultivation
of chena. (76)

> If land were placed within the reach of all classes
> upon such terms, and a supply of water assured, the
> plea for chena cultivation - the most wasteful and ex-
> travagant of all cultivations especially in the Eastern
> province where whole forests have been swept away by it
> - would cease.

The 'metabolism' between the capitalist and the precapitalist economies, necessary for the accumulation of capital (Rosa Luxemburg), generally did not take place within
the boundaries of the nonsettler economies.

The problem of a labour supply in different socio-historical situations has been solved in different ways. In
the classical industrial economies, as Kuczynski tersely
stated, 'the machine was the forceps which delivered the
working class'. In the settler colonies labour was prised
out of the precapitalist economy by force and administrative intervention. In the nonsettler colonies, such as
Sri Lanka and Malaysia, the problem of a labour supply
which plagued the planters and mine-owners over several
decades was met by siphoning off labour from the great
human reservoirs, India and China. For reasons which I
cannot go into here, this labour could virtually be
scooped off the land with a minimum of administrative
pressure. Export production was thus able to expand without integrating itself with the rest of the economy;
there was virtually a Chinese wall between them. The
peasant sector, though severely strained by the growth of
the export economy, was neither absorbed nor annihilated.
(77)

Such a pattern of development impulses, which either
bypassed the peasant economy (the plantation case) or proceeded within the framework of peasant production, leaving
the peasants substantially in possession of their land,
was reflected in the politics and governmental policies of
the nonsettler colonies. The political involvement of the
foreign investors, as expatriates, was on a limited scale.
In the absence of a fundamental clash between the foreign
and the indigenous interests, the colonial administration
needed to intervene or adjudicate between them only within
minor limits. The administration, without seriously jeopardizing European interests, was able to take a relatively
independent stance, endeavouring to hold the scales evenly
between metropolitan and colonial interests - between
planters and plantation labour or between planters and
peasants.

If in the nonsettler colonies the process of economic development was not wholly amenable to market forces alone, in the settler colonies the development process was practically wrought by the political power of the settlers. The government for its part threw its weight heavily on the side of the settlers - against the indigenous interests. Hobson's dictum that 'the true riches of the newly discovered lands are their people' was perceived by the settlers and acted upon without restraint. They came 'without question to regard the native as simply one of the factors entering into the making of money, a factor to be treated in the same objective way as water, soil, or any other non-sentient or inanimate object'. (78) The indigenous economy was virtually denuded of both its land and labour. In South Africa by 1956 about 89 per cent of the land was owned by the Europeans; in Swaziland and Rhodesia 49 per cent; in Kenya the proportion, though only 7 per cent, included about 'half the land that is worth cultivating'. (79) In Algeria the French colons at the beginning of this century held over 40 per cent of the cultivated land, generally in the most fertile tracts. (80) By contrast, in the nonsettler territories of Africa, including Rhodesia and West Africa, the Europeans usually held 5 per cent of the land and in some cases less than 1 per cent. (81)

Labour was far more formidable a problem than land. Settler agriculture was less labour intensive than either plantations or peasant-based cereal crops. It was of the 'homestead' type, partially mechanized, and its labour requirements were seasonal. Yet there was an absolute scarcity of labour. In regard to labour supply the settler colonies were in an anomalous position. As explained in an earlier chapter, interrace relations in these colonies impeded a substantial influx of European workers (whereas to the regions of new settlement a white working class migrated). The far more limited size of the indigenous population in these regions than in the settler colonies precluded complex interrace problems and made the settlement of a white working class possible. In the settler colonies at the same time, though the indigenous population was larger than in the regions of new settlement, a local or regional labour supply was virtually unavailable. These colonies were thinly populated, they were distant from the cheap-labour belts of South India and China, and their indigenous, invariably tribal economy was not yet falling apart. In the regions of new settlement high wages induced an inflow of European workers, and an altogether different pattern of development. But in the settler colonies the prejudice that the 'native' is

cheap and idling in the reserves forestalled any market
incentives for a labour supply. This prejudice was a convenient rationalization for violating indigenous interests
to an extent unknown elsewhere, and was effective because
of the natives' incapacity to resist. (82) Labour was
thus extracted by dismantling traditional economic structures - through taxation, land expropriation and by outright coercion.

For instance, the Kenya government, having from 1908
encouraged the movement of Africans out of the reserves,
intervened blatantly in 1919 to ensure a compulsory labour
supply for the settlers. The Registration Ordinance required the compulsory registration of male Africans from
16 years of age. In 1919 the well-known Northey Circular
directed officers in charge of what were termed 'labour-
supplying districts' to obtain labour by 'every possible
lawful influence'. The circular warned of the necessity
for 'other special measures to meet the case' 'should the
labour difficulties continue'. The Governor was given the
names of chiefs and headmen who helped to obtain labour.
There was already legal provision to obtain labour for
projects of national importance: for public utilities -
roads and railways - and for porterage. Now the Northey
Circular practically established a system of compulsory
labour for the settlers. (83)

The labour needs of the settlers even influenced the
government's attitudes towards the productivity of African
farms. The direct pressure on Africans to work for the
settlers was accompanied by measures to disable African
farmers. For example, they were paid lower prices for
their products, and charged higher freights on the railway. In Kenya, where African peasants were engaged in
coffee cultivation, the government introduced a licence
fee of 30 shillings (under the Coffee Planters' Registration Ordinance of 1918) and did not issue licences to
Africans. They were also denied technical assistants even
when the agricultural results would have justified it. An
official report in Kenya stated in retrospect: 'If some
of the expenditure which had been incurred by the Agricultural Department on behalf of European settlers had been
spent in the interests of the Kikuyu and Kavirondo, it is
likely that a speedy return would have resulted.' (84)
The success of such measures was reflected in a decline in
output on land farmed by the Africans. (85)

These policies created a binding nexus between the administration and the settlers; the administration's need
for revenue, said Wrigley, dovetailed exactly with the
settlers' demand for labour. The mission of government in
this situation was explained by Sir Harry Johnstone: (86)

All that needs to be done is for the Administration ...
to introduce the native labourer to the European capitalist. A gentle insistence that the native shall contribute his fair share to the revenue of the country by
paying his tax is all that is necessary on our part to
ensure his taking a share in life's labour which no
human being shall avoid.
According to one European farmer, 'the ideal reserve is a
recruiting ground for labour, a place from which the able-
bodied go out to work, returning occasionally to rest and
to beget the next generation of labourers'. (87) As time
went on the settlers increased and their involvement in
the economy and society became irrevocable. Their political influence then increased beyond the degree that government had initially allowed from a sense of obligation
for having encouraged settlement or for the sake of revenue.

Part two

The plantation system and underdevelopment

7 Plantations and their metropolitan orientation

The character of the plantations, both as a production system and with respect to their international aspect, was moulded by the agrarian and social changes which had occurred from the mid-seventeenth century in the British colonies in the New World. In the West Indies, the spread of sugar cane led to cultivation in extensive land units. However, the availability of land created a labour problem. White servants who were originally brought to America and the West Indies received land as 'freedom dues' at the expiry of their term. Access to land and a diffusion of landholdings resulted in a class of white farmers based on a homestead type of agriculture. In this 'open resources' situation 'no one need[ed] voluntarily [to] offer himself as a labourer to another since he might easily take up land and farm for himself'. A ready-made workforce had therefore to be brought in from outside.

The use of unfree labour, of one form or other, with a highly authoritarian structure of labour relations, as an answer to this problem was the mainspring of the plantation system. The introduction of slave labour led to an exodus of the poorer white colonists and the growth of absenteeism among planters; the displaced whites were mostly tenants who were easily got rid of. (1) To control this process of a depletion of whites, which was causing insecurity among the resident planters, the Deficiency Acts required each plantation to have a minimum proportion of whites. The Acts failed in their purpose - they were annulled in 1674, and the absentee interest prevailed. Europeans who lived in the West Indies were now mostly managers, not proprietors; the wealthy and influential West Indian interest was in England - gentlemen planters, London merchants trading with the islands, and colonial agents. (2) The exodus of white labour was initially from Barbados to the other islands, but in each of these the

pattern of change was repeated: large landholdings,
unfree labour, absentee interests, and the dominance of
one or a few export staples.

The cultivation of sugar and later indigo, which had
become more profitable than tobacco, lent themselves
easily to this change. These crops could be cultivated by
a routinized and regimented workforce, whereas tobacco in
many ways was a free man's crop; it required attention to
the minutiae of cultivation and its labour requirements
were seasonal. The unit of tobacco cultivation was thus
relatively small in Virginia as well as in Cuba and Puerto
Rico. Unlike in the plantations of the West Indies, land
was not consolidated nor was there a concentration of
ownership. The farmer in Virginia, even when he employed
slave labour, 'came to live a life far different from that
of the indolent West Indian planter; he worked long hours
and was close in his supervision. The ... [farmer's] wife
acquired new and hardly ornamental tasks'. (3) All the
same, it was not the agronomic features of the plantations, established at this time in the West Indies (based
on sugar cultivation), that distinguished them from the
small farming systems based on resident proprietors in
Virginia and the Middle Colonies of North America. In the
one case unfree labour was available in the form of transplanted Africans, and in the other white labour could
neither be enslaved nor prevented from acquiring land.

The use of unfree labour moulded the character of the
plantations in several respects. It conformed with the
simple methods by which plantation crops could be produced. Though not indigenous to countries where they came
to be extensively grown, plantation crops required only
minimum adaptation to local conditions. The ecology of
these countries was favourable to their cultivation, and
the crops as a rule also fitted easily into the traditional peasant system. As perennials they could, after reaching maturity, withstand long periods of neglect, and relatively little care was needed to obtain a product of acceptable quality. For instance, cocoa cultivation in West
Africa got very little attention beyond thorough weeding
during the first four or five years. Palm oil production
was mostly 'collecting and preparing sylvan produce' and
actual cultivation was limited to only a few small plantations. The cracking of the palm kernels and the extraction of oil were done by women, using a large stone or
anvil and a smaller one as a hammer - 'a very tedious process'. (4) Small hand presses were introduced comparatively recently. In Malaysia peasant-based cultivation of
rubber expanded alongside large plantations. Though European investors, to pre-empt the best land, claimed that

plantation agriculture was of a 'scientific nature', there
is, as J.H.Drabble said, 'no particular mystique about the
basic technique required ... [for rubber] which the Europeans possessed and the Chinese did not'. (5)

High yields per acre on the plantations were achieved
by means of a large volume of working capital - in the
form of fertilizer, superior planting material, and regular maintenance and upkeep. Smallholders could themselves
achieve comparable agronomic standards, as is seen by the
success of tea smallholdings in Kenya. While smallholders
were not intrinsically precluded from developing high
agrarian standards, the low yields which prevailed were
offset, and often more than offset, by lower costs due to
smaller overheads and a lesser volume of production
inputs. Far from plantations driving out peasant production through the operation of market forces, except when
it was hampered by institutional obstacles - mainly a lack
of credit - the economic advantages enjoyed by smallholders enabled them to coexist and compete with plantations.
Most plantation crops can then be grown on a non-plantation basis, and there are no exclusively plantation crops.
Bananas are generally grown on plantations, but in Ecuador
smallholdings seldom larger than fifteen acres constituted
nearly half of the total cultivated area in 1960-1. For
cocoa, plantations are dominant in Brazil and smallholdings in West Africa. Rubber is divided between plantations and smallholdings, plantations being in the lead in
Malaysia and Sri Lanka while smallholdings dominate in
Indonesia and Thailand. In Kenya, tea smallholdings have
expanded rapidly. Coconut is as a rule grown on smallholdings. Similarly for cotton, peasant production in
East Africa was economically viable, as the British Cotton
Growing Association realized. In West Africa the superiority of the plantations was only in palm oil production -
and this only in South-Eastern Nigeria. 'In other West
African staples the competitive efficiency of peasant
methods has not been seriously challenged.' (6)

While all plantations, as the term is used, are large
units, size (despite what is thought) is not crucial to
the production of plantation crops. As Ida Greaves
stated: (7)

Although they are regarded as a large-scale method of
production, and are readily distinguishable from smallholdings of the peasant and tribal types, plantations
are not easy to classify on the basis of size.... Most
of the plantations in the West Indies in the eighteenth
century were only family-size farms.... There is,
moreover, a great deal of large-scale agriculture in
the world which is never regarded as being plantation.

In the absence of indivisible equipment in the cultivation
of these crops and, with one or two exceptions, in their
processing prior to export, economies of scale are not
significant. The large size of plantations is the result
of the historical and institutional circumstances in which
the plantation system developed, with high overhead costs
due to absentee ownership and the use of immigrant labour.
In America and the West Indies, the capital cost of slaves
transported from Africa was five times as much as that of
white servants, (8) and the larger outlays set a minimum
size to a plantation. The question of scale economies
will be taken up in a later chapter, in which I shall also
discuss in detail the effect of institutional factors as a
determinant of the large size of plantations.

A distorted perception of plantation agriculture, apart
from the importance given to its large-scale nature and
export orientation, is also that plantation agriculture is
a specialized form of production, conforming to the distribution of the world's natural resources. For example,
R.C.Buchanan stated that, plantations are a 'particular
type of large-scale, specialised agriculture'. (9) J.C.
Jackson regards plantation production as involving 'a
sharp division of labour with a highly centralised management, a high degree of specialisation, frequently amounting to monoculture'. (10) N.G.Silvermaster and M.M.Knight
refer to 'a high degree of specialization [in plantation
agriculture] coupled with a large initial investment and
heavy fixed costs'. (11) According to P.R.Courtenay, 'the
plantation crops on which many of ... [the underdeveloped
countries] specialise still probably remain the best basis
... [for] their "take-off" into self-sustaining economic
growth'. (12) Likewise Ida Greaves: 'Another characteristic of plantations is that, typically, they specialize
in the production of a single commodity for export ...
[resulting in] a high degree of regional specialization.'
(13) In all these writings specialization is taken to
mean merely the opposite of a diversified production pattern, production for the market instead of for self-con-
sumption, leading to international trade in different
types of products. Since specialization involves a division of labour, with improved skills and a higher productivity, the plantations are also presumed to be a dynamic
form of production.

However, the extensive cultivation of one or a few
crops in a region (monoculture) does not connote specialization, if it does not enhance productive efficiency.
Specialization, involving economies of scale, requires an
extended division of labour within a sphere of production
operations appropriately defined. For the adoption of

such a division of labour, giving rise to the use of specialized equipment and skills, large-scale production is only one precondition. If mere preoccupation with one or a few activities were to mean specialization, the more primitive an economy is, with a drastic limitation in its range of activities, the more specialized it becomes. But a man who does nothing but pick wild berries or catch fish is hardly a specialist if he does so in a rudimentary way, say with his bare hands. His work is not part of a larger, and more complex production operation, the splitting up of which into separate production processes facilitates the use of specialized equipment. He does not contribute to greater productive efficiency than if he were to perform numerous activities, each of them on a small scale. He neither generates external economies nor does he enjoy any.

In the case of plantations the size of production units increased as individual proprietors gave way to corporate enterprises whose management was further centralized under agency firms; this involved no change in production methods or in the division of labour. The impressive improvements that occurred in crop yields, based as they were on a higher level of fertilization, the use of superior planting material, and plant stimulants in rubber, could have been achieved just as well within the framework of small-scale units; they were what Hobsbawm has called 'improvements rather than a transformation of production'. If the plantations were specialized in any sense, this specialization had none of the advantages of growth which the classical economists attributed to world trade and the division of labour.

Furthermore, the notion of specialization, as indicated already, is meaningful only in relation to an appropriate unit of production operations (not necessarily defined by geographical or political boundaries). The USA and the Soviet Union are considerably more self-contained, and diversified, than any plantation economy; yet their individual branches and individual enterprises or firms are highly specialized. The US economy in the present day is more specialized than during its early stages, but also more diversified than when production was limited to a few export staples. The plantations are no more specialized than the agricultural systems in the peasant-based export economies of West Africa (producing cocoa, groundnuts, oil seeds, etc.) or in the rice-exporting economies of Burma and Thailand, all of which are limited to one or a few crops and participate extensively in international trade. It is the subdivision of the production process - within the firm among its different departments, between firms,

and between industries - which enables the various production units to specialize, limiting themselves to one or a
few production processes or commodities in a related network. Thereby the various production units, comprising
separate elements of the broader complex, benefit from the
external economies they confer upon each other. Specialization increases with the proliferation of industries or
firms which are functionally related, either vertically or
horizontally. Initially enterprises produce components
for their own final products, but later the production
processes become increasingly differentiated and are
operated as specialized units.

While the plantations do not differ from other forms of
agriculture in developed economies or from peasant-based
agriculture in underdeveloped economies for the reasons
commonly adduced, one determining feature of the plantations is the technology of the plantation system and its
production relations including methods of labour recruitment, control and retention. Plantations everywhere are
phenomenally labour intensive. Production techniques are
primarily extractive - the bulk of the labour applied is
in harvesting. Considerable uniformity prevails in techniques, and therefore in labour productivity, between one
country and another. The low labour productivity, due to
a virtual absence of capital equipment in the cultivation
process, is linked to the social relations of production,
based on resident labour, recruited and employed in family
units, lacking occupational or geographical mobility and
subjected to varying degrees of duress. I shall reserve
for later chapters a discussion of the technology and
social relations of plantation production.

This internal dimension of the plantation system is as
vital to an understanding of it as are its external relations based on sharply defined markets for plantation products confined to the industrialized countries, and the
limited processing of such products prior to export. As
a politico-economic phenomenon, the plantations were also
characterized by their domination by merchant capital.
The specific historical circumstances in which this domination was established, linked to the absentee nature of
the investors, also underlay the problem of underdevelopment as I shall discuss later. The plantation system,
that is to say, conditioned the total economy and society
of the territory in which it functioned. Its low wage
structure went hand in hand with an almost total lack of
secondary production, giving the economy a pronounced
export-import bias, thereby symbiotically linking the
territory's economy to the centre.

The form in which plantation products are exported and

the range and character of their markets differ from those
of the grain-producing export economies of, say, Burma and
Thailand. Contrary to what is usually thought, (14) their
export orientation per se is not a basic characteristic of
plantation products. The export staples of the non-plantation economies are consumed widely in economies of varying levels of development, causing a geographical diffusion of trade. On the other hand, the consumption of
plantation products is extremely limited in the countries
where they are grown and in the underdeveloped world as a
whole: raw materials for obvious reasons, and foodstuffs
and beverages grown on a plantation basis because they are
most in demand in the high-income countries. Tea and
coconut are exceptional in this respect, though most of
the tea consumed in the producing countries is of the
lower grades. Coconut is consumed as a food either directly or as a vegetable oil. Coconut fibre, a by-product, is, however, exported for use as an intermediate
good in the industrialized economies; its production,
based on a simple decorticating process, is done both on
a cottage basis and in large enterprises. The relatively
limited consumption per head of plantation foodstuffs and
beverages in the producing countries is a reflection of
their low wage economy. The predominantly export bias of
plantation products thus conforms with the underdeveloped
condition of the plantation economies, making it possible
to expand output far beyond the limits imposed by low potential demand within these economies themselves.

    What is specific about the plantation crops, and which
also underlies their role in the world economy, is neither
the large-scale nature of their production nor their
export orientation but the limited extent of processing
which takes place in the producing regions, either because
little processing is required before final consumption or
because the processing is carried out only in the metropolitan centres. A special relationship is thereby established between plantation economies and a metropolitan
centre. The production and trade of plantation crops are
intertwined with the sharp division of productive forces
on a world scale between the developed and the underdeveloped economies. The non-utilization of plantation products as also of other primary materials in the plantation
economies defines the underdeveloped condition of these
economies. Furthermore, the markets for these products
are 'narrowly controlled' and involve a 'dependent, symbiotic and carefully circumscribed relation ... with a
patron nation'. (15) The inclusion of plantations within
the general rubric of export agriculture detracts attention from the international or political aspects which de-

termine the exportable form of plantation products,
serving mainly as primary inputs for the industries of
advanced countries. A corollary to the commercial attachment of plantation economies to a metropolitan country is
a severe limitation on their intra-regional trade. Much
of this, consisting of a traffic in labour and, in Asia,
of rice exports from Thailand and Burma to the plantation
economies, was subsidiary to the basic trade flows between
the industrial and the non-industrial economies.

An aspect of plantation production which is even more
fundamental than the limited degree of local processing
and the metropolitan markets for which the crops are produced is the dominance of merchant capital in their production and marketing. Merchant capital mediates between
two sharply differentiated production structures in the
plantation economies in the periphery and the industrial
economies in the centre. These production structures correspond to two different modes of production. Whereas
capitalism was the mode of production in the centre, merchant capital being its agent, in the plantation situation
merchant capital remained dominant. Absentee production
capital in the periphery and the pronounced export-import
bias of the underdeveloped economies created lucrative opportunities for the merchant, not merely as the managing
agent for the absentee investors but also in various activities connected with the marketing and sale of export
produce - transporting, warehousing, shipment and sale of
plantation crops, and originally in their short-term financing; an additional source of profit was the supply
of plantation inputs and materials. Merchant capital
throve on the long-distance trade, arising from the world
division of labour between the production of plantation
crops and of other primary materials in the periphery and
their industrial utilization in the centre; in the period
when transport and communications were relatively undeveloped, merchant capital reaped prolific gains.

The dominance of merchant capital and the export-import
bias were common to all countries of the periphery, including the peasant-based export economies such as Nigeria, Ghana and Burma. In the later instances merchant
capital was less pervasive in that cultivation was in the
hands of indigenous small farmers who were relatively less
integrated into a production and marketing network dominated by merchant capital and linked in a single chain to
the metropolis. Whether this situation allowed greater
leeway for the growth of an indigenous bourgeoisie with
an internally oriented problem of production and investment compared with the plantation economies such as Sri
Lanka, Malaysia, Indonesia, and the West Indies is a theme
deserving of a separate study.

By its dominance over absentee production capital, merchant capital was able to realize and to appropriate a large portion of the surplus value generated by the plantation economy, in its production, exporting and importing aspects, as it had done in earlier centuries in the countries of Southern Europe and the Mediterranean. The great trading corporations of Tudor and Stuart times had tended to relegate these countries, especially Spain and Portugal, to a peripheral relation to the emerging industrial economies of Western Europe. With the development of the plantation staples, the new investment opportunities for merchant capital that arose successively in the American colonies, the West Indies and Asia were a powerful stimulus to its continued expansion on a world scale. At a certain stage merchant capital shifted its principal area of operations to countries which were later to become the periphery. This perhaps contributed to a relaxation of the grip of merchant capital in the countries of Southern Europe and to its debilitating influence on the underdeveloped world. Southern Europe, though remaining backward in relation to Western and Central Europe, escaped a fate similar to that of the underdeveloped world.

I have discussed in a brief way, foreshadowing a detailed exposition in later chapters, some aspects of the plantations as a system of production. The backwardness of the plantations which these attributes signify, involving the underdevelopment of the plantation economies, underlay the role of the plantations in a world economy dominated by the metropolitan nations. Thus the significance of plantations lay fundamentally in their international aspect. With the plantations, the Europeans began to organize production overseas. Though capital was still used to expand trading activities by 'opening up new labour fronts' and annexing markets by physical means, economic expansion now required the investment of production capital. Landes stated: 'The decision of certain European powers ... to establish "plantations", i.e. to treat their colonies as continuous enterprises whatever one might think of its morality, was a momentous decision.' (16) What was important, however, was not the permanence and stability of European enterprise but the growth of absentee interests and the dominance of merchant capital in the periphery, marking a turning point in the history of centre-periphery relations.

European colonialism, having ended physical violence and simple exchange as the basis of exploitation, developed in two different forms. In the West Indian islands, the presence of slave labour and the exodus of Europeans made the plantations no longer a settler enterprise, although originally a planter was one who established a colony or settled - i.e. a colonist - and the Crown officials had even regarded the American colonies as plantations. Now a clear differentiation arose between colonies of settlement and 'colonies of exploitation'. The settler colonies reproduced, in varying degrees, the economic and social structures of the metropolitan country. They developed along autonomous lines, and underwent advances in technology, labour productivity and incomes. They competed economically, and ultimately broke away. The non-settler economies were complementary and subordinate to that of the metropolitan country. Manufacturing industry was almost nonexistent, and the use of land was extensive and inefficient. These colonies (aptly termed the 'colonies of exploitation') fitted into the imperial division of labour far more closely than the colonies of settlement. As Pares commented, they 'employed more shipping, produced more valuable goods, and consumed more English manufactures'. (17) The West Indian sugar islands were thus the most promising colonial market. Though they had a large white population till about the eighteenth century, the dominance of export staples in the economy created a two-way traffic with the mother country involving the export of plantation produce and the import of materials and provisions. In contrast to the pliability of colonies whose economies were easily subordinated in the metropolitan interest, the settler colonies competed with England in the sale of foodstuffs to the West Indies. The settler entrepreneurs had a propensity to manufacture substitutes for imported goods, and thus these colonies also competed with England in their domestic market for manufactures. The settler colonies in North America were 'viewed with a great deal of suspicion'; they were also politically unreliable. To make these colonies complementary to the economy of the mother country, export staples were deliberately introduced into them, such as the production of naval stores in the Middle Colonies and New England. This reduced England's dependence on non-Empire resources, enhanced imperial self-sufficiency and also enabled the colonies to pay for English manufactures.

It was in the nonsettler colonies that the plantation system developed as a form of agriculture distinguished by its organization and technology and by its role in the world economy. The plantations developed a narrow symbiotic relation with the metropolitan economy - a relation which was sustained both by the exercise of political control and by a division of production activity based on sharply unequal levels of productive forces. For a long period the cotton plantations of Southern USA had served

as a 'colony' of the Manchester mills. The influence of
the plantation system on the broader territory in which it
functioned, and the relations between that territory and a
metropolitan centre, conditioned the economy of the territory as a whole, making it a plantation economy. Plantation crops, while not competing with production in the
metropolitan countries, furnished opportunities for the
investment of capital: both short-term funds to finance
current production and long-term funds to create a whole
framework of facilities for storing and transporting these
crops and for expanding the plantation. The production
and export of tobacco and sugar in the American colonies
'served excellently' the interests of the English mercantile system; the colonies were 'to be always the producer of the raw material which the industry of the mother
country should work'. (18) The English merchant capitalist provided the planter with funds against the mortgage
of his land and slaves, and acquired the business of supplying plantation materials and articles of personal consumption. The marketing of these crops also conferred a
bounty on English shipping and on 'commission men, factors, financiers, processors and distributors'.

A policy of 'enforced bilateralism' turned the early
plantation economies into a market for British manufactures and limited their exports almost to a single market.
Competitors were excluded from this trade, and enumerated
products could be exported only to England or had to be
sent there for trans-shipment. This pattern of production
discouraged the development of industries or of alternative trade links. The territorial allocation of activities (between the plantation economies and what were at
this time the industrializing economies) was backed by
legislative measures. Even an expansion in the money
supply and banking and credit institutions were controlled
so as to restrain industrial investment. (19)

The development of plantation economies was linked to
the rise of industrial capitalism in Europe, which depended on organic raw materials - such as natural fibres,
vegetable oils, dyestuffs and rubber. There was an ever-
mounting hunger for these materials in Europe. Improved
incomes and an expanding population caused a parallel
demand for tropical foodstuffs and beverages produced on
a plantation basis - such as tea, coffee, cocoa, sugar and
bananas. It was this 'overflow of demand' in the industrial countries, rather than the competitive efficiency of
primary producers emphasized by Myint, (20) which underlay
the boom in plantation products in the nineteenth century
and the first decades of the twentieth. Inorganic substitutes were still unknown. At the same time, the pressures

of the capital-accumulating process in the metropolitan
countries, with a constantly advancing technology, led to
a conversion of the plantation and other noncapitalist
economies into markets. The growth of plantations dovetailed into the economic transformations that were occurring in the metropolitan centres.

The localization of plantation crops in the underdeveloped regions was not merely due to geographical conditions specific to these regions, but was also linked to
the politico-economic structures of the plantation economies including their labour situation and wage levels.
Natural prerequisites were a necessary but not sufficient
premise and, as Bukharin said in a somewhat broader context, they interact with 'prerequisites of a social
nature'. J.H.Drabble appropriately referred to 'non-
environmental factors' in the development of the plantation system, but they were not what he presumed: the
'business confidence of investors resulting from metropolitan control' and the encouragement given to Empire
sources of raw materials. (21) Such factors may explain
why British capital flowed into Malaysia and, say, not
Indochina, or why French capital did not flow into Malaysia. The overriding question is why Malaysia 'specialized' in plantation products and minerals, producing them
to the exclusion of industrial goods - a pattern of investment and production activity which underlies the division between the developed and the underdeveloped economies. A subsidiary issue is why the same crops are grown
on a plantation basis in some instances and by peasants in
others. 'The unequal development of productive forces
creates different economic types and different production
spheres.' (22) Of the social prerequisites which conditioned the localization of plantation crops, I shall now
refer to the labour situation and wage levels in the plantation economies.

In a developed economy it is the high wage level which
militates against the plantation form of production.
Southern USA, an exception, had access to cheap, docile
Negro labour whose wages and working conditions were similar to those in underdeveloped countries. By the same
token, the industrialization of the plantation economies,
leading to higher productivity and wages and the spread of
capitalist labour relations, would undermine the plantation system, in the way that rising wage levels in the developed economies are causing a transfer of the labour
intensive branches of manufacturing production to underdeveloped regions. The plantation system thus depends for
its viability on the lack of new investment in other sectors which would raise the average level of labour produc-

tivity and of wages in the economy as a whole. Such stagnation was in the interests of the plantation sector. An
illuminating contrast, referred to in an earlier chapter,
was in the regions of new settlement, where the export
staples not merely declined in importance as the economy
developed but also generated technological change and a
rise in wages.

The primary consideration in the operation of the plantation system was the 'availability of cheap labour' as
Bruno Lasker wrote, drawing on the work of Carl J.Pelzer.
'And indeed, often the new enterprise in Southeast Asia
was a direct transplantation of one [the slave labour
system] closing down elsewhere.' (23) The wage rate for
plantation labour is low in absolute terms and in relation
to incomes in the peasant sector - a circumstance which
inhibited the Lewis style of labour transfers. This low
wage rate is obscured by a possibly larger income per
family than in the peasant sector, since a plantation provides employment for the entire family including children
from the age of 12 or 14 - and even below that. There is,
moreover, greater continuity of employment. Child employment influenced the income-fertility relationship on plantations, resulting in large families. (24) According to
an International Labour Office survey in 1960, the living
conditions of plantation labour were 'often very poor'.
The workers 'are nearly always badly fed and their diet
is monotonous and unbalanced ... their earnings do little
more than provide a bare existence. They have very little
furniture - usually the bare minimum. Cooking utensils
normally represent the bulk of their possessions'. (25)
An official inquiry in Sri Lanka in 1923 reported that the
standard of food consumption among plantation labour 'compare[d] favourably with the jail diet'. (26)

The dominance of the plantation sector per se discouraged complementary forms of production. The labour
intensiveness of the plantations, making a low wage structure imperative and resulting in a large component of wage
costs, led the plantation interests to attempt to keep
wages down by preventing an increase in living costs.
They were thus opposed to protective tariffs on the imports of manufactured consumer goods and of foodstuffs
which might have been produced locally. (27)

Therefore, so the argument goes, nothing must be done
to raise the cost of living through such practices as
increased tariffs; there must be cheap imports of
'wage goods'.... Also there is the traditional rubber
growers' attitude, rarely expressed openly, that manufacturing expansion is not desirable because it would
offer alternative employment for labour, and so bid up
wage levels.

For instance, in British Malaya attempts at levying an import duty on rice, whether to protect domestic producers or as a revenue measure, were administratively rejected. Any increase in rice prices was seen as detrimental to the employers of both Chinese and Indian labour. (28)   The encouragement of local rice production in British Malaya was also not compatible with the interests of British capital in promoting the export trade in Burmese rice.   This 'rubber-tin mentality' in Malaysia was paralleled in other plantation regions;   the 'sugar men' and the 'banana men' were attached to their respective crops to the exclusion of other branches of production. (29)   The nature of the resistances to developing manufacturing production out of the profits from the plantations has been discussed in an earlier section of this book.

The rationale of the plantation system must therefore be seen in terms of the total structure of the plantation economy and the role of the latter in the world economic framework, inclusive of the political relations between the developed and the underdeveloped regions.   Within this relationship there was, as stated before, a narrow bilateralism, which reduced the various plantation economies to the rural hinterland of the respective metropolitan powers.   For example, in order to monopolize the supply of palm kernels from West Africa, Britain in 1917 levied a discriminatory duty of £2 per ton on exports outside the Empire.   Two years earlier the export of palm kernel oil from Nigeria was subject to a duty of £2 per ton, which remained even after the differential duty on palm kernels was revoked in 1922.   'It is ... difficult to escape the conclusion', wrote Charlotte Leubuscher, 'that the duty [on palm kernel oil] has been retained as a safeguard against the setting up of crushing machinery in Nigeria.' (30)   The pre-emption of the supplies of these economically and strategically important products led generally to political control.

Control over the production and marketing of other plantation primary products later shifted to private investors but metropolitan governments never wholly renounced their responsibility. (31)   The encouragement given to the production of naval stores (mentioned already) was to make Britain independent of the Baltic states which had a virtual monopoly over supplies of tar, pitch, hemp and timber.   The production of indigo, used as a dye for British naval uniforms, was an active concern of the East India Company.   There was also a political background to tea growing in India.   Though the tea gardens started by the East India Company were transferred in the early 1830s to the Assam Tea Company, the British govern-

ment attached great importance to tea growing. The planters were given tax concessions, land at nominal rates,
subsidies for the transport of labourers on government
steamers, etc. At this time, when the consumption of tea
was expanding in Britain, its supply which was entirely
from China had become uncertain. Conditions in the Far
East affected Britain's trade in this region. The East
India Company's monopoly had ended, Japan had broken off
trade relations with the West, and the Chinese government
was resentful of European trading companies. Tea production in India was thus seen as a 'better guarantee ... for
the continued supply of this article than at present
furnished by the mere toleration of the Chinese government, which although the Chinese have at present a monopoly, it will be easy for us to destroy'. (32)

In rubber the British government intervened to exclude
American ownership of rubber land in the British Empire.
In collusion with the planters and the Rubber Growers' Association in London, Britain prevented the United States
Rubber Company in 1916 from purchasing rubber land in the
Federated Malay States (FMS). The company wanted, according to a spokesman, 'merely to achieve a degree of independence from market price fluctuations in supplies of
raw rubber'. Sterling plantation companies in Malaysia,
subjected to restrictions on capital issues in Britain,
expressed fears of overproduction if American investments
were allowed. But in fact the opposition to American
ownership was politically oriented. The Rubber Growers'
Association wanted the Colonial Office to check the intrusion of American capital into 'what is at present a
British industry'. The High Commissioner of the FMS felt
that American ownership of the acreage envisaged carried
no risk of monopoly control. Yet the Secretary of State
for the Colonies wanted 'to retain maximum control of
rubber as a strategic commodity'. (33) By the Rubber
Lands (Restriction) Enactment of July 1917, alienation of
land of over 50 acres to non-Empire interests was prohibited. American attempts to grow rubber in Sarawak were
likewise thwarted by the British government. (34) The
Stevenson Rubber Restriction Scheme, according to Drabble,
set the seal on this policy whereby 'the fortunes of the
rubber industry in Malaya came to be regarded as of Imperial, as well as of local concern'. (35)

With the economic depression of the 1930s raw materials
policy acquired an overtly mercantilist outlook and the
metropolitan powers began to systematically pre-empt supplies. In rubber, the political separation of the raw
material producers from the manufacturers aggravated the
conflicts between metropolitan powers. The producers were

mainly British and the manufacturers mainly American. Despite restrictions, the major rubber companies in America acquired small acreages of rubber which marginally reduced their dependence on the world rubber markets. (36) For the same reason, to be free of dependence on British sources, France encouraged rubber production in Indochina by subsidies and export bounties to the planters. The restrictive policy applied to raw materials in general. For instance, in 1934-5 a new prohibitive duty was levied on tin ore exports from British Malaya except for smelting in Singapore, the UK or Australia. The barriers to trade and the 'selfish exploitation' of raw material sources by colonial powers caused concern in the League of Nations. But nothing came out of this concern.

In recent decades technological developments in the production of inorganic substitutes have reduced the need for organic materials, which had led metropolitan governments to monopolize or control their supply. An early expression of the shift from organic to inorganic materials, which is characteristic of industrial technology, was the substitution of coal for wood as a source of heat and mechanical power; and the most buoyant industries, excepting cotton, were those which substantially changed over to inorganic materials. 'The searcher is not constricted by the characteristics of raw material won from nature; rather, he makes his own stuff, and in the long-run his possibilities are limitless.' (37) The relative lack of dependence of industrial processes on organic materials later had a suffocating effect on the primary exports of underdeveloped countries, beginning with the invention of chemical dyes which rooted out the indigo plantations of Bengal. The tendency to replace plantation products was more pronounced in the period between the two world wars, with the development of synthetic substitutes in Germany, Italy, Japan and, to a lesser extent, the USA. (38) The raw material base of the textile industry changed overwhelmingly. The displacement of organic materials made extraordinary headway after the Second World War. As industrial products, the inorganic substitutes are more durable and versatile and have a capacity to reduce labour costs; also, their production is more easily regulated.

The recent decline in the demand for primary products is not in any way due to a loss of their original efficiency, contrary to what Myint has suggested. According to him, a neglect of export production by the newly independent countries, allegedly and unjustifiably preoccupied with manufacturing industry, was the cause of this decline. (39)

> The United States may have a general technological
> superiority over Malaya, but provided Malaya applies
> sufficient capital and modern technology to improving
> her rubber production, there is no reason why she
> should not be able to hold on to her competitive ad-
> vantage in that commodity.

Myint does not explain the nature of the technological improvements that would enable plantations to maintain their
former competitive position, or the feasibility of such
improvements within the framework of the plantation
system. Pending a detailed discussion of this issue in a
later chapter, a brief exposition may be helpful here.
Technological improvements are of two kinds. First, there
are those which conform to the institutional basis of the
plantation system - raising the yield per hectare without
a basic change in capital-labour ratios or in the organic
composition of capital. The prodigious use of labour has,
despite low wage rates, caused such improvements to have
little or no effect on the unit costs of output and therefore in the competitiveness of plantation products. It is
improvements of this kind that have been adopted on plantations in the past and for the most part still continue.

A second type of improvement is the substitution of
capital for labour, with a concomitant rise in labour productivity and a decline in the unit cost of output.
Higher labour productivity is also the source of wage increases; and where a rise in productivity is not fully
offset by wage increases, the resulting decline in production costs strengthens the competitive position of producers - enabling them to withstand a fall in price or to
enlarge their market. Such technology is characteristic
of production in the developed economies, both in manufacturing industry and in agriculture, and it differs qualitatively from that adopted by the plantations. It is, in
fact, incompatible with the plantation system, as will be
seen in a later chapter. Embodying a distinct set of
social relations and technological levels, which gives it
coherence and stability, the plantation system has inherent limits to the assimilation of cost-reducing technology.

The plantations also lacked a powerful spur to innovation in the form of a labour scarcity and of a free labour
market. In the first place, once the plantations were established in a region, they had their private labour force
which reproduced itself over time. An integral element of
the plantation system is also its institutional mechanisms
for retaining virtually for their lifetime the labourers
on whom the plantation invests capital, in the form of the
expenses of recruiting and settlement. Its enclave nature

gave the plantation a lien on the offspring of the labourers whom it recruited and settled. Second, there was no
competition between plantations and producers in advanced
economies, except in the case of cane sugar - which responded by upgrading its technology. Likewise the settler
colonies which sought to develop forms of production competitive with those in the metropolitan countries felt a
compulsion to improve efficiency when production outgrew
a small home market. Despite cheap African labour, the
settler investors could not enter export markets without
advancing their technology. Plantation producers, on the
other hand, were able to operate on the same platform of
costs; expansion took the form of extensive investments,
replicating already existing techniques. Third, and more
fundamentally, technological stagnation resulted from control of the plantations by merchant interests seeking to
maximize not net profits but the gross proceeds of the
plantations (on which the income of these interests depended).

The supersession of organic by inorganic materials has
had a twofold effect. There has been a contraction of
world trade and its diversion away from the underdeveloped
countries - with a change both in the geographical pattern
of trade and its commodity composition. The trade in
primary products has declined and a growing share of the
trade is among the developed countries. Britain's imports
of primary products not merely declined substantially but
also shifted to a great extent to Europe, North America,
Australia and New Zealand. (40) An increased volume of
exports by the underdeveloped countries has thus been accompanied by a relative stagnation in demand and in
prices, compared with the primary products of the developed countries - e.g. wheat and other temperate cereals,
meat, dairy produce, and animal and vegetable oils and
fats. The value of the traditional exports of underdeveloped countries (with the exclusion of petroleum) has
fallen markedly from the beginning of the 1950s, and likewise their terms of trade. The commodity boom after the
1974 oil price rise checked this trend in the case of
certain primary products.

The prevailing commodity relationship between the developed and the underdeveloped economies is compounded of
different elements. Commodities which are supplied exclusively by the underdeveloped countries retain their
prospects: beverages (tea, coffee and cocoa), edible oils
and fats (coconut, peanuts and palm kernels), and bananas.
These commodities for which the industrialized countries
still depend heavily on external supplies are, however,
not very important, strategically or economically. A

second group of primary commodities are those confronted
by synthetic substitutes or alternative supply sources,
the demand for which has diminished; broadly, they comprise cotton, natural rubber and industrial fibres.   A
third group of primary commodities, e.g. oil and mineral
ores - finite natural resources - as well as timber, have
improved their export prospects very substantially.   The
diminished dependence of the metropolitan economies on
primary products has involved a shift in importance from
agricultural raw materials to minerals and basic energy
resources - oil and fissionable materials.   The demand for
petroleum has grown immensely, with its chemical uses as
an industrial raw material and the widespread displacement
of coal as a source of energy.   The production of these
commodities requires large capital investments and advanced technology which only the industrialized countries
could provide.   The utilization of many of these commodities is virtually confined to the highly industrialized
countries.

The declining prospects for primary commodities, with
the exception of the last group, have been accompanied by
an increasing dependence of the underdeveloped countries
on imported inputs for the growing of even the traditional
crops, both plantation products and staple foodstuffs.
Whereas industrial production has become less dependent on
organic materials, agriculture which dominates the economy
of underdeveloped countries requires greater quantities of
inorganic materials (fertilizers, pesticides, weed kill-
ers, etc.) and equipment that must be imported.   The old
division of labour on a world scale is thus continued in
a more intensified form.   A corresponding change has been
in the pattern of foreign investments, both commodity-wise
(41) and by countries.   Alongside a decline in investment
in plantations and in plantation economies as a whole,
foreign investment has expanded considerably in the production of strategic minerals in countries such as Indonesia, East Malaysia and the Philippines.

8 Problems of labour supply and the recourse to migrant labour: I. Labour shortages and the non-availability of indigenous labour

The major problem in the growth of the colonial 'export economies' arose from a phenomenal demand for labour. The manual weeding of plantations, their harvesting, and the porterage of the crops were highly labour absorptive. For example, in Sri Lanka in the middle of the nineteenth century coffee was conveyed from the estates to Kandy by pack-bullocks or by labourers carrying it on their heads. (1)   Rice and other stores for the provisioning of the labourers were also carried by bullocks or by hand. Labour requirements on this scale were not easily met.   A steady supply of local labour was not available, and labour migration from India was affected by a lack of transport and the hazards of the journey. (2)

> Depressed and wretchedly poor [the migrants] ... trekked hundreds of miles throughout the arid plains of South India and the steamy jungles of Ceylon, banding themselves under leaders called kanganies, the victims of both their own countrymen at home and any Sinhalese in Ceylon who chose to relieve them of their hard won earnings.   Death picked them on jungle tracks;   cholera and malaria completed what the privation of the march had begun.

In 1846 public meetings were held and a draft resolution presented to the Ceylon Legislative Council 'for the protection and encouragement of Indian labourers to Ceylon'. (3)   In 1861 the planters in Badulla, the principal coffee-growing district, warned the Duke of Newcastle about the effect of transport difficulties on the labour supply. (4)

In the 1890s labour troubles were back again. With the steady displacement of Chinese tea in the British market, tea cultivation expanded both in India and in Sri Lanka. A large labour migration into Sri Lanka in 1891 was absorbed by an extraordinary demand, causing a labour scarcity 'in many parts of the country [in] individual estates in almost every district'. (5)   In 1895 'The Economist' wrote: 'Labour is becoming scarcer and more expensive both in India and Ceylon, and as new areas which have been planted in recent years begin to bear, this labour diffi- culty may increase.' (6)   'Wild and reckless' extensions in the plantation acreage aggravated this scarcity.   In 1900 there was a tendency to overproduction, leading to a fall in prices and profits, with the prospect of a reduced demand for labour.   The average dividend of forty-five re- presentative sterling tea companies declined steadily from 9.0 per cent in 1894 to 2.7 per cent in 1901. (7)   A beautiful thought then was that 'nature might step in and ravage the gardens by storms or earthquake, or parch them with drought'. (8)   However, a tea boom averted overpro- duction and intensified the labour problem.

In 1908 there was a resurgence of labour difficulties which the Governor of Sri Lanka observed 'have shown a tendency to become acute'. (9)   A boom in rubber created an additional demand for labour.   Rubber prices increased almost fourfold in less than eighteen months, between Feb- ruary 1908 and September 1909.   The high company dividends nourished the expansionary process.   'The prospectuses pour out, the subscriptions pour in', said 'The Economist' in February 1910, and in the London stock market there were such scenes of excitement as have rarely been wit- nessed.   The introduction of the 2-shilling share brought the 'most unlikely' people into the market. (10)   At this very time there was an intolerable strain on the planta- tion labour supply, due partly to the use of Indian labour for rice growing in Burma.   In Sri Lanka, the annual re- quirement of migrants was thrice that of the preceding ten years.   The rubber estates were able to pre-empt labour, placing the brunt of the crisis on the tea estates, with the likelihood of a 'general trek' of labour from up coun- try to low country such as occurred on a similar scale in 1907. (11)   The labour scarcity marred the prospects for tea in both Sri Lanka and India.   'Until blights disap- pear, droughts cease and coolies multiply, expansion could be hoped for but cannot be relied upon.' (12)

The demand for labour caused fears about a permanent rise in wages and a crisis in the plantation economy amidst a boom of astonishing proportions.   For the first time wages showed a tendency to rise.   'It is now more difficult to get Indian labour to Ceylon than 25 years ago.   Even a good coolie who is working 5 to 6 days and gets his rice at Rs. 4.80 per bushel and whose pay is 33 cents, finds conditions insufficiently attractive.' (13) 'Cooly wages have already gone up.   In Pussellawa the rate

for pruners [on tea estates] is 36 cents, [rubber] tappers
and factory coolies 40-45 cents.' (14)   Another report
referred hastily to 'fabulous wages paid to the Sinhalese
in the low-country'. (15)   Payment for the supervision of
labour also increased.   'Extra names are put down for
looking after work;   any kangani with 5 coolies gets his
name for looking after work.' (16)   The kanganies pressed
for bigger advances.   The planting member in the Ceylon
Legislative Council stated, 'Planters have of late years
... not only suffered shortness of labour, but they have
also suffered to a very considerable extent by the large
advances now demanded by kanganies and coolies.' (17)   Un-
recorded advances were a growing liability to planters.
'Apart from the loss inevitable when the cooly dies or
escapes he invariably creates a bigger debt each month
than he repays.' (18)   By 1911, as labour got 'scarcer
and more expensive' production costs rose. (19)   In the
sellers' market in labour that now prevailed the kanganies
were 'crimping' labour.   They moved their gang to estates
that paid bigger advances, financing the debt to one employer out of the money received from the next.   Estate
agents and superintendents were instructed by the proprietors 'to get labour at any price'.   The planters were
losing control over the labour supply, despite the Labour
Federation which was formed to eliminate competition. (20)
In Malaysia wages rose higher than in Sri Lanka.   According to the Penang correspondent of 'The Economist',
'Native Labourers were hard to get in many of the un-
healthy parts;   they could command practically any wage,
and went on getting it for a considerable time.' (21)

In Assam, where the British government was anxious to
promote tea cultivation, the planters were harassed by
labour shortages from the first day. (22)   Under a policy
of state-aided migration Chinese labour was brought into
Assam.   But they proved unsuitable, and were all dismissed
except the most expert tea makers.   A batch of 'Dhangar
coolies' who were recruited did not remain long.   Labourers from Chittagong refused to stay on the plantations.
The problem of labour - this riddle of the Sphinx - was
reflected in the Calcutta Board's Report in 1841, when,
under the laconic heading 'labour, lost and unproductive',
a debit of Rs. 123,279 was entered.   The government intervened to force local labour on to the plantations by
raising the rent on peasant farms 'progressively and
systematically' and by small grants of land offered as a
bait to land-hungry peasants. (23)   But these measures did
not produce sufficient results.   By 1859 'only some 14 per
cent' of tea land held by planters was cultivated 'and
that too with a thin spread of the scant labour-force'.

(24)   In 1868 a commission of inquiry into tea cultivation
in Assam stated: 'The whole matter /of plantation agri-
culture/ may be reduced to the question of labour. If
this can be achieved in sufficient quantity, and at a
reasonable cost, gardens properly planted and locally
managed ought to return a fair profit on the outlay.' (25)
In India, the labour problem was the concern of practically all plantation inquiries and commissions, and the
earliest labour legislation was to safeguard the planter
against financial losses through the defection of his employees.

The foregoing sketch of the labour situation on plantations raises two questions. How was a low wage economy
created in the face of persistent labour shortages, and
why did indigenous peasants not take up plantation employment? I shall discuss the latter question here, reserving
the former for the next chapter. The refusal of the
peasants to take up plantation employment is generally
ascribed to a value system which did not accord with a
'modern' ethos. They are reputed to have lacked economic
maturity at the time the European investors arrived. This
question is of considerable historical and sociological
significance. In the case of Sri Lanka, 'whether the
Sinhalese were given an economic incentive to work on the
estates', Snodgrass asserted, 'is a very difficult question'. (26) In line with the conventional view he, however, attributed the non-availability of indigenous labour
to two drawbacks in the outlook of the peasants: first, a
lack of acquaintance with a money economy and Western culture and, second, an aversion to arduous or disciplined
work. 'The indigenous inhabitants of the plantation area,
the Kandyan Sinhalese, had been under European domination
for only about 20 years when the coffee industry began and
their acquaintance with the money economy was slight.'
(27) Myint had a similar perception about 'the peoples of
backward countries'. They 'have had shorter periods of
contact with "money economy" so that the habits of mind
and the symbolism associated with monetary accounting may
not be deep rooted in their minds'. (28) In the case of
India, Wilbert Moore referred to 'some inelasticity of
wage aspirations ... but more among mine and tea garden
workers who have had the least contact with Western culture'. (29) Even when such assertions are qualified by
the view that the payment was insufficient, an aversion
of coloured workers to wage labour is supposed to make
them demand unreasonably high wages. In all these arguments there are both logical and historical difficulties.

The notion that it was a lack of contact with 'money
economy' and 'Western culture' which precluded wage labour

seeks to explain people's acceptance of a money economy by
their past acquaintance with such an economy instead of by
the factors governing the transition to a money economy
from a non-monetary one. It seeks to explain the rise of
a money economy by a pre-existing receptivity to monetization instead of the real historical sequence, in which the
monetization of an economy was a product of certain social
forces which required this form of exchange as a pervasive
and versatile one. It is as though an economy develops
along capitalist lines, because of its previous acquaintance with capitalism. This is a veritable non sequitur of
bourgeois scholarship. There are some other reasons of an
a priori kind which undermine this notion. The peasants
from South India who constituted the plantation labour
force practically throughout the world were as remote from
the modernizing effects of Western organization and culture as were the Sinhalese who rejected such employment.
The Chinese wage labour in tin-mining enterprises in
Malaysia were no different in this respect. In Sri Lanka,
the plantations failed to draw labour even from the maritime districts, which had a long history of European rule.
According to a historian of the Dutch colonial period,
these districts 'on balance ... became more cash-conscious
during the eighteenth century, despite many drawbacks of
the Company's policy and other circumstances'. (30) The
people here also displayed considerable mobility. Soon
after the British conquest small traders from the low
country set up businesses in the plantation areas, taking
with them shop assistants and other employees. Plumbago
mining was based partly on labour from the low country.
In the Dumbara mines, at Yatiyana across the Kalu Ganga,
the Assistant Agent of Ratnapura stated in 1884, 'The
coolies and miners who are working are all Galle men and
seem to thrive on the industry.' (31)

To take the view that precolonial societies were unfamiliar with the use of money is almost to assume that
the handling of money was a natural propensity of Europeans and that it was this uniqueness that conditioned their
economic breakthrough. It also implies that the growth of
wage labour in Europe was a spontaneous process to which
the Europeans by their attitude or personality were attun-
ed - a development which would then spread to a precapitalist community coming into contact with European investors. A corollary of this is that in underdeveloped regions the growth of capitalism must be externally induced.
This means that the development of these regions requires
the 'opening up', or in today's context their reopening to
foreign capital. The possibility of an indigenous capitalism is excluded. But in Japan's experience cultural

contact was not a precondition for the emergence of wage
labour and a money economy or of a fully-fledged capitalism itself. In fact, an important factor in its innovative industrialization was the sealing off of Japan completely from Western influence prior to the Meiji Restora-
tion. The gimmickry of monetization, as Professor M.M.
Postan wrote, 'has been repeatedly called in to help with
recalcitrant problems of economic growth'. (32)

In conventional wisdom the unresponsiveness of the indigenous peasants to the monetary incentives offered by
European investors is tied up not merely with a primitive
stage of evolution but also with idleness and inertia.
For example, the Malays, reported Governor Bort in 1678,
'were of that independent nature that will not for a considerable time submit to the strict discipline of civilised nations'. (33) When·they did not respond to the advances for tin ore which were given by the Dutch East
India Company, Bort stated in dismay, 'The people being
so idle and lazy that they mine no more tin than the
amount necessary to pay for the goods they have already
received.' (34) Nearly a century later an official
British report declared: 'The Malayan peasantry are
slothful, ignorant and unenterprising, difficult to wean
from old habits and ideas.' (35) (This image of the work
habits of the Malay was even introduced into novels, as
for example in Pierre Bouille's 'Sacrilege in Malaya'.)
In Sri Lanka, this same view found expression from the
outset of colonial rule. J.Deane stated in 1820: 'The
insuperable aversion of the Sinhalese to personal exertion
renders it impractical to procure labour for Public
Service other than by compulsion.' (36) William Granville
said: 'The greatest calamity which infests the country is
idleness ... there are no people in the world so much its
slaves, except the Cingalese as not to toil for base subsistence.' (37) The partners of a British commercial firm
in Sri Lanka, wrote to Thomas Eden, Secretary to Government, in 1828, about 'the natives, who are naturally indolent.... A few such gentlemen as Mr. Bird who is now
growing coffee on an extensive scale, would stimulate,
animate and encourage the natives to work'. (38) Another
such comment was that of Edward Sullivan, after holidaying
with some planters in the early 1850s: 'The Cingalese are
of that miserable race that will not work unless forced to
do so. Even gold that all powerful persuader, fails in
producing the desired effect.' (39)

Those unwilling to probe deeper have found in the concept of the 'lazy peasant' or in his lack of motivation an
appealing explanation for the lack of a ready labour
supply for mines and plantations. For example, Snodgrass

attributed the refusal of the peasants in Sri Lanka to
work on plantations to their aversion to arduous or disciplined toil.   'Coffee, perhaps more than any other
estate crop, required a large disciplined labour force.
An alternative source of supply had to be found if the
industry was to grow.' (40) The assumption that the
Sinhalese peasants were generally unwilling to engage in
intense physical effort or that they lacked labour discipline is also subject to the logical and historical difficulties I referred to earlier in connection with the non-
receptivity of peasants to monetization. Before the Europeans came the Sinhalese had constructed massive labour-
intensive projects (aqueducts, religious monuments, palaces and mausoleums), requiring physical stamina and the
coordination and synchronization of effort. Labour organization on so large a scale and the task of supervision
and management were formidable, in the absence of a
machine-centred process for establishing the tempo of
labour and a proper sequence of operations.
     As a case study I shall in section 2 examine the view
that the unresponsiveness of peasants to plantation employment was due to their non-acquaintance with a monetary
economy, by considering the case of the Kandyan kingdom of
Sri Lanka, where the coffee and later the tea plantations
were established. As in comparable situations, the recourse to migrant labour on these plantations is attributed to the indigenous villagers' unacquaintance with
trade and money transactions. I shall argue that this was
not so, and that even before the plantations trade and
monetization had already developed in the Kandyan kingdom.
It will be shown in the next chapter that the Sinhalese
were not averse to wage labour as such but to their being
absorbed into the plantation system where labour was held
virtually under duress, and where for several decades the
planters defaulted on wage payments, the labourers were
subjected to the fraudulent practices of the kanganies or
labour contractors, and, finally, the wage level itself
was usually lower than the rate of earnings in the peasant
sector.

1 TRADE AND MONETARY EXCHANGE IN A PRECAPITALIST ECONOMY
   - THE CASE OF THE KANDYAN KINGDOM OF SRI LANKA*

The non-availability of indigenous labour for the plantations pertains especially to the attitude of the Kandyan

* A glossary of terms used mostly in this section is
   given at the end of the chapter.

Sinhalese to being drawn into the plantation system, since
it was in their areas that the coffee and tea plantations
were mainly set up. Though this attitude is conventional-
ly explained by their unfamiliarity with trade and the use
of money at the time of the British occupation, the evidence that I now present shows the existence in the
Kandyan society of a variegated criss-cross of commercial
relations mediated through monetary exchange. The
peasants themselves engaged in monetary exchange. A pronounced acquisitive spirit among the class of senior
Kandyan officials even resulted in illegal levies on the
mass of the people. Several different currencies were in
circulation, and a significant volume of money existed if
judged by the cash hoards of considerable value which were
seized by the British. Money transactions in this situation assumed a complexity beyond a simple use of money.

The complexity of commercial dealings is shown by the
proceedings of the Board of Judicial Commissioners set up
by the British for the settlement of disputes. There were
credit transactions, and these were expressed in different
interchangeable currencies. Interest payments prevailed.
(41) Land was mortgaged and jewellery was pawned. Loans
were advanced on personal security and bonds executed.
Just before the British annexation, the Kandyan king himself had borrowed money from several persons - among other
purposes to meet expenses incurred for his aunt's funeral.
A sum of 500½ Porto Novo 'pagodas' was outstanding. He
requested the British government to help him to settle
these debts in return for forgoing a payment for joys
(jewellery) which the British had promised him; or else
he wanted to sell the 'few Joys his wives now wear to
enable him with the proceeds to satisfy the debts'. (42)

Transactions in property and in money were characterized by a high degree of complexity and flexibility; different forms of transactions dovetailed into each other.
The system of adjudication was suited to deal with an assortment of disputed transactions that seemed to be mixed
up in rich profusion. Unlike under the Roman-Dutch law
where different transactions are considered as falling
into distinct classes and governed by discrete laws, in
the Kandyan society there was a fluidity of transactions.
For instance, a fine or a money debt was commutable into
a land transfer (43) and even into the produce of a crop
season. In contrast to the complexity of transactions in
property and in money, the resolution of disputes was
based largely on a fairly general acceptance of sanctions
by the chiefs, and the appeal to commonsense. The Kandyan
chiefs had authority to pass and execute decrees, and to
decide on land claims. The adjudication of any transac-

tional nexus was governed by the general principle of
equity. In one instance, equity was held to override the
mistaken discharge of a bond, and the bond was revalidated
by the court and the consequent debt obligations were adjusted. (44) The simplicity of this system did away with
the need for an extended legal profession.

A reasonable volume of both internal and external trade
existed in the Kandyan kingdom, and much of this was on a
cash basis. There were three components of trade: first,
the internal trade within the Kandyan kingdom; second,
the trade with the maritime provinces; and, third, trade
directly outside the country. The Kandyans sold produce
in their own villages where they had a choice of articles
of exchange. They were accustomed to trade on the normal
principles of mutually beneficial exchange. In some of
the productive districts, the Agent of Government stated
in 1818, 'a very considerable quantity of produce' was obtained from the Kandyans for cash and salt. A portion of
the grain and cattle was disposed of direct to traders,
bypassing the needs of the British fort at Ratnapura.
This led to a beef shortage for the troops, and the com-
missariat wanted to compel the inhabitants to trade their
rice and cattle for salt. The Agent of Government, however, saw no need for such a step, because of the readiness of the Kandyans to trade if they were 'civilly treated and received full value of their produce'. (45)

> I would recommend to your Department and what I adopted
> myself was to send people through the country to buy
> what cattle the people were willing to dispose of and
> found no difficulty of procuring them. From your es-
> tablishment, from your command of challiè money and
> salt I would think you would be at no loss whatever
> in procuring cattle for the use of the Troops. (46)

The trade of the Kandyan kingdom with the maritime provinces was of a relatively long-distance nature and it had
a wide geographical spread. Salt, salt fish, cloth and
arrack were brought in and pepper, cardamoms, cinnamon,
arecanuts, wax and paddy were taken out. The maritime
trade extended to the district of Mannar, the focal point
of 'tavalam' roads along which convoys of hawkers carried
goods. One of the roads led to Wertittvoe, which was another centre of tavalam traffic. (47) Salt, fish and
cloth were brought in and paddy, sesame and cotton were
sent out. (48) An extension of this traffic was with
Jaffna. The high value and volume of the commodities
carried through the passes (Elephant Pass, Cutchery and
Colombogam) made the management of the Pass Rent in the
Jaffna district a lucrative source of income - the Renter
levied a duty on merchandise. 'The produce of the

Carratro ... Pomeryn and other distant salt fields' were
brought by the tavalams and disposed of at the Kandyan
frontier. (49)   Salt and salt fish were brought to the
Kandyan kingdom from sources varying from Puttalam on the
northwest coast to Hambantota and the Giruwapattu in the
extreme south.   Salt was produced mainly in Hambantota and
dried or salted fish in the fishing villages of the south
and on the eastern coast in Batticaloa and Trincomalee.

It was the dependence of the Kandyan kingdom on these
staples that induced the British to suppress the trade in
them as a way of forcing the Kandyans to capitulate.   'We
must endeavour to distress the enemy by every means in our
power', declared Robert Arbuthnot in 1804, 'and none can
be more effectual than cutting them off from supplies of
salt.' (50)   The carrying of 'salt or other articles' to
the Kandyans was made a political offence, punishable by
death or banishment;   and judicial procedure was amended
to have offenders arraigned before the Sitting Magistrate
instead of the Supreme Court, the proper tribunal for such
cases.   However, it was difficult to suppress this trade
and there was extensive smuggling.   A clandestine traffic
in salt at Balangoda was noted by H.Wright in 1818:   'The
Mahawallatenne Dissawe has thus reported to me that the
merchants convey it beyond the station into the neighbouring villages, from whence he long had reason to believe
that the cause of government has suffered accordingly.'
(51)   The Kandyans also began plundering the salterns of
Maho, Hambantota and the stores at Kandagolla, and when
these stores could not be defended the British ordered
their destruction. (52)   After the embargo ended the trade
soon regained its usual proportions;   and merchants from
the low country purchased salt from the government store
in Kalutara to be traded with the Kandyans for arecanut
and other products.   Arrangements were even made for the
sale of stocks lying in the stores of the Kandyan king,
the 'inhabitants of Uva within the mountains ... [being]
in the greatest want of salt'.

Kandyans also bought iron ore in a village in Kirime in
the Matara district to supplement supplies from Matale and
in the vicinity of Kandy.   The 'excellent iron' for agricultural implements which was produced in Kirime was 'a
considerable source of traffic with the Candians who came
down to purchase it for grain and other articles of consumption'.   The iron (53)

> in cakes of 9 or 10 pounds dross ... sells amongst the
> Candians for a Cooerene of paddy.   From these furnaces
> the whole of the Moruw Corle is supplied with imple-
> ments of husbandry.   These are also constructed at
> Kirime and sold to the people of our Corle as well as
> to the Candians.

The iron ore mined within the Kandyan territory was bought
by the cultivators for cash 'at 3 and 4 fanams a lump' at
the furnace. (54)

In spite of the restrictions imposed by the Kandyan
monarchs on access to their kingdom from the seaboard,
there existed numerous trading routes, of which the
British were unaware. 'I have every hope', wrote W.Mal-
colm, Agent of Government, 'that it has not been through
this province that gunpowder etc. have been forwarded into
the interior.' (55) Arbuthnot in a letter to John D'oyly
in 1804 referred to 'the extreme difficulty of guarding'
the boundaries of the Kandyan territory and claimed to
'have been tolerably successful in preventing smuggling'.
(56) The external trade of the Kandyan kingdom was thus
not easily suppressed. In one instance of a sale of gunpowder to the Kandyans in 1815 the Sitting Magistrate of
Colombo was directed by the Secretary, Kandyan Provinces,
to make inquiries 'particularly with the view of discovering the channels through which ammunition is ... fraudulently embezzled from the store'. (57)

The third component of the trade of the Kandyan kingdom
was a direct trade overseas, constituting a part of Sri
Lanka's external trade. Some of the produce of the
Kandyan kingdom was shipped in dhonies to the Maldive
coast. There was a flourishing export trade with the
Coromandel coast in arecanut, considered 'far superior to
that grown in any part of India', and fetching a premium
price. There was a falling off in exports in the 1820s,
due to increased production in Coromandel and the levying
of a prohibitive duty in India of 102.5 per cent by value.
(58) The exports of pepper by the Dutch East India Company came mostly from the Kandyan kingdom. One estimate for
1750 gives 75,000 lb out of 96,000 lb, (59) but according
to a memorandum sent in 1828 by Messrs Beaufort and
Hensham, two British merchants in Colombo, to Thomas Eden,
Secretary to the Government, 'Formerly the Dutch exported
nearly a thousand tons of pepper annually from this Island
to Holland'. (60) The exports of cardamoms, which increased steadily in the early part of the eighteenth
century, were supplied mostly from the Kandyan kingdom.

Much of the external trade of the Kandyan kingdom was
controlled by Moormen from the maritime provinces. They
brought their produce by boat along the Kaluganga to
storehouses at Tiruwanaketiya, 2½ miles from Ratnapura, at
the convergence of roads leading to Balangoda, Marapane,
Matara and Galle. From here the partners of each boat
proceeded to different districts where they bartered their
goods for paddy, cattle and arecanuts. The Moormen often
pre-empted the paddy surplus before the harvest by ad-

vancing cloth and salt. Sinhalese from the low country
also engaged in the Kandyan trade. For instance, a
'merchant from Moorette' [Moratuwa], about 15 miles south
of Colombo, was arrested in 1818 and had his boat seized
for selling cartridges to Kandyans in Batugedera. The
court which interrogated him was surprised to hear that
the cartridges were stolen from the British army! He was
found to have been trading in Sabaragamuwa for about
twenty years, in cloth, salt, rice, coconuts and salt
fish. (61) The view expressed by Ralph Pieris, that 'The
Sinhalese had an antipathy for commerce which until recently was regarded as degrading', (62) is either incorrect or must be interpreted as reflecting the absence of
a specifically trading class among the Kandyans of this
time. Much of the trade with the Kandyan kingdom had
been, for certain historical reasons, pre-empted by the
Moors who before the intrusion of the Europeans were commercially dominant in the East. But the lack of an indigenous trading class is not to underrate the volume and
scope of trade and money payments. Their pervasiveness or
significance is in no way diminished by the ethnic origin
of those who controlled such transactions.

Though the admission of aliens into the Kandyan territory was controlled by having certain checkpoints or
'gravets' on the border, there was in this no desire for
isolation or a dislike of commercial activity. It was
mostly a security measure and constituted a reversal of
an earlier policy of tolerance towards foreigners. In Sri
Lanka, as elsewhere, the Europeans were prone to threaten
the sovereignty of those with whom they came to trade.
Events later confirmed the shrewd suspicions of the
Kandyan kings. (63) The Moors, essentially traders by
occupation, were exempt from restrictions of entry and
travel in the Kandyan kingdom. According to an account
by Odorado Barbosa in 1519, which Emerson Tennent cited,
'Moors from the Malabar coast were continually arriving to
swell their numbers, allured by the facilities of commerce
and unrestrained freedom enjoyed under the government'.
(64) A recent historian has stated that the Kandyan
rulers even in ancient times 'far from opposing the Moors
actually tolerated if not encouraged them'. They were allowed to have a mosque in the capital, and travel freely
within the country. (65)

The explanation of Snodgrass, to which I referred
earlier, with regard to the refusal of the Kandyan Sinhalese to constitute themselves as a plantation labour force
is based on the view that they, unlike the inhabitants of
the maritime provinces, had not been long enough under
'European domination'. The suggestion that in pre-British

times the Kandyan kingdom and the maritime provinces were
like sealed compartments is one which I must jettison.
There was considerable social and commercial contact between the Kandyan kingdom and its outlying territories,
through a regular movement of goods as well as of people.
A regular influx occurred from the maritime districts to
the Kandyan areas for trade, cinnamon peeling, to collect
cardamoms for sale to the Dutch Company and for timber
felling. 'Prior to our occupation of the Territory', a
British official noted in 1815, 'it frequently happened
that our people obtain[ed] leave from the Headman of a
village in Kandy to cut a number of trees and upon bringing them down the river were charged the same duty as if
cut in our Dominions.' (66)   A duty was levied on timber
taken out of the Kandyan territory. (67)   Timber felling
gave rise to sawing and wood working in which apparently
the Kandyans were not very proficient, and carpenters were
hired from the southwestern coastal areas. 'After due
enquiry, I find there are neither saws nor sawyers amongst
the natives of Saffregam [Sabaragamuwa] for cutting planks
to complete that work [the repair to bridges]', wrote the
Agent of Government, H.Wright, to George Lusignam, Secretary, Kandyan provinces. 'I request to know whether
government will authorise instruction of the Kandyans in
this useful art. It would render their services hereafter
not only available to government but of general advantage
to themselves.' (68)   People also migrated seasonally to
cultivate 'chenas' in the Kandyan areas, especially after
the company prohibited chena in its territories so as to
encourage cinnamon growing. (69)

The collection and processing of cinnamon was a well-
organized activity in the hands of the Dutch East India
Company, and led to regular commercial and social contact
between the Kandyan kingdom and the maritime districts.
The cinnamon was cut mostly from the jungle by the Chaliya
caste - émigrés from the Malabar coast who lived in the
maritime areas. (70)   They came in a brigade of 1,000
organized in several groups, or 'ranchoo', each under a
petty headman.   They were well acquainted with the Kandyan
country and knew 'where good cinnamon most abounds and
also the roads leading from village to village'.   Heavy
rains which frequently interrupted the collection and
drying of the cinnamon and delayed transportation caused
the peelers to spend several months in the Kandyan kingdom.   'The difficulty of the pathways and bridges and
really in many instances the weight of their bundles of
cinnamon 60 and 65 lbs. each [make] 15 or 20 miles in the
Kandyan territory ... more laborious than double the distance here.' (71)   The cinnamon was taken to stores or

depots constructed on the bunds of navigable rivers, and
then by boat to Colombo, Kalutara, Galle and Matara, where
it was inspected and lodged before being transported for
shipment abroad.

Furthermore, geographically or culturally, there was no
sharp dividing line between the Kandyan territory and the
extensive tracts comprising the Sabaragamuwa district.
The district in turn was contiguous with several other
districts in the extreme South and on the West coasts of
Sri Lanka, such as the Giruwapattu of Hambantota,
Morowakorle or Matara and Gangabode Patto of the Galle
district and the Pasdun, Raigam and Hewagam Korles of the
Colombo district.   The ancient limits of Sabaragamuwa had
included lands which at the time of the British conquest
were under Kandyan jurisdiction.   'The Revenue District of
Saffregam [Sabaragamuwa] comprises the old Dissawany of
that name held under the Kandyan Government.' (72)   A
portion of the former area of Sabaragamuwa on its eastern
flank, later known as Kandepolle Korle, and a section of
the Kadawate Korle, were encroached on by the people of
Uva during their struggle with the Portuguese when they
captured the Portuguese fort at Ginigatyala.   Mahawella-
tenne Dissawe, with a view to enlarging his own authority
after the occupation, proposed that these lands be restored to Sabaragamuwa. (73)   H.Wright, recommending this
proposal, referred to the political advantage of detaching
from the Kandyan territory 'a population so long noted for
its contumacy and disobedience'. (74)   The movement of
people between the Kandyan kingdom and the rest of the
country was not exclusively a one-way traffic.   At the
time of the British embargo on salt, the Kandyans, besides
raiding the salterns in the vicinity, ventured out into
the maritime districts to purchase salt and salt fish.

The shifting to and fro of the political boundary between the Kandyan kingdom and Sabaragamuwa had caused
common socio-cultural influences to permeate over a large
extent of border territory.   The inhabitants of the
Sabaragamuwa district, while being essentially Kandyan and
governed by Kandyan law, had 'adopted many of the habits
and customs' of the maritime provinces.   The diversity and
cosmopolitanism of Sabaragamuwa were partly due to the
pressure of numerous Moor and Chetty traders who, the Assistant Agent observed in 1864, were 'scattered throughout
the district and one native village of Moormen exists,
introduced during the Kandyan rule'.   In their struggle
with the British invaders, the Kandyans were supported by
people outside their territory.   Those who assisted them
included people of the Matara district;   and Arbuthnot in
a letter to John D'oyly in 1804 mentioned a scheme for

sequestering the property of the allies of the Kandyans, some of whom were sojourning in the Kandyan territory. 'He [the Governor] is of opinion', wrote Arbuthnot, 'that the property of all these inhabitants of the District of Matura [Matara], who decidedly joined the Kandians should not be returned to them....' (75)   'It is the intention of the Governor that the property not only of those who were still in the Kandian territory but of all those who even joined the enemy should be sequestered.' (76)

The external trade of the Kandyan kingdom was based partly on cash. 'On my journey I met many parties from the Northern parts of the Galle district on their way to Candy to exchange Sicca rupees, Dutch doits, salt fish and other articles of consumption for Candian grain.' (77) The Kandyan kingdom had apparently a favourable trade balance, resulting in a net accretion of coin. The exist- ence of a large supply of foreign currency is evident from the treasure seized by the British government immediately after the conquest. This was part of the money hoarded during the conquest and the years of insecurity preceding the Kandyan surrender. In numerous places large quanti- ties of coins of varying descriptions were found. For example, Robert Brownrigg recorded in 1815: 'Besides the property taken by Major Kelly further captures to a con- siderable amount have been made and information has been received of many places where more treasure is hid.' A total sum of 60,000-70,000 Rix dollars was found, a major portion of which consisted of 'challies' or Dutch copper coins. A second deposit found at Hangurankette and opened was computed at 60,000 Rix dollars 'and a third has been pointed out and visited at a village called Motale but there are no authentic data from which to state a probable conjecture of the amount'.

The cinnamon enterprise was an important source of foreign currency for the Kandyan kingdom. The cinnamon peelers sent by the Dutch spent about two or three months each time in the Kandyan kingdom. Food and other provi- sions were bought 'for ready money' from the Kandyans 'at a fair and reasonable rate'. The peelers obtained lodgings in the Kandyan villages, especially when wet weather delayed the drying and preparing of the cinnamon. 'The bad roads, distance at which [the peelers] are em- ployed, rains and in many instances the weight of their bundles all of which I lately witnessed at Batugedera', wrote Maitland, (78) 'caused great delays in bringing all the cinnamon to the Depots.' The Kandyans were employed to carry cinnamon - an activity for which 'he [the peeler] must make or pay remuneration of some sort'. Each peeler was given a cash advance amounting to two or three months'

pay, with which he also hired a Kandyan to carry his
second or third bundle of cinnamon. In 1815 Maitland
arranged to advance three months' pay to the peelers at
the rate of 6 'pice' for every pound wieght delivered into
the store; after 1822 the quality of the cinnamon supplied was also taken into account. (79) To expedite the
transport of cinnamon to the ferries the Dutch Company in
1766 pressed into the 'Cinnamon Service' about 400 persons
from the Galle and Matara districts; they were paid 8
doits or 2 pice per day more than the usual allowance.

The supply of arecanuts from the Kandyan territories
was a well-organized activity based on cash payments. The
Renter of the arecanut monopoly was advanced money by the
Kandyan treasury to buy arecanuts at a stipulated price.
The major arecanut-growing districts furnished specific
quantities annually. For example, the supply from Lower
Bulatgama was 50 'amunams' for which 300 'ridi' were advanced in copper challies. The Adigar of the Korle advanced the Renter 2,400 Rix dollars, and was responsible
for setting up 'booticks' or 'tavalams' in all the villages. He provided the Renter with the necessary articles
of trade from Colombo to be distributed to the tavalams
for sale, the proceeds of which financed the purchase of
arecanuts. After selling the arecanuts in Colombo the
Renter would remit to the Adigar the sale value less
transport charges and, as his own remuneration, the duty
collected at the gravet of Idangodde. (80) The trade in
arecanuts was considerable. A British official noted in
1815: 'A very great trade is carried out at this place
[Ruanwella] in arecanuts such as possibly government is
not aware of.' The supply of other products, viz. pepper,
coffee, cardamoms and wax, was subject to similar arrangements.

In Sri Lanka as a whole several species of coin were in
circulation. In the Kandyan kingdom ridis and copper
challies were used predominantly, and in the maritime
areas Rix dollars, fanams and pice. Despite a seeming
complexity in trade and money transactions, the traders
were perceptive of fluctuations in the purchasing power
of the different currencies. For instance, when the
British government announced a slight increase in the
value of challies in terms of pice, from a rate of 16
challies to 5 pice to a rate of 12 challies to 4 pice, the
Kandyans declined to accept the official exchange rate.
The reason was that in Kandy and the Kandyan provinces the
challie was not purchasing more than before the announce-
ment of the new rate. The challie price of arecanuts remained unchanged, the amount that could be bought for 12
challies at the new rate being less than the amount that

could earlier be had for 16. John D'oyly appropriately
commented: 'The Kandyans ... will attend only to that
which experience teaches, that the true value of any coin
is the quantity of commodities it will purchase.' (81)
Soon after the British occupation there was a shortage of
money in circulation, especially of the lower denominations, and there was 'great distress ... in small dealings
for want of exchange'. The British then issued a coinage
of silver fanams besides releasing some of the copper
money which it had earlier seized. According to Brownrigg, the action was (82)

> received with avidity by the public, and had removed
> much of the difficulty formerly experienced and after-
> wards by the capture of a considerable quantity of
> Dutch Copper Money in the Kandyan Country which had
> been taken by the Prize Agents on account of govern-
> ment.

The foregoing sketch of the Kandyan economy at the time
of the British arrival deviates from the idyllic picture
of a primitive rustic society untainted by the base metal.
Apart from its internal trade the Kandyan kingdom had
trade connections and social contact with the maritime
provinces, and some of the local produce was shipped
abroad to the Maldives and to Europe. The cash basis on
which a certain portion of the external and internal trade
of the Kandyan kingdom was conducted is also evident from
the presence of several types of 'foreign' currency. An
outcome of these developments was the amassing of wealth
among the privileged strata consisting of the courtiers
and state officials. Chandrika Rekawe, a mistress of the
last Kandyan king, left an estate which included a cash
fortune of 4,322 Rix dollars. In 1815 this sum was deposited in the government treasury by J.D'oyly, the
British Resident in the Kandyan provinces who took over
the administration of her estate. (83)

The wealth of the Kandyan upper class was largely based
on a rentier income, from landholdings. The king, by his
ownership of royal villages, drew an income in the form of
grain rent, either one half of the produce, as in Uva, or,
as in Sabaragamuwa, the amount which ordinarily accrued to
a private owner. Analogous to the royal holdings were the
'vidhani villages' and 'nindagam' fields - obtained at
various times as gifts from the king. Proprietary rights
over them were held by the 'Dissawe' of the province
during his tenure of office. He exacted fees and fines as
well as personal services, and got a revenue in grain from
the 'muttettu' fields. Fields that were the private property of the villagers were cultivated either in 'ande',
or on the basis of 'ottoo'. From the former the landowner

received half of the produce; from the latter, he levied
an ottoo duty, which was paid in paddy, or exempted on
account of personal service, or commuted for money.
    Both the king and the Kandyan chiefs received what was
largely a tributary income from the subordinate officials
in consideration of their appointments or reappointments,
made soon after the Sinhalese New Year. Numerous appointments were subject to additional dues. The appointment of
subordinate officials was a lucrative source of cash
income for the chiefs, and shortly before the British occupation they were found to be appointing headmen 'whenever they please', to the detriment of the inhabitants.
The payments for the annual renewal of appointments were
calculated at between a half and a quarter of the incomes
which the appointments were supposed to bring, and in addition the chiefs received a gift in the form of
'bulatsurulu'. At a festival called 'däkum mangallya' the
chiefs assembled before the king to present their first
offerings, consisting of cloth and other articles. These
were taken to the treasury and valued and any balance due
was paid in cash before the end of the year. (84) One
statement of these payments from the districts under the
king's rule shows a total sum of about 32,000 ridi. The
scale of payments was revised periodically. A schedule of
payments during the time of King Kirtisiri drawn up around
1755 on the advice of the elder Migasteynne Adikar, the
king's treasurer, and chiefs of Dumbara led to a considerable increase in the royal revenue. It was on the fixed
däkum which the chiefs had originally paid for their respective appointments to the royal treasury that the
British administration based its allowance to the principal chiefs of districts, in lieu of fees, etc.
    The annual payments made to the king by the chiefs as
distinguished from the däkum mangallya offerings, were
predominantly if not solely in cash. Thus the dues included in the schedule of around 1755 were stated in different currencies (fanams, challies and ridi). Conversion
rates were specified and they remained in force regardless
of the actual rates of exchange. (85) A commission comprising former Kandyan chiefs reported to the British (86)
in 1815 that the king's revenue from the Seven Korles comprised a supply of articles from the different villages
and 'pattoos', such as silver chunam boxes, apparel, iron
tools and foodstuffs - grain, coconut oil, jaggery, etc. -
as well as an estimated 1,780 Rix dollars in cash. The
Dissawe of the Seven Korles received a total cash income
of 920 Rix dollars, and a further 169 Rix dollars in cash
as duty on the paddy fields. The income obtained by the
Dissawe of Uva was noted in the Lekam Mitiya as 5,000

ridis, but this sum was reduced to 3,419 ridis by King
Kirtisiri. Simon Sawers believed that the collections of
this Dissawe both in fees and dues did not exceed 14,000
ridis, or 5,333 Rix dollars, out of which he paid his own
dekum to the treasury, leaving him net emoluments of about
3,500 Rix dollars. Sawers recommended that a sum of 525
Rix dollars per month be given to him to compensate for
the loss of this income. (87) In certain districts as in
Gokuwela in the Nawadum Korale the dues payable by the inhabitants to the Dissawe were entirely in cash; they consisted of what was termed 'maha nadappu', amounting to
337½ ridis, and a much smaller sum called 'panam nadappu'
of about 20 ridis per month. (88) Several lesser administrative officials, such as the Dissawe Mohottal and the
Nilames, levied fines and served as revenue collectors
both on behalf of the Dissawe and on their own account.

The wealth of this class was also based on commercial
activity over which it exercised a virtual stranglehold.
The chiefs had an income of considerable value from the
management of the arecanut trade (explained earlier) and
from trading monopolies in coffee, pepper, wax and cardamoms. The Wanniar (a provincial official) who administered the four gravets in Nuwerakalawiya at the limits of the
maritime settlements levied a duty of 10 per cent on goods
that crossed the border - and for this privilege he paid
into the royal treasury a certain tribute annually. Also,
'merchants of respectability' who visited the territory
were accustomed to exchange expensive gifts. (89)

A final source of accumulation of the Kandyan chiefs
was clandestine profits involving the misappropriation of
state funds and improper exactions of money from subordi-
nates. They retained a portion of the collections which
they made on the king's behalf. In Sabaragamuwa the
Renter of the arecanut monopoly defrauded the treasury,
'the King being kept in ignorance of what [i.e. the amount
of arecanut] the province was capable of producing'. (90)
The collectors of the grain tax did the same, taking advantage of the vagaries of the paddy harvest. The excessive amounts of grain they collected led to regular complaints by the cultivator. 'It is plain from various
passages in the Kandyan papers that the 'Weebädde Lekams'
were in the habit of exacting bribes and of misappropriat-
ing the revenue they collected.' (91) The Adigars took
money from the headmen as 'travelling expenses', and those
failing or delaying to pay were fined in addition to their
having to discharge the original liability. A petition
submitted by some headmen to the British in 1815 complained against Molligoda Adigar for his arbitrary impositions.
(92) Likewise the Kandyan Dissawes demanded presents and

forcibly gathered the produce of other people's lands.
(93) Soon after the Kandyan surrender Katoogaha Dissawe,
one of the collaborators with the British, embezzled grain
and appropriated the property of those who had sought his
protection before their capitulation to the British. He
also defrauded the British. Sawers wrote that this man
totally neglected 'the best interests of Government in the
securing of grain ... a greater share [of which] is supposed to have been appropriated by himself as well as much
property exacted from the people who claimed his protection preparatory to their submission'. (94)

2   WAGE LABOUR IN THE PRE-PLANTATION AND THE EARLY PLANTATION PERIODS

I have shown how in Sri Lanka the extensive and relatively
complex commercial and monetary transactions in the
Kandyan kingdom before the British conquest invalidate the
commonplace view that it was an unfamiliarity with money
which made the Kandyan peasants reluctant to be drawn into
the plantation system. This brings me back to the question of the so-called aversion to wage labour among people
of precapitalist economies. Wage labour in these economies assumed several forms without the specific characteristics of wage labour under capitalism. As is explained
in detail in a later chapter, capitalist wage labour is
more than hired labour and is the product of a specific
capital-labour relation which the capitalist production
process continually reproduces. In this capital-labour
relation not merely is labour dispossessed of individual
means of production but it is free and mobile. Hired
labour, i.e. labour working for money wages, was not
lacking in precapitalist societies, and such labour was
already prevalent in Sri Lanka at the time the British
arrived. Furthermore, at various stages in the development of the plantations the Sinhalese villagers sought and
obtained plantation employment, even neglecting their traditional activity - paddy cultivation. The discussion in
this concluding portion of the chapter will relate to the
prevalence of wage labour in Sri Lanka prior to the plantation economy and in its early years.
  In 1825, the government fixed a schedule of daily payments for labour. (95) The payments were classified by
revenue districts, and by occupational groups, such as
'fishers employed as boatmen', persons engaged in collecting salt, 'common coolies or day labourers' (including
women and boys), palanquin bearers, bricklayers, tank dig-
gers, 'cadea or whitewashers', masons, carpenters, black-

smiths, stone cutters, etc. Wage rates were also differentiated by types of work: for example, masonry work was
divided into 'rough work, such as tiling houses' and 'assisting the fine workmen in building walls', carpentry
into cutting or clearing timber and 'assisting the fine
workmen'. A classification of occupations in such detail
is in itself significant. According to the Collector of
the Colombo district, this graded schedule of wage payments had a twofold purpose: 'to preserve the public from
imposition and ... to prevent the coolies being compelled
to a service they are unequal'. (96) Far from being indifferent or averse to cash incomes, the workmen of this
time were demanding higher rates of pay than those which
had existed for some time. The schedule of 1825 explained
that for a few groups, viz. palanquin bearers, 'coolies
carrying burdens from one place to another', and boatmen,
'the usual and customary hire' was retained.

A willingness of the Sinhalese to engage in wage labour
even outside their traditional occupation was noted by
Philip Anstruther, Collector of the Colombo district in
1830. In view of the possible transfer to private owners
of the government's cinnamon lands, revoking its monopoly
over the cinnamon trade, the Colebrooke Commissioners
inquired whether 'prospective tenants or proprietors of
these lands supposing them to be Europeans or Burghers
would be able to procure labourers'. Anstruther replied:
(97)

> If the gardens were in the hands of individuals they
> could probably procure labourers of all castes in the
> maritime divisions of this district (i.e. in all places
> where there are cinnamon gardens) at a rate varying
> from four pence to a shilling per day.... There would
> be much greater difficulty in procuring peelers, [but]
> people of any caste could be procured to labour in the
> gardens only.

Even caste injunctions were liable to be disregarded, at
least in some cases. Anstruther knowingly observed: (98)

> It appears to me the native of Ceylon generally avails
> himself of the prejudices of caste as an armour against
> the calls of Government for labour. I do not observe
> that in cases where Government is not concerned [i.e.
> involved], the majority of natives shun any mode of em-
> ployment which would otherwise be easy and profitable
> on the score of caste only.... In case the Government
> were positively and unequivocally to renounce all
> interferences with the cultivation of cinnamon, the
> prejudices of caste would perhaps be gradually thrown
> aside, and natives of all castes begin to peel cinnamon
> if they found it profitable.

The social prejudices of the Kandyans were reasonably
flexible to admit of rational behaviour. For instance,
when it was thought that they would not sell cattle to
meet the demand for beef by the British garrison, the
Kandyans were helped to overcome their scruples by the
offer of gold pagodas. To avoid moral censure it was made
out that the British army was to use the cattle as draught
animals! The people of the Southern Province had even
more mundane values. Stolen cattle were driven by night
from Ahangama to Galle and sold to the beef contractor to
augment the meat supply for the troops. (99) The Collector's Report for Tangalle for 1827 stated: 'The confirmed
and crying abuse of this part of the country seems to be
cattle stealing.' (100)

Prior to the British conquest Kandyan artificers, while
holding lands which were subject to service, like other
occupational groups, were also paid money wages: workmen
2 ridis per 12 days and the 'mulacharyia' or overseers 1½
ridis. It was on the basis of these payments received by
the Kandyan artificers 'under the King's Government' that
Sir John D'oyly recommended the payment of 2 fanams a day,
and to the overseers 2½ fanams. (101) In the early years
of British rule, Kandyans were employed by the commissari-
at, as building labour and in the porterage of grain and
other provisions for the troops. For the transport of
rice between Alliput and Badulla the rate of hire was 6
fanams a trip or 3 fanams for every 'marakkal' of rice,
together with a ration of rice and salt. (102) 'The
Kandyans are satisfied with the Hire allowed them', wrote
Sawers, 'and I hope and trust the business will now go on
well.' (103) In 1815 'Cingalese Artificers' - carpenters,
bricklayers, blacksmiths and hammermen, were also employed
by the Public Works Department on a daily wage. They were
'natives of the Interior [i.e. the Kandyan provinces] who
had grants of land for their services under the government
of the deposed Rajah'. (104) In other instances, as when
the British army had to transport 'a large quantity of
grain from the confiscated stores of the rebels in many
parts of upper Uvah', Sawers thought it possible to employ
people from the Chilaw, Colombo, Kalutara and Galle districts on the same pay as that of Malabar labour. 'A
corps of Cingalese', he wrote, 'might be procured which
would be infinitely more valuable than the Malabars, for
taking them in general a Cingalese cooly in point of
strength, courage and willingness is worth two of the
others.' (105)

Later the Kandyan Sinhalese were employed on the preparatory work on plantations. The axemen practised an
ingenious method of clearing jungle land for coffee plant-

ers with the aid of rudimentary tools. In dense jungle
'40 native workmen with the assistance of a plough [could]
clear an acre in a month'. (106) The houses of the estate
labourers and of the planters were constructed by the
Kandyans working for wages. The Assistant Agent of the
district of Sabaragamuwa noted in his report for 1864:
(107)

> The coffee estates, which are daily increasing in im-
> portance, are worked principally by coast labourers
> [Indians] but in felling, and all the preliminary
> operations of an estate, the people of the district are
> found to be most useful, and readily available, while
> numbers of them yearly migrate to estates in all parts
> of the Island for similar employment.

The Sinhalese had grown coffee - mostly in the Kandyan
districts - and they continued doing so even after the
plantations were developed. They were also employed on
some of the earliest European estates, during slack
periods of the paddy cultivation cycle or when the paddy
crops failed. In a report on agriculture in the Kandyan
provinces, George Bird, one of the first planters, asserted that the Sinhalese were not averse to wage labour,
but because of alternative means of livelihood they could
not regularly work on the plantations. 'Have you had any
difficulty in procuring labourers?' he was asked. Reply:
(108)

> I have people come up and stay for a month or two with
> me and then go away to their own grounds. The wages I
> pay them are 6½d. per diem, the people finding their
> own subsistence. I cannot induce them to stay longer.
> They return to their own lands. In seasons when their
> own crops fail, they are willing to take work in any
> numbers and more than I could employ. I have employed
> 270 at a time.

The villagers took to wage employment on the tea plantations as well. They cut firewood for use in tea factories on a contract basis and were employed directly as
estate labour. The Assistant Agent of Nuwera Eliya, the
principal tea-growing district, was convinced that where
payment was assured or when the villagers were not cheated
by kanganies and contractors they were ready to work on
estates. (109)

> Mr.Whitford of Maha Uva estate ... wrote to say that he
> was prepared to take Sinhalese labour - men and women -
> for tea plucking etc. ... I wrote to Mr.Whitford to say
> that if he paid them himself everyday and avoided all
> middlemen, I had little doubt he would get as much
> labour from the villagers as he wanted.

The Colonial Secretary, who read the Assistant Agent's

diary, minuted: 'Good advice. I am curious to know if it
was followed.' The Assistant Agent minuted: 'Yes it was
and he got more labour than he wanted at once.' A few
days later he wrote, 'A great many of the villagers have
already accepted Mr.Whitford's offer of services on the
Maha Uva estate.' (110) In the following year, on a tea
estate in Gampola there were 'some hundreds of villagers'
employed, and 'the same thing is perhaps true in other
parts of the island where tea estates are close to the
villages'. (111) Even land-owning peasants were accepting
plantation employment, including those whose paddy fields
were 'especially productive'. 'Where they are now certain
of constant employment on good wages', it was noted, 'the
villagers are gradually selling their fields to Moormen
and are not cultivating them.' (112) A fear that paddy
cultivation was being neglected even before the prospects
for tea were assured caused the Assistant Agent to suggest
the abolition of the grain tax so as to make paddy cultivation more profitable. 'What [would] the consequences
be, supposing the tea industry to collapse, or to be
hindered for a time by some such calamity as a European
war and these people to be thrown out of employment and
to have nothing to fall back upon.' He added: 'there is
no doubt ... [the employment of villagers] will increase
as the tea industry requires more hands'. (113) A similar
situation arose when rubber planting began.

Throughout the 1880s and 1890s Sinhalese were employed
by tea estates, in the transporting of tea from the estates down to the cart roads and in carrying 'shooks' for
tea bags on the return journey. In fact, they were employed alongside Indian labour. According to reports obtained by the Assistant Agent in 1894, 11 per cent of the
'able-bodied residents' in the Kegalle district were 'prepared to work on tea estates'. (114) In 1892, out of a
total estate labour force of 30,000 in this district, 26
per cent were Sinhalese. (115) The Planters' Association
found the prospect hopeful. (116)

    In many of the lower [elevation] estates Sinhalese vil-
    lagers continue to be increasingly employed, and per-
    haps in this way the labour difference [i.e. insuffi-
    ciency] may to some extent in time be solved. The
    Sinhalese villager is capable of improvement and when
    judiciously treated offers some advantage over his
    Tamil rival.

The presence of Sinhalese labour on tea estates in Nuwera
Eliya is seen from a comment by the Assistant Government
Agent in 1898 with regard to a proposal to commute the
'Gansabhawa' tax, which imposed ten days' work on a public
project. Commutation, he argued, would discourage the

villagers from 'leaving lucrative work on Estates, or
having to quit their paddy fields or chenas at critical
moments.... The Planters also would gain by not losing
their Sinhalese labour force at very short notice for 10
days at a stretch'. (117)

The Kandyan Sinhalese were responsive to wage payments
and also to wage differentials. In 1889, the villagers of
the Uda Dumbara district were reluctant to work as road
labourers for sixpence a day in spite of a local famine.
According to an official report, 'only six men turned up,
and ... they did not continue working, asking "why should
we work on the road for 6 d. when we can get 8 d. on the
tea estates?"' (118) Later, when the rubber estates were
opened up, the lure of a wage income was turning small
peasants into day-labourers. Thomas Villiers deplored
this tendency. (119)

> The villager found himself in possession of cash ...
> and rather than till his small paddy fields, he neg-
> lected these, bought imported rice, raised his whole
> standard of living, and when hard times came ... in
> many cases his means of living had gone.

The villagers found rubber tapping congenial, not so much
as a work operation different from that on a tea estate
but because the work schedule was more suitable. Work on
a rubber estate ends around midday, allowing the villagers
to attend to their own crops. Thus the Sinhalese were
among the pioneer labour on some rubber estates. From 150
to 200 of them were employed daily on a new rubber estate,
'in an hitherto unopened corner of the Province'. (120)
The same estate, in Viyaluwa, had later a workforce of 500
Sinhalese and 'has had as many as 700 at one time'. (121)
The Estate Superintendent stated that the Sinhalese on the
estate accounted for 58,000 labour days of men, women and
children, and Rs 35,000 on contracts for timber felling
and clearing. (122) On another rubber estate, 25,000 days
of Sinhalese labour were recorded for 1907, with a wage
bill of over Rs 15,000. (123) Yet another estate employed
160 Sinhalese who 'received 62 cents per head per diem
paid weekly, and barring a little fever are doing well and
seem contented'. (124)

The Sinhalese also performed wage labour outside the
plantations: on irrigation projects, on the railway, and
in cutting firewood for estates. At the time the tea
plantations were opened up the Assistant Agent for the
Nuwera Eliya district sought to dispel a belief that the
villagers disliked wage labour. (125)

> I should like to record how untrue is the report pro-
> mulgated sometime ago that the villagers who are not to
> be benefited by this [the Waduwawela ela] and the

Bodi [ela] will not work for hire on it and that the
P.W.D. have had to import Tamil labour for the purpose.... They have worked and are working most cheer-
fully on those channels. In fact in many cases they
have done far more than could ever have been expected
from them.

For repairing the Kalawewa Dam the Government Agent of
Anuradhapura in 1885 recommended that villagers be employed because immigrant labour was slow and uneconomic.
(126)   Contracts for supplying firewood to tea estates
were given to the villagers. (127)   From about the beginning of this century, Sinhalese were employed in desiccated coconut and fibre mills in the North Western Province as well as in plumbago mines. One of the mills in
1901 employed 130 Sinhalese men and women. (128)   In the
'large desiccating and fibre mills belonging to Vavasseur
& Co.' the Sinhalese worked alongside the Tamils and
Cochins. (129)   The 'Ratemahatmaya', on a suggestion by
the Government Agent, was 'sending a group of [Sinhalese]
labour to work on the railway under the local headman'.
(130)

In plumbago mining a relatively large Sinhalese labour
force was employed from the 1880s. 'There are as many
Kandyans as low country men in the pits.' (131)   At the
Dodantalawa mine on the Kandy road, in 1885, 'the digging
and carrying of plumbago gave employment to large numbers
of men and women'. (132)   Women workers removed refuse from
the pits and also carried the ore to the road. Some mines
were worked on a twenty-four-hour basis. The pits were
very deep and water was emptied by hand. The mine-owners
neglected the safety and health of the workers. (133)   The
miners had to go 60 to 80 fathoms down the sides of the
timber shafts relying chiefly on their toes. (134)

The steps of the ladder or timbers are as slippery as
glass with the plumbago grease and there is nothing -
no rope to save a man if he slips. It says a good deal
for the prehensile toe of the Oriental that more accidents do not occur. Accommodation for coolies is extremely bad.

In one mine, no extra wage was paid for night work;   'it
is always night on the pits!'

Despite the hazardous and exhausting conditions in the
mines, the wages paid ensured an adequate labour supply.
'Wages are high, no man getting less than 50 cents a day.
They work in shifts day and night.' (135)   In another
instance where over 2,000 were engaged at the pits 'the
men earned 50 cents a day and Re. 1 for night work in digging at the pits, and the women 25 cents a day for carrying'. (136)   'A great deal of ready money ... [is being]

thrown into the district.' (137)   At the Dodantalawa mine,
the wage bill was over Rs 1,500 per month. (138)   In 1899
it was feared that the 'rush to plumbago mining' was
causing a labour scarcity for estates on which Sinhalese
labour was employed. (139)   A few years later some villages even abandoned paddy cultivation - conventional
models of peasant behaviour notwithstanding. Near the
village of Panagoda 'several old paddy fields had been
abandoned, being covered with grass and bushes'. They had
not been cultivated for some time, for the reason that
'the villagers found plumbago digging more lucrative'.
Another comment by the Agent expresses the villagers' response to changing market prospects. 'I suppose they will
revert to their fields when plumbago digging ceases.'
(140)

   To dispose of the prevalent arguments explaining the
non-availability of village labour in the plantations in
terms of attitudes, values and mores or the innate racial
characteristics of people, I have examined in some detail
the level of trade and monetization in the relevant case
of the Kandyan kingdom and have also adduced evidence of
the prevalence of wage labour in Sri Lanka before and
during the period which saw the establishment of plantations. An interpretation of the non-availability of an
indigenous labour supply that needs to have recourse to
subjective factors must necessarily be superficial and
ahistorical. The problem, in fact, resolves itself into
a much broader and more complex one concerning the prevailing character of the peasant economy in which a potential labour supply may have existed. The prerequisite
for the release of such labour is appropriate institutional changes in the peasant economy enabling the existing
labour resources to be used in a more rational and efficient way - thereby throwing up a labour surplus seeking
employment elsewhere. The peasant sector would have shed
its labour in much the same manner as the enclosure movement in England, which heralded the rise of capitalism,
caused the mass transfer of labour rendered surplus. (141)
Such a change implies the development of capitalist agriculture. I shall highlight a few basic aspects of the
problem of why the peasant economy in the underdeveloped
countries failed to evolve on capitalist lines. However,
before doing so I shall consider very briefly the objective factors which conditioned the growth of a wage proletariat in the classic model of the transition to capitalism in Europe. Both in Europe and in Japan the creation
of a wage proletariat was the result not of culture contact, as is presumed necessary in the case of people of
colonial lands, but of objective factors connected with
the rise of capitalism.

The proletariat did not spring ready-made out of
nothing, as Athena is reputed to have sprung fully armed
from the head of Zeus. The transfer of labour outside the
family workshop or farm was a deliberate and long drawn
out process, accomplished earlier in England than on the
Continent. The transfer was not simply a demographic
phenomenon but the result essentially of social forces.
There were definite institutional changes which historically produced and moulded a working class from the precapitalist forms of labour and social organization.
Within an appropriate class structure, the ruling class
began to increase surplus extraction by a greater use of
fixed capital in production, and the resulting improvement in techniques dispossessed the small producer by
making obsolete the tools with which he worked. Technological change had always been taking place, but a point
was reached in the different branches of production when
such changes demanded more efficient equipment, on which
only a few could afford the outlay. The small producer,
unable to compete, became wholly dependent on the owners
of capital, and was forced on to the labour market. He
was free to move and compelled to move - to compete with
other workers for employment. The wage worker was a
creation of the capital-labour relation which prevailed
from then onwards.
    As is to be expected, the process was hardly peaceful
or voluntary. As Marx commented, 'the labouring classes
had little impulse to self-expropriation for the glory of
capital'. In England, the handicraftsmen and peasants who
eventually composed the proletariat did not gladly leave
their traditional pursuits and way of life but were
wrenched out by the competition of the factory and by land
enclosures respectively. Under the domestic system of
production the labourer's position was akin to that of
share-cropping tenants who even when oppressed by the
landlord and usurer had a free hand in organizing cultivation. The meanest peasant or domestic producer had a
robust independence which set him apart from proletarians.
As a wage worker, however, he lost his freedom to decide
the pace and pattern of work; and work discipline was now
externally imposed in the interests of the capitalist.
Furthermore, wage labour was socially demeaning. Workers
in the centralized mills which were the forerunners of the
factories became an 'out-group', without property of their
own. The miners, an important group among the early
working class, were ostracized when mining became a specialized activity confined to mining settlements. (142)
Young women in wage employment were considered little
better than 'beggars or street girls'.

Capitalist changes in agriculture, as in industry, were linked fundamentally with the progressive application of fixed capital in production and a corresponding increased use of wage labour. While the development of capitalism in agriculture is a far more complex and slower process than in industry - the reason for which I shall presently suggest - the growth of capitalist relations in paddy production has been extremely tardy. Agricultural and ecological risks, especially in monsoon lands, resulting in the uncertainty of harvests, inhibited fixed capital investments. The use of wage labour (which constitutes a fixed financial commitment) is also discouraged, apart from by the instability of harvests, by the uneven and sporadic demand for labour during the crop cycle. A concomitant of this situation is the absence of a class of wage labourers and the characteristic form in which surplus labour manifests itself in the peasant economy. A fairly large volume of surplus labour exists, but in a condition of underemployment, trapped among a proliferation of small family farms; it is not a totally unemployed and mobile workforce available for employment in other sectors.

The slow growth of capitalism in agriculture generally has much to do with the difficulty of rationalizing the use of labour in conditions where work conforms to a specific sequential pattern governed by the natural crop cycle, in contrast to a machine-centred operation where a simultaneity of operations enables a fuller and planned utilization of a given labour force. This difficulty is aggravated in the case of paddy cultivation by the nature of the discontinuities in the pattern of labour demand both inter-seasonally and intra-seasonally. These discontinuities in labour demand, which are very pronounced and are also influenced by the vagaries of the weather, cause the timing of labour inputs to be unpredictable. The paddy economy consequently requires a large labour force employed at various degrees of intensity during different times of the year. The peak demands necessitate a standby labour force, whose actual labour input during the year is considerably less than its overall potential - in contrast to a production pattern which could utilize a smaller workforce fully and on a more continuous basis. An appropriate response to this situation is the resort to sharecropping, based on smallholdings and the exploitation of family labour.

In Sri Lanka this phenomenon is reflected in the contrasting tenurial patterns in the Wet Zone and the Dry Zone. In the Wet Zone, where paddy cultivation depends on direct rainfall, and harvests are uncertain, there is a preponderance of smallholdings and share-cropping, not necessarily due to a relatively high population density. In the Dry Zone large-scale irrigation ensures relatively stable harvests. Holdings are consequently of a large size and are owner-operated with fairly widespread use of wage labour. Furthermore, land rent is usually a fixed volume of produce or is payable in cash. In the paddy tracts of the Eastern Province and in the Hambantota district of the Southern Province such forms of production which are transitional to capitalism developed from the middle of the nineteenth century.

The penetration of capitalism is contingent upon a control by the capitalist of the labour process, including an ability to regulate the flow of labour into the productive process with a minimum of idle time. This may require a reordering of the sequence of work operations, based partly though not entirely on technological changes. Whereas in most forms of production an efficient labour utilization pattern could be achieved by a relatively simple reordering of production, in the case of paddy the natural constraints to which I have referred preclude a stable labour demand without a major organizational and technological change. (143)

The relative absence of landless wage labour was also due to the nature of the pressures to which the peasant economy was subjected. As referred to in an earlier chapter, these pressures emanating from the growth of the plantations undermined the infrastructure of the paddy economy, through a decline in irrigation facilities and the loss of access of the peasants to forest land and pastures. While damaging the peasant economy they were insufficient to create a supply of landless wage labour. The peasant economy settled at a lower equilibrium with a more impoverished peasantry. The impact was not comparable, for example, with what occurred in the settler colonies of Africa, both north and south of the Sahara, where a labour force for the capitalist sector, consisting of mines and settler agriculture, was extracted by a virtual dismantling of the traditional, often tribal economy. In the nonsettler colonies while the commercialization of the village economy led to a concentration of land ownership, and there has been a growing social differentiation of the peasantry brought about by debt, usury and mortgage, the dispossessed peasants became, in the absence of the development of capitalist agriculture, entrenched as share-croppers on the land which they previously owned. The risk element in the investment of fixed capital in the types of grain cultivation which predominated in the peasant sector, being far too great for merchant and

usurer capital to undertake, inhibited the transformation
of merchant and usurer capital into industrial capital.
The ramifications of the dominant capital in the peasant
economy, its sources of strength, and the specific circumstances which impeded its transformation, however, need
more probing than has been done here.

GLOSSARY

ADIGAR - a minister.
AMUNAM, amuna - a measure of grain; also a measure of
    arecanuts; 24,000 arecanuts = 1 amunam.
ANDE - a type of tenancy of land provided by the pro-
    prietor to another to cultivate on a share-crop basis.
BOOTICKS, boutiques - small native shops or booths.
BULATSURULU - literally 'a bundle of betel leaves'. A
    fee, or gift, of money is usually presented to a chief
    or proprietor wrapped up in such a bundle; and the
    fee, or gift, has come to be referred to by this term.
CHALLIE, salli - the eighth part of a fanam; also used
    generally to mean money.
CHENA, hena - high jungle land, cultivated at intervals -
    'slash and burn'.
COOERENE, kuruni - measure of grain, approximately one
    eighth of a bushel.
DÄKUM - the gift given by a subordinate to his chief or
    lord at an annual appearance ceremony.
DÄKUM MANGALLYA - the festive occasion when a chief or
    lord makes his annual appearance.
Dessave, DISSAWE - an official in charge of an administra-
    tive district.
DHONY (pl. DHONIES) - a small flat-bottomed sailing craft.
DISSAWANI - an administrative district.
DOIT, duit - Dutch term for a part of a fanam.
FANAM - a gold coin; one tenth of a pagoda, and one
    twelfth of a Rix dollar.
GANSABHAWA - Village Tribunal.
GRAVETS, kadawatha - a check point at the boundary of a
    kingdom or district.
KANGANI, kankany - an overseer of a number of coolies, on
    an estate or public works site.
KORALA - an official in charge of a minor administrative
    division.
KORALE - a minor administrative division.
LEKAM MITIYA - Register of Lands of the Kandyan govern-
    ment.
MARAKKAL - a traditional measure of capacity and also of
    land which varied in different regions of the country.

MULACHARYA - headman or group leader.

MUTTETTU - field which is sown - on account of the king
     or other proprietor, temporary grantee or village chief
     - by other persons, with only seed paddy being pro-
     vided.

NINDAGAMA - 'a village which for the time being is the
     entire property of the grantee or temporary chief ...
     it generally contains a muttettu field which the in-
     habitants, in consideration of their lands, cultivate
     gratuitously for the benefit of the grantee, and,
     besides are liable to the performance of certain other
     services for him.'   H.W.Codrington, 'Ceylon; Glossary
     of Native, Foreign, and Anglicised Words' (Colombo,
     1924).

OTTOO - a tithe of produce paid in acknowledgment of over-
     lordship.

PAGODA - a gold coin.

PATTOO - a collection of several villages for administra-
     tive purposes.

PICE - a copper coin.

RANCHOO - a gang or group.

RATE MAHATMAYA - minor administrative official.

RIDI - a larin; a coin consisting of a silver wire twist-
     ed into the shape of a hook, stamped with an Arabic
     legend on either side.

SICCA RUPEE - a silver coin.

TAVALAM - a caravan of carriage bulls.

TUNDU - a chit or small note; on estates, a discharge
     note.

VIDHANI VILLAGES - villages under a Vidhane, usually in-
     habited by people of low caste and liable to public
     services.

WEEBÄDDE LEKAM - an officer who collected the grain tax.

9 Problems of labour supply and the recourse to migrant labour: II. The response of indigenous labour to the plantation system

The preceding chapter dealt with the apparent anomaly of indigenous labour in Sri Lanka not responding to the abundant work opportunities on the plantations. The conventional explanation of this, in terms of their non-receptivity to money and of an innate aversion to wage labour, was shown to be not in accordance with the evidence. The emphasis commonly attached to the attitudes, motivation and values in a precommercial society as causative factors in this situation made it necessary for me to probe the state of commercial activity in the Kandyan kingdom before the arrival of the British. I also referred to the existence of wage labour among the Sinhalese before the plantations were established as well as outside the plantations at a time when the Sinhalese were generally rejecting plantation employment. Further, evidence was adduced to show that there was no absolute rejection of plantation employment and that in certain periods and in certain circumstances the Sinhalese worked even on plantations.

I shall now show that there were definite deterrents to the Sinhalese villager joining the plantation workforce, and that his reaction was not to wage labour as such but against the plantation system. Low wages and the infrequency and irregularity of wage payments were aggravated by the extortion of the kanganies and of the traders who had dealings with plantation labour; furthermore, in the adjudication of labour disputes the state machinery was loaded in favour of the planters and against the labourers. A belief of employers and of the colonial state in the peasants' supposed aversion to wage labour and to physical toil was part of a supporting ideology which, having served as a moral basis for the commercialization of slavery in the New World, was made use of to justify the low wage economy and the coercive labour practices of

European investors. In the final analysis, these beliefs
and policies were linked with a 'North-South' division on
colour lines and the domination of the coloured races by
'white' capital.

On the plantations in Sri Lanka the level of wages was
lower than in South India from which labour was drawn, and
the plantation wage level was a fortiori less than the
rate of earnings in the surrounding peasant economy. In
the Lewis model of labour transfers, subsistence earnings
set a floor to the wage level in the capitalist sector,
and the 'capitalist wage' exceeds the subsistence wage by
a labour transfer premium. A voluntary transfer of labour
which this implies is the premise on which propositions
regarding the behavioural limitations of indigenous
peasants who refuse plantation employment are predicated.
In the plantation-peasant situation, the acceptance of
this model has led to the assertion that the plantation
labourer was economically better off than his village
counterpart. This view that the plantation wage exceeded
the average rate of earnings in the peasant sector has no
foundation in theory or fact. I shall maintain - again
questioning the model - that though South India was a
great labour reservoir, the transfer of labour was hardly
voluntary but was brought about by various forms of extra-
economic pressure, applied even during periods of acute
economic distress in South India.

Though the conditions in the South Indian economy were
themselves conducive to labour migration, extra-economic
pressures were applied to ensure an adequate flow of migrants. Indicative of these pressures is the word 'recruiting' itself, which is almost equivalent, in the
actual context, to press-ganging or dragooning. The
Plantation Convention, 1958 (No.10), included under the
term 'recruiting' any measures taken for 'obtaining or
supplying the labour of persons who do not spontaneously
offer their service at the place of employment or at a
public emigration or employment office'. (1) In India
'labour-hunting' was a term used in government reports.
The use of force and deception for obtaining labour for
mines and plantations was prevalent throughout the underdeveloped world. The 'agent, operating at a distance,
could get away with monstrous misrepresentation which even
a watchful labour inspection service in the sending area
might not always detect'. (2) The wage levels and labour
conditions were not known in the places of recruitment;
those already employed were prevented from going back, as
in the case of Indian labour recruited in the 1830s for
the sugar plantations in the West Indies, Mauritius and
Fiji. They were bound beyond their initial period. Small

plots of arable land were also granted, if the labourers
commuted their return passages.

The government of India, agreeing with a commission of
inquiry in the 1830s on plantation labour in Mauritius and
Demarara, stated that 'immigrants ... have been in too
many cases, entrapped by force and fraud, and systematically plundered of nearly 6 months' wages, nominally advanced to them but really divided on pretences more or
less transparent, among the predacious crew engaged in
the traffic'. (3) The deceiving of labourers was acknowledged in the Tea Commissioner's report of 1886, and in
the Assam Labour Enquiry report of 1906. 'The same tale
is told of deception, of misrepresentation, of trapping
people on bazaar days, when they had something to drink
and of cajolement of single women, who were offered various inducements.' (4) Even the supervising officials were
deceived; for example, advantage was taken of family
quarrels and young men were enticed by the promise of
marriage on the plantations. (5) Those who were prey to
the wiles of the recruiters had no idea of the journey to
the plantations; they expected reasonable wages, agreeable work, and thought they could come home when they
liked.

The resort to duress in the recruitment and retention
of labour was flagrant in Assam. A report of 1868, which
one official said was an understatement, described their
plight. (6)

    In a swampy jungle, far from human habitation, where
    food was scarce and dear, where they had seen their
    families and fellow labourers struck down by disease
    and death, and where they themselves [were] prostrated
    by sickness, [the labourers] have been able to earn far
    less than they could have done in their homes.
Those who survived the journey to the plantations arrived
emaciated. Supposedly free men, their chances of self-
assertion were hardly more than those of the slaves in the
American South. They were hemmed in by dense jungle and
guards (chowkidars) posted at possible outlets from the
'cooly lines' which were enclosed in some instances by
high palisades. As migrant labourers they incurred the
illwill of the local villagers, who were enlisted to track
down fugitives. If caught, they 'were tied up and flogged', and a reward of Rs 5 paid to the captor was deducted
from the labourer's earnings. (7) This is reminiscent of
the shoot-at-sight standing order issued to the guards
around the diamond-mining reserves of South Africa.

The rapacity of the labour agents continued, despite
the Act of 1863 passed by the Bengal Legislative Council
to regulate the 'coolie trade' and to lessen mortality

among labourers. Between May 1863 and May 1866, the death
toll among 85,000 labourers was 32,000. (8) The legislation was ineffective, as pointed out by the Deputy Commissioner of Manbhum. (9)

> Very few coolies leave the district, knowing really
> what they were going for ... I consider that ... [the
> Act of 1863] is not in any case calculated to bring
> what, is its real object, protection of the coolies as
> well as of the planters' interest [as against those of
> the recruiting agency].

According to the Tea Commissioner, 'The protection which
the Act was designed to afford has been little more than
nominal.' (10) The legislation was basically in the
planters' interest. In 1862, 'desertion' and 'insolence'
were made punishable offences; planters were assigned
police powers, and empowered to arrest absconding labourers; the time spent in prison was added to the period of
the labour contract. (11) The Act of 1863 gave legal recognition to the indenture system, by specifying a five-
year term. An amending Act in 1865 made no real change,
though it stipulated a monthly wage and reduced the indenture period to three years.

The 'coolie trade' from South India was not a voluntary
response to market forces but an organized business, with
capital outlays by shippers, recruiting agents and planters. A recruiting agent and several sub-agents scoured
the villages, drumming up hopes of a bright future and
using every possible stratagem to increase their catch.
Recruitment for the plantations in Malaysia was of two
types. One type of recruitment was akin to a consignment
sale and financed by a shipper and a recruiting agent, and
the other was contractual, on orders placed by planters at
a stipulated price. (12) These recruitment practices continued even after the abolition of indenture in 1909. The
migrants were forced into debt in order to bind them, and
few of them reached the plantations as free labourers. In
1922 a Malayan government official stated: (13)

> in many cases, sums have been debited to coolies on the
> strength of the kangany's account which they certainly
> never received and which were not expended on their
> behalf. There has also been a tendency to detain unin-
> dentured labourers against their will on estates until
> the sums debited against them have been paid off.

Even in periods of acute labour scarcity the planters
were in control over the labour market. The planters and
the state in combination took measures to insulate the
wage rate from possible market pressures both by elimi-
nating competition for labour and by concentrating most
recruitment in periods of acute distress in South India.

When indentures were abolished, a semi-official agency was
established in South India in 1908 to serve as a centralized recruiting organization, thus preventing competition
for labour. The government's role in devising appropriate
institutional measures for curbing wages was also apparent
in legislation in Sri Lanka to exempt kanganies from the
liability of imprisonment for debt. Indebtedness to
traders and moneylenders had caused kanganies to move with
their labour gangs from one estate to another, collecting
ever increasing advances. The new legislation induced
defaulting kanganies to remain on their estate. Measures
were also taken to loosen the kanganies' hold over the
labourers by reducing the indebtedness of labourers.
Planters were required to pay wages monthly instead of
within sixty days of the month for which wages were due.
Furthermore, the notice given by a kangany on a labourer's
behalf had now to be confirmed by the labourer himself.
Finally, a system of legalized discharge tickets was introduced for labourers seeking re-employment. (14)
     These measures aimed at freezing wages while allowing
capital outlays on recruiting to fluctuate according to
the demand for labour. An increase in recruiting outlays
was preferred to wage increases which were liable to
become permanent. (15)

     Wages once raised - unlike advances - would be almost
     impossible to reduce. We therefore think that an ir-
     reparable blow may be dealt to up country tea estates
     if the question of the best means of competing on more
     equal terms with the F.M.S. /Federal Malay States/ and
     of inducing a larger influx of coolies into Ceylon is
     much longer postponed.

'If competition by offering increasing wages starts in
Ceylon, as it has already to some extent, where will it
end?' Planters were given free passage tickets to obtain
Indian labour, and the British India Steam Navigation
Company was guaranteed a sale of 8,000 tickets a year.
(16) The improved migration facilities were purposely
designed to 'blunt tendencies for wages to rise' consequently. As J.N.Parmer stated with reference to the
rubber plantations of Malaysia, 'wages were generally low
and bore no real or sustained relationship to the actual
demand for estate labour'. (17)
     Labour recruitment was greatest when distress in the
South Indian economy was abnormally acute. For instance,
in Sri Lanka, the Government Agent for the Central Province stated in his Administration Report for 1877: 'The
labour supply of Uva /one of the principal plantation dis-
tricts/ for 1877 was, as a rule, greater than the demand,
owing to the famine in India, and from the coolies having

come over from the [South Indian] Coast in a weak and
emaciated state, there was more sickness among them than
in previous years.' Again, in 1892 when South India was
ravaged by famine labour migration increased sharply, 'no
doubt ... greatly aided and assisted by the prevailing
scarcity [of food] on the coast of India, where nearly the
whole of our labour force is derived'. (18) In 1905, when
the failure of the monsoons caused a 'serious state of
affairs' in the districts of Changlepet, North Arcot and
Vellore, the Ceylon Labour Commissioner reported 'there is
no doubt that this year should be an exceptionally good
one for recruiting labour, with every prospect of a great
reduction in advances'. (19) Recruitment also fluctuated
with the state of the grain market in India; and bad
harvests, while being favourable to labour recruitment,
depressed real wages by raising the price of rice - the
staple food. 'The continued drought now prevailing in
South India [in 1892] is a very important circumstance for
us in Ceylon dependent as we are both for food and
labour.... Should a really serious famine ensue we may
expect an abundance of labour and little rice.' (20) In
such periods when conditions in the South Indian economy
plunged numerous peasant families below the poverty line,
making them potential migrants to the plantations, the
real wage of plantation labour declined, because of the
increased price of rice, below average earnings in South
India and considerably below those in the peasant sector
of Sri Lanka. Though plantation labour was cushioned
against the full impact of such price rises by the inclusion of a certain amount of rice as a part of the wage,
the consumption standards in the peasant sector were
hardly affected because of the large subsistence component
of the paddy output. The migrants were the sub-marginal-
ized segment of the Indian peasantry and the relaton between the plantation wage and earnings per head in the
sector from which labour was drawn appears to be the converse of what the Lewis model envisaged.

According to data available, in India plantation wages
were much lower than, for instance, the wages paid by the
government on construction projects. In 1864, while
labourers in the Public Works Department could earn Rs 7
per month, the average wage in the tea plantations of the
Assam Company was Rs 4 to 5 and in many others it was
about Rs 3.50. A similar disparity existed between plantation wages and the wage rate of 'able-bodied agricultural labour'. In Lakhimpur, for example, agricultural
labour was earning Rs 9.37 per month in 1873 and thereafter never less than Rs 6 except in 1875 and 1876, and
in most subsequent years till 1901 between Rs 8 and Rs 11.

Only rarely did estate labour earn even Rs 6.50. The
minimum wages stipulated by government for male, female
and child labour on plantations were Rs 5, Rs 4 and Rs 3,
respectively. The provision of housing and subsidized
rice made little difference to plantation wages compared
with wages in other sectors. Throughout the 1860s and
1870s plantation labour was receiving almost half the wage
earned by non-plantation labour. The Tea Planters' Association of India formed in 1881 was concerned mainly with
keeping down plantation wages in the face of rising wage
rates in jute mills, textile factories, railways and the
Public Works Department.

If the plantation labour migrants, as the sub-marginal-
ized segment of the South Indian peasantry, were paid
lower wages than the average earnings in South India's
peasant sector, in Sri Lanka, Assam and Malaysia these
wages were considerably less than comparable earnings in
non-plantation employment. In Sri Lanka for this reason,
from about 1848, a preference was shown for Indian migrants for repairing irrigation tanks in the Eastern Province. The migrants' wages were lower than those of the
Jaffna Tamils. 'Formerly Jaffna people were employed, but
since the system of the Coast people coming over here in
such numbers commenced the employment of Jaffna people has
been discontinued as the Coast people [from South India]
work for lower wages.' (21) According to an Assistant
Agent in 1884, the peasants demanded higher wages for
estate work than those payable to Indian labour. 'I find
that the people from some of the villages go and work on
the estates at Uda Pussellawa doing such work as digging
holes for the planting of tea but they require higher
wages than the Tamils, poverty stricken as they are.' (22)
Having access to land whether as small proprietors or as
tenants, they set a higher price on their time and effort.
(23) The villagers who worked on the rubber plantations
from about 1910 were paid more than the migrants. A
writer on the labour situation commented: 'It is ... a
question of how long the Tamil will be content to work
alongside a Sinhalese labourer - who is paid 10-15 cents
per day more.' (24)

One important element in the wage policy of plantations, to which I referred, was the increase in labour
recruiting outlays. Another element in this strategy was
payments in kind which were built into the wage structure
- notably housing, a kitchen garden and facilities for
grazing cattle, and subsidized rice. Rice was originally
supplied because of the remoteness of estates from trading
centres. In Malaysia, soon after the First World War, the
planters responded to wage demands by increasing the rice

subsidy, and some even reimbursed labourers the extra cost
of remittances to India due to a depreciation of the
Straits dollar. Again, at the end of the Second World
War, the planters insisted on supplying food in lieu of a
wage increase. In East Sumatra, in 1959, when inflation
was rampant, 85 per cent of the wage of permanent male
labour on the estates was paid in foodstuffs and provisions, but temporary labour was paid entirely in cash.
(25) The direct-consumption component, while serving as
a real wage cushion in the short run, depressed wages and
consumption standards in the long run.

The coercive elements which underlay the supply of
plantation labour which I have described so far show the
inapplicability of the Lewis model. Despite an enormous
manpower potential in India, the plantations lacked an
elastic supply of labour such as envisaged in this model.
In the absence of a 'pull' into the capitalist sector,
there was also lacking a transfer margin which, according
to Lewis, was partly to compensate those leaving 'the easy
going way of life of the subsistence sector' for a 'more
regimented and urbanized environment'. The plantations
were hardly the free labour market implied here. In spite
of the collapsed condition of the South Indian economy, a
labour supply was not had, or retained, without compulsion
of one form or another; it was extracted by crafty recruiters during recurrent disasters in the peasant economy. Plantation wages, consequently, were even lower than
the distress wage at which the peasants and artisans may
have opted to join the plantations. The low wage rate per
unit of working time and effort, compared with the earnings per head in the peasant sector, was obscured by
fuller and more continuous employment for the plantation
worker and his family. If the frontier of competition between the plantation and the peasant sectors, as Lewis
said with reference to the capitalist and the subsistence
sectors, was a cliff, not a beach, the wage differential
which defined the relation between them was in favour of
the subsistence sector.

There is a second difficulty in applying the Lewis
model to wage levels on plantations. The assertion that
the wage rate in the capitalist sector is governed by
average and not marginal earnings in the subsistence
sector holds good only when the total produce of the farm
is shared among its members. In a situation of labour
surplus, the average product being greater than the marginal product, the consumption of every individual regardless of his labour contribution is somewhat higher than
bare subsistence. 'The product of ... *[the family farm]*
goes into the same pot and the members of the household

eat out of the same pot.' (26)   If, on the other hand, the
total product of a farm family falls abnormally because of
harvest failure or a loss of the farm itself due to dispossession, consumption would also fall abnormally below
the average level of the farming community as a whole -
except in the unlikely circumstance of the rural product
being shared among different families. With the family's
total product tending towards zero, it would hardly be
able to consume at all. In South India, from which plantation labour was drawn, conditions in the peasant sector
did not conform to the Lewis-type situation, in which marginal consumption exceeds the marginal product; output
and consumption levels were determined by events which
deprived entire farm families of livelihood. Contrary to
the model, consumption levels were not determined merely
or significantly by increases in the size of farm families, resulting in disguised unemployment or underemployment. The situation periodically was rather one of 'com-
munalized' destitution. The plantations drew their labour
not from a surrounding peasant economy, as the Lewis model
envisages, but from a completely different geopolitical
region in which conditions were abnormally depressed.
During the last quarter of the nineteenth century, when
in Sri Lanka the tea plantations were being established,
in all districts of Madras excepting Tanjore agricultural
wage rates declined markedly. The fall in living standards was even greater owing to a decline in the volume of
employment. (27)

A transfer of labour from the traditional economy to a
'capitalist' sector 'à la Lewis', was limited to a number
of urban enterprises engaged in processing activity and in
transport and other services. In Sri Lanka only in very
recent years has there been a transfer of indigenous
labour to the plantations and this was confined to the
rubber estates where the conditions of employment of such
labour differed from those of the classical plantation
labour force - the latter resided on the plantations, they
were controlled by kanganies, lacked mobility, and were an
enclave cut off from the surrounding economy and society.
Though working alongside Indian labour, the Sinhalese were
paid higher wages, like the Chinese labour which worked in
the Malaysian rubber plantations on a contract basis.
Where the Sinhalese could not be employed on these terms
they repudiated plantation employment.

From this conceptualization of the wage relation between the plantations and the peasant sector of South
India, from which plantation labour was drawn, I shall now
proceed to a discussion of the contrasting wage levels and
working conditions in the plantations and in the surround-

ing peasant sector. The discussion will draw mainly on
historical facts pertaining to Sri Lanka. Without entering into an assessment of relative returns in the two
sectors I shall point out the numerous factors which deterred the indigenous peasants from seeking employment on
the plantations. These included low and stagnant wages,
uncertainty about wage payments, the subjection to the
kanganies, and the extortion of traders in a situation of
insufficiently developed markets; and the harsh and arbitrary work regime including physical chastisement as a
means of enforcing work norms and discipline.

Plantation wages remained unchanged over long periods.
According to the Silver Currency Commission of 1894, they
had not increased during the eighteen years from 1876.
(28) T.N.Christie, a spokesman of the planters, stated in
evidence before the Indian Currency Committee of 1894:
'During the last 20 years, or last 24 years, ... the rate
of wages has not varied.' (29) Ludowyk suggests that the
wage rate had remained at 6d. a day for fifty years from
the 1840s, (30) though a Government Agent commenting in
1889 on distress in the Uda Dumbara district suggests a
wage rate of 8d. on the tea estates. A decline in real
wages resulted from a depreciation of the rupee in the
1880s and 1890s, and 'an inflation of considerable proportions'; prices of 'the necessaries of life' increased
by 20-50 per cent during 1873-4. (31) The rise in the
prices of food and clothing, which were mostly imported
from India, greatly influenced the cost of living of plantation labour. The development of the tea plantation
'took place against a background of a continuous depreciation of the exchange'. (32)

The living standards of plantation labour in Sri Lanka
were also affected by delays in food supplies from India,
due to crop failure and to interruptions in rail traffic
from Colombo to the plantation districts. Food prices in
Sri Lanka rose during famines of even average intensity in
India and traders then raised prices without restraint.
'They are ready enough to raise prices unnecessarily high
on the slightest excuse', wrote the Assistant Agent. (33)
In 1897, following a railway slip and an Indian famine, a
sharp rise in the prices of basic foodstuffs led virtually
to a riot by plantation labourers at Pundaloya bazaar,
which was checked by the 'energetic interference of Mr.
Curtis, the unofficial P.M. [Police Magistrate] with the
aid of a police sergeant and two constables sent from outside'. (34) 'Threatening disturbances' were reported from
Ramboda and Maturata, two other leading tea-planting
areas. The labour unrest resulting from such price increases was condoned privately by the Assistant Agent.

'I have ... very little sympathy with the boutique keepers, and shouldn't be sorry to see a few of them looted.
It is a good oriental custom which helps to regulate
trade, though it looks bad in official returns.' (35) Recurrent scarcity and price increases were aggravated by
false accounts maintained by traders of credit sales of
food and other provisions. In addition, the traders used
short measures, as the Government Agent noted with reference to 'several of the large rice stores at Padiyapelella'. (36)

> The cooly purchasers were being deprived of a consider-
> able portion of rice.... In three of the principal
> rice stores ... a 'striker' was used which ought by law
> to be round like a ruler, but which had a piece of iron
> attached to the lower side which projected into the
> measure and scooped over a fair allowance of rice each
> time.

In another case, a storekeeper at Kandepola, against whom
'there had been constant complaints of short issues from
his store', was convicted for 'having a bushel measure
considerably short of proper capacity'. (37)

Though these malpractices were fairly widespread, it
was not easy to proceed against errant traders. In
Padiyapelella, the rice merchants tried to bribe the
Mudaliyar with Rs 500 not to press charges, but the Assistant Agent had the false measures in his possession;
he wrote in his diary, 'I fancy there will be trouble for
the merchants.' At other times the problem was inadequate
police vigilance. In 1890 a European police officer who
was in Nuwera Eliya to test weights and measures had allegedly taken money from traders in complicity with the
local police sergeant. The Assistant Agent, though
'averse to "cases" in court against the Police', thought
the evidence good enough for a conviction. But to his
dismay the accused was acquitted. The facts of this case,
carefully described by the Assistant Agent, (38) illustrate the defenceless position of plantation labour vis-à-
vis the individual employer and also the whole phalanx of
social and political forces that were arraigned against
them. In adjudicating wage disputes the police magistrates themselves took the side of planters.

The low earnings of plantation labour were further
reduced by the extortions of the kangany. The paternalism
of the kangany system helped him to establish a stranglehold over the labourers. In the early decades of the
plantation system the kangany would even collect the wages
and distribute them to the labourers in their homes. The
labourers were as a rule in debt to the kangany, and no
proper accounts were made. Delays in wage payment - on

most estates wages were paid every two months - obliged
the labourers to borrow on the accumulating balance with
the employer, and the kangany usually withheld a whole
month's pay on account of the advance he had given. On
pay day they received only the second month's pay or part
of it - often no money at all. The extortions by the
kangany were an impediment to the supply of indigenous
labour to the plantations. 'What deters Sinhalese so
often from going to work on estates close to their homes
is the kangani system', an Assistant Agent explained in
1889. (39)

    They get advances from the estates on account of the
    kangani who charges them exorbitant rates of interest
    for such advances and keeps the account with the result
    that their pay goes to the kangani in the matter of
    'advances' etc. and they get nothing.

Malpractices of labour contractors were widespread in this
period. The Government Agent of Anuradhapura wrote in
1885 that 'so long as the labourers were promptly paid'
their re-employment on construction projects would be absolutely advantageous. (40)   Cheating and wage defaults
were likewise mentioned by the Agent for the North Western
Province in 1900. (41)

    I have told Mr. Kirkwood [the Chief Assistant Irriga-
    tion Engineer] that I am quite prepared to assist him
    with labour, but it is necessary that the villagers
    should be paid by responsible Government Officers for
    work done and they must not be left to the tender
    mercies of contractors who cannot work on a profit, on
    the rates allowed, without cheating their labourers.

On one Sinhalese-owned estate the labourers were also defrauded by what was virtually a truck system of payment.
(42)

    The managers have engaged in trade and keep boutiques
    at which they compel the coolies to deal, preventing
    them from dealing elsewhere by paying them pewter
    tokens to represent 25 cents but only accepted at a
    less value at the boutiques.

In another case two employees of a British firm (Messrs
Nowell & Co.) were prosecuted for 'cheating in regard to
coolies' pay and rice'. (43)

    Thus it was not wage labour which was resented but the
fraud and oppression which were inherent in the system of
labour relations. On the railways and the Public Works
Department, where the Sinhalese villagers found employment
from the beginning of this century if not before, employment conditions were closer to a capitalist labour market
than in the plantations. The Government Agent of the
North Western Province in 1901 ascribed the employment of

Sinhalese on the railways to the fact that 'the system on
which they work is more satisfactory as the villagers have
their own Kanganies, who do not cheat them as the former
contractors did'. (44) The agent was informed by the
railway engineers that the villagers 'turn out in large
numbers, but irregularly', and he was hopeful that the
'headmen will correct' this. (45) From the first decade
of this century the Sinhalese began to be employed in
large numbers on the low-country rubber estates but here
Superintendents dealt directly with the labourers, without
kanganies and other labour recruiters. (46)

> Much less confiding than the Tamils, they are keenly
> suspicious of the kanganies and recruiters, and have a
> rooted objection to go-betweens separating them from
> their superintendent. Proof of this is to be found in
> the fact that numerous Sinhalese are to be found on
> every estate where the manager speaks fluent Sinhalese.

Considerable discord prevailed between migrant Indian
labour and the villagers in the vicinity of plantations.
In the eyes of the villagers the plantation labourers represented an institution whose interests were basically in
conflict with those of the village economy. Village tanks
and pasture reserves had been sold to estates, paddy
fields and irrigation channels were silted up by the
cutting of estate roads, and straying cattle were shot on
estates. The wretched economic condition of the migrant
labourers and their supposed social inferiority increased
the alienation. In the 1880s and 1890s there were actual
clashes in the tea-growing areas of Nuwera Eliya. For
instance, in October 1889 a 'general fight' occurred in
the Padiyapellela bazaar, and Sinhalese boutiques were
looted by estate labourers. The Government Agent wrote:
'There were two factions in the bazaar - Tamil and Sinhalese and they are constantly fighting and leading the
coolies of the adjoining estate into mischief.' (47)
Where irrigation channels ran through the estate, the
villagers were denied access to these channels, apparently
to prevent thefts of estate produce. (48) There was a
complaint by villagers that when gathering fence sticks in
the Crown jungle they were molested by the labourers of
Medacumbura Estate. (49) The Government Agent in 1884
ordered the Gansabhawa (village council) not to try cases
in which estate labour were involved, owing to its inability to conduct inquiries in the Tamil language. This decision, the Colonial Secretary noted, 'is equivalent to
one that petty complaints ... against coolies are not
heard at all'. (50)

To round off this discussion I shall set out the experience of plantation employment of a group of villagers

from Walapane, whom the Assistant Agent had met during a
field circuit.   The Walapane district was one which the
British had wantonly devastated after an uprising in the
Uva province, and the paddy tax had been a further source
of distress.   The district had been in poverty for a
generation and the villagers whom the Assistant Agent met
were without work, but they would still not take up plantation employment.   The cold facts brought home to the
Assistant Agent provide an answer to the puzzle. (51)

Went on to Kurundu Oya.   I have met during this circuit
whether by accident or by design I cannot say, more
than my usual number of destitutes - villagers who have
lost all their lands and are now vagabonds in the same
district.   Their story is usually the same.   It is
somewhat as follows:-

Q.   Who are you?
A.   We are people of Walapane.
Q.   Why have you left your village?
A.   Because we have lost all our property.
Q.   How did it happen?
A.   We were allowed to run into arrears with our
     paddy tax for two or three years.   It was then
     called up all of a sudden.   No mercy was shown
     to us and all our property was sold.*
Q.   What are you doing now?
A.   We are in search of employment and means of
     livelihood.
Q.   Where are you going?
A.   Nowhere in particular.
Q.   Why do you not go and work on a tea or coffee
     estate?
A.   We have tried this, but never get anything for
     our work.   Our earnings were taken by the
     Kanganies 'for debts'....   It is 'debt', 'debt'
     always 'debt' with us....

  *   This is strictly true.   The people were allowed
to run into arrears because it was felt that the
[paddy] tax was such a heavy one.   Then a lenient form
of recovery was adopted - i.e., my plan of recovery by
degrees.   Then all of a sudden Government turned round,
reversed their previous decision and sold up the fields
wholesale.

Three years later the Assistant Agent made a similar comment, entitled 'Employment of Sinhalese on estates and the
railway': (52)

I wish to mention an interesting fact in connection
with this question as far as Walapane is concerned.
The people who leave their villages to work on estates
and the railway very rarely bring anything in the shape

of earnings back with them and generally return in
rags.

At about the beginning of this century, the demoralizing effect of indebtedness and delays in wage payments
made labour less responsive to wage payments, and even
attendance at work declined. 'To hold a pay-day at which
no money is actually handed over to the coolies', the
government came to realize, 'would be to run grave risk of
trouble, owing to the discontent which would result.' (53)
A commission of inquiry recommended a statutory pay day so
as to reduce the labourer's recourse to credit on the
basis of money which much of the time the planter owed
him. From 1908 planters were required to declare to the
Government Agent that wages were paid every month. The
reason for this intervention in plantation labour relations was explained by the Governor: (54)

> The payment once monthly must be real, not merely
> nominal.... Unless, however, steps be taken ... to
> insure that a monthly pay-day shall actually be held,
> and that on these occasions the balance of wages due
> shall really be tendered to the labourers, the old
> practice of paying cash to coolies once in two months
> only will, in my opinion, inevitably continue.

In the preceding decades a more serious aspect of the
labour situation on plantations had been the non-payment
of wages, which led to the promulgation of the Cooly Wages
Ordinance of 1884. In 1846 a correspondent from Colombo,
in a letter published in 'The Economist', referred to 'Malabar [estate] coolies, who are cheated and defrauded of
their wages by the European Superintendents to an extent
which few know of.' (55) Likewise Torrington stated in a
dispatch to Lord Grey in 1848, 'Much of the difficulties
[regarding plantation labour in Sri Lanka] must be attributed to the natural reluctance of coolies to return to
estates on which they have been irregularly paid, and that
a portion of the crops will be lost upon some few of the
estates, owing to the refusal of coolies to work until the
arrears long due to them have been settled.' (56) Official concern over this and other matters arose from a possibility that the conduct of individual planters might
jeopardize labour recruitment to the plantations. Migration at this time had fallen off, 'the cause apparently
being the bad name which Ceylon has got through the many
instances in which coolies had lost their wages'. (57)

Before discussing the extent or frequency of wage defaults, as revealed by the Cooly Wages Ordinance, I must
refer briefly to the earlier history of wage labour,
during the first years of British rule. The villager even
at this time does not seem to have lacked a positive re-

sponse to monetary incentives, but the stark truth was
that those who were hired were not paid. One recorded
complaint was in 1815, by the inhabitants of the Three
Korles, which John D'oyly confirmed. 'They suffer from
our People [i.e. British officials] at Ruanwella.' The
grievances were (58)

> that the Country People coming to Ruanwella to purchase
> or sell commodities in the Bazaar have been frequently
> pressed as Coolies and carried Burthens without re-
> ceiving any pay. That some coolies employed in Govern-
> ment works at Ruanwella have not received the full pay
> which is due to them.

Later, the Kandyan Sinhalese undertook the felling and
clearing of forests for the planters, and till the early
1840s low-country Sinhalese migrated seasonally to work on
coffee plantations. As a rule, they performed specific
jobs on a contract or piece-work basis, (59) but avoided
joining the regular workforce. In 1847, Sir Emerson
Tennent inquired into this matter by means of a question-
naire sent out to the police and the magistrates in the
Central Province. The results of his inquiry, conveyed by
him to Lord Russell, make the planters' labour problems
easier to understand than do most sociological constructs
based on the mores and personality traits of people or
their alleged indifference to money. The Superintendent
of Police in Kandy, Colepepper, denied that the Sinhalese
were work-shy but admitted they were reluctant to work on
plantations. This, he said, was not without a reason.
(60)

> I have been informed even this season [in 1847] some
> Estates have applied to them [native villagers] with
> success. The villagers demand only to be paid at the
> end of the day and not once a week. The villagers do
> this from experience, most of them having been employed
> at the opening of Estates and having suffered the same
> treatment and disappointment to which the Malabar
> labourers have been reduced.

The Police Magistrate of Gampola had a similar tale:
'Several Headmen of this District tell me that the villagers have so often been duped and cheated out of their
due that some have given up work and others daily become
more averse to work on the Estates.' (61)   Governor
Torrington in 1848 agreed with this view. Many of the
difficulties of labour were due 'to the reluctance of
coolies to return to estates, in which they have been irregularly paid ... [and] their refusal to work until the
arrears long due have been settled'. Commenting on Colepepper's report, Ludowyk says, 'In other words they [the
labourers] were paid no wages and were beaten for their
impudence in demanding them.' (62)

The question of indigenous labour on estates has been briefly commented on by Michael Roberts. 'Many planters', he wrote, 'did not pay the wages regularly or withheld them altogether - a feature that was most common in 1847-8 when the coffee industry had slipped into a serious depression.' (63) There is some ambivalence in his view. The Kandyans, while resenting the 'treatment meted out to the labourers' in the 1840s, 'regarded estate-work as degrading [and this] contributed to their antipathy to such work'. He then asserts: 'In the final analysis their access to land must have been the crucial factor.' In Part II of his article he further argues that from the 1850s the treatment of plantation labour in Sri Lanka 'was satisfactory and certainly much improved'. The villagers' alleged dislike of estate work because of its 'degrading' nature and the significance of caste, as against monetary inducements, are matters on which I shall have something to say later. Roberts enumerates several factors which underlay their attitude to plantation employment, some of which are in keeping with my analysis. Yet, he fails to emphasize that it was the non-payment of wages which made the Sinhalese peasant stop working on plantations. This was the 'crucial factor' and not access to land, which diminished progressively from the 1840s, along with a decline in irrigation facilities. His statement that the wage defaults were a feature only before the 1850s, after which the situation 'was satisfactory and certainly much improved', is not borne out. The available evidence is that long after the 1850s the planters continued to default on wage payments.

Wage defaults were a serious drawback of plantation employment in this period. As mentioned already, by the 1880s this had become a concern to government which in 1884 enacted the Cooly Wages Ordinance. The number of estates that had not paid wages, the periods of default or the sums involved are not known in detail. According to the quarterly returns made by planters under the ordinance, a good number of estates were in default. For the last three quarters of 1884, out of 621 wage returns there was not one which showed that wages had been 'promptly paid'. For the second quarter of that year, one third of 199 estates that submitted returns had not paid wages for a period of three to six months, and eight estates were in arrears for over nine months. For the third quarter, 41 per cent of the estates which sent returns were in arrears for three to six months and in the last quarter of that year 46 per cent were in default for a similar period.

The information on unpaid wages presented on Table 9.1 is the result of a less than complete search of the avail-

TABLE 9.1 Arrears of pay of plantation workers, 1884-6. Compiled from the official diaries of the AGA for Nuwara Eliya

Date of AGA's diary entry	Name of estate	Wages not paid since	Period for which wages were unpaid at the time of scrutiny of quarterly returns	Remarks of Assistant Government Agent
5 July 1884	Stain	June 1883	12 months	–
	Gracelyn	May 1883	13 months	–
7 July 1884	Brookside	Jan. 1883	18 months	'Mr. Moorhouse states that he is throwing up the Estate to the Mortgagees. The 3 months' full pay will in this case be equivalent to a full settlement for 6 months. For the rest of the arrears the coolies will I believe be without a means of recovery.'
18 July 1884	Stafford	Sept.1883	10½ months	–
16 Oct. 1884	Oliphant	Aug. 1884	2½ months	'This Estate at the end of the previous quarter showed one of the worst returns and the clearance of arrears ... has only been effected in consequence of anticipation of possible action.'
1 Nov. 1884	Clarendon	June 1882	2½ years	–
28 Nov. 1884	Gomalia	Nov. 1881	1 year &	'The non payment of wages during this period was not mentioned in the Wages Return. The Estate could not
		June 1883	7 months	produce the Accounts later than March 1882. Mr. Moorhouse's affairs /he had a quarter share of the

TABLE 9.1 (continued)

Date of AGA's diary entry	Name of estate	Wages not paid since	Period for which wages were unpaid at the time of scrutiny of quarterly returns	Remarks of Assistant Government Agent
				Estate] are in a state of inextricable confusion. He can give no definite information about the Gomalia wages beyond saying that they are in the same state as those of Waldemar.... That is no wages were paid of the period Nov. 1881 to June 1883.'
24 July 1885	Rossiter			'The Rossiter coolies are still without a settlement of wages due to them.'
18 May 1886	Mahakelay 'and other Estates of Mr. Smith'	Oct. 1885	7½ months	—
20 July 1886	Kadawatte; Ella-mule; Lamaliera; Caldeonia; Dim-bulle; St John's; Uda Pussellawa; Yoxford; Dim-bulla; Kadawatte Uda P.		10 months 'very much in arrears to other [?] coolies'	'Reported to G.A.' 'Found that a large no. of estates in the district were not in my lists. They have not sent in returns for a long time and therefore /had/ been struck off. On my insisting that returns should be sent in for them I found that several /those mentioned/ were very much in arrears to other coolies.'

29 July 1886			'The coolies sued and obtained judgment in Dec. 1885 for wages due from Oct. 1884-June 1885. In the meantime they [the owners] have allowed the arrears to run several months again.'
8 July 1887	Ederapola	Sept.1886	9 months	'For the recovery of ... [their wages] the coolies have taken a case in the Avissawella Court. The plaint is for the recovery of wages since 1886. ... The Superintendent in his return for the Quarter ending 31 March last declared that no wages whatever were due on 31 March 1887.'
30 Aug. 1886	Hazelwood Ferryland		9 months	'Reported the wages in Hazelwood and Ferryland - owned by Mr. Rossiter as being in my opinion in jeopardy. Nine months wages are due.... Mr. Rossiter's arrangements to pay them [the labourers] as reported are not I consider satisfactory. Mr. Rossiter has already had 2 cases instituted against him for similar arrears, i.e. Lawston and Sommer-ville, in both of which the estates were sold.'

able records. In 1886 and 1887 the Assistant Agent noted
the names of some of the defaulting estates, with related
particulars, for the period 1884-6. The scope of this
information varied considerably between districts and over
different periods, according to the thoroughness with
which the officials were able, or were inclined, to carry
out their duties under the ordinance. Thus the instances
of non-payment which came to the notice of the Assistant
Agent, and were recorded in his Diaries, do not reflect
the full extent of wage defaults. The provincial admin-
instration could not cope with the work relating to wage
inquiries under the ordinance. In the Nuwera Eliya district the Assistant Agent excluded estates whose period of
arrears was less than six months. (64) Not all estates
submitted returns regularly. Some others, serious in default, were not in his records. (65)

> Found out that a large number of estates in the dis-
> trict was not in my lists. They have not sent in
> returns for a long time and [have] therefore been
> struck off. On my insisting that returns should be
> sent in for them I found that several were very much
> in arrears.

The Cooly Wages Ordinance was a far-reaching piece of
legislation compared with the Assam Regulations in India
whose aim was similar, but there were hindrances to imple-
menting it. One reason, already mentioned, was administrative bottlenecks which prevented proper checking of the
quarterly wage returns, probing likely cases of unpaid
wages, and instituting legal proceedings; there were even
delays in disbursing to labourers the money recovered from
the estates. 'There is much extra work in connection with
[quarterly labour] returns.' (66) At first, estates were
allowed a grace period of six months, after which the
Agent would instruct his Assistant to induce the Estate
Manager to come to a settlement quickly. (67) 'The planters [thus] felt safe from enquiry if they allow wages to
run into arrears provided 6 months were not exceeded.'
(68) The period for which arrears could accumulate without resulting in a special inquiry was later reduced to
four months 'as it is not desirable that the impression
should be allowed that the government will not notice
arrears unless they extend beyond six months'. (69) But
this encouraged the planters to shorten the period of
default or even falsify the wage returns. The number of
estates showing arrears beyond the period which invited
action then declined, with an almost corresponding increase in those where wages had run into arrears up to
the end of that period.

The information given in the wage returns was question-

able. Many plantations at this time were managed directly
by the proprietors, who had a scant regard for truth and
justice; a compulsion to pay labourers for work done
seemed to them a strange injunction. The planters would
even deceive the officials. In one instance, 'the Superintendent in his return for the quarter ending 31 March
last /1889/ declared that no wages were due on 31 March
1877' whereas the labourers had last been paid in February
1876 and 'perhaps not in full'. (70) In 1898 the Superintendent of an estate in the Kegalle district sought
police protection against his labourers. The Assistant
Agent who went to his aid found the real cause of the com-
motion: 'The coolies had not been paid for some months
and on receiving their pay today they objected apparently
to the amount of the deductions.' (71) On another estate
workers who had not been paid for seven months had 'de-
tained a large amount of /cinnamon/ bark (some 12,000
lbs.)' which on intervention by the Assistant Agent they
released for sale. The Superintendent promised to use the
proceeds to settle the arrears of wages, but after the
sale disregarded his pledge. (72) The Government Agent
who filed proceedings against him for cheating observed
ruefully, 'I doubt - disgraceful as his conduct had been -
whether it will fall within the definition of cheating in
the code.' (73)

The ineffectiveness of the ordinance was due, secondly,
to the plantation labourers being incapable of taking
legal measures to defend their interests during the prescribed time when a wage claim was actionable in court.
The kanganies of Naltakelly estate 'should enter an action
before the end of the present month', wrote the Assistant
Agent. 'They have already lost valuable time by not
taking the remedy open to them.' (74) Moreover, the
labourers lacked proper legal advice. A provision under
the ordinance for a proctor to watch their interests does
not seem to have been carried out. The Assistant Agent
drew attention to this lapse, in regard to overdue wages
on the Nattekelly and St Coombs estates: 'The kanganies
and coolies might have entered the case themselves and
have lost by not doing so. Mr. Smith says that they got
into the hands of outdoor proctors who took payment from
them for services and did nothing for them.' (75) And two
months later: 'Suggested to the G.A. that Government
should direct a proctor to watch the interests of the
coolies as provided by the Ordinance 16 of 1884.' (76)
There is no trace in the Diaries of the Agents when or
whether this requirement was fulfilled.

Third, the courts made a defective ordinance even more
difficult to enforce. The courts began insisting on -

apart from the names of unpaid workers - the sums due, and
proof of employment on the estate. This information could
only be had from the estate Superintendents. 'Supposing
as is possible the Superintendent of the Estate refused to
furnish [this information] I cannot force him to', wrote
the Assistant Agent, 'nor can I summon the kanganies and
coolies before me to examine them on this point.' (77)
Since neither workers nor kanganies kept a record of their
wages in a form that the courts would not dispute, access
to the estate check roll was needed. But the planters had
no legal obligation to furnish it. Some would not even
submit the quarterly returns of wages under the ordinance;
two estates refused saying that the labour on their estates was paid daily and not monthly. (78)   In one instance the Assistant Agent explained, (79)

> The matter is a serious one ... as there are I believe
> large arrears of wages due on the estate.... Owing,
> however, to the refusal of the Court to entertain the
> case without a statement of the names of the coolies
> and the sums due to them being furnished and the ab-
> sence of any means of gathering this statement, this
> matter has remained a status quo for some months and
> will probably remain so - until the law is altered.

The ordinance by not putting teeth into its own implementation virtually blocked all proceedings under it, and
estates continued to default.

The courts by their insistence on particulars of non-
payment before proceedings were begun placed an undue
burden on the Crown. 'It appears to me', wrote the Assistant Agent, (80)

> that where the Attorney General is the plaintiff all
> that is necessary is to give the total number of
> coolies and an appropriate estimate of the total due.
> The Court then issues processes and can force the
> Superintendent to appear with his check-roll and from
> this determine how much really is due and decide ac-
> cordingly. Otherwise a dishonest or obstructive pro-
> prietor or Superintendent can always prevent any pro-
> ceedings being instituted by the Attorney General or
> at any rate delay them until the time when the 'first
> charge' on the estate shall have been prescribed.

One magistrate began insisting that the Government Agent
of the province or the Assistant Agent of the district
should be present when planters were being prosecuted even
for not submitting a quarterly return on wages. 'Hitherto
it has been the custom for the clerk in charge of those
returns to do this but Mr. Northmore [the Magistrate] told
that the return might have been lost between the G.A. or
A.G.A.' (81)   The Assistant Agent felt this ruling by the

magistrate to be ludicrous. 'He might as well insist on
the attendance of the postal authorities or the peon who
brings the letters to prove the non-delivery of the
packet.' (82) The Colonial Secretary saw the anomaly:
'He is strictly in his legal right but he reduces the
Ordinance to an absurdity.' (83)

   The courts, apart from making a successful prosecution
difficult, imposed only nominal fines. The lax treatment
of planters in court was a recurring complaint of one
Assistant Agent. 'A planter was fined one rupee only for
failing to send in his cooly returns by Mr. Wartmore because it was his first offence. It is of little use
entering prosecutions in such cases if this is all the
punishment inflicted.' (84) Subsequently, when the Police
Magistrate had again imposed a fine of R. 1, the Assistant
Agent wrote: (85)

   It is, as I have remarked before, of very little use my
   insisting on these returns if such ridiculously small
   fines are to be inflicted on conviction - and what
   makes matters worse in this particular instance is that
   I had no less than four cases against one [Estate]
   Superintendent, so that he could hardly plead that it
   was his first offence.

Another planter, convicted for the fifth time, was fined
just Rs 25. (86)

   The partisan nature of colonial institutions was sharply felt in the sphere of labour relations. Planter-
labourer relations in Sri Lanka, observed Ludowyk, were
(87)

   weighed against the unfortunate wage slave in the open
   market. He now had the full force of the law invoked
   against him by the planter who could, in rare cases,
   even be both accuser and judge.... The coolie who
   dared betake himself from the estate when he was ill-
   treated would find himself before a friend, or crony of
   his employer and suffer accordingly for his temerity in
   breaking the law.

In Mauritius, the magistrates and police were hostile to
plantation labour. Until 1878 the vagrant laws were enforced so as to compel old immigrants to renew their indentures. These vagrant hunts involved the arrest of
labourers spuriously declared to be vagrants. (88)

   In Sri Lanka during the rise of the coffee plantations,
the government officials themselves had a business interest in the plantation economy, which affected their impartiality in disputes between the planters and the villagers and between the planters and plantation labour. In
such disputes, observed George Ackland in 1849 in evidence
before a committee of the House of Commons, 'the European

will push his interests with a degree of impunity that the
native will not', and the European official to whom the
villager could present his grievances was, almost invariably, a planter himself. (89)   (Ackland was connected with
coffee planting from 1834 and had managed thirty-four estates.) A ruling by the Secretary of State for the Colonies in 1844 that civil servants who already held investments should either dispose of them or retire (90) did not
immediately apply to all public servants. The order did
not extend to judges of the Supreme Court, officers of the
Customs, surveyors, military officers - many of whom possessed land and cultivated coffee. (91)   The Governor,
when enforcing the order, found himself 'in opposition to
the individual interests of all those who ought to advise
and assist him'. (92) A few years later the prohibition
was applied to all government officials. This removed the
private interests of government officials, though it
cannot be assumed, as Ludowyk does (op.cit., p.7) that
there was then a fundamental change in the relationship
between them and the planters.

In the West Indies, until the West India Committee was
set up at the end of the eighteenth century, sharp differences in interest and outlook prevailed between the planting and the mercantile interests and between the resident
planters and the absentee planters, (93) whereas in Malaysia, Sri Lanka and India from the outset there were among
the European community close bonds of association and
interests. (94) An extraordinary degree of cohesion between commerce and plantation enterprise was reflected in
the development and functioning of the managing agency
system which is discussed in later chapters. Social differences generally prevailed among planters, merchants and
officials as reflected in their different clubs and hospital wards. For instance, the Colombo Sports Club drew
its membership from the merchant class, whom the planters
and administrative personnel viewed with some disdain.
The planters had their own clubs in the provinces, and in
Colombo they and the administrators belonged to the
Queen's Club. In spite of these social differences the
Europeans in general conformed in their attitude towards
the native.

A few provincial officials tried to mediate impartially
between European and indigenous interests, but they had
little impact on the colonial order. They could hardly
deal with planters who defied the law, and could do
nothing about court decisions that were blatantly prejudicial to plantation labour. Furthermore, the intervention of the colonial government did not necessarily
arise from a concern for the rights of non-Europeans. As

in the case of the Cooly Wages Ordinance, such intervention served to protect the long-run interests of the
planting community from the intemperate actions of individual planters. Sometimes the partisan feelings of a
single official tilted the scales in favour of the planters. A notable case was the administering of the Forest
Ordinance in the Nuwara Eliya district during 1889 and
1890. The proper management of Crown forests had become
important in those years, owing to the demand for firewood
by tea factories and the railway. But the head of the
Forest Department was conniving with the planters. He
'had on more than one occasion given planters permission
to cut trees and in one instance after I had expressly
refused this', wrote the Assistant Agent. (95) The Assistant Agent reported to the Government Agent: 'He
denied having done so, but I have ascertained for a fact
that he ... gave Mr. Tunbridge of Preston [estate] permission to cut down trees in the jungle.' (96) Later he
allowed another planter to fell timber without a permit
and before royalty was paid. (97) Forest rangers were
harassed and threatened with dismissal for bringing to
notice instances of illicit felling 'over and over again'.
(98) 'It was due to information from these patrolmen that
the illicit felling at Gonapitiya (Mr Steuart) and at
Morgavilla (Mr Bagot) was discovered. It was due to them
that extensive encroachments were discovered at Dutron-
field and at St John's estates.' (99) Even those comply-
ing with the Assistant Agent's instructions were intimi-
dated. (100)
     The planters had almost sovereign power in their dis-
tricts. Two labourers from a tea estate were once sentenced to a whipping for attempting to crimp labour, and
had the word 'crimp' written in tar across their clothes.
The planter told the Assistant Government Agent that this
was how he invariably dealt with 'coolies'. The Assistant
Agent admonished him against the use of such methods. 'I
felt bound to point out that ... there were humble individuals called magistrates, told off [sic] by Government to
try such cases, and so I fined him Rs. 20 for each offence. I shall be amused to see what is the verdict on
my verdict.' (101) The minor officials were treated by
the planters with impunity. In a case of illicit felling
of Crown timber by a planter, the Assistant Agent noted:
(102)
     He [the planter] seems to have grossly insulted the
     Fiscal's Officer and one of my clerks whom I sent out
     to point out the property. Among other things he made
     them take off their boots before he would allow them
     to enter the house - although they were dressed in
     European costume.

On another occasion the planter threatened the Fiscal's
messenger with physical injury. 'Mr. Bagot had fired a
couple of shots at or near him and had ordered his dogs
to be slipped at him while he was trying lately to serve
a summons on him.' (103)
   In court cases where planters and other Europeans were
on trial the impartiality of the judiciary was open to
question. The implementation of the Cooly Wages Ordinance, it has already been shown, was virtually thwarted
by the magistrates, and in the rare event of a successful
prosecution the sentences imposed on planters were so in-
ordinately light that the effort of prosecuting them
seemed hardly worthwhile. Court decisions generally condoned breaches of the law by planters. For the illegal
cutting of a channel through Crown forest, a planter 'was
mulcted in Rs. 8.45 and costs of suit', the Assistant
Agent noted facetiously. 'If this judgment is to stand,
Mr. Bagot has got off very cleaply as our claim was for
Rs. 3,000 odd. The District Court seems to have fixed an
arbitrary price.' (104) Magistrates were clearly reluctant to convict Europeans. A planter accused of assault-
ing a Fiscal's peon was acquitted in the police court
merely on his own evidence. The Assistant Agent commented: 'Mr. Northmore [the Police Magistrate] prefer[red]
to believe Mr. Bagot instead of the peon. Mr. Northmore
held the charge to be entirely false and, if this is so
[the Assistant Agent wrote sarcastically] the peon should
now be put on trial for perjury.' (105) In the case of
the police officer accused of extortion (referred to
earlier), the Assistant Agent wrote: (106)
   I see by the Newspaper that the man has got off - a
   gross miscarriage of justice, and what makes it worse
   is that the unfortunate P. [Police] Sergt. who acted as
   Moore's go-between has been dismissed after making a
   clean break of it. Now I hope the Inspector will be
   dismissed, for though he has been acquitted of the
   charge of bribery, it was grossly irregular to make a
   wholesale seizure of nearly all the weights and
   measures in the town, without authority and so making
   it possible for the bribery to be carried out. For
   that there was bribery is admitted, only he seems to
   have been able to make the jury believe that it was the
   Sergt. who was bribed and not himself.
As summed up by an official report in Assam in 1900, (105)
   Europeans being administrators of justice in all disputes between Europeans, planters and labourers, it was
   impossible for them to be altogether uninfluenced by
   their natural feelings towards their fellow countrymen.
   ... There is an undoubted tendency among magistrates

in Assam to inflict severe sentences in cases in which
coolies are charged with committing offences against
their employers and to impose light, and somewhat inadequate punishment, upon employers when they are convicted of offences against labourers.

In India after the Mutiny most of the magistrates and
the English press were uncompromisingly for the planters.
For instance, when one of them had sadistically beaten up
his goatherd and shot him dead, the Calcutta press
clamoured for clemency. (108) In another instance there
was reluctance to convict a planter who had beaten a
labourer to death. 'Judging from experience of such
cases', the Commissioner of Assam stated, (109)

a conviction is not very probable. In Assam the life
of a coolie hangs at best by a slender thread; with a
climate that so saps his vitality, it unfortunately
takes very little to kill him; and the shock of such
a flogging as would elsewhere be borne with impunity
might prove fatal.

The planter was allowed bail, and later sentenced to
prison for one year and fined Rs 500 by a jury composed of
planters. Plantation labourers in Assam were subjected to
'cold-blooded revolting cruelty'. They were beaten and
kicked, a punishment from which female labourers were not
exempt. Similar treatment of the labourers was mentioned
by a Captain Lamb after inspecting the gardens of the
Assam Tea Company. (110)

Found 7 men in one of them, who had the marks of having
been unmercifully beaten with a cane on their backs.
They state that short rations had induced them to abscond, and about a fortnight ago, they had been brought
back to the garden, and the assistant in charge of it
had tied them up and given each of them a severe
beating.... From further enquiries, I gather that
often these unfortunate men had had their backs cut to
pieces with a cane, oil and salt had been rubbed into
their wounds.

In lower Bengal indigo production which preceded the development of tea was carried out by 'a rather rough set of
planters' including some who had operated slave labour in
America. (111)

I have up till now explained mainly in the context of
Sri Lanka the gross abuses of the planters in their treatment of wage labour - low wages, irregularity and default
of wage payments, and coercion and physical cruelty.
These abuses of a largely economic origin are common
enough in capital-labour relations of a primitive character. However, the low wage structure which came to be established in tropical regions was not exclusively an eco-

nomic phenomenon. The pressing down of wages and living
standards almost to limits beyond which labourers could
not live was accomplished through a broader process connected with the political domination of the coloured races
by European colonizers. There was also a certain rationalization of the prevalent system of labour relations by
beliefs about the indolence of the 'native' and his inability to adjust himself to a commercial economy. The
supporting ideology of cheap labour was linked with the
organization of the world economy on colour lines. Even
today North-South is conterminous with white-coloured. In
this division between 'white' capital and 'coloured'
labour and what seemed to be an acceptance of the situation by the latter, racial feelings were a strong current.
   A discussion of the impact of such ethnic attitudes on
the labour relations in the plantation system requires a
brief reference to racism as a specific historical phenomenon connected with the colonization and exploitation of
what was to become the underdeveloped world. Racism, involving claims of superiority based on physical attributes, especially lightness of skin, though prevalent in
earlier human societies, was either of a mild form or was
compounded largely of ethnocentrism and religious bigotry,
as in the case of Portugal and Spain. After an inflow of
African slaves into Portugal from about the 1450s, there
was racial intermingling between them, resulting in the
Negroid features of the Portuguese that are even now apparent. (112) In this period the mixing of races extended
from Spain and Portugal to Italy. The English, before
they began to profit from the slave trade, had themselves
been free from racist feelings. The unfavourable portrayal of Moors in Elizabethan and Jacobean masques can
scarcely be compared with the demoralizing social disabilities which were later imposed on the coloured races.
Moors were 'evil' because their skins were of the devil's
colour. Flirtations between black and white boys and
girls were acceptable episodes in English poems and plays
of the early seventeenth century. (113)
   The first contacts of the Europeans with coloured
people had no rationalization of innate human inferiority.
The Portuguese - the earliest European colonizers - did
not at this time develop any racial feelings against their
captives. The colonization of Goa soon after 1498 was effected, wrote L.S.S.O'Malley, 'not so much by immigration
as by marriage with Indian women. There was no colour bar
and the children of mixed marriage were under no stigma of
inferiority'. (114) In Sri Lanka, too, the Portuguese
intermarried freely with the indigenous people. In their
forays on the African coast, the Portuguese had encounter-

ed Moors who were not as good fighters as they were themselves. But the 'superiority' which the Portuguese
evinced arose from their 'Christianity', not from their
'whiteness'. Christian ideology tended to hold racial
antagonism in check. The Church drew Africans into its
fold, and segregation or 'cultural parallelism', if it
existed, was not put to any commercial use. The equality
of men which the Church recognized also extended to their
economic rights.

Religious influence in other instances, too, controlled
racial antagonism as in the early colonization of New
Zealand. The missionaries safeguarded the Maoris from
despoliation of their lands by European settlers. They
often acted as witnesses in land transfers, and the Maoris
respected the impartiality of the Church. The confidence
in the missionaries was noted by Marsden in 1815. 'During
the wars which were to follow the Maoris, though they
might destroy the houses of a settlement, respected the
Churches and the houses of the missionaries.' (115) In
the transfer of Maori lands, when the transaction had not
been explained to the rightful owners, the missionaries
declined to sign as witnesses. In later years when Maori
lands were being fraudulently taken, the missionaries
began to doubt the moral aspects of colonization. They
felt 'that the needs of many of the colonists, professing
Christians though they were, would appear inconsistent
with the doctrine and the precepts of Christianity'. (116)
At this stage the influence of the missionaries waned, and
they were considered an obstacle to European interests.
In the colonization of Australia a similar situation
arose, when the 'lower-class whites deliberately undermined the missionary efforts' on behalf of the aborigines.
(117)

Racism in its modern form was a specific historical
phenomenon, connected with the economic development of the
New World based on slave labour. Slavery itself, in its
earlier phases, was different from that which came to be
practised later. The use of slaves as a source of commercial profit was exceptional, even on the agricultural
estates of the Dahomean kings. Slaves enjoyed social
mobility. In the kingdom of Benin in coastal Nigeria,
slaves were permitted to earn enough to buy their freedom,
and in Dahomey, Ashanti and the Niger delta they commonly
achieved free status through adoption by their masters.
Among the Ashanti the slaves could marry free people, and
they owned property as well as other slaves. African
slaves who were brought into Spain and Portugal in the
fifteenth century had the protection of the state and the
Church, and their descendants were socially absorbed into

the general population. In the Islamic countries, a slave
was like a servant or a personal valet - the Khalif Ali
sat for meals with his slaves. Debt slavery as existed in
Malaysia was a system whereby a man pledged himself, like
mortgaging his land or leaving goods in pawn. Many of
these practices replicated usages regarding slaves which
developed out of the evolution of ancient slavery under
the Romans. In these instances, the treatment of slaves
was relatively humane. Above all, the slaves did not
inherit a lasting disability like original sin. There was
no institutionalized stigma which removed them outside the
pale of human society.

The traffic in slaves to supply the plantations in
America changed the social character of slavery. The
first Negroes who landed at Jamestown in 1619 had shared
the status of indentured white servants. But within fifty
years of this date the condition of the Negro was one of
institutionalized slavery and black-white relations had
changed. The stages of this progression have been sketched by Meir and Rudwick. (118) In 1630 a white man was
sentenced to a whipping for having sexual relations with a
black woman, and a decade later there was discrimination
in the punishments meted out to three runaway slaves. Two
of them who were whites were sentenced to four years of
servitude but the other, a black, to servitude for life.
By 1640 black servants in Virginia began to suffer legal
disabilities in relation to white bondsmen; a relaxation
of the terms of indenture specially excluded Negroes. In
1643 black female servants over 16 were included among the
tithables. Negroes were now treated as 'property', and
listed in estate inventories as more valuable than white
servants. From the early 1650s the terms of sale of black
servants specified life servitude which their offspring
would inherit. In the 1660s a rudimentary slave code was
enacted, and in 1667 Negro servitude was acknowledged by a
decree so that baptism and conversion to Christianity did
not alter the status of a slave.

After the replacement of the white servants by Negroes
the status of the former began to improve. For deserving
cases the term of binding was reduced from the usual five
years, and the master was expected to assist these 'useful
men' in other ways. (119) As the social condition of
white labour improved, the position of the Negroes grew
steadily worse; it was seemingly a peculiar kind of compensatory balancing mechanism by which the total benefits
to the employers from white and black labour remained
intact. The first Negro immigrants were mostly indentured
servants; but later a slave code gave legal recognition
to their social disabilities. Occasional revolts by Ne-

groes led to greater repression, and by the second decade
of the eighteenth century slavery was institutionalized.
Though the great majority of whites were still relatively
poor, a social superiority of the whites came to be explicitly recognized. White women who 'to the disgrace of
our nation do intermarry with Negro slaves', it was decreed, 'shall serve the master of such slaves during the
life of her husband';   and the children of such unions
became slaves like their fathers. (120)   The Negro was
now forbidden to own or carry arms and was denied the
right of assembly;   he could not leave his owner's plantation without permission;   for striking a white the punishment was forty lashes, though a master was free to kill a
slave. (121)

A correlated aspect of the economic use of slave labour
was the moral justification which was developed. Slavery,
in the context of the American plantations, was seen as a
historically progressive institution. The enslaving of
the Negroes, it was urged, raised them from savagery and
they were better off in a Christian land - this, despite
Thomas Ashley's view that if the Negroes benefited from
American slavery it should be left to them to make the
choice. (122) The slave raiders in their work invoked
religion. And in this context it has to be said that
religion and not patriotism turned out to be the last
refuge of the scoundrel. The flag ship of Hawkins in
1563, which led a convoy of vessels loaded with African
slaves for the West Indies, was called Jesus. (123) The
Portuguese in this period baptized their captives before
enslaving them. (124) The tobacco planters of Virginia in
the eighteenth century built places of worship for slaves
on the plantations. In New England, slaves were admitted
into the Congregationalist Church, though they could sit
only in the rear section of the gallery.

However, religious conversion was not allowed to affect
the economic value of the slaves or to improve their position in society. An earlier law against enslaving 'christian servants' including Negroes who were baptized was
annulled in Virginia in 1667. Baptism, it was decreed,
'doth not alter the conditions of the person as to his
bondage or freedom'. The church services held out salvation only to those who obeyed their masters, with no
claims to social justice on the ground of professing a
common Christian faith. (125)

Many slaves in the U.S. retreated into a compensatory
other worldliness;   for them Christianity served the
function it had so well served for the slaves among
whom it first spread in the Roman Empire. Christian
doctrines exalted the meek and the lowly, making a

virtue of accepting without resistance the persecution
that the slaves were forced to endure.
Unlike the proselytizing zeal of the Church before this
time, religion gave the planters a certain control over
their slaves.

With the commercialization of slavery in the eighteenth
century racism assumed a new form, which was later to
become widespread as the European nations extended their
dominion abroad. 'The Western [i.e. West European] strain
of the virus had eclipsed all others in importance', wrote
Pierre L. van der Berghe. (126) The pervasiveness and
intensity of racist feelings from then onwards were 'not
even remotely approached by any previous cultural tradition'. (127) He might have added, without detracting from
reality, that the virulence of the virus was unsurpassed.
Though slavery was later abolished, racism, its offshoot,
continued to affect labour and indeed all sections of
people under European domination. And like slavery racism
came also to be supported by a complex mythology and ideology, with its 'familiar themes of grown up childishness,
civilizing mission, atavistic savagery and arrested evolution'. (128) A certain psychological mechanism was needed
to justify the jettisoning of the ancient idea of the
fundamental equality of human beings. All this, of
course, does not exclude the discrimination against various gradations of whiteness considered to be inferior;
such was the case with the mixed populations, the poor
whites of South Africa, the Puerto Ricans of the USA and
the Irish in the UK. It is to this generalized form of
exploitation of and discrimination against so-called
'free' wage labour, so often as not laced with ethnic
overtones, that I now turn.

When after the abolition of slavery European investors
in colonial lands had to employ free labour, the same ideology which had governed the treatment of Negroes was
used, bereft of religious pretensions, to explain and
justify the cheap labour policies and the recruitment and
management practices which verged on semi-servitude. On
the plantations of Asia and Africa there emerged, just as
with the presence of the Negro in the New World, a sharp
ethnic separation between employers and employees, circumscribed by a 'dominant-dependent' relation representing
the basic division of the world into economically unequal
segments. Notions regarding the indolence of the 'native'
and his unresponsiveness to material reward, which were
advanced by colonial administrators and by planters and
mine-owners faced with labour shortages, soon crystallized
into a system of thought. That coloured labour is content
with low wages was a view expressed at different times by

both employers and colonial governments.   For example,
Ludowyk refers to an English planter who said the high
rate of wages in the 1840s was 'proved by the circumstances that a labourer in Ceylon can live on one-third of his
pay, and save two-thirds'.   An English visitor to Sri
Lanka in about 1890 wrote of the good fortune of the Tamil
cooly 'whose pay of sixpence a day [which had not gone up
since the 1840s] is so enormous that he can afford to
dress his children in this astonishing way (i.e. with
silver rings on their toes, etc.)'. (129)   The stereotyped
(and extremely profitable) image of coloured labour was
comparable to that which had developed much earlier in
Europe and America, where compulsion and propaganda, respectively, played their part in the creation of a factory
labour force.

A growing impatience with labour and their supposed indifference to work was felt by the employer class at various times in history.   Defoe was just one of the many pub-
licists to express such beliefs during the half century
which preceded the industrial revolution.   He 'castigated
the worker for the sloth that made him waste his time in
idleness and low diversions, and the vice that led him to
squander his scanty resources in alcohol and debauchery'.
(130)   Arthur Young regarded the pernicious effect of high
earnings of workers on their readiness to labour as axio-
matic that it was 'idle to think of proving it by argument';   Mandeville had shown that 'there were riches ...
in the poverty and necessitous state of the masses'. (131)
English workers were thought of in the same character and
tone which was later reserved for coloured workers only.
'British employers then, like South Africans now', Hobsbawm pointed out, 'constantly complained about the lazi-
ness of labour or its tendency to work until it had earned
a traditional week's living wage and then to stop.' (132)
Tawney had noted earlier: 'The denunciations of "luxury,
pride and sloth" of the English wage-earner of the 17th
and 18th centuries are, indeed, almost exactly identical
with those directed against the African native today.'
(133)   Poverty was evidence of ungodliness, and workmen
had to be forced into virtue. (134)

The manpower situation and the significance of a cheap
labour supply was a leading concern in Mercantilist
thought;   Sir Josiah Child, even before becoming Governor
of the East India Company, had rejected the settlement of
white labourers in the colonies, on the ground that emigration deprived Britain of workers and consumers. (135)
Davenant clearly suggested that aliens be encouraged to
settle in Britain so as to make up for any emigration of
Britons.   By the end of the seventeenth century, with the

intensification of commercial rivalry in Europe, a new
cost-consciousness developed, in which the cost of labour
was more important than that of raw materials. Wage costs
could be lowered by increasing the labour supply and reducing wages, and some of the Mercantilists, including
Mun, even put forward a subsistence theory of wages. (136)
Low wages as a means of stimulating exports became a
matter of such concern as to lead to a change in the conception of Britain's demographic status - from an over-
populated country, which she was thought to be in the
sixteenth century, to a belief in the seventeenth century
that she was underpopulated. 'The desideratum was a population as large as possible, as fully occupied as possible, and living as near as possible to the margin of subsistence.' (137) While Englishmen emigrated to America,
England's chief commercial rivals, Holland and France, it
was alleged, had a 'greater output at lower costs because
they were well populated'. (138)

Thus the curbing of wages was first applied to labour
in Europe. The disintegration of the precapitalist economy had caused the transformation of independent peasants
and artisans into wage labour, leaving no option to those
involved; and society as a whole was conditioned into
condoning and accepting the wage levels and working conditions which resulted. In the early stages of capitalism, as labour became an important item of cost, influencing profits and the competitiveness of the national
economy, the extraction of the last ounce of effort from
labour was the concern of both employers and the state.
As Eli Heckscher explained, 'By forcing down wages ... the
export of such goods as contained relatively more human
labour could be increased. The corollary was that efforts
had to be made to obtain an abundant supply of labour at
as low a price as possible.' (139) With increased competition in world markets, the state arraigned itself on the
side of employers to maintain a pressure on wages. Its
intervention was invariably in favour of the employer and
official wage-fixing as a rule proscribed maximum wages.
The state now began to protect the employer against
actions taken by labour in defence of its interests.
Women and children were employed, especially in the manufacture of textiles, with a view to cutting down costs.
To pay them lower wages, the employers even explained that
the factory system gave children disciplined habits and
allowed them to support their parents, and that children
and most females who were not taken into the factory would
be exposed to vice and immorality. (140) In England the
living standard of large numbers thus declined during the
first period of industrialization. (141) 'Without any

alteration in the juridical relationships prevailing in
society, the working regime acquired characteristics of
duress such as had not been known in Europe for the entire
preceding thousand years.' (142)

However, a low wage ideology in the West proved to be
only a transitory phase. The 'virtuous indignation'
Landes spoke of, and which hardened the employers' attitude towards the labouring poor in the late seventeenth
and early eighteenth centuries, seemed 'to have softened'
from the middle of the eighteenth century, and thereafter
it was argued that 'labour was not incorrigibly lazy and
would in fact respond to higher wages'. (143) The manpower problem in both its aspects - i.e. inadequacy of the
total supply, and the employer's lack of control over the
worker - was being overcome by a change in the technology
of production. This, according to A.W.Coates, provided a
definitive solution to the labour problem. (144) Though
the exact circumstances in which this occurred cannot be
discussed here, the pivotal element in it was the use of
machinery and the adoption of capitalist production relations. There was in consequence an improvement in the
quality of labour, and a rise in productivity.

The widespread belief among employers regarding the unresponsiveness of the labouring class to higher wages,
having originated in the West, acquired a universality as
the Europeans established their dominance over the economically less developed regions. An early recognition
of this was by James Stephen, Permanent Under-Secretary of
State at the Colonial Office in 1841. When Lt Gen. Colin
Campbell, the Governor of Sri Lanka, referred to 'the
great advantages likely to arise from the reduced wages of
labour', Stephen minuted: (145)

So the rich invariably argue in all parts of the World.
Whatever gives them a greater command of the labour of
the poor on lower terms, they, who hire such labour,
will always regard as a public benefit.... One would
think wages were low enough in Ceylon where you can
hire a day labourer for three pence, and men live in
Wigwams with clothing and food not much better than
those of an Aboriginal New Hollander.

The more or less conscious development of an idea, even
supported by audacious claims, is necessary only in its
formative stages, after which it acquires a credibility
that is independent of any conscious element. Thus do
ideas acquire a life of their own. Human attitudes, conditioned as they are largely by social factors, are prone
to accept what is advantageous to the dominant groups in
society, although it is true ideas do not visibly appear
in the garb of sectional self-interest. The moulding of

society as a whole by the ideology of the ruling interests
is doubly easy with regard to doctrines which are not
verifiable without systematic evidence or study. Or else,
what is demonstrable in some situations, as, for example,
the 'backward sloping supply curve of labour', is seized
upon and applied indiscriminately to other situations.

One element in the conventional characterization of
coloured labour, that it is used to a customarily low
standard of living, leads quite easily to its central
tenet that such labour accepts such a standard and even
welcomes it - preferring to work less if wage rates rise.
This theory of the insensibility of 'natives' to monetary
inducements is said to have two aspects. One is that
given the opportunities 'natives dislike spending money;
the other is that though not averse to spending money they
will not earn it'. The former is a crude version of the
theory of limited wants which I.C.Greaves thought not even
its rashest exponents now hold. (146) The distinction she
makes between the two aspects of the 'theory' is, however,
not always appropriate, since one follows closely on the
other. The central premise in the theory as a whole as
applied to peasant societies is that the consumer aspirations of the peasant are transfixed on a traditional
horizon, limiting the attractiveness of earnings through
work. Though widely discredited in recent times, this
view of peasant behaviour even in its crude form has been
remarkably tenacious among administrators and planning officials when explaining the failure of peasant agricultural programmes. In the observation by James Stephen, which
I quoted, on the ethics of low wages what is most pertinent is the indication it gives of the 'prime mover' which
underlies this social attitude. In the crisp comment of
Ludowyk, 'Those who preach the virtues of work have tended
to profit from the labour of others.' (147)

The application of such ideas, which in the case of
capitalism in the West proved limited in the long run,
persisted more firmly in the colonial lands where domination proceeded on racial lines. The refusal of people to
accept wage labour on the terms and conditions imposed by
the employers was attributed to drawbacks in their outlook
and personality. The image of the Africans as a set of
'indolent, berry-picking natives' conformed to this
notion, as much as did the later characterization of the
peasants in Sri Lanka and Malaysia when they failed to
offer themselves as wage labour to the owners of plantations and mines. Compulsory labour on European enterprises was invested with an educational value - a view
even accepted by the British Colonial Office. The African, it was said, must be 'convinced of the necessity and

dignity of labour' and that the European's task was to
teach him to work! These attributes of colonial labour as
seen by employers were also the basis of its thoroughgoing
and more intense subjection long after the degradation of
the European working class had declined to tolerable
limits. Various forms of compulsion and fraud were adopted by the plantation employers to avoid paying such wages
as the state of the labour market would have required.
The disdain in which the labourers were held aggravated
the injustice and cruelty inflicted on them. 'Besides the
clash of interest under most trying circumstances', wrote
D.H.Buchanan in regard to the tea plantations in Assam,
'racial and social antipathy were ever present.' (148)
   At one time the feelings of the planters as a body towards their imported labourers was most deplorable....
   Among the worst sort of planters this feeling of
   aversion deepened into a mingling of hatred and contempt that led ... to systematic and gross ill-treatment.
Such feelings were not confined to labour in mines and on
plantations. Racial discrimination, as I have mentioned
elsewhere, was also applied to skilled or educated labour
and to those in technical, administrative and managerial
positions. As O.C.Cox stated, 'the whole people is looked
upon as a class - whereas white proletarianization involves only a section of the white people.' (150) The
process of rationalization of the relations between the
colonizers and the colonized was so extensive in its scope
as to involve what he termed the proletarianization of the
coloured races.

10   The scale of plantation operations and productive efficiency — a distorted image

The image of the plantations as an efficient productive system is to a great extent based on the large scale of their operations. Extensive land units and a large labour force, processing facilities for each estate, with centralized management and business operations by agency houses, are commonly supposed to reflect economies of scale which smallholders lack. The scale of operations, and the fact of metropolitan-based investors and management, are in turn presumed to result in a high level of economic efficiency. A belief in the inherent efficiency of estates over smallholders, as D.H.Penny and M.Zulkifli pointed out, is sustained by the fact that (1)

> estates develop and adopt improved practices; estates
> are orderly, e.g., the trees are in rows; estate
> managers are well-educated, have cars and live in big
> houses; estates use large-scale modern methods, and
> estates have profit maximisation as their goal and
> therefore must make more economic use of resources than
> peasant farmers.

In the penultimate chapter of this book I shall discuss the plantations as a production system; one of my concerns in this chapter is whether the kind of capital equipment used for the processing of plantation crops, with the exception of sugar cane, conferred scale economies.

I shall argue, in section 1 of the chapter, that the large scale of plantation production was determined by the heavy overhead expenses resulting from absentee ownership and its concomitant - the agency house system; and that in the case of crops such as tea and rubber the processing facilities on a plantation, though of a much larger capacity than required for production on a smallholding, were of a divisible type and therefore not functionally related to the scale of cultivation. The economies of scale were

certainly not those associated with technologically determined industry or modern farming systems, as is also
evident from the marketing strategy of plantation companies to which I have earlier referred. The plantations
sought to improve their gross proceeds by a maximizing of
output and price, rather than to reduce the unit costs of
output. In the context of absentee ownership, centralized management by agency houses was a potential source
of economies of scale. But these economies, exclusively
in the sphere of management, were mostly appropriated by
the agency houses themselves. In section 2 of this chapter I shall, in a sense, continue to demystify the plantation system by showing that the resident labour force,
which by raising overhead costs also contributed to the
large scale of operations, was not an agronomic or technical necessity. If the hallmark of the plantation system
was its pattern of labour utilization and control, this
pattern, based on resident labour, determined a number of
key attributes of the plantation system - the continuity
of production activities throughout the year, the reliance
on cheap labour, and the investment of capital in acquiring and retaining labour rather than in the techniques of
production.

1 THE LARGE SCALE OF PLANTATION OPERATIONS - THE RESULT
   OF INSTITUTIONAL RATHER THAN ECONOMIC FACTORS

The nature and magnitude of the overhead expenditure which
had an important effect on the scale of production was influenced by absentee ownership and its subordination to
merchant capital. The heavy overhead expenses arising
from the agency system were in the form, first, of inflated prices payable by the plantations for materials and
inputs supplied by the agency - fertilizer, agricultural
implements, tea chests, etc. - and, second, of payments to
persons in an 'elaborate hierarchy' drawing salaries, commissions and fees. (2) The managerial posts were confined
to Europeans and they were paid very liberally. In the
Assam Company in 1844 the salaries of twenty-five European
officers accounted for about a quarter of the production
cost of tea. (3) Agency charges not directly related to
estate management were also quite substantial. These were
not disclosed in the published accounts of plantation companies; the agency's commission (the best part of its
income) was lumped under 'marketing expenses'. In addition to a 'sizeable management fee' and the profits made
by the agency as buyer of estate stores, large amounts
were paid to the agency as commissions on the marketing

and sale of plantation produce and on insurance and shipping. 'The lack of competition for these services tended
to render them expensive.' (4) Payments on this scale
could be borne only by estates with a sufficiently large
acreage and output. Their effect on production costs was
noted by a rubber company in Sri Lanka in 1909: 'Owing to
the relatively heavy charges for superintendence etc. consequent on the small area, the cost of the planted areas
was somewhat heavy.' (5) The heavy proportion of overhead
charges was also seen by K.E.Knorr to 'weigh heavily on
the smaller estates'. (6)

The institutional nature of the factors underlying the
large size of plantations in Malaysia seems to have been
recognized by J.H.Drabble. 'Rubber cultivation was first
developed along estate lines in Malaya because of a particular conjunction of historical circumstances.' (7)
Some of the factors which raised overhead costs were
specific to Malaysia. In certain rubber-growing districts
expenditure was incurred on drainage and malaria eradica-
tion. Estate hospitals were needed after the government
ended the free treatment of labourers in March 1906.
Labour recruitment expenses were also higher in Malaysia
than in Sri Lanka, owing to the greater distance from
Southern India.

Institutional factors rather than economies of scale
were also evident in the growth and decline of plantations
in America. In the tobacco plantations of seventeenth-
century Virginia, though cultivation did not require expensive equipment or fixed structures, production units
were of large size. The abundance of land and the relative cheapness of labour (indentured white servants and,
later, Negro slaves) as well as the extreme labour intensiveness of tobacco cultivation led to large-scale
operations. To raise foodstuffs for the resident workforce, and to fell timber for construction and fuel,
labour was required beyond the direct needs of cultivation. The large size of the production units was also due
to the 'centre-periphery' relations of that period, which
depressed the producer's price for tobacco, through trade
monopolies and the high freight rates consequent on the
Navigation Act of 1660. (8) The reshipment of colonial
produce from Britain was subjected to heavy duties, besides extra charges - porterage, brokerage, warehouse
fees, agents' commissions, etc. All this was beyond the
means of small planters. The big planters with sufficient
credit and an agent in London to supervise sales had their
private docks from which tobacco was loaded directly on
the ship. (9) Thus the typical production unit, three
times larger than that for staple crops, became a plantation rather than a farm.

The scale of plantation production was also influenced by its pattern of labour utilization and control, as seen in the transfer of the plantation belt from the Northern states to the Southern states of America, and in the subsequent decline of the plantation system. By the close of the eighteenth century the plantation was no longer the dominant form of agriculture in the Northern states. With soil exhaustion and the loss of export markets during the French wars, tobacco cultivation declined. But hemp, cereals and livestock which replaced tobacco did not lend themselves to the plantation style. They needed far less labour and a greater variety and spontaneity of effort, for which relatively small farms were better suited. Consequently, the slave population became dispersed among numerous farmers instead of being held in large batches by planters. (10)

The spread of short staple cotton from about 1800 gave a totally new direction to Southern agriculture. Whereas in the Northern states by the 1850s large-scale cultivation, and even the term 'plantation', had almost disappeared, in the South (the land of cane and cotton) 'the plantation, with its broad acres, mansion, "quarters", and gangs of slave labour, stood regnant'. (11)   A large volume of slave labour at hand, pressed down to the plantation under physical duress, organized in gangs and capable of routinized physical effort made cotton a viable plantation crop. While in the North the whites began articulating humanitarian ideals, in the South slavery was too good to be questioned.

When slave labour was abolished the plantations were broken up. The average cultivation unit declined from 199 acres in 1860 to 134 acres in 1880 (12) and 'little farmsteads sprang up by the dozen on what had been large single plantations'. (13)   This 'revolutionary break-up of the Southern plantations' (Allan Nevins) was due partly to a fall in land values after Emancipation and the acquisition of land by small farmers. It was also due to a change in the basis of Southern agriculture, with the replacement of resident labour by share-cropping tenants. The wiping out of the capital value of slaves, and the curtailment of overhead expenses due to nonresident labour, made large-scale operations unnecessary.

In the plantations of underdeveloped countries, the large scale of operations was determined by factors similar to those in the case of tobacco cultivation in Virginia and of cotton in the Southern states. As mentioned already, these factors were related to the large overhead expenses associated with foreign ownership, and comprised broadly payments in various forms to agency houses and the

investment in labour.   In consequence, the production unit
became the plantation, with a larger land acreage than had
prevailed earlier when cultivation was carried out by individual proprietors;   and the entrepreneurial unit represented by the plantation company was even larger than that
of the individual estate.   Before discussing these factors
in detail, it would be helpful to distinguish the unit of
entrepreneurial operations, i.e. the plantation company,
from the physical unit of production, i.e. the estate.

    While the scale of operations of a plantation company
was quite large, the acreage and output of individual estates were limited by the way in which the plantation
economy developed, erratically and in short spurts.   In
Sri Lanka only small acreages were opened up at a time,
and increases in factory capacity took the form of a
series of modifications and extensions.   Starting off with
a relatively small acreage, plantation companies owned
scattered blocks of land rather than extensive or compact
properties.   After a time the non-availability of contiguous land limited the size of estates, though not the total
acreage and output of a plantation company. (14)   In other
words, land belonging to any given entrepreneurial unit -
a single plantation company - became scattered over different districts, i.e. there was fragmentation.   (A tea
company in Assam to which V.D.Wickizer refers owned seven-
teen estates situated in different parts of the province.)
(15)   Even the land constituting an estate may have been
dispersed, thereby impeding access from one portion of an
estate to another. (16)

    This haphazard development, with a wasteful deployment
of buildings, bridges and estate roads, raised overhead
expenses including management costs.   Road mileage on estates was unnecessarily great, and construction and maintenance costs were high per acre of plantation land and
per unit of output.   Some plantation companies subsequently began disposing of inconvenient blocks of land in
favour of consolidated tracts.   The United Planters Co. of
Ceylon Ltd, which sold its Campden Hill estate, explained
in its report for 1944:   'The estate was an isolated one
and far from the company's other properties, which made
the management of it difficult.'   It later sold Kaloogalle
estate and negotiated for the purchase of a property in
place of this.   The company's report for 1951 stated that
Kaloogalle estate 'was a small one ... and was an expensive producer on account of its size'.   In a few cases the
faulty siting of tea factories in relation to the road
network was overcome when factories destroyed by fire were
rebuilt in more appropriate locations.   But attempts at
rationalizing holdings were not always successful.   In

1905 the Kalutara Rubber Co.Ltd 'applied for a further
block of some 200 acres which it proposed to purchase
should it be procurable at a reasonable figure'. But the
next year (1906) the Chairman stated:

In view of the fact that any considerable expansion of
the company's acreage would require an increase of
capital, which the Directors think in the present state
of affairs would not be in accordance with the wishes
of the majority of the shareholders, they decided not
to bid for the block of about 200 acres referred to in
the last report.

In 1920 the Wellandura Tea & Rubber Co.Ltd stated: 'There
is plenty of land available for planting and this shortage
will be made up when the financial position of the Company
permits of extension being resumed'; and in 1923:   'There
is a large quantity of good reserve land available for
planting.' The same point was repeated in the statement
for 1924. In 1911 the Kaluganga Valley Tea & Rubber Co.
Ltd stated: 'The directors have reluctantly been compelled to abandon the project of opening the Katiapola Valley
in Tea owing to the want of financial support. They have
decided to dispose of the tea plants. The sub-lease of
1,000 acres in the Pasgan Valley is under consideration.'
In 1925 this company sub-leased to the Katiapola Co. 'two
outlying blocks aggregating 25 acres' and accepted as rent
half the net profits of the rubber harvested. When suitable land was available the financial position of the companies may have militated against acquisition or the price
may have been deemed too high, or else when funds permitted land may have been scarce. (17)

    I have already discussed the historical and institu-
tional factors which raised overhead expenses and enlarged
the size of individual estates. The large size of the
plantation companies (the ownership and entrepreneurial
unit), it was explained in an earlier chapter, was also
due to the recourse to capital abroad and the heavy payments to agency houses which acted essentially on behalf
of absentee shareholders. I shall now examine the nature
of the scale economies both in the cultivation of crops
and in their processing. It will be contended that economies inherent in the production process, as distinct from
those imposed by absentee ownership, were minimal, and
were confined to the processing of the crops. An entrepreneurial or organizational separation of the cultivation
and the processing phases would thus remove the advantages
enjoyed by estates vis-à-vis smallholdings; furthermore,
while the capacity of the machinery and equipment installed in the tea and rubber factories may have been large,
this capacity was made up of divisible units, making the

economies of scale even in processing far less than is
commonly supposed.

In tea production there are two factors which are supposed to reflect the existence of scale economies: first,
the price variations for tea produced by different estates
and, second, the use of machinery on plantations for processing. Price variations, it is held, reflect differences in quality as determined by the size of estates. A
larger estate can enforce 'careful supervision in minute
detail of each stage' of the production process, (18) and
conform to standard production practices ('regularity of
manuring, composition of fertilizers, pruning, plucking
of tea leaves, withering, rolling, fermenting and blending', etc.). However, the relation between estate size
and the quality and price of tea cannot easily be established because of the interplay of numerous variables.
These include natural factors (elevation, weather and
soil), the age distribution of the plants, and management
practices in the field and in the factory which have
little to do with the land acreage. Price is also influenced by the intensity of demand for tea of particular
grades and flavour and by market imperfections introduced
by tea blenders and distributors.

The absence of a positive relation between the size of
a cultivation unit and the quality of produce is evident
in Kenya. Aided by the Kenya Tea Development Authority
(KTDA), smallholders achieve yields comparable with those
on estates, and the processing of tea is done in large co-
operative factories. The KTDA also enforces quality standards for the green leaf purchased from smallholders. (In
Sri Lanka, on the other hand, the estate factories readily
purchase smallholders' produce irrespective of its quality, but pay very low prices.) In Kenya since the early
1960s, and in Malawi more recently, tea production has
been increasingly on smallholdings. 'Formerly, [Africans
were] prevented ... from growing tea [even] for the internal market.' (19) The disabilities of the smallholders
had less to do with economies of scale than with the 'dis-
economy' of being an African. 'Technical, legal, financial and administrative' disabilities were imposed on
smallholders. Until the Second World War there were legal
sanctions against tea growing by Africans just as in Sri
Lanka, during the early years of this century, village
headmen were instructed to destroy rubber trees planted
by the peasants - ostensibly to discourage theft of planting material from estates. The performance of the Kenyan
small producer in recent decades led D.M.Etherington to
conclude: 'Certainly, wherever else the advantages of
scale exist they would not seem to lie in the production
of green leaf in the field.' (20)

Though Etherington ruled out scale economies in the cultivation process, he attributed to smallholders a management deficiency. This he regards as 'a more reasonable and more satisfactory application of the observed differences in performance of tea farmers than a purely mechanistic scale effect'. (21) According to him smallholders tend to neglect maintenance and upkeep, and are slow to respond efficiently to unfamiliar and novel opportunities in Kenya tea growing. 'Consequently, even among the farmers who "accept" tea (i.e. plant tea stumps) there is a wide range in the degree to which the total package of innovations is accepted.' (22) But peasants in numerous instances have been successful innovators, and Etherington's worry about the smallholders' lack of perceptiveness or initiative is possibly exaggerated. In fact, the view expressed by him in the article on economies of scale does not accord with the assertion in his book that the Kenya smallholders have produced tea of 'surprisingly high quality'. If the comparison is between the European and the native entrepreneurs, it is useful to recall that in Malaysia the Chinese took to rubber growing at a time when the Europeans were still hesitating.

'Maintenance and upkeep', on the basis of which Etherington grades the marginal efficiency of farmers, is a question not of managerial acumen but essentially of the available credit facilities. An analogous case is the small paddy farmer in many Asian countries who neglects intensive cultural practices - especially transplanting and weeding; though maximizing the input of family labour, he is unable to finance sufficient hired labour and material inputs. A second reason is that the smallholder divides his efforts between the growing of plantation crops and his other interests. He is typically a man with multiple interests which compete for labour and other resources. For instance, in Malaysia most smallholders handle more than two cash crops though rubber is dominant, and in Indonesia both rubber and tea are interplanted with foodstuffs or have a secondary importance. As one writer observed, 'These other activities require and justify diversion of attention away from rubber production during certain periods of the year.' (23) Diversification, besides stabilizing aggregate income - an important consideration at lower income levels - enabled smallholders to sustain themselves during the pre-maturity period of any individual crop. Both in Malaysia and in Indonesia, smallholders were able to replant their rubber lands with a minimum of governmental assistance. The lower level of maintenance and upkeep on smallholdings is due, third, to a pattern of resource allocation which, while resulting in a sub-optimal return on any single activity, maximizes the overall income of the smallholder per unit of time, effort or resources. This, to be sure, implies a scale economy in respect of the unit of ownership and management of each activity. Nevertheless, the size of the tea or rubber holding which would induce him to divest himself of his other interests, and to devote himself entirely to one crop, is obviously less than the acreage of an estate.

As indicated earlier, the disabilities of smallholders arose fundamentally from the vested interests in the estate system, both at a private and official level. The price paid for green leaf by the tea factories was barely remunerative. The financial condition of smallholders (with their constant need for cash), and a deterioration in the quality of green leaf within about six hours of being plucked, weaken their bargaining position in the market for leaf. In Indonesia, smallholders were even obstructed by estate-owners from selling green leaf, for fear that a successful smallholder industry would divert labour from estates; and in the early decades of this century attempts to set up co-operative factories were misrepresented by the planters as a 'communist plot'. The control of processing facilities by the estates and the monopolistic practices of traders typically affect peasant producers who have to face a small group of exporting and processing firms.

In Malaysia, rubber smallholders were subjected to 'legal-institutional barriers'. With a commitment 'to uphold vested economic and institutional interests', the government intervened on behalf of the large, British-owned estates. The policy was to 'remove peasants from rubber to other, non-competitive, less remunerative crops'. (24) The restrictive schemes of the 1920s, though professing merely to regulate the market, were prejudicial to smallholders. 'One of the primary objects of the Rubber Control Scheme', the Chairman of the British North Borneo Company stated, 'was to protect European capital in plantation companies in Malaya, Borneo and the Netherlands East Indies from competition arising from the production of rubber by the native at a fraction of the cost involved in European-owned estates.' (25) Production permits were based on an 'iniquitous system of differential assessment'. Replanting funds given to smallholders specifically excluded new plantings though this did not apply to estates. The smallholders contributed a large portion of the rubber export duty collections and of the cess which financed the Rubber Research Institute though its research work did not benefit them. Along with the Land Regulations which sought to confine the Malays mainly to paddy cultivation, the discrimination against

smallholders had also the political objective of impeding
the modernization of Malay society.
Rudner sought to explain this pro-plantation policy in
terms of the mental preconceptions of Western colonial administrators. They had 'an ingrained bias in favour of
neat, well-ordered Western-style plantations'. 'To the
colonial mind Western-style, large-scale, estate-type
rubber plantations were inherently preferable to alien,
native, smallholdings.' (26) However, in Burma, West
Africa and Uganda the 'colonial mind' was prepared to
accept export crops grown on 'native smallholdings'. In
Southern Nigeria, British administration in the early
1920s adopted what has been termed an 'anti-plantation
policy'. (27) As Stephen Hymer showed, in West Africa the
British Colonial Office was cautious not to interfere with
indigenous interests; they were 'fully aware of the stiff
native political resistance towards any attempt at interference with land ownership or mineral rights'. (28) In
West Africa, plantation agriculture could not be introduced because of the difficulty of obtaining labour and
the competition of Ghanaian farmers. In all these instances it was not an attitude of mind or the desire for
order in the abstract which underlay British policy but a
conscious pursuit of economic and political interests in
accordance with the specific conditions that prevailed.
The favoured treatment of the plantations, predominantly
European-owned, seems to validate Knorr's contention about
the Stevenson rubber restriction scheme: 'In view of
their generally lower output costs there could be no doubt
that, in the absence of restriction, the native planters
[i.e. smallholders] would have captured a gradually increasing share of the world's rubber market.' (29) The
competitive ability of the peasant producers of plantation
crops was also referred to by Myint: 'Frequently the
peasant methods are found to have lower costs than the
"modern" scientific methods, and that is the reason why
peasant production has been able to withstand the competition of the plantation system in some countries.' (30)
   My discussion shows that plantation crops could have
been grown on smallholdings as cheaply and effectively as
on the plantations themselves, but that the plantation
interests together with the colonial state actively impeded the development of smallholdings. The necessity for
such discrimination was the high overhead expenses of the
plantation system and its inherent disability vis-à-vis
the smallholding. The competitive strength of the plantations is attributable, first, to the import of cheap
labour. The study by Penny and Zulkifli on rubber in
Indonesia suggested that 'if local labour had had to be

employed there is some doubt that the plantations would
have been viable'. (31)   Likewise in the cotton plantations of Southern USA, there were economies in the maintenance of a slave labour force. Second, much of the research and extension work carried out by government sponsored institutes had an estate bias. The competitive
strength of the plantations lay, finally, in their control
of processing facilities.

Whereas scale economies in plantation production have
been attributed in the first instance to efficient management systems compared with smallholdings, resulting in the
superior quality of plantation produce, the second factor
is the use of capital equipment in the processing of
crops. According to one writer, rigidities of factory
capacity imposed a lower limit upon individual acreages,
so that 'tea plantations generally had to be large'. (32)
Another explicitly stated: (33)

economies of scale in tea production are considerable.
Wickizer puts the optimum size at 500 acres. Besides
the economies realised in the field, there are also
very considerable economies available to the larger
estate in the processing of green leaf.

The processing of plantation crops as is done on the estates has been regarded as an industrial activity. (34)

While there has been little mechanisation of the field
work over the years, the factory work - drying,
grading, rolling and packing the tea - has long been a
mechanised operation. This essentially industrial work
is traditionally done on the estate and only a large
estate can afford a factory.

A third writer, Samir Amin, in describing plantations as
'an ultramodern sector' with high productivity ... 'comparable to those found in the advanced countries', (35)
implies a considerable use of capital on plantations. The
specific relation between the size of the landholding and
the processing capacity will be examined later in this
chapter.

The question of scale economies involve two issues.
One is that, contrary to the views cited above, empirical
studies on tea and rubber production refer to scale economies only in the processing of crops but not in their cultivation. For example, for rubber in Malaysia: (36)

The physical size of an estate does not itself appear
to have exerted any important influence in tapping
costs per pound.... The principal influence on processing and smoking costs was level of production....
The main economies of scale were exhibited by expenditure on labour in processing and smoking.

'With given yield per acre, however, area of rubber land

makes little difference to financial performance and success. An exception to this is the high cost of processing
and low product quality on the smaller farms.' (37) For
Indonesia, a direct comparison of rubber estates and
smallholdings showed that 'the efficiency differential in
favour of the estates is probably less than generally
believed'. (38) For Sri Lanka, an analysis of input-
output relations in rubber smallholdings led to a similar
conclusion: 'It seems that there is no "economic" justification for increasing the existing land area [of individual holdings] in view of the constant returns to scale as
far as land area is concerned.' (39) In tea growing in
Kenya and Malawi, smallholders have been increasingly dominant, with a level of productive efficiency approximating
that of estates. While the capital coefficients in cultivation have undergone hardly any change, the processing of
plantation crops has involved new types of capital equipment and significant scale economies. In tea production,
and far more in rubber, the capacity of processing equipment exceeds the amount of green leaf and of rubber latex,
respectively, which a smallholding can supply; the level
of financing and of technical and managerial know-how has
been correspondingly high. The technology of manufacturing block rubber has expanded processing capacity far
beyond a smallholder's output; the marketing standards
and quality of the new varieties of rubber, viz. concentrated latex and block rubber, are also markedly superior
to smoked sheet rubber which can be made in 'processing
sheds with simple and often primitive equipment'.
     The second issue regarding such economies has some
theoretical relevance in that the concept is meaningful
only in terms of an appropriate phase in a larger production process, which can be technologically demarcated from
other phases even though they are entrepreneurially
linked. If economies of scale are limited to processing,
the prevalence of large units in cultivation is due merely
to the linking of cultivation with processing. The linking makes it appear that scale economies apply to cultivation as well. If, on the other hand, cultivation is
detached organizationally and entrepreneurially from the
processing of crops, the size of production units in the
two phases would differ markedly; cultivation would then
be essentially a smallholders' enterprise and processing
a large-scale one. In plantation crops the integration of
the cultivation and the processing phases under a single
ownership or management is not a technical necessity. (40)
     Just as the individual wheat grower does not produce
     his own flour or the beet-sugar grower his own sugar,
     there is no compelling reason why the individual rubber

planter should prepare his own rubber. Large modern
mills in central locations, perhaps run co-operatively,
would promise greater uniformity of product and hence a
better price for the average ton of rubber.

In rubber production in Malaysia the Group Processing
Centres involve a separation of this kind. The production
of concentrated latex and block rubber at these centres is
a 'mechano-chemical process', involving a large output
capacity, and high capital intensiveness and technical
expertise. Smallholders produce latex for sale to these
factories or their collecting agents. It was a differentiation of this kind between cultivation and processing
that caused sugar cane and coconut to become predominantly
smallholders' crops. The circumstances in which the sugar
mill was separated from cane growing have been referred to
in an earlier chapter. Likewise, desiccated coconut and
coconut oil mills became large-scale enterprises based on
an industrial or a quasi-industrial process. The mills
are relatively few, and hardly any of them are located on
the land from which they draw supplies of the crop or are
entrepreneurially linked to it. The mills are highly
capitalized and have an enormous capacity in terms of the
land acreages from which they obtain fresh nuts and copra
for conversion, respectively, into desiccated coconut and
oil; to achieve even minimum efficiency a desiccated
coconut mill must be fully automated. The separation of
cultivation from processing also overcomes a problem of
logistics, since a desiccated coconut mill if served by
its own coconut plantation would require an unmanageably
large land acreage. By comparison, the size of a tea or
rubber estate, and its processing capacity, are dwarfish.
In the case of tea, it may be advantageous for an estate
to have its own factory to facilitate the speedy processing of green leaf before its quality deteriorates, but
this advantage is unrelated to economies of scale. Even
so, there is no compelling reason for combining cultivation and processing under the same management - as is
evident from the comparable case of sugar production, in
which the sugar mill regulates the quantity and quality of
the cane and ensures its speedy delivery by numerous small
cane growers, and it is also evident from the case of
smallholders' tea in Kenya.

In tea and rubber production, the entrepreneurial unification of cultivation and processing enabled estates to
control the market for unprocessed crops. The depressed
prices for green leaf and rubber latex paid by factory-
owners and middlemen undermined the competitiveness of
smallholders. In the context of the colonial economy this
meant barriers to indigenous enterprise. In Sri Lanka,

consequently, whereas tea and rubber production were dominated by foreign capital, in coconut cultivation, which
entrepreneurially is a separate activity from the milling
of the coconuts, smallholdings predominate. (Likewise, in
the rice economy of Burma, whereas European capital was
dominant in milling, the growing of paddy was a Burmese
enterprise.) The higher profitability of estates vis-à-
vis smallholders is, in fact, partly due to their monopoly
of processing facilities. The profits differential between estates and smallholders thus contains a rent element and, to this extent, reflects the depressed prices
for unprocessed produce. While there is no agronomic or
technical reason for combining the ownership of the cultivation units and the processing facilities, the feasibility of doing so is due to the relatively low capital cost
of the processing unit, and the absence of a sufficient
level of complexity in its operation and management to
warrant a separation. The entrepreneurial unification of
cultivation and processing, in other words, shows that
scale economies even in processing are relatively limited.
(41)

I shall now argue, contrary to the supposition that
factory size imposed a lower limit on the acreage of an
estate, that in the relationship between factory size and
acreage it was the latter rather than the former which had
the constraining factor - that factory size was a function
of available land, not the other way round. The area of
individual estates could not easily be expanded for
reasons already discussed; and, far from consolidated
acreages being linked to individual processing units, the
haphazard way in which land was acquired and cultivated
resulted in a fragmentation of the landholdings of plantation companies. The supply of tea leaf or of rubber latex
- the crucial determinant of manufacturing capacity -
could increase only within the limits provided by the unutilized land on the estate and by increases in yield per
acre. While a plantation company owned estates in different districts, the scale of operations of an individual
estate was consequently limited by the size of its land
acreage. The type of tea and rubber equipment in use permitted flexibility in manufacturing capacity, reducing the
scope of scale economies.

Both tea and rubber machinery were of different capacities, so that the minimum size of a manufacturing unit
(and hence the scale of factory operations) varied considerably. For example, Parnell's Tea Cutters 'fitted for
hand or power' were available in the 1890s in capacities
of 60 lb, 120 lb, and 240 lb; Barker's Patent Sifter
could be fitted with either a single cylinder having an

intake of 75-100 lb per hour or a double cylinder which
took in 150-200 lb per hour; Scott's Challenge Propellers
were manufactured in several sizes. (42) 'Multiflu' Tea-
drying Equipment 'comprised a range of driers designed ...
to cater to every type of climate and every size of crop'.
The tilting tray-type of 'Multiflu' equipment was suitable
for the crops of smaller tea estates, and the endless
chain suction pressure-type to those of larger estates.
(43) The Sirocco Endless Chain Tea Drier was available
in several sizes, its two main units being the semi-auto-
matic 'Minor' drier, with an output of 100 lb of made tea
per hour, and the 'Major' drier, with an output of 155 lb
per hour. In rubber manufacture also there were variations in capital intensity. 'Standardisation had admittedly not gone far in Ceylon', wrote the Colombo correspondent of 'The Economist' in 1913. 'The various methods
of preparing exist side by side; every kind of coagula-
tion is used; every kind of machinery.' Flexibility in
production capacity was a feature of tea and rubber manufacturing equipment till very recently. These variations
in capacity made factory extension a gradual process, conforming to increases in the supply of tea leaf or of
rubber latex. For instance, High Forests Co.Ltd, in 1910,
having to cope with larger crops, decided on 'an extension
of the factory and sundry additions to the machinery'.
(44) In the same year the visiting agent of the Uvakelle
Tea Co. of Ceylon Ltd wrote: 'I would urge on the Directors that they should at once sanction ... additions to
the factory and machinery. The company's profits have
suffered this year for the want of room and machinery.'
(45)

Furthermore, the relative unimportance of processing
costs in the total production cost reduced the impact of
scale economies in processing on the combined plantation
activity and therefore on the production cost per unit of
output. For instance, in Sri Lanka and in India the processing costs of tea have been, respectively, around 3 per
cent and 5 per cent of the total production cost. (46)   In
the absence of a major improvement in the technique of
producing green leaf or rubber latex, which would raise
processing costs in relation to cultivation costs, the incentive for cost-reducing investments in processing is
weak. Such investments involve changes in the composition
of capital rather than extensions to capacity which repli-
cate existing equipment. As mentioned earlier, the effect
of innovations already introduced in processing has been
to improve the marketability of plantation produce rather
than to lower production costs. In sugar production, the
milling of cane had always constituted a far bigger compo-

nent of the total production cost than did the 'factory'
operations in tea or rubber.   But while cultivation
methods were also improved, there was a piling up of capital investment on the sugar mill from about 1900, after
the introduction of the sugar central.   An increase in the
ratio of fixed costs to variable costs in the operation of
the mill caused a decline in the cost of milling sugar
cane per unit of output relative to that of cultivation.

In plantation crops other than sugar cane, though factory capacity was by no means static, expansion was purely
quantitative.   There was an increase in the existing units
of equipment rather than qualitative changes involving
higher capital-labour ratios and changes in work methods -
the source of scale economies and cost reductions per unit
of output.   The processing units, in these circumstances,
were not impelled to reach out to vast crop acreages as a
source of supply, as the sugar mill did - assimilating
small mills in the neighbourhood and pre-empting cane
supplies by means of private railways and the economic
subjection of the colono.   While all plantation crops
enjoy certain economies of scale, the level of output
which gives rise to such economies does not require an
individual acreage which is as large as a plantation.   The
plantation scale of operations, as explained earlier, was
determined by the inflexibility of overhead costs, comprising both management expenses and capital outlays on
labour.   In turn, the heavy management expenses arose from
the framework of extra-territoriality in which the plantation system developed.

2   THE SIGNIFICANCE OF RESIDENT LABOUR

The scale of plantation enterprise has already been attributed to its high level of overhead costs, arising from
large payments to agency firms and the investment in
labour.   The characteristic labour system on a plantation,
resulting from the investment in labour, distinguishes it
from any other enterprise.   As Fraginals said with reference to the latifundia, a plantation is not a quantitative
concept or an agronomic one, but essentially a system of
labour relations with its associated levels of wages and
technology. (47)   The use of resident labour tied to the
plantation by duress or by social mechanisms was the key-
stone of its labour system. (48)
    The labourer's home is bound up with his job, and both
    are directly dependent upon the planters.   Workers do
    not commonly live outside the estate, the land of which
    they cultivate, but upon it;   and the conditions and

arrangements of life and recreation, as well as of work
fall to a very large extent within the bounds of the
territory possessed by the planter, and hence are subject to his authority.
The plantation was a form of settlement in a situation of
'open resources' - the local population was too sparse or
could not be induced or coerced into supplying labour.
This circumstance called for a migrant or transplanted
workforce, socially and culturally differentiated from the
surrounding society, employed in family units, and subjected to the plantation system of wages and labour control and discipline.

The investment in labour recruitment created a need for
estate housing to minimize the risk of the labourer de-
serting, a major problem for the planters. In Malaysia,
the Planters' Association stated in 1911: 'Many of the
large companies have recruited with much difficulty and at
a considerable expense ... only to see a large percentage
[of the labourers] drift away in the course of a few
months to other employers.' (49) The acquisition of
labour entailed money, time and effort. The cost and difficulties of obtaining immigrant labour were particularly
great on plantations in Malaysia. Larger sums were payable to labour recruiters (50) and travel expenses from
India were higher than to Sri Lanka or Burma. The planters as a body were averse to 'local recruiting' because it
led to competition for labour. Local recruitment enabled
some employers to acquire 'labourers introduced into the
country by other[s] at considerable expense'. (51) The
Planters' Association stated in its Annual Report for
1910, 'The free labour forces [as opposed to indentured
labour] which characterise the older estates have taken
years to build up and the difficulty of young estates is
to find reliable men to send as recruiters.'

The provision of estate housing, apart from helping to
retain labour whose recruitment entailed a capital cost,
conformed with the enclave nature of the plantation
system. Labourers, brought from long distances, were cut
off from the surrounding peasant economy and bound to the
plantations by their conditions of employment, if not
juridically. In Sri Lanka an alien workforce was foisted
amidst a wholly Sinhalese population - yet removed from
the latter and living aloof. (52)

Here besides a land-owning or rice-growing peasantry,
Sinhalese Buddhist, enjoying a comparatively fair standard of living, was planted a large group of badly paid
wage slaves, Tamils, Hindu, completely isolated from
the peasant and his life, maintaining within the confines of the estate a hard life reminiscent of condi-

tions in South India in everything but the mode of
making a living and its terrain.
The commercial interaction of plantation labour with the
villagers was curtailed by the facilities for growing
vegetables and grazing cattle on the estate and by the
provision of basic articles of consumption from an estate
store. The plantations were an enclave, whether they were
close to or distant from populous villages and urban
centres. Their economic and social isolation was also due
to the road system created by the estates, which afforded
no links with the surrounding areas. Furthermore, the
plantation workforce had a separate linguistic and cultural identity and was occupationally immobile.

In turn, the residential basis of the plantation labour
force determined the profile of labour inputs, ensuring a
continuity of work through the year. (53) While residential labour necessitates the spreading of labour inputs
during the year, a wide discontinuity in labour demand, or
a sharp seasonality, making resident labour impractical,
would rule out the plantation system altogether - as in
the case of cereal crops. A plantation's ability to provide regular employment (for reasons which I shall later
explain) makes monoculture possible in the plantation
system, whereas smallholders and cereal growers must
resort to multicropping or engage in several production
activities if they are to fill in the slack periods in any
one crop or activity and to derive an income throughout
the year. What is essential to the plantation system is
the specific time pattern of labour utilization, and not
the agronomic characteristics of the crop, including its
long growing period, or the scale of the enterprise and
its export orientation. Ulrich Phillips on this basis
classified plantation and non-plantation crops in America
- restricting the former to the 'five great Southern staples', viz. cotton, tobacco, sugar, rice and indigo. (54)
The pattern of labour utilization is interlinked with
several other elements of the plantation system: residential labour - immigrant or transplanted - low wages,
labour intensiveness, and the investment of capital on
labour recruitment and retention rather than on the techniques of production. While none of these elements could
be taken in isolation, all of them were organically interrelated to constitute the plantation system. Though
Phillips's inclusion of rice among the plantation crops in
the American South may possibly be justified by the specific conditions in that region, utilizing slave labour,
the sharp seasonality in the labour requirements excludes
the production of rice under basic plantation conditions.
A discontinuity in labour demand, if it does not ex-

clude the plantation system, modifies it. For instance,
in sugar cane, when slavery was abolished and vast capital
outlays had made the sugar mill a specialized enterprise,
cultivation was separated from processing, entrepreneurially and financially. Likewise in coffee growing in
Puerto Rico, resident labour was not feasible owing to
sharp fluctuations in the pattern of labour utilization
during the year; two major production seasons are separated by a clear period of two to three months of inactivity. The labour required at harvesting time is almost
equal to that during the remainder of the year. (55) The
hacienda was a device for 'stabilizing the necessary
labour supply', making labour available without being
resident. Such labour, though nominally independent, was
induced to offer itself for employment by means of a set
of indirect compulsions including credit sales made by the
hacienda store. When not wanted by the hacienda it maintained itself by other means.

The flexibility of the work regime on a plantation, and
the factors underlying different work regimes, are seen in
the marked changes that occurred in cane sugar production
in Puerto Rico. Slave labour was kept active throughout
the year, fed and provisioned at a minimal level. (56)
Though sugar, like coffee, is a distinctly seasonal crop
(with a well-defined 'dead season') a resident labour
force was made feasible by staggering the cane harvest
over a fairly long period and by the availability of work
not directly connected with cultivation; there was the
felling of timber, the preparation of charcoal for the
mill, the repair of irrigation facilities and the growing
of food for the labour force. The emancipation of slaves
and subsequently the heavy capital investment in the sugar
mills compelled a change in the volume and profile of
labour inputs. The milling of cane had always accounted
for an overwhelming share of the production cost of sugar.
But from about 1900, after the introduction of the sugar
central, a plantation was no longer able to provide work
throughout the year; and the disruption of the traditional pattern of work severed the nexus of sugar cane labourers to the plantation.

A sugar central, while requiring a vast cane acreage
and output, shortened the period of employment. To ensure
maximum utilization, the mill was worked twenty-four hours
a day, six days a week for only a short period, after
which it remained closed until the next harvest. The
mill's grinding period declined from 159 days in 1940 to
123 days in 1946, and the harvesting period to five and a
half months, compared with eight to nine months prior to
1900. (57) Though the labourers still lived on plantation

lands and were very dependent on the sugar central, their
ties with the plantation were not the same as before.
They became semi-independent small farmers, having a contractual grinding agreement with the central. The change
in labour relations was also reflected in harvesting, for
which 'temporary or transient' labour was partly employed;
such labour lived outside the plantations, and were free
to work on different farms or to seek other work.

Resident labour, and the ability of a plantation to
provide regular employment, along with the large-scale
operations, were clearly the result of institutional factors that were alluded to before. Continuous, day-to-day
attention is not an agronomic or technical requirement,
nor is the timing of any cultural operation 'quite so
crucial' as in seasonal crops, such as cereals or sugar
cane. For instance, the plucking of tea (by far the most
labour absorptive phase in its cultivation) (58) can be
postponed by two or three days without adverse effects on
yield. In fact, each tea plant is plucked at intervals of
five to fourteen days, depending on the season. Pruning,
fertilizing, weeding, forking (aerating the soil), and
draining on a given portion of the estate are carried out
at very long intervals; pruning (the most important activity in the maintenance and upkeep of a tea plantation)
is done every five years, and the pruning cycle is flexible.

Furthermore, plantation crops, though perennial, are
subject to fluctuations in output and hence in the volume
of labour required for harvesting. In tea, the pattern of
output fluctuations depends on the 'flush' or the rate of
sprouting of green leaf, and in all tea-growing regions
there is a dormant period. The seasonality is greatest in
North India, where about 90 per cent of the annual output
is during the six months June-November. Seasonal fluctuations also prevail in South India, Sri Lanka and Kenya,
where tea is produced almost throughout the year. In Sri
Lanka, the average monthly output of tea during April-June
is in some years more than 50 per cent higher than during
July-September, and while the national output of tea is
relatively stable, in specific districts the fluctuations
are considerable. The fluctuations are greater for high-
grown than for medium-grown tea, and they are least for
low-grown tea. In the Uva district, nearly 50 per cent of
the crop is plucked in the four months March-June. (59)
In Malawi, 80 per cent of the crop is produced during five
months. (60)

Fluctuations in output and in the pattern of labour
demand are also a feature of rubber production. Two
thirds of Sri Lanka's rubber crop is harvested during

July-December. The remainder of the year is virtually a
non-cropping period, when there is leaf fall followed by
the monsoon. In districts with a high rainfall rubber
tapping is done on an average of only 140 days in the
year. (Rain washes off the latex, and the collection of
latex is not practical until the tree panel is dry.) For
agronomic reasons, rubber trees on estates are tapped on
alternate days. With high-yielding clones a larger resting period is needed, and tapping is limited to every
third day.

The patterns of output fluctuations in tea and rubber
are reflected to some extent in their respective work
schedules and in the proportion of resident and nonresident labour. In tea, the output fluctuations are more
pronounced but comparatively regular. Production varies
seasonally and therefore from month to month, whereas
rubber may vary from day to day haphazardly, depending
mostly on tapping done within limited hours - early
morning to about midday. Yet, resident labour is characteristic of the tea plantations both in Sri Lanka and in
Assam, whereas the rubber plantations have a fairly large
component of nonresident or village labour. Rubber is
widely cultivated by smallholders, though individual estates in Malaysia are larger than in Sri Lanka owing to
the historical reasons which I mentioned earlier. (In
Malaysia the estates also employ nonresident Chinese or
Malay labour on a contract basis, whereas the resident
labour comprising the classical plantation labour force
is Indian.)

The use of resident labour on tea plantations has been
made possible by two circumstances. The somewhat uniform
pattern of output fluctuations affords flexibility in the
deployment of labour on a tea estate. The labour used at
peak periods (for plucking) is diverted at other times to
the maintenance and upkeep of the estate, so as to ensure
continuous work. On a rubber estate, though production is
more stable from month to month, a rotation of labour
cannot be worked out as easily, since less labour is
needed for maintenance and upkeep; e.g. extensive weeding
is confined to the first five years - after that cover
crops drastically reduce the need for weeding. (A tea-
cum-rubber estate affords more flexibility in the pattern
of labour inputs than a rubber estate.) The relative difficulty of rotating labour on a rubber estate is also due
to fewer work days per month and their irregularity.
Rubber tapping is suspended during rain, to prevent water
getting into the cut bark and into the latex drawn out,
and during the drought (in Sri Lanka for about a month)
when latex flow is minimal; furthermore, the tapping of

rubber takes place for only five hours each day. This
discontinuity of work and the fewer workdays suit nonresident or village labour, and such labour in turn fits into
the pattern of rubber production - combining estate work
with other employment. In rubber, there is consequently
a preponderance of smallholdings and the average size of
estates is smaller than for tea. The smaller size of cultivation units is linked to a lower level of overhead
costs; the processing facilities are relatively inexpensive and a smaller complement of resident labour on
rubber estates curtails the expenditure on housing and
related amenities.

The greater employment of nonresident or village labour
on rubber estates in Sri Lanka is reflected in a wage disparity between the rubber and the tea estates - the proportion of nonresident labour on rubber estates has been
increasing in recent years with the repatriation of Indian
labour in the Kelani Valley district. The wage rates on
the rubber estates are significantly higher. As at November 1978 a rubber tapper earned a total wage of about
Rs 17 per diem as against Rs 9 received by a tea plucker.
(61) If account is taken of the shorter hours of work on
a rubber estate (the normal working day is around five
hours ending by 11 a.m. or noon), the disparity is even
greater. The price-wage supplement for rubber workers is
somewhat higher than for tea workers - and in their case
the supplement is limited to a maximum of 30 cents per
diem. The higher wage rate of rubber workers can hardly
be explained by the fewer days of employment on the estate
and the irregularity of work, since these workers do not
wholly depend on the estate. Tea estate workers though
larger in number, have apparently less bargaining power
than rubber estate workers, among whom there is a higher
proportion of nonresident workers with greater mobility
and alternative employment opportunities. Furthermore,
the structure of production costs in rubber, with its
lower proportion of wage costs, enables the rubber producers to bear an increased wage rate more easily than tea
producers; a given increase in the wage rate has a smaller impact on production costs. Though nonresident labour
fits into the pattern of rubber production, the planters'
ideal is transplanted Indian labour. What the planters
see as negative qualities of village labour are merely the
expression of the greater options of such labour, which
enable them to resist the classical system of plantation
management and control, including low wages and residence
on the plantation.

Though unequal intervals exist between different cultural operations, a plantation arranges its work regime so

as to meet the employment needs of its resident labour
force. Round-the-year employment is made possible by
several factors. First, the nature of plantation crops
(which are usually perennial and have a long maturation
period) allows flexibility in the timing of labour inputs,
unlike crops with a short growing period and seasonal
harvests, in which the pattern of labour utilization conforms with the biological cycle of plant growth. With a
simultaneity of work rather than a rigid sequential pattern, the labour force can, at any given time, be distributed among several activities: e.g. in the case of
tea - harvesting, pruning, fertilizing, weeding, forking
and draining. Though harvesting requires less labour on
certain days each month and during dry weather, the total
labour demand is relatively stable, owing to a range of
work connected with maintenance and upkeep: e.g. pruning,
draining, forking, road maintenance and repairs, and
weeding. Each of these activities, except weeding, needs
to be carried out at long intervals, and can be spread
throughout the year. The large scale of plantation operations also enables the workforce to be rotated every few
days, if not daily, from one division of the estate to
another or from one activity to another. Accordingly,
each production activity is staggered over a longer time
span, so as to create a more regular work pattern, albeit
in different operations, than would be available if these
operations were completed sequentially, with long spells
of inactivity in between. (With a sequential pattern the
whole of a tea plantation would be harvested, weeded or
pruned or its soil aerated within a relatively short
period. In this event the workforce would be discontinu-
ously employed - as in grain cultivation or even when
plantation crops are grown on a peasant basis.) In its
ability to utilize the available number of labourers unin-
terruptedly, in a smooth and continuous region of work, a
plantation resembles a factory. (62)
     Second, continuous employment - a prerequisite of resi-
dent labour - is made possible by an interchangeability of
work units, though on tea plantations there is a certain
sex-specificity of work. In Sri Lanka and India tea
plucking is done by women, but in Kenya by juvenile
labour. On the sugar cane fields in Peru adult males are
usually employed for the arduous work of cane cutting, and
such labour is nonresident. But on plantations generally
an absence of heavy manual tasks or specialized skills
makes for an overall flexibility of the workforce. Practically all members of the family (barring the very young)
belong to the workforce, so that despite low wages there
is a relatively favourable income for the family unit. In

India, about 45 per cent of tea plantation workers are
women, in coffee about 40 per cent and in rubber 25 per
cent. The employment of children is also greater than in
other occupations. On the plantations in Assam about 15
per cent of the workers are children, and in Bengal 20 per
cent; but in South India, where nonresident labour pre-
dominates, the proportion of children is only 10 per cent.
(63) Family groups function as work teams and the plantation workforce is typically an aggregation of family
units.

Third, a plantation stabilizes its aggregate labour
input during the year by a system of crop control (which
also overcomes bottlenecks in processing capacity). (64)
A portion of the estate is rested for a period longer than
is agronomically necessary. On tea plantations, this control system takes the form of lengthening the interval between plucking rounds. By various skiffs or light prunes
(which remove two or three inches of leaf three weeks
before the peak growth), the distribution of yields is
evened out. The skiffing of tea plants reduces the loss
in yield. The extended period within which harvesting
could be carried out and variations in the frequency of
harvesting reduce fluctuations in the demand for labour.

A different view regarding the need for resident labour
is that of Dr K.S.Sandhu. Plantation labour, he observes,
was 'lowly paid, unskilled and manageable', yet he makes
out that long-period employment was due to a need for
training and skills. The labourer had to remain on a
plantation 'for at least a few years, if not for the rest
of his life' because 'it took a year to train a labourer
to be a reasonable worker in a specific job such as tapping or factory work'. (65) In an earlier chapter I explained the almost life-long employment of labour in terms
of the capital outlay on the recruitment and retention of
labour, which the plantation sought to recoup by the payment of a lower wage than the market price of labour. But
even in Malaysia, to which Dr Sandhu's perspective is
limited, the workforce had a certain component of nonresident Chinese labour. Such labour was employed for short
periods at a time, on a contract basis, and they were not
committed to plantation employment. Many transferred
themselves from tin mines to the rubber estates; they
moved from one estate to another, and even out of the
rubber estates - an option denied to the Indian labourer.
'At least 25% of the nominal [Chinese] labour force never
engages in steady work, but moves from place to place
doing an odd job here and there, and cheating contractors
and managers as frequently as it can.' (66) Another component of plantation labour was Malay - in 1916 they were

a 'not insignificant part' of the rubber tappers in North
Perak, Province Wellesley and Kedah. Like the Chinese,
Malay labour also lived outside the estates, in their
traditional villages; and 'in many cases ... [they]
proved reliable and efficient workers'. (67) In Sri
Lanka, a small number of Sinhalese throughout the 1880s
and 1890s worked on tea plantations as nonresident labour
and later increasingly on rubber estates. In East Sumatra, rubber estates employed resident labour as well as
temporary nonresident labour. Those resident were Javanese immigrants recruited by the Sumatra Planters' Association (the 'Gappersu') and paid mostly in kind. On the
other hand, the nonresident labour combined estate employment with peasant farming, and they were paid solely in
cash.

While the employment of nonresident labour on a short-
term basis undermines the view that plantation work required long-term training and skills, the preference for
workers who were permanently attached to the plantations,
as already mentioned, was plainly due to the low wages
payable to such labour. The 'training' was the conditioning of the labourer to adverse pay and working conditions
involving the relentless routine of simple, repetitive
tasks. The Planters' Association of Malaya stated in an
Annual Report: 'Plantation workers are trained in a
matter of days or even hours, depending on the type of
work involved.' (68) Harvesting alone requires a certain
skill on the part of the individual worker, though a lack
of skill merely reduces the pace of work - a contingency
which the system of labour remuneration based partly on a
piece rate provides for. The tapping of young rubber
trees must be of a high standard to avoid wounding the
bark; but this work is assigned to the experienced tappers, who are initiated as 'sundry workers' on the old
rubber - which could withstand somewhat rough handling.
(69) These workers take the place of the regular tappers
when they fail to turn out for work. In an industrial-
type organization (which includes certain agricultural
enterprises) most workers are entrusted with equipment
which is expensive and complex, and neglect by or inefficiency of an individual could impair the overall result.
In such a productive organization the use of equipment necessitates responsibility, alertness and care, just as the
interrelatedness of the work must lead to the co-ordination and the synchronization of effort.

On plantations, while the nature of the work did not
require long-period employment, the system of work organization facilitated supervision of large numbers of workers, untrained and illiterate. Labour gangs carried out

routine tasks under the eye of an overseer. The physical
layout of a plantation enabled a single European manager
traversing the area on foot or on horseback to supervise
the entire field-operation, involving sometimes a thousand
workers. 'Besides being unskilled, the work is of such a
character that if improperly executed the error can be de-
tected and the worker required to correct it.' (70) A
South Indian planter at the beginning of this century
noted the salutary effect of punitive measures on careless
tea pluckers: 'When the day's work is done the women
bring the leaves to be weighed and if any of the baskets
be found to contain unduly coarse leaves, the whole day's
work should be confiscated; if this be done once or
twice, it will operate very beneficially upon the careless
pluckers.' (71) 'Tasks' which required relatively more
attention were paid on a piece rate, and negligence was
severely penalized. The word 'tasks' was suggestive of
a moralistic basis on which work was extracted. The expression originated in the plantations of the New World
where the slaves had to be made obedient and industrious.
(72)
     The care and responsibility exercised has been found to
be a function of the wage and other incentives offered.
On the rubber estates in East Sumatra where both permanent
and temporary, nonresident workers are employed, most of
the tapping is carried out by the permanent labour, and in
this more than in any other estate work incentive payments
are adopted with beneficial effects on work efficiency.
Likewise on some of the palm oil plantations where as a
result of piece rate payments and a system of wage premiums 'the labourers have [even] shown interest in maintaining estate equipment since their productivity is related
to the conditions of the tools with which they work'. (73)
On the other hand, 'the reported shortage and the indifferent work performance of borongan [contract] labour on
the rubber and palm oil plantations in North East Sumatra,
has been attributed to insufficient incentives'. (74)
     Despite the large-scale nature of the plantations
labour specialization is lacking. There is little differentiation in production processes when compared with those
in other enterprises of an acknowledgedly precapitalist
nature. For example, in Asia the cultivation of paddy has
several distinct processes, viz. ploughing, the preparation of field bunds, fencing, transplanting, soil aera-
tion, water distribution, weeding, the application of
fertilizer, pest control, harvesting and threshing. (75)
A rather complex aggregation of separate processes was a
feature of even mining and shipbuilding in Europe in the
eighteenth century. In tea and rubber production the

number of distinct field operations is limited to harvesting (the tapping of latex or the plucking of tea), weeding, and soil conservation (mainly the digging of drains).
The same workers can perform a variety of tasks, moving
'from the field to the factory and back again'. Work
units are often interchangeable and rubber tappers or tea
pluckers could also carry out weeding or soil conservation. In rubber cultivation, the tappers are almost the
only distinct category of workers but they perform a
variety of tasks including weeding, maintenance and
upkeep, and the application of chemical stimulants to the
trees. The limited labour specialization in the cultivation of plantation crops is reflected in the absence of
capital equipment other than light hand tools. The field
operations engaging almost nine tenths of the labour force
involve rough physical toil. The estate labourers, though
organized on a rigorous system of routine and work discipline and functioning within a wage economy as part of a
vast rationalized operation, do not require any but the
simplest manual skills. 'We have in the Tamil coolie a
perfect machine for the cultivation of our tea, coffee, or
other tropical produce', declared L.B.Clarence in 1896
when celebrating the centenary of British rule in Sri
Lanka. (76)

A resident labour force which is characteristic of the
plantation system originated in the conditions of labour
supply as elaborated earlier. The system of recruitment
and retention, involving a capital outlay, necessitated
the attachment of labourers to the plantation for long
periods, and this system was in turn linked with a low
wage policy. The rudimentary physical work which was
mainly required would have made the plantations tolerant
of a high turnover of labour. Nevertheless, the loss of
a labourer who had been 'recruited' (not necessarily
trained) was as prejudicial to the plantation if he left
the day after he was taken on (before he could even gain
any work experience) as, say, a year later. The skills
required are minimal, and are no more complex than in exclusively peasant crops (e.g. for transplanting or reaping
paddy). (77) 'Factory' work on plantations requires a
moderate amount of mechanical knowledge but such work engages a minuscule portion of the workforce. In discus-
sions on the problems of labour supply or in the protests
against the government for employing labour which the
planters had recruited, the question of trained labour was
never an issue. As mentioned earlier, the plantation preferred 'raw' labour direct from South India, who could
easily be assimilated into the social structure of the
plantation, to non-assisted migrants who had been employed
locally, outside the plantations.

The argument in this chapter has been directed towards
showing that the largeness in the scale of plantation
operations is not an agronomic necessity; plantation
crops can be grown just as efficiently on smallholdings.
Neither is it a technical necessity; cultivation is essentially labour intensive, while processing requires a
certain amount of capital equipment, but since the equipment generally in use is of a divisible type it did not
lead to significant economies of scale. Rather, it has
been shown that the large scale of plantation operations
resulted from the heavy overhead costs of management and
of the extra-economic measures for acquiring and retaining
labour. In turn, these heavy management expenses arose
from the absentee nature of the investment, while the
capital outlay on labour was the result of the employment
of migrant labourers and the low wage structure on which
the plantation system was based. The rationale of this
arrangement will be discussed in the next chapter. That
plantations have survived is solely due to the disabilities imposed by plantation dominated states on smallholdings. The view that they are a modern, efficient
form of organization is illusory.

11 Plantations and technological stagnation

In the common conception of plantations, the processing facilities for the crops requiring a 'factory' and machinery of some sort or another carry with them the presumption of a technologically advanced form of production. The foreign ownership and management of the plantations are presumed to have required technology and management practices which pertain to a developed economy. Though the plantations are also regarded as a capitalist enterprise, the actual nature of the technology used has not been taken account of. The technological changes have been partly agrobotanical, based on (a) high-yielding plant material, (b) improved agronomic practices and (c) horticultural techniques (for instance, by yield stimulation the full genetic potential of trees could be realized regardless of age and variety). Whereas the agrobotanical changes have greatly increased yields, the changes in processing methods which have been equally impressive took the form mainly of product innovations, i.e. changes in quality, presentation and grading. In tea, there has been a better control over factory operations - with almost perfect regulation of temperature and humidity during the tea-drying process, a uniform withering of green leaf, and advances in factory hygiene. Improvements in processing machinery have resulted in lower fuel consumption, increased speed of drying the green leaf, and a saving in factory space. In rubber, parallel achievements have been made in latex-processing systems and in grading and marketing - including the production of concentrated latex, block rubber, and Standard Malaysian Rubber (SMR). (1)

These changes have sought to raise yields and output per acre, and to improve marketability and prices, rather than to reduce the unit cost of output. There was hardly a substitution of capital for labour. Such substitution was confined to the processing activities (which consti-

tute only a minor proportion of total production cost).
(2) The reduction of the labour intensity on plantations
has been marginal. The industrial revolution type of
technology, with a sharp fall in production costs due to
a change in factor proportions, was lacking. Generally no
distinction is made even, in the context of the plantation
system, between output-increasing technologies and those
which reduce costs per unit of output, and technological
change has been associated merely with the former. (3)
The increase in labour productivity and the economies in
cost that were achieved were not significant in an overall
sense. The improvements were comparable with those in the
production of peasant crops - especially paddy. Technology in the so-called backward peasant sector underwent at
least the same kind of evolution as that in the plantation
sector; in some respects it displayed an even greater
dynamism. There have been improvements of a botanical
type, involving planting material and the control over
plant pests and diseases, as well as an increased use of
capital in depth, by the introduction of mechanized
ploughing (a change from the animal plough to the tractor). The shortening of cultivation periods has led to
multiple harvests. In rice milling, a production phase
comparable to the processing of plantation crops, there
has been a substitution of capital for labour. (In Indonesia, the use of the sickle instead of the hand-held
knife halved the demand for harvesting labour, and an
equally significant change has been from the hand pounding
of paddy to the use of the mechanical huller.) (4) In
peasant agriculture in Japan, improvements of this kind
led to a phenomenal increase in productivity per worker -
not just per hectare - by 2.6 per cent annually from 1878
to 1917. (5) The changes in plantation technology in
crops such as tea, rubber, coconut or oil palm could not
dislodge peasant cultivators who have continued to supply
the world market in their own fashion. The stagnation in
productive forces in the plantation system went hand in
hand with low wage levels and a basically precapitalist
pattern of labour relations.
    Cane sugar alone, among plantation crops, underwent
significant technological and social changes. Though
their developmental impact on the economy was hardly felt,
a discussion of the changes that occurred in cane sugar
production is a useful basis for examining the viability
of plantation production in general. Sugar production
initially was no different from other plantation-crop production. Expansion was purely quantitative. Mills and
cultivation units proliferated; the equipment was bigger
and better - made from more durable materials and capable

of being used intensively. The use of high-yielding cane
varieties and even partial mechanization of the mill required no change in work methods or in social relations.
Slave labour remained the basis of production. The mill
could not cope with the quantity of cane available, and it
was the bottleneck in the expansion of production. Though
cane production was limited to only five months in the
year slave labour fitted into the pattern, because of a
large amount of off-season work - the growing of maintenance crops, woodcutting and cattle tending. After a
while this equilibrium was disturbed. Technological improvements in the sugar mill caused a 'qualitative change
in the capital stock'. (6) At the same time a phenomenal
increase in overhead costs limited the operation of the
mill to a very short period. Furthermore, the subsistence
plots lost their rationale, with the sugar mill's competing claims for cane land and the availability of imported foodstuffs. The reduction in off-season work
undermined the residential labour system, making wage
labour cheaper to employ than slave labour. (7)

There was also a separation between the agricultural
and industrial aspects of cane production. Planting, cultivation and harvesting were left to the small-scale cane
growers who supplied a sugar mill owned by a corporate
body. But with the emergence of central factories (the
land-and-factory combine), the cane growers became vassals
of the sugar mill owners. As the size of mills and their
cane requirements increased, rival mills extended their
sources of cane supply by means of private railways. Thus
the sugar mill acquired control over vast extents of cane
territory and was able to depress the price paid to the
grower. In cane sugar production technological progress,
apart from the competition of beet sugar producers, was
due to certain agronomic reasons. The bulk and heaviness
of the raw cane carried to the mills presented formidable
problems in materials handling and in the recovering of
sugar. The seasonality of the crop and the difficulty of
storing the unprocessed cane also required a whole year's
production to be milled in a short period. A large mill
needed to meet peak demand lay unutilized during the rest
of the year. (8)

The displacement of individually owned mills, and the
subordination of small farmers, involved concentration and
centralization of production. (9) Land belonging to
thousands of small farmers was consolidated into immense
agrarian units. From the ranks of independent small
farmers a proletariat arose - other plantation crops did
not generate their own labour supply. The cane workers
also became related to the mill on a contractual basis in-

stead of by direct physical coercion. Wage payments were
exclusively in the form of cash. The workers functioned
within the framework of a labour market, and planter
paternalism was ended. Cane workers, as Mintz wrote with
reference to Puerto Rico, became politically conscious,
and 'formed not only a class but a class with a culture,
an ethos and ideology'. (10) Even before the abandonment
of slavery, technology had begun to create a new labour
system in the sugar mill. To operate the vacuum pan
evaporator introduced in the early 1840s a 'free labour
cell' emerged within the slave establishment. Slaves continued to be used but only in processes 'up to the machine
and after the machine'. (11)
    An almost complete break with the traditional produc-
tion system was reflected not merely in the technological
levels and in the pattern of labour relations; there was
also a fairly high degree of work specialization both in
the cultivation process and in the mill. Cultivation consisted of a large number of separate activities - e.g.
planting, 'weeding, ditching, irrigating, cane cutting,
wagon loading, aligning, cane trash'. Even before large-
scale mechanization, slaves were made to concentrate on
specific tasks. They 'stayed in the same place, repeating
a thousand times the same exhausting motions' (12)
throughout the day. Later specialization increased considerably in the field and in the factory, and a hierarchy
of labour developed.
    Though my concern here is the nature of plantation
technology, a fleeting reference may be made to another
branch of colonial production in which technological
change was just as spectacular as in cane sugar. In tin
mining in Malaysia, the use of hydraulic machinery led,
over a ten-year period, to a fourfold increase in the capacity of the dredge, and its depth of working increased
from four to six times. (13) Labour productivity increased more than one and a half times between 1939 and 1961.
From the late 1920s there was consequently a vast expansion in the ore deposits which could be economically
mined. The improvements in mining and in cane sugar production, though qualitatively different from those which
generally occurred in plantation crops, were hardly analogous to the progress in techniques which continually
transformed the economies of the developed countries.
They were essentially improvements of a mechanical nature,
in sugar cane to a far lesser extent. Though representing
a higher phase of mechanization based on inanimate energy,
they were based on mechanical contrivances per se as distinguished from rationalization or the use of science.
(14)

In the advanced economies, while technological changes
in the several branches of production required the direct
application of capital in production as well as the use of
science, it was the latter type of development, based on
what Veblen called the 'technology of physics and chemistry', which continually transformed the productive process. This type of development was also far more complex
and took a longer time to achieve than 'mere mechanical
ingenuity'. The recognized views on this issue were expounded by Marx. 'Science and technology', he wrote,
'give capital a power of expansion independent of the
given magnitude of the capital functioning.' (15) Growth
acquires a qualitative dimension relying upon technique
and less on capital formation as such. A saving in both
labour and capital involves economies in the use of constant capital, per unit of output and in relation to variable capital; there is an increased durability of plant
and equipment, a saving in raw materials and fuel, fuller
utilization of waste materials and by-products, and a
rationalization of production. These improvements were
the nodal point of a technological impulse which had the
ability to transform and expand productive capacity all
round, creating a long line of development possibilities.
The improvements had an impact far beyond their immediate
boundaries. The 'multiplication of production branches'
extended the frontier of growth and gave it a self-propagating quality, both increasing demand and reducing costs;
each branch of production generated external economies
while benefiting from those generated by other branches.
(16) Concomitantly there was a diffusion of scientific
knowledge among the workforce and the community as a
whole. The rational manipulation of the environment was
pervasive in its effects. 'He who is rational in one area
is more likely to be rational in others.' (17)

An admirable example of such progress is the use of applied chemistry by the brewing industry in France and
England in the second half of the nineteenth century.
This illustrative comment is based on research by E.M.
Sigsworth. (18) The brewing industry produced a train of
changes some of which were fundamental. The diseased fermentation of beer had been causing a loss in output of
about 20 per cent until laboratory research and studies,
from the 1870s, resolved this problem as well as some
others which pertained not merely to the breweries. Louis
Pasteur's identification of bacteria alien to the pure
fermentation of yeast broadened scientific knowledge on
the nature of fermentation when barley was converted into
malt and malt into sugar. The role of the nitrogenous
content of barley in the extract derived from it was de-

termined. Qualified chemists were now required in the
breweries. The Institute of Brewing was founded in the
1890s and ten years later Birmingham University started a
School of Malting and Brewing. A partiality for light
sparkling bottled beer drew attention to the problem of
secondary infection in the bottle and the technique of
dealing with it 'practically revolutionised the bottling
trade'. A bottle-machinery industry drastically cut down
production time and costs. Two other innovations were the
'crown cork' and pressed glass tumblers. These advances
in manufacturing had their effect on the agricultural
side. Hop harvests were stabilized, and yields doubled
within five decades.

The improvements that occurred in sugar cane production
and in mining, while being largely of a mechanical nature,
were not part of a general advance nor of a cumulative
kind. They were very specific improvements, limited in
their impact, without the ability to transform neighbouring branches of production through link effects. In comparing the introverted nature of this technology with the
pattern of scientific improvements in the developed countries, we may even consider the changes in rice cultivation which occurred in nineteenth-century Japan, based on
small farming. Each move in technology produced several
related moves, whose cumulative effect was substantial.
The innovations, stated T.C.Smith, 'rarely if ever came
singly; they hung together in clusters by a kind of inner
logic; one innovation brought others in its train, and
often could not be adopted independently of them'. (19)
For example, with the use of inorganic fertilizer, the
labour released from the collection of organic manure was
used for multiple cropping; labour was also re-absorbed
in intensive weeding required by the increased use of
fertilizer. The replacement of the spade by the animal
plough induced improved drainage and water control.
Finally, larger crops required more labour for harvesting.
A chain reaction of a somewhat similar nature, to which I
referred in an earlier chapter, was that brought about by
the introduction of the stirrup in medieval warfare in
Europe.

Though technological progress in one branch of production does not per se lead to the development of the economy as a whole, it is still necessary to examine the resistances to technological advance in the plantation system.
I shall take up first some existing explanations. The
stagnation was attributed by Myint to an unstable demand
for plantation products, which made investors 'unwilling
to take the risk of locking up their capital'. (20)
Further, during the booms, output had to be expanded as

quickly as possible along existing lines and there was
no time to wait for the fruits of a longer term labour
policy; during the slumps it would be difficult to
raise capital for this purpose. This is an understand-
able account of why the cheap labour policy continued.
The question, however, is not the aggregate volume of
fixed investments which the plantations involved but that
these investments were basically not of the cost-reducing
kind. One component of them was the value of land, including the planted areas and capital improvements, e.g.
estate roads, superintendent's bungalow, etc. A far more
important component was the expenses of labour recruitment
and the overhead costs of maintaining a resident workforce, by the provision of amenities such as housing. The
investment in labour was a substitute for capital-deepening investments. In short, capital outlays were directed
towards an extensive rather than an intensive use of
labour.

Myint's presumption that it was an unstable demand for
plantation products which discouraged the improvement of
production techniques is at variance with his assertion
about a stable rate of expansion of colonial export agriculture over fairly long periods, covering years of high
and low prices. 'Once the opening-up process had got into
its stride, these countries generally experienced long
waves of economic expansion, lasting for at least two or
three decades, but frequently for longer periods.' (21)
In the case of tea, though inelasticity of both demand and
supply contributed to price fluctuations as in most plantation products, the centralization of production and
marketing and of entrepreneurial and financial policy of
the plantations in the hands of a comparatively few groups
made the control of supplies relatively easy; and thus
'the potential stability of the tea industry [was] even
greater than that experienced during recent decades'. (22)
'Booms and slumps notwithstanding the tea plantation industry has come to be regarded as one of the most stable
industries and tea shares are bought as an investment
rather than for speculation.' (23) Irrespective of the
stability of markets, technological stagnation was common
to all plantation products excepting sugar.

Plantations by their very nature accustomed investors
at the outset to take a long view of their investments,
forgoing dividends until new plantings attained maturity
or until estates were expanded or improved and placed on
a viable footing. As mentioned elsewhere, dividends of
tea and rubber companies were withheld for several years.
The shareholders, according to a company chairman, acquiesced in a 'self-denying policy', and 'the profits earned

year by year [were] steadily returned to meet the cost of
capital expenditure'. The question then is not that plantation investors were averse to 'locking up capital', as
Myint makes out, but that they preferred to use capital in
one way rather than another, in capital-widening instead
of capital-deepening investments. Capital was invested in
acquiring and maintaining labour rather than in aids to
production. The reasons for this will be discussed at a
later stage.

Another explanation of technological stagnation is the
physical environment of plantation crops and the nature of
the harvests. In tea cultivation the difficult terrain -
steep and rocky slopes - and the need for selective plucking of the tea leaves are regarded as impediments to
mechanization. For example, Youngil Lim: 'It seems that
mechanisation has been prohibited on technical grounds
rather than on the "cheap labour policy" of the foreign
plantation owners as Myint asserts.' (24) Even allowing
for the fact that not all tea land is situated on undu-
lating hillsides that would prevent the use of tractor-
type machines, there is another view of this problem. The
real obstacle to mechanizing field operations is much less
the nature of the terrain than the traditional arrangement
of the tea bushes - which are planted too close together
for the manoeuvring of any mechanically propelled equipment. The only appliance that could be used is one which
the labourer could carry, including the engine which
drives it. Moreover, if new planting were done on the
contour the difficulty resulting from steep slopes and
field drains would be reduced. S.J.Wright, who on an invitation under the Colombo Plan examined the problem of
mechanizing tea cultivation in Sri Lanka, found that, with
an appropriate bush pattern and layout of drains, fairly
straightforward mechanization was possible that would
reduce existing labour requirements by at least 50 per
cent. Experiments over an eighteen-month period indicated
that bush management (i.e. maintenance of yield) was not a
problem, and Wright felt that if this was indeed the case
'any short-comings on the manufacturing side will not be
difficult to rectify'. 'There is a very strong case for
giving serious attention to mechanisation in direct association with replanting, and for instituting further enquiry and experimentation necessary to bring it to practical fruition.' (25)

In assessing the purely technical obstacles to mechanization, two general considerations must be taken into account. One is that in agriculture technical and scientific progress has been complex. Such progress began much
later, and was slower than in industry - Marx referred to

the 'earlier' and more rapid development of the mechanical
sciences and their application compared with that of
organic sciences. (26) The problems of mechanizing agriculture that have arisen at various stages in its development are not unique to the cultivation of tea. The cotton
plant, for example, lacks the uniformity and the cultural
simplicity of cereal crops and its mechanical harvesting
requires very complex equipment. The cotton picker could
not easily accommodate the technical adaptation in agricultural machines made possible by a series of inventions
from McCormick's reaper to the modern combine harvester.
The mechanization of sugar reaping in Hawaii, impelled by
labour shortages, required a great deal of improvisation
and even of adjustments in the harvesting operations - in
the absence of specially devised reaping machines. (27)
For picking 'unassailable' crops such as grapes and
tomatoes prototypes of machines have been developed. On
many Brazilian plantations mechanical cultivators and tree
trimmers are becoming commonplace. Tree crops are being
subjected to 'tree shakers' in California. Tea is largely
machine picked in the Soviet Union. (28)

The second point to be considered is that scientific
and technological advances are not independent of social
needs. The nature and pace of these advances are conditioned by the capacity of different producers to profit
from them. Technological change is both encouraged and
limited by the prevailing economic and social milieu and
its ruling interests. (At a time when England, faced with
the growing fuel needs of industry, was using the steam
engine to drain out flooded coal mines, a feudal prince in
Germany, having obtained one of these machines, employed
it to operate the fountain in his manorial park.) (29)
When inventors were ahead of social needs as expressed by
the dominant interests (businessmen, government and the
military), their ideas were ignored and the fruition of
innovative ideas and the pace of scientific advance were
delayed. At the same time, there could be autonomous impulses to technological progress which would influence
entrepreneurial policy.

The technological backwardness of the plantations was
inherent in their structure. As a system of production,
the plantations had an anti-technology bias. Their framework of labour relations, including the pattern of labour
utilization, control and retention, aimed for a low wage
structure which was central to the plantation system. A
relevant factor in this connection is also the relation
between merchant capital and productive capital in plantation enterprise, which, as explained earlier, encouraged
technological and marketing strategies that were geared to

maximizing the gross proceeds of a plantation rather than
to reducing costs of production and enlarging its net
profits. Absentee ownership, and the significance of the
purely commercial operations at the time the plantation
economy was founded, made the plantation very much of a
merchant's game - in which profits were wrung from controlling spheres of production and engrossing markets
rather than from the investment of capital in depth and
a lowering of production costs.

Though my concern is with the institutional resistances
to technological change in the underdeveloped countries, a
useful analogue will be the problems of factor substitutability on the cotton plantations in Southern USA. The
labour conditions and production technology were similar
to those in tropical plantation colonies. The parallelism
was also due to the transplanted Africans who lent themselves 'to ready exploitation by the white planters'. (30)
Share-cropping, which later became the basis of cotton
production, enabled the planters to retain control over
the production process, the share-cropper merely providing
the labour of himself and his family. He worked at the
existing technological level and at the lowest rate of
earnings in America. The crop lien and the food and
clothing furnished by the landlord, which kept the share-
cropper persistently in debt, became a substitute for the
slave driver's whip. The tying of labour to the plantations by means of this 'highly unequal power relationship'
was reinforced by the 'continued absence of alternative
employment opportunities', the denial of credit for any
purpose other than cotton growing, and the refusal of
white landlords to sell arable land to blacks; labour
recruiting in the Southern states for employment outside
was also disallowed. With a cheap, stable and docile
labour force, the economy of the American cotton region
therefore preserved much of its original character.

This system of labour relations on the cotton plantations delayed the mechanization of production long after
the advent of the tractor. 'The principle of the cotton
stripper, now widely used in the High Plains of Texas,'
wrote J.H.Street, 'was known in 1874, but did not arouse
serious interest until the critical year of 1926, and
thereafter only intermittently until the reduction in
migratory labour during the second world war made a technological solution imperative.' (31) A mechanical cotton
picker was patented in 1850 and soon after that several
hundred patents were filed; in the 1930s an automatic
picker was developed that could pick in seven and a half
hours as much as could be done by hand in five weeks. (32)
Yet the manual picking of cotton continued. Though the

planter's lack of interest in this invention was attributed (in an official report) to the fear of unemployment,
there was a reluctance to dismantle the plantation system
when there existed a cheap and docile labour force. 'A
routinised, poorly educated and politically ineffective
rural labour force ... rendered sustained inventive and
developmental interest in labour-saving farm machines
economically pointless.' (33) Only during and after the
Second World War did 'the stultifying effect of southern
social and economic institutions' weaken. A sharp increase in the demand for labour led to a large exodus from
the South and to improved wages and working conditions of
those who remained. Along with the disappearance of cheap
labour, the intervention of the federal government induced
planters to overcome the technological lag in cotton cultivation.

In the case of tea and rubber plantations, there is no
evidence of the kind which Street has furnished in regard
to cotton production in the American South where labour-
saving devices that were already available, or with known
potentialities, were not made use of. However, in the
technology of tea processing a study of such changes that
have taken place indicates a strong reluctance to disturb
established methods. The conservatism was stronger in Sri
Lanka than in India and Kenya. The traditional methods of
tea processing persisted longer in Sri Lanka, as seen in
the delay in adopting the trough system of tea withering.
The trough saves both factory space and labour; it has a
much bigger capacity for leaf, about 7 lb per square foot
or three to four times more than the older system based on
tats. (34) In 1962-3 the Colombo Commercial Co.Ltd, an
agency firm which also made tea machinery, adopted the new
withering device on the few estates it owned, but for
several years no other agency firm did so. India and
Kenya were at this time rapidly installing withering
troughs, but in Sri Lanka they did not gain prominence
until increased crops made the existing withering capacity
a serious bottleneck. The CTC machine ('crush-tear-curl')
as a replacement for the traditional tea roller encountered far more resistance. The CTC is a continuous process
of manufacture and produces tea of uniform size (in only
two or three grades). Its greater standardization, poor
'appearance' but good liquor and a quick infusion, make
CTC tea very suitable for the tea-bag market. The economies of scale are also far greater than those in the manufacture of 'orthodox' teas - which is a batchwise process,
based on the wringing action of a tea roller. Despite the
lower cost and a strong demand for CTC teas which prevailed in the world market (of which the Kenyan producers

took advantage), the orthodox methods of tea rolling have
persisted. In India and more particularly in Kenya (a
late developer) tea producers adopted the CTC machine, and
consequently factory capacity was enlarged and the manufacturing process on the whole was far more mechanized.
(35)

At a general level there were several factors which
militated against a vigorous search by the plantation
interests for technical alternatives to customary production methods. First, the large overhead·expenses which
had been incurred in securing and housing a labour force
ruled out labour-saving innovations. These expenses, consisting partly of 'coast advances' paid to the kangani or
recruiting agent, increased in periods of labour shortage,
as in the first decades of the century when the rubber
plantations in Malaysia began competing for labour. A
more substantial item of overhead cost was estate housing
and related amenities which enabled each plantation to
function as a separate entity from the rest of the rural
economy and society. The plantations preferred to invest
in the recruitment and settling of migrant labour rather
than to obtain its labour supply, in a free market, at a
higher wage but without the need for a capital investment.
(36) The production methods on plantations were thus
interwoven with the system of labour relations. This is
to say, the plantation invested capital in labour, whose
capital value was liable to be lost by a labour-displacing
technology. Though unamortized capital is not always a
barrier to innovation, the amount and proportion of overhead capital on plantations which was committed to the
traditional method of production was a disincentive to
change.

The resident labour system ruled out a piecemeal devaluation of the capital that had been invested in labour
recruiting and settlement. As long as one or a few work
operations remain unmechanized, a reduction in the labour
force would create a relative scarcity of labour; alternatively, the retention of the full complement of labourers, some of whom are not needed for the rest of the year,
would raise overhead costs. The impracticality of a
gradual or partial mechanization of production in a situation of resident labour was referred to by Zimmerman in
the context of the American cotton plantations. (37)

If cotton must be picked by hand labour that must live
on the plantation there is no incentive to introduce
mechanical means of plowing, cultivating and chopping.
But if, as in many parts of our western cotton belt,
migratory labour is available for picking, mechanisation can proceed piecemeal even though mechanical
pickers have not yet been perfected.

For a similar reason the sugar plantations in the West
Indies persisted in using the hoe from the seventeenth to
the early nineteenth century; some of the resident
labourers needed to meet the crisis demand for labour
during the five harvesting months would have been wasted
for the rest of the year if the hoe was replaced by the
plough. (38) To adopt piecemeal mechanization some planters in the Southern states of America did away with resident labour and adopted a system of quasi share-cropping
labour. Wage payments were combined with either share-
cropping or the granting of subsistence plots. In either
form the non-wage income was insufficient for a living,
compelling the workers to be available for plantation work
as day labourers. (39)

A second barrier to technological change has been the
structure of the market for plantation products. Technology is the child of competition; the individual firm
under competitive conditions must innovate, in order to
keep in line with go-ahead rivals or to inflict losses on
others. (In the absence of competition, enterprises try
to conserve the value of past investment unless new techniques would more than cover losses from the replacement
of existing equipment.) It is the competitive element in
monopoly firms which induces even them to carry out research and innovation. Owing to their access to capital
and control over the market, they are, in fact, well
placed to risk making these investments. The 'monopolist'
of the real world (being rarely the sole firm but merely
one giant among a few) competes to maintain and strengthen
his relative market share - both by sales promotion and by
cost-reducing innovations. He works on two fronts -
minimizing competitive price reductions and raising productivity. In this connection the production monopolist
must be distinguished from the trading monopolist. The
former protects himself by reorganizing the production
process or by putting out new products (i.e. differentia-
ting his market). The latter resorts to extra-economic
restrictions and vested interests, including trade licences, royal charters, legal privileges and, in the heyday
of merchant capital in Europe, physical violence. In the
production and marketing of plantation crops (excepting
sugar cane), where management and control is centralized
in a handful of agency houses, the prevalent monopolies
are of the trading type, not vulnerable to annexation
through the market. They are not a 'resultant of the
stresses inherent in the process of capitalist development' which encourage technological research and innovation. (40)

The production of and trade in plantation crops were

determined by trading monopolies consisting of agency
houses, brokers, shippers and the marketing combines in
the metropolitan countries. I have demonstrated elsewhere
how these monopoly interests perpetuated their control
over the plantation economy, and I shall show in later
sections of this chapter their influence on the technological and marketing strategies of plantations so as to
maximize gross revenue instead of minimizing production
costs. In the case of tea, an important factor making for
market imperfection is heterogeneity of the manufactured
leaf - appearance, colour, flavour, briskness and the
strength of the liquor. The quality of tea is determined
by natural factors (climate, soil and altitude), and thus
plantation profits include an element of rent. The quality of tea is also determined by management policies connected with plucking standards and manufacturing processes, as well as by seasonal variations in the atmospheric
conditions. For example, the Uva teas of Sri Lanka,
which have a distinctive flavour, are produced during a
period of between one and a quarter and two months when
weather conditions are optimal; likewise the Dickoya
teas, the Maskeliya teas, and in India the Darjeeling
teas. The quality of tea as a determinant of brokers'
valuation is itself not a homogeneous attribute but is
influenced by individual judgments. (41) By gradual changes in the composition of the leading brands, the large
tea-blending companies could influence consumers' choice
and the pattern of demand. Blending and the use of trade
names (often the 'garden marks' of different estates)
result in considerable product differentiation even within
the broad categories that are traded in the different markets. The Middle East countries consume mostly low-eleva-
tion tea, America, Europe, Australasia and South Africa
high- and medium-grown teas, and the producing countries
mostly tea dust. The market imperfection due to these
complexities is intensified by the control over the market
exercised by the larger tea-buying interests, having close
connections with tea brokers, shippers and distributors.
    The presumption made by P.P.Courtenay, (42) that plan-
tations compete among themselves, compete with substitute
products and, in some instances, with smallholders is unrealistic. In beverages and vegetable oils and fats, the
substitute for one plantation product is another product
which is also plantation-based and shares the same technology (e.g. tea and coffee; coconut oil, palm oil and
groundnut oil). The location of the plantations exclusively in the underdeveloped world placed them on the same
technological platform, without a compelling need for
technological change. An 'opportunity' of this kind was

not open to settler agriculture in Kenya, Rhodesia and in
the lands of the Maghreb, whose products - wheat, dairy
product, livestock, fruit and wine - had to face competition from efficient producers abroad. When the settler
farmers outgrew the sheltered domestic market a revision
of their production methods became imperative. In plantation crops, competition did not extent to the mode of production. Furthermore, while the demand for most plantation crops has a low price elasticity, the strong world
demand for these crops which prevailed over long periods
dampened the effects of low labour efficiency on the value
productivity of labour. Where demand is strong and competition limited 'even primitive production methods might
rank high in measured "efficiency"'. (43)

In plantation products competition has arisen in the
past from outside the sphere of plantation production;
that is, not from other plantation products or plantation
regions, but from inorganic substitutes in the industrial
economies. However, the development of these substitutes
took place mostly in periods when the supply of plantation
products was, or was likely to be, cut off rather than in
the course of normal trading conditions. (44) (An exception to this was the invention of synthetic dyes which
crippled the indigo plantations of Assam - they were the
outcome of a continuous progress in industrial chemistry.)
The wartime shortages of organic raw materials fostered
technological advances which continued long after, yielding a crop of synthetics which were highly competitive;
they were durable and versatile, had considerable cost advantages, and their supply could easily be controlled.
However, plantations to some extent could tide over a
crisis by wage cuts, without altering their production
technology. The high labour intensity of production
causes a slight lowering of the wage rate either directly
or by increasing work norms ('task sizes') to have a significant effect on the overall cost of production. For
instance, the rubber planters in Malaysia did so in the
1930s to meet the competition of smallholders. As the
Planters' Association of Malaysia explained, (45)

each cent saved [by a reduction in wages] is another
lease of life to those [estates] approaching the
margin. Therefore, there are today estates in tapping
which already would have discontinued had it not been
for the respite granted by the general reduction of
labour costs.

Many estates increased the working time of rubber tappers
from seven to nine hours - the maximum allowed by the
Labour Code. (46)

In the case of raw materials, the low proportion which

their value constitutes in the cost of the final goods
makes technological advance and cost reduction in the
primary stages of production far less significant than at
the manufacturing end. The reluctance of plantation interests to effect cost reductions at the raw material
stage is demonstrated in Malaysia, where they strenuously
opposed the first replanting scheme, recommended by the
Mudie Commission in 1954 and supported financially by
government. (47) At this time some of them had also made
stable forward contracts (extending in some cases over
three or four years) with the big rubber manufacturers in
the USA. To some extent, these manufacturers were interlocked, as in Liberia, with the plantation rubber interests. It was the threat from synthetic rubber which induced natural rubber producers, in the 1950s, to begin replanting with superior clones. Replanting on a systematic
basis was put off until competition from synthetic rubber
caused a displacement of natural rubber and a steady decline in prices.

The positive effects of market structures on technology
and production costs are demonstrable in the case of cane
sugar. An impetus to improvements in cane sugar production was competition from the beet sugar industry in
Europe. A brief run-through of developments in beet sugar
production in Europe would be helpful. The beet sugar industry, established during the Napoleonic blockade of the
Continent, had the support of powerful interests and of
government bounties during the rest of the century. Beet
sugar production at first was handicapped, in comparison
with cane sugar, by the need for annual planting, the
careful washing of the beet and a complicated slicing and
maceration process. The resolution of these problems required technological improvements and the growth of capitalist farming. In Russia, where the development of capitalism occurred relatively late, the sugar beet industry
was a trail blazer. The first steam ploughs were used in
the growing of sugar beet, and the processing of the crop
became 'highly concentrated in big capitalist enterprises'. (48) The 'competitive edge' which the beet sugar
industry gained set the pace for productivity growth in
cane sugar. As early as the 1820s the sugar producers in
Cuba were compelled to work their rollers by steam and to
use imported equipment for clarifying the cane juice.
Likewise the system of vacuum concentration which came to
be used in Cuba originated in Europe's beet sugar factories. Mechanization brought into the sugar mill a free-
labour cell which led eventually to a change in both the
technology and the 'juridico-institutional' relations of
production. (49)

The third factor which dampens innovation is the specific business and financial relationships between the
managing agency firms and plantations. The agencies
'rarely hold substantial investments in the operating
companies, [and] ownership often is virtually divorced
from control'. (50) The net profits of the plantation
companies (which technological changes would influence
through a reduction in costs) are thus irrelevant to the
business interests of the agency firms. The cleavage of
interests between the agencies and the shareholders of
plantation companies was discussed in an earlier chapter,
in terms of the purchasing policy of the agencies, the
exorbitant payments to the agency firms and the difficulty
of transferring agency rights. Here I shall confine
myself to the impact on plantation technology of the different entrepreneurial interests between the agencies, qua
agencies, and the plantation-owners.

As also pointed out earlier, the basis of remuneration
of the agency house was the gross proceeds of the plantation company. The rationale of such a system related to a
period when commercial risks were high, because of shipping delays and the lack of timely information on market
conditions. Consignment sales were then the dominant form
of business transaction with commercial risks being borne
by the producer on whose behalf the merchant acted. The
application of this system to the plantations meant that
the agency's income was unrelated to net profits/losses of
a plantation, on which dividends of capital depend.

In a study of the financial accounts of plantation companies in Sri Lanka, N.Ramachandran mentioned that the
companies (51)

> are managed, for the most part, by agent-directors
> whose commissions vary with the quantity of tea or
> rubber produced. They therefore appear to favour
> maximum output even if the cost of winning it is high,
> i.e. they seem to maximise production rather than
> profit.

While expressing the conflict of interests between agencies and the plantation-owners, this statement, which G.L.
Beckford has also quoted, (52) is misleading. What the
agencies would wish to maximize is not output but gross
revenue (a combination of price and output); i.e. it is
maximum revenue that they would favour 'even if the cost
of winning it is high'. In the case of tea a larger revenue might be obtained from a larger output and a lower
price; but in rubber production, since the yield of latex
does not influence quality and prices, maximizing output
per se would maximize revenue. Ramachandran's exposition
also needs clarification on a few details. The 'agent-

directors' of the plantation companies are paid a fixed
fee just as are the other directors of these companies.
The commission payable by the companies is to the managing
agency firm of which the 'agent-directors' are invariably
principal shareholders, and this commission is usually
based on sale proceeds - not on the quantity of tea or
rubber produced.

The payments to the agency were a first charge on the
revenue of a plantation - in India the managing agents of
manufacturing firms, significantly, were usually paid on
a profits basis. Thus, while the plantations kept wage
rates as low as possible (creating a bias in favour of
labour intensity), the level of production costs and the
possibility of lowering them through technological changes
were not of direct interest to the agency compared with
maximizing the gross revenue. As K.E.Knorr stated, (53)

the size of the [agencies'] remuneration did not,
except in periods of very high or very low rubber
prices, vary with the profits of the rubber companies.
This seems unfortunate in view of their control over
management. The agencies were interested in lengthening the life of the operating rubber companies rather
than in maximising their net profit at any given price.
In general, their influence was one of caution and
conservatism rather than of progressive enterprise.

The same system of payment prevailed in the West Indies
and the American colonies where the plantation system
first developed. Richard Pares commented: (54)

Many overseers were paid by a percentage of the crop.
... This led them to neglect the future for the present, and to encourage expenditure without considering
whether the plantation could really afford it - that
was somebody else's business. Some, especially among
the attorneys, encouraged expenditure for its own sake,
*for they were merchants drawing a commission on stores
supplied to the plantation, which yielded them a handsome income, besides the 5 or 6 per cent* on the crop
which they took as commission.

In the guano export economy in Peru during the mid-nineteenth century, a similar divergence prevailed between the
interests of the consignment contractor who carried out
the 'loading, charter, storage and final sale' of guano
and those of the Peruvian government as owner of the guano
deposits. The contractor was reimbursed the costs incurred and also paid a 2 or 3 per cent commission on the
gross sale proceeds. The consequence of this financial
arrangement, as pointed out by J.V.Levin, was the steady
rise in the cost of transporting and marketing guano; and
the contractor had an interest, besides raising intermedi-

ate costs, in lowering (or raising) the sale price 'to the
point necessary for the maximisation of gross sales proceeds'. (55) Under the guano consignment sales system
rising costs, lower prices and outright fraud reduced the
government's revenue and aroused increasing public resentment in Peru. (56)

The policy of maximizing gross revenue determined both
the technological and the marketing strategies of plantations. Technology is geared to achieving greater output -
through increased productivity per acre (not per worker).
A typical response to rising costs was expressed by the
Marigold Tea Estates Ltd in its Chairman's report for
1968: 'Rising production costs can be effectively contained only by increasing yields [per acre] through sound
agricultural practice and by replacing the old tea with
new and vigorous V.P. [vegetatively propagated] material.'
The technology also seeks to maintain or improve quality,
partly by changes in processing methods. In so far as the
attributes of quality originate in natural conditions (57)
or are determined and propagated by the tea trade itself,
such attributes cannot be replicated, and plantation
profits contain an element of rent. On the other hand,
the prevailing marketing strategies for tea require a
multiplicity of grades which compose the various blends
and the maintenance of quality differences between grades.
Thus mechanical devices in either cultivation or processing which affect these attributes are ruled out. For instance, the partially mechanized shears used for tea
plucking in Japan (58) and the fully mechanized ones in
the USSR do not allow selective plucking; the mechanical
spreading of tea leaf for drying would bruise the leaf;
the CTC machine reduces flavour and involves greater standardization; and likewise the marketing of tea in the
form of tea-bags minimizes the influence of appearance and
colour of the leaf on consumer attitudes. The use of
quality teas as additives (much like essences) to improve
the flavour of the blended product gives it premium
prices. The specificity of these teas and their limited
substitutability give their producers an oligopolistic
position in the market.

In the case of tea, since quality (apart from the
effect of natural factors) is achieved by a relatively low
level of mechanization, the technological and marketing
strategies of plantations are interlinked. Thus Indian
and Sri Lankan teas are produced in a large number of
grades and at a much lower level of mechanization than
Kenyan teas; the latter are also far more standardized
(sometimes even artificially flavoured - e.g. mint teas).
The oligopolistic market catered for by tea producers in

Sri Lanka and India, with their resulting bias against
cost reductions through a rationalization of production,
is also seen in their response to a decline in profitability (due to a fall in price and/or to a rise in wage
rates). They would seek to maintain profits by expanding
output at the existing level of technology, preferring investments which increase marginal revenue than those which
reduce marginal costs. The policy of maximizing output
is, however, constrained by the system of wage payments
conforming to government policy. For example in Malaysia,
'task sizes' for rubber tappers could be increased only up
to a limit of 600 trees at a given wage rate. In excess
of 600 trees the tapper is entitled by a Court Award to a
tree bonus of 5 cents per ten trees. (59) But in Sri
Lanka the wage system on the tea plantations reduces wage
costs as output increases. The statutory 'price-wage supplement' is lower than for rubber plantation workers and
is subject to a ceiling of 30 cents per diem. Furthermore, the payment to tea pluckers for 'over pounds', i.e.
an output above the norm, is less than the notional piece
rate for the eight-hour working day (contrary to the over-
time principle). The rate for 'over pounds' is negotiated
between employer and employees and varies from district to
district. A bigger output than the daily norm thus involves an effective lowering of the wage rate without a
change in the physical productivity of labour.

Thus plantation technology, characteristically agrobotanical, enhances the profits of agency houses in two
ways. It involves increased inputs of fertilizer and
other agrochemicals, packing materials, etc., which are
purchased through the agencies. The expansion in complementary inputs that is characteristic of plantation technology is demonstrated clearly by the use of Ethyrel as a
yield stimulant in rubber. Though increasing output phenomenally, the use of Ethyrel requires a higher volume of
both fertilizer and harvesting labour. Also involved is
the cost of the chemical and of the labour for applying it
(including the preliminary work of scraping the tree
bark). A final item of expenditure, varying directly with
the volume of rubber sales, is the agent's commission -
categorized in plantation accounts under 'marketing expenses' and excluded in estimates of production cost.
While such technologies, involving a package of complementary inputs, reduce unit costs less than proportionate-
ly to the increase in output, their adoption also serves
the interests of industrial capital in the metropolis
which produce some of these inputs, viz. agrochemicals.
The circumstances in which Ethyrel was adopted as a yield
stimulant by plantations in Sri Lanka bear this out.

First, Ethyrel was adopted by plantations before its agronomic and economic implications were fully investigated,
at a time when the Rubber Research Institute was attempting to dissuade growers from using it except for old
rubber which was soon due for uprooting. (60) Second,
plantation technology, by its effect on output/revenue,
increases the agencies' income from commissions on marketing, shipping and insurance. These forms of income derived from the management of plantations conform with the
interests of the agencies as representatives of merchant
capital - concerned with the volume/value of transactions
rather than with productivity. A marketing orientation
gains precedence over cost consciousness. The emphasis
on output/revenue maximization also subserves the interests of the suppliers of material inputs which the high-
yielding technologies entail. (61)

The agrobotanical or chemical-based technologies involve an increase in complementary inputs (of materials
and labour), so that variable costs increase as output
expands. As R.W.Palmer-Jones observed of tea production
in Malawi, the inputs and outputs are related in a most
complicated manner. A single input (a fertilizer application) 'requires inputs of labour for plucking, and for
drying etc.'. (62) The nature of the technological
changes while expanding the output and revenue of the
plantation, on which the agency's commissions depend,
reduce costs per unit of output but only less than pro-
portionately to the increase in yield per acre. An increase in yields (with a greater flush of tea on each
plant or a larger volume of latex per rubber tree) reduces
the harvesting effort per unit of output. In the case of
tea there is a greater reduction in labour input with
vegetatively propagated plants because of uniformity in
the tea flush and a larger continuous leaf surface. But
generally the reduction in labour inputs is less than proportionate to the increase in output. In rubber, the
effect of an increased yield on production costs is partially offset by higher collection costs - additional
labour being needed to transport the latex to collection
centres either by hand or on bicycles. When the critical
carrying load is reached, the tapper who usually performs
this work or part of the tapping operation has to be assisted. On many rubber estates in Malaysia the maximum
load that a tapper can manage was reached nearly a decade
ago. (63) Likewise in the case of coconut; higher yields
(with bigger clusters of nuts) reduce the labour input
needed for plucking, but not for transporting the nuts to
a central point - and payment for transport is by the
number of nuts. In all these situations an expansion in

output enlarges the total volume of labour. This is to
say, the overall cost reduction is not a linear function
of increased productivity either per acre or per worker.
(64)

In plantations the technology of production, their
marketing strategies as well as the system of remuneration
of the agencies reflected fundamentally the domination of
merchant capital over productive capital in a precapitalist situation. The agency houses as representatives of
merchant capital appropriated surplus value from the plantations by being the suppliers of plantation materials and
inputs and by their control over the marketing and sale of
plantation produce. The commercial activities of the
agencies in relation to the plantations were discussed
earlier, in terms of the purchases made by the agencies on
behalf of the plantation companies and of the restraints
placed by them over the sale of plantation assets. Merchant capital was interwoven with productive capital - but
all the same it was entrepreneurially and financially independent. Treating commodity production merely as an accessory to its trading functions, merchant capital subordinated productive capital; it drew out surplus value
without developing the forces of production and, consequently, expanded relative surplus value - 'the direct aim
and determining motive' of the capitalist mode of production.

The non-technological factors connected with the dominance of merchant capital which constrained the scope and
impact of technological improvements on the plantations
had effects on the economy as a whole. The emergence of
an autonomous and inwardly oriented investment pattern was
hindered. Colonial export production as an offshore operation of the metropolitan interests was not permitted to
have linkage effects with the territorial unit where such
production was carried out. Thus technological change was
contained within the sphere in which it was relevant to
these interests, while imposing on the host economy a condition of 'modernized dependency'. The siting of the
capital equipment and knowledge industries in the developed countries made the application or utilization of such
technology by underdeveloped countries a very limited
exercise in scientific know-how. The monopoly of the
machine-building industry by the developed countries increased the dynamism of these countries and their profi-
ciency in discovering scientific knowledge; it widened
the technological distance between them and their underdeveloped trading partners, increasing their economic
hegemony and undermining the latter's growth potential.

The technical and economic transformation of sugar cane

production is enlightening when, compared with most plantation crops, it is viewed as arising from the diminished
importance of merchant capital. The short maturation
period of the sugar cane and extraordinarily high prices
made sugar producers relatively independent of outside
sources of credit. Nevertheless, in Cuba merchant interests had at the outset exercised control over the producers; they were Spaniards and the producers were
Creoles with 'potentially nationalist attitudes'. The
merchants controlled transport, warehousing and credit,
the supply of sugar boxes, equipment and provisions, and
the importation of slaves - and these activities, though
subsidiary to the main business of producing sugar, over-
shadowed it in importance and profitability. (65) But
from about the beginning of the nineteenth century the
power of the merchants over the production and marketing
of sugar diminished, after the producers won control of
the Real Consulado. After an initial compromise the producers tilted the producer-merchant power balance in their
own favour. For example, provision was made for extending
bank loans to sugar producers; the export duty on sugar
was to be removed (as well as taxes on the sale of land
and sugar mills); the tax on sugar boxes was to be administered by the producers; and the supply of Negroes
was to be increased and their price lowered. (66) Fundamentally the sugar producers freed themselves from the
grip of the merchants by a drastic change in the techno-
economic framework of production, with a large-scale substitution of capital for labour and of free labour for
slaves.

   In Cuba, while industrial capital took priority over
merchant capital in the sugar industry, in the economy as
a whole it remained subordinated to merchant capital.
Though the techno-economic transformation of sugar production involved a subordination of merchant capital to industrial capital, at the same time the sugar industry by
promoting the export-import character of the economy preserved a large sphere of activities in which merchant
capital dominated. Technological change in the sugar
plantations was thus compatible with the underdevelopment
of the economy. The by-products of the sugar industry
which offered immediate development possibilities were
wasted or else utilized abroad. The production of high-
grade molasses was principally for export - to be used in
the USA for manufacturing industrial alcohol. The price
of molasses was kept down by three or four American dis-
tillers who controlled the export trade in sugar. A livestock industry was not developed, though the sugar mills
owned large herds of cattle and though cane flour (ground

sugar cane) mixed with peanut oil cake was a source of
rich livestock food. Bagasse - a base for high-grade but
low-cost plastics materials - was not utilized. (67)
Also, sugar production was expanded to the exclusion of
everything else, and the sugar industry lay idle for six
or seven months in the year (the dead season). The control of social overhead capital by the sugar interests inhibited the growth of other branches of the economy. The
tariff structure encouraged imports of manufactured goods
as against raw materials - a policy which was slightly
modified in the 1920s. In return for the sugar quotas,
the USA kept the Cuban market for finished goods as its
preserve. 'Cuba went into a long sugar orgy which might
be called "the first dance of the millions".... The sugar
society was born - the semi-plantation which continued
with few essential changes into our times.' (68)

12   Labour relations in plantations

The technological stagnation in the plantation system, involving a low level of labour productivity, went hand in
hand with low wages. In a later chapter I shall discuss
the precapitalist nature of the plantations in terms of
the composition of their capital investment; capital was
invested on the acquisition and maintenance of a labour
force rather than on the techniques of production. A
corollary of the composition of capital investment was the
use of non-market mechanisms for the retention of a resident labour force; along with the encapsulated nature of
the plantation labour force, labour organization and control were designed to retard the mobility of labour and
stifle wage increases. The discussion in this chapter
will show that despite certain outward capitalist forms,
labour relations in plantations were essentially precapitalist in nature. The plantations of Malaysia, which will
furnish the background to much of the discussion, had a
dualistic pattern of labour relations within the precapitalist mode of production. Semi-serf labour coexisted
with labour of a more capitalist type. South Indian
labour, numerically predominant and constituting, as in
other regions, the classical plantation workforce was
semi-serf in character. The mechanisms of labour organization and control of Indian labour ensured a captive
workforce and a low wage structure amidst a potential
labour scarcity. Chinese labour, recruited and employed
under conditions resembling more those of a capitalist
labour market, and paid significantly higher wages, were
not fully integrated into the plantation system. While a
mode of production can include more than one set of labour
relations, the dominant form of relations on the plantations involving South Indian labour was precapitalist.
     The use of wage labour (even though wages were not
wholly paid in cash) was per se a break with the system of

labour relations in the peasant economy. Yet, the framework of recruitment, retention and disciplining of plantation labour was antithetical to the conditions of a free
labour market which it had been the historic role of
capitalism to establish. The distinguishing feature of
such a market, besides payment of a money wage, is the
determination of that wage by market forces. This meant
that the worker was free to move, to compete with others
in the labour market; he could benefit from a temporary
scarcity of labour as much as his employer could benefit
from temporary surpluses. The worker was mobile, because
he was unencumbered by property, and institutionally free;
unlike the serf, he was not bound to one employer or occupation. Alternatively, if he remained permanently in an
occupation it was because he had developed specific
skills. In other words, capitalism 'transformed labour
into a commodity being available for purchase (in theory
at any rate), being offered on the market to the highest
bidder, withdrawable at the discretion of the worker and
paid for in money'. (1) Such labour is free in a 'double
sense'; they do not, as in the case of peasant-proprie-
tors, own means of production, nor do the labourers 'themselves form part and parcel of the means of production, as
in the case of slaves, bondsmen, etc.'. (2) The possibility of wage increases in such a situation induced technological improvements, with a greater use of capital in
the production process.

The freedom of movement which was central to the
mechanics of wage determination under capitalism, and
indeed to the whole system of capitalist labour relations,
was lacking in the plantation system. A central element
in the plantation system was its captive labour force, on
which I shall elaborate, and the corresponding pattern of
labour recruitment, organization and control. While the
reliance on extra-economic pressures to secure and retain
a workforce was linked with the inability of the plantations to compete for labour with the peasant sector, the
retention of a labourer on the estate, permanently if possible, was not due to any occupational specialization
requiring technical skills or work experience. As explained in an earlier chapter, despite the large land area
and output of individual plantations, and the centralization of capital ownership in plantation companies and of
the management of companies by agency houses, there was
little specialization of production activities, even when
compared with certain enterprises of an acknowledgedly
precapitalist nature.

What was chiefly required was a conditioning of the
labourer to the living conditions and work regime on a

plantation. 'People ... who are accustomed to subordination, to permanency of abode, and who have moderate expec-
tations in regard to a livelihood' were thought to be
ideal. (3)   In Malaysia, a distinct preference was for
'raw recruits' from India or for those who had not been
outside a plantation. Immigrants who were on their own
or who had been employed by government, especially on
public works, were considered unsuitable. Compared with
those brought directly to an estate, they were more independent, assertive, less tolerant of chastisement, and
liable to abscond. 'Useless, undisciplined black-
guard[s]'! (4)   Efficiency on the part of the plantation
labourer meant adaptation to a way of life which regimented him completely both as a work unit and as a human
being. The style of living imposed upon estate labour -
even the architecture of their living quarters and the
regulations for their upkeep - left no room for individuality. Simple extensions to his house were prohibited.
(5)

> For instance, no labourer occupying a line may plant
> flowers in front of his residence. Similarly, a
> labourer risks his job if he puts up a tin shed to
> serve as a bathroom. The labour lines ... thus present
> a stereotyped appearance; line after line and row
> after row, built to a common plan and maintained in the
> same fashion.

Labour relations on a plantation were conditioned by
the capital investment in labour, consisting of the commissions payable to recruiting agents and the expenses of
transporting the worker over long distances and of housing
him; and the planter expected to recoup these expenses
through a lower wage rate than that in the free market.
The economics of this arrangement dictated the retention
of a labourer for as long a time as was possible; the
general absence of skills may otherwise have made the
plantations accept a high turnover of labour. The capital
outlay on a slave, as that on a horse, represented his
purchase value, but the operating expenses in both cases
were low, being limited to their metabolic needs. 'The
slaveowner buys his labourer as he buys his horse. If he
loses his slave he loses capital that can be restored only
by new outlay in the slave market.' (6)   A slave in an
economic sense was no different from a horse, and an indentured labourer differed from a slave in that he was
temporarily the property of the owner; during this time
he got a wage higher than the subsistence cost of a slave
but lower than the market price for labour. The plantation worker was a form of private property for at least
the period necessary for the owner to recover his investment.

The indentured labour system explicitly enabled the
plantation to recover the capital investment on labour.
In times of labour shortage, desertions and crimping increased so that both the recruitment of labour and its retention were difficult. Free and spontaneous emigration
was for this reason unacceptable to both planters and the
colonial state. The Labour Commission of 1890 regarded it
'necessary to sanction a contract of specified length, so
as to enable the employer to recover by the labour of the
coolie the sum advanced for the expenses of his importation'. (7) R.N.Jackson, when quoting this passage, explained, 'It was feared that the labourers and kanganies
would keep moving on from employer to employer, leaving
the importing employer in the lurch.' (8) Indenture,
which made fugitives criminally liable, was itself no
guarantee against desertions, and large numbers evaded
recapture. On the Malaysian rubber estates in Selangor
and Negri Sembilam in 1906, out of a total labour force
of 19,354, 3,182 absconded. (9) Precautions against
labour mobility included late payment of wages with a lag
of at least a month or two. (10)
     The plantation system was structured so as to retain
labour by extra-economic means, by placing impediments on
its free movement from one estate to another or outside
the plantations altogether. The first of these impediments was the role accorded to the kangany in labour relations;   second, management paternalism;   and, third, the
enclave nature of the plantations. The plantation system
vested in the kangany authority far beyond that of re-
cruiter and foreman. The labourer's lack of access to the
estate manager made the kangany the link between the
estate management and the labourers;   in the early years,
he even distributed wages on behalf of the employer, and
till recently a labourer's notice of resignation required
the kangany's endorsement. His ties of caste and kinship
with those whom he recruited gave a moral basis to his
authority. He mediated in their family affairs and was
their representative and spokesman in labour disputes.
Combined with this patron-client relationship between the
kangany and his labour gang was a creditor-debtor relationship, which placed the labourers in financial bondage
to him, and consolidated his leadership. As an intermediary the kangany was not a neutral element but a prop in
the power structure of the estate community. In the eyes
of the labourers he was effectively their employer.
     Apart from the debts which the labourers usually owed
him, the kangany had a financial interest in keeping the
labourers on the estate. He was paid by the estate partly
in the form of 'head money', based on the daily turnout of

labourers for work; 2 cents a day in Malaysia. When the
kangany wished to leave, he took his labour gang with him,
moving within the 'same restricted employment system'
(i.e. from one estate to another). The kangany's power
and control over the labourers was greater in Sri Lanka
than in Malaysia and, of course, greater during the
kangany system of recruitment than after. But regardless
of these different situations, the mere presence of the
kangany and his role in labour relations curbed the
labourer's freedom. In Malaysia, despite the abolition
of the kangany system in 1938 and the growth of trade
unions, 'the kangany never actually disappeared'. 'More
often than not - [he] remained a person whom the ordinary
Indian estate labourer preferred to avoid, at least not to
antagonise and always to appease.' (11)

The caste and family affiliations of plantation labour,
the use of the labour gang as a work unit, and the attachment of labourers to their respective kanganies, both
financially and morally, held the labourer on the estate.
The ending of the indenture system freed labourers from a
contract to serve for a specified period, making them
liable only for the financial advances given at the time
of recruitment. Yet, the mobility of the labourers was
not necessarily any greater. The planters seldom insti-
tuted civil proceedings for unrecovered advances but instead relied upon the kangany's influence on the labourer.
The advances given to the labourers were entered up as a
charge against the kangany, so that he was liable for
their repayments. The pattern of labour relations based
on the subjection of labourers to their kangany thus out-
lived the system of indenture. The kangany remained an
integral element in the plantation structure.

The lack of labour mobility was closely linked with the
enclave nature of the plantations: a 'total institution',
within which labourers 'not only produce [say] rubber for
export but also grow up, marry, save, and consume,
quarrel, cooperate and die'. (12) The planter's control
and authority permeated far beyond employer/employee relations to include all aspects of the labourers' lives, and
on the sugar plantations of Cuba such control and authority reached an extreme limit; they were a 'huge feudal
territory practically outside the jurisdiction of public
law'. 'There is not a small holding nor a dwelling that
does not belong to the owner of the [sugar] central, nor
a fruit orchard or vegetable patch or store or shop.' (13)
Despite specific forms, the authoritarian tradition and
labour control mechanisms of the plantation set it apart
from other forms of production. Its institutional qualities were not fully apparent in the mere scale of its

operations, the nature of the crops, its export orientation or in the formal status of labour - slave, indentured
or free.   Ultimately the plantation, 'like Christian
science, became a state of mind'. (14)

In whatever region it developed, the plantation was
separated from the rest of the economy and society - with
its own place of worship, shops, taverns, dispensary,
school and 'law courts';   as an entity, the plantation
insulated the labourer from outside influence. As Jain
has stated: 'Whether a person was born into it or was
introduced into it as an immigrant, he found it difficult
to escape from the closed world of the estate.' (15)   Many
of those who leave the plantations are eventually drawn
back. A girl who married outside may return to the estate
when her family grows since she cannot easily find employment. The institutional and cultural autonomy of the
plantation communities and their social remoteness even
from other rural communities, 'often separated from each
other by great distance and by the jungle', contributed to
the isolationism of the plantation labourer. This ghetto-
like atmosphere compressed his social life and even his
mind. The plantation workers were very much of an 'out-
group', a mere aggregate, without an organic unity, like
Marx's sack of potatoes. The non-wage concessions, including small allotments for stock grazing and fuel
gathering, essentially for 'stabilizing and holding' the
workforce, minimized interaction with the surrounding community. The adverse effects of plantations on the surrounding village economy even caused antipathy towards the
labourers;   they were the interlopers. The clash of
interests between estate and village in Sri Lanka was discussed in an earlier chapter. There was official discrimination in favour of estates and in numerous ways
estate expansion was detrimental to the village economy.

The isolation of the plantations from the surrounding
countryside, economically, culturally and socially, was
strengthened by their 'symbiotic relationship' with the
labour-recruiting areas. The Indian homeland had a strong
social influence, even serving as a haven for dishonest
union leaders (16) and a place to which the government
could deport union militants. (17) The plantations in Sri
Lanka and Malaysia drew labour from restricted areas in
South India, mainly Trichinopoly, which were also the home
of the kanganies. The migrants were brought solely as
plantation labour, and they lived and worked in compact
groups. Their supposedly transitory stay, intended as a
means of saving money to buy a plot of land at home or
redeem the family property, made them eager to retain
their ethnic ties. In Sri Lanka and Malaysia, the links

with the homeland were also preserved by its relative
proximity and by the familial basis of migration.
    The institutional mechanisms whereby the plantation
system conserved its labour force, by restraining the
labourer's movement, were buttressed by state intervention
on behalf of the planters. At various times when a scarcity of labour was thought likely to lead to a wage rise,
the state sought to forestall such a situation by elimi-
nating competition among estates for labour. These impediments to labour mobility perpetuated the low wage
structure of what was termed in Malaysia the 'Indian
sector' of the economy consisting overwhelmingly of Indian
plantation labour. The planters justified this low wage
policy, saying that Indian labour was not responsive to
wage increases. 'The higher the wages paid to the Tamil
labourer, the fewer days does he desire to work ... the
higher the wages, the higher the percentage of lazy men.'
(18) They exaggerated the non-wage benefits that were
given -

    expensive lines [i.e. housing], hospital and dressers,
    maternity allowance, midwives, line amahs and so forth
    - all of them costly, all of them for the benefit of
    the Tamil, and all of them forgotten in these bald com-
    parisons of Tamil and Chinese basic earnings.

In refusing to share the benefit of the high rubber prices
at this time, they even suggested, like employers nowadays, that low wages safeguarded the worker against an inflationary increase in the prices of consumer goods.
'Having regard to the quantity theory of money, the increase of money necessarily deprecates [sic] the purchasing value of wages.' Finally, to keep down wages, the employers made out that mobility was not in the workers'
interest. When at the outset of rubber planting in Johore
small groups of Indian labour went from one estate to another, 'perchance because better wages are offered or the
conditions seem better', this movement was attributed not
to higher wages but to a 'love of change', a.'migratory
restlessness' which causes labourers to forfeit wages due
after the period in respect of which they were last paid.
There was usually a lag of three weeks between any wage
payment and the month for which this payment related, and
the law prohibited them from leaving without giving a
month's notice. (19)
    Though the planters rationalized their wage policy on
these grounds, what was fundamental to the situation was
the labourers' inability to bargain with the employer. A
significant aspect of wage policy was the suspension of
the market mechanism generally in times of labour scarcity. Plantation labour was exposed to wage cuts in times

of labour surplus but excluded from the beneficial pressures of the market when labour was scarce; during these
periods the employers combined to prevent 'crimping' or
the competition for labour. As seen by J.N.Parmer, 'wages
were to be kept from rising too high but were permitted to
fall as low as they might. When it suited employers'
interests, the labourers' liberty was defended'. (20)
Evidence of this policy is the contrasting wage levels of
Indian and Chinese labour on the Malaysian plantations.
In Johore (where mainly Chinese were employed at the
outset of rubber planting) in 1912, the wages of Indian
labour ranged from 40 to 50 cents a day while 'free Chinese coolies' were paid a minimum of 50 to 55 cents a day.
(21) For Malaysia as a whole, in 1915 the maximum daily
wage of Chinese plantation labour employed on a time basis
was 50 to 55 cents and that of Javanese and Malays around
40 to 45 cents; in districts where Indian labour predominated it was paid generally around 30 to 40 cents. (22)
The wage disparity between Indian and Chinese rubber
tappers before the Second World War was estimated by K.S.
Sandhu as being in the order of 200 per cent, which he
slashed to about one third to take account of housing and
medical amenities given to the Indians. (23) The stagnation in the wages of Indian labour is no less apparent;
at the end of 1940 their wages were at the 1928 level of
50 cents, whereas the Chinese were paid from 70 cents to
over $1 a day. The wage disparity persisted after the
Second World War and, according to Stenson, was 'probably
greater in 1946 than in 1941'. (24) An explanation of
this disparity between the two segments of the labour
force will provide a further insight into the plantations
as a mode of labour organization and control.

A consistent wage disparity of this magnitude is not
attributable to productivity differences or to the non-
wage benefits of resident Indian workers. The relative
efficiency of the Chinese and Indians as estate labour is
an unsettled question. The Chinese, it was thought, were
(25)

> stronger, healthier and better workmen, although they
> require better food and do not perhaps stand prolonged
> exposure to the hot sun as well as the natives of
> India, and the price of their labour is consequently
> too high to enable them to compete successfully with
> the Klings.

The Bukit Kanjong Rubber Estates Ltd regarded the Chinese
as 'excellent tappers, better than Tamils'. (26) On the
other hand, the Tamil labourers were reputed to be more
disciplined and easier to manage. The Visiting Agent of
the Gedong (Perak) Rubber Estates Ltd for this reason pre-

ferred Tamil labour. 'Those of us who have had experience
of Eastern labour, I think, generally believe, ... that
Tamil labour is in every way most amenable to discipline
and preferable to Chinese or other labour.' (27) A general consensus was that the Chinese rubber tappers were more
productive, though this was not necessarily due to superi-
or skills. The Chinese usually started work earlier in
the day, when the flow of latex was greater, and they made
a deeper incision in the tree; they thus obtained a
higher yield of latex but there was also a greater consumption of tree bark. (28)
     Even when account is taken of the saving in overhead
expenditure on housing and related amenities when the Chinese were employed (on a non-resident basis), there is no
doubt that Indian labour was under-priced. Sir Malcolm
Watson, a government medical officer who was later employed by estates, estimated that the cost of tapping and
collecting a pound of rubber was halved when Indian labour
was substituted for Chinese. (29) A leading British
planter in Sri Lanka who had visited estates in Malaysia
also referred to the dearness of Chinese labour in terms
of relative efficiency levels - and this alone, he felt,
made them unsuited for estate work in Sri Lanka. (30)
     If a harbour block occurred again and business was ac-
     tually at a standstill, for want of labour, then would
     be the time to go in for Chinese. As an agricultural
     labourer, I don't think the Chinaman can compete with
     the Madrasi, because he is too dear.
In Malaysia itself, in the early 1880s, Indian labour displaced Chinese on the sugar and coconut estates in Province Wellesley; (31) again during the rubber phase,
though Chinese labour was predominant at the outset, as
the plantations became stabilized Indian labour was increasingly employed. (32)
     The higher wages of Chinese labour, which was not fully
integrated into the plantation system, were determined by
conditions of labour supply and demand and by the state of
the rubber market. A general conformity between the wages
of Chinese labour and fluctuations in the market price of
rubber is seen from the data assembled by Parmer for the
period 1925 to 1940. (33) The impact of market forces on
the wage rates of Chinese labour was evident during the
fall in rubber prices between 1920 and 1922; the average
wage of Indian labour declined by about 14.6 per cent and
that of Chinese labour by 60 per cent; (34) and in periods of labour scarcity Chinese wages rose appreciably.
The fixity of money wages of Indian estate labour, on the
other hand, exposed them to a fall in real earnings as
food prices rose; for instance, soon after the outbreak

of the Second World War their cost of living rose by 24
per cent while their wages remained constant even though
the volume and value of rubber exports expanded.

This disparity between the wage rates of Chinese and
Indian labour was connected with their respective modes of
recruitment and their relative mobility. The wages and
working conditions of the first Chinese employed in
Malaysia from about the 1890s were almost similar to those
of the mass of Indian labour. But by the 1930s the economic condition of Chinese labour had improved considerably when the abolition of indentures made European employers depend on Chinese labour contractors. Whereas the
Chinese and the locally recruited, i.e. non-assisted,
Indian migrants held comparable positions in the labour
market, and therefore had comparable bargaining strengths,
there was a sharp difference between them and the assisted
Indian migrants. The non-assisted Indian migrants, like
the Chinese, were paid higher wages than those recruited
by the kangany. They were employed on a 'comparatively
large number' of estates in Johore, having worked before
in Singapore and the Federated Malay States, many of them
on the railway and in the Public Works Department. Even
as plantation labour they were very mobile, often leaving
one estate for another. On estates where the non-assisted
migrants worked alongside kangany recruited labour, the
former were paid 50 cents to 55 cents a day and the latter
40 cents. (35)

Chinese labourers in this period were paid on a piece-
work rate under a contract system, with which their high
wage structure was linked. Before examining the factors
underlying this distinctive pattern of wage payments, the
prevalent explanation baeed on ethnic categories must be
disposed of. 'The Chinese coolie', wrote Shirle Gordon,
'worked better under his own kind.' (36) Dr Kernial Singh
Sandhu felt that the Chinese 'seemed to prosper better
under the employ of their own countrymen and consequently
did not cherish the idea of serving under an alien employer'. (37) Victor Purcell in the same manner explained
differences in the system of wage payments: 'The Chinese
were intense individualists and would only work satisfactorily as tappers when they were paid by piece work.' (38)
Dr Wong Lin Ken in his study of the tin industry gives a
similar interpretation of the different employment patterns; there was a preponderance of 'tribute labourers'
among the Chinese - much like share-croppers, they rented
out a piece of mining land for a fixed percentage of the
output. According to him the Chinese had a flair for
entrepreneurship which prevented them from being good
wage labourers. They preferred to work for themselves,

whereas the Indians 'worked better for wages'. (39)   Dr
Saw Swee-Hock discovered among Indian women a 'natural in-
clination' for rubber tapping: 'Owing partly to these
historical developments and even more to natural inclina-
tion, Indian women are extremely well suited to work as
tappers in the rubber estates.' (40)   In Sri Lanka Sinhalese labour, like the Chinese in Malaysia, carried out the
preliminary work on the plantation (jungle felling, land
clearing, hut building, etc.) on a contract basis.   But
social scientists have been perceptive enough not to read
into this pattern personality differences. (41)
    Such explanations rely on a limited chain of causation.
Wage labour is not a spontaneous creation but a very definite socio-economic process involving the subjection of
independent small producers to a capitalist employer.   The
resort to ethnic stereotypes fails to explain the objective circumstances which gave different social groups the
option of alternative employment patterns.   The established pattern of thinking on the relation between ethnicity
and economic behaviour makes a somewhat extended discussion of this aspect necessary at this stage.   Before advancing more specific reasons for the contract labour
system among Chinese plantation labour - the question
which really concerns us - it should be noted that after
the Second World War Indian and Malay rubber tappers were
increasingly employed on the contract labour system.
Also, the Chinese labour contractor on the estates has
been transforming himself from an independent employer on
his own account to a mere labour supervisor, paid a wage
instead of a commission. (42)
    In the first place, the view that for ethnic reasons
Chinese labour preferred to work directly under a Chinese
excludes the socio-historical factors which underlay this
work pattern.   The nature of Chinese labour migration into
Malaysia obliged employers to rely heavily on the contractor for the recruitment and control of labour.   He paid
the passage expenses of migrants, and supplied them with
'food, lodging, opium and sundries' during their employment, deducting whatever he wished from their wages.
While the employer's dependence for labour on the Chinese
contractor and on the Indian kangany, respectively, increased after the formal abolition of indentures in June
1914, the entrepreneurial role of the Chinese contractor
was far greater than that of the kangany in relation to
Indian labour. (43)   Whereas the Chinese employers in
Malaysia did not need to obtain labour through the Protectorate, European planters, lacking direct contact with the
sources of labour supply in China, were impelled to do so.
    Second, the contract system grew out of a reluctance of

Chinese labour to work directly for European employers -
this was no ethnic prejudice but was influenced by a specific historical experience. On the Deli tobacco plantations in Sumatra where Chinese labour had been employed
under European assistant managers, (44) despite a stricter
control, in theory, of labour conditions than in the
Straits Settlements in the 1870s, the Chinese had suffered
'an unusual degree of personal humiliation, if not physical cruelty'. (45) The ill-treatment of labour sometimes
erupted in assaults on Europeans, as in the 1890s, forcing
the Dutch to intervene officially. (46) Chicanery and oppression by the recruiting agents aggravated these conditions. Whatever the cause, the Deli plantations began to
be shunned by the Chinese immigrants. There was then a
partial replacement of Chinese labour by Javanese, with a
decline in the numbers of Chinese recruited from the
Straits Settlements for work in the Dutch colonies; the
average for 1889-92 was 8,000 compared with an annual
figure of 21,000 for 1887 and 1888. (47) In the Straits
labour market, a general aversion developed among the
Chinese to direct employment under European planters. (48)
'A sinkeh with absolutely no experience of the "red-haired
devils"', observed Anthony Reid, 'felt less secure in
placing himself in their power than in that of an employer
with shared standards of behaviour.' (49)

     Third, the contract system was financially advantageous
to Chinese labour because of the different role of the
contractor compared with that of the kangany in Indian
labour. The kangany as the employer's man had no interest
in the wages that were paid. The Chinese contractor - an
independent middleman - bargained with the employer over
the amount payable for a given work task and set the wages
of the labourers in his gang, making a profit for himself.
In negotiating with the employer he took into account the
demand and supply of labour, the yield and production
costs of rubber, and even the prevailing state of the
rubber market. The relevance of market forces to the
wages paid to Chinese labour induced them to become acquainted with economic conditions including the trend of
commodity prices. (50) In the early years the contractor
grossly underpaid his labourers, but by the 1930s they
were in a position to avoid being exploited by him. (51)
The planters themselves favoured the contract labour
system for nonresident Chinese labour. Far less supervision was required, and regardless of a sudden scarcity
of labour a given work task would be completed before the
labourers left.

     While the contract labour system was advantageous, for
different reasons, both to the European planters and to

Chinese labour, the government's immigration quotas in
1930 improved the position of the Chinese in the labour
market. Even earlier, from about 1917, immigration was
affected by the civil war in China and a sharp rise in
fares. Sailings became fewer and ticket brokers rigged
the prices of sea passages. With a buoyant rubber market,
the wages of Chinese labour thus remained at a very high
level. (52) The scarcity of Chinese labour continued in
1921 - 'difficulties of an almost unsurmountable nature'
were complained of by the Malayan Planters' Association.
(53) An amendment to the Aliens Ordinance, giving planters special permits to get labour direct from China, did
little to relieve the situation as the scheme was improperly availed of by non-labourers. (54) Even in 1938 the
quotas, while curbing the influx of Chinese, checked 'the
type [of migrant] Malaya wants and needs for its estates
and mines'. The excessive prices of steamship tickets allotted under the quota made it 'well nigh impossible' for
peasant would-be migrants to purchase them. (55) The
tightness in the labour market also caused a change in
recruitment procedures, and undermined the contractor's
position. His access to 'customs bound, docile' recruits
from rural China virtually ended; he had now to obtain
labour from the Chinese 'lodging houses' in Malaysia,
which came thereby to serve as employment exchanges.

With a view to highlighting the extra-market forces
which conditioned the wage levels and working conditions
of Indian labour in plantations, I have used as a point of
comparison the relatively high wage structure of Chinese
labour. The disparity in wages and working conditions between the two was explained fundamentally by the way in
which the two categories of workers were recruited, organized and controlled. Emphasis was also placed on the respective roles of the Chinese labour contractor and the
Indian kangany in relation to the employer. In rounding
off this discussion of the degree to which market forces
impinged upon wage levels and working conditions of the
Chinese, I shall refer finally to the political position
of the Chinese in colonial Malaya, and their relative
autonomy which enabled them better to withstand the depressive forces to which Indian labour was subjected.

It is thus necessary to discuss here how the ties of
clan organization protected the Chinese. Organized in
territorial dialect groups, the Chinese migrants developed
an internal solidarity based on a vertical division of
their community instead of on a horizontal division as in
the caste society of the Indians. Though different clans
clashed with each other, for instance over the mining
rights of contending Malay factions, the clan organization

was an integrative force vis-à-vis the outside world. The
secret societies with which the Chinese clans were sometimes allied from the early years of British rule had a
law enforcement machinery and a system of protection for
members. These societies were not wholly devoted to ter-
rorism and blackmail, gambling, 'brothel-squeezing', theft
and the trafficking in opium as is commonly made out. The
Chinese labourer was 'controlled and protected' by them.
(56) Some, as essentially mutual aid societies, were made
use of by the small entrepreneurs. The Hock Hin, a predominantly Hokkien society, provided banking facilities,
lent money on mortgage and arranged for cash remittances
to relatives overseas; 'benevolence, charity and mutual
assistance' were the main objects of another. (57)
     The secret societies had an anti-European streak -
brought about by the British commercial domination of
Malaysia at the expense of the Chinese. In some cases
the political strength of the societies was due to a
'merger of Malay and Chinese' interests. The Toh-Peh Keng
and the Ghee Hin were allied, respectively, with the Red
Flag and the White Flag societies consisting entirely or
mainly of Malays. In 1867 the murder of a Red Flag
diamond merchant in Penang caused a violent feud between
two Malay factions, which was taken up by their allied
Chinese societies. Membership of the Chinese societies
even included Malay chiefs. Such Malay-Chinese collaboration was a matter of concern to the British. Under instructions from the Governor, the Chief Kathi of Penang
warned the Malays to keep out of the secret societies.
Malays who joined them were declared traitors to Islam,
and the virtuous were those who were faithful to the
British. (58) A few years later a British official commented: (59)

    It is not the first time that I have heard of Malay
    Rajahs becoming members of Chinese Kongsees. If it
    really obtains, the practice is well worthy of notice,
    suggestive as it is of political arrangements that are
    likely to arise when - as no doubt will be the case -
    the immense resources of the Peninsula attract a vast
    population of Chinese to the present uninhabited terri-
    tories.

As a result the Chinese were treated circumspectly by the
British and the immigration control from 1930 was politically motivated. In 1920 action was taken under the
Registration of Schools Enactment to control the activities of the Chinese medium schools. In 1928 four Chinese
night schools were proscribed 'for allowing their premises
to be used for political purposes'. (60) In the precarious balance of interests which the British fostered among

the several ethnic groups, (61) the Indians were cast in
the role of a counterpoise to the 'troublesome Chinese'.
(62) Though China's sovereignty in that period was nominal, her moral defiance of the Westerner influenced even
the overseas Chinese and imbued them with a sense of independence and ethnic solidarity. It was in this context
that Chinese labour came under the sway of the labour
market, but without the depressive effect on wages of an
uncontrolled flow of migrants.

Indian labour, on the other hand, continued to be depressed for a number of reasons. The caste society of the
Indians was hierarchically stratified within each caste
and between castes, and it lacked the solidarity of the
Chinese clan organization. The Indian Immigration Committee, a semi-official agency, administered and partly
financed by government, made it possible to augment the
supply of migrants as required. Estate housing and the
familial pattern of employment of Indian labour were an
impediment to their bargaining. Plantation conditions,
with large numbers of low paid workers living and working
close together, under a system of regimentation and discipline, would normally have been conducive to collective
action. Nevertheless, they failed to pursue their interests as a class; the result of an unsuccessful tussle
with the management was too grave a risk. Occupational
and social immobility doomed the labourer to permanent unemployment if he was turned out of the estate. Dismissal,
possible even now at very short notice, caused the whole
family to be unemployed. The odds were too great - the
loss of the family income and of a place to live.

As a result, Indian and Chinese labour in Malaysia have
shown divergent levels of consciousness as a proletariat.
The first serious labour uprising was by the Chinese in
March 1937, in Selangor. Several estates were involved,
with sympathy strikes at the rubber, match and pineapple
factories in Klang as well as in the Malayan collieries
at Batu Arang. The upsurge, which J.N.Parmer has written
about, (63) was formidable in scale and militancy. Over
a hundred plantation workers were arrested and at the collieries armed troops and police were attacked with crow-
bars, axes and poles. There was a certain solidarity
among plantation workers as well as between them and the
industrial workers. Aware of prevailing economic conditions, the strikers contended that the level of rubber
prices could easily accommodate a wage increase. The
demands included welfare benefits and a curtailment of the
power of the contractors. But throughout this conflict
the Indian plantation labourer was conspicuous by his non-
participation, and this was duly appreciated by the Plant-

ers' Association. 'It speaks well both for Indian estate
labourers and their employers that the strikes among Chinese labourers and their employers which occurred in March
1937 did not spread to them.' (64)

The socio-political conditions of Indian labour compared with Chinese, which underlay their respective levels
of consciousness as a labouring class, as well as the
divergent patterns of labour relations, require discussion
at this point. In the first place, Indian labour migration was for the most part organized by British officials
and planters solely for supplying unskilled labour for the
plantations and public works, whereas the settlement and
employment of Chinese labour were arranged largely through
their own associations and secret societies. They migrated not as balanced communities with lineage and local
groupings intact (65) but as individuals seeking a new
life. As Jain expressed it, 'they were not "groomed" for
their role as labourers'. (66) Spatial and occupational
mobility gave the Chinese a relative independence and led
to better wages. Their wide range of occupations emancipated them socially, while the possibility of urban residence offered education and upward mobility for the
children. Furthermore, the clan leadership of the Chinese
protected them from aliens, including Europeans.

Second, Indian labour was absorbed into the broader
power structure of the plantations, which left them isolated and oppressed on all sides. The Asian 'staff' on
the plantation, i.e. the kirani, looked down on them. As
Malayalees from Travancore-Cochin or else Jaffna Tamils
from Sri Lanka they kept aloof. The kangany, who came
from the same village in South India as the labourers and
lived with them on the plantation, held an ambivalent position. In Sri Lanka, the solidarity of the kangany with
the estate labourers and his position primus inter pares
diminished greatly after the 1850s when the traffic in
labour became a highly organized business. A 'new class'
of kanganies emerged (67) who were professional recruiters. While retaining patriarchal control over the labourers the kangany was now 'a mere planter's agent with no
personal interest in the gang'. (68) The artisan class on
the plantations - drivers of vehicles, generator attendants, carpenters, engine operators and mechanics -
also kept apart from the labourers. They lived separately
and their position occupationally and socially was mid-way
between the labourers and the Asian 'staff'.

Third, though the transformation of labour into a commodity was partially achieved under the plantation system,
socially and culturally the plantations were a projection
of the caste-ridden society of the South Indian village.

The Indians were brought to the plantations with the whole
integument of the Hindu caste system intact. Migration
was in caste groups who acknowledged the social superiority of the kangany and regarded him as their patriarchal
head; the sub-kanganies had the same role with smaller
groups. Caste-based occupations prevailed, such as those
of the barber and the washerman; the lower services were
performed by the untouchables. The employers for their
part recognized and fostered the distinctions and loyalties of the South Indian village along with the cruder
manifestations of Hindu religion. The kangany's caste was
stated in the printed form which estates had to submit to
the Labour Recruiting Agency. (69) The allocation of
housing, and the household work which labourers did for
the European manager and the 'staff', conformed with caste
divisions. (70) The plantations also catered to the religious needs of its exclusively Hindu workforce. A temple
in the vicinity of his residence was one of the first
social amenities with which the estate labourer was provided, and 'modest little shrines dedicated to one or the
other of the Hindu pantheon' littered the plantation districts. (71) At these shrines a whole range of deities
could be propitiated, according to the type of divine intervention sought. In India religious reform movements
fostered a more humanistic and non-sectarian outlook, but
on the estates in Malaysia Hinduism's ritualistic aspects
were preserved, including self-mortification and blood
sacrifices. Religion had psychological compensations for
the labourers. When everything else was lost, it sustained a nostalgia for the past, a binding link with the homeland. Religious orthodoxy was in the management's interest. It ensured greater control over the labourer. Religious worship and discussion were the only form of public
meeting permitted on the plantations, and in British
Guiana the priests were chosen by committees on which the
management was represented. (72) There was no possibility
that religion might encourage a sense of equality between
labourers and planters, as in North America, where the
Negroes began to profess Christianity (the religion of the
planters). On the estates religious differences persisted. Hinduism and Christianity never mixed.

As in all precapitalist situations, management paternalism underlay the system of human relations on the
estate, obscuring a fundamentally exploitative situation.
It ensured a docile and cheap workforce amidst a potential
labour shortage. In early industrial Europe with its
'strong feudal and manorial tradition', the employer
'placed himself in loco parentis, treated his workers as
minors in need of a firm tutorial hand, and felt a certain

responsibility for their job security and welfare - always
of course at the very modest level suitable to their
station'. This concern, not wholly idealistic, was partly
'a response to the danger and inconvenience of losing a
work force collected with difficulty and only too easily
dispersed'. (73) On the cotton plantations in the Missis-
sippi delta the planters spoke of 'my tenants' or 'my
labourers', emphasizing the inferior status of the workers
(than poor whites); this also won sympathy for the planters' labour problems while disguising the severity of the
labour contract. (74) Paternalism, finally, helped to
create in oppressed groups a dependent psychology. Colonizers, by making out that subjugated people were like
children, immature, could take harsh measures, demand
obedience, and exact labour from them. 'The father of a
family', wrote Crawford Young, is one of the most familiar
metaphors in the colonial lexicon. (75)
     On the plantations management paternalism had two
elements. Rudimentary social benefits were provided -
free medical attention, maternity leave and grants,
crèches for children while the mothers were at work, an
estate school, and donations for births, funerals and religious festivals. This welfare package had a bias in
favour of child bearing - children born and reared on the
estate being an ideal source of labour. In Malaysia in
1930 the planters sought to reduce infant mortality and
provide amenities for children. (76)

     Every child born on the estate should have the best
     possible chance of developing into a healthy labourer.
     This can only be done if the fostering care of the
     mother (whose labour the estate requires for several
     hours a day) is replaced by the fostering care of the
     estate management.

Crèches were recommended for the proper feeding of the
children. They 'need not be an expensive item.... All
that is required is a suitable shed not far from the
lines'. The moral aspects of this arrangement were compounded by very mundane considerations. (77)

     From a purely business point of view, apart from its
     humanitarian aspect, the care of the young is a sound
     proposition. It ought in the years to come if largely
     or universally adopted to result in a healthy, sturdy,
     locally-bred labour population.

The other element of paternalism was the estate manager's
role as a 'benevolent father figure'. (78) The manager
and his European assistants were honoured guests at the
marriage ceremonies of labourers and at religious festivi-
ties. At one Dipavali celebration the manager was 'gar-
landed with jasmine and marigold and sprayed with attar of

roses', and on the next day the labourers carried gifts to
the residence of the European manager, in symbolic reaf-
firmation of their tie. (79)

   While giving their patronage to the social and religious activities of the labourers, the European estate
staff confined themselves to 'planning and administration,
and top level supervision'. They wielded effective power
as though from a distance (much like the British imperial
authorities who controlled millions of people from a
remote centre without confronting them directly). The
kangany and the Asian office staff, as the 'punitive
counterparts' of the European, had an invidious role. (80)
The kangany supervised the field work, enforced work
norms, and was responsible for the capture and chastisement of 'bolters'. His disciplinary role extended to the
labourers' community life. He dispensed justice in the
labour lines, and enforced petty regulations: for example, the extinguishing of all lamps after 9 p.m. - to
compel the labourer to rest and be fit the next day - and
maintaining the uniformity of the 'lines', by seeing that
no labourer made any alteration to his house. The kangany
could resort to physical coercion. Latterly, his intervention declined, but not his high-handedness. (81) Likewise the duties of the Asian office staff impinged directly on the lives of the plantation labourers; these duties
included the weighing of the rubber latex brought in by
tappers and the allocation of houses, some of which were
built better or more advantageously situated than others.

   Fourth, the pattern of employer-employee relations was
of a semi-feudal nature. The status of the plantation
worker in one respect was that of a proletarian - he had
no independent means of livelihood - but he was not wholly
a proletarian. Although juridically free, he was half
serf, half proletarian. A lack of property was an attribute which the plantation worker shared with both a proletarian and a serf. In certain other ways his position was
that of a serf, not a proletarian. (82) The attitude of
estate managers in Malaysia to the rubber tappers' strike
of March 1937 typified plantation labour relations. They
admitted the workers' claims but resented the collective
orientation which the workers displayed for the first
time. As Stenson explained, the prestige of the estate
manager was at stake. He wanted grievances to be presented separately like a petition to a feudal lord, so
that he could redress them as a privilege out of his gra-
ciousness but not from compulsion. (83)

   The techniques of work organization and discipline on a
plantation were designed to browbeat the labourer and bend
him into subservience. In Malaysia, even after the Second

World War, the dismissal of a labourer deprived his family
of housing. Outsiders had no access to the labourers'
quarters. (84) Trade unionists who met workers in their
homes could be charged for trespass - to prevent 'political activity of a possibly inflammatory nature'. (85)
Until the 1930s errant labourers were liable to be
flogged. In 1923, out of seventy-four complaints which
the Labour Department received from plantation workers in
Malacca, twenty-five were classified as 'assault of
labourers by manager or assistant or by clerk or kangany'.
(86) To curb labour unrest the incorporated Society of
Planters in 1947 recommended a 'ruthless application of
the sentences of death, banishment and particularly flogging'; (87) plantation companies in their annual reports
advocated similar action. According to Stenson, physical
punishment probably decreased during the 1930s and largely
disappeared after the war, 'although estate staff still
talk of taking a stick to the labourers'. (88)
    A campaign by the Klang Indian Association in February
1941 brought the social relations on the plantations into
sharp focus. The association inveighed against the vic-
timization of workers who tried to express their grievances. It demanded, besides freedom of speech and assembly,
that Europeans and 'black' Europeans should stop molesting
the labourers' womenfolk, and that the labourers should
not have to dismount from a bicycle when a European was
present. (89) These lord-serf relations are still prevalent. For instance, male workers as a sign of deference
to the estate manager must remove the shawl from their
neck and tuck it under their arm. The superordinates in
the plantation hierarchy are paid homage even at temple
festivals and social functions. By this 'etiquette of
deference' inequalities were institutionalized - as Banton
has shown with reference to the North American plantations. (The Negro was not supposed to overtake a white
man even when driving a motor car, or to contradict him or
to use correct 'college' English when talking to him.)
(90) On the Malaysian plantations, those refusing to conform or to accede to the wishes of the Asian 'staff' are
harassed. They may be assigned a 'task' on a portion of
the rubber estate where the trees have a low yield of
latex or are far from the latex collection point (which
reduces daily earnings), family members may be separated
while at work, or the nonconformists may be discriminated
against in regard to communal facilities and welfare benefits. The favours expected of the labourers may even be
their women.
    Finally, the encapsulated nature of the plantation
labour force left it with no means of advancement except

through formal education that would qualify for employment
outside the plantations. But education was not a part of
plantation culture; it was neither technically necessary
nor did it have any survival value. Education has con-
flicting interests within the plantation community. For
the labourers' children, education is a means of emancipation, but to the planter it is a potential threat to the
labour supply. There was even a conviction among planters
that education incapacitates people for work. The estate
school has thus been a 'typically one-room, one-teacher
affair', whose medium of instruction - the Tamil language
- in Malaysia has no vocational value. Large numbers
forgo this education. The drop-out rate of pupils following the Tamil medium (virtually restricted to the
estate schools) in 1969 was twice that of the Malay and
the Chinese streams and eight times that of the English
stream. The National Union of Plantation Workers had
sought to change this situation by means of scholarships
and grants for plantation children and, since 1969, by
loans. Assistance was confined to secondary school and
university education. The potential beneficiaries from
this scheme were the 'freaks' who somehow managed to go
through primary and secondary school. (91)
    In this deprived environment parents regard their
children as an income-earning asset. Soon after the
Second World War planters in Malaysia employed child
labour even though unprofitable, because adult workers
preferred estates where their children were given work.
The retarded physique of plantation children made it difficult to say by mere observation whether those employed
were below 10 years (the statutory minimum age for employment). 'The inspecting officer was confirmed in his
opinion that it was almost impossible in his opinion to
judge the ages of Tamil children between the ages of 9 and
14.' (92) Schooling is further hampered by a lack of
books as well as a home environment. Most of the labour
'lines' have no proper lighting, sanitation or washing
facilities. The necessity for the parents to be at the
work site by 6 a.m. leaves children unsupervised - an
older child gives them their breakfast.
    While those born to this situation tended to accept it
without question, their hopelessness and lack of horizon
were reflected in their off-work preoccupations - promis-
cuity, drug abuse, and alcoholism and harmless but trivial
pastimes to the exclusion of any serious interests. The
seclusion and monotony of the plantation made many of the
labourers addicted to drink. Toddy shops were part of the
infrastructure - they served both to lure labour and relieve the tensions which plantation life made latent. (93)

In the 'early days' the National Union of Plantation
Workers took a strong stand against this - but time
seems to ferment all things. Employers, or, should I
say, absentee owners, who do not build community
centres or lounges for the workers' relaxation and possible enlightenment, nor libraries, nor anything
towards the liberation of the working community, do
contract out toddy shops that are ever so convenient
to the labourers after a day's work.
Estate housing, family employment, and the incorporation
of the labourers' social life in the plantation community
gave them relative security. But unlike other migrant
groups they were essentially 'abyss dwellers' with virtually no opportunities for education or advancement. The
cultural backwardness and political passivity of plantation labour were fostered by the plantation system in
which they were absorbed. The backwardness of the plantation labourer was the backwardness of the plantation as an
economic and social institution.
   The influence of external circumstances on the condition of the labourer, over which he had no control, may be
seen by the marked differences between the patterns of
social behaviour of plantation labour in Mauritius and in
British Guiana. The large majority of their labour migrants were not from South India, whose people Dr Sandhu
regards with derogation as 'almost ideal labouring material for capitalist endeavours'. They came mostly from
Bihar, Bombay, the North Western Province and Uttar
Pradesh. On the plantations in Mauritius (as in Sri Lanka
and Malaysia), Indian labour recreated their traditional
village society based on caste and kinship, but in British
Guiana they underwent a major cultural and social change.
The caste system disintegrated, and notions of ritual
status based on degrees of pollution were abandoned. Respect for the traditional culture was confined to a refusal to accept Christianity (though one estate on which
South Indians were heavily concentrated had the highest
proportion of Christian converts). In British Guiana, the
Hinduism of the South Indians was free from caste or sect
variations; 'Madras' rites were practised only by a
minority. (94) Furthermore, the isolation of the plantations declined when many Indian labourers, after their indenture, settled in the vicinity. They developed close
relations with Negroes and other ethnic groups, and dropped traditional social practices, including the use of
Hindi. This acculturation was due partly to the residential shift of labourers outside the plantations and also
to an acute shortage of Indian women.
   The conditions and social outlook of Indian plantation

labour as given in this background may also be contrasted
with those of Indian labour migrants outside the plantations and with those of the indigenous peasants. The non-
estate migrants in some degree or another became immersed
in the local society. The main kin groups they formed
were flexible enough to allow interaction with other
people and strata - some of the Malayalee migrants in Sri
Lanka cohabited with Sinhalese women. They acquired economic and social mobility, joining a variety of manual occupations and trades: cooks, gardeners, tailors, barbers,
domestic servants, railway and dock workers, shop assistants, hawkers, dealers in castaway goods - old newsprint, jute bags, clothing, bottles and tin cans. These
migrants were not necessarily endowed, ab initio, with
commercial talents, nor were their resourcefulness and
diligence due to ethnicity or any 'natural disposition'
as is often said. (95) Like the Chinese migrants, their
position enabled them to explore types of employment from
which plantation labour was precluded. The uncertainty
and irregularity of earnings in the occupations they
adopted created in them a compulsion to save. For these
people accumulation was a condition of existence - unlike
plantation labour which had a regular cash income besides
housing and some modest amenities. The predicament of
these people sharpened their wits, while separation from
relatives or dependants made them oblivious of social
mores which may have hampered personal advancement.
Pirenne's description of the petty traders, or 'mercatores', who made their appearance in the cities of medieval Europe, at the first dawn of bourgeois civilization,
provides a fitting analogy. They were 'adventurers, relying only on themselves.... Men without possessions who
were seeking their fortune.' (96)
   The economic success of the non-estate migrants was
also not entirely due to their severance from the feudal
society in their homeland, as Professor Alatas said about
the Chinese in Malaysia. According to him, the Chinese
acquired the right values by a 'complete political administrative severance ... from their own feudal past', while
the Malays, whose religion, Islam, was much more in accordance with the requirements of a commercial ideology,
remained entangled in their feudal past and so failed to
develop the capitalist ethic. 'It is this value system,
a hangover from the feudal past and consolidated by colonial influence, that forms the greatest obstacle to
modernisation in contemporary South-East Asia.' (97)
Ideas of values, however, are not a causative factor of
primary importance; per se they neither give rise to
capitalism nor prevent its emergence. 'Capitalism' and

'modernization' are more than a condition of mind or of
mores and values.

Ideology is not moulded in vacuo, but a particular
ideology is pendent on a specific economic and social
structure to which it is relevant, perhaps giving it
legitimacy. As Christopher Hill states, 'Men did not
become capitalists because they were Protestants, nor
Protestants because they were capitalists. In a society
already becoming capitalist, Protestantism facilitated the
triumph of new values.' (98) Ideologies tend to change
when they no longer accord with the economic demands of
the age. A notable case is the position of the mendicant
in Europe, to which Pirenne referred. (99) The 'magnificent impulse of Christian charity' which the Church had
inspired in the Middle Ages came to an end. The mendicant
lost the halo of sanctity, and began to be chastised for
his idleness. A puritanical lawyer, in the English House
of Commons in the fifteenth century, spoke of the 'horrible abuses of idle and vagrant persons, greatly offensive
to both God and the world'. (100) The classical economists' dislike of unproductive output, including Ricardo's
impatience with the extravagance of the Catholic Church
and Adam Smith's abhorrence of standing armies and large
bureaucracies, developed during a crucial period in
capitalism's growth. A more topical example of the
mutability of values is the effect of technological innovations in rice production on the cultural pattern of
peasant society. The introduction of the new high-yielding varieties of paddy is found to have disturbed village
festivals. A shorter interval between the cultivation
seasons has discouraged time-consuming customs after the
harvest. (101)

The mere fact of being migrants or their ethnic identity did not create the heroic qualities of the Chinese in
the Straits Settlements or of the Indian Moslems in the
port towns of Malaysia. They were qualities that were
bred in the society of artisans or traders which the migrants joined. The economy gave these groups a handicap
over others while placing a limit on what they could
achieve. Even as homines novi they failed to make the
transition from commercial to industrial capital, and
remained for the most part traders, money lenders, middlemen and real estate owners. In a different setting the
migrant groups may have recreated their feudal past or
remained impoverished like the Indians in the rice economy
of Burma. Though not generally from South India, their
condition was probably worse than that of their compatriots on the plantations in Malaysia, Sri Lanka and Assam.
Indian labour on the plantations were an investment; and

the planters could not let their conditions sink below a
level required to maintain work efficiency over a lifetime. This obligation was one from which employers in
Burma were exempt, owing to the casual or seasonal nature
of the workforce in rice cultivation and in milling. The
condition of Indian labour in Burma was noted by the
Public Health Committee in 1928: (102)

> In one room we counted 50 coolies, the number allowed
> by the regulation was 9.... Every inch of the floor
> space is occupied by a sleeping human being, and
> others are to be found on shelves and bunks along the
> walls ... the exhalations from over-crowded seating
> humanity, lying actually on top of one another and
> breathing the same foul atmosphere over and over again
> is [sic] sufficient to turn the strongest stomach....
> There are thousands of such houses, huts and hovels....

A few years later, during the Depression, the consumption
of rice per capita in Burma fell drastically. In such
cases 'the struggle for survival under conditions of hard-
ship', which Professor Alatas, for one, associates with
the overseas Chinese, did not yield comparable results.
That is to say, while an alien environment might create in
people the qualities making for success, the realization
of such qualities is contingent on the opportunities open
to them - the outcome in each case depending on the interaction between 'values' and the external environment.

In the style and pattern of economic activity of the
non-estate migrants, their severance from feudalism was a
negative factor: a necessary, not a sufficient condition
for their relative success. It was not so much their
heroic personal qualities which decided this outcome as
the economic opportunities in the new land. The expansive
urban economy of Malaysia, while having no place for
feudal values, afforded positive opportunities for advancement such as were lacking in the environment of the
plantation labourers or of the Malay peasant. In the
heterogeneous tertiary sector there was occupational
fluidity; the skills acquired in any one line of employment were relevant to a whole range of others. A shop assistant, a hawker's boy or a garage hand, after collecting
a little savings, could set up on his own, later to
expand his scale of operations or branch out into allied
trades - linkages being ever-present in the world of commerce. The slow process of growth which was open to small
businesses at that time aided capital accumulation. Savings could be converted into capital in small amounts, at
least by investing them in the enterprise from which the
savings arose. Gradualism was the order of the day; it
was possible to advance from low beginnings, in short

spurts fed by small increments of capital. The environment was less competitive than now, and opportunities for
petty trade proliferated as the colonial economy expanded.
The market also produces in those subjected to it a corresponding set of norms and attitudes. They found themselves buffeted by the tides of the market, not over-
whelmed by natural calamities; and a stern pragmatism
gained precedence over magical animism in social behaviour. In this milieu, the way to heaven was not what it
seemed in the peasant economy or among migrant labour on
the plantations. Salvation lay not in divine worship,
submission to the patriarchal authority of the landlord or
the kangany, or a conformity to customary values, but in
an assertive self-confidence and the correlated traits
composing the capitalist ethic.

The position of the resident plantation worker was inferior to that of the peasants. Socially and culturally,
if not economically, the latter were relatively free.
Though dominated by a landlord, they were not constantly
watched or liable to be punished like the plantation
worker; they could decide the rhythm and tempo of their
work subject to the constraints of natural forces or the
growth cycle of the crop. The peasants, unless wholly
subsistence producers (few were), underwent a cyclical
metamorphosis as consumers and as social beings. Whenever
there was a favourable harvest or a turn of the market
they could break out of their traditional world - visit
the town, purchase new goods, go on a pilgrimage and
extend their social horizon which receded when slack times
returned. In Malaysia after independence those on the
rural-urban fringe underwent a more far-reaching change.
They interacted closely with the urban economy, reaping
the spillover benefits of urban expansion. The opportunities in question were also of a new type in petty trade
and industry, transforming their traditional locus and
opening up new vistas however modest.

The plantation workers, by contrast, were held in an
immutable mould regardless of the upswings in commodity
markets or of developments in other sectors of the economy; they even fulfilled their socio-cultural obligations
within the precincts of the plantation (barring a journey
outside at the time of the Thaipussam festival). The
growth of urban centres to which trade and manufacturing
industry gravitated, drawing labour from the urban periphery, had no impact on the estate population. They did not
participate in the internal migration that followed this
urban expansion. Improvements in their condition achieved
through the National Union of Plantation Workers were
minimum benefits of a welfare kind, to be enjoyed within

the plantation system. As concessions granted by the employers and encouraged by government, they precluded the
worker from leaving that framework and contained him in
the role which the colonial economy had assigned him.
J.A.Barnes asserts that plantation workers 'are not necessarily proletarians in perpetuity, for their favourite
form of capital investment is land in India'. (103) They
did migrate with the hope of buying land or redeeming the
family property, but how many succeeded? For instance,
during the large-scale retrenchment of plantation labour
in 1920-2, unemployed Indians had to be accommodated by
the government in camps and assisted with free repatriation, whereas the Chinese 'found most aid within their
own community'. (104) In the end some of them were affected by the fragmentation of estates. They lost social
amenities such as estate schools, clinics and crèches and
also came outside the Workmen's Compensation Ordinance.
(105)
    It would now be evident that the depressed state in
which Indian plantation labour remained was not primarily
due to a failure as individuals (compared with the Chinese
or the South Indian Moslems who forged ahead in the colonial cities). The plantation economy constrained this
labour both spatially and occupationally. Mobility, at
best, was from one estate to another on which the pattern
of work and social life was replicated in nearly every
detail; such transfers were familial, and usually involved all members of a labour gang led by the kangany.
Occupational mobility was nonexistent within the plantations system or outside. The labourers were ineligible
for any position on the estate which called for more than
merely manual effort. Appointments to such positions required ascribed qualifications, including a cultural and
social differentiation from the labourers, on which depended the 'ability to control labour' within the institutional framework of the plantation. Jain highlights this
issue: 'It is unlikely that any of those who do get
through secondary school will ever be offered a job as a
probationer conductor or a typist on Pel Melayu. Indeed,
it is doubtful if labourers' children would even apply for
such positions.' (106) Plantation labour was thus neither
exposed to heterogeneous social situations from which
other migrant groups benefited, gaining new skills and a
broader outlook, nor could they advance within the plantation system. The financial savings of the plantation
worker, unlike those of the petty craftsman or trader,
could not be converted into capital by being invested in
either his existing employment or in related spheres. His
savings could merely be set aside for deferred consump-

tion. An official report in 1928 on the need for savings
societies on the Malaysian plantations observed that the
Indian labourer 'has few opportunities for investing his
savings and is largely at the mercy of the estate shop-
keeper. He can hide or hoard his savings or deposit them
with the "kangany", tindall or foreman or with the shop-
keeper'. (107)

The semi-servile condition of plantation labour and the
indignities they suffered diminished after the Second
World War. The politicization brought about by the war in
Malaysia, as in some other countries, had an impact on
them. The postwar generation of plantation labour, in the
terms of an official report, had 'experienced great up-
heavals and ... developed a consciousness of their political and economic position'. (108) By this time large
numbers of plantation workers had also been born in
Malaysia. Yet there has been no serious action to improve
their position. This failure has been due to the growth
of both management paternalism and of a trade union leadership which is under the influence of the employers and
the state. In most plantation frontiers employers made
use of the cultural and religious ties of the labour force
as a means of control. In Malaysia the fear of Communism
made the employers play up the religious and social activities of the workers as an alternative to industrial
action. They relied on welfare temple committees on the
estate, assisting them financially and holding the executive positions in these organizations. In one instance
assistance was given for the building of a Hindu temple
which cost $(M) 20,000. (109) In another, a Panchayat
Board was set up on instructions from the company's head
office. The European Superintendent became the Chairman
of this Panchayat Board, the Asian Estate Assistant its
Vice-chairman, and the senior estate conductors the division secretaries. This paternalism has encouraged extreme
deference to the management. Invitations to the annual
temple festival are carried to the European manager and
the Asian 'staff' on a tray laden with fruits. He and the
staff are treated during the ceremony according to their
positions in the plantation hierarchy. They are fed with
rice cooked in ghee, the others get plain rice; they are
accommodated at a table draped with white cloth, the
others sit on the floor; and they are served first. (110)

Though plantation labour soon after the Second World
War attained some improvement in their economic condition
through strike action, the union leadership became heavily
welfare oriented. Programmes of 'self-help' have been
promulgated to the neglect of basic issues - such as
housing, educational facilities and employment - which

are far more than a problem in industrial relations to be
resolved within the framework of the plantation system.
The National Union of Plantation Workers, with imposing
buildings in Kuala Lumpur, professional executives and a
public relations service that releases magazines and news-
letters, has become dominated by an affluent bureaucracy,
some of whom are connected with the establishment and have
outside business interests, and personal incomes and life-
styles totally removed from those of the plantation workers. (The General Secretary, formerly a field conductor
on a rubber estate, is a director of several joint stock
companies including a commercial bank.) The reformism of
the union complements the plantation system as a production mode dependent on cheap labour.

I have dealt elsewhere in this book with the domination
of merchant capital over production capital and with plantation technology as determinant aspects of the precapitalist nature of the plantations. The investment of capital in the recruitment and retention of labour rather than
on the techniques of production resulted in the tying of
labour to the plantations by means of institutionalized
impediments on their mobility. My concern in this chapter
has been with labour relations in plantations as the other
determinant aspect of their precapitalist nature. The
prevailing system of labour exploitation involving both
technological stagnation and precapitalist labour relations, in turn, imposed limits on wage increases. Using
as my touchstone the classical form of plantation labour
as it was represented in Malaysia by the Indian segment of
the workforce, I have accounted for the low wages and the
semi-servile status of this labour, in terms not of their
ethnic origins but essentially of the plantation system
itself. A corollary to this is the lack of a class consciousness, the final expression of which is the reformist
nature of the plantation unions which seem to function in
the interests of plantation capital rather than in the
interests of labour.

Part three

Towards a theory of underdevelopment

13 The framework and mechanisms of metropolitan control

Foreign capital in the colonies inevitably conformed with the interests of the metropolitan economy. The manufacturing and commercial enterprises based in London differed in their entrepreneurial interests and focus from the locally domiciled British firms. The former constituted the metropolitan interest and their interests contradicted sharply those of the colony as a national entity; the latter were relatively free to respond to local profit opportunities. A sharp division of interests prevailed between the shareholders of plantation companies - a scattered mass of individuals owning small parcels of shares - and the essentially mercantile groups represented by the agency houses. The general framework of their relationship, involving a subordination of plantation interests to merchant capital, was discussed in the two preceding chapters. Production capital in the colony was subordinated to merchant capital, which in turn was the agent of metropolitan industrial capital.

The foreign investors in London and those resident locally were in conflict on matters such as imperial preference, the Crown Agents system, and freight rates. Their conflicts were generally resolved in favour of the absentee interests based in London. In the Straits Settlements in 1918, after abortive attempts by the resident British firms to develop Singapore as a centre of the world's rubber trade, the 'Straits Times' asserted: (1)

> Practically the whole of the Sterling companies are ruled from London and to a very large extent the boards of these companies are under the influence of principal cliques which are not friendly to a great development of Singapore as the world's chief rubber centre.

The locally established British interests were overridden by the foreign shareholders, boards of directors and head offices in London. 'The men out here can scarcely call

their souls their own because the dictation from London
locks and fetters them at every turn.' (2) Entrepreneurial authority was not shared with the local agents, and
only limited responsibility was given to them even in administrative matters;   for example, the branches of
British banks in Sri Lanka could not recruit staff or determine their responsibilities and functions. In a study
of extra-territorial enterprise in Nigeria, it was shown
that the London interests (3)
    are rather jealous of their power ... and do not ap-
    point agents with greater authority than area managers
    within each colony.... Their mere routine duties such
    as the monthly stocktaking, prevention of fraud, super-
    vision of clerks, take up by far the greater part of
    their time.
The structure of metropolitan control on a general
plane consisted of organizations that were set up in the
UK to pursue and promote British interests in the individual colonies. Sterling companies in Sri Lanka were
represented by the Ceylon Association in London, those in
the West Indies by the West India Committee, and those in
Malaysia by the Association of British Interests. The
Ceylon Association, conscious of its influence, claimed
that it 'provided the means whereby the voice of those who
have financial or other interests in Ceylon can be heard
in the appropriate quarter on matters of current concern'.
(4) The locally registered British companies had their
own organizations; in Sri Lanka they were the Ceylon
Estate Proprietors' Association, the Planters' Association, the Ceylon Chamber of Commerce and the European Association - all of which liaised with the Ceylon Association in London. In the case of sterling plantation companies, one or more of their directors were resident in
Britain, and they were assisted by retired colonial officials who were taken as advisors to the London offices
of these companies. The board of directors in Britain
acted in concert with the subscribers of capital and
sought to influence the home government when necessary.
    The centralization of policy and business operations in
London is exceptionally great in the case of firms that
are branches or subsidiaries of a metropolitan business.
Even when incorporated locally and having a formal individuality, these firms are tied organizationally and financially to the parent concern. It owns their fixed
assets - land, buildings and machinery - and takes a certain proportion of the profits. The several departments
of these firms - e.g. exporting, importing, estate agency,
etc. - deal directly with the corresponding department in
Britain, bypassing the local managing director. For

transactions with the parent concern or head office the
branch maintains a separate account, and credits to this
account dividends, head office administrative expenses,
rent, interest or depreciation on the property of the
parent firm, commissions and payment for goods supplied
by (or through) the head office. A branch may have to
advance funds free of interest (i.e. on 'current account')
to the parent concern or finance new branches elsewhere.
(5) Interbranch transactions are settled through a
clearing house arrangement. The export documents for
produce would be negotiated by the London office, and the
proceeds debited against payments due from the branch.
These paper transactions, apart from cutting out bank commission on a two-way transfer of funds, help to unify
branch accounts with those of the parent firm. This pattern of accounts integration, while facilitating disguised
'periphery to centre' financial flows, impinges on the
sovereignty of the branch firm.

     In the plantation-cum-mining economies, where invest-
ment was essentially of an absentee nature, the managing
agency system was the central element in metropolitan
control and direction. Sterling plantation companies were
managed by parallel agency houses, one in the metropolis
and the other in the colony, and the division of authority
mirrored clearly the structure and mechanism of metropolitan control. The two agencies, though nominally servants
of the plantation company to which they were responsible,
were not on the same footing. Their relationship inter se
was that of a principal and an agent. In the case of the
sterling plantation companies in Sri Lanka, the London
agency had a branch in Colombo or else engaged a separate
agency firm to attend to its affairs. The Colombo agency
acted merely as 'agents' for the plantation company and
the London agency as 'agents and secretaries'. It was unusual for the Colombo agency to be a branch of a London
agency firm (e.g. Harrisons & Crosfield Ltd, James Finlay
Ltd and Colombo Commercial Co.Ltd), and most agency houses
incorporated locally were independent British firms.
Though organizationally separate, the London and Colombo
agents in some instances were financially interlocked.

     In the management of a sterling plantation company, de-
cisive entrepreneurial control was with the London agency,
and the work of the Colombo agency was mainly technical
and supervisory in scope. The financial and business
policy of the plantation companies was determined by the
London agency in conjunction with the directors in the UK.
Policy originating abroad involved capital programmes,
dividends, reserve funds, trade investments, and the adjustments necessitated by changes in taxation, exchange

control or political conditions in the countries of investment. The London agency, though distant from the
scene of investment, directed the company by means of
regular and timely information obtained from Colombo on
all estate matters; it was assisted by retired plantation
superintendents who were familiar with local conditions.
The more significant administrative and secretarial work
also devolved on the London agency. It prepared the
annual financial statements, maintained the head office
registers, records and accounts, and furnished the directors and auditors with any information they required.
The locus of decision making which lay with the London
agency extended to relatively small matters including the
gratuity payable to a labourer.

The marketing and sale of plantation produce - a source
of vast commercial profits - was vested in the London
agency. The establishment of produce auctions in Colombo
and in Singapore increased the commercial role of the
local agency. But the perquisites of the London agency
did not diminish. As the sole consignee of the company,
it received a commission on the gross proceeds of tea and
rubber 'wherever sold'. The exclusive rights to marketing
commissions were written into the service agreements between the agencies and the companies.

The Company shall immediately after any sale of produce
which may not have been consigned to the [London]
agency supply the agency with full particulars of such
sale and of the proceeds realised thereby and with such
other information as the agency may require in relation
thereto.

This service agreement was between the Kadienlena Tea
Estates Ltd and its London agent, the Rubber Estate Agency
Ltd; such agreements are kept confidential but this is
one of a few that became available for inspection.

The principal-client relation between the London and
the Colombo agencies was such that the Colombo agency
managed the estate, the London agency managed the company.
In the dealings of the plantation company with the Sri
Lanka government on matters such as exchange control and
taxation, the Colombo agency served mainly as a receiving
and forwarding office for correspondence. A mimeographed
note used by one of the largest Colombo agencies when responding to official inquiries is revealing: 'This serves
merely to acknowledge receipt of your letter ... the con-
tents of which we are conveying to our Principals in
London. We shall revert if necessary, on hearing from
them.'

The centralization of management and business policy in
the UK was supported by the constitution of the sterling

companies and the legal framework within which they operated. Their articles of association required 'management
and control [to] be exercised in the U.K.' and that 'Directors must be citizens of the U.K. and Colonies and
ordinarily resident in the U.K.'. (6) Legislation governing the service agreements between sterling companies and
their local agents was that of the metropolitan country.
For instance, the service agreement between Rosehaugh
(Ceylon) Tea Co.Ltd and its Colombo agency, the Consolidated Commercial Agencies Ltd, stipulated: 'This Agreement shall be construed and shall take effect in accordance with the Laws of England.' The resolution of any
dispute would be in accordance with the constructions
given to these laws by the jurisdictional and arbitration-
al tribunals in England. The law enabling such processes
to be included in a contract was promulgated in 1859,
after which Britishers could transfer property in Sri
Lanka or execute mortgage bonds without recourse to the
Sri Lanka courts. The need for this legislation was explained by William Loader in a dispatch to Herman Merivale, dated 10 February 1859.

Two merchants in the City of London cannot, as the law
is in Ceylon, make a coffee plantation in that colony
the subject of a sale or mortgage between them. The
instruments of sale and mortgage must be entered into
before local officers, forwarded to the Secretary of
the Court of the District within a month. Such a
system of law is a barrier to a merchant in London,
although a trader with the colony, buying an estate
in Ceylon or advancing money on the mortgage of one.

Sterling companies in Sri Lanka continued to function outside the legal framework of the country even after it had
achieved its independence. The agency houses in 1964,
when called upon by the Central Bank to make available for
examination, for exchange control purposes, their service
agreements with the plantation companies, declined on the
grounds that they were not legally obliged to do so.

Metropolitan productive capital which the foreign
interests represented consisted of (a) plantation investments in the colony and (b) manufacturing industry in the
metropolis; metropolitan merchant capital consisted of
(a) merchant capital based in London (represented by the
London agency houses) and (b) merchant capital based in
the colonies (represented by local agency houses - in the
case of Sri Lanka the Colombo agency). The relation between these different interests was such that merchant
capital based in the colony was subordinate to merchant
capital based in London, as was made evident in my earlier
discussion on the allocation of entrepreneurial power and

responsibility between the London and the Colombo agency
houses. While merchant capital in London predominated
over locally based merchant capital, foreign merchant
capital as a whole exercised a dominance over absentee
production capital in the plantations; such capital invested in joint stock companies was held by numerous small
investors, scattered and disunited. As discussed in an
earlier chapter, the lavish commissions and fees appropriated by the agency houses for the management of the plantations were the price which production capital had to pay
for operating on an absentee basis in the colonies.

The subordination of the colonial economy to the merchant and manufacturing interests in Britain was supported
by the Colonial Office and by the subscribers of capital
in London. Two examples of such intervention in Sri Lanka
may be cited. When in 1909 Governor Ridgeway proposed a
higher duty on imported cotton manufactures, purely as a
revenue measure with no anticipated reduction of imports,
the Secretary of State espoused the interests of the
Lancashire cotton industry. In rejecting the Governor's
proposal, he explained: 'I would rather leave cotton
goods severely alone, as whether the duty is likely to be
felt or not it is very probable that it might lead to
protests or something more from Lancashire exporters of
cottons and we should avoid this if possible.' (7) On the
other hand, the British cotton industry was eager to use
Sri Lanka as a possible source of raw cotton. In 1861,
when the Cotton Supply Association of Manchester favourably reported on a sample of cotton grown in the Badulla
district of Sri Lanka, the Board of Trade recommended that
facilities be developed 'for irrigating the lands and for
carrying the cotton to the nearest shipping place'. Production was to be encouraged only if it could subserve the
interests of British industry. Sir J. Emerson Tennent
drew the 'special attention' of the Colonial Office to
'the duty of the Colonial government to give its early attention' to this because of 'the vast importance not only
to the Colony itself but to the manufacturers of the U.K.
of obtaining a supply of cottom from our possessions'. (8)

Governor Sir Henry Ward's proposal in 1855 to tax salt
imports into Sri Lanka - again only as a revenue measure -
was rejected for reasons similar to those that prevailed
in the case of Governor Ridgeway's attempt to tax cotton
manufactures. British manufacturers, merchants and shipowners stood to gain from a free trade in salt. Vessels
sailing to the colonies carried salt as 'rough freight' so
as to reduce the shipping rates on Britain's industrial
exports. A Liverpool shipowner wrote to the Secretary of
State against interfering with this trade. (9)

I am concerned in the shipment of manufactured goods to
Ceylon and in common with all engaged in that Trade
owing to the obstacles the shipowner experiences in obtaining the proper proportion of Rough Freight necessary for the loading of his vessel, the whole expense
of the voyage thus being thrown in many instances upon
the freight on fine or manufactured goods.... If we
could increase the earnings of our vessels by enabling
them to take a proportion of salt freight instead of
ballast we could be in a much better position for
bringing produce in return to this country [i.e.
Britain] at less expense.

Salt was carried as ballast until the 1870s, after which
the volume of 'outward' cargo began to exceed the 'homeward' cargo. (10)

In resolving the issue the Committee of Privy Council
for Trade, to whom the proposal to tax salt imports was
referred, took refuge in the sanctity of market forces
which in such matters suited the metropolitan interests.

Whether the Sinhalese will cling to their own produce
or evince a decided preference for the purer European
Article, and whether the latter can be introduced and
disposed of in such terms as will remunerate the exporter in this country [Britain] ... must be left for
the determination of commercial experience.

The anxiety that such imports would affect domestic production was brushed aside in favour of Britain's economic
interests. (11)

The higher question is whether the British trader
should be excluded from legitimate enterprise and the
native consumer from the option of purchase.... If as
my Lords have reason to hope the British exporter may
find it in his interest to avail himself of the opportunity to take part in the trade, additional employment
will pro tanto be given to capital [in Britain] and
labour in Ceylon if displaced, will re-adjust itself
as elsewhere.

The Secretary of State concluded the issue: 'I entirely
concur in the view of their Lordships as adopted in this
letter.'

Intervention by the British government in the relation
between metropolitan investors and the indigenous interests varied according to the nature of the threat to
British interests. This intervention was active or explicit where a potential indigenous industrial class
existed as in India, or when the British industries that
were threatened were those which relied on colonial markets, such as cotton textiles and iron and steel. Furthermore, as A.K.Sen has added, the metropolitan interests

were not homogeneous. For instance, the sellers of British textile machinery to Indian mills had aims which were
different from those of the textile manufacturers and exporters. All the same, sectional rivalry was moderated by
the climate of opinion in Britain which those affected by
the sellers of textile equipment could easily build up
against their errant countrymen. Thus, though British
capital contributed only slightly to the development of a
textile industry in India, any British mill-owner in India
was stigmatized, even civil servants who were 'investing
their spare money'. Such people violated an ethic which
the British in the outposts of the Empire had to uphold.
The strangling of the Indian textile industry by tariff
measures was regarded as an act of patriotism. 'We are
often told', explained Sir John Strachey, (12)

> that it is the duty of the government of India to think
> of Indian interests alone, and that if the interests of
> Manchester suffer it is no affair of ours. For my
> part, I utterly repudiate such doctrines.... The
> interests of Manchester at which foolish people sneer,
> are the interests not only of the great and intelligent
> people, engaged directly in the trade of cotton, but of
> millions of Englishmen.

Similar obstacles confronted the growth of the indigenous iron and steel industry in India. A ready domestic
market existed for steel and wrought iron; imports in
1880-1 were valued at £3.3 million (of which one third was
by government). Iron ore of suitable quality was available close to coal deposits or to forests which could provide charcoal. The Finance Department of the government
of India in 1882 resolved that 'no reasonable doubt can be
entertained [about] the capabilities of the Indian iron
measures to fulfil all that is required of them ...'. (13)
Accordingly, the government under Lord Rippon held out a
ten-year guarantee to purchase locally made steel, at a
price equal to the landed cost of imports. The local correspondent of 'The Economist' himself wrote in favour of
the subject. When the plans for an iron and steel project
were becoming a reality, public opinion in Britain was
roused. Catching up with events, 'The Economist' accused
the Indian government of 'travelling beyond its province',
and in the next issue returned to the fray more fiercely.
(14)

> A great zeal for the encouragement of private enter-
> prise seems to have taken possession of them, and to
> be fast hurrying them on to very slippery ground....
> State patronage [is] being employed as a cork jacket
> to float over the difficulties attending their initia-
> tion, enterprises which promise to promote native in-

dustries. And where are schemes of this kind to end?
Of course, no such policy should be tolerated. The
Home government may be trusted not to permit the interest of India and of this country to be imperilled.
The Indian government abandoned its plans for the project
when the Secretary of State, Lord Hartington, had expressed 'serious objections'. As Dr Rungta notes, the development of this industry was thus held back nearly three
decades. Further research is likely to yield fresh evidence of impediments placed on industrialization in the
colonies.

Though colonies in their role as markets were restrained from setting up industrial enterprises, some
writers have doubted that the colonies were of economic
value to the metropolitan power. The trade and investment
flows to the colonies are contrasted with the considerably
larger flows to the white dominions. Such a view, which
this would seem an appropriate place to discuss, has been
advanced by both Harry Magdoff and Michael Barratt Brown.
The former asserted: 'The commonly held notion that the
theory of imperialism should be concerned largely with investment in underdeveloped countries isn't correct....
Profitable investment opportunities in such countries are
limited by the very conditions imposed by the operations
of imperialism.' (15) Barratt Brown thought 'there was an
obvious contradiction in the idea that capital could flow
to impoverished colonies, except to enclaves of direct raw
materials extraction'. Taking the view that capital
flowed mainly to the rich lands and rich markets, Barratt
Brown asserted: 'It was rather the development of the
white dominions than the exploitation of the colonies that
expanded British industry's markets and productivity in
the nineteenth century.' (16) In their critique of the
established 'theory of imperialism' these authors fail to
consider the qualitative significance for metropolitan industries of the trade and investment flows into the colonies. These flows, though limited in volume, were more
amenable to control in the best interests of the metropolitan economy than its financial and commercial dealings
with other developed countries. Colonial markets - as
well as raw materials - were of strategic importance to
the different metropolitan powers, being their virtual
preserve, not an open field like the trade with independent countries and the white dominions. A revealing
comparison is that between the import of iron and steel
products into Canada and into India - the two largest importers within the British Empire. In 1913, 85 per cent
of Canada's imports of these products were from the USA
but 60 per cent of India's imports were from Britain. The

markets for British locomotive engines in Canada and New
Zealand were highly competitive - in Canada there was com-
petition from local producers as well; in New Zealand
British manufacturers sold only few engines. But the
Indian market was dominated by British firms. (17)

Furthermore, the capital and trade flows among the developed countries (the 'cross investment' which made them
each others' best customers) could seldom be relied upon,
since the developed countries as politically sovereign
units could regulate these flows in the national interest.
Foreign loans were sometimes conditional on the purchase
of materials and equipment from the creditor nation
(Bukharin mentioned a German loan to Serbia and one by the
French government to Russia after the Revolution); (18)
yet, the imperialist element in these transactions was obviously not pushed too far or too frequently. The politico-economic mechanisms for creating dependency and backwardness were not operative. Trade and investment flows
among these countries were more mutually advantageous than
the sharply one-sided relations between the metropolis and
the colonies, and were liable to be changed from time to
time by national policies. On the other hand, the colonies, as sources of and markets for raw materials, were a
constant element in the stability of the metropolitan economy; and it was to the colonies that the metropolitan
economy turned in times of crisis.

Britain's economic policy in the interwar years highlights the importance of the colonies in this respect.
Soon after the First World War, and on and off until 1939,
export markets were a major problem. The switch to
autarky by other European powers and their increased technological competence seriously affected Britain, the
oldest industrial nation. In the context of unemployment
and the threat of social unrest, the potentialities of the
Empire gained renewed attention both as 'soft markets' and
raw material sources; this resulted in closer economic
ties with the colonies. Leo Amery assessed the situation
as follows: 'We are in fact no longer the sort of country
that can compete industrially in the open market.... It
really comes to this, that we can carry out social reform,
and develop an immense trade, but mainly if not almost
entirely within the Empire.' (19) Much earlier, in 1897,
a delegate to the British Trades Union Congress - who was
also 'a merchant in the Manchester trade' - recognized the
importance of Empire trade. This was a time of chronic
trading crises, due to rising tariffs in Europe and America. The 'great [African] continent might not only become
our chief outlet for manufactures, and a great field for
railway and steamship development', but it could also

'prove a reservoir for supplying all sorts of raw materials for manufacturing'. Another speaker saw the possibility of 'work for engineers, iron founders and every description of workmen imaginable'. (20)

Britain's dependence on non-Empire sources of raw materials became a matter of official concern soon after the First World War. Cotton, sugar and tobacco were specially mentioned by the Committee on Commercial and Industrial Policy. 'A large number of raw materials are not produced at all, or are produced on a scale altogether incommensurate with our requirements within the British Empire.' (21) The hazards of this situation were felt even earlier, 'but it is doubtful', the committee added, 'if they were at all widely known or if *their significance for the industrial position of this country in times of internal disturbance was generally appreciated*'. (22) The Lancashire cotton industry was threatened by the increased prices of American cotton in 1919 and 1920. Britain then looked to the colonies as a way out of an impending economic impasse. A very definite policy was begun of encouraging primary production in them. The Colonial Research Committee, the Imperial College of Tropical Agriculture in Trinidad (1921), the Empire Cotton Growing Corporation (1923), and the Empire Marketing Board (1923) were set up. Economic and political problems were kept under general review, through commodity studies by the Imperial Economic Committee, and commissions of inquiry on the production and marketing of colonial produce. Furthermore, official loans and grants were given to the colonies. There was also enacted the Colonial Development Act of 1929 - which 'despite its title had as its primary objective the relieving of unemployment in Great Britain'. (23)

I have so far considered the importance of colonial investments and markets in a critical phase of Britain's development. The importance of such investments and markets for specific economic interests must not, however, be neglected. The two are not necessarily separate because different economic interests or sectors were paramount in specific phases. For example, from 1750 onwards the greatest beneficiary of colonial markets was the British cotton industry. India, from being a major cotton manufacturer, was turned into a market for Lancashire exports. 'The cotton industry', wrote Hobsbawm, (24)

was ... launched, like a glider by the pull of the colonial trade to which it was attached.... Between 1750 and 1769 ... the overseas market, and especially within it the poor and backward 'underdeveloped areas' not only expanded dramatically from time to time, but expanded constantly without apparent limit.

'Semi-colonial and colonial markets' became increasingly
important for Britain's textile industry between 1814 and
1850.
     Colonial investment and markets were far more crucial
for the development of heavy industry in Britain. Unlike
colonial export agriculture, the infrastructure investments (ports, railways, bridges, warehouses and telecommunications, etc.) were highly capital absorptive. British investment in overseas railways was extensively diffused, but it was concentrated during different periods in
different regions and countries - on the European continent, Russia, America, the white dominions and the colonies. When investment in other areas was faltering, the
colonies were the main field of investment. Rosa Luxemburg shows that the maximum growth of the permanent way in
Europe was during the 1840s; in America it was in the
1850s, in Asia in the 1860s, in Australia in the 1870s,
and in Africa during the 1890s. In the period 1890-1910,
95,000 kilometres of railway line were constructed in Asia
and Africa compared with 90,000 kilometres in the whole of
Europe and 12,000 in Australia. (25)   In 1875 nearly £75
million of Indian guaranteed railway securities were held
in England. (26)
     The colonial infrastructure investments had a bigger
impact on the metropolitan economy than the mere volume of
capital would suggest. For instance, railway building
created an immediate demand for capital goods, comprising
a wide range of equipment and industrial materials.
Unlike the consumer goods industries which, because of
relatively limited scale economies, could well have done
without the captive markets in the colonies, the industries connected with railway construction were based on
costly and long-range investments and therefore required
a massive demand to get started and to be kept going. (27)
The railways also facilitated the development of export
products and of markets in centres remote from seaports,
particularly in India and Africa. Furthermore, they
helped in the annexation and pacification of colonial
territories. The demand for armaments was in turn a
stimulus to heavy industry. Africa became a dumping
ground for obsolete weapons to be used by Africans to
fight each other but which were ineffective against European adversaries. (28) Finally, colonial export production was a fillip to the shipbuilding industry in Britain.
The carriage of bulky goods of low unit value promoted
technical improvements in shipping which resulted in
metal-built ships at the close of the nineteenth century.
     The market for capital goods which these investments
generated was the preserve of metropolitan suppliers,

unlike the consumer goods market to which the different
nations had freer access. For instance, the first major
expansion of British locomotive exports, in 1875-85, was
based largely on Indian orders; the second big spurt,
ending in 1908, was based on the demand from South America
and South Africa 'as well as India'. The sales pattern of
British firms making locomotive engines shows that the
pioneers had the home market but latecomers relied essentially on colonial markets. 'In general huge orders from
India dominated the industry.' (29) During 1860-89, 23
per cent of the total sales of British locomotive engines
was in India, and in 1890 to 1913 the proportion was 31
per cent. In 1860-89 Neilson, one of nine leading manufacturing firms, effected 40 per cent of its total sales
in India; and another, Vulcan Foundry, in 1890-1913 had
two thirds of its market in India. (30)
   The infrastructure investment in the colonies and the
resulting demand for capital equipment, contrary to what
Magdoff felt about colonial investment fields and markets,
were compatible with the 'conditions imposed by the operations of imperialism'. Since these investments catered
mainly for the production of export staples and for military needs, they could proceed independently of the level
of domestic purchasing power. Moreover, the investors,
with fixed interest-bearing securities guaranteed by colonial governments, were indifferent to the viability of
these projects. As one British official said, those who
held Indian railway stock could not care whether their
funds went into brick and mortar or were dumped into the
Hooghly. In East Africa it was found that the firm chosen
by the Crown Agents to construct the Uasin-Gishu railway
line had charged fabulous prices for materials; it had
hired surplus administrative staff some of whom were remunerated lavishly. The settlers challenged the railway
interests in London over the expenditures incurred, and
the Kenya government which then took over the project was
able to reduce the cost per mile on the remaining portion
of the Kenya-Uganda railway by more than half. (31) Although in Kenya and other settler colonies the settler
bourgeoisie had a 'national' focus and were vocal and
powerful enough to resist the metropolitan interests, in
the nonsettler colonies and in the semi-colonies, these
interests had a free hand.
   In China, with every railway concession, excepting the
Peking-Kalgan line, firms in Europe obtained the right to
supply building materials and equipment and to recruit
professional staff. (32) In the construction of the
southern trunk line, principally from Hankow to Canton,
the recruitment of engineers was shared between Britain

and Japan. The creditors held mortgages over the property
and revenue of the railway, with full authority over the
disbursement of funds. Chinese government officials and
the trading and manufacturing firms which opposed these
contracts were overridden by the intervention of the
foreign powers. In the case of the Hukuang railway loan,
the Vice-president of the Board of Posts and Communications denounced the companies for their refusal to use
local materials including iron and steel. China was help-
less against this rampage of foreign railway investors.
The Director General of the Hankow-Canton railway could do
nothing. He said: (33)

> First ... [Bland, the representative of a consortium of
> financial and shipping houses] wanted to place the con-
> struction on a contract basis, aiming at monopolising
> the construction rights; then he wanted the chief en-
> gineer to sign for all expenditures, aiming at inter-
> fering with China's authority in appointment[s] and
> purchase. His demands were so improper that they were
> really beyond the bounds of reason.

The successful integration of colonial enterprises with
the metropolitan centre did not require constant inter-
cession by the Colonial Office or the Board of Trade. By
means of the Crown Agents system Britain made itself virtually the sole supplier of colonial governments. In the
early stages the Crown Agencies 'afforded a means of
rewarding long and able services in the Colonial Office'.
(34) Apart from retired civil servants, the agencies had
on their staff merchants and army officers who were not
debarred from following their usual occupations. Colonial
governments were required to purchase through the Crown
Agents' office 'articles, the produce or manufacture of
this country [i.e. Britain] or Europe'. (35) 'They had
no alternative even under protest', (36) whereas the
dominion governments selected their own financial and
purchasing agents overseas. The colonies were permitted
to borrow only from Britain, and foreign exchange reserves
were held in sterling securities, while the British
government itself and the dominions raised funds outside
the Empire - e.g. from the USA. The placing of colonial
government loans in the City was a 'family affair'. (37)
They were not tendered directly in the open market and the
rate for any particular loan was decided on the advice of
'favoured financial houses' who then sold the loan to
certain other financial houses that dealt with the public.
When making purchases or allocating tenders the Crown
Agents dealt only with a few 'approved' firms, so that
competition was restricted. The warehousing, packing and
shipping of stores were shared between two firms dependent

largely on colonial business. Requisitions for the colonial stores were obtained through the agents, (38) though the regulations required goods to be bought locally whenever possible. From 1904 the Crown Agents were allowed to 'interpret orders' and exceed prices stipulated in indents. This discretionary power enabled a handful of firms to profit at the expense of the colonial treasuries.

The Crown Agents system, far from effecting economies of centralized buying, caused unnecessary payments. Even when the supplier's price in England was the same as that of local dealers, the final cost of articles was higher, owing to the Crown Agents' commission of 2½ per cent - besides freight, insurance and other charges. In Sri Lanka drugs and medical equipment supplied through the agents were found to be costlier than when these were sold by private importers. The Principal Civil Medical Officer in 1908 explained to the Colonial Secretary: (39)

As far as I remember I was asked by some of the official members of the sub-committee [of the Legislative Council] if I obtained drugs locally and at a cheaper rate than through the Crown Agents and I replied in the negative.... I was then asked if any drugs could be obtained at a cheaper rate than through the Crown Agents and I replied in the affirmative.

In the Federal Malay States, a member of the Federal Council, Colonel Rae, asserted during a debate on the Crown Agents' purchases: 'My enquiries into this business have revealed situations which are difficult to describe in moderate language.' (40)

The Commission on the Trade of the Straits Settlements in 1933 found several grounds for complaint - apart from the high prices. Supply delays and the uncertainty of delivery dates compelled government to hold large stocks. Machinery and other equipment supplied by the Crown Agents could not be serviced or repaired owing to the lack of local agents. The Crown Agents had no first-hand knowledge of local requirements, and so could not use their discretionary power to deviate from specifications given in the indents, unlike the overseas agents of a private trader. Moreover, the Crown Agents' supplies were ex-ship and damages or losses in transit had to be met from insurance, whereas the prices of private importers were ex-godown and they were bound to make delivery in good order; government thus saved the trouble and delay in negotiating insurance claims - which in any case did not cover the full damage. (41)

The placing of tenders in Britain for supplies and construction projects discriminated even against British firms based in the colonies. Messrs Walker, Sons & Co.,

a British engineering firm in Colombo stated: (42)
> All those who are acquainted with the capabilities of
> the many well-equipped engineering establishments in
> the colony simply smile at the idea of the government
> having to call in the Crown Agents to obtain the plans
> and estimates for so simple a piece of constructional
> work as the grain sheds.

In 1909, representations were made to the Ceylon Chamber
of Commerce: 'Singapore is weary to death of the Crown
Agents system, and like Ceylon asks for a wholesale reform
of an antiquated system.' (43) A few years earlier the
Singapore Chamber of Commerce had stated: 'The advantage
[to the Colony] of asking for local tenders has been repeatedly brought before the government but without much
effect.' (44) To ward off the Crown Agents, the Ceylon
Chamber proposed joint action with the Chambers of Commerce in Hong Kong and Singapore. (45) Five leading firms
protested: 'We do not claim preference, as might well be
accorded to us; we seek the opportunity of competing on
level terms as permanent factors in the colony's progress
and welfare.' (46) The Ceylon Chamber of Commerce wrote
to the Colonial Secretary of 'many past instances' where
local firms were kept out of government projects. In 1908
the Crown Agents Inquiry Committee referred to the monopoly given by the Crown Agents system to the metropolitan
interests as 'the most fruitful cause of discontent' among
the British engineering and construction firms in Sri
Lanka.

The result, if not the deliberate intention of the
Crown Agents system, was 'to confer upon U.K. industry the
chief benefits of the loan expenditure'. (47) For instance, 95 per cent of foreign borrowing by the Indian
government in 1923 was spent on purchases in the UK. An
East India bill in the British Parliament in the same year
wanted 'at least 75% of any such sum, so raised [to] be
expended in Great Britain'. (48) An indiscriminate range
of orders was channelled through the Crown Agents: from
capital equipment for colonial railways, bridges, piers,
docks, telegraphic and other utilities to articles worth
only a few pounds - such as clothing, bedsteads and stationery. Every item of stores required by the civil and
military establishments of the Indian government 'from the
biggest machinery to the smallest door nail' was got from
Britain. (49) Railway materials alone were of considerable value - 'engines, rolling stock, permanent way materials, workshop machinery, coal and everything else necessary for their equipment and maintenance'. But for the
Crown Agents' purchases the decline in Britain's exports
after the First World War would have been much greater.

(50)   The stimulus given to British industry by investments in the colonies became self-propagating. The supply
of plant and equipment from Britain forced the colony into
a dependence for spares from the same source. The employment of British executives and technicians in colonial
enterprises consolidated this advantage. 'Through goodwill, prejudice or actual arrangement', wrote A.K.Cairn-
cross, these men 'tended to specify British machinery for
new construction and replacement'. (51)   For instance,
in India, the railway managers 'as a matter of course'
ordered every item of equipment and spare parts from
Britain, including 'right down to the 1920s ... [those]
that were, or could be made in India'. (52)   The system of
'buying British' as a matter of habit was reinforced by
pressure on the Crown Agents, consulting engineers and
contractors to place orders in Britain. 'Any difference
in price unfavourable to British manufacturers was explained in terms of the inferiority of foreign mills.'
(53)
     During the First World War the British government in
India was obliged to concede the need for a stores department. The Industrial Commission in 1917-18 explained how
a properly constituted stores department, with facilities
in the chief industrial and commercial centres to inspect
goods tendered for sale, could divert to Indian mills and
workshops the large indents on government and railway account that were being sent to London. (54)   However, the
stores department that was set up was ineffective and of
limited scope. The Indian railways, far from stimulating
heavy industry by creating a demand for rails, locomotives, passenger cars, etc., destroyed more occupational
opportunities than they opened. According to Vincent A.
Smith, the railways 'administered the coup de grâce' to
the traditional industries of India which were already declining. (55)   In the case of Russia, Engels foresaw
clearly the basis of the economic dynamism of railway
building. 'It is necessary that you should be able to
mend and repair your engines, coaches, railways and the
like, but to do this cheaply, you must also be in a position to make at home the things needing repair.' (56)   The
dynamic effects of railway building in India were appropriated by the metropolitan economy. In a different historical context, the industrialization of the periphery
which the multinationals are now fostering plays the same
role.
     The interests of the metropolitan manufacturers, which
colonial policy espoused, were shared by the subscribers
of overseas capital in Britain - influenced as they were,
said S.H.Frankel, by a 'combination of sentiment, patriot-

ism and opportunities for gain'. (57) Investment was promoted when it brought opportunities for British industry
and trade. For instance, a proposal in 1925 to spend £50
million on railways, harbour and transport generally in
the Crown colonies found favour in Parliament because of
its 'very close connection' with the demand for British
manufactures. Sir Alfred Mond explained: 'That at the
beginning would mean contracts for railways, bridges,
locomotives and rolling stock.' (58) The steady increase
in official loans and grants to the colonies after the
First World War was viewed by the Board of Trade in 1923
in terms of 'immediate orders' for British goods. (59)
When the capital market was temporarily tight, the railway
companies in India were given financial advances by the
India Office. (60) On the other hand the British capital
market, with its informal links with the Foreign Office,
(61) withheld financial support to enterprises which might
compete with the production and export trade of domestic
industry.

The largely one-sided advantages derived from colonial
investment accrued, directly or indirectly, to wide sections of the British community, not merely the investors.
For example, in the construction of the Indian railways,
a welter of interests stood to gain. When the first railway projects were mooted in the 1840s, (62)

the provincial governors had their eyes on the economy
of military resources, the British mill owners had
hoped that the opening up of the interior would mean
larger markets and new sources of raw cotton supply,
and the British shipping companies and the British and
Indian merchant houses saw in improved communications
a means of vastly extending their business operations.

The gains were even shared by the British working class -
despite what Barratt Brown thought. (63) In his view,
imperialism was of limited benefit to the metropolitan
country and was detrimental to the working class, because
capital exports starved metropolitan industry of capital
(an implication that is analogous to the present day surplus leakage model); the investment income was confined
to the property-owners; and the impoverishing of the
colonies - by the large profits of foreign investors and
declining terms of trade - made the colonies of little
value as investment outlets and markets. The contention
about capital exports seems contradictory. They could not
have been insignificant if at the same time they deprived
British industry of capital; nor could the colonies have
been of little value as investment outlets and markets if
large profits accrued to the foreign investors. The rate
of return on colonial investments was very high though the

aggregate volume of profits was small. The profits to the metropolitan interests from plantations and mines were higher if one allows for the exactions of merchant capital - in the form of management and marketing commissions, inflated prices of materials and inputs and the high insurance and freight charges. The market prices of plantation and mining produce and the resulting profits also contained an element of rent based on a monopoly of natural resources.

Much of my discussion pointed to the colonies as a source of dynamism to the metropolitan economy and to the range of interests that benefited. The overall gains were diffused though not evenly shared; the degree to which they accrued directly to their recipients, or could be identified in an accounting sense, no doubt varied. From this dynamism which the colonies imparted to the metropolitan economy the working class of the metropolis also received its share of gains - by way of expanding or more stable employment and wage levels that were supported by rising productivity. Both Barratt Brown and Magdoff appear to have overlooked the symbiotic relation between colonial investment and export orders for metropolitan industry. Though, as Barratt Brown said, 'the importance of British overseas investment' must not be confused 'with its colonial direction', colonial investment had a pronounced imperialist element, resulting in much higher gains than the non-colonial component of overseas investment. In emphasizing the growth of productivity in metropolitan industry as the source of its wealth, Barratt Brown also detracts from the framework of imperialism in which productivity growth occurred. (64)

Though it was mostly the capital goods sector which profited from colonial investment, through increases in the scale of output and productivity, (65) the colonial market for consumer goods was in no way insignificant. Just as the growth of export production in the colonies and the related infrastructure were not dependent on the level of local purchasing power, the consumer industries of the metropolis benefited from imperialist relations despite the impoverishment of the colonies. The market in an individual colony may have been insignificant, but not the market in each colonial empire. Low purchasing power per head was offset by the large number of consumers. Furthermore, the limiting factor in colonial investment, contrary to what Barratt Brown and Magdoff suggest, was not a lack of markets, but, in the case of the export sector, the low organic composition of capital. And even in the consumer goods sector, the limits to investment were not the size of the market but the imperialist divi-

sion of labour - leading in varying degrees to the 'deindustrialization' of the colonies. Their resulting impoverishment occurred within the framework of imperialism,
enabling the metropolitan country to pre-empt and monopolize the available market. Alternatively, had there
been no imperialist relations, the metropolitan country
would scarcely have been able to control these markets.
Both the impoverishment of the colonies and their controlled development in metropolitan interests were facets of a
single process.

Moreover, the income from foreign investment sustained
a flow of commodity imports into Britain, and the assurance of this income was an important concern of Britain's foreign economic policy - more in evidence in some
periods than in others. 'If [this] ... income ... were to
fall', The Economist' wrote in 1937, 'the whole structure
of British trade and industry would be shaken. Dividends
and interest on our capital abroad are a vital part of our
national income; they are the fund which makes it possible for us to have both guns and butter.' (66) Political
and economic aims were closely interwoven. Overseas investment by British nationals made the rule of the British
government in the colonies more effective, and colonial
rule served to advance the interests of British commerce
and industry. (67)

Whether it was plainly a matter of financial calculation (or otherwise) ... the feelings and decisions of
the investors showed substantial identity with those of
the government in power. Capital went primarily to
those lands from the development of which the British
people hoped to benefit in the way of new resources for
raw materials and foodstuffs, new markets which brought
orders to British industry.

14 The domination of plantation interests by merchant capital: agency house-plantation relations

The mercantile interests were so dominant in the colonial export economy that they even affected the exclusively plantation interests with which they were linked. The general framework of their relationship, which subordinated the plantation interests to merchant capital is discussed later in this book in the chapter on merchant capitalism and underdevelopment. Here I shall adduce some specific evidence of the functioning of the agency system in relation to the plantations. I shall deal first with two aspects which express this subordination sharply. One of them concerns the purchasing policies of the agency houses in respect of materials and inputs required by the plantations. In making these purchases, which were a lucrative source of commercial profits and commissions to the agency, the interests of the agency overrode those of the plantations. The other aspect I shall consider is the restriction placed on a plantation company in the disposal of its assets where this affected the interests of the agency house. I shall show in the concluding portion of the chapter how the subordination of the plantation interests stemmed fundamentally from the control exercised by the agency firms over the plantation companies. This control even restricted plantation companies from transferring the agency rights from one agency to another, let alone freeing themselves from agency control. The discussion in this chapter, though dealing specifically with the functioning of the agency system in Sri Lanka, illustrates the dominant position of merchant capital in colonial export economies in general.

As regards purchasing policies, agency houses were expected to purchase estate requirements on behalf of plantation companies at the most advantageous terms available in the open market. Some service agreements expressly stated this. Yet in the actual conduct of purchases,

practice differed considerably from matters of form.
Whereas owners of private proprietary estates, who maintained an active interest in the affairs of their estates,
would specify the sources from which the estate agency
must purchase, the shareholders of plantation companies,
whose individual financial interest was limited, left the
agency a free hand. Where the estate agency was not
itself an importer, and derived no special gain from
fostering any particular trade connections, its purchasing
policy would be guided by price considerations alone. But
often the estate agency is also the agent of a particular
supplier or manufacturer, or acts as a principal in the
sale of such goods. The choice is then influenced by the
interests of the estate agency as an importer; and orders
could be placed with firms from which the agency drew
trade discounts or supplier's commissions. As Kathleen
Stahl circumspectly wrote, 'obviously cases will arise
when a purchase could be made to better advantage or more
cheaply outside this channel'. (1)

The divergence of interests between the plantations and
the agency houses over the prices charged for plantation
materials was noted during the early years of the agency
system in Sri Lanka. In an essay, on The Causes of the
Great Increase of Expenditure on Coffee Estates [during
1865-6] and the Means to be Adopted for Reducing It, a
British planter named Woodhouse discreetly referred to the
purchasing policy of estate agents. (2)

> Another minor item is what might be saved on the pur-
> chase of Bags, Tools, Cumblies, Medicines, Baskets,
> etc., by a little more attention to the subject by
> Estate Agents. Without for a moment imputing other
> than the most strictly honourable motives to those
> gentlemen, it must be very evident to even a casual
> observer how very inferior and unsuitable are many of
> the articles referred to, compared to what they might
> be, and in many cases used to be, or to what their cost
> entitles the purchaser to expect.

A more explicit comment was that made by another planter,
Mr Peter Moir. 'The larger the disbursements, the better
are the agent's commissions. In other words, the agent
gains by increased expenditure, the Proprietor suffers.'
(3) A third planter, Mr Millie, urged that 'Agencies in
Colombo and Kandy should combine more in keeping down
prices of articles for Estates'. (4) In Malaysia where
the plantations developed much later, the commissions
taken by agency houses for the supply of stores, machinery, etc., to rubber estates and for arranging the shipment of produce met with 'a good deal of criticism'. A
commercial correspondent of the 'Straits Times' wrote in

1911: 'there is a natural tendency among managers of the
these agencies to make the store bills as heavy as possible, so that their own profits may be increased'. (5) The
report referred to 'a good deal of friction over the indenting of estate supplies even in the case of few agency
firms of good repute'. (6)

The excessive prices paid for plantation materials are
the result of the trading interests of the agencies and
their exclusive business connections with manufacturing
firms in Europe. A recent instance which gained official
cognizance in Sri Lanka related to the import of nylon
netting used as withering tats in tea factories. Up to
1965 two agency houses, Carson Cumberbatch & Co.Ltd and
the Colombo Commercial Co.Ltd, were importing nylon netting at Rs 4 a yard, c.i.f., from Elastic Nets Ltd, a
manufacturing firm in England, while some other agency
houses, including Whittall Boustead Ltd, were buying from
Japan at prices nearly one third lower. Carson Cumberbatch & Co.Ltd and the Colombo Commercial Co.Ltd were importers on their own account; the former bought direct
from manufacturers, the latter through its parent firm in
Britain, the Colombo Commercial Co. (Export) Ltd, which
acted as intermediary. The netting supplied by these two
agencies to the estates which they managed, besides being
more expensive, was technically inferior (7) according to
the Tea Research Institute of Sri Lanka. Following this
disclosure, the government for foreign exchange reasons
imposed an import price ceiling of Rs 3 a yard (for
stretched net of stipulated dimensions), based on the
prices of Japanese netting. The administrative intervention eliminated the UK as a supplier.

The disregard of plantation interests by the agency
houses was also seen in the import of tea chests, in which
the agencies were aligned with powerful trading concerns
in Britain. An exposition of this issue requires a background comment. The supply of tea chests for the plantations in Sri Lanka had been a monopoly of the London
Plywood Chest Association, a buying agency, whose member
firms secured orders through their local representatives,
many of whom were managing agents for plantations; e.g.
Acme Tea Chests Co.Ltd was represented by James Finlay;
Harrisons & Crosfield Ltd by its branch in Colombo;
Venesta Ltd by the Colombo Commercial Co.Ltd. Several
plantation companies which were outside the trading sphere
of these agency houses were supplied by their London agencies. The London Plywood Chest Association obtained plywood boards mainly from Finland and re-exported them to
Sri Lanka and other tea-producing countries. During the
Second World War supply sources shifted to the USA and

Canada, but after the end of the war the association re-
verted to its traditional suppliers. The growth of Sinhalese proprietorship in plantations and the entry of Sinhalese into the import trade led to imports of lower-
priced Japanese chests. Supplies from Finland (imported
through the association) consequently declined from 75 per
cent of the total value soon after the war to around 50
per cent in 1959. Finnish chests were exclusively bought
by the agency managed estates, which were served by the
members of the London Plywood Chest Association.

A change in trading procedures occurred in 1962, when
the USSR started selling tea chests direct to importers in
Sri Lanka and Indonesia. The c.i.f. price of these chests
in Sri Lanka was 71 pence, as compared with 92 pence for
Finnish chests and 78 pence for Japanese chests. (8) The
importer of Russian chests - a Sri Lanka firm - offered
them in the market at correspondingly low prices, but the
leading agency houses desisted from buying them. The
agency managed plantations, which accounted for about 60
per cent of the total imports, continued to be supplied
from Finland on orders placed with the London Plywood
Chest Association. As in the case of nylon netting, the
government had to intervene on account of the wide disparity in c.i.f. prices. Imports were regulated on the
basis of a ceiling price of 71 pence. After a time exporters in Japan lowered their prices in line with those
of Russian tea chests, while the London association was
priced out of the Sri Lanka market. Imports of tea chests
from Finland fell to Rs 0.4 million in 1964 from an annual
average of Rs 4.7 million during 1955-61, while those from
Russia increased to Rs 7.6 million from 0.6 million.

The reaction of the London Plywood Chest Association to
the price ceiling was significant. The association, along
with the agency houses, protested vehemently through the
British Board of Trade. It was urged by them that Russian
deliveries were unreliable and that Russian chests were
inferior in regard to size and to the quality standards
required by tea buyers overseas. The price ceiling, because of its adverse effect on British firms, was also
construed as trade discrimination and a breach of GATT
principles. Actually Britain was never a producer of tea
chests but a middleman booking orders from Finland. What
was at stake was Britain's entrepot trade with Sri Lanka
which had been a virtual monopoly of the London Plywood
Chest Association, served by the agency houses. (9)

The price ceiling ended the purchases of tea chests
from Finland, but the agency houses continued to buy
battens for these chests through their principals in the
London Plywood Chest Association. The import control

order had used the term 'tea chests' which the agencies
conveniently interpreted to exclude battens. Like tea
chests earlier, the battens imported from Sweden by the
London Plywood Chest Association were more costly than
those from Japan. The price disparity in 1964 was nearly
40 per cent; the c.i.f. cost of full battens imported
from Sweden was 16s. 4d., and of half battens 14s. Od.,
compared with 11s. 8d. and 10s. 1d., respectively, for
those from Japan. In 1964, four of the five agency houses
which were the representatives of the London Plywood Chest
Association made almost all their purchases from Sweden,
(10) while the rest of Sri Lanka's requirements was met
from Japan. These were imported by Sri Lankan traders and
by one agency house, Mackwoods Ltd, which had no connection with the London Plywood Chest Association.

An attempt by the Controller of Imports to impose a
price ceiling on imported battens was thwarted by the
British dominated Ceylon Chamber of Commerce. The Chamber
argued that if Swedish supplies were excluded, plantations
would have only one source, Japan, as Russia did not sell
battens; the quality of the Japanese battens would affect
Sri Lanka's tea exports. This argument was hardly valid.
A proper timing of imports would have ensured uninterrupted supplies despite typhoon damage in Japan, to which
the Chamber referred. Any doubts about the quality of
Japanese battens were unfounded as they were already being
used by exporters of tea to the London auctions. (A similar fear about the quality of tea chests made in the USSR
was disproved by a technical report which the Controller
of Imports obtained from the Ceylon Institute of Scientific Research.)

The subordination of the plantation interests by merchant capital has so far been discussed in terms of the
prices of materials purchased by the agencies on behalf of
the plantation companies. The trading interests of agency
houses also resulted in a distribution of purchases among
firms in the UK on economically irrelevant grounds. Plantation companies under the same agency in Colombo were
made to patronize different suppliers in the UK according
to the commercial affinities of the managing agents in
London. For example, four sterling plantation companies
whose Colombo agent was Whittall Boustead Ltd were supplied with tea chests from three different sources. The
Dickwella Tea Co.Ltd was until 1963 supplied by Bobbins
Ltd (London) on orders placed by the Dickwella Tea Co.'s
London agent, James Warren & Co.Ltd. The United Planters
Co. of Ceylon and the New Dimbulla Co.Ltd were supplied by
Westman's Woodexport, Gothenburg, Sweden, on orders placed
on their behalf by Robert Brooks & Co., and the Bandara-

pola Ceylon Co.Ltd was supplied by K.T.Lewis (London) on
an order by Lyall Anderson & Co. The placing of orders by
the London agency rather than by the Colombo agency caused
a foreign exchange loss to Sri Lanka, in the form of commissions, and lower tax revenues. Since a London agency
has fewer plantation companies under its management in any
one country, compared with most local agency houses, the
vesting of purchasing rights in the London agency also
caused a proliferation of suppliers - forgoing the economies of centralized buying which are one of the potential
advantages of the managing agency system.

The sale of estates belonging to plantation companies
was another area in which there was a conflict of interests between the agencies and the plantation shareholders.
Agency houses have obstructed plantation companies from
disposing of their assets in view of the loss of agency
rights or a fall in the agency income, as in Malaysia
after the Second World War when a boom in land values made
the fragmentation and resale of certain estates very profitable to their owners. Some of these estates were
managed by agency houses in Colombo; and two of them
intervened to obtain amendments to the articles of association of the plantation companies, in order to prevent the
sale of the estate lands. Among the Gordon Frazer group
of companies any sale for which the consideration exceeded
Rs 100,000 was made subject to a special resolution con-
sented to by at least 75 per cent of the shareholders who
were represented or present at a meeting. Concomitantly
the directors' powers to appoint and remove agents and
secretaries were curbed. The exercise of these powers was
made dependent on a resolution by three fifths of the directors instead of by a bare majority as before. For
plantation companies under the agency of Carson Cumberbatch & Co.Ltd, the value of property, the sale of which
required a special resolution, was lowered in 1957 from
Rs 100,000 to Rs 25,000.

The Lower Perak River Coconut Co.Ltd, a company registered in Colombo but owning estates in Malaysia, had three
separate offers during 1959 and 1960 for the purchase of
Blenheim estate. These were successively rejected at the
instigation of the agency house, though the price offered
was increased from $(M) 1,000 an acre in January 1960 to
$(M) 1,500 in November 1960. Before the final offer was
discussed at a general meeting of the company, its managing agents, Gordon Frazer & Co.Ltd, sought to influence
shareholders against a sale, stating that at $(M) 1,500 an
acre the break-up value per share was only Rs 19.45. When
this figure was challenged by shareholders in favour of
the sale, the agents submitted a revised figure of

Rs 21.27 as against an estimate by the shareholders of a break-up value of Rs 23 per share.

The resolution for a sale failed to obtain the majority of votes required by the company's amended articles of association. The group in favour canvassed the absentee shareholders, many of whom resided in Britain, giving reasons why the sale of the estate at that time was most opportune. (11) First, capital transfers permitted from Sri Lanka had already been reduced from Rs 100,000 in 1957 to Rs 25,000 in October 1960, and owing to balance of payments problems exchange control was likely to further restrict the remittance of liquidation proceeds abroad. Second, the offer of $(M) 1,500 per acre was thought to reflect a peak value for Malaysian coconut property. Third, the possible introduction of anti-fragmentation laws and of exchange control in Malaysia would, respectively, reduce land values and affect the transfer of sale proceeds abroad. The resolution to sell was, however, defeated by a block vote representing 42,214 shares, or 27 per cent of the total. The first two prognostications were soon borne out. Capital remittances from Sri Lanka to nonresidents were totally suspended from January 1962, and after November 1962 the share value of the Lower Perak River Coconut Co.Ltd declined from Rs 12.50 to Rs 7.75. Fundamentally, the episode confirmed the dominant position of the agency houses vis-à-vis the plantation owners, and the ability of the agencies to mobilize voting power in their interests.

The block of votes which decided the issue was held by four investors, viz. the Perak River Coconut Co.Ltd (16,764 shares), Ceylon Financial Investments Ltd (22,750 shares), Gordon Frazer & Co.Ltd (1,700 shares), and two directors of the Lower Perak River Coconut Co.Ltd who were also directors of Gordon Frazer & Co.Ltd (1,000 shares). The first two of these shareholders, viz. the Perak River Coconut Co.Ltd and Ceylon Financial Investments Ltd, could alone have vetoed the sale; at the time of the general meeting they held 39,514 shares or 25.6 per cent of the total issued capital, or slightly more than was needed to reject a special resolution. These dissenting votes belonged to a business group which always espoused the interests of the agency house. Both the Lower Perak River Coconut Co.Ltd and the Perak River Coconut Co.Ltd had Gordon Frazer & Co.Ltd as their managing agents, and the majority of directors of Perak River Coconut Co.Ltd were also directors of Gordon Frazer & Co.Ltd. Ceylon Financial Investments Ltd had Gordon Frazer & Co.Ltd as its agents and secretaries, and their directorates were identical. (12) Furthermore, Ceylon Financial Investments Ltd

held 49 per cent of the issued capital of Gordon Frazer
& Co.Ltd, as at 5 August 1960. The interlocking between
them was not merely due to almost half of the capital of
one being owned by the other. Ceylon Financial Investments Ltd invested 66 per cent of its capital (book value
as at 1 April 1962) in plantation companies under the
Gordon Frazer agency, while 24 per cent of its capital was
invested in Gordon Frazer & Co.Ltd. Between them they had
financial control over twelve rupee plantation companies
in Sri Lanka and two Malaysian companies registered in Sri
Lanka.

The voting power which the agencies mobilized against
the sale of estates was mustered at the time when offers
were being made to purchase Blenheim estate. It was then
that both the Perak River Coconut Co.Ltd and Ceylon Financial Investments Ltd built up their shareholdings in the
Lower Perak River Coconut Co.Ltd, with a view to acquiring
the critical block of shares to prevent the sale. Between
31 December 1959 and 30 November 1960, the period when the
offer of $(M) 1,500 per acre was being considered, Perak
River Coconut Co.Ltd increased its holdings in the Lower
Perak River Coconut Co.Ltd from 12,602 shares to 16,764
and, by 31 December 1961, to 21,140 shares. Likewise,
Ceylon Financial Investments Ltd expanded its holding to
22,750 shares by 30 November 1960, the date of the special
resolution. Taken in conjunction with the common financial interests of these two corporate investors and the
agency house, their action in buying up shares in a company, some of the assets of which were likely to be sold,
and in voting against the sale shows a vested interest in
keeping the plantation company intact. After their acquisition of large shareholdings in the Lower Perak River
Coconut Co.Ltd, the market price of the company's shares
fell by nearly 40 per cent between December 1960 and
December 1962. The gain to Gordon Frazer & Co.Ltd, qua
managing agent, may have outweighed the fall in the value
of its investments.

In a similar instance, in June 1951 a special resolution to authorize the sale of the Opalgalla Tea and Rubber
Co.Ltd, whose agents and secretaries were Carson Cumberbatch & Co.Ltd, was defeated; 42,267 voted in favour of
a sale and 39,668 against it. Carson Cumberbatch & Co.Ltd
had taken steps to defeat the resolution for sale by a
timely increase in its voting rights. In the months preceding the meeting at which the resolution for sale was
voted upon, Carson Cumberbatch expanded its holdings in
the Opalgalla Tea and Rubber Co.Ltd from 4,393 shares to
10,042 shares. Those present at the voting were three
directors of the company and only four other shareholders.

Eight shareholders were represented by attorneys and for
ninety-three others the agency house acted as proxy. At
the meeting one shareholder questioned the impartiality of
the agency house in regard to the sale and even the way in
which the voting was conducted. He complained to the
Registrar of Companies that the Chairman of the plantation
company (who, as in other cases, was also a director of
the agency house) refused to disclose the names of shareholders represented by attorney or proxy and of those
voting for or against the resolution. (13)   The Companies
Act did not, however, provide for the investigation of
such a complaint.

The ability of the agencies to override the exclusively
plantation interests entrusted to their care was due to
the absolute power which they had over the management and
business policy of plantation companies. The existence of
such power is contrary to the image put up by tea and
rubber associations in Britain. The agents, it is
claimed, 'merely carry out the instructions of the boards
of these companies and they cannot influence policy on an
unwilling directorate' since usually a plantation company
would not have more than one director who is also a director of the agency. (14)   To pose the question of control
in these terms presupposes that the influence of the
agency is confined to that of its own director or directors on the board of the plantation company, and that investors take an active interest in the running of their
companies. Modern joint stock organizations are known for
the growth of a rentier element drawing income from the
negotiable titles to ownership while surrendering business
control to a 'managerial' group. 'Small stockholders
often do not care much about what for most of them is but
a minor source of income and, whether they care or not,
they hardly even bother, unless they or some representatives of theirs are out to exploit their nuisance value.'
(15) The diffusion of the ownership rights of corporate
enterprises has merely the effect of increasing de facto
control by a minority, through its command over a certain
marginal block of shares. There is in these enterprises
a large body of disunited shareholders content with merely
collecting their dividends. A narrow financial oligarchy,
by mobilizing and manipulating the voting rights of the
small shareholders, partly through the exercise of proxies
and powers of attorney, dominates immense spheres of production.

The directors of the managing agencies, though owning
only a small capital in any single company which they
managed, were persons with substantial financial power and
close connections with share brokering, trade, insurance

and shipping interests. The control they exercise over
plantation enterprise was also influenced by two important
developments during the first decades of the present
century. One was that the majority of shareholders were
expatriates and away from the scene of their investments,
leaving management completely in the hands of resident
directors and agency houses. This passivity was a feature
even of the rupee companies although many of the shareholders lived in Sri Lanka. A correspondent writing to
the 'Times of Ceylon' in 1910 thus declared, 'Owing to
[the] apathy of shareholders who fail to attend meetings,
those who have the financial control of tea companies are
able to do as they please.' (16) The other factor which
contributed to the centralization of power was the small
par value of the shares of plantation companies. By the
1930s there was a distinct tendency for the issue of plantation shares to be in small denominations. For example,
in 1930, for thirty-five rupee plantation companies chosen
at random, with an ordinary capital of Rs 27.5 million,
the proportion of shares with a par value of Rs 15 and
less was 94 per cent (the par value of the remaining
shares being Rs 50-100), whereas in 1910 for eighteen companies with a capital totalling Rs 6.6 million, the proportion of low denomination shares was 53 per cent. The
spreading of ownership, while facilitating the raising of
capital, fostered the dominance of a small group. The
preponderance of the smaller shareholders, mere coupon-
clippers, enabled a resolute group to gain control easily.
(17)

Alongside the passivity of the shareholders of plantation companies the agencies exercised financial and administrative control over the companies. This control was
based partly on the investment in the plantation companies
of the surplus funds of enterprises managed by the agencies and partly on interlocking directorates between the
agencies and the plantation companies. In Sri Lanka, the
enterprises whose surplus funds were used in this way included insurance firms, which after 1948 were statutorily
required to retain locally a portion of the premium reserves of non-life business. The bulk of such funds was
channelled into holding companies and investment trusts
sponsored by the agency houses (and managed and controlled
by them), and these funds were in turn invested in plantation companies. For the sake of spreading risks any
single investment trust holds only a small percentage of
the capital of any one plantation company.

The relationship between investment trusts and the
plantation agencies is set out in Tables 14.1 and 14.2.
The trusts investigated had a paid-up capital in 1959 of

about Rs 16 million, but their total capital inclusive of
retained profits exceeded Rs 23 million; and almost the
whole of the latter sum was invested in agency managed
plantation companies. The directorships of these investment trusts were held by eleven persons, eight of whom
were directors of agency houses. In the Ceylon Investment
Co.Ltd and Ceylon Guardian Investment Trust Ltd (the two
largest trusts, with investments totalling Rs 22 million),
a majority of the board members were directors of Mackwoods Agency; and they were also on the board of Rubber
Investment Trust Ltd. The boards of three other trusts,
viz. Ceylon Financial Investments Ltd, Darton Development
Co.Ltd and Pembroke Estates Ltd, were composed entirely of
directors of Gordon Frazer & Co.Ltd, while the board of
Investment Holdings Ltd consisted of directors of four
agency houses. As agency house nominees, their directoral
appointments were due to the financial control which the
agencies exercised over the trusts, for they had themselves subscribed only a nominal value of the share capital of the trusts. Six of the investment trusts had a
total of eighteen directorships, held by eight individuals. The directors' total shareholdings (at par) were
less than Rs 40,000 (inclusive of shares held by the wives
of directors), compared with a paid-up capital of Rs 15.8
million. The shareholding per directorship was thus about
Rs 2,000. The remaining investment trust (Investment
Holdings Ltd) was financed entirely by agency houses, and
its directors were officially agency house nominees.
    The financial relation between the agency houses and
the investment trusts was similar to that between the
agencies and the plantation companies. While wielding
financial control the agencies had invested little or no
capital of their own, except in the case of Investment
Holdings Ltd and Pembroke Estates Ltd, whose paid-up capital was, however, less than Rs 0.5 million. The capital
of Investment Holdings Ltd was subscribed by eight agency
houses, and 93 per cent of the capital of Pembroke Estates
Ltd by Gordon Frazer. On the other hand, in the Rubber
Investment Trust Ltd and the Darton Development Co.Ltd the
agencies held no capital at all; in the Ceylon Investment
Co. they held 6 per cent of the capital but controlled at
least 47 per cent (invested by plantation companies under
their management); and in the Ceylon Guardian Investment
Trust they held only 2 per cent whilst controlling at
least 36 per cent. Almost the entire capital of the
Rubber Investment Trust was subscribed by two other in-
vestment trusts - the Ceylon Investment Co.Ltd and the
Ceylon Guardian Investment Trust Ltd. Thus in the Ceylon
Guardian Investment Trust Ltd, 36 per cent of the capital

TABLE 14.1 Control of investment trusts by agency houses, 1959

Investment trust	Agents and secretaries	Directors of investment trust	Membership of directorates of agency houses	Value of investments (at cost) (b)	Paid-up capital	Capital of investment trust controlled by agency houses						
						Total	Ownership of such capital				
							Plantation companies	Insurance companies	Individuals	Agency houses	Investment trusts
1 Ceylon Investment Co.Ltd	Investment Managers and Secretaries Ltd (a)	G.N.Russell (c) O.B.Forbes G.K.Newton	– Mackwoods Mackwoods	Rs 11.3 m	Rs 6.4 m	Rs 1.6 m	47%	3%	34%	6%	7%
2 Ceylon Guardian Investment Trust Ltd	Investment Managers and Secretaries Ltd	G.N.Russell O.B.Forbes G.K.Newton	– Mackwoods Mackwoods	Rs 10.6 m	Rs 8.7 m	Rs 3.5 m	36%	55%	2%	6%	–
3 Rubber Investment Trust Ltd	Investment Managers and Secretaries Ltd	O.B.Forbes G.K.Newton P.R. Candappa R.J.Barrow	Mackwoods – – –	Rs 451,000	Rs 245,000	Rs 242,000	–	–	2%	–	98%
4 Investment Holdings Ltd	George Steuart & Co.	G.K.Newton R.J. Gilmour B.W.J. Anthony L.S. Boys E.C.E. Shattock	Mackwoods George Steuart Bois Bros Gordon Frazer Gordon Frazer	n.a.	Rs 305,000	Rs 305,000	–	–	–	100%	–

5 Ceylon Financial Invest-ments Ltd	Gordon Frazer & Co.Ltd	L.S. Boys P.R. Walton A.L.de Montfort	Gordon Frazer Gordon Frazer	n.a.	Rs 150,000	Rs 150,000	–	–	100%	–	–
6 Darton Develop-ment Co. Ltd	Gordon Frazer & Co.Ltd	L.S. Boys P.R. Walton A.L.de Montfort	Gordon Frazer Gordon Frazer Gordon Frazer	Rs 347,000	Rs 200,000	Rs 200,000	–	–	100%	–	–
7 Pembroke Estates Ltd	Gordon Frazer & Co.Ltd	L.S. Boys P.R. Walton	Gordon Frazer Gordon Frazer	Rs 347,000 Rs 189,000	Rs 88,000	Rs 88,000	–	6%	93%	1%

(a) Investment Managers and Secretaries Ltd in 1959 had four directors, all of whom were partners of Turquand Youngs & Co., a British accountancy firm having a large volume of business with the agency managed plantation companies; but earlier - for example, in 1951 and 1952 - the board of Investment Managers and Secretaries Ltd consisted of only two directors, both of whom were directors of the estate agency firm Boustead Bros Ltd.

(b) Paid-up capital plus permanent reserves.

(c) Formerly a director of the estate agency firm Boustead Bros Ltd.

n.a. = not available.

TABLE 14.2 Financial control of investment trusts classified by agency houses, 1959

	Ceylon Investment Co.Ltd	Ceylon Guardian Investment Trust Ltd	Rubber Investment Holdings Ltd	Investment Holdings Ltd	Ceylon Financial Investments Ltd	Darton Development Co.Ltd	Pembroke Estates Ltd
Paid-up capital	6,400,000	8,700,000	245,000	305,000	150,000	200,000	87,500
Capital subscribed by:							
(1) Agency houses:							
George Steuart	123,000	505,000	–	38,700	–	–	–
Bois Bros	29,260	–	–	38,700	–	–	–
Whittall Boustead	469,060 (a)	376,020 (b,c)	–	38,880	–	–	–
Mackwoods	276,756	684,500	–	–	–	–	–
Gordon Frazer	59,040	107,000	–	38,600	149,995	200,000	87,500
Carson Cumberbatch	78,230	568,000	–	38,800	–	–	–
Bosanquet & Skrine	90,000	146,890	–	34,500	–	–	–
Leechman	101,900	65,000	–	–	–	–	–
Shaw Wallace & Hedges	110,000	137,500	–	38,700	–	–	–

Harrisons & Crosfield	8,500	850,000	–	–	–	–
Aitken Spence	30,000	10,000	–	38,000	–	–
Colombo Commercial	44,250	–	–	–	–	–
Other agency houses	10,340	–	(e)	–	–	–
(2) Investment trusts	133,320 (d)	–	241,650 (e)	–	200,000	87,500
Total	1,563,656	3,449,910	241,650	304,880	149,995	200,000	87,500

Source: Registrar of Companies.

(a) Excludes Rs 416,000 held by the National Mutual Life Association of Australasia, Colombo, whose manager, Mr J.H.Newton, in 1960 was also a director of the Rubber Investment Trust Ltd. (When Newton went on leave in 1960 he was temporarily succeeded on the board by R.J.Ireland, Acting Manager, National Mutual Life Association of Australasia, Colombo.)

(b) Includes Rs 196,500 controlled by Lewis Brown & Co.Ltd, which became a financial subsidiary of Mackwoods from about 1960. But even in 1959 there was a unified management between Mackwoods and Lewis Brown, as is seen from the composition of their directors. Mackwoods: G.K.Newton (Managing), R.J.S.Bean, N.S.O.Mendis. Lewis Brown: N.S.O.Mendis (Chairman), S.A.Chitty, P.B.Rowson, G.K.Newton, T.C.A.de Soysa (P.B.Rowson was employed as an assistant at Mackwoods).

(c) Excludes Rs 363,000 held by the National Mutual Life Association of Australasia, Colombo.

(d) Of this sum Rs 45,740 was held by the Rubber Investment Trust Ltd, Rs 72,420 by Ceylon Guardian Investment Trust Ltd, Rs 15,060 by Investment Managers and Secretaries Ltd (the managing agents of Ceylon Investment Co.Ltd, Ceylon Guardian Investment Trust Ltd, and Rubber Investment Trust Ltd).

(e) Of this sum Rs 120,460 was held by Ceylon Investment Co.Ltd, and Rs 118,740 by Ceylon Guardian Investment Trust Ltd.

belonged to plantation companies and 55 per cent to insurance companies; in the Ceylon Investment Co.Ltd, 47 per cent of the capital, was held by plantation companies and 34 per cent by individuals connected with the agencies in some way or other. They were directors of either the agency house or of plantation companies managed by the agency, or else employees or ex-employees of the agency, or the wives and other close family members of such persons. (Only shareholders of investment trusts whose connection with the agency could be determined were included in this calculation.) (18) In the case of Ceylon Financial Investments Ltd and the Darton Development Co.Ltd, all of their capital was held by individuals who had proprietary interests in the agency firm Gordon Frazer & Co.Ltd. (19)

TABLE 14.3 Agency house affiliations of the directors of plantation companies, 1964

No. of interlocking directors	No. of stg plantation companies having on their board directors of the London agency	No. of R. plantation companies having on their board:		No. of plantation companies whose Chairman is a director of the agency house: (a)	
		Directors of the Colombo agency	Shareholders or employees of the Colombo agency	Sterling companies	Rupee companies
0	9	11	4	30	17
1	31	68	49	17	62
2	34	69	64	29	69
3	10	4	29	8	4
4	6	1	5	6	1
5	1	-	2	1	-
	91	153	153	91	153

(a) London agency for sterling companies and Colombo agency for rupee companies.

An analysis of interlocking directors between plantation companies and their agents in London and Colombo is
given in Table 14.3. Out of a total of 111 sterling plantation companies operating in 1964, the boards of ninety-
one companies were examined, in respect of which it was
possible to ascertain the directors of their respective
London agencies. (20) In nearly nine tenths of these
sterling companies at least one director was also a director of the London agency, while one half of the companies
had at least two agency house directors on their boards.
In nearly three quarters of the sterling companies which
were interlocked the board chairman was a director of
their own agency. For sterling companies as a whole 48
per cent of the directorships were held by agency house
directors. The extent of interlocking of the London agencies with sterling companies was generally less than that
between the Colombo agencies and the rupee companies.
Since the London agencies manage plantation companies in
several countries the control they exercised over the
production and marketing of plantation produce was quite
considerable.

The rupee plantation companies investigated were all
those existing in 1959. The management of 153 of these
companies was exclusively by agency houses registered in
Sri Lanka and having locally resident directors. Twelve
companies were managed by the local branches of three
London agency firms, (21) and all of these companies were
interlocked with the agency; four of them had one interlocking director on their boards, and eight of them two
interlocking directors. Interlocking in these cases was
through directorships in the companies which were held by
employees of the Colombo agency houses (not shown in Table
14.1). Out of the 153 companies managed by such agency
houses more than four fifths had on their boards at least
one director of the agency house, (22) who almost invariably was chairman of the plantation company's board. The
managing agency was represented on the boards of rupee
companies not merely by one of its own directors but also
by shareholders of the agency house or else by visiting
agents or superintendents of a plantation company under
the same agency. As employees of the agency or by working
under its direct supervision, they were also practically
its nominees.

An alternative measure of the control over plantation
companies by the agency houses is given by the distribution of directorships (shown in Tables 14.4 and 14.5). In
the rupee plantation companies, 44 per cent of all directors were the representatives of agency houses or their
nominees as already defined, each of whom held a relative-

TABLE 14.4   Multiple directorships in Ceylon's plantation companies

No. of director-ships per person	STERLING COMPANIES (1964) No. of directors			No. of directorships			RUPEE COMPANIES (1958) No. of directors			No. of directorships			No. of directors		No. of directorships	
	Total	Agency nomi-nee	Non-agency	Total	Agency nomi-nee	Non-agency	Total	Agency nomi-nee	Non-agency	Total	Agency nomi-nee	Non-agency	Ceylon-ese	Brit-ish	Ceylon-ese	Brit-ish
	148	29	119	148	29	119	114	24	90	114	24	90	57	57	57	57
1	148	29	119	148	29	119	114	24	90	114	24	90	57	57	57	57
2	38	14	24	76	28	48	31	14	17	62	28	34	18	13	36	26
3	15	8	7	45	24	21	17	10	7	51	30	21	7	10	27	24
4	18	14	4	72	56	16	16	13	3	64	52	12	2	14	8	56
5	3	3	-	15	15	-	8	6	2	40	30	10	3	5	15	25
6	3	2	1	18	12	6	2	2	-	12	12	-	-	2	-	12
7	1	1	-	7	7	-	5	4	1(a)	35	28	7	1	4	7	28
8	1	1	-	8	8	-	4	4	-	32	32	-	1	3	8	24
9	-	-	-	-	-	-	6	6(c)	-	54	54	-	-	6	-	54

	30	20	3	2	20	30	50	2(b)	3	5	–	20	20	–	2	2
10	30	20	3	2	20	30	50	2(b)	3	5	–	20	20	–	2	2
11	–	–	–	–	–	–	–	–	–	–	–	–	–	–	–	–
12	12	–	1	–	–	12	12	–	1	1	–	12	12	–	1	1
13	39	–	3	–	–	39	39	–	3	3	–	–	–	–	–	–
14	14	–	1	–	–	14	14	–	1	1	–	–	–	–	–	–
15	15	–	1	–	–	15	15	–	1	1	–	–	–	–	–	–
16	–	–	–	–	–	–	–	–	–	–	–	–	–	–	–	–
17	–	–	–	–	–	–	–	–	–	–	–	–	–	–	–	–
18	18	–	1	–	–	18	18	–	1	1	–	–	–	–	–	–
Total	434	178	124	91	194	418	612	122	93	215	210	211	421	155	75	230

(a)+(b) Two of these three directors are partners of a prominent legal firm conducting a large volume of business for agency managed plantation companies. For the purpose of this table they have, however, been regarded as non-agency men.

(c) Includes a senior partner of the legal firm Julius Creasy & Co., who in 1959 was a shareholder of the managing agency firm Aitken Spence & Co.Ltd.

TABLE 14.5   Income from directorships of plantation companies classified by directors who are agency house nominees and others, 1959

	AGENCY HOUSE NOMINEES								INDEPENDENT DIRECTORS (NON-AGENCY)			ALL DIRECTORS		
	Shareholders of agency houses		Visit-ing agents	Employees of agency houses		Total	Ceylon-ese	Brit-ish	Total	Ceylon-ese	Brit-ish	Total	Ceylon-ese	Brit-ish
	Direc-tors of agency houses	Other		Estate super-in-tend-ents	Execu-tives									
No. of directors	44	4	12	21	11	92	12	80	88	56	32 (b)	180	68	112
No. of directorships	272	20	36	45	37	410	51	359	142	101	41	552	152	400
Total income (Rs OOOs)	309	21	48	50	32	460	39	421	173	124	48	633	146	469
Income per director (Rs)	7,028	5,275	4,053	2,360	2,927	5,003	3,267	5,264	2,000	2,222	1,500	3,516	2,410	4,190
Capital held by directors in plantation companies: All companies (Rs OOOs)	753	111	201	155	73	1,292	246	1,046	6,954	5,783	1,171	8,246	6,029	2,217
Average per directorship (Rs)	2,768	5,536	5,583	3,432	1,970	3,152	4,823	2,914	48,972	57,260	28,555	14,939	39,666	5,543

Capital invested in
agency houses:

Total (Rs 000s)	5,898	143	–	–	6,041	3,451	2,590	–	–	6,041	3,451	2,590
	(a)					(b)						
Average per planta-tion company direc-tor (Rs)	134,052	35,669	–	–	65,663	287,619	32,369	–	–	33,561	50,756	23,121

Sources: The Table refers to public rupee plantation companies. The directors' incomes have been compiled from the published accounts of plantation companies by dividing the total sum paid as directors' fees by the number of directors. The share capital of plantation company directors in these companies and in agency houses was based on the par value of shares held by them as stated in shareholders' lists filed with the Registrar of Companies.

(a) Includes the share capital of Rs 3.3 million held in Mackwoods Ltd by one of the directors of Mackwoods Estates & Agencies Ltd. The latter firm (which is an agency house) is a wholly owned subsidiary of the former.

(b) Includes two directors who, in fact, may be regarded as agency house nominees; one of them was formerly a visiting agent and the other an estate superintendent in agency managed plantation companies. Each of them held four director-ships each.

ly large number of directorships. These agency nominees,
though forming a little more than two fifths of the total
number of directors, held more than two thirds of the
total number of directorships in the rupee companies. The
average number of directorships held by the agency nominees was 4.5, as compared with 1.6 by the non-agency directors. The multiple directorships, distributed mostly
among agency nominees, were further concentrated among a
minority of influential persons. Thus while 80 per cent
of those who held single directorships were non-agency men
(90 out of 114), 93 per cent of those with multiple directorships were nominees of an agency house (93 out of 101).
At the apex of this pyramid stood 16 agency men holding
30 per cent of the total number of plantation company
directorships (an average of 11 directorships per person).
(23)

    The domination of rupee plantation companies by the
Colombo agency houses is paralleled in the case of sterling plantation companies by membership of their boards
by the directors of London agencies. Owing to a lack of
information on the business affiliations of directors of
the sterling companies, other than their connections with
agency houses, the term 'agency nominee' as used in the
Table excludes, in respect of these companies, persons not
directly associated with the agencies. One third of all
directors of the sterling plantation companies were directors of London agency houses, and the latter held half the
total number of directorships of the companies. As in the
rupee companies, these directorships were confined to a
small number of agency house directors. Whereas 80 per
cent of the directors who held only one directorship each
were non-agency men, 56 per cent of the multiple directorships were held by agency men; and of their number 24
held 30 per cent of the total number of directorships (or
5.4 directorships per person).

    Agency house nominees on the boards of plantation com-
panies owe their loyalty to the agency house as agency
house executives and also because of their direct financial interests in the agency. Most agency house nominees,
though holding only a nominal amount of capital in any
single plantation company, usually to satisfy the formal
requirements of membership, hold significant investments
in the agency house. They differ in this respect from the
partners of legal, accountancy, estate, engineering,
brokering or trading firms whose membership of the boards
of plantation companies confers merely a business advantage. Since almost all the agency houses are partnerships
or private limited companies (whose shares are not freely
negotiable), shareholding, however small, denotes a somewhat exclusive proprietary relationship with the agency.

Table 14.5 sets out, both for agency house nominees on
the boards of plantation companies and for independent
directors, their financial connection with the plantation
companies and with agency houses, in terms both of the
capital invested by them and of their income qua directors. Out of ninety-two agency nominees on the boards of
rupee plantation companies, more than half were shareholders of the agencies. The value of their investments
at par in the agency houses was Rs 6 million compared with
Rs 864,000 in the plantation companies in which they held
directorships. The average investment in agency houses of
those who were directors of plantation companies was
Rs 125,854 while their average investment per directorship
in the plantation companies was only Rs 2,957. The financial interests of the agency house nominees on the boards
of plantation companies were thus overwhelmingly in the
agency house, and the directors of agency houses were far
more sharply divided in their interests than were the
plantation company directors who were mere shareholders
of the agency house. As seen from Table 14.5, the average
investment in agency houses of their directors was
Rs 134,052, compared with an investment per directorship
in the plantation companies of only Rs 2,768.

The loyalty to the agency house of its nominees on the
boards of plantation companies was also ensured by the
multiple directorships of these companies which they
secure as agency men. The number of directorships each of
them held depended essentially on their business connections with the agency. The value of the plantation company directorships which they held, qua agency house men,
cannot be measured in terms of directors' incomes alone.
A concentration of authority and managerial control is the
basis of various perquisites and advantages as well as
patronage which they could extend - for example, in the
appointment of visiting agents and superintendents of estates. But the direct financial gain from multiple directorships is in itself considerable. As directors of plantation companies the agency nominees drew an average
annual income of Rs 5,003, compared with Rs 2,000 for the
non-agency directors. Among the agency nominees the highest incomes from directorships of plantation companies
were drawn by those who were also agency house directors.
Out of fifteen directors of plantation companies with
annual incomes from those directorships exceeding
Rs 10,000, there were fourteen agency house nominees;
nine of them drew more than Rs 12,000; three more than
Rs 16,000.

The income of the agency house personnel as directors
of plantation companies is lucrative both in absolute
terms and in relation to their work and the capital they

have invested. The conduct of managerial and administrative functions of plantation companies by the full-time
executive staff of the agency houses minimizes the work of
the directors of these companies; and board meetings are
infrequent - usually two or three a year. As mentioned
already, the investments made by agency nominees in the
plantation companies whose directorships they held were
negligible; their average share capital at par in a plantation company being Rs 3,152 compared with an annual
income from directors' fees of Rs 5,003. The incomes of
the agency house directors were a windfall compared with
those of the non-agency directors; the latter invested
Rs 48,972 per directorship with an average income of only
Rs 2,000. (24)

The control of plantation companies by the agency
houses was accompanied by a growing monopoly in agency
business. The changes in the volume of business of the
Colombo agency houses during 1950-64 are given in Table
14.6. There was both a decline in the total volume of
agency business and its redistribution among fewer agency
firms. The redistribution involved a decline in the
number of agency firms by almost half, from twenty-three
in 1950 to thirteen in 1964; of the firms that existed
in 1950, five became fully owned subsidiaries of other
firms, four were liquidated, and one ceased estate agency
work. (The figures exclude one agency firm which was set
up after 1950 and liquidated before 1964.) The concentration of agency business, on the other hand, is seen by the
fact that whereas in 1950 the four leading agency houses
managed 161 plantation companies (or 44 per cent of the
total), in 1964 they had 179 companies (or 65 per cent of
the total). The business of some firms expanded in absolute terms while others showed only a relative increase.
Five agency firms, George Steuart & Co., Whittall Boustead
Ltd, Shaw Wallace & Hedges Ltd, Mackwoods Estates & Agencies Ltd, and Colombo Commercial (Agency) Ltd, managed 171
companies in 1964, compared with 101 in 1950; their relative share of the total number of companies increased from
28 per cent to 61 per cent.

A more comprehensive picture of the distribution of
agency business among firms in 1964 is given in Tables
14.6, 14.7 and 14.8. Plantation acreage and output are
classified in these tables by sterling and rupee interests, and the data relate to agency managed companies and
proprietary estates. As seen from Table 14.8, four firms
controlled 64 per cent of the tea acreage and 70 per cent
of the rubber acreage of the agency managed plantations,
and roughly the same proportions of the output of tea and
rubber respectively. Three of the agency firms, on the

other hand, controlled 56 per cent of the tea output and
63 per cent of the rubber output of the agency managed
plantations. The concentration of control was greater in
rubber, with one of the firms managing 32 per cent of the
acreage and 31 per cent of output; in the case of tea the
leading agency managed 23 per cent of acreage and 25 per
cent of output. Five agency firms controlled 74 per cent
of this acreage, and 76 per cent and 80 per cent of the
output of tea and rubber, respectively. The distribution
of agency business among the London agency houses (in
respect of sterling plantation companies in Sri Lanka) is
shown in Table 14.9. Compared with the Colombo agencies
there were more than twice as many London agency firms
which managed plantation companies in Sri Lanka, and most
of them controlled only one or two companies in Sri Lanka.
    This process of centralization involved in some cases
the liquidation of an agency house or its abandonment of
agency business. In other cases an agency firm, though
not formally wound up, preserved merely its nominal identity. Such an arrangement not merely avoids liquidation
expenses but also passes on the goodwill and business connections of the firm taken over. For example, when Lee
Hedges & Co.Ltd was acquired by Shaw Wallace & Co.Ltd in
1954, the prospectus of the 'new' company (called Shaw
Wallace & Hedges Ltd) stated that 'whilst retaining their
separate entities ... the business of the company and of
Lee Hedges & Co.Ltd., shall be as closely integrated as is
possible'. The liquidation of certain agency houses in
the 1950s and 1960s was due to specific problems affecting
their individual businesses. Thus Rosehaugh Co.Ltd, whose
agency business in Sri Lanka was limited to three plantation companies in which its parent firm in London had a
financial interest, was 'seriously affected' by rising
costs of administration as well as by the nationalization
of insurance in Sri Lanka, which wiped out a portion of
its income. (25) On the other hand, the progressive enlargement of a few of the remaining firms was a measure of
further rationalization of the agency system. The take-
over of Lee Hedges & Co.Ltd by Shaw Wallace & Co. was thus
expected 'to effect considerable savings in the [latter's]
Estates Departments'. (26)
    While the persistent 'mismanagement' of a plantation
company carries with it the remote penalty of a loss of
custom, several factors render the position of an agency
invulnerable in the short or medium run. First, the
boards of plantation companies, rarely having full-time
working directors, allow substantial powers of management
to the agents. Though managerial responsibility is borne
by the entire directorate of a plantation company, the

TABLE 14.6 Number of plantation companies (sterling and rupee) managed by Colombo agency houses, 1950-64

	1950	1951	1952	1953	1954	1955	1956	1957	1958	1959	1960	1961	1962	1963	1964
George Steuart & Co.Ltd	43	44	44	44	42	41	38	52	51	53	53	52	52	52	53
Carson Cumberbatch & Co.Ltd	58	52	52	49	48	46	44	44	41	41	40	40	41	52	52
Whittall Boustead Ltd (1)	30	30	30	29	29	30	30	30	56	53	53	52	52	49	48
Shaw Wallace & Hedges Ltd (2)	3	3	3	3	12	12	10	11	11	12	9	9	9	30	30
Gordon Frazer & Co.	30	30	30	30	29	29	28	28	28	27	26	26	26	26	26
Mackwoods Estates & Agencies Ltd (3)	12	12	12	11	11	11	11	12	12	12	25	25	23	23	22
Colombo Commercial (Agency) Ltd	13	12	12	12	12	12	11	11	11	11	10	15	15	15	18
Aitken, Spence & Co.Ltd	22	22	18	17	16	17	16	15	14	13	13	14	14	12	12
Harrisons & Crosfield Ltd	11	9	8	8	8	8	8	8	8	8	8	8	8	8	8
James Finlay & Co.Ltd	8	8	8	8	8	8	8	7	7	7	7	7	7	7	7
Brooke Bond Ceylon Ltd	5	5	4	3	3	3	3	3	3	3	3	3	3	3	3
Darley Butler & Co.Ltd	1	1	1	1	1	1	1	1	1	1	1	1	1	1	1
Henderson & Co.Ltd	6	6	5	5	5	5	5	5	4	4	4	1	1	1	1
Walker Sons & Co.Ltd	1	1	1	1	1	1	1	1	1	1	1	1	1	1	1
Bois Bros Ltd	23	23	23	21	22	20	19	20	21	21	21	21	21	-	-
Bosanquet & Skrine	22	22	23	23	23	23	21	21	(b) -	-	-	-	-	(a) -	-
Boustead Bros	6	6	6	6	6	6	6	6	-	-	-	-	-	-	-
Galaha Ceylon Tea Estates Agency Co.Ltd	9	9	7	7	7	7	7	7	-	-	-	-	-	-	-
Leechman & Co.	11	11	11	11	11	11	11	11	10	11	10	11	11	-	-

Lee Hedges & Co.	8	9	9	9	–	–	–	–	–	–	–	–	–	–	–
Lewis Brown & Co.	22	20	18	19 (d)	19	17	17	16	15	14	–	–	–	–	–
J.M.Robertson & Co.	18	17	17	16	16	16	16	–	–	– (e)	–	–	–	–	–
Rosehaugh & Co.	3	3	3	3	3	3	3	3	3	3	3	3	3	3	–
Rowewans & Dimid Agencies Ltd	–	–	–	–	–	–	6	5	5	5	– (g)	–	–	–	– (f)
Total	365	355	345	336	332	327	314	318	302	300	292	289	288	283	281

Source: Based on names of plantation companies listed under Agency Houses in the Mercantile List of Ferguson's 'Directory'.

(1) Until 1958 this was Whittall & Co.Ltd.
(2) A reconstruction of Shaw Wallace Ceylon Ltd.
(3) Until the estate agency work was performed by the parent firm, Mackwoods Ltd.

(a) In 1963 Bois Bros Ltd became a subsidiary of Shaw Wallace & Hedges Ltd.
(b) In 1958 Bosanquet & Skrine became a subsidiary of Whittall Boustead Ltd.
(c) In 1963 Leechman & Co. became a subsidiary of Carson Cumberbatch & Co.Ltd.
(d) In 1954 Lee Hedges & Co. became a subsidiary of Shaw Wallace & Hedges Ltd.
(e) In 1960 Lewis Brown & Co. became a subsidiary of Mackwoods Ltd.
(f) In 1964 Rosehaugh & Co. wound up business in Sri Lanka and transferred its estate agencies to Colombo Commercial (Agency) Ltd.
(g) In 1961 Colombo Commercial Co. became the managing agents in Ceylon for the business of Rowewans & Dimid Agencies Ltd.

TABLE 14.7 Estate Agency business of Colombo agency houses, 1964

Colombo agency	No. of companies			Total acreage (a) (thousand acres) (b)			Sterling (thousand acres)			Rupee (thousand acres)			Total output (million lb)		Sterling (million lb)		Rupee (million lb)	
	Stg	Rs	Total	Tea	Rubber	Total	Tea	Rubber	Total	Tea	Rubber	Total	Tea	Rubber	Tea	Rubber	Tea	Rubber
Aitken Spence & Co.Ltd	2	8	10	4.4	6.0	12.6	1.4	0.7	2.1	2.9	5.3	8.4	4.5	3.9	1.6	0.3	2.9	3.5
Carson Cumberbatch & Co.Ltd	16	36	52	47.5	43.4	90.0	20.2	28.0	48.2	27.3	15.4	42.7	47.0	25.8	21.6	17.6	25.5	8.2
Colombo Commercial Co.Ltd	14	5	19	28.2	5.7	34.5	23.3	5.3	28.6	4.9	0.4	5.3	29.8	2.3	26.7	2.2	3.1	0.1
James Finlay & Co.Ltd	4	2	6	18.1	5.4	23.5	15.3	4.4	19.7	2.9	1.0	3.9	12.3	4.3	9.5	3.6	2.8	0.8
George Steuart & Co.Ltd (c)	29	24	53	69.6	18.4	88.0	46.0	12.8	58.8	23.8	5.6	29.4	80.6	12.7	53.0	8.0	27.6	3.9
Gordon Frazer & Co.Ltd	7	15	22	13.8	11.2	24.9	10.1	4.7	14.8	3.7	6.4	10.1	13.5	6.8	9.0	3.4	4.5	3.5
Harrisons & Crosfield Ltd	2	6	8	16.3	3.7	20.1	12.5	3.7	16.2	3.7	-	3.7	18.0	1.4	13.1	1.4	4.9	-
Mackwoods Estates & Agencies Ltd	5	16	21	20.1	5.7	25.8	7.5	3.1	10.6	12.6	2.6	15.2	23.4	2.9	8.9	1.6	14.6	1.3
Shaw Wallace & Hedges Ltd	9	21	30	27.5	11.19	39.8	12.7	1.8	14.5	11.8	9.3	21.1	31.2	7.1	16.9	1.2	14.3	6.0
Others (d)	4	3	7	7.3	2.7	10.0	4.1	2.7	6.8	3.3	-	3.3	6.7	2.1	3.9	1.1	2.9	-

Total	108	165	273	301.9	135.0	441.4	179.5	77.0	256.4	122.6	57.9	182.1	318.6	82.9	189.8	48.4	128.9	34.7
Bois Bros	8	12	20	19.2	5.3	24.5	14.4	1.8	16.2	4.8	3.5	8.3	21.0	2.9	15.4	1.2	5.6	1.8
Bosanquet & Skrine	5	10	15	12.5	2.8	15.8	5.9	-	5.9	6.6	2.8	9.3	12.2	1.6	6.2	-	6.0	1.6
Leechman & Co.	7	5	12	17.0	2.6	19.6	14.5	1.5	16.1	2.5	1.1	3.6	16.5	1.1	15.7	1.1	0.9	-
Lewis Brown & Co.Ltd	3	6	9	3.3	3.0	6.3	0.4	2.5	2.9	2.9	0.5	3.4	3.7	1.4	0.4	1.2	3.4	0.3
Total	23	33	56	52.0	13.7	66.2	35.2	5.8	41.1	16.8	7.9	24.6	53.4	7.0	37.7	3.5	15.9	3.7

Sources: Based on figures supplied on request by the agency houses, with the exception of Brooke Bond Ceylon Ltd for which information was taken from Ferguson's 'Directory'.

(a) Including sterling proprietary estates and rupee proprietary estates.
(b) Including small areas under coconut.
(c) Includes Namunukula Tea Estates Ltd, which in August 1964 was transferred from the agency of Walker Sons & Co.Ltd to George Steuart & Co.Ltd.
(d) Brooke Bond Ceylon Ltd, Henderson & Co., and Darley Butler & Co.Ltd.

TABLE 14.8 Estate agency business of Colombo agency houses, 1964 (percentages)

Colombo agency	Total acreage (a)			Sterling			Rupee			Total output		Sterling		Rupee	
	Tea	Rubber	Total (b)	Tea	Rubber	Total	Tea	Rubber	Total	Tea	Rubber	Tea	Rubber	Tea	Rubber
Aitken Spence & Co.Ltd	1.5	4.4	2.8	0.8	0.9	1.4	2.4	9.2	4.6	1.4	4.7	0.8	0.6	2.2	10.1
Carson Cumberbatch & Co.Ltd	15.9	32.1	20.6	11.3	36.4	18.7	22.3	26.6	23.4	14.7	31.1	11.4	36.4	19.8	23.9
Colombo Commercial Co.Ltd	9.3	4.2	7.8	13.0	6.9	11.4	4.0	0.7	2.9	9.4	2.8	14.1	4.5	2.4	0.3
James Finlay & Co.Ltd	6.0	4.0	5.3	8.5	5.7	7.6	2.4	1.7	2.1	3.9	5.2	5.0	7.4	2.2	2.3
George Steuart & Co.Ltd	23.0	13.6	19.9	25.6	16.6	22.7	19.4	9.7	16.1	25.2	15.3	27.9	18.2	21.4	11.2
Gordon Frazer & Co.Ltd	4.6	8.3	5.6	5.6	6.1	5.7	3.0	11.1	6.5	4.2	8.2	4.7	7.0	3.3	10.1
Harrisons & Crosfield Ltd	5.4	2.7	4.6	7.0	4.8	6.3	3.0	-	2.0	5.6	1.7	6.9	2.8	3.8	-
Mackwoods Estates & Agencies Ltd	6.7	4.2	5.8	4.2	4.0	4.1	10.3	4.5	8.3	7.3	3.5	4.7	3.3	11.3	3.7
Shaw Wallace & Hedges Ltd	9.1	8.2	9.0	8.6	2.3	6.8	9.6	16.1	11.6	9.8	8.6	8.9	2.5	11.1	17.2

Whittall Boustead Ltd	16.3	16.1	16.2	13.0	12.7	12.9	21.0	20.6	16.2	16.2	16.4	13.5	12.8	20.2	21.3
Others (c)	2.4	2.0	2.3	2.3	3.5	2.3	2.7	–	1.8	2.1	2.5	2.1	4.3	2.2	–
Bois Bros	6.4	3.9	5.6	8.0	2.3	6.3	3.9	6.0	4.6	6.5	3.5	8.1	2.5	4.3	5.2
Bosanquet & Skrine	4.1	2.1	3.6	3.3	–	2.3	5.4	4.8	5.1	3.8	1.9	3.3	–	4.6	4.6
Leechman & Co.	5.6	1.9	4.4	8.1	1.9	6.2	2.0	1.9	2.0	5.2	1.3	8.3	2.3	0.7	–
Lewis Brown & Co.Ltd	1.1	2.2	1.4	0.2	3.2	1.1	2.4	0.9	1.9	1.2	1.7	0.2	2.5	2.6	0.9

Source: Based on Table 14.5.

(a) Including sterling proprietary estates and rupee proprietary estates.
(b) Including small areas under coconut.
(c) Galaha Ceylon Tea Estates Ltd, Henderson & Co., and Darley Butler & Co.Ltd.

TABLE 14.9   Estate agency business of London agency houses, 1964

London agency (no. of plantation companies under each agency is shown in parentheses)	Cultivated acreage (thousand acres)			Output (million lb)		Gross proceeds (£000s)	Total paid to agent (£000s)	Percentage					Gross proceeds	Total paid to agent
								Cultivated acreage			Output			
	Tea	Rubber	Total	Tea	Rubber			Tea	Rubber	Total	Tea	Rubber		
1 Arbuthnot Latham & Co.Ltd (3)	9.7	1.5	11.2	9.6	1.5	2,090	42.3	5.5	2.1	4.4	5.0	3.2	7.3	7.6
2 Boustead Bros (2)	1.8	0.8	2.6	2.0	0.4	395	15.3	1.0	1.1	1.0	1.0	0.9	1.4	2.7
3 Ceylon & Eastern Agency Ltd (4)	8.1	23.2	32.5 (a)	7.8	15.1	1,947	32.4	4.5	32.2	12.7	4.0	33.1	6.8	5.8
4 Colombo Commercial Co. (Agency) Ltd (10)	15.2	–	15.2	16.7	–	2,687	41.4	8.5	–	5.9	8.7	–	9.3	7.5
5 Crabbe & Co.Ltd (1)	3.8	–	3.8	5.1	–	941	12.1	2.1	–	1.5	2.7	–	3.3	2.2
6 Dickson Anderson & Co.Ltd (1)	6.6	–	6.6 (b)	7.4	–	813	17.8	3.7	–	2.6	3.8	–	2.8	3.2
7 Harrisons & Crosfield Ltd (1)	11.3	3.0	14.4 (a)	12.2	1.1	935	9.9	6.3	4.2	5.6	6.3	2.4	3.2	1.8
8 H.B.J.Jarvis (1)	9.2	2.7	14.4	10.3	1.6	255 (c)	n.a.	5.2	3.8	5.6	5.3	3.6	0.9	–
9 Lyall Anderson & Co.Ltd (6)	5.8	3.9	9.7	6.2	2.6	953	20.3	3.3	5.4	3.8	3.2	5.8	3.3	3.6
10 McMeekin & Co.Ltd (4)	4.2	2.5	6.7	5.7	2.6	854	9.8	2.4	3.5	2.6	3.0	5.7	3.0	1.8
11 Pryor Tindall (1)	4.7	–	4.7	6.2	–	1,525	38.8	2.7	–	1.9	3.2	–	5.3	7.0
12 Robert Brooke & Co. (1)	5.9	–	5.9	6.2	–	1,146	23.6	3.3	–	2.3	3.2	–	4.0	4.3

13 Robertson Bois & Co.	(20)	31.9	2.6	34.5	34.8	2.0	6,696	759.2	17.9	3.6	13.5	18.1	4.3	23.2	28.6
14 Rowe White & Co.Ltd	(5)	8.2	1.7	9.9	8.3	1.2	1,297	22.5	4.6	2.4	3.9	4.3	2.7	4.5	4.1
15 Thompson Alston Ltd	(6)	9.2	6.3	15.5	10.8	4.4	2,041	26.7	5.2	8.8	6.1	5.6	9.7	7.1	4.8
Others (d)	(44)	44.1	23.9	69.6	45.4	13.0	4,232	84.5	23.8	32.9	26.6	22.6	28.6	14.6	15.0
Total	(110)	179.7	72.1	257.2	194.7	45.5	28,807	556.6	100.0	100.0	100.0	100.0	100.0	100.0	100.0

(a) Includes coconut.

(b) Includes cardamom.

(c) Excludes sale proceeds in Ceylon - not available.

(d) Anglo-Ceylon General Estates Co. (2), Aurea Agency Ltd (1), Bolton Pitt & Breden (1), Brinkworth & Co. (1), Eastern Produce (Holdings) Ltd (2), Estate & Agency Co.Ltd (1), M.P.Evans & Co.Ltd (2), Francis Peek & Co.Ltd (2), H.E.Goulter (1), J.G.L.Harding (1), J.R.Henderson & Co.Ltd (1), James Finlay & Co. (2), James Warren & Co.Ltd (2), Martin Currie & Scott (1), Meredith & Co.Ltd (1), E.A.Mimms (1), W.M.Nevett & Co. (1), Pannel Fitz Patrick Graham & Crewdson (1), Richardson & Co.Ltd (1), Rosehaugh Agency Ltd (3), Rubber Estate Agency (2), Shar Estail & Co.Ltd (3); R.G.Shaw & Co. (1), Spence Wallis & Co. (1), Taylor Neble & Co.Ltd (3), H.E.Trueman (1), Walker Bros (London) Ltd (1), George White & Co.Ltd (1), Williamson Ltd (1), Wilson Smithett & Co. (2).

n.a. = not available.

concentration of management and technical functions in the
agents leaves de facto authority with those directors who
are also agency house directors. (The boards of plantation companies do not as a rule have a chief operating
executive in the form of a managing director, since the
executive functions are performed by the agency house.
The senior director of a plantation company, who is a
director of the agency, serves as chairman.) The agencies
also maintain the financial accounts, advise the company
on dividends and on capital expansion programmes and
possess so complete a knowledge of the company's affairs
that rarely would the non-agency directors be in a position to intervene.

Second, in common with most public joint stock enterprises, the information required for a proper appraisal of
the efficiency of management is not available to plantation shareholders. A significant omission is the total
remuneration of the agency house and the basis on which
it is computed. The agency income comprises a fixed
annual sum as secretarial services, and a commission based
on the gross sale proceeds of the company's produce. (27)
The secretarial fee alone is shown in the published accounts of plantation companies but not the commissions
based on the output of plantation produce or its sale proceeds. The profit and loss statements of sterling plantation companies as a rule show merely the net proceeds representing the (undisclosed) gross proceeds less certain
charges including the London agent's commission. (28) In
the very few instances where the gross value of sales is
shown, the agent's commission as an item of expenditure by
the company lies concealed under a head such as 'Production and Marketing Cost', 'Freight, Wharfage and Selling
Expenses', or simply 'Expenditure'. The gross proceeds of
direct sales in London and hence the commission of the
London agency on such sales would not generally be known
even to the Colombo agents of a plantation company. This
commission, along with freight, insurance, broker's
charges, etc., is deducted from each sale transaction. On
produce sold in Colombo (ex estate or at the Colombo auctions) the London agency takes its commission from funds
which accrue from the company's direct sales in London.
In the quarterly cash statement which sterling companies
submit to the exchange control, the agency commission on
sales in Colombo is included as head office expenses.
Along with certain other sums which provide for dividend
payments and taxes in the UK, these expenses are deducted
from the net proceeds of London sales, and the balance is
repatriated to Sri Lanka.

The shareholders of plantation companies have also no

knowledge of the agent's and secretary's service agreements, which lay down the terms and conditions of service,
and which in some cases bind the plantation companies to
their existing agency for long periods. Nor are the
shareholders informed of changes in such agreements even
when they involve an increase in the rates of agency commission. For example, in 1960 the Aurea Agency Ltd, who
were the London agents and secretaries of the Carolina Tea
Co. of Ceylon Ltd, amended the basis of their remuneration
from £2,000 p.a. as secretarial fees plus 0.25 per cent
commission on all produce sold to £750 p.a. as secretarial
fees plus 1.25 per cent commission on sales. The new arrangement involved, on the basis of the Carolina Tea Co.'s
gross proceeds for 1964, an additional payment to the
agency of nearly £3,000 p.a., or nearly double the sum
payable earlier. The increase represented 15 per cent of
the pre-tax profit of the company for the year ended 30
June 1963, sufficient to pay a 6 per cent dividend less
income tax on the ordinary share capital of the company.
This revision in management charges, which had significant
implications for the shareholders of the plantation company, was effected merely by an informal exchange of
letters between the directors of the company and the
agency.
    The original articles of association of a few planta-
tion companies require some of this information to be disclosed to members. For example, in the case of the Indo-
Malay Estates Ltd and the Perak River Coconut Co.Ltd, it
was stipulated that the annual statement laid before the
company 'shall show arranged under the most convenient
heads, the amount of gross income distinguishing the
several sources from which it has been derived and the
amount of the gross expenditure, distinguishing the expense of the establishment, salaries and other heads of
expenditure'. (29) In later years, however, amendments
to the articles removed such an obligation. Company law
allows directors to determine the kind of information to
be supplied in the interests of the company as a whole;
withholding 'any matter which is or may be in the nature
of a trade secret, mystery of trade, or secret process'.
This safeguard - hardly relevant to the cultivation and
sale of plantation crops - is made use of by agency houses
and company directors to deny shareholders the information
needed for appraising managerial efficiency. The discretionary power of the directors (virtually the agency
house) in regard to the disclosure of information is far
more than the interests of shareholders warrant.
    Apart from the very limited information available to
shareholders, the annual financial statements which the

plantation companies publish are based in many cases on a
partial audit confined to the books and accounts kept by
the agency house in Colombo. The estate accounts as well
as the superintendent's monthly reports, for which the
Colombo agency is responsible, are not seen by auditors.
(The accounts of the rupee companies are audited in
Colombo and those of the sterling companies in London.)
Auditors' reports on many plantation companies are subject
to the qualification that 'returns from estates, as signed
by the superintendent, have been accepted as correct'.
While the Sri Lanka Companies' Ordinance (no. 51 of 1938)
does not compel an auditor to accept returns merely because they are signed by the estate superintendent, auditors refrain from inspecting books of a company kept on
the estate. In the absence of definite statutory requirements, plantation company directors and managing agents
encourage partial audits, ostensibly to save on the audit
fee. In the case of the Kinnersley (Kalutara) Rubber Co.
Ltd, where only partial audits were carried out, the
Registrar of Companies urged the importance of a complete
audit; for auditors 'would be failing in their duty if
they examine only some of the books of the company as they
appear to have done'. (30) But the agency house upheld
the prevailing practice, claiming in support that qualified audits satisfied shareholders. In the case of the
Biddescar Rubber Co.Ltd, a perceptive shareholder pointed
out that, if this view is valid, then some of the shareholders may even decide to dispose of the audit altogether. 'I am quite convinced', he wrote to the Registrar
of Companies in 1952, 'that the opposition to a full and
proper audit of a company's accounts proceeds entirely
from the Agents & Secretaries of the Company and is solely
and entirely mala fide. One audit report which I have
studied made staggering revelations.'
     The third factor which safeguards the agency is the
alignment of the directors of the plantation company with
the agency rather than with the general body of shareholders. The main interests of the directors, that is to
say, are not based on their position as shareholders but
run parallel with those of the agency. The tie-up between
them is more than a broad focusing of interests. For although a managing agency stands in a contractual relationship with the companies it manages, as defined by an
'agency agreement', there is, as I have shown, much over-
lapping between the directors of the agency and those of
the plantation company. In a majority of cases, their
relationship conforms to the situation in India, where
'except in law, the agency and the operating firm /their
principal personalities/ are indistinguishable'. (31)

The almost unassailable position of the agency houses vis-à-vis the plantation companies which they manage is due, then, to their exercise of continuous and full-time powers of management over a plantation company, the unfamiliarity with the affairs of their enterprise of most shareholders and particularly those who are nonresident, the insufficiency of information for appraising management costs as distinguished from the overall financial results, and the predominance of agency house nominees on the boards of the plantation companies.

Furthermore, these agency directors are not a class of salaried managers in the hands of the owners of plantation capital, easily removable by shareholders as are, for instance, the auditors and accountants of the company. Unlike independent directors who retire in rotation (but are, as a rule, re-elected), agency appointments run for long periods, and there have been no instances of the removal of those appointed. Agency rights over plantation companies are set out in legal form in a 'Secretaries' Service Agreement' which is treated as confidential. An attempt by the Central Bank of Ceylon in 1964 to obtain copies of these agreements, for exchange control purposes, was generally resisted by the London agencies. Notwithstanding provisions in Sri Lanka's exchange control law, one of the agents held out on the plea that he was awaiting legal opinion, until the bank withdrew 'special account facilities' for companies under this agency. Many others merely submitted extracts from the agreements, relating to the agency commission, which they surmised was what the bank wanted. Out of three agents' and secretaries' agreements between sterling plantation companies and the London agency that were submitted to the bank, two were to be valid, 'in the first instance', for fifteen years and ten years respectively after their dates of negotiation. (32) Two other agreements stipulated that if the plantation company were to sell any of its estates to a new company promoted by it, it would use its best endeavours to procure for the agency the management rights over the new company. (33) In some cases, however, there is no formal agreement and the agent's function and remuneration are governed by an exchange of letters. A fiduciary relationship of this kind expresses a close commercial intimacy between the companies and their managing agency.

Historically, the agency houses and plantation company directors belonged to a narrow group, and the relationship between them has not substantially changed. The boards of the plantation companies, for the most part, remain linked with the agency houses by close ties of business interest.

A short résumé of the development of the agencies will
demonstrate the control which these purely mercantile
interests came to exercise over the plantation economy.
The managing agency system did not emerge full grown at
any point of time but reflected the changing financial and
organizational needs of the plantation economy. In Sri
Lanka two phases in the development of the system are distinguishable, corresponding broadly to the period of the
coffee plantations (from the 1840s to the 1880s), and,
subsequently, to the production of tea and rubber. In the
first period, the agencies were basically purveyors of
working capital to the coffee estates. In the second
period there was a radical enlargement in the fixed capital of plantations, necessitating access to the British
capital market and consequently a change in the organization of plantation enterprise - from sole proprietary concerns or partnerships to joint stock companies. In fostering this change the agencies developed from mere outsiders to become organically connected with tea and rubber
companies, often intervening at their birth. This union
was brought about by interlocking directorates. During
this period the plantation companies were able to reduce
their financial dependence on the agencies, because of the
growth of banks, the quicker realization of plantation
proceeds, and a gradual accumulation of funds. Despite
the decline in the financial role of the agencies, the
growth of absentee ownership led to an increase in their
management functions. The centralization of these functions, whereby several plantation companies owning vast
acreages came under a single agency, with economies of
supervision and control, led to the institutionalization
of the agency system.

15 Merchant capitalism and underdevelopment

The manner in which capital is utilized, wrote Orest
Ranum, is as important a question as how capital is acquired. (1) All societies, except the very primitive,
have a surplus of production over and above subsistence
needs, and their economic dynamism relates to their capacity for productively utilizing the surpluses currently
generated. The concern of classical economics with this
question caused it to distinguish between productive and
unproductive consumption. (Ricardo and Say were dismayed
by the improvidence of the English landed aristocracy and
its regressive effect on accumulation and investment.
Smith was dubious about the 'rich merchant' who, though
employing capital productively, appeared by his expenses
to resemble a feudal lord. Military expenditure and large
bureaucracies were considered by him to be equally dis-
agreeable.) The way in which the current surplus is
utilized and, in turn, the pattern and rate of development
are determined by the interests of those into whose hands
the surplus accrues. More specifically, this means the
relation of the dominant class to the productive process.
In this respect the contrasting roles of the merchant and
the industrial capitalist will be discussed later. They
are the principal actors in the investment process.

The dominant social classes have influenced investment
patterns in different historical situations. J.M.Gullick,
commenting on the expenditure of the Malay chiefs before
the British occupation, showed how 'political values can
distort the use of economic resources and run counter to
purely economic considerations'. The size of the armed
followings of the chiefs, as the basis of their power,
caused peasant incomes to be diverted to achieve military
power and prestige instead of being invested. (2) In
Europe, 'The Commons of England, the Tiers-Etat of France,
the bourgeoisie of the Continent generally ... were a

415

saving class while the posterity of the feudal aristocracy
were a squandering class'. (3) Puritanism was the philosophy of the rising bourgeoisie as much as conspicuous
wealth and ostentation were both the hallmark and the
ultimate solvent of the effete aristocracy. A prime example of the effects of the pattern of capital utilization
was the economic decline of the Netherlands during the
seventeenth century. With an extensive trading empire,
resting on 'snug monopolies', the Netherlands perfected
the machinery of international finance and accumulated
prodigious wealth but failed to advance production techniques. This, as Ranum remarked, was not for lack of
capital. The inability of the Dutch merchantmen as a
class to use their wealth for industrial development is
a question which I shall take up later.

Different modes of production can be distinguished according to their manner of appropriation and utilization
of surpluses. This is determined by and in turn determines class formations. In the colonial export economies
the dominant groups were the mercantile interests, for
whom production served merely as an accessory rather than
an independent objective, valued for its own sake. An
indication of the specificity of merchant capital was
given by Richard Grassby: 'What was peculiar to the merchant was the form in which his capital was held and the
use which he made of his assets.... There was something
special about commercial capital.' (4) Merchant capital,
as the agency which mediated on behalf of production capital in the metropolis, shaped the economic structures in
the periphery and its condition of underdevelopment.
Underlying this condition is the prevalent relation between merchant capital and production capital, just as the
economic transformation of the metropolis was contingent
upon the supremacy achieved by production capital over
merchant capital.

The character of merchant capital compared with that of
industrial capital, in terms of the relative importance of
fixed and circulating capital, will be explicated in the
next chapter in an attempt to expound the 'colonial mode
of production'. Here I shall set out, taking England as
the classic case, the changing relation between the two
varieties of capital during the transition to capitalism.
The historical research which I shall draw on is that of
George Unwin into the relation of merchant capital and industrial capital in the two centuries preceding the English industrial revolution, though Unwin did not explicitly distinguish between these two varieties of capital.
'Merchant and production capital', he wrote, were 'two
forms of capital', and their 'rivalry' was that of 'two

classes nearest to each other on the social scale, stimulated by the larger opportunities opened up to both of
them through the expansion of industry and commerce'. (5)
Distinguishing more sharply between merchant capital and
industrial capital, on the lines of Marx, I shall conceptualize the phenomenon of underdevelopment in terms of
the persistence of precapitalist structures in the periphery, based on the independent existence of merchant capital and its predominance over industrial capital.

The role and significance of merchant capital in the
periphery is best seen in terms of the historical process
whereby in Europe, and particularly in England, merchant
capital established itself and later lost its dominance.
Merchant capital was the historic premise for the development of capitalist production. It disturbed the equilibrium of the feudal social order by expanding trade and
commodity production and redistributing money wealth.
'The merchant was the revolutionary element in this society where everything else was stable - stable, as it were,
through inheritance.' (6) Merchant capital later spawned
several related activities. Merchants 'doubled as
bankers' and dealt in foreign exchange. They were revenue
farmers, contractors, agents and commissioners for sale,
and they invested in land and in urban property. Though
'liquidity' was the hallmark of merchant capital, merchants were not averse to risk taking. They gave out
bottomry loans subject to the risk of total loss and
therefore at very high rates of interest. The liquidity
and relative ease of disinvestment of merchant capital
gave it a significant advantage over production capital
tied up in land, mining property and capital equipment;
merchant capital even enabled the owners of production
capital to realize the value of their fixed assets. (7)

In the original accumulation of capital, merchants
played a key role by concentrating wealth through windfall
profits, usury, speculation on scarcity, etc. Some of
this wealth was channelled as credit for producers.
Before the industrial revolution capital flowed outwards
from commerce to industry, especially in textiles and
mining. The Manchester cotton industry in the sixteenth
century depended heavily on credit given by the Irish merchants; (8) and the metal trades in many towns 'seem to
have been fostered as a rule in the interests of the shop-
keeping class'. (9) Some of the early industrial enterprises got started in this way, or were helped to tide
over the interval between production and sale by the
financial patronage of the merchants. The merchant also
initiated the process of proletarianization of the producer and his subjection by capital. This occurred when

the merchant took on the extra role of a 'contractor' by
supplying raw materials to be made into finished goods on
the merchant's account. He appropriated surplus value by
cutting down the rate of payment to the producer. At the
same time he lowered prices, for the sake of a quicker
turnover and a larger profit - thus 'donating' a small
portion of surplus value to the buyer. (10)

   Though in this period of transition to capitalism merchant capital was interwoven with production capital,
there was a clear differentiation of interests. The differentiation did not wholly correspond to that between
fixed capital and circulating capital which signified the
respective activities of the producer and the merchant.
Merchants, too, needed fixed investments - warehouses,
docks and transportation facilities - and they also held
urban property. The differentiation lay partly in the
rentier nature of the merchant's investments including the
other bases of his wealth, such as usury, licences and
government monopolies. It was in this precapitalist soil
that merchant capital arose - and from which it never
wanted to be uprooted completely. During the period of
its independent existence merchant capital was thus prone
to become 'allied with feudal reaction'. Engels saw the
contradictory nature of merchant capital in its genesis.
'Into this [feudal] world then entered the merchant with
whom its revolution was to start. But not as a conscious
revolutionary; on the contrary, as flesh of its flesh,
bone of its bone.' (11)

   Though trade expansion required the development of
productive forces, and encouraged division of labour, the
role of merchant capital in the development of productive
forces, compared with that of industrial capital, is both
indirect and limited. The stimulus given by merchant
capital to commodity production is through a widening of
markets and a territorial division of labour, rather than
through a deepening of markets by a splitting up of the
production process into a greater number of distinct and
specialized products or production operations. The merchant trades in products as he finds them without influencing the way in which they are produced. While financing the purchase of raw materials and carrying out the
sale of finished goods, the merchant did not invest in
the fixed capital of the producer. He appropriated surplus value primarily to expand trade and not to develop
the techniques of production. Where the merchant organ-
izes production, his relation to the direct producer is
one of externality. He has no proprietary involvement in
the production capital which he controls.

   The existence of merchant capital as an exogenous ele-

ment in the production process was due to the nature of
merchant capital itself.   Capital applied in circulation -
i.e. in transportation, communications and selling - increases the mass of products which enters trade and passes
through the merchant's hands ('handling charges' being
typically one element of his profits);   the merchant's
profits do not depend on the lowering of the costs of production through increases in productivity.   Historically,
the rate of merchant's profit was 'necessarily high' because of the monopoly which he exercised.   Marx adduced
reasons for the prior emergence of concentration in trade
rather than in production;   the same function (e.g. the
making of purchases and the services of bookkeepers and
other commercial workers) 'requires the same labour-time,
whether performed on a larger or a smaller scale'. (12)
Costly investments were also needed for the outfitting of
ships or caravans, partly as a protection against piracy,
and there was a risk of the total loss of cargo.   On the
long haul turnover was slow and contractual obligations
were uncertain.   Merchants were backed by the emerging
nation states, and trading companies were given monopoly
privileges, in return for subscribing to government loans
and performing fiscal and diplomatic functions.   In this
period, as Engels wrote, the merchant (13)

> was by no means an individualist;   he was essentially
> an associate like his contemporaries....   And the same
> holds good in no less degree of the merchant companies
> which initiated overseas trade....   [They] formed com-
> plete trade associations;   they were closed to com-
> petitors and customers;   they sold at prices fixed
> among themselves.

The merchants used their monopoly power to depress the
prices paid to the producers of exportable commodities and
to raise the prices of imports. (14)

The detachment of merchant capital from the production
process conformed to the investment opportunities it had
exclusively in the sphere of circulation.   In the period
of its growth, merchant capital throve on the long-distance trade, based on commodities of high value and low
bulk/weight.   The sale price of spices, for example, was
several times more than the production cost and the price
paid to the producer.   In this milieu 'selling was more
profitable than manufacture ... marketing more difficult
and more vital than production [and] the distributor commanded the greater profit'. (15)   Merchant capital had no
compulsion to apply capital in depth so long as new lines
of trade could be opened up and investment opportunities
existed outside the sphere of production.   As I shall
later explain, the opening up of the periphery was to afford such opportunities par excellence.

Under the merchant manufacturer, the metamorphosis of
the traditional system of production was thus far from
complete. 'In themselves neither merchant nor usurer's
capital represents a sufficient premise for the rise of
industrial capital (i.e. capitalist production), they do
not always disintegrate the old mode of production and
replace it by the capitalist mode of production.' (16)
The merchant by interposing himself between the producer
and the market, both for finished goods and for raw
materials, and through usury subjects the producer to a
relation of personal bondage. He depresses the producer's
economic condition below that of an 'outright wage
worker'. The surplus appropriation process is based on a
tighter work regime and a lowering of the producer's earnings per hour or per unit of output. Without an improvement in productivity (in which the merchant has no interest owing to the nature of his relation to the production
process), the extent to which accumulation could take
place is constrained by the producer's subsistence needs.
    Merchant capital, while having a more or less dis-
solving influence on the precapitalist mode of production,
is 'incapable, by itself, of promoting the transition' to
capitalism. In fact, it strengthened and prolonged the
precapitalist mode of production even in Europe, where the
growth of trade and money payments rekindled feudalism -
the 'second serfdom' about which Engels spoke. The
strengthening of the old forms of exploitation by merchant
capital was evident in thirteenth-century England. As
Dobb explained (basing himself on Kosminsky's research on
the agrarian history of England), it was in the economically most backward areas - in the north and west - that
the process of commutation was rapid. Labour services
persisted longer in the areas of the liveliest circulation
of money. (17) Likewise usurer's profit depended on the
backward, rather than on the advanced features of the
economy. It was based on the 'extravagance of the land-
owning classes, and ... the perpetual bankruptcy of the
peasant and the small artisan'.
    The change from a subsistence to a market economy,
while giving the producer a bigger demand for his products, subjects him to both ecological and market uncertainties which the landlord, usurer and merchant take advantage of. In the period preceding the rise of capitalism, without any change in juridical or economic status,
the small producer suffered a sharp deterioration in his
work regime and wages - a condition which he accepted for
the sake of his nominal independence and to avoid becoming
a proletarian. As a home worker he also had access to a
garden plot. This partial independence was eroded when he

became 'restricted ... little by little to one kind of
work'. Eventually he was entirely 'dependent on selling,
on the buyer, the merchant and ... produce *[d]* only for him
and through him'. (18) The old forms of exploitation were
intensified, contrary to what Sweezy said, not merely in
agriculture and in the periphery of the exchange economy
but also in the proximity of towns. (19) Marx referred to
the contrast within one and the same country between the
'specifically merchant towns' and the industrial towns;
the former have 'far more striking analogies with past
conditions'. (20) Lenin referred to the attempts of merchant capital in Russia to preserve forms of production
which incorporated the medieval and the modern. (21)
Trotsky demonstrated how in Russia merchant capital throve
'on the basis of ... extremely primitive and in many respects barbaric economic relations'. (22) While fostering
commodity production - a necessary premise for the development of capitalism - merchant capital thus retards its
development. 'The degree of development of merchant capital is in inverse proportion to the degree of development
of industrial capital.' (23)

Industrial capital comes into its own when the extensive forms of growth which merchant capital fosters are
superseded by investment in depth. Improved production
methods per se lead to an enlargement of markets by the
lowering of unit costs and selling prices. The change
usually occurs through competition among both producers
and traders, even before the extensive forms of growth
peter out. 'Industrial capital is the only form of existence of capital, in which not only the appropriation of
surplus-value or surplus product but also its creation is
a function of capital. Therefore, it gives to production
its capitalist character.' (24) At this stage 'it is not
commerce ... which revolutionizes industry, but industry
which constantly revolutionizes commerce'. (25) The expansion of the economic universe, territorially and demographically, on which merchant capital feeds, was itself
a product of industrial capital, in so far as this expansion was due to technological improvements in transport.

The divergent roles and results of merchant capital and
industrial capital relate basically to their modes of exploitation. 'The pure form of merchant capital is the
purchase of a commodity, in order to sell it in worked-up
form, hence the purchase of raw materials, etc., and the
purchase of labour-power which subjects the material to a
process of working up.' (26) Merchant capital, dominating
the sphere of exchange, does not create value. Except for
transportation (a productive activity), the merchant's
activities involve a change in ownership rights. By

buying in order to sell, the merchant realizes surplus
value, and in a precapitalist economy in the course of
doing so he appropriates for himself a good portion of the
surplus value without concern for production methods and
the investment of capital in depth. Merchant capital can
function whatever the mode of production. The interaction
between different territories which it promotes on the
basis of their prevailing modes of production was referred
to by Trotsky. The economic power of Andreyevich Chernykh
the 'merchant dictator' came from an 'odd marriagè between
a primitive nomadic economy and a shiny brand new alarm
clock made in Warsaw'. (27) In the colonial export economies the development of export production required little
more than a reorganization of precapitalist production
techniques; and merchant capital, therefore, was able to
'manage' and control these economies, mediating between
them and industrial capital in the metropolis.

Production capital, having started historically from a
position of dependence on merchant capital, overcame this
dependence in the countries where capitalism developed,
relegating merchant capital to the sphere of distribution
and exchange. In England from the sixteenth century onwards merchant capital began to lose its dominance.
Crafts were formed into separate organizations over which
the merchants had no control. A differentiation arose between the activities of craftsmen and merchants as markets
and raw material sources expanded and became far flung.
The concentration of production capital, due to technological change, caused capital to accumulate within the
enterprise; and the producer, freed from financial dependence on the merchant, was able to meet him on equal
terms. In fact, the relative importance of trading capital diminished. With increasing specialization, the combination of trade, finance and rentier investments as the
basis of merchant wealth began to fall apart by the end
of the seventeenth century. As credit institutions developed, private usury declined and a separate moneyed
interest arose bringing to a close the economic dominance
of the merchants. (28)

There was no historical inevitability in this course of
events. The outcome was decided by a struggle between
merchant capital and industrial capital, which at one
level became a contest between town and country. In England, after the first half of the sixteenth century, the
growth of the textile industry in rural districts had encouraged the sale of cloth to export merchants, bypassing
both the town draper and the finishing and dyeing industry. But a series of governmental measures imposed a
check on the country interests who were allied to the

export merchants. The Tudor monarchs arraigned themselves on the side of the 'relatively small but powerfully organised bodies of cloth finishers and dyers' in London and the chief industrial towns. The Statute of Artificers, 1551, forbade country weavers to sell cloth or other wares except to the town draper. The Weavers Act discriminated against the country clothiers - they were prevented from having more than one loom or from hiring looms to others. Furthermore, to offset the competition of cheap country labour municipal policy encouraged the employment of the urban poor.

Industrial capital, besides arresting the growth of the textile industry in the rural districts, demanded control over the export trade, since the merchants were sending out woollen yarn and unfulled cloth to be finished and dyed in the industrial cities of the Continent. An Act of 1566 forbade cloth made in Suffolk and Kent, the two textile districts nearest to London, to be exported before being finished and dyed; merchants exporting cloth from other districts were required to carry one finished cloth to every nine unfinished. (The industrial interests represented in the Clothworkers' Company even arranged for an official 'search at the waterside of all cloth about to be exported'.) The merchants were seen to be profiting from the 'necessities and misfortunes of the rest of the country'. (29) A campaign against 'the ill advised activity of the merchant', (30) to whom the economic evils of the time were largely attributed, strengthened the national appeal of the town industries. (31)

> It was not merely the 'merchantys which carry out thynges necessary to the use of our people and bring in agayn vayn Tryfullys and conceytys only for the folysch pastime and pleasure of man' who fell under condemnation, the merchant staplers, who had been chiefly engaged in the export of raw material, were fast giving place to their rivals the merchant adventurers, who were largely concerned with the export of cloth; yet the pamphleteer of the period looked upon the adventurer with feelings scarcely less hostile than those with which he regarded the stapler.

The 'popular outcry against the merchant class' was also based on the unproductive nature of employment which the merchants' activity sustained. 'The merchants' calling [was] regarded as drawing off the most promising artificers to swell the ranks of an unproductive class.' (32) In their wider context, the measures to undermine merchant capital were directed towards achieving England's industrial hegemony - as Unwin said, removing by 'artificial means' its position of economic inferiority vis-à-vis the Continent. (33)

By checking the export of raw materials to regions outside their influence and control, the Tudor monarchs
sought to alter what Unwin described as 'the relation of
England as a whole to the chief industrial centres of the
continent'. (34) They seem to have perceived what
present-day development economists refer to in their well-
worn parlance as linkage/leakage effects. In the thirteenth and fourteenth centuries England supplied wool,
hides and tin to the industrial centres of Ghent, Bruges,
Cologne and Florence. The backwardness of English industries compared with those of the Continent involved a
centre-periphery type of relation; in textiles this was
based on the export of white cloth to be finished and dyed
in the cities of Flanders and Italy. The export of raw
materials or semi-manufactured goods was now regarded as
the loss of so much potential treasure to the realm and
caused a popular outcry against the merchant class. Restrictions were then placed on the export of woollen yarn
and unfulled cloth in 1467, which in 1487 were extended to
cloth which had not been 'rowed and shorn'. The prohibition was re-enacted several times by Henry VIII, and special measures were taken for its enforcement. As a
result, the export trade in wool declined while the export
of cloth increased considerably. But for these measures
England's economy may have been totally different and she
may have continued in a peripheral role in a flourishing
European economy.

At another level, industrial capital directed its
attack against syndicates of merchants who controlled
trading circuits and depressed the producer's price.
Foreign trade was confined to 'mere merchants' (35) among
whom a privileged handful operated within a framework of
'restrictions and vested interests'. For instance, the
staplers from the mid-fourteenth century had a monopoly
granted by the government in consideration of their fiscal
and financial services. The Merchant Adventurers' Company
in the sixteenth century became a closed corporation controlling the trade between England and the Netherlands.
These foreign trade monopolies ran counter to the interests of the producers of exportable commodities and of the
majority of the small merchants. There was now a demand
for freer trade as well as for the removal of restrictions
of the craft guild, which were hindering the growth of
capitalist production.

The dislodging of merchant capital from its dominant
position over the producer (apart from the political
forces which secured this result) was due to the growing
independence of industrial capital to which I earlier
referred. An accumulation of funds within the enterprise,

as productivity increased, and the growth of banking as a
specialized activity ended the financial role of the merchant. Furthermore, the producer began to confront the
market on his own. Instead of producing for some individual merchant or for special orders, he was able to
create his own markets by improved productivity and the
lowering of costs, and latterly by adding saleable appearances to his products. Markets were no longer dependent solely upon factors exogenous to the production process. Marx explained: it is 'not commerce (in so far as
it expresses the existing demand)' which restricts the expansion of markets, 'but the magnitude of the employed
capital and the level of development of the productivity
of labour'. 'As soon as manufacture gains sufficient
strength, and particularly large-scale industry, it
creates in its turn a market for itself, by capturing it
through its commodities. At this point, commerce becomes
the servant of industrial production.' (36) The phenomenon of demand generation had its corollary in the subordination of marketing to production. Capital and credit now
flowed from industry to commerce instead of the other way
round. The concern of industrial capital about productivity and costs arose from its mode of exploitation,
based on increases in relative surplus value, unlike merchant capital which seeks to maximize sale proceeds and
annex already existing markets by extra-economic means.
    In the developed economies, therefore, the rule of mer-
chant capital proved to be merely a prelude to the rise of
capitalism. 'With capitalist production', wrote Marx,
(37)

    merchant's capital is reduced from its former indepen-
    dent existence to a special phase in the investment of
    capital, and the levelling of profits reduces its rate
    of profit to the general average.... The independent
    and predominant development of capital as merchant's
    capital is tantamount to the non-subjection of produc-
    tion to capital.... The independent development of
    merchant's capital, therefore, stands in inverse pro-
    portion to the general economic development of society.
When the subjection of industrial capital by merchant's
capital ended, there developed a mutuality of relations
between them. Merchant capital, no longer in control over
production, specialized in distribution and exchange,
serving as the agent of industrial capital.
    However, a development now occurred that was to have a
momentous consequence for the periphery. Merchant capital, having lost out politically and economically to industrial capital in Europe, expanded its operations in the
overseas empire. Its relationship here to production was

in many ways analogous to that which existed in Europe
before the industrial revolution. It played an independent role, mediating between precapitalist forms of production in the periphery and capitalism in the metropolis.
While subordinating to its own interests metropolitan
capital invested in the periphery, it throttled the development of indigenous production capital. From its
management and agency function in the production and sale
of export crops, merchant capital appropriated large surpluses. Improvements in labour productivity leading to
cost reduction and to the maximizing of net profits rather
than total turnover - characteristic of the capitalist
mode of production - were outside its frame of interests.
In some earlier chapters I explained in respect of Sri
Lanka and Malaysia the cleavage of interests between plantation shareholders and the essentially mercantile interests represented by the managing agency firms. In the
case of Latin America, a similar pattern was noted by
J.E.Ripply: 'English bankers, brokers, shipping companies
and agents, exporters and manufacturers and grafting Latin
American bureaucrats profited at the expense of British
investors.' (38) The absentee nature of the investments
which were entrusted to the care of merchant capital
removed the possibility of a collision between the two
fractions of metropolitan capital. Their relation was not
necessarily a contradictory one. Its subordination to
merchant capital was the price which metropolitan production capital had to pay for operating on an absentee basis
in the periphery.
    Even before the Industrial Revolution merchant capital
had secured a hold over the colonies, based on the plantations in America and the West Indies and on the import
trade in textiles from India. The historical process
whereby merchant capital became dominant overseas is helpful in understanding the nature of its overseas involvement and its relation to production capital. In the
seventeenth century the volume and composition of overseas
commerce changed radically with the sudden cheapness of
plantation staples, especially tobacco. The plantation
staples were of a mass consumption nature and the trade
in them gave English commerce a long-distance range. Furthermore, a large re-export trade based on the production
of the southern colonies of America and the West Indies
increased the middleman's role; in 1699-1701 re-exports
were nearly a third of the total value of England's exports. (39) 'The profits of this trade ... seemed to have
limitless possibilities for growth which English merchants
were determined to keep to themselves, along with its
corollaries of export trade to the plantations and a ship-

ping industry to carry their products.' (40)   The 'revolution' was a commercial one.   There was a phenomenal increase in output typically unaccompanied by technological
improvements or by a growth of industrial capital.
Merchants in Britain financed the development of the
American plantations.   They advanced credit for constructing stores and warehouses, for the purchase of plantation
supplies and, in South Carolina and Georgia, for the purchase of slaves.   In the late seventeenth century the
tobacco plantations in Maryland and Virginia began using
slave labour.   The larger credit requirements for the production and marketing of plantation staples were financed
by British mercantile houses.   At first the produce was
sent abroad on a consignment basis by the London merchants
and the proceeds were remitted to the planter after the
cost of materials supplied had been deducted.   In the
eighteenth century a change in the system of export marketing strengthened the position of the merchants vis-à-
vis the planters.   The consignment system was replaced by
direct sales to factors resident in Britain and the merchants became responsible for all matters connected with
the shipment and sale of produce.   From now on they were
not mere representatives of the planters, but acquired
ownership of the produce when it left the plantations.
By their control of finance and marketing the merchants
gained the 'upper hand' in plantation enterprise. (41)
Lured by the profits created by the export staples, the
commercial and maritime interests in England became involved in colonial policies.   These interests were 'ubiquitous and influential'.   They were responsible for the
Navigation Acts, they favoured the production of naval
stores in America, and discouraged tobacco growing in
England so that the colonists would have a monopoly of the
metropolitan markets. (42)   The English shipping industry
until the revolt of the American colonies was a favoured
child of imperial policy. (43)   Though the profits gained
by the shipowners from restrictions on the carrying trade
were at the expense of the purely merchant interests, they
both had a common goal in subordinating the economy of the
colonies to that of the mother country.
The policy of organizing production in the colonies was
also a more effective means of supplying the mother country than that of compulsory deliveries of produce, often
requiring trading posts and protective establishments
against rival European powers.   Soon this policy became
an imperial division of labour rather than one of mere
empire self-sufficiency.   English manufacturing industry
in the eighteenth century was emerging from the swaddling
clothes of the domestic system, and stood to gain from

controlled markets in the colonies. Even earlier, expanding woollen manufacturers felt the need for 'depend-
able' export outlets instead of the 'precarious' foreign
markets. For the mother country the colonies were a
'natural' market (in which she held a monopoly position),
compared with the 'artificial' trade with Europe; they
were a very useful outlet for 'low-grade commodities' that
were not easily sold in a competitive foreign market. In
this scheme the metropolis was to be the industrial
centre, on which the colonies must depend for manufactured
goods while supplying raw materials to the mother country.
'According to the prevalent doctrine of the value of plantations - the profits of Empire depended exactly on the
perpetuation of this division of labour.' (44)

To realize their potential, colonial markets had to be
protected from competitors including the colonists themselves who were a threat to the mother country - they
would even trade with the enemy in wartime. It was thus
necessary to incapacitate the colonies from developing a
manufacturing sector and to tie them in relations of dependence. From the turn of the seventeenth century the
North American colonies were restrained from engaging in
production which was competitive with the mother country.
Their attempts to do so were squashed by punitive legislation; e.g. the Woollen Act of 1669, the Hat Act of
1732, the prohibition in 1705 of shoe manufacturing in
Pennsylvania, in 1706 of the oil cloth industry in New
York, and in 1756 of linen manufacture in Massachusetts.
(45) Any 'interference' with British manufacture was declared improper by the Board of Trade. Monetary, banking
and credit policies favourable to industrial investment
were proscribed, (46) and even the establishment of towns
- for fear that urban communities would encourage manufacturing. Jefferson clearly saw the meaning of this policy:
'This is to say, iron which we made must not be wrought
into ploughs, axes, hoes, etc., in order that the shipowner may have the prospect of carrying it to Europe.'
(47) Small wonder that the Boston Tea Party had to take
place!

The organizing of production overseas led to a flow of
capital from the metropolis to new areas of the periphery. Though capital, as Mandel said, 'by its very nature
tolerates no geographical limits to its expansion', production capital till very recently was relatively immobile
and in the periphery was confined mostly to plantations
and extractive investments. The high value of fixed
assets and their long gestation period commits production
capital to a national unit, competing with production
capital elsewhere. For reasons discussed in an earlier

chapter, the immobility of production capital is greater
in manufacturing industry than in plantation agriculture.
Thus capital for manufacturing industry rarely moved
across national boundaries, except to the settler colonies, where it moved along with the owners and became
'indigenized'; there thus developed in these colonies an
autonomous investment pattern on the lines of the parent
economy. In the nonsettler colonies (which constituted in
a sense the periphery proper) the movement of production
capital without recourse to merchant capital as its agent
occurred only in the initial phase in the development of
export production, when the small scale of operations was
conducive to the proprietary planter. After this initial
phase, metropolitan capital for plantations and mines was
mobilized only under the aegis of merchant capital. The
institutional framework in which this occurred, dominated
by the managing agencies, was discussed in detail in an
earlier chapter.

Compared with the nature of production capital, which
is committed to a fixed locus, merchant capital has traditionally had a high degree of mobility. Merchant capital is characterized by an insignificance of fixed assets.
(The accounting treatises and account books of the
eighteenth century said nothing about depreciation costs
and reserves.) (48) In trade what was important was circulating capital, and thus banking and the instruments of
credit developed long before the advent of capitalism.
Unencumbered by fixed assets, the merchant could realize
his investment quickly. His liquidity was like quick-
silver. Even in maritime commerce where a large volume of
finance was involved, the capital was recouped after a
fairly definite period. At the end of one voyage the ship
was sold and the partnership dissolved. (49) The lack of
fixed investments and of a long-term capital involvement
gave trade 'its advantage over industry as a magnet for
funds'. Furthermore, the extensiveness of trading activities, straddling territories and productive systems, gave
merchant capital an outlook which transcended national
barriers. (50) During a certain stage in its development
merchant capital promoted the nation state, to further its
interests against the old feudal order. It also utilized
the military power of the state to destroy rival traders.
Yet, unlike industrial capitalists, merchants have no
national focus, and the concept of a national bourgeoisie
is scarcely applicable to them. Basically the merchant is
a peregrinator - a 'man without a country'. As Grassby
said, the mobility of commercial capital was 'both its
source of strength and the instrument of its own destruction'. Commercial capital had 'great influence but no
sustaining power'. (51)

While capital for manufacturing industry hardly moved
to the nonsettler colonies, it fulfilled its expansionary
potential by promoting a world market for commodities.
Manufacturing industry in the metropolis relied on merchant capital, through its control over the productive
apparatus consisting of plantations and mines, to secure
orders for industrial goods. (Colonial governments also
provided captive markets, especially for the goods of
heavy industry for the building of an infrastructure.) In
this phase the world economy involved the internationalization of markets rather than of production, and internationalization even in its trading aspects was somewhat
constricted by the existence of different colonial empires
and the zoning of markets and raw materials spheres. Dis-
parate centre-periphery networks arose, with a division of
labour that was optimal only from the standpoint of each
metropolitan power. The uneven growth of these spheres of
influence over markets and raw material sources intensified the rivalry between them. The militarism and armed
conflicts resulting from this rivalry were an aspect of
the international order which was of substantial concern
to Lenin in his study of imperialism.

Merchant capital, no longer supreme in the metropolitan
economies, predominated in the periphery. The managing
agency system created a nexus between merchant capital and
(a) production capital in the colony and (b) the manufac-
turing-cum-trading interests in the metropolis. In the
case of the plantation economies, it was shown in an
earlier chapter how merchant capital, while being the
agent of production capital, overrode the latter's interests. Three aspects of their relationship which I considered (Chapter 14) were the heavy management charges of
the agency houses, the excessive prices that were charged
for plantation materials and inputs, and the inability of
a plantation to change its agency. To safeguard its
income the agency even resists the sale of land by a plantation company under its management. The rise of the
agency houses and the manner in which they blanket and
control production capital in the colonies will repay detailed examination. Though performing ostensibly a
managerial function, the agencies were a key element in
the apparatus of ownership and control by absentee capital
in the periphery. Local interests were subordinated to
foreign interests and production capital to merchant capital. There has been no proper assessment of the agency
system in these terms. (52) The following discussion,
based on a study of the agency system in Sri Lanka, ap-
plies mutatis mutandis to the export economy of India and
Malaysia.

The historical basis of the managing agency system lay
in the resident agents (the descendants of the old 'super-
cargoes') (53) who managed a merchant's business in a
foreign land. The transformation of these coastal 'residents' into managing agencies was associated with the investment of capital in production as distinguished from
trade. The comparative non-liquidity of production capital made it far more risky than trading enterprises.
Plantations and mines had a slower turnover of capital and
a larger value of fixed assets. The geographical separation of the investors from the scene of their enterprise
increased the risk. The likelihood of mismanagement and
fraud called for a locally based institution which was
reliable and commercially experienced. The managing
agency system met this need. With connections both in
the country of investment and in the metropolitan centre,
the agents later assumed a wide variety of functions including the promotion of companies.
    While the agency system was a product of absentee
ownership, a specific factor which underlay its growth was
the dependence of the early planters on established merchant firms for liquid funds. In Sri Lanka in the mid-
nineteenth century the coffee estates borrowed their working expenses in the form of 'block advances' (54) from
mercantile firms in Colombo, just as in India the indigo
planters borrowed from firms in Calcutta. As a basis for
advancing credit, the firms often employed a 'visiting
agent' to assess the standing crops 'almost before the
blossoms had set'. (55) In return for their financial advances, the mercantile firms acquired marketing rights for
the crop, with a seller's commission and interest on the
capital lent.
    The dependence of the plantations on outside sources of
credit was due to several reasons. A long interval
elapsed between cultivation expenditure and realization of
the proceeds. The coffee crop was sold in London nearly a
year after harvesting 'so that financing was an all important part'. (56) The working expenses of the estates
were considerable, owing to the heavy costs of weeding and
the porterage of the harvested crops and of provisions for
the workforce. (57) Furthermore, the early plantations as
sole-proprietor concerns or partnerships had little capital of their own. 'Men, with only a few hundreds [of
pounds] where thousands are needed rush[ed] into Coffee
... merely to yield to London capital a good interest, and
to Ceylon Agencies handsome commissions.' (58) In the few
coffee companies that were formed later equity investment
was small and they depended on loan capital. The commercial value of an estate was enhanced if it had regular
sources of credit.

Agronomic and commercial risks in this period aggravated the financial exigencies of the planters. The
coffee plant, apart from sensitivity to weather, had a
yield cycle of its own which resulted throughout the
nineteenth century in an 'anarchic succession of overproduction and under-production'. Fluctuating exchange
rates and delays and difficulties of shipping imposed
other risks. In a dispatch to Earl Grey, Sir Emerson
Tennent wrote from Colombo in May 1847: (59)

> Many mercantile houses have still to ship two-thirds of
> their crops, and those two-thirds must necessarily be
> deteriorated by 5-10% in addition to the interest at
> 9% on the value of its produce thus detained; in ad-
> dition to which, as the season advances, shipping is
> becoming scarcer and freights are becoming higher.

In view of the 'very great' banking losses on the advances
given to indigo planters in Calcutta, 'The Economist' in
1843 cautioned British banks to accept only 'securities
available within short periods and not those which involve
funds for a long or indefinite time'. (60) In 1847 'The
Economist' (61) called plantations 'the most objectionable
of all fixed securities' - a quotation used by Marx in his
discussion of merchant capital. The Bank of Ceylon, set
up in 1841 to finance export agriculture, was prevented by
its rules from advancing to planters except upon crops.
The collapse of this bank during the coffee slump in 1847,
with nearly all its capital locked up in land, was a harsh
lesson to errant colonial banks which flouted the banking
traditions of their time.

In contrast to the risks confronting banks which went
beyond 'strict banking business', the 'commercial agency
houses' took to the financing of plantations as an adjunct
of their trading activities. 'Their more accurate knowledge of every circumstance connected with markets', 'The
Economist' noted in 1843, 'must make ... advances upon
factories, plantations, growing crops etc. safe to them
which would be very unsafe for a bank with its more limited knowledge or power of superintendence.' (62) The
financial dealings of these agencies had already become
evident. 'In 1840-2 many small capitalists purchased land
which they are only able to carry on by borrowing money
from England or Colombo through the agency houses, i.e.
the old West Indian plan of advances on crops.' (63) The
normal trading activities of these firms were not a sufficient outlet for their liquid funds and, despite initial
discouragement from their head offices, they therefore
regarded plantations as a good investment. The Imperial
Economic Committee referred to the merchant houses of this
time as being more properly merchant bankers. (64) When

the first commercial bank was set up in 1841, they aligned themselves against it, for fear of losing business. 'Difficulties were created by the Merchants then in Trade in Ceylon holding themselves entirely aloof from the project. ... None of them, with only one exception, were originally Subscribers for a single share, and even after the Bank was in full operation, it was long before any of them ... would give it any cordial support.' (65)

The financing of plantations was attractive for its own sake and for the agency appointments which this secured. One of the biggest agency firms recalled how 'a number of agencies went to the mercantile firm which was willing to make advances'. (66) This firm expanded its agency business 'apparently as the price of financial support'. The policy of one of its early partners was 'to make advances to estates in order to secure agency appointments'. (67) Another commented that 'the opportunities of finance enabled the firm to build up an Estate Agency business'. (68) The control acquired by the Colombo agencies over the rupee plantation companies as the price of financial support was replicated in the relation between the London agencies and the sterling companies. At first, when the capital of tea companies was privately subscribed, shareholding was confined to the stock brokers' own clients, including merchants and agency houses, among whom prospectuses were circulated. Being connected with the tea trade in one way or another, these groups evinced an active interest in their companies. Later, many of the companies were sponsored in the capital market by the London agency, which then became represented on their boards. The conversion from private to public companies also brought in a broader class of shareholders who were inclined to leave managerial responsibility to the agents-cum-directors. The basis of the domination of the plantation companies by the agencies was explained by the Imperial Economic Committee in 1913: 'In many cases the parent tea producing companies were established by these agents who financed the original planters, and they were not only represented on the Board but in reality control the companies of which they are nominally the servants.' (69)

Plantation finance spawned a whole series of related activities. As stated earlier, when money was advanced under the prevailing system of crop bonds, estates were obliged to assign their produce to the agents for shipment and sale. (70) The agent also got the orders for estate requirements, thereby expanding his import business. By his role in the financing and sale of export produce the agent became the local representative of banks and investment trusts and of insurance and shipping concerns. (71)

The necessity of securing finance sealed the relation between trade and plantation enterprise. As purveyors of
finance the agencies, however, fastened themselves to the
plantations which they then subordinated to their mer-
chanting interests. The ensuing relation between merchant
capital and production capital was already noticed by one
planter in 1865: 'If [estate proprietors] are dissatis-
fied with their Agents, [they] cannot [be] change[d], because the Borrower is Servant to the Lender.' (72)
    The involvement of the agencies in plantations increas-
ed dramatically after the coffee crash in the 1880s. When
through non-payment of debts estates passed into the hands
of creditors, many of the new owners were not themselves
active planters, and they entrusted the control and
management of the properties to an agency, hoping to save
something from the wreckage. At the same time, individual
planters began to combine into partnerships or private
companies. Broad-based forms of ownership helped those
who wanted to retrieve what little capital remained or
else to redeem their liabilities. The proceeds were drawn
partly in cash and the rest held as shares in the new companies. The estate agencies which provided the funds had
also to estimate the capital value of estates and the
costs of bringing them into bearing. (73)
    Later the character of the agency system changed, when
a diminution in working capital requirements of plantations caused a decline in the financial role of the agencies. First, improvements in transport reduced the wage
bill of plantations. Ferguson stated: (74)

    A great economy of labour has taken place with in-
    creased facilities of transport, and the introduction
    of spouting, shoots and machinery generally on the hill
    plantations. Only in a few exceptional cases have
    coolies now to carry coffee and rice on their heads for
    any considerable distance.

Second, with the cultivation of tea and rubber, planters
were able to finance themselves to a great extent out of
current profits because the harvesting and sale of these
products went on practically throughout the year. Third,
there was a lessening of the financial risk, due to more
uniform harvests, the availability of shipping, and relatively stable exchange rates. Alongside the spread of
banking facilities, a smaller and less frequent need for
credit reduced the financial and risk-bearing functions of
the agency house, and its responsibility was confined to
plantation management in the more technical sense of that
term.
    Not merely did plantations become largely financially
independent of agency houses but there was also, in later

decades, a reversal of their earlier relationship; the
agencies came to be in a position to borrow from plantation companies the latter's short-term surplus funds. The
basis for this development was the control by the managing
agency over the local sale proceeds of plantation companies. Although the agency, upon receipt of these funds
from the brokers, deposited them in the bank accounts of
the companies, through its powers of attorney the agency
could operate on these accounts. It was thereby enabled
to have a clearing-house arrangement, matching temporary
deposits and surpluses in the respective accounts of the
group. Companies whose idle funds were used to finance
deposits in others earned interest at the prevailing rate
on the amounts so drawn out. Such deployment of surplus
funds was also advantageous to the borrowers, because it
saved them the cost and inconvenience of bank loans.
Funds borrowed by the agency in this manner were used to
finance other plantation companies and Ceylonese proprietary estates under its management; having smaller resources than the better established companies, these estates were in frequent need of advances. But a portion of
these funds may have been used by the agencies themselves
for their direct business needs, such as the financing of
imports or exports traded on their own account.

In distinguishing between the two phases of plantation
economy in terms of the financial role of agency houses,
it must not be supposed that there was in this respect a
break in continuity which corresponded to the abruptness
with which land cultivated with coffee was brought under
tea. At the boundary the economic qualities of each phase
were necessarily blurred. The role of the agency houses
as the source of working capital for plantations did not
end in the 1880s, when coffee was replaced by tea, but
remained important until around 1910 or 1915. Indeed,
while working capital was much less of a problem than for
coffee, in the first two decades of the tea economy the
financial dependence of plantations on the agencies temporarily increased. The larger credit requirements arose
mainly from 'cash advances' to labourers - there was at
this time a serious competition for labour. The Kandyan
Hills Co.Ltd explained in its report of 1905: 'To secure
a force sufficient for all the requirements of the estate,
the issue of additional advance had been necessary. With
regard to coolie advances, it seemed quite impossible to
keep them down.' The Colombo correspondent of 'The
Economist' referred to this in 1913. 'In Ceylon every
estate is burdened with advances to coolies, which have
grown in recent years.' The advances (Rs 50 to Rs 100 per
labourer) often could not be recovered. Two other items

of cost, absent in the case of coffee, raised the minimum
scale of investment. One was the overhead expenses of
housing a resident labour force. The Caledonian (Ceylon)
Tea Estates Ltd mentioned in its report for 1908 that
apart from paying larger 'advances to coolies' it had
erected 'new buildings on three of the estates for their
better accommodation. This expenditure is necessary to
keep the labour force adequate, as well as content, notwithstanding the keen competition for labour'. Capital
outlays on recruitment made it imperative to restrain
labour and to bind it to the plantation. The other item
of cost was the construction and equipping of tea and
rubber factories.

   The long-term nature of capital investment at this
stage caused the plantations to resort to capital markets
abroad. There was consequently an increase in the unit
size of plantation investment. At first small properties
were merged into private limited companies and later, to
enable a larger body of investors to subscribe, public
companies were floated in London and Edinburgh. The trend
towards corporate ownership, while minimizing the financial role of the agents, strengthened their position in
other ways. To be successful in the capital market, a
plantation company had to be sponsored by the 'right
people', and the reputation of its agency influenced the
company's financial prospects. 'The management will be in
the careful hands of Messrs. Lyall Anderson & Co., agents
of the Consolidated Malaya and other successful companies'
was typical of the prospectuses of this time. (75) 'Companies with a good connection and a powerful board may
have the offer of good "propositions"', said 'The Economist' in a review of market floatations in 1910 (2 March).
'Without considerable influence ... /they/ will be lucky
if ... /they/ succeed.'

   The formation of companies was actively encouraged by
the agencies. In both Malaysia and Sri Lanka in the first
decades of this century, the agencies having acquired land
and prepared it for rubber planting, or after 'preliminary
negotiations for land with the government', turned the
property over to a plantation company. (76) They profited
from the resale price of the land and received promotional
fees and underwriting commissions. The management of the
companies which they promoted brought the agencies a permanent income as secretarial and agency fees and expanded
their trading business. 'The supply of every sort of
agricultural equipment, machinery, tool, fertilizer,
building materials and household necessity both for the
estate as well as its labour force would then become the
exclusive business of the agency firms.' (77)

With foreign financing there was also a definite need
for agents who could act on behalf of absentee owners.
Agency work increased as fresh transfusions of metropolitan capital took place or when the leading shareholders
of partnerships and rupee companies retired from the
colony and incorporated their businesses in Britain, entrusting the management to an agency. The later generations of shareholders even of locally registered companies lived abroad. On behalf of absentee owners, the
agencies had to perform work that was of a responsible and
trustworthy kind, though not onerous in a technical or
entrepreneurial sense. They collected and remitted dividends, exercised powers of attorney and safeguarded the
principals against misappropriation or fraud. For such
work the agents had to be paid very lavishly. In insurance and shipping they performed similar services, accepting business and collecting premiums on behalf of principals abroad.

My account of the development of the managing agencies
shows how, through the mediation of merchant capital, production capital in the metropolis gained access to raw
material sources and markets in the periphery. Merchant
capital, the earliest source of short-term funds for colonial export production, fostered production capital in its
own interest, as it had done in Europe in previous centuries. Unlike the metropolitan countries where merchant
capital was only the historical premise for the development of capitalist production - becoming later subordinated to production capital - in the periphery the power
and pervasiveness of merchant capital was far greater and
has persisted till almost the present day. It failed to
transform itself into industrial capital while at the same
time it blocked the emergence of an indigenous industrial
class. More generally merchant capital determined the
economic structures of the periphery and its pattern of
interaction with the metropolis. The colonial state
intervened to uphold these relations.

Through the device of the managing agency system, the
control of the productive organization consisting of plantations and mines became vested primarily in the hands of
merchants and financiers, tending thereby to freeze
trading activities into monopolized spheres and to increase the profits to be wrung from the purely commercial
operations. The export-import business which the agencies
acquired from their management of export production in the
colonies was but one aspect of a broader commercial operation, involving a ramified group of metropolitan interests - manufacturers, shippers, exchange banks and insurance firms and a network of dealers and sub-dealers, com-

mission agents and brokers. Special interests profited
more than others: for instance, agency houses far more
than the plantation shareholders; manufacturing and commercial enterprises in the metropolis far more than the
locally domiciled metropolitan firms. Major beneficiaries
were also the shipping interests. In the Straits Settlements, (78) after 1896 the Straits Homeward Conference had
a virtual monopoly in the shipping of produce. The conference had the support of the bigger merchants, in consideration of which shipping space was reserved for them
at a preferential margin of 8.1/3 per cent over their
rivals. (79) The sequel to this arrangement was that the
freight on shipment of tin trebled in 1897 and 1898 compared with that in the preceding five years; the rates on
gambier and copra, and on black pepper, respectively, were
20 per cent and 27 per cent higher. (80)

The control over production by the mercantile interest
and the multifarious activities involved in the financing
and export of primary produce gave rise to what Maurice
Dobb in an analogous case called a system of 'exploitation
through trade'. (81) Yielding surpluses to carriers, commission agents, financiers and distributors, foreign trade
became a mould in which economic activity tended automatically to settle. The organization and expertise required pertained essentially to trading operations including transportation, insurance and finance and made little
demand on the production system, in the same way as the
colonial banking systems specialized in exchange transactions and the financing of foreign trade without providing capital for production. The dominance of trading
activities supported numerous commercial and financial
interests which were opposed to production for the domestic market, as Richard Graham described in the case of
Brazil. (82)

The British banks were primarily tied to the export
sector rather than the industrial one. The shipping
companies and insurance firms facilitated the concentration of export commodities.... British imports
cheapened the cost of coffee production and emphasised
the monocultural nature of the Brazilian economy....
Coffee interests were usually against tariffs, government loans to industries, crop diversification, land
reform and education.... Once industrialisation had
begun in Brazil the export economy - to which the
British were so closely tied - often slowed the pace
of change.

To the trading interests the flow of exports is valuable not merely for its own sake but also because it involves an element of reciprocity with the flow of imports,

from which the remainder of their earnings comes. In
reverse, imports were valued for the sake of exports. The
combining of import and export business by many of the
trading firms enabled the profits from either exporting
or importing to find an investment outlet without leaving
the foreign trade sector. A certain portion of the imports of a firm 'specifically contributed to increasing
[its] exports' so that the two sides of the trade were
complementary. The financial return on capital invested
in the import-export business and its ancillary activities
is so lucrative that progress towards self-sufficiency of
a colonial economy is naturally liable to injure these
enterprises. 'Merchants tend to think mainly of marketing; they want to live by buying and selling alone.' (83)
But as merchants engage exclusively in foreign trade they
are not interested in production other than for the export
market. That industrialization would lead merely to a
change in the composition of imports, in which consumer
goods are replaced by the import of machinery and intermediate goods, is a prospect which appeals very little to
those who hold the reins of the existing economic arrangement. The uncertainty of a smooth change-over and the
likely disruption of their trading connections both
strengthen the tendency for established entrepreneurs to
favour the status quo and fear the unknown and the incal-
culable.

It is pertinent to contrast the vitality of merchant
capital in the underdeveloped countries with the weakness
of merchant capital in Japan during the transition to
capitalism. From the seventeenth century there was an
extensive monetization and commercialization of the economy which enabled the merchant class to accumulate capital
rapidly. Social sanctions against commercial involvement
by the daimyo and the samurai left commerce entirely to
the merchants. (84) On the other hand, the heavy expenses
of the nobility caused it promptly to encash their rice
revenues and to rely on the merchants for loans. By the
end of the Tokugawa period between half and two thirds of
the agricultural output was marketed. (85) Grain transfers between Osaka and Edo (now Tokyo) were financed by
drafts and bills of exchange issued by the money brokers.
The growth of these transactions led to a market in the
credit slips issued as advance payments for rice, from
which arose the world's first commodity exchange. The
merchants held current accounts with the money brokers, on
which cheques were drawn, and net balances were settled by
a clearing house arrangement. The rice market in Osaka
influenced rice prices in the country, through market information carried by express messengers. (86) But after

this lively precapitalist development, the accumulation of
merchant capital suffered a setback.

   Jon Halliday pointed out that this retardation was due
not merely to the rigid control of foreign trade during
Tokugawa rule but also to the trading structures and patterns which emerged. The government, in carrying out both
diplomatic and foreign economic relations, influenced the
volume and the composition of imports. 'The imperialist
bourgeoisies tried to push Japan towards a "consumer
society", but Japan cut out both the kind of people who
push consumer items and the actual items themselves.' (87)
Furthermore, the import business became centralized in a
few trading companies and zaibatsu banks. Merchant capital, 'driven inwards into rural commerce', thereby acquired a purely domestic orientation; and its political
and social position was one of dependence on the nobility.
There is here an important contrast with the merchant
bourgeoisie of Western Europe prior to the Industrial
Revolution and with that in the underdeveloped countries.
The bourgeoisie in both these instances throve on international commerce, and was supported by sources outside
the national economy. (88) In Japan, merchant capital
never acquired a position of autonomy; and, in consequence, the constraints imposed on effective industrialization by commercial supremacy were totally lacking.

   As Trimberger concluded from her model of capitalist
development in Japan, the underdevelopment of the periphery was due not merely to the impact of external forces,
within a framework of imperialism, but also to its internal social structure. In Europe, the countries in
which the transition to capitalism was delayed or was not
fully accomplished included some which were themselves
metropolitan nations: the Netherlands, France, Spain and
Portugal. Thus external influences were not the whole
story. The importance of the social structure is also
important from those instances in which the urban mercantile and banking oligarchy in these countries had political power, and accumulated vast surpluses but failed over
a long period to make the transition. The Netherlands and
the leading cities in Italy and Flanders had a promising
start centuries before England, but faltered. Dobb was of
the view that they found their progress retarded by 'the
very success of maturity of merchant and money lending
capital'. (89) The merchant capitalists of the Netherlands were lending abroad, and earning lucratively by
manipulating their holdings of foreign stocks, instead of
making an industrial revolution at home. 'So far from
stimulating Dutch industrial development', wrote C.H.
Wilson, 'Holland's 18th century loans almost certainly ob-

structed and postponed it, directly and indirectly....
Dutch economic development was postponed by a leakage of
capital into international finance.' (90) The merchants'
interests lay in an open economy and only after 1816, when
the Dutch foreign trade had declined, was protection given
to certain branches of industry. (91)

The tendency for the growth of capitalism was not universal nor was any country predestined to tread the capitalist path of development. While a model of the transition to the capitalist mode of production can be built up,
such a model must take account of the specificity of the
forces which underlay the transition in different historical situations; this is evident from the unevenness of
the transition - its timing and pace - within Europe
itself. There was no automaticity about the process. The
triumph of capitalism was conditioned both by the external
relations of a country and by its internal politics -
specifically class relations and the political alignment
of the state in various periods. Furthermore, the related
elements in the transition, such as the role of government, a technological lead, a large surplus to be invested, or the innovative propensities of the dominant class,
proved significant not in and by themselves, but only in a
specific set of circumstances. For instance, the scale of
state intervention that would be effective at any given
time, or the appropriateness of shoring up an indigenous
bourgeoisie to accomplish a breakthrough, would be relative to the strength and resistance of the countervailing
forces both international and local. It is not as though
the dynamic elements are accumulated within the old order
preparing for a general concatenation when the appropriate
volume or proportion of these elements is reached. False
starts and throwbacks have been as much the order of the
day as unimpeded advance. To put it differently, the
total circumstances had to reach a 'critical mass' before
the qualitative change occurred.

The non-transformation of merchant capital, which is
the crux of the problem of underdevelopment, is a question
which must continue to claim attention. I have referred
to it in a general way in terms of the unusual strength of
merchant capital in the nonsettler colonies. In contrast
to the historical situation both in Western Europe and in
Japan, the vitality of merchant capital derived from its
role as the agent of absentee production capital, and its
monopoly profits based on a control over the investments
and productive facilities in the colonial export economy.
The specific relation of merchant capital to the plantation system caused it to be disinterested in the development of productive forces; merchant capital though manag-

ing and controlling the plantation system was yet entrepreneurially independent. In this relationship its interests lay in the maximizing of plantation output and therefore the gross revenue of plantations rather than net
profits. Furthermore, the technological disparity which
had already arisen between Europe and the colonies at the
time they were opened up forestalled any attempt at establishing competitive production systems. The failure of
the peasant sector to transform itself along capitalist
lines is likewise attributable to the dominance of mer-
chant-cum-usurer capital in the village economy; though
not exhaustively dealt with in this book, this failure has
been highlighted in some of its basic aspects.

Thus the growth of capitalism in these countries was
retarded both by the class structure dominated by merchant capital, and by the impact of external influences.
These were not separate and independent forces but were
the two blades of a scissor. (92)

> The course of development of non-Western societies has
> not been determined only by the impact of external
> capital, but as much by the social relations in the
> pre-capitalist social formations, and how these rela-
> tions both helped structure the imperialist challenge
> and were themselves altered by it.

A final word on this issue comes from Baran: 'The principal impact of foreign enterprise on the development of
the underdeveloped countries lies in hardening and
strengthening the sway of merchant capitalism, in slowing
down and indeed preventing its transformation into industrial capitalism.' (93) In the periphery merchant capital
subsisted, in its relation to foreign production capital,
as a parasite on a parasite.

16 Plantations, economic dualism and the colonial mode of production

The ruling theoretical model of underdevelopment in the plantation or plantation-cum-mining economies refers to a 'capitalist' sector and a 'subsistence' sector. This model of economic dualism, according to one writer, is 'an apt analytical tool for exploring the colonial heritage of a large area of the underdeveloped world'. (1) The categorization of plantations as 'modern'/'developed'/'capitalist' forms of production is a widely held notion. For example, Higgins and Eckaus group plantations with mines, oil fields, refineries and transportation as the 'modern' sector. (2) Myrdal classifies plantations as a type of industrialization - 'capital-intensive highly specialised commercial enterprises'. (3) Samir Amin refers again and again to plantations as 'modern', 'highly productive modern', 'ultramodern', 'modern capitalist'. (4) The effort to vindicate the thesis of unequal trade relations as the determinant of low wages requires him to presume that the level of productivity in plantations is the same or is comparable with that in advanced industrial countries.

Plantations and peasant agriculture, as productive systems, were also distinguished by Myint. 'While the mining and plantation sector represents the extension of modern economic organisation and technology, the peasant sector seems to be an extension of the traditional economic organisation and technology of the subsistence sector.' (5) Arthur Lewis refers to 'a few highly capitalised plantations, surrounded by a sea of peasants'. (6) D.R.Snodgrass on the same lines regarded the underdeveloped economies as being 'split ... into two sectors, one modern in organisational structure and technology, producing for the world market, and the other traditional in both these regards, producing for the immediate village market'. (7) Clifford Geertz referred to 'increasingly

severe' economic dualism in Java, based on plantations,
with 'increased capital inputs', and peasant agriculture
with 'increased labour inputs'. According to him the sec-
toral division of the economy was so sharp that it excluded even any intermediate stages. (8) Likewise, J.I.
Clarke spoke of 'vivid contrasts' between modernity and
tradition in colonial economies. 'The modern sector was
localised in towns, mines and plantations and estates.'
(9)

The problem of underdevelopment, according to this
model, is due to the enclave nature of the export sector.
The impulses to growth, in the export sector, failed to
spread. Depending on the peasant economy neither for markets nor labour, the plantations were able to expand without integrating themselves with the rest of the indigenous
structure, with a Chinese wall between them. The relatively limited size of the export sector was claimed by
Lewis to explain the low rates of saving and capital formation in underdeveloped economies. They save so little
'because their capitalist sector is small'. Unless it is
taken to mean only that the export sector was developed
relative to the peasant sector - a qualification which is
not made and would not be analytically helpful if it were
- this implies that had the export sector expanded sufficiently to swamp the peasant sector, taking over all of
its land and labour, the economy would have become a
modern or a developed one. A legitimate corollary of this
viewpoint is that if the peasant sector were to be geographically detached from the national entity to which it
currently belongs, leaving behind only the export sector,
the result would be a developed economy! The average
income, technological skills and labour productivity of
its workforce would, however, be no higher than those of
a present-day plantation worker. A 'developed economy' of
this kind is an anomaly without precedent.

The dual economy hypothesis also postulates that plantations constitute capitalism. A.G.Frank, while rejecting
the dualism hypothesis, carried the presumption about the
existence of a capitalist sector even further by asserting
that the whole of the underdeveloped economy was capitalist, 'from its toe bone to the collar bone'. Others have
employed terms such as 'colonial capitalism', 'dependent
capitalism', 'peripheral capitalism' and 'agrarian capitalism'. 'There are two types of capitalism - capitalism
of the imperialist countries and colonial capitalism....
In the colonies capitalism is not a product of local conditions and development but is fostered by the penetration
of foreign capital.' (10) Though this diversity of expression obviously reflects an awareness of a certain com-

plexity in the colonial mode of production, it implies
that what exists in these economies is capitalism however
distorted. There is here an unwitting departure from the
classical notion of capitalism and a failure to look
closely at the colonial economy as a conceptual category.
The idea of capitalist 'penetration' implies also a trans-
ferability of capitalism spatially like a concrete object,
or the possibility, shall we say, of practising capitalism
within a cordoned off space (a plantation or mining enclave). Later, in discussing the essential nature of
capitalism as a mode of production, I shall show how inap-
propriate is this view.

Marx, from whose vocabulary the basic categories of the
colonial mode of production - as capitalism or some variant of it - have been taken, was not centrally concerned
with colonialism and underdevelopment. In line with his
belief in the universalizing and homogenizing tendency of
capitalism, he at first was of the view that capitalist
agriculture was developing in Ireland and that in India
British rule would 'lay the material foundations of
Western society'. (11) He recognized different colonial
situations. In some the conquering nation 'refrains from
interfering in the old mode of production and ... [is]
content with tribute', and in others 'interaction may take
place between the two, giving rise to a new system as a
synthesis'. Or else 'the conquering nation may impose its
own mode of production', as in Ireland, and 'to some
extent' in India. (12) Marx and Engels later abandoned
this prospect in regard to Ireland, and emphasized the
retardative effects of colonialism. Ireland was 'stunted'
in its development and 'thrown centuries back'. There was
a total absence of any and every industry, and the Irish
landowners themselves have been 'demoralized' instead of
taking on 'bourgeois qualities'. (13) They even saw a
centre-periphery type of relation. 'Ireland is at present
only an agricultural district of England, marked off by a
wide channel from the country to which it yields corn,
wool, cattle, industrial and military recruits.' (14) As
a secure outlet for absentee capital, it sustained an
annual flow of revenue to England. The degradation of
Ireland was an 'artificial' condition, induced by English
domination.

Marx and Engels at this stage saw clearly the underdeveloping aspects of colonialism in Ireland, and that a
capitalist transformation was unlikely. In exploring the
genesis of capitalism as a mode of production Marx devised
analytical tools and lucid concepts which can be used to
unravel the nature of underdeveloped economies. In
'Capital', volume I, Marx ended his discussion of primi-

tive accumulation with a short chapter entitled The Modern
Theory of Colonization. But this was a finale to his exposition of capitalism as a conceptual category. By
referring to the problem of a labour supply in the regions
of white settlement, he showed how the expropriation of
the labourer is a fundamental condition for the capitalist
mode of production and accumulation. Neither he nor
Engels expounded a model of the colonial economy or of
underdevelopment. For one thing, the Irish Question was
of only specific concern to Marx - as a strategic element
in the revolutionary struggles of the English proletariat.
A blow delivered in Ireland 'against the English ruling
classes ... will be decisive for the workers' movement [in
England and] all over the world'. (15) Second, it was too
early to advance a model of colonialism and of underdevelopment. The plantation economies had not fully developed except in the West Indies, and the domination of
merchant capital in the colonies was not widely apparent.
The settler/nonsettler dichotomy had not yet emerged, with
divergent patterns of internal class formations and symbiotic relations with the metropolis.

Colonial problems first gained the attention of social-
ists at the Amsterdam congress in 1904 but, like Marx's
interest in Irish politics, their concern was a practical
one - that of the attitude of communists to bourgeois
democratic groups and nationalist movements. As against
the view propounded, among others, by Rosa Luxemburg in
1916, which regarded the liberation movement in colonies
as an adjunct to the socialist revolutions in Europe,
M.N.Roy at the Comintern's second world congress in 1920
held that the colonial question was important in its own
right. Having India especially in mind, he asserted that
since the First World War there had occurred in some of
the colonies a 'fairly high level' of capitalist development. Their indigenous bourgeoisie, already threatened by
the proletariat, would collaborate with imperialism. A
concomitant of this view, which was basically accepted by
Lenin, was the distinction between 'bourgeois democratic'
liberation movements and 'revolutionary' movements of
liberation - and the latter deserving the support and
leadership of the communist parties. In other colonies
precapitalist relations were dominant, and the bourgeoisie
was 'weak, underdeveloped and oppressed'. But most colonial countries, Roy implied, had a kind of economic dualism. The foreign owned industrial, commercial and banking
enterprises, 'the most important means of transportation,
the latifundia, plantations etc.', were contrasted with
'precapitalist forms of exploitation' in the peasant
sector. (16)

Looking at the world economy from the vantage point of
a more recent period, Trotsky envisaged a tendency for a
unification of separate production structures on a world
scale, levelling out productive forces and reducing the
economic distance between nations. 'The penetration of
capitalism to new territories ... brings about their
rapprochement and equalises the economic and cultural
levels of the most progressive and the most backward countries.' (17) Capitalism hampers and throws back development in countries, yet 'drawing them closer to one another'. (18) Backwardness 'permits or rather compels, the
adoption of whatever is ready in advance of any specific
date'. (19) 'Theoretically, "inevitable" stages [in a
historical process] can be compressed to zero by the
dynamics of development, especially during revolutions,
which have not for nothing been called the locomotives of
history.' (20) He even spoke of 'the industrialisation of
the colonies, the diminishing gap between India and Great
Britain'. (21) The 'natives' are driven 'from their
primitive environment straight into capitalist civilization'. (22)

Trotsky's prognosis of uneven and combined development
was part of a wider polemic in which he combated the doctrine of 'socialism in one country'. In the regions of
new settlement, the European colonists overcame with one
stroke the precapitalist structures which they encountered, and even Russia had the 'most primitive beginnings and
the most modern European endings'. (23) Uneven and combined development expresses the necessity for capitalism
to bring new territories and resources within its orbit.
The 'uncontrollable expansion of capitalism', its 'universality, penetrability and mobility', about which Trotsky
spoke, does not, however, match the economic reality in
the periphery. Imperialism, as the agency by which capitalism expanded its sphere of influence, has had little or
no transformative effect on the periphery; rather than
developing capitalist social relations and productive
forces, imperialism stifled them and intensified unevenness of development on a world scale. In countries that
came under the hegemony of the established capitalist
centres there was for the most part merely a reorganization of their precapitalist structures, retarding a real
transformation of these structures. Baran thought that
these countries were transfixed in a twilight world which
is neither feudalism nor capitalism.

Lenin, Bukharin, Luxemburg and Trotsky, in applying and
extending Marx's thought seem to have been influenced by
his view of capitalism's ability to propagate itself in
societies with which it came in contact and even subordi-

nated. Though Marx modified his thinking on this matter
from about the end of the 1860s and totally changed his
earlier view in regard to Ireland after, as he said, 'occupying [himself] with the Irish question for many years'
- the possibility of capitalism as a transforming agent on
a world scale lingered in the minds of Marxists. For instance, Bukharin, while denouncing imperialist activity in
the colonies, asserted in a book to which Lenin wrote a
preface: 'The gigantic growth of maritime transportation
has made it possible to unite the organisms of several
continents and to revolutionise pre-capitalist methods of
production in the most backward corners of the world.'
(24) In another volume which Bukharin wrote, three years
later, in 1920, he again stressed the international nature
of modern capitalism: 'Capitalist relations of production
dominate in the entire world and ... they connect all
parts of our planet with one strong economic bond.' (25)
However, Lenin in his marginal notes on Bukharin's manuscript underlined the words 'entire world' and wrote 'not
everywhere'. (26) The prospect of a capitalist development in the periphery was formally rejected at the sixth
congress of the Comintern in 1928. Nevertheless, there
has been among both Marxists and non-Marxists an amazing
convergence of views with regard to the 'capitalist'
nature of the colonial export economies. This sector,
which came into direct contact with capitalism in the
metropolis, has been regarded as historically progressive
and advanced.

The analysis of most underdeveloped economies, as already referred to, is based on the notion of economic
dualism, with its presumption that the plantations were a
capitalist form of production. A rejection of the central
postulate of dualism, which ascribes underdevelopment to
the failure of the peasant sector to respond to the growth
impulses emanating from the plantation sector, would imply
the possibility that the plantations had no dynamism to
spread; in fact that the plantations were themselves a
precapitalist form of production. Underdevelopment would
then be seen as a pervasive phenomenon, not confined to
the peasant sector but engulfing the whole of the economy.
The mode of production which the plantations constitute
does not easily fit into the usual Marxist schema of
social formations. But a suitable label is less important
than an explanation of the content of this mode of production. This is not a problem in semantics as those professing or assuming inability to investigate social formations more closely seem to hold. The importance of a
proper characterization of the colonial mode of production
has been lost sight of owing to the neo-classical tradi-

tion of expressing development and underdevelopment in terms of statistical indicators - such as income per capita, labour productivity, or the proportion of industrial production in the GNP. In countries which preserve the institutional basis of capitalism, resting on private ownership, underdevelopment is in reality the expression of their failure to accomplish the transition to capitalism.

The colonial mode of production also has an important political dimension; it was Frank's attempt to perceive this political dimension that led him to his choice of the term 'capitalism'. The political attitudes and strategy of communist parties towards the local bourgeoisie have depended upon the question of whether feudal, precapitalist elements persist. If they do, an alliance of the left with this emerging bourgeoisie, liberal and progressive, and cast in an oppositional role to imperialism, is a necessary prelude to a socialist programme. Alternatively, in the absence of feudalism, a socialist programme should immediately take its place on the political agenda. Frank's characterization of an underdeveloped economy as capitalist was a political reaction against attempts by the communist parties in Latin America, as elsewhere, to foster a 'national' bourgeoisie which would hopefully play an oppositional role to imperialism. While this may be in the diplomatic interests of the Soviet bureaucracy, it limits the mobilization of the masses in an anti-capitalist struggle. The futility of such a policy is theoretically demonstrable by the impracticality of a belated development of capitalism in the present day, without having to assert (erroneously as I shall point out) that the economy is already capitalist. Very recently the colonial mode of production has been the subject of lively controversy relating to India's agricultural economy in its post-independence phase. Whereas this polemic focused on non-plantation agriculture, my discussion relates to the plantations whose claims to being a capitalist form of production have not been questioned.

The categorization of plantations as a modern/developed/capitalist form of production has been due to their more obvious economic attributes: exchange relations (involving wage labour and market orientation), the generation of a surplus, the large scale of operations and, finally, the use of capital in production. I shall later examine the appropriateness of this categorization, in terms of the nature of capitalism as a mode of production. Before doing so I must, however, observe that the attributes of the plantations which have been thought, explicitly or otherwise, to denote their capitalist linea-

ments were not exclusive to the capitalist mode. Money
and market relations as well as surpluses had existed well
before the establishment of plantations. It was shown in
an earlier chapter that trade and money payments, and an
export trade, had developed in the Kandyan kingdom in Sri
Lanka during the eighteenth century. Prior to European
colonialism, there were well-entrenched systems of sea
trade in the Indian Ocean. (27) I have already discussed
the case of Tokugawa Japan whose feudal society had made
an extraordinary advance in commerce: by the latter half
of the seventeenth century a business philosophy had developed - with an emphasis on diligence, frugality, economy (avoidance of waste), the adoption of bookkeeping techniques and, in large enterprises, a double entry system.
(28) The bill of exchange appeared in Italy in the first
half of the fourteenth century, and bookkeeping by double
entry was adopted in Europe apparently in 1394. (29) In
the Ottoman Empire, credit, foreign money transactions
and long-distance trade existed from the mid-fifteenth
century. (30) Foreign trade was based on partnerships or
joint ventures. Bursa, as a centre of the silk industry,
developed an entrepot trade for Persian silk which was
bought by the Jewish merchants for the Italian market. In
the textile industry of Bursa there was an incipient differentiation between commercial and industrial capital.
The provision of raw materials and the export of cloth
were left entirely to merchants, but weaving was carried
out, to a certain extent, independently, by the owners of
the looms - in some instances in workshops. 'The masters
of looms with much capital invested' differed sharply from
the journeymen and workmen. As Eugene Genovese said,
'Many precapitalist economic systems had well developed
commercial relations, but if every commercial society is
to be considered capitalist the word loses all meaning.'
(31)
     A second aspect of the dualism hypothesis is surplus
generation by plantations but not by the peasant sector.
The peasant sector is presumed to produce little or no in-
vestible surplus. Nurkse contended that 'the peasantry
[in underdeveloped countries] is incapable of producing a
surplus of food above its subsistence needs', (32) and
likewise D.R.Snodgrass asserted in regard to Sri Lanka:
'The villager grew paddy to feed himself and his family.
His idea was self-sufficiency and the ideal came close to
being realised in practice.' (33) The view that the
peasant sector is subsistence-based rests partly on the
fact that its produce is not marketed in the same way as
that of the plantations; also the surplus of the plantations being easily identifiable and measurable, is subject

to accounting procedures, and accrues as profits and dividends. The idea that rural economy lacks a surplus may also have been influenced by the demonstrably low level of consumption of peasant producers. This presumed relation between consumption levels and surpluses, if applied to the plantation sector, would lead to an obviously inadmissible conclusion, since the living standards of the labourers (estate coolies!) are not markedly different from those of peasants.

The traditional, non-market economies did, in fact, produce a considerable surplus, though its magnitude can only be conjectured. In the ancient riparian societies of the Indo-Gangetic plain, the Nile valley, and Mesopotamia, productivity was high even without the use of heavy or metal implements. The natural fertility of these lands, continually replenished by silt from the flood waters, led to crops that were far in excess of the peasants' domestic needs. It was the existence of a production surplus which furnished the basis for the growth of trade and the early manifestations of an urban culture. In Egypt the pharaohs could not consume all of this product, 'however lavish their banquets and extravagant the reserves buried in their tombs.... Quite a lot was redistributed to support a whole new population of non-farmers, from labourers to clerks, and some was used directly to pay for the imported raw materials'. (34) By force or custom, through taxes or tribute, the surplus was centralized, and used for infrastructure projects - such as irrigation and flood control schemes, which in monsoon lands were a prime requisite of stable agriculture. The surplus was also absorbed in warfare, conspicuous piety and ostentation - for palaces, temples, monuments and mausoleums. Another portion of the surplus was extravagantly consumed by a non-producing class of lay or ecclesiastical dignitaries and their retainers. The tertiary sector - personal services in particular - loomed large in the urban employment pattern. The upper class gathered around it a large body of attendants, including domestic servants, concubines, artists, musicians and singers. One of the Mogul emperors kept a seraglio of 5,000 women. (35) The Han emperors were served in varying capacities by more than 2,000 Manchu girls and women. (36) Each of the dogs brought from England as presents for one of the late Mogul emperors had four human attendants. (37) As Gideon Sjoberg said, the preindustrial city was unquestionably a 'node of consumption'.

I have shown that the distinction made between plantations and peasant production in terms of capacity to generate a surplus is unreal. Whether such a surplus is

unproductively employed or diverted outside the peasant
sector is another matter. The diversion of the rural surplus and the forms in which this occurred substantiate
further the existence of a surplus and its possible
extent. Sometimes a portion was skimmed off by taxation -
for example, in Sri Lanka a grain tax was imposed during
the nineteenth century, the proceeds of which were used to
finance an infrastructure for the plantation economy. Another portion of the surplus was taken as rent, interest
and trading profits by a village rentier class. (For
India as a whole K.N.Raj estimated rent and interest incomes in the rural economy as varying between 20 and 45
per cent of gross output. (38) In the Philippines during
1960-1 more than one fifth of the total rice crop was
taken by landlords. (39) There were several groups who
gathered the economic surplus of the village. A resident
landlord-cum-merchant bourgeoisie combined trafficking in
grain and other village produce with rice milling, money
lending and land transactions. With a monopoly over rural
credit, they were short-changing the peasants in their
commercial transactions - by keeping false accounts, using
short-weight measures, etc. In pre-communist China, 'the
landlords', wrote Professor Chen-Han-Seng, 'are often
quadrilateral beings. They are rent collectors, merchants, usurers, and administrative officers'. (40) There
was, second, a languishing aristocracy, whose more enterprising members gravitated to the towns, entrusting their
lands to intermediaries, but drawing income from the village. They lived on the village without living in it.
The situation of surplus transfers out of the plantation
sector is thus replicated within the country in a drain
from village to town. The third of the groups preying
upon the village economy was the professional ranks - the
village physicians, school teachers and petty officials.
They supplemented the income from their substantive employment with the rent from their paddy holdings.
    In the peasant sector there has also been a consider-
able volume of capital formation which existing concepts
and statistical indicators tend to understate. Grain production in monsoon regions required the construction,
maintenance and repair of hydraulic devices including
ditches, dams, dykes and water gates. These infrastructure investments, which in earlier times were based on the
gratuitous labour of the peasants, as well as the cost of
land clearing and of the houses of peasants, were made
over a long period and, though not reflected in company
balance sheets, may have been considerable. In the rice
economy of Burma, the clearing of several million acres of
swampy forest involved an enormous capital cost, financed

mainly by the chettiyar money lenders. What was admittedly lacking in the peasant economy was productivity-raising investments; and, as on the plantations, there was a stagnation in labour productivity. This failure to invest in directly productive assets has nothing to do with the prevailing level of savings or even the capacity for saving. Basically it involves the social relations in the village that precluded the growth of a rural bourgeoisie and a rural proletariat. While precapitalist production was not devoid of surpluses, what it lacked was a social mechanism in the form of an appropriate class structure for capitalizing the surplus on an expanding scale. To discuss the critical or key factors which militate against such a development would take us too far out.

The third reason why plantation enterprise has been regarded as a capitalist form of production is the large-scale nature of its operations. However, like exchange relations and production for export markets, large-scale production is not exclusive to capitalism. Certain projects, whatever the mode of production, required a conglomeration of labourers - as in land reclamation and in the construction of irrigation schemes and of roads and canals, where work is performed over an extended physical space. In preindustrial Europe there were yet other enterprises with hundreds of workers and capital outlays comparable with those of plantations, in copper, tine and coal mining, in the manufacture of paper, and alum, in gunpowder mills and cannon foundries, and in salt making, sugar refining and saltpetre works; by 1640 'large enterprises were the rule'. (41) Nef refers to a salt works which at the time of the English Civil War 'employed about 1,000 men', and had an 'original investment of many thousands of pounds'. In the eighteenth century even the charcoal furnace for producing cast iron required 'control over considerable resources', (42) and involved several different operations - digging ore, cutting and charking wood, the transport of materials, and smelting. (43) The medieval shipyards were 'large and costly establishments'. The naval arsenal at Chatham had over a thousand men, whose work was carefully assigned and regulated. Defoe observed that 'you see the whole Place as it were in the utmost Hurry, yet you shall see no Confusion, every Man knows his own Business'. (44) The Venetian arsenal is referred to by Ruggiero Romano (45) as a 'genuine industrial concentration'. It carried out several manufacturing processes, and had its own supplies of hemp and timber yards and gun foundries. In the period 1560-70 there was an estimated workforce of three to four thousand, comprising sailmakers, artillery-men, ships' carpenters and sawyers.

Outside Europe, irrigation works and the construction of palaces, temples and public monuments required the combined efforts of a mass of people. In ancient India, though the dominant unit of enterprise was the craftsman working at home, 'large-scale production for a wide market was not unknown'. (46) The sandstone quarries of the Mauryan period supplied material for the giant monolithic columns of buildings that were not dissimilar to the famed Egyptian and Chinese edifices. Large spinning and weaving workshops were established by the Mauryan state, as well as enterprises where weapons and armaments were produced by salaried craftsmen. In Sri Lanka, in the cinnamon enterprise from the second half of the eighteenth century, brigades of Sinhalese from the maritime provinces were dispatched to the Kandyan kingdom to peel and transport cinnamon. A brigade, comprising about a thousand, was divided into groups (ranchoo), each under a supervisor.

While large-scale undertakings existed long before the rise of capitalism, a distinction which Marx brought into clear focus was that between capitalist and precapitalist large-scale production. In precapitalist large-scale production, though the labourer 'strips off the fetters of his individuality', labour co-operation is in its elementary form, and 'division of labour and machinery play but a subordinate part'. (47) A conglomeration of labourers, and their mere proximity to each other, while improving labour efficiency would not basically change the labour process. Thus shipping, mining and the production of textiles 'as early as the Middle Ages' contained the 'rudiments of industrial capital', but the virtual absence of machinery imposed rigid limits upon the degree of labour exploitation and therefore upon the rate of surplus value. Though co-operation 'is a necessary concomitant of all production on a large scale', in its elementary form (48)

it does not, in itself, represent a fixed form characteristic of a particular epoch in the development of the capitalist mode of production. At the most it appears to do so, and that only approximately, in the handicraft-like beginnings of manufacture, and in that kind of agriculture on a large scale, which corresponds to the epoch of manufacture, mainly by the number of labourers simultaneously employed, and by the mass of the means of production concentrated for their use.

In capitalist large-scale production, the effects of a concentration of capital and of the amalgamation of individual production units are partly technical and partly economic and social. The use of machinery leads to a differentiation of activities, which in turn facilitates the

use of machinery. In the capitalist development of
Russian agriculture, as Lenin said, the small producer
'with his patriarchal and primitive methods' was driven
out. The differentiation of labour gives agriculture a
social character - ending the isolated existence of individual farms and production units. Production costs are
lowered, and there is a release of surplus rural labour,
leading generally to a flight of labour from the countryside. The rise in the organic composition of capital
causes a shift in the basis of exploitation from absolute
surplus value to relative surplus value, the latter being
based on the increased use of fixed capital in production.
It is then that the (49)
    separation of the producer from the means of production
    reflects an actual revolution in the mode of production
    itself. The isolated labourers are brought together in
    large workshops for the purpose of carrying out sepa-
    rate but interconnected activities;   the tool becomes
    a machine.
Technological change rules out irrevocably a relapse into
petty commodity production. 'The mode of production
itself no longer permits the dispersion of the instruments
of production associated with small property;   nor does it
permit the isolation of the labourer himself.' (50)
    Furthermore, in determining the scale of production in
agriculture, the size of landholdings is not always the
same as the size of enterprises;   nor does extensive
landed property - which also existed in feudal times - by
itself signify large-scale production. The land area of a
farm, both Lenin and Kautsky pointed out, was a superficial index of the scale of production. A large landholding can be extensively farmed, but with intensive
farming a smallholding becomes compatible with large-scale
production. In Europe, though the area of farms diminished, the increasing use of fertilizers, machinery and
higher grade non-manual employees - e.g. managers, overseers, bookkeepers and technicians - resulted in a scale
of cultivation which was not necessarily smaller than in
America. In Ireland, on the other hand, the scale of production was low despite large landed property. The change
from forestry and pastoral farming to tillage, and from
tillage to livestock farming causes a diminution in the
area of farms. But an increased intensiveness of farming
causes an increase in output both per unit of land and per
worker. That is to say, large landed property is not a
necessary condition of large-scale production.
    In the discussion so far, I have shown that the charac-
teristics of plantations which are brought forward as evidence of their capitalist nature were also prevalent in

precapitalist forms of enterprise and do not make a conclusive case for so characterizing them. I shall now go
further and consider the generic features of capitalism in
terms of which it would be possible to examine theoretically the conventional notion of plantations as a capitalist form of production. Capitalism, according to Marx,
the most perceptive elucidator of this concept, has two
main features. The first is a specific capital-labour relation based on wage labour; the second is the production
and accumulation of surplus value as the 'direct aim and
determining motive of production'. (51) The capital-
labour relation is personified in the capitalist and in
the worker - the two main agents in this mode of production. Capital is not purely a technical category, consisting of the physical means of production, but is essentially a relation between the capitalist and the
worker. The extra-economic coercion to which the labourer
was subjected earlier is replaced by a system which creates a labour supply via the market, without the need to
bind the labourer personally. Capital, as an instrument
of social control, also determines the employer's authority over the worker and hence the basis of the latter's
collaboration in the production process. The condition of
the labourer is one of dependence on the capitalist.
'Cheaper and more subservient labourers - ... a class to
whom the capitalist might dictate terms, instead of being
dictated to by them', is an attribute of wage workers
which Herman Merivale saw was lacking among the early
migrants to Australia. 'In ancient civilised countries
the labourer, though free, is by a law of Nature dependent
on capitalists; in colonies his dependence must be created by artificial means.' (52) In Marx's clear language,
'Capital is not a thing but a social relation between persons.' (53)
     The creation of a labour supply is not a once-for-all
process but a continuing one. Regardless of exogenous
factors, such as population growth or the impoverishment
of peasants due to natural disasters, capitalism has its
own mechanism for both creating and augmenting the labour
supply. This it does by the increasing use of fixed capital in production and a lowering of the amount of labour
per unit of capital. Without such a mechanism for repro-
ducing the capital-labour relation even an existing labour
supply might cease to be available. For instance, in the
regions of white settlement, labourers brought from Europe
'vanished from the labour market'. They became independent farmers, or artisans, working for themselves. (54)
'The great beauty of capitalist production consists in
this - that it not only constantly reproduces the wage-

worker as a worker, but reproduces always in proportion to
the accumulation of capital, a relative surplus-production
of wage-workers.' (55)

The basis of this increase in the labour supply is the
tendency to increase the productivity of labour. While
capitalism requires an appropriate structure of production
relations, involving wage labour and commodity production,
these production relations acquire a specifically capitalist character only by 'the development of the social productive power of labour'. (56) Capitalism requires free
labour not for its own sake, but as the basis for a more
complex form of labour co-operation, with an increasing
use of fixed capital in production. For instance, in
agriculture ecological risks may inhibit the use of fixed
capital and of wage labour - both of which involve the
producers in a fixed commitment. When the social and
physical conditions exist for the use of fixed capital in
production, accumulation and technical progress (coupled
with the social relations of production) acquire a self-
reinforcing quality and the two became mutually dependent.
As D.S.Landes wrote, 'The man who lived by the machine was
more likely to be interested in and save for mechanical
improvements than the merchant who relied on cheap cottage
labour.' (57)

Primitive accumulation or the 'pre-historic stage of
capital' (by which Marx referred to the expropriation of
direct producers) was essentially a process for the transformation of money wealth into capital. (58) A dispossession of the petty producers had occurred even earlier,
whether by legislative action or by their financial impoverishment through debt, usury and mortgage. In these
forms of production the subordination of labour to capital
was merely a 'prelude to the history of capital'. (59)

Both the ruin of rich landowners through usury and the
impoverishment of the small producers lead to the formation and concentration of large amounts of money-
capital. But to what extent this process does away
with the old mode of production, as happened in modern
Europe, and whether it puts the capitalist mode of production in its stead, depends entirely upon the stage
of historical development and the attendant circumstances. (60)

In forms of production dominated by merchants' and usurers' capital 'capital has not yet acquired the direct
control of the labour process'. There is only a 'formal
subjection of labour to capital', which fails to reproduce
the capital-wage labour relation. 'The predominance, in a
society, of this form of exploitation excludes the capitalist mode of production: to which mode, however, this

form may serve as a transition, as it did towards the
close of the Middle Ages.' (61)   In other instances, a
whole epoch of merchant capital might intervene and abort
the prospect of a capitalist transformation.

The emergence of industrial capital as a category in
its own right signified a change in the character of capital investment to which I have already referred.   There
was an increasing use of capital in the actual production
process, in contrast with investments in factory buildings, warehouses, workers' housing, improved transportation, etc.   These investments were mostly supportive to
the production process, enabling production to be carried
out on a large scale, or extending the radius of the
market, without necessarily raising productivity.   They
were more within the ambit of merchant capital.   Thus
Ricardo stated: (62)

Different occupations require very different proportions between the fixed and circulating capitals employed in them.   The capital of a merchant, for example, is altogether a circulating capital.   He has occasion for no machines or instruments of trade, unless
his shop or warehouses be considered as such.   Some
part of the capital of every master artificer or manufacturer must be fixed in the instruments of his trade.
Though the difference between merchant capital and industrial capital in terms of the relative importance of circulating and fixed capital was perceived by the classical
economists, (63) they nevertheless regarded merchant capital as a particular variety of industrial capital akin to
the different varieties of industrial capital as reflected
in different branches of production.   Marx made a critical
distinction between merchant capital and industrial capital and made use of this in explaining the development of
the capitalist mode of production.   In distinguishing between the two forms of industrial capital - fixed and circulating - he used a slightly different classification:
constant capital and variable capital, based not on the
mere fact that one is 'fixed' and the other 'circulates'
but on their productive roles or their respective contribution to the creation of value.   Labour creates value
while constant capital, i.e. raw material and machinery,
transfers existing values to the commodity.

Later economists abstracted the process of capitalist
production from its underlying system of social relations
which, as I sought to explain earlier, rests on the increasing dominance of fixed capital in production.   In
doing so they jettisoned even the distinction between different varieties of capital.   By concentrating merely on
the use of capital in production, they disregarded the

specific elements and peculiarities of capitalism as a
mode of production. They deserved Bukharin's taunt about
those who might even attribute the beginnings of capitalism to the savage's club. 'By "explaining" everything it
explains absolutely nothing. This is the "method" of
bourgeois historians and economists. They gloss over the
fundamental difference between the slave-holding system of
"antiquity", with its embryo of trade capital and artisan-
ship, and "modern capitalism"'. (64) Only recently, as
statistical data became available on capital formation in
Britain during the early phase of the Industrial Revolution, has there been a revival of attention to the shift
from circulating to fixed capital in the growth of capitalism. (65)

The new composition of capital investment signified a
change in the basis of exploitation and appropriation from
the sphere of exchange to the sphere of production. The
merchant producer who earlier dominated production had
resorted to fraud and extra-economic measures: 'outbar-
gaining and cheating'. The growing importance of fixed
capital corresponded to a functional separation between
merchant and industrial capital, which economists before
Marx had in their analysis thrown 'indiscriminately together', overlooking the characteristic peculiarities of
each. 'Nothing could be more absurd than to regard merchant's capital, whether in the shape of commercial or of
money-dealing capital, as a particular variety of industrial capital.' (66) Marx distinguished between the two
forms of capital, merchant and industrial, operating at
different levels, related differently to the productive
process, having different bases of exploitation, and personified in two different categories of capitalists. With
this distinction it was possible to get beyond the 'superficial phenomenon of exchange' and to probe the internal
structure of capitalism as a specific mode of production,
based on its capital-labour relations. 'The real science
of modern economy only begins when the theoretical analysis passes from the process of circulation to the process
of production.' (67)

The change in the composition of capital which underlay
the capitalist mode of production was preceded by a
greater use of capital, but predominantly in the form of
working capital - as in Britain during the sixteenth and
seventeenth centuries. Even in relatively capital intensive industries the vast bulk of the capital represented
stocks of raw material and goods awaiting sale. (68) For
example, in the tanneries, fixed capital consisting of
buildings and machinery was less than 3 per cent of the
total value of investments. In iron smelting, working

capital predominated - charcoal for the furnace accounted
for 70 per cent of all production costs. In textiles the
capital composition was similar. These industries with a
high ratio of working capital to fixed capital used up a
large volume of raw materials, and the conversion process
from raw materials to finished goods was either limited or
technologically simple. During this period, though the
factory system made 'remarkable headway', there was no
major change in the technique of production. (69)

In the transition to a modern growth trajectory, a decline in the relative importance of working capital was
due partly to its substitution by fixed capital investments. Improved transport and distribution facilities,
all-weather roads, central warehouses, vehicles, and the
relocation of industry, reduced the optimal level of
stocks of raw materials and finished goods in which working capital was tied up. Together with the speeding up of
production time and the quicker realization of proceeds,
this led to a displacement of working capital and the diversion of funds to fixed capital. Alongside a subordination of merchant capital to industrial capital, they
become differentiated from each other - with specialized
functions. While capital accumulation was itself nothing
new, the qualitative changes pertained to the structure of
investment. Fixed capital now sprang into prominence, and
a necessary adjunct to this was a 'revision of the concept
of risk'. (70)

Flexibility had been the hallmark of the older pattern
of investment in which the value of raw materials and
labour predominated. When demand slackened the entrepreneur could reduce output without being burdened by expenditure on overheads. The merits of this arrangement,
epitomized in the putting-out system, were, of course,
outweighed by the difficulty of expanding production as
demand increased. Its flexibility was a one-way street.
Nevertheless, the traditional merchant manufacturers could
readily withdraw their involvement before bankruptcy and
business liquidation smote them down. Hereafter the
entrepreneur was caught in a cage; he was 'the prisoner
of his investment'. (71) The increased use of fixed capital enabled output to expand without the rigidities inherent in the domestic system of production but it also
introduced a new framework of risks which spurred the
capitalist to continually intensify the production process, stepping up the rate of accumulation and leading to
a further concentration and centralization of capital.

In the rise of capitalism there was a second development, more crucial in its effects than changes in the
relative proportions of fixed and working capital. This

related to the content of fixed capital itself. As mentioned before, much of the fixed capital earlier was supportive to the actual production process or else it enlarged the distance over which goods could profitably be
carried; the former included, for example, factory buildings and the latter improved transport. Fixed capital of
these two types did not make investment intrinsically more
productive. The factory system in its early phase was
merely a regrouping of equipment which had been dispersed
among several producers. A change in the content of fixed
capital occurred when a rising volume of investment began
to be made on plant and machinery - 'the kind of capital
assets that offer continuing scope for technological improvement'. (72) Capital accumulation and technical
change went hand in hand with investments that are capital
deepening (i.e. which use more capital per unit of output)
rather than capital widening. Output expansion was no
longer based on a repetition of the previous scale and
level of technology but on improvements in productive
forces with a consequent increase in surplus value. Accumulation involved the setting apart by the capitalist of
a definite quantity of surplus labour for the progressive
expansion of the forces of production. Marx referred to
this as 'one of the civilising aspects of capital' compared with the preceding forms of slavery, serfdom, etc.
The costliness of the new types of equipment, linked with
their greater sophistication and enlarged minimum capacity, accelerated the concentration of ownership and the
division of society into contending classes. In Britain,
the 'modernizing' of the capital stock, compared with its
mere augmentation, began from about the 1830s.

    The new investment had a marked propensity to reduce
costs. Parallel with a reduction of labour in relation to
output, there was specialization of labour and of capital
investment. The production process was split up into
several independent though related processes - which furnished both internal and external economies. Whereas
large-scale production was not altogether absent in precapitalist economies, capitalism created a qualitative
difference between small-scale and large-scale production.
Specifically associated with these changes was a shift in
the organic composition of capital - i.e. the ratio of
constant capital to variable capital or that of machinery
and raw materials to the value of wage payments. In both
manufacturing industry and agriculture, expansion took the
form of increases in the productivity of labour. The production process, while losing the flexibility that resulted from a minimal use of fixed capital assets, acquired an internal dynamic.

The cost reductions and lower prices, apart from their
direct effects on demand, enabled producers to create
demand or appropriate existing markets. By improving real
wages, especially in the production of mass consumption
goods, the price reductions had also a feed-back effect on
demand. As Dobb asserted, capital accumulation and technical progress were the heart of these changes - whether
or not they were also exogenously derived - in the sphere
of population and markets. (73) Lenin explained that
market expansion was partly determined by 'the degree to
which the social division of labour becomes ramified', and
by this he expressed concisely the employment-creating
potential of balanced growth which R.Nurkse propounded in
the 1950s. An 'overall enlargement of the market' results
from 'a more or less synchronized application of capital
to a wide range of different industries', to 'a number of
complementary projects [which] become each others' customers'. (74) The primacy of production relations over
exchange was also expressed by Professor H.Heaton: 'The
story is not one of insistent demand compelling changes in
production methods; it is rather one in which changed
methods and lower production costs resulted in a commodity
which created a new big demand.' (75) The Communist Mani-
festo recognized these potentialities of capitalism: 'The
cheap prices of its commodities are the heavy artillery
with which it batters down all Chinese walls.' (76) At
the same time, 'production for production's sake', with an
inadequate release of purchasing power, was a continual
check to the process of accumulation, productivity growth
and market expansion. 'The more the productive power develops, the more it enters into contradictions with the
narrow basis on which the relations of consumption rest.'
(77)

These changes in the character of capital investment,
while giving it a self-expansionary power, had also an
enduring and pervasive quality, in contrast with the innumerable false starts in development based on a mere expansion in output and incomes. Landes spells it out in
some detail. Until the industrial revolution (78)

the advances of commerce and industry, however grati-
fying and impressive, were essentially superficial;
more goods, prosperous cities, merchant nabobs. The
world had seen other periods of industrial prosperity -
in mediaeval Italy and Flanders, for example - and had
seen the wave of economic advance recede in each case;
in the absence of qualitative changes, of improvements
in productivity, there can be no guarantee that quantitative gains would be consolidated.

In the Orient, one such surge of commercial activity was

the rise of the salt trade of Yang-Chou in the eighteenth
century. Much of the wealth so accumulated was lost in an
orgy of conspicuous extravagance, for which the Liang-huai
merchants became known in their time as the 'salt fools'.
(79) The technological and economic advances of the Industrial Revolution, on the other hand, were cumulative
and self-sustaining. The countries which underwent this
revolution began to differ profoundly in their development
of production forces from those which did not. The productivity and income gap between these two groups of countries can hardly be expressed in terms of an unevenness of
development; it has assumed awesome proportions.

The comprehensive nature of these changes, permeating
all branches of the economy, is now generally recognized.
Agriculture itself was transformed into a rationalized,
capital-based operation akin to manufacturing industry in
some ways. The production process became based on 'the
application of technology and of mechanical and electrical
power to supplement human effort'. (80) As Harry Johnson
wrote, industrialization 'is an economy wide phenomenon,
applying to agriculture and the service trades as well as
to manufacture; the essence of it is not the production
of products typically considered as "industrial" but the
rational approach to the production process itself that it
embodies'. (81) What another writer has called the 'industrialization of agriculture' (82) was referred to by
Marx a century earlier: 'Agriculture to an increasing
extent becomes just a branch of industry and is completely
dominated by capital', unlike the preindustrial economy
where 'manufacturing, its structure and the forms of property corresponding thereto [and] even capital ... [which]
consisted of traditional tools, etc. ... retained a specifically agrarian character'. (83) A concomitant of such
a change has been a narrowing of the gap in the productivity of labour between industry and agriculture, between
the town and the countryside, and consequently in income,
consumption patterns and even the social outlook of corresponding classes of people. Though even in the developed
economies the countryside is still not conterminous with
the city economically and demographically, 'rurbaniza-
tion', as this process has been called, signifies an admixture of rural habits with the basic characteristics of
the urban world and culture. (84)

The 'transformation of technique', with a 'development
of the productive forces of social labour', was an aspect
of the development of capitalism in Russian agriculture
which Lenin considered important. (85) The key element in
the transformation from a patriarchal to a capitalist
agriculture, beginning from about the 1890s, was the use

of machinery. There was fundamentally an increasing use
of fixed capital relative to variable capital, which
raised the productivity of labour and shortened working
time and reduced costs. Along with the use of wage
labour, which constitutes a fixed financial commitment,
this composition of investment gave a new dimension to the
problem of risk associated with the capitalist entrepreneur. The varying pace of these changes in different
crops related partly to ecological risks and partly to the
pattern of labour inputs during the crop cycle. The developments were more pronounced in those branches of production which required a considerable degree of processing
or working up of products, e.g. beet sugar and potatoes
and their conversion into treacle and starch, and in flax
growing. The processing of crops led to a two-way technical interrelationship between agriculture and industry.
There was in this process an interlocking of changes which
spread out like ripples on a lake. (86)

> The keeping of dairy cattle calls forth the cultivation
> of grasses, the change-over from the three-field system
> to multi-field systems, etc. The waste products of
> cheese making go to fatten cattle for the market. Not
> only milk processing, but the whole of agriculture
> becomes a commercial enterprise.

As stated earlier, what is important in the capitalist
mode of production, whether in manufacturing industry or
in agriculture, is not capital investment as such but the
character of the investment, involving basically the distinction between merchant capital and production capital;
there is both an increasing use of fixed capital in production and a change in the content of fixed capital
itself - from investments which are merely or mainly supportive of the actual production process to investment on
plant and machinery which raises the productivity of
labour. As would be apparent by now, the notion that the
plantations constitute a capitalist sector derives basically from a failure to distinguish between forms of capital investment. While the total quantum of investment in
plantations and in peasant agriculture, including the
capital value of irrigation facilities, rice mills and the
dwellings of the peasants, would be comparable in magnitude, it is not the total quantum of investment that is
important but its composition. On the latter basis the
plantations as a system of production would indeed differ
very little from traditional agriculture. While the plantations required a considerable volume of investment in
the aggregate, much of it was working capital - a point
repeatedly made in my analysis.

The dominance of working capital - typical of precapi-

talist forms of production - has been a feature of investment in colonial economies, though recognition of this, it
would seem, has been only in respect of their 'opening up'
phase. Thus (Myint): 'With the possible exception of
mining the bulk of the foreign investment made during the
opening-up process took the form of circulating capital
rather than that of fixed capital.' (87) Myint would
appear to argue that in the subsequent phase of investment
fixed capital became more important. 'In the mining and
plantation sector ... the major part of capital investment
took the form of expensive durable equipment and fixed
capital. In contrast, apart from land, peasant production
required very little durable capital equipment.' (88)
Myint's assertion may apply, but only to the mining
sector; in the rest of the colonial economy, including
the plantations, fixed capital was throughout insignificant, not merely during the opening up phase. Higgins and
Eckaus, in their concept of technological dualism, referred to sharp differences in factor proportions, i.e. the
capital-labour ratio, between plantations and peasant
agriculture; and he classified plantations, along with
mining, oil refineries and transportation, as the modern
'sector'. (89) But the fact is that plantation technology
remained stagnant and highly labour intensive. The expansion in output was due at first to acreage increases, latterly to increases in crop yields; and in either case, a
large portion of total investment was in the form of wage
payments.

Whereas in the capitalist mode of production the increasing use of fixed capital, by reducing the employer's
dependence on the domestic producer, ensured a better control over supply, the bigger risks which fixed capital entailed gave an entirely new complexion to the production
process; besides encouraging a more businesslike attitude
to the production process, because of the higher proportion of fixed costs, they constrained the capitalist to
embark upon a continual cycle of accumulation and reinvestment. In the plantations, however, the relative insignificance of fixed capital reduced the financial risk
of investment, minimizing losses through interruptions to
output due to vagaries of the weather (90) or fluctuations
in demand. Though the reliance on working capital for
financing wage payments was usually larger, such expenditure varied with the level of output. Flexibility was the
great virtue of such enterprises; they were less affected
by variations in output, total costs being regulated according to the scale of productive operations. The stability of output required by larger fixed investments,
which cannot withstand fluctuations in demand, may even be

illustrated by the contrasting pattern of Chinese and
European tin mining in Malaysia. European enterprises
which had a larger proportion of fixed capital invested in
expensive machinery and equipment sought to ensure stable
and continuous production by acquiring large areas of
mining land. The Chinese who used labour intensive
methods could cope successfully with fluctuations in
demand even on smaller extents of mining land. (91)

The fixed capital of plantations, mostly in the form of
land, estate roads, and housing, was external to the
actual production process. Like the price of land which,
Marx explained, is 'merely capitalised rent', and the
price of a slave which is the 'capitalised surplus-value
to be wrung out of the slave', investments of this kind
have 'absolutely nothing to do with capital invested in
agriculture itself'. (92) They do not 'enter as capital
into the price of production of the product ... [as do]
machines and raw materials'. (93) As in the case of the
slaveholders to whom Marx referred, the investment on
estate housing and on recruiting labour is capital which
the planter 'has parted with, it is a deduction from the
capital which he has available for actual production. It
has ceased to exist for him just as capital investment in
purchasing land has ceased to exist for agriculture'. (94)
In plantations, the use of machinery and other aids to
production was confined to the processing of crops prior
to export. The value of such investment was minimal, both
in absolute terms and as a proportion of total costs. (95)
Furthermore, even the investment in processing equipment
and machinery was capital widening, not capital deepening.
More capital was not used per unit of output, but the
amount of capital used grew pari passu with the increase
in the output, i.e. in constant technical conditions.
Though the total installed capacity of tea and rubber
machinery conformed to a volume of output that was considerably greater than that on a smallholding, this
machinery (with the exception of that adopted recently in
the manufacture of block rubber) was of varying sizes and
made up of divisible units. In tea production, the kind
of technical change which took place resulted in improvements in the quality of manufactured tea rather than in
lower production costs. The improvements on the agricultural side have been primarily land saving, based on improved planting materials, control of plant pests and diseases, and intensive fertilization. The consequent increase in yield per acre causes a less than proportionate
decline in costs per unit of output - since the ratio of
variable to fixed costs is relatively unchanged and harvesting and certain other expenses increase directly with

total output. Wages remain by·far the largest item of
plantation costs, and the improved labour productivity due
to increased yield per acre could barely keep pace with
the secular rise in wage rates. This relationship between
changes in cost per acre and in the cost per unit of
output is fundamental to plantation technology.

As output expanded, a relative decline in the volume of
fixed capital was accompanied by àn increase in the total
capital employed, since working capital grew in almost the
same proportion as the expansion in output. The working
capital needed for achieving an increased output consisted
of both labour and agro-inputs. The virtual absence of
increasing returns to scale is due not merely to a low
ratio of fixed capital to working capital but also to the
nature of the fixed capital itself, which is mostly of a
non-labour saving type. It comprised, besides land,
estate roads, housing and amenities for a resident, enclave labour force, factory buildings and processing
equipment. The investment in migrant labour, including a
fixed capital component in the form of housing, was an
alternative to reorganizing production techniques. Whereas capitalism in agriculture reduced labour requirements
as output expanded (thereby influencing the urban-rural
ratio), on the plantations a permanent surplus of labour
arose only in recent years when alongside a natural increase in the resident labour population the plantation
acreage either ceased to expand or, as in Malaysia, actually declined.

Cost-reducing investments, involving fixed capital,
were almost confined to the infrastructure facilities,
financed by the state. These investments, especially
transport, were merely a prerequisite for the development
of a plantation economy; they did not lower the 'farm-
gate' price of export produce; they were also a once-for-
all type of investment. Moreover, export agriculture was
not in all instances dependent on a costly transportation
network. In the Gold Coast· and Nigeria, natural waterways
led to a large export trade in palm oil even without the
railway or motor transport. (96) Rivers such as the
Tanosu and the Ankobra gave access to the forest, and in
other areas human porterage and barrel rollers were used
to convey produce to the coast. The Ogan river and the
creeks of the Niger delta opened up the 'vast oil palm
regions of the east'. In Burma, the numerous waterways
that link the coast and the main paddy-growing tracts in
lower Burma have been used for conveying paddy to the
mills in Rangoon and other parts. The railway is the exclusive means of transport only in the Mid-Zone and in
Upper Burma. (97)

In the plantations reinvestment was essentially in
labour and land, on the same lines as the original investment. Thus, as Genovese said of the cotton plantations in
the American South, 'economic progress is quantitative' in
contrast to the qualitative nature of progress in capitalism. (98) The plantation system's production relations
and techniques caused the market for its products to
expand geographically (horizontally) but not in depth.
Apart from a sharp fall in the cost of ocean transport in
the second half of the nineteenth century, this expansion
in the market was exogenously derived from population
growth or an increase in income abroad; it did not reflect nor did it impart any real dynamism to the productive process. Expansion was achieved by enlarging the
total resources employed in production. The plantation
system had no power to create its own markets by raising
productivity per unit of investment, and lowering costs
and prices. Technological stagnation has also made the
plantation system vulnerable to economic progress in industrialized countries, leading to inorganic substitutes -
as, for example, in indigo, natural rubber, vegetable
oils, jute and cotton. On the supply side, the inflexibility of costs means a narrowing of profit margins when
a cheap labour supply runs out, or when statutory minimum
wages are fixed to conform with standards in the economy
as a whole. In Malaysia, while the value of output per
worker on the rubber plantations increased between 1959
and 1970 by 23 per cent, at a much faster rate than in the
smallholding sector, plantation wages increased by almost
40 per cent.
     The low organic composition of capital in plantations
limited its surplus-generating capacity. The plantations
produce a relatively large mass of surplus but only by
employing a large labour force at a small surplus value
per head. The low rate of surplus value nevertheless is
linked with a high rate of profit, i.e. the mass of surplus value related to the total investment - both constant
and variable capital. In other words, in plantations the
mass of surplus value, while being low in terms of the
variable capital, i.e. wage payments, is high in terms of
the capital invested; the former expresses the rate of
surplus value and the latter the rate of profit. (99) The
high rate of profit on plantation investment is also due
to the quick turnover of capital comprising mainly working
capital; and in this respect plantation investment resembles merchant capital and is far removed from industrial capital.
     The low organic composition of capital on plantations
also retards capital concentration - a process that is

closely linked with the capitalization of surplus value,
increases in the productivity of labour, and the falling
rate of profit. (100)

> Essentially, the capitalist process of production is
> simultaneously a process of accumulation.... Accumula-
> tion itself, however, and the concentration of capital
> that goes with it, is a material means of increasing
> productiveness ... applying methods which yield rela-
> tive surplus-value (introduction and improvement of
> machinery).

In plantation investment there was merely a centralization
of ownership without an enlargement in the operational
unit of production - the only exception to this was sugar
cane. Generally there was a fragmentation of plantation
property, with several scattered estates under single
ownership. The noncapitalization of the surplus was
linked with the absence of technical progress and of
changes in the technical composition of capital, accompanied by qualitative changes in the capital stock and a
rising productivity of labour. The possibility that the
plantation surplus was capitalized somewhere else, outside
the plantations, is not pertinent to this issue. If, as
Alavi explained, the colonial mode of production was capitalist since a good part of its surplus was capitalized in
the metropolis, by analogy every small peasant economy is
capitalist because some of its surplus may be invested in
trade and in urban undertakings of a capitalist nature.

The presumption about a high surplus generating capacity, on the basis of which plantations are regarded as an
'advanced' or 'developed' sector, fails to distinguish the
mass of surplus value from the rate of surplus value and
the overriding significance of the latter in the process
of accumulation and growth. (101) While the rate of
profit, as the amount of the profit divided by the total
volume of capital (both constant and variable), may be
higher in an underdeveloped country than in a developed
one, on account of the larger volume of variable capital
associated with a smaller rate of surplus value, the rate
of dividends is even higher because of the fact that it
relates the given mass of profits (less certain deductions
for taxes, reserve funds, etc.) to only one component of
the total capital of the enterprise, viz. the equity capital of shareholders; such capital, being more or less
limited to the financing of the fixed assets, represents
a small capital base. Though the relevant mass of profits
which is used for dividend payments is less than the gross
profit, the capital base to which it is related is usually
even smaller.

The small volume of equity capital invested by the

shareholders limits the size of the fortunes which they
could make. Despite a high rate of profit/dividends, a
plantation on the basis of its prevailing technology and
capital composition cannot also withstand an appreciable
wage increase, since even a small increase in the wage
rate applicable to a large number of workers would eat
heavily into the volume of profit. The volume of profit
is low in relation to the size of the labour force which
produces it, a given amount of constant capital being 'set
in motion' by a large number of labourers. That is to
say, low wages are not fundamentally a distributional
problem. Whereas a given percentage of wages if transferred to profits would add considerably to the profits component, a large transfer from profits to wages would leave
the volume of wage payments, and still more the wage per
worker, practically unaffected. The low labour productivity on a plantation, while being a constraint on wage
increases, is compatible with a high rate of return on
capital. Arghiri Emmanuel, in attempting to explain unequal exchange between the developed and the underdeveloped
countries, in terms of comparable levels of productivity
but divergent wage levels, was cautious enough not to
speak categorically of high productivity in the export
sector of underdeveloped countries. Appropriately he
referred only to sugar cane. (102) Samir Amin, less perceptively, lamented, 'Unfortunately, Emmanuel does not
make enough of this fact' that 'exports from the periphery
... come from ultramodern sectors where productivity is
high.' (103)

A concept of plantations which conforms with the foregoing discussion was given by Hacker: (104)

The plantation system flourishes in those regions where
land is relatively cheap and plentiful, where extensive
rather than intensive operations can be carried on, and
where a permanent labour force can be called or retained. Its leading hallmarks are the production of
staples for a market and the *investment of capital not
so much in land and the improvement of its techniques
as in the maintenance of its labour force*. Hence,
plantations grow tobacco or cotton or rubber or tea;
and they utilise an unfree labour force, whether its
specific characteristic is indenture or slavery or
peonage or sharecropping [or so-called 'resident'].

The low ratio of fixed capital to working capital on plantations, and the capital-widening character of the fixed
capital, was the very antithesis of the capitalist mode of
production. Capital investment of the kind referred to
was either a substitute for a more intensive use of capital or was merely a prerequisite of production, enabling

production to take place in the first instance without
enhancing the productivity of labour. I will now cite one
of Marx's rare comments on plantations, chiding those who
'discover a capitalist mode of production in every monetary economy' and therefore even in the agricultural
economies of classical antiquity. He said that a formal
analogy these agricultural economies had with the capitalist mode of production was 'completely illusory'; their
'similarity to a plantation economy is greater than to a
form corresponding to the really capitalist mode of exploitation'. (105) For the emergence of capitalism in
agriculture, the precapitalist mode of production must
'extricate itself from the mere subordination to capital,
and [it does so] as soon as agricultural improvement and
the reduction of production costs [take place]'. (106) It
was this lack of any improvement in production techniques
and of a consequent reduction of costs which depressed the
level of dynamism of the plantation-based export economy,
as H.J.Habakkuk observed: (107)

> International trade as an engine of growth did not
> generate enough power to stimulate a cumulative expan-
> sion.... Why did these [underdeveloped] economies fail
> to respond to the stimulus of foreign demand? ... I am
> inclined to [attribute it to] ... the technological
> characteristics of the production functions of the com-
> modities which these areas produce for export.

I argued that the plantations did not conform to a
capitalist mode of production - in their system of production relations and their technological level, in their
composition of capital or in their surplus generating
capacity. The system of labour recruitment, retention and
utilization had an institutionalized apparatus of extra-
economic coercion which obstructed labour mobility and
labour's organizational cohesiveness. But even free wage
labour does not of itself mean the arrival of capitalism,
though it is a necessary condition. Though in agriculture
capitalist development is a more complex process than in
manufacturing industry, the decisive changes in both are
those that proceed from capitalist relations of production; they comprise wage labour together with a shift in
the composition of investment. The dominant strands in
the texture of capitalist agriculture were connected with
what Marx called the 'industrialization of agriculture'.
He clearly differentiated the 'specifically agrarian
character' of equipment and tools in precapitalist forms
of agriculture with that under capitalism. Where a branch
of production comes increasingly under the domination of
capital, a point is ultimately reached when the various
changes react on each other to give the capitalist mode

of production a distinctive quality, causing productivity
levels and income to assume a kind of 'runaway equilibrium'.

The commercialization of the colonial economy consequent on its involvement in international exchange is
presumed to have marked a departure from the traditional
system, transforming it into a capitalist mode of production. This is a line which A.G.Frank, its popular expo-
nent, takes along with other non-Marxist writers (Lewis,
Myint, Myrdal, Geertz et al.). Frank's conceptual scheme
appears to differ from that of the others, but in the
characterization of the colonial economy they are all on
common ground. While they reserve the sphere of operations of capitalism to the export sector, Frank rejects
'dualism' and regards the whole of the colonial economy as
capitalist, with the proviso that it was an 'underdeveloped' capitalism. Those who regard the colonial mode
of production as capitalist, because of its commercial
nexus with the metropolis, locate the capitalist mode of
production in the sphere of exchange relations rather than
in production. But commodity production, though it involves wage labour and the realization of the surplus on
the market, does not of itself constitute the capitalist
mode. As Takahashi said, 'The question to ask as to a
given social situation is not whether commodities and
money are present, but rather how these commodities are
produced.' (108) Exchange relations and surplus generation, on the basis of which the colonial mode of production is claimed to be capitalist, were but a continuation
on a bigger scale and perhaps at a faster tempo of tendencies already prevalent at the time of the colonial impact.
The trading of colonial produce in the world market and
surplus appropriation by the metropolis, under whose aegis
the colonial economy developed, did not create a capitalist mode of production notwithstanding any proviso that
what came about was a deformed capitalism. George Novack
explained: (109)

> The rule that the same causes [in this instance capi-
> talism in the metropolis] produce the same effects is
> not an unconditional and all-embracing one.... The
> same basic cause can lead to very different and even
> opposite results [when the historically produced con-
> ditions are different for each country and constantly
> changing and interchanging with one another].

The aborted economic development of the periphery
cannot properly be expressed, far less explained, by
calling the colonial mode of production a 'dependent capitalism'. The nature of this dependency has not been elaborated beyond saying that the colonies were a hinterland,

appendage, or backyard of the industrial economies;   for
example, Egypt was 'a cotton farm of Lancashire' and Sri
Lanka 'Lipton's tea garden'.   The economy of New Zealand
and, until recently, that of Australia, though overwhelmingly based on exports of food and agricultural products to the Western world had, on the other hand, developed a mode of production comparable with that in the
economies from which they initially drew their capital and
on whose markets they were 'dependent'. (110)   In the
countries of the periphery, unlike the regions of new
settlement, international exchange led merely to a 'restructuring' of their economies, (111) not to the reproduction of the same mode of production as in the centre.
The difference in the productive systems between the
centre and the periphery was so profound, in their level
of dynamism and in their productive relations, that they
could be regarded only as different production modes - not
variants of the same mode as the terms 'dependent', 'backward' or 'peripheral' capitalism would suggest.

While the concept of dependency has not been clearly
expounded, except to say that it connotes some incapacity,
a cognate idea is that of 'deformed' capitalism. The de-
formity apparently lay, according to Alavi, (112) in the
appropriation of economic surplus by a metropolitan bourgeoisie for investment in the metropolis and not in the
colony.   In a somewhat different sense, Che Guvera meant
by deformation a pronounced disproportionality in the
growth of different sectors or branches of production,
resulting in a 'monstrously distorted economy'. (113)
Surplus extraction, with its appealing visual effect,
underlies most models of underdevelopment which have
metropolis-colony relations as their framework. According
to Amin, (114) 'primitive accumulation' is proceeding in
the periphery of the world economy. But the capital so
accumulated is transferred to the metropolis by various
mechanisms of unequal exchange. In Frank's phraseology,
the 'thesis of underdevelopment' is the 'expropriation by
a few metropolises of the economic surplus generated by
several satellite capitalisms and its utilization by the
metropolitan for their own development'. (115)   Lacking
access to their own surplus, the satellites remain underdeveloped.

Underdevelopment as seen by us is essentially a system
whose capacity to both generate and absorb surpluses is
limited at every level and sector of the economy including
the export sector where the surplus mainly originates.   It
would also be misleading to imply, as by Frank et al.,
that the colonial surplus was appropriated by the metropolitan bourgeoisie, indiscriminately and without re-

straint. The growth of the plantation and mining economy
was based on a recurring ploughback of current profits.
In other words, the surplus currently appropriated by the
metropolis arose out of earlier investments. What a model
of underdevelopment must identify and explain is the cut-
off point in the chain of reinvestments and, furthermore,
how the particular mode of generating surpluses constrained the surplus generating capacity. In the plantations,
certainly, investment was of a capital widening form resulting in technological stagnation and hence in sharp
limits to surplus generation. The question why the metropolitan bourgeoisie who owned and managed the export
sector reinvested the surplus in one way rather than the
other has been explained in the chapter dealing with the
technology of plantation production. Contrary to the
dualistic model and also to Frank's contention, the export
sector was not transformed into a capitalist sector.

The limitation on the economy's surplus-generating
capacity cannot be explained by the loss of surpluses as
such. While a large portion of the surplus is taken by
the metropolis, the remainder (not insignificant in relation to the existing stock of capital) is unproductively
consumed by landlords, merchants and usurers. Thus, even
if the whole of the surplus had been retained locally one
cannot presume that any more of it would have been productively employed. The unproductive use of the surplus, or
else its investment in the metropolis - which is a misdirection from the standpoint of the surplus generating
country - is due to a complex combination of forces.
These forces which militate against an alternative use of
the surplus were, no doubt, conditioned by the metropolis-
colony relationship. In the post-colonial phase, the
former metropolis may continue to appropriate surpluses
almost by invitation. (116) Surplus appropriation is not
the cause of underdevelopment, any more than feudalism, as
a socio-economic system, was due to the presence of the
feudal lord and the robber baron. The stability of a
socio-economic system over long periods is not due merely
to its controlling agents but also to its internal coherence and the absence of major tensions and conflicts.
Furthermore, the unproductive use of the surplus, or its
misdirection, was not specific to the colonial mode of
production but was a feature of precapitalist societies
and those in which merchant capital remained dominant. In
the colonies, the effects of imperialism were to develop
and strengthen the role of merchant capital and to stifle
its transformation into industrial capital. The factors
impeding this transformation may well provide a more
fruitful framework of analysis than an attempted classi-

fication of capitalism into such varieties as 'deformed'
or 'backward' or 'dependent'.

The particular pattern of surplus utilization in the
underdeveloped economy stemmed from the dominance of merchant capital, both in the export sector and in the
peasant sector. In the export sector, where foreign merchant capital was firmly entrenched, the generation and
disposition of the economic surplus was in the hands of
managing agency houses, import-export firms, brokers,
bankers, shipowners and so on. The strength of merchant
capital, vis-à-vis a potential colonial industrial class,
was drawn partly from its international ramifications and
partly from its role as the agent of an established capitalist mode of production in the metropolis. Thus merchant capital, suitably modified in the metropolitan
interests, became not a disintegrative but a binding element of the essentially precapitalist economy. Merchant
capital instead of being merely a transitional phase retained its control, stifling a movement in the direction
of industrial capital. The historical distinction between
merchant capital and industrial capital and the tendency
of merchant capital to conserve the precapitalist mode of
production was comprehensively stated by Dobb: (117)
    If we are speaking of capitalism as a specific mode of
    production, then it follows that we cannot date the
    dawn of this system from the first signs of the appear-
    ance of large-scale trading and of a merchant class....
    The appearance of a purely trading class will have of
    itself no revolutionary significance. Since its for-
    tunes will tend to be bound up with the existing mode
    of production, it is more likely to be under an induce-
    ment to preserve that mode of production than to trans-
    form it. It is likely to struggle to 'muscle in' upon
    an existing form of appropriating surplus labour; but
    it is unlikely to try to change this form.
Capitalism as a world phenomenon expressed itself in
the type of participation of the different national entities in the world economy. While the developed economies
substantially overcame economic unevenness within the
national economy (between the town and countryside, between the different branches of production, e.g. agriculture and industry, and within the industrial sector
itself), economic unevenness internationally was intensified. The underdeveloped economies whose mode of production was essentially precapitalist were drawn into the
world economy without their mode of production being
transformed into a capitalist mode. In this process of
incorporation a few countries which had already achieved
a perceivable degree of industrial advance were 'deindus-

trialized' in the interests of the metropolis;   India was
converted from an exporter of textiles into a market for
Lancashire goods. The 'restructuring' of their economy
and society entailed by this process, the resulting orientation towards the metropolis, and the mechanisms of
metropolitan control were discussed in earlier chapters.
An important aspect of the metropolitan orientation was
the vertical division of the world economy into self-sufficient compartments, as spheres of influence of the various metropolitan powers. A division of labour emerged
within each of the empires rather than in the world economy as a whole. The allocation of resources was optimal
within each compartment, but such optimality was only from
the standpoint of each metropolis. While the metropolises
could engage in trade and economic relations among themselves, the colonies lacked unfettered access to the world
economy. As Ingrid Palmer wrote, (118)

> if the boundaries of the empires were altered, or if
> the empires were to exchange European 'mother econo-
> mies', the existing allocation of resources in the
> colonies and indeed in the 'mother economies' too would
> no longer be considered optimal according to the above-
> mentioned goal.

Trotsky described this restructuring, which was not
tantamount to a dissolution of the old mode of production
nor even a transition towards a capitalist mode, as 'not
... a simple reproduction of development of advanced countries, England or France with a delay of one, two or three
centuries ... but an entirely new "combined" social formation ... creating peculiar relations of classes'. (119) A
similar assertion was made by J.C.F.Fei and G.Ranis: 'In
general, colonialism can be said to have intervened and
thus prevented the occurrence of a parallel transition [as
in Western Europe] to industrial capitalism.' (120) Capitalism in the metropolis extended its sway overseas, har-
nessing for its own use precapitalist formations and relations. It implanted African slavery in the New World,
making the slave trade a branch of capitalist commerce and
slave labour the basis of commodity production. The same
system, with further modifications, was later adopted as
indentured labour for plantation agriculture in Asia. The
resulting mode was a fusion of commodity production for a
long-distance market with precapitalist technology and a
semi-free labour force.
    In the restructuring of the colonial economy to meet
the demands of the export sector, there came into being
certain specific features which removed the prospects of
a possible transformation of its production process. The
incorporation of the economy in the metropolis, through

the growth of export production, did not require a capitalist transformation of either the export sector or the peasant sector of these economies. The experience of the colonial economies was quite different in this respect from that of some regions of Europe, where the first step towards capitalist development caused a short-lived relapse into feudalism which only hastened its collapse. What Kosminsky called a 'general offensive against the peasantry', (121) and Ashton 'a tightening of lordly exploitation', (122) provoked a crisis through a flight of serfs from the land and the further growth of towns, trade and industry. In the peasant sector of the colonial economies, commercialization based on usury and petty trading capital strengthened merchant capital and parasitic landlordism. As Barrington Moore said in regard to India, these changes (123)

> more significantly still ... formed the basis of a
> political and economic system in which the foreigner,
> the landlord and the moneylender [who] took the eco-
> nomic surplus away from the peasantry, failed to invest
> it in economic growth and thus ruled out the possibili-
> ty of repeating Japan's way of entering the modern era.

This hybrid formation (occupying a twilight zone between feudalism and capitalism) derived its viability partly from the high rate of profit which was possible from a production technology which combined relatively little fixed capital with a large mass of semi-free labour pressed down to an almost subsistence standard. Thus Marx observed: 'Capitals invested in colonies, etc. ... may yield higher rates of profit for the simple reason that the rate of profit is higher there due to backward development [i.e. the low organic composition of capital].' He also gave the added reason that 'slaves, coolies, etc. permit a better exploitation'. (124) They were, to use an expression of Bukharin, 'the little peoples of the colonies'. Like the silver and sugar of the New World, indigo, coffee, tea, rubber, tin and palm oil and other tropical products were not carried to Europe without the taint of blood. 'It is in the colonies that all the blood and the filth, all the horror and the shame of capitalism, all the cynicism, greed and bestiality of modern democracy are concentrated.' (125) The plantation system, while keeping the economy backward, could market its products in the high-income metropolitan regions. The colonial export economy, based on a realization on the world market of the products of a precapitalist technology, conformed to the role of the colonies as peripheral units of a world economy, dominated by capitalism at the centre; this export economy was in no sense a resolution of the internal contradictions in the precapitalist economy.

Although in Britain capitalism was to a large extent
self-induced, growing out of the contradictions of the
feudal society, the bourgeois transformations which occurred later needed the state or, as in France, revolution as
their midwife. The rise of capitalism was inexorably
linked with the nation state and its exercise of political
and diplomatic, as well as military, power on behalf of
the national bourgeoisie. State sponsorship of a belated
capitalism was greatest in Japan, where it exercised a
massive initiative in industrialization. But for this
intervention Japan's destiny would have been no different
from that of most of the underdeveloped nations of today;
she would have been 'tied into the world capitalist
system, but with an extremely underdeveloped internal
capitalism'. (126) In the settler colonies, which developed more viable production structures than the nonsettler colonies, this advancement was contingent upon the
partial political sovereignty which they exercised. Rhodesia is the classic case where, even with a metropolis
ethnically akin to the settler bourgeoisie, the continu-
ance of the colonial relationship showed itself as a
fetter on further capitalist development. Hence the phenomenon of Ian Smith and the UDI. On the contrary, in the
'semi-colonies' - e.g. Persia, Thailand, Egypt (from
1922), China (till 1949) - there was also a political dimension to the non-emergence of the capitalist mode of
production. The independence of such countries was merely
juridical. The intrigues of rival European powers maintained effete local governments and dynasties, dependent
on these powers for advice, subsidies and arms. This was
the era of client states. China's semi-colonial status
arose from its control by several countries instead of by
a single country (through the unique device of 'concessions' and 'extra-territoriality') and from the disunity
which prevailed both among the imperialist powers and
within the ranks of China's own ruling class. (127)
Whereas in Western Europe and Japan state power was used
to secure concessions for the national capitalists, in the
colonies and semi-colonies, the state, as the political
expression and instrument of a coalition between imperialism and a fragmented ruling class, precluded an economic
transformation. Alternatively, it was unable to resist
the encroachments of foreign capital, through trading concessions, fiscal exemptions, legal privileges and the
like; the international 'settlements' in China were
flourishing centres of tax evasion. In Egypt, the Anglo-
Egyptian Agreement of 1936 conceded large military and
strategic advantages to Britain.
  In the politically sovereign states the growth of capi-

talism dismantled the traditional economy, creating a
national market and a national economy, but internationally capitalism preserved precapitalist forms. The outcome
of this 'internationalizing' process was a 'hierarchy of
production modes' (Jairus Banaji), generating sharply different levels of productivity and incomes. In the sovereign states, the unifying effect of capitalism was also
felt politically, in a considerable degree of national
homogeneity despite regional diversity and various forms
of sectionalism. Acute commercial rivalry has been the
constant undercurrent in capitalism's history, with each
capitalist nation securing at the other's expense 'concessions' and privileged spheres of trade and investments,
by political manipulation, military pressure and territorial conquest. By the time capitalism turned its attention to the present underdeveloped world, it had already 'eliminated from the economic race some areas which
had been formerly dynamic and advanced - e.g., Italy and a
large part of Central Europe - leaving, in effect, only
the Dutch, the English and possibly the French in the
race'. (128) Whereas the hostility of one capitalist node
to another was an expression of the contradictions of
capitalism on the international plane, between the capitalist and precapitalist nodes complementarity and 'harmony' were made to prevail. The metropolitan economy provided the rationale for an underdeveloped country's precapitalist status; it decided upon the stimuli to which
she responded, the compulsions to which she submitted and
the pattern of priorities that was established.
     The link between colonialism and underdevelopment may
appear to be tenuous when one considers Thailand. Its
underdevelopment in Myrdal's way of thought was independent of colonialism, because of Thailand's strictly non-
colonial status. By contending that Thailand 'did not
become more developed than Burma', Myrdal (129) discounts
the role of colonialism as a generating force in underdevelopment. Though Thailand was not an outright colony, it
was not entirely free of foreign political influence and
economic domination. The Franco-Siamese treaty of 1893
gave the French virtual suzerainty over the Luang Prabang
districts - a situation like the extra-territoriality of
the Chinese coastal concessions. Following upon the
killing of a French agent, three French gunboats had
earlier sailed up the Menam and anchored near the Royal
Palace in Bangkok. The manner in which this incident was
resolved and its aftermath revealed the foreign pressures
to which Thailand had perforce to submit despite her
nominal 'independence'. 'Most of all, diplomatic problems
which surrounded the events were negotiated not in Bangkok

but in London and Paris, and Thailand did not have the
power to insist on her own opinion as an independent country.' (130)   By the border treaty with the British in 1905
the Thai government yielded more than it gained. These
political pressures were reflected in exclusive commercial
privileges assumed by foreign interests, such as the task
concessions of the Bombay-Burmah Corporation. The reforms
of Chulalongkorn, nationally significant in some ways,
were planned and carried out by English 'advisers', some
of whom had earlier been British officials in India or
Burma. The orders, regulations and gazettes of the Thai
government were translations of memos written by them.
Thailand, though juridically free, was subject to the same
kind of economic domination as a colony; nevertheless,
among the underdeveloped countries, Thailand has probably
come nearest to a capitalist transformation. The factors
underlying this forward advance have to be sought not in
its semi-colonial status which Myrdal by his comparison
with Burma seems to discount.

While the colonial mode of production - with no forward
development - was locked within the strait-jacket of merchant capital, what was crucial for the survival of this
mode was the aegis of metropolitan capitalism under which
it was introduced and maintained. As an arm of the metropolis the colonial administration could not foster a competing capitalist node to that of the patron nation. As
Barrington Moore, Jnr, observed, the English did not come
to India to carry out an industrial revolution. (131)   In
fact, British interests dictated that any possibility of
industrial development be stifled. This retardation of
industrialization is a theme that is extensively pursued
in this book.

17 The political economy of underdevelopment

Modern colonialism differed from the preceding forms by its preoccupation with production as opposed to merchandising. Earlier colonialism had two phases. In the first - the pure appropriation phase - colonialism was the collection of wealth in the form of tribute or booty, or of compulsory deliveries of peasants' produce. The dynamic of expansion was expenditure on piracy and warfare, causing a redistribution of income from one political and military unit to another. Treaties were signed with petty rulers, through force or deceit, and forts and garrisons were set up whereby the European powers protected themselves from each other. No attention whatever was given to how commodities were produced. In the second phase - that of simple colonial trade - the Europeans were 'facilitators'. Though not entrepreneurs, they ensured that production was carried out and that a surplus of commodities was available to them. To some extent they encouraged the production process, and the element of fraud or force was now confined to the European's manipulation of his knowledge of the profits to be made in distant markets. The procurement of commodities was from unsuspecting peasants who were totally unaware of conditions in foreign markets and lacked access to these markets. The distinction basically is between the direct or forcible appropriation of an existing surplus and appropriation by indirect or subtler means of a surplus which they partly helped to create. In neither of these phases did the Europeans engage directly in organizing production overseas.

The expansionary potential in this commercial traffic was low. Spices, silk and cotton textiles, as luxury goods of high unit value, encouraged restrictionist devices to maximize profit per unit of sale rather than to expand turnover. The strategy was one of 'keeping the

market hungry'; its watchword was scarcity value. There
was also a lack of control over supplies. Extra-economic
compulsions on producers did not eliminate the hazards and
uncertainties or the high cost of procurement. Factories,
depots or collection centres on the coast had to be defended against marauding rivals. Furthermore, this pattern of interaction with the periphery was limited by
Europe's inability to offer much in exchange for foreign
produce, resulting in a drain of bullion. The China trade
alone was unaffected because of opium exports from India.
European capitalism in this phase led a nomadic existence
overseas, without a stable involvement or a regular economic return. The benefit which Europe drew from it was
in the nature of windfall gains - Hobsbawm called it 'a
single bonus rather than a regular dividend'.

Though the period of modern colonialism was characterized by the organization of production in conquered lands,
until recently there was little more than a 'reorganization' of production. Surplus value was appropriated
through the labour process, but the organic composition
of capital was low; working capital predominated, and
labour relations were of a quasi-capitalist form. The
task of organizing production was one which merchant capital could carry out on behalf of absentee investors, supported by control of the apparatus of the colonial bureaucracy. In the nonsettler colonies it was only in the
early phase that there was a migration of production capital from the metropolis along with the owners of such
capital. In this phase export production was carried out
by proprietary planters. Later, capital for plantations
and mines flowed out under the aegis of merchant capital
represented by managing agency firms. The capital was
subscribed mostly by small investors organized in joint
stock companies - unlike the great trading companies in
Europe from the fifteenth to seventeenth centuries, which
were composed of big capitalists enjoying monopoly privileges and protecting themselves by force of arms. In the
plantation and mining enterprises, production was labour
intensive, and investment units were of a relatively small
size; absentee ownership and the scattered and disunited
nature of the investors laid them open to control by merchant capital.

The structure of centre-periphery relations based on
the colonial export economies, which corresponded to the
prevailing development of world capitalism, was seriously
weakened politically and militarily in the decade and a
half following the Second World War. Apart from the
socialist revolutions in Eastern Europe and China and the
development of anti-imperialist struggles, there was pres-

sure by the USA to open up the formerly exclusive or semi-
exclusive spheres of influence. (After encouraging the
decolonization movement, the USA later organized the suppression of national forces wanting a complete break in
centre-periphery relations.) At this time the leading
colonial powers were engaged in rehabilitating their home
economies. US capital, more powerful after the war than
that of any other nation, was feverishly propping up
Western Europe and to a lesser extent Japan, Taiwan and
South Korea, as bastions against the onrush of communism.
The postwar reconstruction boom in its character, magnitude and duration was unprecedented in capitalism's history. It was underpinned by a very high level of spending
on arms and by rapid technological innovation which yielded a crop of new products and raised productivity levels
in several existing branches of industry.

The period of decolonization between the end of the
Second World War and the advent of the multinational corporations in the periphery in the mid-1960s was a formative one in the development of the socio-economic structures and class relations that were to determine the politics of different countries in the present day. Though
this period is commonly regarded as the beginning of neo-
colonialism, it lacked a distinctive quality of its own.
It marked the transition to a definitive stage in the
internationalization of capital as opposed to the internationalization of markets. The internationalization of
capital until then had been constrained by the very structure of imperialism based on the division of the world
into separate colonial empires. The stage of development
of capitalism in the centre, and the level of productive
forces, did not require nor did they permit the centralization of capital on a world scale. While not totally
devoid of consequence, the period of decolonization was
something of a hiatus in the history of imperialism.
There was, in fact, a tendency for a loosening of centre-
periphery links. It was only with the advent of the MNCs
in the periphery that a new form of imperialist relations
emerged, when the integrative tendency of capitalism began
reasserting itself globally and at a more advanced level
than during the period of the classical export economy.
Centre-periphery links now assumed a distinctive character.

Some of the countries of the periphery, e.g. Malaysia,
entered the post-independence phase without interrupting
their links with the centre but merely internationalized
them. India, with a relatively developed national bourgeoisie, sought (though not too successfully) to create an
economy that was competitive with that of the centre.

Some others were impelled by recurrent crises to disengage themselves partially from the centre. Investment propensities in them were reorientated in favour of a nascent industrial class. The resulting 'inwardly oriented' policies threatened the interests of foreign capital in varying degrees through import-substituting industrialization, the state monopoly of certain branches of foreign trade, and the partial indigenization of capital and management. However, in the absence of a political revolution these countries failed to disengage themselves fully from the imperialist system. After abortive attempts at autonomous development they were then relinked with the centre. I can illustrate this relinking process and its implications by referring to the Philippines and, in somewhat more detail, to the case of Sri Lanka.

The Philippines, in the throes of a balance of payments crisis, adopted trade and payments control in 1947. Under a regime of import and foreign exchange control, which lasted up to the end of 1961, the economy underwent a vigorous expansion. Earnings from traditional exports were channelled into the manufacturing sector. A whole range of industries developed, and there was an annual growth of industrial output of nearly 13 per cent from 1952 to 1961. There was a Filipinization of the economy, and the period was one of remarkable price stability. But the half-hearted and purely administrative nature of the intervention produced results that were at variance with the professed development objectives. The controls were in conflict with the prevailing structure of incomes and market demand. With the collusion of corrupt officials the investment and output pattern which the controls envisaged was sacrificed to meet the consumer preferences of the rich, and even the goal of conserving foreign exchange lay unachieved. The crisis strengthened the anti-controls lobby backed by American interests. In this, as in other instances to which I shall later refer, exogenous forces made use of the crisis to subvert the attempts to develop a relatively autonomous political and economic structure. With the failure of such attempts a shift of policy occurred from import substitution to export oriented industrialization, reincorporating the Philippines fully into the world capitalist network but with political control through a pliant local bourgeoisie.

In January 1962 the peso was devalued by nearly 50 per cent. The US government underwrote the new policy with a loan of US $300 million. Incomes were now redirected from the industrial class to the traditional export-cum-trading interests, and the Filipinization process of the preceding twelve years was checked. Manufacturing industries were

generally handicapped by foreign competition, high interest rates and the increased cost of imported materials and
equipment. While the periodic commodity booms brought
profits to a few, the condition of the masses slumped.
The real wage rate for skilled labour in Manila and its
suburbs (index, 1965 = 100) declined almost continuously
from 1959, with a drop of 31 per cent between that year
and 1973. Consumer prices rose sharply and income disparities widened. Above all, the relinking of the economy
failed to avert recurrent cycles of currency devaluation
and foreign indebtedness; there was a mounting repayments
schedule, with a steep rise in the debt-servicing ratios.
Persisting foreign exchange and economic crises have since
characterized the Philippines' economy.

In Sri Lanka, trade and payments control - as in the
Philippines, primarily a reaction to foreign exchange
problems - lasted from about 1960 to 1977, with a relaxation during 1968-70, the last two years of the Senanayake
government. In 1977 the controls were swept away by a
government that was voted into power in place of a liber-
al-left wing coalition which had failed economically and
was repressive and corrupt. There was now a relinking of
Sri Lanka's economy with the centre with all the elements
of the standard package: trade and payments liberalization,
currency devaluation, high interest rates, an open door to
foreign capital and the setting up of a Free Trade Zone,
and the virtual removal of social welfare subsidies. The
state sector, comprising industrial and trading corporations, the plantations and transport, though juridically
intact, has come increasingly under the influence and control of private business. There has also been a 'tidying
up' of the labour market, with an informal repression of
militant unionism and a whittling away of democratic
rights.

Paradoxically, the bourgeoisie that is benefiting from
the rightward political swing was nurtured by the profes-
sedly left wing policies of the coalition government,
under which the economic controls reached their high
point. Though a large segment of the import trade was
nationalized, market scarcities created abnormally high
profit margins on the trade that still remained in the
hands of private importers and retailers. Tax privileges
in tourism and the gem trade provided new bases of wealth.
A genuine industrial development was inhibited by the extreme profitability of outright trading activities. The
profit margins on the import of industrial raw materials,
components and equipment for almost final assembly exceeded those on finished goods imported earlier. The
commercial-cum-industrial or pseudo-industrial class had

had virtually a mandate to enrich themselves. In the
plantation sector, land reform emasculated the traditional
monied groups. An expansion of state activity in selected
manufacturing industries and in trade (the so-called non-
capitalist road to socialism) involved the grafting on of
a state-owned and inefficiently managed investment enclave. On balance, the path of development was a capitalist one. What generally occurred in these years was an
overhauling of the existing class structures.

All the same, the coalition government, having nourished the process of private accumulation, constrained it at
a certain level. The controls caused a decline in investment outlets, aggravated by a ceiling on house ownership
and on landholdings; and shortages of imported equipment
and materials led to unused capacity. The licensing
system, whereby established importers and 'approved' industries alone were eligible for foreign exchange, concentrated surpluses in existing enterprises - thus retarding
the mobility of capital. The structure of both trade and
industry became involuted, with effects analogous to those
of a guild system.

By the current liberalization of the economy, the process of concentration of incomes has gained a coherence
and consistency which it lacked earlier. Investment and
entrepreneurial interests have spread beyond their original spheres. An osmosis of funds across a wide range of
enterprises has enabled the bourgeoisie to expand its
wealth without let or hindrance. A fillip to this process
has been a tax amnesty on undeclared wealth and the repeal
of punitive laws against foreign exchange and tax viola-
tions. However, the process of accumulation that is
taking place is substantially one of money wealth, whose
transformation into productive capital is hindered by the
trading and rentier activities which the open economy has
spawned. As in the parasitic cities of the underdeveloped world, the service trades, the urban land market, and
the construction of commercial buildings and luxury dwellings have enjoyed a phenomenal boom. The seeming buoyancy of the economy has been confined to such enterprises
catering essentially to the conspicuous indulgence of an
affluent enclave. The very framework within which wealth
is generated inhibits its transformation into productive
capital.

Income disparities generated by the new policies have
diverted an expanding component of employment and production to counterproductive activities. Domestic manufactures have been affected by the removal of protection, by
the higher cost of imported inputs and of credit, and by a
price inflation, officially estimated at 35 per cent annu-

ally (but probably in the region of 40-60 per cent) - all
of these have made imported goods more competitive. The
demise of the 'high employment oriented handloom textile
industry' was noted by the Central Bank in its report for
1978. The effect of export oriented industrialization,
relegating indigenous enterprise to the role of subcontractors to the foreign firms, will be discussed later in
this chapter. In Sri Lanka export oriented industrialization, the fullest expression of which is the Free Trade
Zone, has had a similar effect. The zone has been dominated by the ready-made garments industry, and the foreign
firms enjoying tax holidays have asserted themselves over
established local firms. Specific evidence for this will
be adduced at a later stage when discussing the effects on
indigenous industrial enterprise of the relinking of the
periphery. A rise in imports, far exceeding the increased
income from tourism and remittances by Sinhalese in the
Middle East, has caused a rapid run-down of the accumulated foreign exchange reserves. The satisfaction of what
the Central Bank has called pent-up demand has turned out
to be an import mania involving non-essential goods and
those that were earlier produced locally - even soap, pen-
cils and erasers (the last mentioned notwithstanding Sri
Lanka's status as a rubber-producing country). A trade
deficit in 1978 was followed by a deficit of massive proportions in 1979, reversing the tendency towards small
surpluses in the two preceding years. A foreign debt explosion has occurred even before the costly investment
projects have really got under way. The full impact of
the debt repayment and servicing charges has only been
postponed by the initial grace periods of the loans. In
lieu of an open devaluation of the currency for the second
time, as the IMF is reported to have advised in its conventional wisdom, recourse is being had to a veiled but
continual depreciation of the Sri Lanka rupee. The
deepening crisis has led the government into strategies
of repression designed to ensure its own political survival as the agent of the financial interests it has so
spectacularly bred. The economic crisis and its political
repercussions conform to a pattern very familiar from the
recent experience of the Southeast Asian countries. In
fact, Sri Lanka's position is worse, since its natural resource base limits the foreign exchange potential to a
narrower range of exportable commodities.
   The relinking of the periphery with the centre highlights a new phase in the development of world capitalism.
Weakened economically and politically after the Second
World War by the defection of several territorial units,
world capitalism regained its cohesion over a shrunken

area of the globe. What remained intact of the periphery
was then gradually subjected once more to the control and
dominance of the centre, this time in a more far-reaching,
subtle and pervasive manner. The imperialist-periphery
antagonisms of the immediate postcolonial period have
receded. In this phase of 'Late Capitalism', as Mandel
calls it, merchant capital is no longer the agency of the
centre's interaction with the periphery. Industrial capital is invested directly through the metropolitan firms'
overseas subsidiaries, which are in effect their own departments, with a complete identity of interests, virtually no autonomy and subserving a single profit centre. The
small investor who had been the mainstay of the colonial
export economy is displaced by the MNC as the unit of
enterprise. Now the internationalization of production,
unlike the mere internationalizing of markets, involves
the transplanting of capitalist social relations. It
opens up the periphery to the capital of all nations, promotes the full and free exploitation of the periphery,
based on the capitalist mode of production, and postpones
the snapping of the weak links in the imperialist chain.
This, as seen by David Rockefeller of Chase Manhattan,
would enable multinational enterprises 'to get on with the
unfinished business of developing the world economy'.

The MNCs by their entry into the periphery have become
the institutional basis of the centre-periphery relations
in the present day. The MNCs carry out the investment of
production capital, without the mediation of merchant
firms. Production capital in the periphery runs little
risk of expropriation, owing to the sheer economic
strength of the MNCs and the fusion of different national
capitals including the collaboration of the MNCs with
local and especially state capital. The MNCs exercise
their countervailing power in devious ways. For instance,
when Argentina imposed price controls on pharmaceuticals
in 1975 the European firms retaliated through their
governments at the 'Paris Club' talks which were to decide
on aid to Argentina. (1) In Sri Lanka the pharmaceutical
firms in 1973 thwarted an attempt by the government to
centralize imports and to encourage local manufacture.
One of them, Pfizer Ltd, later foiled a nationalization
threat by exerting political pressure through the US
government. The American Ambassador intervened personally, reportedly bringing up the matter of US food aid to
Sri Lanka. (2) The conglomerates infiltrate international
agencies, including the United Nations system; with their
effective intelligence networks, they can even destabilize
governments. While making use of the military and diplomatic power of international capitalism as represented by
the USA, (3) they in turn serve its political interests.

To a large extent the conglomerates can defend their interests abroad without colonialism based on conquest of territory, for the reason that they can control activities by their monopoly of technology and markets. First, a good portion of their income is in the form of technological rents, royalties, licensing rights, technical assistance fees, etc. The technology is rarely transferred, and its diffusion outside the orbit of such corporations is rigidly controlled. When deprived of this technology and marketing know-how, the natural resources and cheap labour of the host countries become idle assets at least in the short run. Second, transfer pricing enables a multinational to siphon away profits from high-risk territories; or by easily inflating accounting costs, it can also minimize local tax liabilities. Third, a 'fairly wide geo-political spread' of production facilities enables multinationals to switch the venue of their operations, treating a large part of the world as their keyboard. The twenty-five biggest American multinational firms in 1967 had production facilities, on an average, in twenty-seven countries. (4)   A parallel feature is the spreading of markets over several overseas territories, any one of which contributes only a small share of the total business. For all these reasons, the bargaining power of a multinational is immeasurably stronger than that of the transnational enterprises of the classical colonial period.

There is in this phase a rationalization in the use of resources on a world scale with a vertical integration of investments over a far-flung empire of production sites. Production capital has acquired a new mobility; previously it had flowed overwhelmingly to the regions of new settlement (for the rest, 'world economy' was a reality only in respect of markets). The enlarged flow of capital exports to the periphery involves a concentration and centralization of capital to an extent unheard of before. In relation to the scale and character of capital exports in the present day, the earlier flow of capital was only the beginning of a trend which Lenin was able to conceptualize long before it unfolded its full potentialities.

The attempt to rationalize the operations of capitalism on a world scale is not entirely or principally in the social interest but involves the elimination of rivals, privileged access to raw materials and markets, a relocation in cheap-labour belts, and transfer pricing. This rationalization is a response to the central dilemma of monopoly capitalism - the disparity between the growth of productive forces and the inadequate spread of purchasing power within the boundaries of the nation state. Both in

the USA and in Europe, a deficiency in purchasing power
has led to a debt-induced demand or a debt inflation of
almost cataclysmic proportions. There has also been a
slowing down of technological innovation, with a decline
in productivity growth and a thinning out of the crop of
new products. In the USA productivity growth has dropped
from 3.4 per cent a year during the 1960s to 2.3 per cent
during the 1970s. (5) Expenditure on research and development (R&D) has declined as well as the relative importance of basic long-term research. The mature industries are the most affected, such as steel, motor cars and
textiles. Sales expenses are tending to outweigh technical innovation as a source of market power. Unable to
meet rising costs through improved productivity, manufacturers resort to price increases, stoking the inflationary
fire which they have already had to contend with.

The rationalization of investment on a world scale,
Another expression of the crisis is a weakening of the
system of labour discipline and control that had been
built up over a long period. Of late, capitalism's work
ethic has been breaking down. As Harry Braverman showed,
a continued fracturing of the work process has led to the
de-skilling of numerous categories of work and a disuse of
the worker's conceptual faculties. (6) A separation between the planning and the conception of work, in the employer's interest, has degraded the worker's role almost
to that of the 'alienated machine slaves' described by
Engels in the English textile mills of 1844. The es-
trangement of the worker has found expression in his off-
work pursuits in an alternation of activism and extreme
apathy. According to H.L.Wilensky, by 1960 at least one
fifth or one sixth of the American labour force was affected. (7) While a restructuring of the work process has
given corporate management greater control over labour,
job performance has been lowered and absenteeism, labour
turnover and unpunctuality have risen to record levels.
Worst of all for the employer, labour's responsiveness to
material incentives has weakened. The current work attitudes and the demoralization of labour represent a relapse
into conditions which at its inception capitalism had
managed to overcome by draconian means.

The rationalization of investment on a world scale,
through a direct control by MNCs of productive capital in
the periphery, is not without its problems. With their
greater entrepreneurial reach, the MNCs are like an army
whose lengthening line of communications makes it vulnerable at an increasing number of points. Every small
device adopted to improve the operations of world capitalism intensifies its ambivalence and potential disequilibrium. To increase their competitiveness, the MNCs are

prepared to create unemployment in their home countries.
But after the setting up of export platforms in the periphery, imports into the centre are restricted, lessening
the viability of these platforms. A rising wave of protectionism in the centre chokes off the periphery's access
to markets. The analysis and interpretation of the capitalist order, as well as prognosis, are themselves becoming difficult, despite vastly improved systems of data
collection and processing. The ramifications of the
crisis have made pump priming on a national scale ineffective; instead 'global stimulation' has to be resorted to.
The policy is one of drumming up demand for certain types
of capital goods by means of large infrastructure investments in the periphery. In this process the periphery
becomes locked in a relentless cycle of foreign debt. The
inability to distribute the goods that it produces, and to
fully realize the productive potential of the technologies
it has perfected, is a congenital defect of capitalism
which only the ending of capitalism could banish.

The export of capital in the present day has several
components: first, mining investments which require technology and capital very much greater than the traditional
export staples; second, industries that are ecologically
harmful, whose transfer to the periphery exempts investors
from installing costly anti-pollution devices that are
mandatory in the centre. These two components include
mineral processing, oil refining, petrochemicals, crude
steel, non-ferrous metals, pulp and paper and forest products. The industries transferred are, third, the labour
intensive ones based on simple assembly line methods:
textiles and garments, footwear, carpets, wigs, plastic
products, scientific measuring instruments, and semi-con-
ductors for the electronics industry. Far more significant - a fourth component of capital exports relates to
multipurpose construction, irrigation and electricity-
generating projects, financed mainly by governments and
international lending agencies. The scale of capital investment and the complexity of technological skills are
incomparably greater than during the opening up phase of
these economies. For example, in Brazil the petrochemicals industry from the 1970s was producing basic inputs
like ethylene and benzene and the growth of the industry
outstripped that in the USA and other advanced economies.
(8) On the whole, foreign investment is characterized by
a high organic composition of capital.

The mining investments in the periphery are related essentially to the raw material needs of the centre, which
are now predominantly in the form of minerals. Certain
characteristics set them apart from the plantation and

mining products which had dominated trade and investment
flows in an earlier age. First, these minerals are of
strategic value; they are not easily substitutable, and
their end products are in demand both by the military and
by civilian industry controlled by powerful business
groups. Second, their production is limited to relatively
few locations and is mostly in underdeveloped countries,
whereas consumption is concentrated in the USA, Western
Europe and Japan. In the USA, consumption per head of the
critical raw materials is twenty times that in the underdeveloped countries, and is based largely on imports. Out
of thirteen basic industrial raw materials imported into
the USA in 1950, imports of four accounted for more than
half of its requirements of them. By 1970 there were six
such raw materials, and their number in 1985 is estimated
at nine. (9) Third, while supplies of the basic raw
materials are dwindling, the world demand for them is increasing fast - in copper it has reached explosive proportions.

The political economy of these materials is different
from that of plantation staples and the traditional type
of minerals. Plantation staples (excepting cane sugar)
had a uniformly low production technology which enabled
both plantation companies and peasants to supply the world
market. Likewise tin mining was possible without costly
technology. In Nigeria, indigenous mining enterprises
could only be ousted by extra-economic means; in Malaysia
until the 1920s Chinese-owned mines, based on intensive
labour, competed with the British mining companies. In
contrast, the dominant primary materials of the present
day cannot be produced by underdeveloped countries on
their own except perhaps by a revolutionary society like
that of China which is capable of an exceptionally high
degree of self-reliance. The inability of other underdeveloped countries to mobilize the required capital and
technology gives centre-periphery relations a new dominant-dependent complexion. (10) Control over the resources and politics in the periphery is no longer based
on overt domination or military suppression, and concepts
of territorial sovereignty have tended to lose their relevance.

The sharp asymmetry between the producers and consumers
of the critical raw materials is a source of phenomenal
power for those who can control supplies - as the Arabs
lately discovered. The struggle for raw materials is no
longer between identifiable national capitals but between
oligopolistic conglomerates which criss-cross state boundaries. In this sense, the change-over is from geopolitics
to geo-economics. The larger framework for this rivalry

is the division of the world between the capitalist and
socialist blocs. The political dimensions of this struggle relate to the existence of the Soviet Union as an alternative source of technology, capital and trade. Access
to Soviet technology enabled some of the oil-producing
countries (e.g. Iran) to expand production without private
foreign investment; Soviet intervention in the world oil
market also weakened its control by the multinationals.

The political economy of raw materials control has
shifted since the end of the Second World War from a
struggle among capitalist nations to one between rival
political systems. 'If Asia, Middle Eastern and African
nationalism exploited by the Soviet bloc becomes a destructive force', the Rockefeller Brothers' Fund reported
in 1958, 'European supplies of oil and other essential raw
materials may be jeopardised.' (11) As Professor Rostow
saw it, a pro-Soviet stance by the resource-rich underdeveloped countries is a threat to America's security. (12)

  The location, natural resources and populations of the
  underdeveloped areas are such that, should they become
  effectively attached to the Communist bloc, the U.S.
  would become the second power in the world ... the economic and military strength of Western Europe and Japan
  will be diminished.... Our military security and our
  way of life as well as the fate of Western Europe and
  Japan are at stake in the evolution of the underdeveloped areas.

Richard Nixon saw Indonesia's role as a supplier of raw
materials for the West: 'With its 100 million people, and
its 3000 mile arc of islands containing the richest hoard
of natural resources, Indonesia constitutes by far the
greatest prize in the Southeast Asian area.' (13) In 1977
Helmut Schmidt, the West German Chancellor, expressed concern about a possible decline in mineral exploitation and
prospecting in the Third World. As a long-term measure,
he called for large capital exports in the form of 'private direct investments' in preference to welfare expenditures, which in many developed countries have reached the
'load limit'. Political stability in underdeveloped countries was important in this connection; 'wars and civil
wars' have an adverse effect on raw material supplies.
(14)

Investment in the extraction and processing of critical
raw materials as one component of capital exports to the
periphery has already been discussed. That symbiosis between the centre and the periphery which is based on the
relocation of labour intensive industries arises from the
uneven development of technology. The technological lag,
symbolized in Landes's remark that it takes as much time

to shave a man as it did a hundred years ago, exists in
the services trades as well as in certain forms of manufacturing production. Their viability is threatened both
by rising wage rates and by the nature of their labour
process - monotonous, fatiguing, uncongenial and harmful
to the workers' nervous equilibrium. In the electronics
components industry the introduction of the silicon chip
is a serious health hazard to the workers. (15) Labour in
the developed countries is unwilling to take on such work.
Another aspect of this problem is the high rates of absenteeism and job dissatisfaction which has been very pronounced in the motor car industry, and has resulted in the
proliferation of assembly plants in the periphery.

The contradiction between low labour productivity and
the level of wages can be resolved in three ways. First,
by a change in consumption patterns occupations with low
production are made redundant. For example, live singers
are replaced by taped music, and there is a use of throw-
away paper plates, cups, serviettes, etc. Second, production activities whose qualities the machine cannot repli-
cate gain an extended lease of life by the presence of
migrants and ethnic outgroups working for low wages and
under substandard conditions. In the capital cities of
Europe workers from Southern Europe, Africa and Asia sweep
the streets, collect garbage or are employed in grimy
jobs, cleaning furnaces and scraping filth off heavy
machinery. Performing unskilled though absolutely vital
work, they are 'one of the saddest and most perplexing
problems of modern capitalism'. Third, as a measure of
last resort industries with low production may be relo-
cated in the periphery, shifting continually from one area
of cheap labour to another, not unlike the slash-and-burn
system in primitive peasant agriculture. These industries
rely on cheap, inevitably non-unionized, female labour
amenable to simple repetitive tasks. In the absence of
expensive fixed equipment, they are organized on the lines
of an international putting-out system. The parent firm
provides them with raw materials and components and pre-
empts their output; in the case of the garments industry
piece goods cut in America are sent abroad to be sewn
('assembled') and then brought back under concessional
tariffs that are lower than on apparel manufactured wholly
abroad. The output of these industries is made up in the
home base into final products, or is sold directly under
the parent's brand name or label as though produced at
home.

The transfer of industrial enterprises to the periphery
involves the spread of the capitalist mode of production.
Capitalist labour relations develop, unlike in planta-

tions, peasant agriculture and in the existing urban
enterprises (the 'informal sector'), where small-scale
units and self-employment predominate; in these enterprises outright wage labour and contractual relations are
rare, recruitment is based on ties of family, kinship or
ethnicity, a high degree of paternalism exists and payments are partly in kind. The industries transferred to
the periphery require a semi-skilled and stable labour
force - urban-based, not prone to absenteeism, adapted to
the machine, and amenable to modern management and factory
conditions. The nature of the labour force necessitates a
high wage level compared with other sectors. For instance, in the soap industry of Kenya, in 1972 the average
monthly wage of the multinational firms was twice that of
local firms. For twenty-four industrial firms the average
minimum monthly wage was double the statutory rate, and
the actual wages paid 'ranged even higher'. (16)   In
Southern Rhodesia, there was a 'steady rise' in the wages
paid by expatriate firms during the 1950s and the early
1960s. (17) Wages and working conditions are linked to a
specific labour relations strategy for creating a privileged but apolitical stratum of workers. The transplanting of an entire production package (input combinations,
marketing policies, technology, factory organization and
labour relations) gives rise to a genuine dualism between
the foreign-based mining-cum-industrial sector and the
rest of the economy.

However, the relocating of industries is not a simple
function of rising wage levels in the centre. The process
of relocation has its limits, but for which there would be
a deindustrialization of the centre. Capital has two
options open to it - to relocate or to automate. The outcome, though not easy to predict, depends on various factors. One of these is the technological possibilities of
different industries, offsetting the effect of high wages.
For instance, the offshore electronics industry has passed
its high peak - recent advances in the technology of
microcircuitry require longer production runs than are
possible in the periphery. Second, relocation is constrained by its effects on the value of capital invested
in the home country. The electronics industry was more
easily moved out than the textile industry; and import
quotas are imposed on textiles but not on electronics components. Third, the pace of relocation is governed by its
effect on the centre's labour market. By creating unemployment at home, and restoring a sellers' market, relocation checks its own impetus. Recent advances in automa-
tion, when applied to manual jobs as well as in the service industries - including office work, banking, insurance

and retail selling - have made a large and permanent
labour reserve an imminent prospect. Trade union pressure
then builds up in favour of protectionism, which is, however, no solution as the crisis is of a structural nature.
Lastly, an anti-capitalist ideology in the periphery is a
deterrent to relocation. Militant dissent and radical
movements have preceded the development of capitalist
social relations and of a proletariat - unlike in Europe,
where the rise of capitalism was aided by a dominant bourgeois ideology. The superstructure in the periphery is
more advanced than its material base. Industrial capital
has thus to struggle on two fronts - against an entrenched
merchant class and against an ethos that is already hostile to private accumulation. In the complex political
situation in the periphery, ethnic conflicts are also a
destabilizing element.

The reabsorption of the periphery in the vortex of
world capitalism is not merely through the new mining-cum-
industrial sector in its role as an export platform for
the centre and a venue for its 'export substituting' industries. The centre gains control over an expanding component of agriculture producing for the domestic market,
based on support prices, subsidized fertilizer, and government outlays on irrigation and peasant settlement.
Production in this sector, while competing with other
underdeveloped countries, develops a strong complementarity with the centre. The narrow genetic 'base' of the
Green Revolution seed varieties provides a shot in the arm
for the agrochemical giants at a time when their markets
in the developed countries are levelling off. The seed
varieties require heavy applications of fertilizer, fungi-
cide and pesticide. In the Philippines, a few years back,
Standard Oil of New Jersey (ESSO) set up 400 sales outlets
for fertilizer and other agrochemicals. Furthermore,
rigid cultivation schedules and exacting systems of water
control require the import of oil-powered irrigation pumps
and tractors. (18) In Indonesia the rice estates that
were set up from 1968 were seeded and sprayed with pesticides and fertilizer by aircraft. This capital absorptive
agriculture, sponsored by multinationals, rules out inputs
and technologies available endogenously within the farm
sector, and which are far less ecologically destructive.

Capital exports have not merely expanded in volume but
have also assumed a qualitatively new form. The multinationals which began investing in the periphery from the
mid-1960s had no historical precedent, though it may be
tempting to see their lineage in the great overseas trading companies of the sixteenth century which commanded
large aggregations of capital, or in the plantation and

mining companies of the nineteenth century financed in the
capital markets of the centre. Though functioning trans-
nationally, these enterprises were owned by the nationals
of a single country, excluding the nations of other countries from participating in their capital and management;
e.g. the USA was debarred from investing in plantation
rubber in Malaysia, in Indochina non-French capital was
excluded, and in the Congo the big corporate enterprises
were reserved for Belgian capital. These enterprises were
an expression of the vertical division of the world among
different metropolitan powers. What is occurring in the
present day is not just an enlarged export of capital, as
the term 'transnationalization' is apt to convey, but the
regrouping of capital across national borders. It is more
pronouncedly a horizontal fusion of transnational capital.
Instead of the bilateral circuits between the metropolises
and their hinterlands, there is now a multilateralization
of trade and capital flows among those which were formerly
competitors. The markets and resources of the periphery
have been opened for business irrespective of nationality.
(19)

The competition among national capitals till the Second
World War reflected the prevailing level of productive
forces, which required the concentration of capital on a
world scale but its centralization only within national
limits. (Concentration is an increase in capital outlays
by the individual enterprise and centralization is the
fusion or common control and ownership of separate entrepreneurial units.) The extent of concentration of capital
was itself limited by two factors. One was the different
spheres of influence which defined the circuit for the
capital of each metropolitan power, and the other was the
low organic composition of investments in the periphery.
Recently, however, concentration as well as centralization
has become international in scope. New industries in the
centre (aerospace, electronics and data processing, scientific instruments, the upstream products of the petrochemicals, etc.) and, in the periphery, capital absorptive
projects in mining and of an infrastructure type have
caused a phenomenal enlargement in the unit of investment.
Competition between national capitals is superseded by
that between multinational conglomerates.

In this process of concentration and centralization of
capital, a novel element is the role played by institutionalized funding agencies, such as the World Bank and
the Asian Development Bank, and by consortia of private
firms. These agencies and consortia act as promoters
mobilizing capital in areas and at levels where individual
MNCs cannot operate. The investors are not mere conglom-

erates but a conglomerate of conglomerates. This is not
to be understood to mean that the MNCs keep aloof or have
no undercover role to play in the functioning of these
agencies. The agencies and consortia provide a security
blanket for private capital from various countries. They
negotiate with a host country for an investment package
which combines finance, technology, capital equipment and
managerial services. The safety of the investments is
further ensured through the involvement of the governments
in the periphery. Investment is in infrastructure projects and, to a lesser extent, in state industrial enterprises producing capital goods. The investment results
in large sales of equipment and machinery and opens up
secondary opportunities for agribusiness and for engineering firms. The predominance of loan capital, unlike
earlier flows of private capital in the form of equity,
results in a periodic repatriation of the invested capital
irrespective of the financial viability of the projects.
The inefficiency and extravagance of the bureaucracies in
the periphery and the vast opportunities for corruption
cause the capital costs of these projects to escalate
sharply. Such investments, nevertheless, have a pump-
priming effect on the economies of the centre, helping to
ward off stagflation in the centre, besides conferring a
direct financial gain on the investors.

The multilateralization of capital is a process that
was first manifest in Western Europe after the Second
World War. The leading European nations, and 'even the
most nationalist of national capitals', could not on their
own exploit the potential of certain branches of production, some of which were strategically important like
aerospace, computers and nuclear energy. The supersonic
Concorde built by Britain and France was an outstanding
case of centralized planning and control in these years,
although it is now regarded as a commercial fiasco. A
fusion of the capital, technology and management skills
of different nations, sometimes under state sponsorship,
was encouraged by the need to stand up to the economic
hegemony of the USA. Unable to catch up with America's
extraordinary technological lead in the most advanced
branches of industry, West European firms began absorbing
American capital. 'When a French or Italian firm gets
into trouble it usually turns for help to an American corporation rather than to another European power.' (20) The
transfusion of technology via American capital spared
Europe the heavy research costs already incurred by
America.

In the periphery, multilateralization of capital occurred both at government level, through 'aid clubs' and

consortia, and in direct investments. For example, in the
Philippines the Atlas Consolidated Mining and Development
Corporation has both American and Japanese capital. American interests in 1971 owned 60 per cent of its equity,
while the Mitsubishi Metal Company of Japan had loaned
$7.8 million in 1963 and again $20 million in 1971 to
finance expansion. (21) (A Philippines government regulation limiting Japanese investments in any enterprise to
60 per cent of the equity was overcome by resorting to
loan capital.) In Indonesia, the Gunung Bijeh copper-
mining project (Freeport Minerals) was financed by the
USA, West Germany, Japan and the Netherlands. A consorti-
um of US banks and insurance houses supplied $70 million,
the Kreditanstalt für Wiederaufbau $28 million, and seven
copper and five trading companies from Japan together
provided $24 million. Government agencies in the USA,
Japan and West Germany guaranteed the investment, and the
Overseas Private Investment Corporation in the USA 'in-
sured a portion of the project (presumably Freeport's
equity investment) for $20 million against expropriation,
war and inconvertibility of [earnings]'. (22) In Kenya,
one half the capital of the oil refinery was shared almost
equally by Shell, BP, Exxon, and Caltex; Fluorspar Company is Swiss, US and British; the tannery has British
capital; the paper mill is financed by the World Bank,
Canada, the UK, the USA and India; and a vehicle plant
assembles Leyland trucks and buses, Land Rovers and Range
Rovers, and Volkswagen vehicles. (23)
    Several factors contributed to the multilateralization
of capital in the periphery. After the setting up of
branch plants, the different national capitals tended to
amalgamate as the local market did not justify separate
production facilities. A second reason for multilateralization, already stated in the case of mineral exploitation, is that the financial, technological and managerial
requirements of investment projects exceed the capabilities of an individual firm or even a nation. For instance, to construct Indonesia's Gunung Bijeh copper-
mining project, estimated at US $120 million, the American
firm Freeport Minerals sought outside financing. Third,
in the case of Japan and the smaller capital-exporting
countries of Europe, or those with limited diplomatic influence, multilateralization enables them to share the allocation of critical raw materials. Lenny Siegal commented on the Gunung Bijeh project: (24)
    The Japanese have angled for years for a shot at Indo-
    nesian deposits. When Freeport (Minerals) nailed down
    the exploitation and developmental deal, Tokyo swiftly
    shuffled plans and requested permission to take part in

the U.S. venture via a Japanese semi-governmental development firm.... Once one party gets the upper hand
- for political or economic reasons - the others seek
cooperation.

The regrouping of capital across state boundaries, as
mentioned before, signifies a new stage in the socialization of investment. The interpenetration and mutual involvement of different national capitals have transcended
the phase in which different national capitals, while expanding beyond their national boundaries, had retained a
basically national character. In that phase, capital's
overseas operations were constrained by the existence of
colonial empires which were symbiotically linked with the
respective metropolises. The present phase, characterized
by multilateralization of investments, is tantamount to a
denationalizing of capital or a lessening of its national
attachments. Each unit of the periphery is now linked,
not with a specific metropolitan country, but with the
centre as a whole, with a criss-crossing network of
centre-periphery relations. Capital has assumed a supranational character which has made it, as Baran and Sweezy
wrote, 'more than a mere collection of national capitalisms'. The interests of capital are represented by an
international bourgeoisie.

The different capitals - for example, American, European and Japanese - have not fully overcome their tensions
and conflicts. There is a constant manoeuvring by nations
for positions of relative advantage. Governments sometimes underwrite or partly finance MNCs so as to strength-
en their national component, thereby pre-empting markets
and raw material sources. Yet, the differences among the
various national capitals nowadays are of a negotiable
kind - they do not lead to armed conflicts or diplomatic
ruptures. The 'major problems' today between Tokyo and
Washington were seen by the Prime Minister of Japan, Takeo
Fukuda, in a subdued light. 'There aren't many. If there
was a problem, it would be over how Japan and America
could jointly address the problems of the world.... The
U.S., after all, is the largest economy in the world and
Japan is the second largest in the free World.' (25)

Soon after the intransigence which the developed countries displayed towards the underdeveloped at UNCTAD V,
Japan and the USA agreed to negotiate on bilateral procurement policies, paving the way for large purchases of
American equipment by the Nippon Telegraph and Telephone
Public Corporation. Bilateral procurement policies had
previously been 'the most friction-filled issue in their
troubled trade ties'. (26) In the Asian Development Bank,
there has been a broad conformity of views and action be-

tween the USA and the lesser Western powers. Likewise in
the World Bank, according to Eugene R.Black, a former
President: 'While we will have about 17 per cent of the
vote here, I think that the marginal [European] countries
and Australia and New Zealand and Japan could have similar
interests to ours, and I think that the vote at all times
would certainly be favourable.' He added, 'As a matter of
fact in fifteen years in the World Bank where I was ...
there never was any question of the underdeveloped nations
ganging up and voting.' (27) The defence of the frontiers
of imperialism has been a major concern of the capitalist
world from the time of the Russian revolution. And this
remains its 'central objective' - what Magdoff called the
struggle of imperialism against the contraction of the
imperialist system.

Whereas in the cold war period after the defeat of
Fascism the capitalist and socialist blocs risked a military confrontation, recently the rivalry between them has
become a struggle over spheres of influence and is losing
its ideological content. This very largely also explains
the present Sino-Soviet struggle. At a time when the
capitalist countries are achieving a greater measure of
accord, there is a burgeoning crisis of capitalism. The
tensions within the socialist societies are comparable in
some ways with those of capitalism. The sense of alienation has not been removed by a mere change in the ownership of the means of production from capitalists to a
state bureaucracy. In the Soviet Union factory organization, despite 'workers' control', has emulated the labour
management practices of advanced capitalism. There has
been a fragmentation of the work process and the infusion
of capitalist motivations and norms, depriving the socialist system of a humanist content. The goal of creating
the Socialist Man has receded. Concomitantly, the national interests of the socialist states have overridden those
of international socialism. A completely contrasting
picture presents itself in the case of the leading capitalist countries; the outlines of their sovereignty as
nation states have tended to be blurred to the point where
nation states continue their separate identities only in
so far as they are the effective handmaidens of the internationalized monopolies.

While there has been more accord among the capitalist
states and differences have emerged in the once monolithic
socialist bloc, in the first half of the 1970s the economic problems of capitalism erupted with a new malignance
and complexity. The crisis embodied elements of a most
diverse and contradictory kind, making even the diagnosis
of the crisis, let alone its management, a problem without

precedent. Some of the signs of this crisis and its repercussions on the periphery were referred to earlier in
this chapter. Amidst a slackening of world tension, there
was also in this same period a decline in the pre-eminence
of the USA while Europe and Japan moved to new positions
of strength. The resulting multipolarity in the international power structure was aided by a rift between the
leading communist states. The dismantling of the bipolar
world involved new political relations between the super-
powers, and in the more fluid political climate that prevailed, a few non-superpowers began to influence politics
and economic relations.

All the same, the balance of power between the centre
and the periphery has not changed. The internationalization of capital has contained the disintegrative effects
of multipolarity on capitalism as a world system. There
still exists a mutuality of interests between transnational capital and the USA as capitalism's most powerful
nation state - the dominant partner in World Capitalism
Inc. Except in the settler territories where capital
migrated together with the owners, and became indigenized,
it is in the centre that capital feels most secure and
exercises its first option. The transfer of industrial
plants to the periphery is more of a strategy than a
policy, undertaken to preserve markets threatened by
tariffs or to take advantage of cheap labour, tax exemptions and lax standards in regard to environmental pollution. Though capital is now far more diffused in its
sphere of activity, and is not uniquely identified with
a parent state, it cannot entirely do without the diplomatic and moral support of a powerful government in the
centre.

Capitalism, while in a state of crisis in the centre,
has acquired a buoyancy in the periphery. While opportunities for investment along traditional lines have grown
markedly narrower, international capital has found new
areas of investment in an incipient industrialization of
the periphery, involving high-technology projects in
mining and of an infrastructure type. The prospects for
world capitalism are no longer dependent on an expanding
geographical and demographic fr,ntier - a dependence which
had led earlier to intensified imperialist rivalry. At
the beginning of the 1950s the USA, rather unsuccessfully,
had sought, under United Nations auspices and partly by
treaties of friendship, navigation and commerce, to remove
legal, administrative and political deterrents to private
foreign capital. In contrast with these efforts, the MNCs
and the inter-governmental lending agencies of the present
day have forged a totally new framework for the mobiliza-

tion of capital, surpassing in its effects the improved
functioning of capital markets which from the middle of
the nineteenth century launched the first great wave of
capital exports. The persisting unevenness in the growth
of productive forces, and sharp wage differentials at home
and abroad, enable capitalism to realize some of its expansionary potential. The relative uniformity of national
wage levels in the centre, despite productivity differentials, is a further inducement to the export of capital.
As Mandel explained, capital is invested abroad, bypassing
activities or regions at home in which productivity lags
behind. 'These "internal colonies" were victims of the
fact that although they were certainly underdeveloped they
were at the same time bunched together with the industrialised areas in a system of uniform production, prices,
profits and wages.' (28)

   With the emergence of a group of relatively developed
countries in the periphery, there is also being created a
centre-periphery relation of a secondary nature. The
status of these countries as capital exporters (and sellers of discarded or second-hand equipment) is evident in
the newer Free Trade Zones. In the garments industry, the
products of Hong Kong, Singapore and Taiwan are those
which have a relatively high value added; they conform
with fashion trends, are well designed, cut and sewn, and
use superior accessories and even packing material. On
the other hand, the garments industry in Sri Lanka, for
instance, is restricted to low-priced utility wares. The
uneven development of the periphery has created divergent
interests: for example, between Singapore (as a virtually
free trade entity) and Indonesia which as a primary producer is concerned with controlling commodity markets; or
between Indonesia as an oil exporter and the rest of the
Association of Southeast Asian Nations. This uneven development in the periphery, without necessarily undermining the centre, stifles the transformation of the more
backward countries - preventing them from realizing opportunities to which they might reasonably aspire. Furthermore, the allocation of import quotas by the centre causes
the periphery to compete against itself for limited markets. The US Trade Preference Act, 1974, hampers collective bargaining by the periphery, retaliating against
countries that engage in collective arrangements. The
import quotas, influenced by quasi-political considerations, are liable to be traded off as concessions by the
centre. A periodic redistribution of quotas prevents the
textile industry in any country from developing its full
potential. Once a significant level is approached, 'down
comes the barrier. Thus newcomers (unless they are tiny

countries like Cyprus) have no prospect that textile exports can become significant'. (29)

A corollary to the consolidation of the centre has been
a weakening of intra-periphery links from about 1973,
after an abortive attempt by the periphery to confront the
centre through militant producers' associations such as
OPEC. The centre, by resorting to bilateral instead of
global negotiations, 'split the Third World Front and
ultimately ... [made] it gradually lose the bargaining
power acquired in 1974'. (30) This disunity of the
periphery has been a source of dismay to UNCTAD officials.
According to A.W.Singham, 'The Western countries seem to
have perfected the art of conference politics in which
they are able to exploit circumstances between Third World
countries and to bring most negotiations to a standstill.'
(31) A few of the periphery's foreign debts have been
written off - at a time when inflation had diminished
their real value. Yet the centre's financial and commercial stranglehold has tightened progressively. Even a
partial reform of the capitalist world market, which
seemed possible at the beginning of the 1970s, is no
longer a prospect. (32)

> Indeed, never before have there been recorded such high
> levels of foreign trade imbalances and indebtedness
> among the non-petroleum producing underdeveloped coun-
> tries, and rarely has the interference of the trans-
> national corporations in the internal affairs of the
> countries which they operate been so much in evidence.

The irrationalities and inhumanity of the world order
are essentially a problem of vested interests both on a
national and on an international scale, not to be resolved
as a problem in logic by argumentation or as a problem in
ethics by appeals to righteousness. (33) A given structural arrangement has certain inevitable compulsions which
make meaningful reform impossible with the best will in
the world. The social relations in the periphery are
themselves historically outmoded, and generate the same
inequities and irrationalities which the periphery wants
abolished on a world scale. The liberal developmentalists
of the Third World, through their studies and experience,
understand the fragility and self-destructiveness of the
present world system - a position that was not admitted by
the developmentalists of the old school who very blatantly
were servitors of the imperialist order. However, the
present-day developmentalists in their exertions seek to
keep the existing system on its moorings while conjuring
away its structural defects by appeals to the former
metropolitan powers for improved prices for primary products, access to industrial markets, and expanded finan-

cial credits. In this they are deluding themselves into
the belief that their efforts will be a surrogate for an
effective change of the system. The developmentalists are
practising a kind of therapy like the placebo in medicine.
The real action to change these societies is being taken
by the ordinary people who are affected as is seen by
recent events in Nicaragua.

Foreign investment in the periphery, as before, is a
function of the economic needs of the centre, and is
linked predominantly with raw materials supplies. A precondition of such investment was often the long-term contracts for the sale of the raw materials produced: as,
for example, in Indonesia and the Philippines in the
mining of copper and aluminium. (The whole of the output
of copper from Southern Luzon has been pre-empted by
Japan.) In Indonesia's Ertsberg copper-mining project the
Japanese investors buy two thirds of the mine's output
over its lifetime, and Norddeutsche Affineris - a West
Germany company with British participation - is entitled
to one third. (34) Investment in these projects, while
meeting the centre's need for critical raw materials, con-
solidates established industries in the centre vis-à-vis
processing or manufacturing plants in the periphery. In
the Philippines, ore-smelting capacity and the growth of
mineral-based industries have, as a result, lagged seriously behind the expansion in the output of ore. The pre-
emption by foreign interests of raw materials in whose
production they invest, and the impediments so created to
the growth of local processing industries, are also evident in the lumber industry. As Robert Coates put it, the
lumber producers in the Philippines are trapped in the
export market. (35) Log exports are the source of funds
for building and modernizing local processing plants; but
increased exports raise the price of logs and condition
the lumber interests to meeting the export demand at the
expense of a domestic wood-processing industry. (In 1972,
after destructive rains in the Luzon area, the government
imposed a ban on log felling in the watershed areas but
this was revoked to maintain foreign exchange earnings.)

To ensure their dominance, the capitalist nations have
embarked on a forward-looking strategy to contain civil
wars and revolution through a controlled commitment to
development in the periphery. The basis of investment and
aid flows had been expanded and multilateralized so as to
involve, besides private investors and governments, non-
profit making organizations. The Overseas Development
Council in Washington, one such organization, placed outside the Congress, has academics, civic leaders, and business executives on its governing board. With more credi-

bility than an official agency it is better able to propagate the new 'development strategies' among the American
public and in the periphery. According to its President,
such organizations (36)

> have greater potential for intervening effectively in
> the domestic affairs of a developing country.... If we
> are to develop a firm deterrent to anarchy and subver-
> sion in two-thirds of the world seized by the revolu-
> tion of rising expectations, something far more funda-
> mental ... [than the Agency for International Develop-
> ment, ODC's precursor] is required.

The ODC sponsors research on employment creation, nutri-
tional needs and the relieving of poverty. The policy of
development as an alternative to revolution has found expression in concepts such as 'participatory development',
'self-reliant development', 'poverty oriented development', and 'basic needs', which dominate the social
science programmes of institutions and individuals funded
by the Western powers. The policies embodying these concepts furnish a survival strategy for the underdeveloped
countries as a condition of their continued subjection.
(37)

The process of reincorporation of the periphery has
involved an 'orchestrated shift' from import substitution
to export-oriented industrialization. There were several
reasons for the limited growth impact of the import substitution policy adopted after decolonization. First, the
type of manufacturing production that was developed consisted mainly of non-essential goods. Second, the persistence of precapitalist agrarian relations limited the
growth of the domestic market and the development of a
symbiotic link between town and country. Merchant capital
remained dominant and was powerful enough to negate the
government's efforts to foster industrial capital. In Sri
Lanka the merchant interests resisted the protectionist
policies with boundless ingenuity. (38) There was, third,
a subversion of the import substitution policy by exogenous forces mediating through agencies such as the IMF,
the World Bank and the Asian Development Bank and consortia of commercial banks, which utilized the debt crisis
in the periphery to impose the preconditions for the entry
of multinational capital. Fundamentally, import substitution was pursued as a policy in itself instead of constituting one among a number of measures for transforming
already established merchant capital into industrial capital. The reason for it was to bring into being a new
class - the industrial bourgeoisie, whose ethos and interests are totally different from those of the merchant
bourgeoisie which has been traditionally dominant; a

class which not merely concentrates money wealth in its
hands - like the landlord, the merchant and the usurer -
but seeks to capitalize this wealth within the capital-
labour relationship. This metamorphosis of capital is
contingent upon a restructuring of both internal class
relations and the relation of the bourgeoisie as a whole
with foreign interests. Export oriented industrialization
and the accompanying policy package which exposes the
economy to foreign competition result in enervation and
emasculation of indigenous industrial enterprises. Indigenous and foreign capital become involved in an unequal
relation; when they are in partnership, the foreign interests control capital flows, technology and production
proceeds, and marketing outlets, subserving a profit
centre abroad.

In fact, what is involved in this outward-looking
policy is not export orientation as such. The expression
'outward-looking' as a euphemism for an economy that is
incorporated in the world capitalist network is doubly
misleading. It emphasizes production for export as
against the domestic market, whereas the converse, an
inward-looking economy, does not exclude the development
of export production. Moreover, the openness or extrovert
nature of the outward-looking economies is only in respect
of the centre. In relation to each other they are inward-
looking and closed. While competing with each other, they
enter into a division of labour with the centre, producing
what the centre wants to buy and buying what the centre
wants to sell. The strategy of export promotion reflects
the incapacity of the bourgeoisie and the state to mediate
the land question, so as to realize the potentialities of
the domestic market and develop a new base for surplus accumulation. The productive process thus develops essentially on the lines of the classical export economy, bypassing the need to revamp agrarian relations and to develop a symbiotic link between town and countryside. The
politico-economic significance of the land reform that was
imposed on Japan by the US military soon after the Second
World War was that it provided Japanese capitalism with an
internal base of this kind, making the pursuit of expansionary interests abroad unnecessary, at least for a
while.

Export oriented industrialization is like a quick fix,
sending a jaded economy high by turning it into an 'export
platform' for selected manufacturing industries of the
centre. In the smaller territorial and demographic units,
such industrialization makes bigger ripples, and the
effect can be dramatic. Though lacking a rural hinterland
and with a very small domestic market, these units could

generate a certain dynamism, even encouraging them to
secede from larger national entities. In Singapore, industrial production grew astonishingly after its political
separation from Malaysia; from 1968 to 1973 employment
increased nearly five times. Delighted by the prospect,
Singapore's Foreign Minister explained: 'We have plugged
ourselves into the world economy.' The euphoria of these
years created an anti-regional bias. The case against
economic regionalism was argued in 1971 by Dr Augustine
Tan - Senior Lecturer at the University of Singapore, a
Member of Parliament and of the Economic Development
Board, and earlier the Prime Minister's Political Secretary. (39)

> For member countries [of ASEAN] which have low trade
> barriers, the formation of a common regional barrier
> could make their trade very inefficient.... [There is]
> limited scope for increasing specialisation within the
> ASEAN framework.... The alternative of catering to a
> world market [has a] scope [which] far outstrips the
> regional one.... Even without regionalism capital has
> flowed into industries ... catering to world or extra-
> regional markets as in Singapore.

The recession of 1974-5 and the communist victory in
Vietnam caused a turn-around in foreign economic policy.
The precarious buoyancy of Singapore was at this time
soberly reflected on by Mr Lee Kuan Yew: 'We hitched a
ride on the expanding world economy in these years.' He
then sponsored a revival of ASEAN as a framework for regionalism.

The more or less self-expanding process of accumulation
in Singapore, Taiwan and South Korea was contingent upon
specific elements, both historical and fortuitous. Singapore was a well-developed entrepot of regional and world
trade. The smallness of the country, demographically and
territorially, accentuated the dynamic impact of its relinking with the centre. It benefited in these years from
the raw materials boom in Indonesia, including the oil exploration work and the vast infrastructure investments, as
well as from the American involvement in the Vietnam war.
Moreover, the absence of a rural hinterland did away with
the problem of removing precapitalist social relations and
structures. In Taiwan and South Korea, the capitalist
transformation was far more complex. Their repressive
political system unquestionably favoured a high rate of
accumulation relative to prevailing consumption levels.
A substantial saving in wage costs was also due to the
mobilization of surplus rural labour within the confines
of the rural economy. As in Japan, a preponderance of
small enterprises in the countryside, involving a disper-

sal of labour, held down wages and thereby expanded the
employment potential of a given marketed surplus of wage
goods. Alongside an inflow of capital, inclusive of
American military spending, large numbers were employed
by the military; this and the setting up of pioneer
export platforms helped to spread purchasing power and to
upgrade technical skills.

In the dynamics of the transition to capitalism in
Taiwan and South Korea only the conditioning factors have
been mentioned. Though the generative forces of this
transition have yet to be unravelled and stated more explicitly than has been done here, it is to the actors in
the development process - and not to the factors conceived
of in the abstraction of the prevailing social relations -
that major importance must be attached. In both countries
there was a shift of power internally from a landlord
class to an emerging industrial bourgeoisie. During
Japanese rule the conversion of Taiwan and Korea into a
granary of Japan involved a partial reorientation of the
traditional landlords from a rentier class to a predominantly entrepreneurial one; from rent and interest as a
basis of income to profits. In Korea the landed aristocracy which had 'owned most of the cultivated land and
held the top positions in the administration' was virtually destroyed and replaced by Japanese landlords. (40) The
latter in turn were expropriated by the US military government, and the process of land reform that was begun was
later completed by the Korean government. The systematic
deprivation of the yangban class of its power base removed
all resistance to the implementation of the reforms. (41)
The success of the land reforms was also due to the weakness of merchant and usurers' capital in the rural districts. In many underdeveloped countries it is the dominance of merchant capital that makes the agrarian problem
less amenable to a conventional land reform; landlordism,
being totally functionless, is more easily eradicated than
merchant capital which, though unproductive, plays a necessary role in the day-to-day functioning of the village
economy.

A release of landlord capital paved the way for the
growth of industrial capital. The land bonds given as
compensation to the Korean landlords were redeemable in
cash, and were partly used by them to acquire real estate
and commercial and industrial property that was held by
Japanese. The smaller landlords sold their bonds at a
discount to the big businessmen. (42)

In this way scattered capital was concentrated in a few
hands, later to be mobilised for investment in large
scale industrial projects such as food processing, tex-

tile and other light industries in the 1950s and early
60s, and in the 70s this capital was invested in heavy
industries.
The existence of rural-based small industries encouraged
the conversion of the redeemed land bonds into industrial
assets. In Taiwan, the process of restructuring the rural
economy was carried out by the migrant mainland government
much more effectively. Furthermore, the virtual transformation of the agricultural sector, and an expanded
national market, induced a domestically oriented investment pattern. The development of productive forces was
far less lopsided, and altogether more extensive, than in
South Korea.

The specific elements which underlay the process of
change in Taiwan, South Korea and Singapore, and its his-
toricity, render their experience non-transferable to the
other units of the periphery. It is not conceivable that
Taiwan, South Korea and Singapore could have carried out
this process in a different period. The leading capitalist economies were enjoying an exceptional degree of buoyancy. The MNCs had not yet become active in the periphery. American and European capital was preoccupied in the
reconstruction of Europe, and Japanese capital was re-
building its home economy. Both in Taiwan and South
Korea, indigenous capital was able to develop sufficiently
in these years. The relatively late entry of American
capital into Taiwan compared with South Korea gave refugee
capital from the Chinese mainland even more time to become
established and to expand. Countries currently embarking
upon a capitalist development find their path almost
blocked by the scale of investment and entrepreneurial
operations needed for an internationally viable enterprise, which is beyond the capability of a fledgling bourgeoisie. The disparity in productive forces on a world
scale, having widened over a long period, has acquired
some qualitatively new elements. The concentration and
centralization of capital on a worldwide scale blankets and
controls very pervasively the development of indigenous
enterprise. In a free and open economy, the growth of
indigenous capitalism de novo is also affected by the decline of capitalism as a world system, in contrast to its
remarkable buoyancy some years ago. There is now a revival of protectionism in the developed countries, a massive debt burden in underdeveloped countries, and the
take-over by multinational corporations of their strategic
raw materials, markets, manufacturing sites and cheap
labour resources.

The economic expansion in the periphery consequent upon
its relinking retards the growth of indigenous industrial

capital. The retardation of indigenous enterprise in the
case of the garment industry in Sri Lanka was disclosed in
evidence before a Select Committee of the Parliament of
Sri Lanka by a local industrial tycoon, who is himself a
member of the Greater Colombo Economic Commission. (43)
This tendency extends even to industries producing for the
domestic market. In the Kenya soap industry the MNC firms
within a decade had ousted a good many of the indigenous
firms. (44) The survivors were forced to conform to MNC
patterns - mechanizing their technology, raising the
import content of products, and resorting to fancy packaging and higher advertising outlays. A few of them
became contractors or agents of the foreign firms. A combination of market power and technological superiority enabled the international soap giants to destroy a local industry and to displace it with a functionally superior
product. (45) The tendency for foreign capital to control
or suppress indigenous enterprise was also evident in
Singapore, despite the existence there of a formidable
class of ethnic Chinese capitalists. In 1970 the solely
foreign-owned firms held 57 per cent of the total value of
industrial assets, the solely domestic firms only 17 per
cent and joint ventures 27 per cent. (46) The size of the
foreign firms and their efficient public relations enabled
them to get concessions from the government. Tax reliefs
stipulated a capital investment that exceeded the size of
the typical indigenous firm. Dr Yoshihara, while appreci-
ating the contribution of the Economic Development Board
to Singapore's industrialization, wrote: (47)

But in one respect it failed. The E.D.B. was not very
successful in stimulating a response from domestic
entrepreneurs.... Singapore's industrialization was
carried out to a large extent by foreign subsidiaries.
... There is no sign that the dominant position of the
foreign controlled companies is weakening.

Indigenous capital settles like a sediment lower down
the investment scale. In the manufacturing sector, it
operates mostly on a small-scale basis, independently in
the niches of a highly monopolized economy, or else as
subcontractors to foreign firms, supplying components
whose production technology favours the small unit. In
this role of subcontractor the indigenous entrepreneur
makes available to the foreign firms his access to sweated
labour. Though stifled industrially, indigenous capital
gains new opportunities in the tertiary sector. After the
relinking of the economy, the closure of many independent
small- and medium-scale manufacturing enterprises gives a
stimulus to imports. The trade expansion, however, does
not wholly benefit the indigenous trading class. First,

the increase in imports takes the form partly of intrafirm
transactions by the multinationals - the goods do not
leave the parent company's own channel but move only 'in
one and the same corporate territory'. (48) While the
trading interests are generally reactivated, there is also
greater competition and lower profit margins. Second,
there is an expansion in activities catering mostly for
the needs of a growing expatriate community. (In Singapore, their numbers and importance have warranted a separate cost of living index for expatriates, computed and
published by a business journal.) Third, a buoyancy in
the real estate market resulting from the urban centred
and extroverted development pattern confers prolific windfall gains on speculators and owners of urban property. A
parallel expansion of investment is in residential construction, consumers' stores, recreational and entertainment facilities, tourism and travel, packing and removal
services. These rentier and purely commercial activities
provide soft options to the indigenous bourgeoisie,
leaving foreign capital a free rein over industry, merchant banking and finance.

The relative disability of indigenous capital in manufacturing industry is as much a question of markets as of
technology. The foreign firms have 'expert and comprehensive entry to the world market', based partly on international brand names under which the goods produced by
them are sold. (49) In the components and intermediate
goods industries, though the importance of technical cri-
teria as a determinant of sales is conducive to the entry
of new firms, the ease with which new designs can be
imitated calls for frequent technological innovations;
but investment in innovation requires an assured market.
Patents and the concentration of R&D in the centre, and
access to markets, give the bigger foreign firms an unassailable advantage. It is for this reason that such firms
direct their investment to products and production processes whose technology is changing rapidly rather than to
those which conform with the local resource endowment or
incorporate the functional aspects of a commodity. Exotic
technology increases the monopoly power of the multinational and ensures a higher rate of profits. (50)

Local collaboration, when resorted to by foreign capital, is merely a precondition for starting ventures. It
is a protective mantle. The admission of local capital
'depoliticizes' the investment, and makes it difficult for
the host government to control it in the national interest. For example, in Indonesia, as in the Philippines,
the abuse of the country's timber resources by the foreign
lumber companies was facilitated by their tie-up with army

officials, politicians and bureaucrats. In the resource-
based industries local collaboration gives the foreigner
access to mining concessions, and in industries supplying
the domestic market it gives him access to sales outlets
and distribution networks which the local partner may have
built up earlier as an importer. In the garments industry, the foreigner avails himself of the host country's
export entitlements. In other instances, joint industrial
ventures are trading operations in disguise, promoting the
sale of machinery, components and raw materials, and the
hiring of technology. In these cases a condition of
foreign participation is that the enterprise purchases
plant and equipment from the foreign partner himself, or
on his advice, and raw materials from tied sources. The
supply of inferior, possibly reconditioned equipment, resulting in very frequent breakdowns requiring large
imports of spares for maintenance and repairs, and an
income in the form of royalties and technical assistance
fees, enables the foreign partner to recoup a portion of
his investment regardless of the profits or losses of the
enterprise. With a high import content even a slight
overpricing of supplies enhances hidden profits. The
local collaborators in these ventures may be 'outright
dummies', and totally unprepared to assert themselves.
Their predominantly trading character may even lead them
to connive with the foreign partner to give a trading
orientation to what is nominally an industrial venture.
The trading proclivities of the local bourgeoisie are
thereby strengthened, retarding its transformation into
a genuine industrial class.

    As a modern version of the classical enclave, the
periphery remains 'tightly bound to the home country, far
away, but loosely connected, except geographically to the
local scene'. (51) In the manufacturing sector, despite
some indigenous capital, and the employment of indigenous
labour and indigenous managers and executives, investment
expands horizontally, over a range of final goods. The
vertical integration of investments is between countries
but not within each country. First, the foreign firms
centralize their raw material purchases abroad, and resell
these materials at grossly inflated prices to their col-
laborative enterprises in the periphery. (52) Second,
even when producing for the domestic market, the actual
production operations, in their input-mix, technology and
packaging, are the reverse of import substitution which is
supposedly carried out. The brand differentiated products
imported are now made locally in a way which serves the
global strategies of the producing firm, regardless of the
local resource potential and technological capabilities or

even of the original tastes of the consumers. Third,
unlike the traditional plantations and mines which were
geographically dispersed because of natural conditions
that governed their location, the MNC industrial firms
are in the capital city. Their heavy reliance on imported
inputs places a high premium on efficient transport and
communication links with the external world. Their products cater mostly for urban, high-income consumers whose
preferences could be artificially induced; and the senior
staff of these enterprises (belonging to the transnational
community) are difficult to retain except in the capital
city where social amenities are at their best.

I have referred in the preceding pages to the attempted
rationalization in the use of resources by multinational
capital, through vertical integration of production sites
on a global scale. The resulting concentration and centralization of capital expands the flow of production
capital to the periphery. This leads to a growth of productive forces through an incipient industrialization and
of capitalist production relations. The inability of
capitalism to resolve its basic contradictions, not merely
within the boundaries of the nation state, but even on the
basis of groupings of capitalist countries which have
begun to be formed, is now no longer a problem of markets
and of the need for supplies of raw materials to expand
production, for the sake of production; it also relates
to a breakdown of the work process, with a serious weakening of the established mechanisms of labour discipline and
control.

The new buoyancy of capitalism in the periphery has
given international finance capital a freer rein, one consequence of which has been a foreign-debt explosion of unusual severity - in Pakistan the rice harvest of 1979 was
mortgaged to a commercial bank in Belgium. Manifestly,
this pattern of development seeks to enhance the viability
of the centre relative to that of the periphery. Investment is directed towards (1) the production of raw materials for the centre, (2) industries or production processes
whose productivity seriously lags behind prevailing wage
levels in the centre, (3) the resource-based industries
and those which cause pollution, (4) export industries of
the centre which are threatened by import tariffs in the
periphery, (5) infrastructure projects and (6) forms of
agriculture which are heavy users of imported inputs. The
rationale of this international economic order, in some of
its aspects, was explained by Japan's Council on Industrial Structure: (53)

> Japan will retain and encourage the branches of the
> machine industry that yield high added value, but pro-

duction facilities which involve a low degree of processing and generate low added value should be moved to
developing countries ... so that Japan can concentrate
on high technology and knowledge-intensive industry.
The industries to be transferred were also the resource-
based ones - such as crude steel, petrochemicals, non-
ferrous metals and pulp.

The reincorporation of the periphery into the centre
brings about a complex dialectical interaction between
change and stagnation; it induces a discontinuity in the
traditional centre-periphery relations as well as a continuity. The discontinuity stems from the compulsion of
capitalism at the centre to invest increasingly in the
periphery. In contrast with earlier periods the periphery
is no longer restricted to 'terminal activity' consisting
of primary production and crude processing or of assembly.
Mining and most of the industrial activities are of a
large-scale nature, highly capitalized, technologically
advanced and supported by improvements in the infrastructure - transport, communications and power, as, for example, in Indonesia. There is inevitably a spread of the
capitalist mode of production, whose scope is, however,
limited by the constraints to which I referred earlier on
the transfer of industries to the periphery. The mining-
cum-industrial sector becomes a zone of high development,
sharply differentiated from the rest of the economy. The
continuity in centre-periphery relations lies in basically
the same division of labour as before. Development in the
periphery is not competitive with that of the centre, but
is conditioned by and ancillary to the development of the
centre. Though the new minerals provide enormous potential for the growth of secondary industry (as downstream
activities), the politico-economic forces which have
created the mineral enterprise prevent the full realization of this potential. The internal manifestation of the
impact of these external forces is a continuity in the
class structure of the peripheral countries, where a dominant merchant-cum-industrial class, while expanding its
wealth, does not make the transition to industrial capital.

The underdeveloped economy, consequently, both develops
and underdevelops. The self-contradictory character of
this process has a useful analogue in the 'conservation-
dissolution' tendencies of merchant capital before being
superseded by capitalism; as seen by Geoffrey Kay, it has
both a revolutionary and a conservative streak, 'stimulating and repressing' the development of productive forces
- both 'opening and blocking the way for the full development of capitalism'. (54) Thus the more the economy de-

velops the more it underdevelops. An absolute advance
brings about a relative retardation. Underdevelopment involves not just an unevenness in development on a world
scale but differences in the degree of dynamism between
modes of development which are spatially separated but
symbiotically linked. The periphery then becomes complementary to the centre within the framework of a world division of labour supported by unequal inter-nation relations. These inter-nation relations include, for instance, the tariff policy of the centre which is designed,
along with a whole battery of non-tariff measures, to prevent the underdeveloped countries from utilizing in manufacturing industry the raw materials they traditionally
exported; the centre levies an almost punitive tariff on
imports of low-priced semi-processed goods. (55)   The
mechanisms of underdevelopment relate to the forces which
underlie and reproduce such a division of labour. They
constitute external elements as incorporated in the notion
of unequal exchange as well as internal elements in the
underdeveloped countries - comprising classes, institutions, ideology, etc. The existing division of labour,
that is to say, is rooted both in inter-nation relations
and in the class relations within an underdeveloped country - or more accurately an underdeveloping country.

    A corollary to this dialectic which highlights the
nature of underdevelopment in terms of a process of growth
and stagnation, which cannot transcend the limits imposed
by the interests of the centre, is the interaction of independence and dependence. The industrialization of the
periphery, as explained earlier, imparts a relative viability to even the smallest territorial and demographic
units, encouraging them to secede from larger national
entities. At the same time the subordination of the
periphery to the global interests of the multinational
corporations, upon which the development process becomes
contingent, is a virtual abdication of sovereignty. A
government which has conditioned the economy to foreign
capital cannot risk a confrontation with the MNCs without
jeopardizing its political prospects. In such a confrontation an MNC is far less vulnerable. It operates in
several locations and can withdraw from any country without detriment to its overall interest, but prejudicing
that country's prospects. The sheer size of the foreign
firms gives them an advantage in their dealings with the
bureaucracy. They also develop close contacts with influential politicians and bureaucrats, often with the help of
the local executives - the 'insiders' whom they recruit.
These executives are Western educated, urban-based and
affluent and are part of the transnational community -
citizens of no country and of all countries.

If in the centre the multinationals have outgrown the framework of their own nation states, their operations are far more incompatible with the sovereignty of countries in the periphery. (56)

> Many decisions once considered the province of the nation-state are now being made by externally based MNCs, particularly in such matters as the nature, location and timing of investment. These decisions may affect the employment level, the rate of economic growth, the balance of payments, or whether a given natural resource is developed.

The functional nature of the activities of multinationals in a foreign territory excludes geographical space as the basis of their jurisdiction. Their hegemony rests on a monopoly of technology and markets and an ability to influence capital inflows including the lending policies of governments of the centre and even of supranational agencies such as the IMF and the World Bank.

The repercussions on the periphery of the expansion of world capitalism, and of attempts to contain its contradictions, have been discussed exhaustively in this book. As indicated in the concluding portion of the chapter on merchant capital, the effects of the centre-periphery relations on the growth of productive forces must be seen, however, in the context of a class structure which is still widely dominated by merchant capital and by landlord and usurer capital. Though capitalist production with its increasing application of fixed capital would yield a bigger surplus, a precapitalist class, left to itself or in the absence of social pressures, would not effect the change to capitalism; and the economic interests and goals of this class determine the prevailing pattern of surplus extraction and 'development'. This is not a question of rationality versus irrationality. The relation of this class to the productive process makes the existing mode of production, with its corresponding system of surplus extraction, perfectly rational from its own standpoint. As Hobsbawm once said, the activities which pay off best are not necessarily those which promote development.

The model which has been sketched out in this concluding chapter needs elaboration and in-depth analysis before it can be further developed to enable us to understand the real forces that determine underdevelopment in any specific situation. A concentration on the external factors conditioning underdevelopment in its present phase is not intended to play down or stifle attention to the internal factors - in terms of class structures in the underdeveloped countries and the response of the dominant class to entrepreneurial opportunities or restraints. These in-

ternal factors are far more complex and less capable of
generalization than the external ones; they vary between
countries and even between sectors in the same country.
It is this complexity and specificity which historically
underlay unevenness of development on a world scale.   The
changing economic relations between England and the leading European countries was referred to in an earlier chapter.   From a position of dependence on the earliest centres of industry in Europe, and having served as a field
for the investment of Dutch capital, England made the
transition to capitalism earlier than those countries.
In Japan the seclusion from external influences was not
decisive by itself, compared with the effect of this seclusion on internal class relations and trading structures;   significantly, it undermined the role of merchant
capital.   Furthermore, there has been no uniformity in the
periphery's response to external forces.   Recently,
Taiwan, Singapore, Hong Kong and South Korea have even
managed to subject the more marginalized countries to a
centre-periphery relation, exporting capital to the Free
Trade Zones of Malaysia, Sri Lanka and Bangladesh.   Clearly the external forces as such are less important than the
way in which these forces condition the internal class
structure, strengthening or weakening the barriers to development.   The necessity to probe these internal forces
and to bring them into focus with the external ones leaves
a vacuum to be filled.   This task needs more research and
understanding before there could emerge a sharper and more
effective instrument of analysis than the paradigms in
vogue.

Notes

INTRODUCTION

1   K.J.W.Alexander, The Political Economy of Change,
    Presidential Address at the 1974 Meeting of the
    British Association, Section 'F' (Economics).
2   J.S.Mill, 'Principles of Political Economy' (London,
    1873), p.v.
3   Ibid. Emphasis added.
4   Engels explained that political conditions, etc., 'and
    indeed even the traditions which haunt human minds,
    also play a part although not the decisive one'. He
    stated that 'without making oneself ridiculous it
    would be difficult to succeed in explaining in terms
    of economics the existence of every small state in
    Germany' (letter to J.Bloch, London, 21 September
    1890, Marx and Engels, 'Selected Correspondence'
    (London, 1943), pp.475-6).
5   Maurice Dobb, Introduction to Karl Marx, 'A Contribu-
    tion to the Critique of Political Economy' (Moscow,
    1977), p.14.
6   B.B.Das Gupta, The Theory and Reality of Economic
    Development, 'Bulletin', Central Bank of Ceylon,
    October 1955, p.11.
7   Eugen V.Böhm-Bawerk, 'Capital and Interest' (New York,
    1932), pp.74-5; cit. Maurice Dobb, 'Political Economy
    and Capitalism' (London, 1946), p.134, n.2.
8   Quoted in H.L.Beales, The 'Great Depression' in
    Industry and Trade, 'Economic History Review', vol.5,
    no.1 (1934); reprinted in E.M.Carus-Wilson (ed.),
    'Essays in Economic History' (London, 1966), vol.I,
    p.409.
9   Alexander, loc.cit.
10 'The Nature and Significance of Economic Science'
    (London, 1932), p.83.

11 Lord Keynes, quoted by C.W.Guillebaud, in Introduction
    to the Cambridge Economic Handbook Series. Marx com-
    mented: 'If I ask the political economist: Do I obey
    economic laws if I extract money by offering my body
    for sale ...? (The factory workers in France call the
    prostitution of their wives and daughters the X th
    working hour, which is literally correct.) ... Then
    the political economic ethics and religion have
    nothing to reproach you with' ('The Economic and
    Philosophical Manuscripts of 1844', edited, with an
    Introduction by Dirk J.Struik (New York, 1964), p.
    149). Professor Lionel Robbins, by describing as 'the
    economics of hired love' the phenomenon to which Marx
    here alluded, blurred the social and moral differences
    between different types of productive activity, as for
    example a brothel and a manufacturing enterprise.
12 Lewis S.Feuer (ed.), 'Marx and Engels, Basic Writings
    on Politics and Philosophy' (Fontana Library, 1969),
    p.41.
13 'The Development of Capitalism in Russia' (Moscow,
    1956), pp.142-3.
14 Marx (1977), op.cit., p.197.
15 Marx to the Editor of the 'Otyecestvenniye Zapisky'
    (Notes on the Fatherland), end of 1877, Marx and
    Engels, 'Selected Correspondence', op.cit., p.355.
16 Pradeep Bandyopadhyay, One Sociology, or Many: Some
    Issues in Radical Sociology, 'Science and Society',
    Spring 1971, vol.35, no.1.
17 Preface to the First German Edition (of 'Capital'),
    Karl Marx, 'Capital' (Moscow, n.d.), vol.I, pp.8-9.
18 Marx to the Editor of the 'Otyecestvenniye Zapisky'
    (Notes on the Fatherland), end of 1877, Marx and
    Engels, 'Selected Correspondence', op.cit., p.353.
19 'European Messenger', St Petersburg; quoted in
    Afterword to the Second German Edition (of 'Capital'),
    Marx, 'Capital', vol.I, op.cit., p.18.
20 Karl Marx, 'Pre-Capitalist Economic Formations' (New
    York, 1965), Introduction by E.J.Hobsbawm.
21 Quoted by E.T.Thompson, 'Plantation Societies, Race
    Relations, and the South' (Durham, N.C., 1975).
22 'Can Science Save Us?' (New York, 1947), p.48; cit.
    Bernhard J.Stern, 'Historical Sociology' (New York,
    1959), p.20.
23 Vera Anstey and Anne Martin, 'An Introduction to
    Economics' (ELBS edn, London, 1965).
24 Josef Silverstein, in G.M.Kahin (ed.), 'Governments
    and Politics of Southeast Asia' (Cornell University
    Press, 3rd printing, 1966), p.76.
25 'A History of Modern Burma' (Cornell University Press,
    1956).

26 'The Burma Delta: Economic Development and Social
    Change on an Asian Rice Frontier, 1852-1941' (Wis-
    consin, 1974), pp.29,34,36,209,222.
27 Marx (1977), op.cit., p.203.
28 'Critical Perspectives on Imperialism and Social Class
    in the Third World' (New York, 1978), pp.35,39-40.
29 'The History of the Russian Revolution' (London,
    1934), p.27.
30 Marx to the Editor of the 'Otyecestvenniye Zapisky'
    (Notes on the Fatherland), Marx and Engels, 'Selected
    Correspondence', op.cit., p.353.
31 Ibid., p.354. For the benefit of his Narodnik critic
    Marx added, 'I beg his pardon. (He is both honouring
    and shaming me too much.)'
32 Engels to J.Bloch, London, 21 September 1890, ibid.,
    p.475.
33 Ibid., p.477.
34 Engels to Turati, London, 26 January 1894, ibid.,
    p.520.
35 D.S.Landes, 'The Unbound Prometheus' (Cambridge,
    1969), p.14.
36 'French Rural Society' (London, 1978), pp.xxiii-xxiv.
    'This is not a question of straining after forced com-
    parisons but of making proper distinctions; we are
    not engaged in some kind of trick photography, which
    would produce a fuzzy conventional image, deceptively
    generalised; what we are looking for are character-
    istics held in common, which will make whatever is
    original stand out by contrast', ibid., p.xxiv.
37 'History of Economic Analysis' (London, 1954), pp.
    12-13. Emphasis in original.
38 Marx (1977), op.cit., p.211.
39 Ibid.

CHAPTER 1   ECONOMIC UNDERDEVELOPMENT: A POLITICO-
HISTORICAL PERSPECTIVE

1 'Trends in the Mogul Empire', vol.II, pp.186,170;
   quoted in Gorham D.Sanderson, 'India and British
   Imperialism' (New York, 1951).
2 A.L.Basham, 'The Wonder that was India' (London,
   1967), pp.21-2.
3 Report of International Bank for Reconstruction and
   Development, 'Economic Development of Ceylon'
   (Colombo, 1953), p.3.
4 Erich Fromm, 'The Fear of Freedom' (London, 1960),
   p.37.
5 C.M.Cipolla, 'European Culture and Overseas Expansion'
   (Harmondsworth, 1970), p.151.

6 War and Economic Progress, 'Economic History Review',
   vol.12(1942), p.36.
7 The new form of mounted combat, capable of violence
   without precedent, required a heavier and more elaborate kind of defensive armour; it thus promoted the
   armourer's craft and the science of metallurgy. A
   heavier breed and a larger number of horses were maintained partly to replace those slain in battle. A
   class of professional fighting men also grew up - the
   feudal knights. The military function of the knights
   had by the twelfth century given them a privileged
   position, economically and politically, strengthening
   the social order that was associated with feudalism.
   (Geoffrey Hindley, 'Medieval Warfare' (London, 1971),
   p.57 ff.; Lynn White, Jnr, 'Medieval Technology and
   Social Change' (Chicago, 1962). Excerpts from White
   are reprinted in The Stirrup and Feudalism: Does
   Technology make History?, in Arthur MacEwan and Thomas
   E.Weiskopff, 'Perspectives on the Economic Problem'
   (Chicago, 1970); Henri Pirenne, 'A History of Europe'
   (London, 1961).)
8 Cipolla, op.cit., p.97.
9 H.Myint, The Gains from International Trade and the
   Backward Countries, 'Review of Economic Studies', vol.
   22, 1954-5, p.129.
10 Amalendu Guha, A Big Push Without a Take Off, Paper
   presented to a staff seminar at the Gokhale Institute
   of Politics and Economics, Poona, 20 April 1968.
11 'The Economic Development of India' (London, New York,
   Toronto, 1957), p.5.
12 'Principles of Political Economy' (London, 1873), p.
   414. 'All the capital employed is English capital;
   almost all the industry is carried on for English
   uses; there is little production of anything except
   the staple commodities, and these are sent to England
   ... for the benefit of the proprietors there', ibid.
   In this discussion Mill referred to the West Indies as
   an example.
13 'Thus in order to push our analysis farther to the
   heart of the problem, it would seem desirable to make
   a clean break with the "underdevelopment" approach and
   to recognize the problem of "backwardness" as a major
   problem in its own right which may occur even when
   there is no important "underdevelopment" of resources', H.Myint, An Interpretation of Economic
   Backwardness, 'Oxford Economic Papers' (June, 1954).
14 'The Tragedy of the Chinese Revolution' (Stanford,
   1950), pp.4-5.
15 After the British had suppressed the Kandyan uprising

in Sri Lanka, the Governor warned the people of other
districts of the consequence of any disloyalty. 'To
the Headmen of the Village ... in the Province of Uva
from the Dessave of the Mahagam patto by order of H.E.
the Governor of Ceylon.... You will do well to benefit by the dreadful experience of your neighbours in
the Walapane and Velasse districts.... The people of
Velasse and Walapane were as you are now, in the quiet
enjoyment of their property and personal security,
until the disturbance of the public peace appeared
among them - and what have they gained by it? Their
houses are burnt to the ground, their gardens and
fields are laid waste, and themselves forced to wander
about the jungles, living on wild fruits' (date inde-
cipherable, June 1818, Sri Lanka National Archives
(hereafter SLNA), 6/562). 'It is by fear alone',
wrote Simon Sawers, 'that the Kandyans are to be won.
We are therefore driven to the necessity of either
carrying fire and sword at every district village or
hut that ... gives shelter to the Pretender' (from
S.Sawers, Revenue Agent, Badulla, to his Excellency,
the Governor. Dated Badulla, 13 November 1817. SLNA
6/548).

16 Elphinstone to Mr Cardwell, dated London, 31 January
1865. Colonial Office Papers.
17 'The Accumulation of Capital' (London, 1951), pp.
370-1.
18 'Africa - The Roots of Revolt' (London, 1960), p.23.
19 W.L.Taylor, Problems of Economic Development of the
Federation of Rhodesia and Nyasaland, in E.A.G.
Robinson (ed.), 'Economic Development for Africa South
of the Sahara' (London, 1963), p.242.
20 Aidan Southall, Imperialism and Urban Development in
Africa, in Victor Turner (ed.), 'Colonialism in Africa
1870-1960', vol.II (Cambridge, 1971), pp.248-9.
21 Cited in James Petras, 'Critical Perspectives on
Imperialism and Social Class in the Third World' (New
York, 1978), p.25.
22 In the Ivory Coast, bread baked in Paris was flown
into Abijan on the 'national' airline Air Afrique, a
wholly owned subsidiary of Air France. In Martinique,
milk from the Vosges was brought by the Air France
milk plane, along with the newspapers from France.
Wrapping paper for the banana growers was supplied in
the form of old newsprint from France. Rum exported
from Martinique to North and South America was shipped
to Paris and then redirected. A freight monopoly held
by the Compagnie Générale Transatlantique between Martinique and France enabled it to carry this cargo back
and forth. The telecommunication network required

telephone calls between two adjacent colonies, e.g.
Mali and Guinea, to be routed through a switchboard in
Paris (V.S.Naipaul, 'The Middle Passage' (London,
1963), pp.199,201).

23   Railway Reports from India, House of Commons Papers,
vol.12, 1847.

24   R.S.Rungta, 'The Rise of Business Corporations in
India' (Cambridge, 1970), p.121, n.2.

25   J.C.H.Fei and G.C.Ranis, Economic Development in
Historical Perspective, 'American Economic Review',
vol.59, pt 2 (1969), p.397.   In India 'it is still
possible', wrote Rungta, 'for crops in part of the
country to rot and for people to starve in another',
op.cit., p.120.   Based on Memorandum by the Bombay
Chamber of Commerce to the Famine Commission.

26   Ibid., pp.173-4;   also p.121.

27   The Bullenger pool, which was described as a 'buying
and selling combination', was reputed to mill one
third of Burma's rice exports in the 1870s (V.D.
Wickizer and M.K.Bennett, 'The Rice Economy of Monsoon
Asia' (Stanford, 1941), p.72, n.7).

28   For the lack of means of transport, paddy straw was
burned to get it off the ground.   This reference is to
the Okkampitiya paddy tracts around Badulla.   'Diaries
of the Government Agent', 16 October 1902.   SLNA,
57/63.

29   'Uva Government Agent's Diaries', 25 August 1895.
SLNA, 47/5.

30   Ibid., 1 December 1900.

31   'Uva Government Agent's Diaries', 28 November 1907.
SLNA, 57/68.

32   Ibid., 29 August 1904.   SLNA, 47/6.

33   Ibid.

34   Ibid.

35   Ibid.

36   Ibid., 14 June 1907, SLNA, 57/68.

37   Ibid., 31 January 1916.

38   Ibid., 28 November 1907.

39   Ibid., 18 December 1916.   Referring to the proposal by
a planter to expand the Committee, the Assistant Agent
remarked: 'His theory that because planters pay the
tax they should have a voice in its distribution ap-
plies equally to the natives who pay by far the larger
proportion, and from where is he going to get independent native members in the district?'   Ibid.

40   Ibid., 7 June 1887.

41   Ibid., 19 December 1886.

42   Ibid., 7 June 1887.

43   'I think I am right in saying that not a penny has

been spent on irrigation in this district since my arrival last October *[more than a year]*; a glorious record', ibid., 4 December 1897.

44 'Diaries of the Assistant Government Agent of Nuwara Eliya District', 7 July 1889: 'The land was once under paddy and was irrigated by a channel that followed much the same course as the one proposed ... it is flat and fertile and there would be very little difficulty in converting it into fields.'

45 Ibid., 22 August, 1901.

46 Ibid., 21 April 1904.

47 Ibid., 27 August 1901.

48 Ibid.

49 'To carry out the provisions of the road ordinance properly also entails upon me such additional work and my attendance is presently required at the working places, 6, 7 or 8 miles from Matale. Travelling there and back occupies the whole of the mornings so that I have not sufficient time on my return to attend to any revenue business, but have to go immediately to Court which I seldom leave before 6 o'clock; ... I cannot, as I am now situated, have that constant communication with the headman or with the people which is desirable' (Report of the Assistant Agent, Matale, for the half-year ending 30 June 1850. Kandy Diaries, 1850).

50 'Diaries', 28 July 1896.

51 A discussion of this problem based on administrative records of the period is by Lim Teck Ghee, 'Peasants and their Agricultural Economy in Colonial Malaya, 1874-1941' (Kuala Lumpur, 1977).

52 Memorandum prepared by the F.M.S. Chamber of Mines for the Tin Commission, 'Straits Times', 1 November 1918.

53 A.N.Anjorin, Tin Mining in Northern Nigeria during the Nineteenth and the Early Part of the Twentieth Centuries, 'Journal of West African Studies', new series, no.5 (April 1971), p.62; Penelope Bower, The Mining Industry, in Margery Perham (ed.), 'The Economics of a Tropical Dependency', vol.III, 'Mining, Commerce, and Finance in Nigeria' (London, 1948), p.8.

54 Ibid., pp.4-5; also Anjorin, loc.cit., p.63.

55 J.H.Drabble, 'Rubber in Malaya 1876-1922' (Kuala Lumpur, 1973), p.74.

56 Yip Yat Hoong, 'The Development of the Tin Mining Industry of Malaya' (Kuala Lumpur, 1969), p.152.

57 'Mining Journal, Railway and Commercial Gazette', vol.66, 29 February 1896, p.277, quoted by Wong Lin Ken, 'The Malayan Tin Industry to 1914' (Tucson, 1965), p.215.

58 G.Myrdal, 'Economic Theory and Under-Developed Regions' (London, 1957), p.56.

59   Ibid., p.57. Cf. the importance attached by Professor
     Nove to any short run expansion: 'Often ... the
     interest of international capital is confined to
     primary products. But while this can cause lopsided
     development, it is surely a great deal better than
     nothing, which is all too frequently the only prac-
     ticable alternative' (Alex Nove, On Reading Andre
     Gunder Frank, 'Journal of Development Studies', vol.
     10, nos 3 and 4 (April-July), 1974, p.446.
60   The Long Term Trends in World Economic Growth,
     'Malayan Economic Review', vol.6 (1961), p.18. Also
     Charles Issawi, Egypt since 1800: A Study in Lop-sided
     Development, 'Journal of Economic History', March
     1961.
61   The Plantation Economy and Industrial Change in Latin
     America, 'Economic Development and Cultural Change',
     vol.18, no.3 (April 1970), p.360.
62   'From Dependent Currency to Central Banking' (London,
     1962), pp.1-2.
63   D.R.Snodgrass, 'Ceylon: An Export Economy in
     Transition' (Homewood, Ill., 1966), p.16.
64   A.Hazlewood, The Economics of Colonial Monetary
     Arrangements, 'Social and Economic Studies', vol.3,
     no.34 (December 1954), pp.299-300.
65   Gunasekera, op.cit., p.v.
66   Op.cit., p.16. 'Ceylon very clearly became [an export
     economy] during the decade of the 1840s and remained
     certainly throughout the rest of the colonial era, and
     in some respects to the present day' (ibid., p.17).
67   Ibid., p.1.
68   Ibid., p.70.
69   Ibid.
70   Ibid., p.21
71   J.R.Levin, 'The Export Economies' (Cambridge, Mass.,
     1960), pp.85-6.
72   Op.cit., pp.1,21.
73   Ibid., p.1.
74   Ibid., p.17.
75   The Economic History of Ceylon in the Nineteenth
     Century, vol.I, Plantations, Land and Capital, unpub-
     lished English manuscript of Sinhalese book, 1961,
     quoted in Snodgrass, op.cit.
76   Myrdal, op.cit., p.55.
77   The Distribution of Gains between Investing and
     Borrowing Countries, 'American Economic Review',
     Papers and Proceedings, May 1950, p.475.
78   'The World's Sugar' (Stanford, 1957).
79   Gunasekera, op.cit., p.205.
80   Op.cit., p.60. 'A widening of markets often strength-

ens in the first instance the rich and progressive
countries whose manufacturing industries have the lead
and are already fortified by the surrounding external
economies; while the under-developed countries are in
continuous danger of seeing even what they have of
industry ... priced out by cheap exports from the industrial countries' (ibid., p.51).

81 Historical Experience of Economic Development, in
    E.A.G.Robinson (ed.), 'Problems in Economic Develop-
    ment' (Macmillan, London and St Martin's Press, New
    York, 1965), p.121.
82 Bipan Chandra, Colonialism and Modernisation, Presi-
    dential Address, Indian Historical Congress, 1970.
83 'Western Enterprise in Indonesia and Malaya' (London,
    1962), p.236.
84 T.C.Smith, 'Political Change and Industrial Develop-
    ment in Japan' (Stanford, 1955); extracts in Jon
    Livingston, Joe Moore, Felicia Oldfather, 'The
    Japanese Reader', I (Harmondsworth, 1973), pp.108 ff.
85 R.Nurkse, International Investment Today in the Light
    of Nineteenth Century Experience, 'Economic Journal',
    1954 (December), p.745.
86 W.K.Hancock, 'Survey of British Commonwealth Affairs',
    vol.II, pt I (Oxford, 1940), p.25.
87 H.Myint, The Gains from International Trade and the
    Backward Countries, 'Review of Economic Studies', vol.
    22, 1954-5, p.132.
88 'An International Economy, Problems and Prospects'
    (London, 1956), p.101.
89 'Asian Drama' (London, 1968), vol.I.
90 'Ceylon in 1903' (Colombo, 1903), pp.82-3.
91 In Sri Lanka, with the imposition of Sterling Area ex-
    change control in 1948, plantation companies were
    requested to remit to Sri Lanka the interest and other
    income from their current reserves held abroad. By
    the transfer of these funds the government hoped to
    foster a short-term money market. However, the compa-
    nies refused to comply. In 1961 many of the companies
    removed these funds from any possible control by the
    Central Bank by shifting them to Holding Companies in
    Britain.
92 L.H.Jenks, 'Migration of British Capital to 1875'
    (London and Edinburgh, 1963), pp.196-7.
93 Multinational Corporations and Dependent Under-
    development in Mineral Export Economies, 'Social and
    Economic Studies', vol.19, no.4 (December 1970), p.
    513.
94 W.O.Henderson, Germany's Trade with Her Colonies,
    1884-1914, 'Economic History Review', vol.9, no.1
    (November 1938), pp.13 and 14.

95 'Capital' (Moscow, n.d.), vol.I, p.714.
96 Robert Brenner, The Origins of Capitalist Develop-
    ment: A Critique of Neo-Smithian Marxism, 'New Left
    Review', no.104 (July-August 1977), p.30.
97 'Educational Strategy for Developing Societies'
    (London, 1963), p.ix.
98 Myrdal (1957), op.cit., p.59.
99 Curle, op.cit., pp.45-6.
100 'The Soul of India' (New York, 1960).
101 'A.G.A.'s Diaries', Kegalle, 25 November 1884.
102 Dated 24 November 1884.
103 'A.G.A.'s Diaries', Kegalle, 9 October 1895.
104 Ibid.
105 The Assistant Agent of the Kegalle District in 1895
    made some revealing notes on the family position of
    some of those who had held office in the Three and
    Four Korales:
    Beligal
    Korale   C.H.Samarasinghe - 'transferred in dis-
                                      grace and resigned;
                                      still lives in
                                      Kegalle.'

    Galboda &
    Kirigoda
    Korales
    (R.M.'S)   Rankotdiwala   - 'retired. 1st class
                                      family - dying out.'
                  Beminiwatte   - '2nd class family -
                                      promising youngster.'
                  Unambuwa   - 'still lives at
                                      Gampola - very
                                      decayed.'
                  Keppitipola   - 'still alive - very
                                      decayed - too much
                                      stimulants.'
    Paranakuru
    Korale   Weragoda   - 'Dismissed 1848. 1st
                                      class family. Gone to
                                      the dogs.'
                  C.Bandaranaike   - 'Does nothing at
                                      Peradeniya - a failure
                                      from the low country.'
                  Marapone   - 'Experiment. 1st
                                      class failure.'
    Source: 'A.G.A. Kegalle Diaries, 1895'. SLNA, 30,
    p.167.
106 Joseph Buttinger, 'Vietnam: A Dragon Embattled' (New
    York, Washington, London, 1967), vol.I, pp.161-2.
107 Helen B.Lamb, 'Vietnam's Will to Live' (New York and
    London, 1972).

108   Ramon H.Myer and Adrienne Cheng, Agricultural
      Development in Taiwan under Japanese Colonial Rule,
      'Journal of Asian Studies', vol.23, no.4, August
      1964, p.570.
109   W.R.Roff, 'The Origins of Malay Nationalism' (Kuala
      Lumpur, Singapore, 1970), p.93. The late ruler of
      Johore, Sultan Ibrahim, engaged in big-game hunting,
      riding, driving and horse racing. Abu Bakar his son
      'travelled abroad, entertained lavishly, ran racing
      stables and was popular with the British Royal
      family' (Donald Davis, Sultan Ibrahim - last of the
      Autocratic Malay Sultans, 'Sunday Gazette' (Penang),
      11 March 1973).
110   Roff, op.cit., p.72.
111   Ibid., p.230.
112   A.C.Burns, 'History of Nigeria' (London, 1942), p.
      303.

CHAPTER 2   THE SETTLER/NONSETTLER DICHOTOMY

1   W.A.Lewis, 'Report on Industrialization and the Gold
    Coast' (Accra, 1953), p.8.
2   Compiled by the Gokhale Institute of Politics and
    Economics. Quoted in C.Meyers, 'Labour Problems in
    the Industrialization of India' (Cambridge, Mass.,
    1958), p.20; also H.Venkatasubbiah, 'The Structural
    Basis of Indian Economy' (London, 1940), pp.114-17,
    Appendix D, pp.149-50.
3   Engels to Kautsky, 12 September 1882, 'Marx and
    Engels Selected Correspondence' (London, 1943), p.
    359.
4   One Hundred Years of British Rule in Ceylon,
    'Proceedings of the Royal Colonial Institute', vol.
    27(1895-6).
5   'Netherlands India' (Cambridge, 1944), p.102.
    Furnivall's comment that the nonsettler territories
    were 'colonized by capital' should not be taken to
    mean that they attracted a large amount of foreign
    capital.
6   O.C.Cox, 'Caste, Class and Race' (New York, 1959),
    p.360.
7   A.I.Levkovsky, 'Capitalism in India' (Bombay, Septem-
    ber 1966), p.124.
8   S.W.Baker, 'Eight Years' Wanderings in Ceylon'
    (London, 1855). In highlighting the essentially
    transient interests of individual Britishers in the
    nonsettler colonies, Baker stated: 'You cannot con-
    vince an English settler [sic] that he will be abroad

for an indefinite number of years; the idea would be
equivalent to transportation: he consoles himself
with the hope that something will turn up to alter the
apparent certainty of his exile' (ibid., pp.98-9).

9   'Ceylon in 1903' (Colombo, 1903), p.82.
10 Suriya Wickremasinghe, South Rhodesia, A British
    Algeria, 'Times of Ceylon', 16 July 1964.
11 Cyril Sofer and Rhona Ross, Some Characteristics of an
    East African European Population, 'British Journal of
    Sociology', vol.2(1951), p.319, n.1. The Europeans in
    Indochina, though more cut off from their homeland,
    had their compensations: 'On the whole, between fur-
    loughs, most ... [of them] lead a life which is easier
    than it is in France - without anxiety, comfortable
    routine and rather stay-at-home' (Charles Robequain,
    'The Economic Development of French Indo-China'
    (Oxford, 1944), p.31).
12 F.S.V.Donnison, 'Burma' (New York, 1970), p.95.
13 Pierre Boulle has brought this out in his novel on the
    life of Europeans on a plantation, 'Sacrilege in
    Malaysia' (London, 1959).
14 David Joel Steinberg et al. (eds), 'In Search of
    South-East Asia. A Modern History' (Kuala Lumpur and
    Singapore, 1971), p.282.
15 L.H.Palmier, 'Indonesia and the Dutch' (London, 1965),
    p.132. Based on 1930 Census for Netherlands India,
    vol.6, p.14.
16 According to the 1930 census for Netherlands India,
    the 'pure-bred Dutch' who were gainfully employed in-
    cluded 22,000 in the railway, tramways, posts and
    telegraphs, 15,000 in sugar estates and refineries,
    and 6,000 in retail trade. A.S.Keller, Netherlands
    India as a Paying Proposition, 'Far Eastern Economic
    Survey', 17 January 1940, quoted in H.G.Callis,
    'Foreign Capital in Southeast Asia' (New York, 1942),
    p.29.
17 Ruth T.McVey, 'The Rise of Indonesian Communism'
    (Ithaca, N.Y., 1965), pp.13-14.
18 The data in this paragraph are based on Robequain, op.
    cit., pp.21-9; Callis, op.cit., p.83; and Geographi-
    cal Handbook Series, B.R.510, 'Indo-China' (Naval In-
    telligence Division of the British Admiralty, December
    1943), pp.250-3.
19 Callis, op.cit., p.80.
20 The Economics of a Tropical Colony, in 'Indonesian
    Economics' (Amsterdam, 1961), p.119.
21 Introduction to Callis, op.cit., p.2.
22 H.W.Arndt, Economic Development: Some Lessons of
    Australian Experience, a lecture delivered in 1954 to

the Economic Development Secretariat of the United
Nations. Published in 'Berichte Weltwirtschaftliches
Archiv', Bd.73, Heft 1, 1954, p.162.

23 'British Economic History 1870-1914. Commentary and
Documents' (Cambridge, 1965), p.424.

24 In Sri Lanka in 1937, the authorities panicked when a
young assistant superintendent of a tea estate, an
Australian by the name of Anthony Bracegirdle, was
found addressing meetings of a plantation labour
union. The Governor, using emergency powers, ordered
his immediate arrest and deportation.

25 Loc.cit.

26 Op.cit.

27 In Ralph Linton (ed.), 'The Science of Man in the
World Crisis' (New York, 1945), p.368, quoted in Cox,
op.cit., p.336.

28 James Crawford Maxwell, a High Commissioner of Zambia
in the 1920s. In L.H.Gann, 'A History of Northern
Rhodesia' (London, 1964), p.214.

29 Robequain, op.cit., p.181.

30 C. de Jong, The Dutch Peasants in Surinam, 'Plural
Societies', vol.5, no.3 (Autumn 1974).

31 Ibid., p.36.

32 George Palmer, 'Kidnapping in the South Seas' (Harmondsworth, 1973), p.192. Originally published in
Edinburgh in 1871.

33 'Sydney Evening News', [no day given] May 1869, quoted
in Palmer, op.cit.

34 Eric Williams, 'Capitalism and Slavery' (New York,
1961), p.22. According to the Australian Medical
Congress in 1920, 'The most rigorous scientific examination failed to show any organic changes in white
residents [in the tropical regions of Australia] which
enabled them to be distinguished from residents of
temperate climates' (H.L.Wilkinson, 'The World's
Population Problems and a White Australia' (London,
1930), p.251, quoted by Williams, op.cit., p.32).

35 Op.cit., ch.11.

36 'Results of Committee of Enquiry appointed to consider
Taxation and Finance', Dispatch No.13 from Grey to
Torrington, 17 July 1848, printed in 'British
Parliamentary Papers', vol.XXVI of 1847.

37 'Trade and Politics in the Niger Delta' (Oxford,
1956), p.100.

38 C.M.Turnbull, The European Mercantile Community in
Singapore, 1819-1867, 'Journal of Southeast Asian
History', vol.10, no.1(1969).

39 Ibid., pp.12-13.

40 J.C.Jackson, 'Planters and Speculators' (Kuala
Lumpur, 1968), p.90.

41 The Colonial Stock Act of 1837 made the Empire a popu-
    lar field for British overseas capital by permitting
    trust funds to be invested in colonial and British
    government securities; and these securities were ac-
    corded a privileged position in the market.
42 Man-Land Relations in the Caribbean Area, in Vera
    Rubin (ed.), 'Caribbean Studies: A Symposium',
    American Ethnological Society (Seattle, 1960), pp.14,
    16.
43 Richard Pares, Merchants and Planters, 'Economic
    History Review' Supplement 4 (Cambridge, 1960), p.16.
44 The Climatic Theory of the Plantations, 'Agricultural
    History' (January 1941), p.60, quoted in Williams, op.
    cit., p.22.
45 Quoted by L.M.Hacker, 'The Triumph of American
    Capitalism' (New York, 1965).
46 V.T.Harlow, 'A History of Barbados' (Oxford, 1926),
    p.302, quoted in Celso Furtado, 'The Economic Growth
    of Brazil' (Berkeley and Los Angeles, 1968), p.21.
47 Abbot Emerson Smith, 'Colonists in Bondage: White
    Servitude and Convict Labour in America, 1607-1776'
    (Chapel Hill, 1947), pp.3-4,30; cit. D.B.Davis, 'The
    Problem of Slavery in Western Culture' (Harmonds-
    worth, 1970), p.152.
48 J.R.Commons et al. (eds), 'Documentary History of
    American Industrial Society' (Cleveland, 1910-11),
    vol.1, pp.329-40,346-8; reprinted as Runaways,
    1736-55, in Oscar Handlin (ed.), 'Readings in American
    History' (New York, 1960), p.76.
49 'Present State of Virginia (1724)', quoted in Commons,
    op.cit., vol.I, pp.339-48, reprinted in Handlin, op.
    cit., p.75, Recruiting and Managing Servants, 1724-39.
50 Pat Tyler et al., A True and Historical Narrative of
    the Colony of Georgia in America, in Peter Force,
    'Tracts' (Washington, 1835), vol.I, no.4, pp.20-3,
    reprinted in Handlin, op.cit., pp.27-8, The Demand for
    Negroes in Georgia, 1735.
51 The English settlers in Georgia found the cost of
    making tar and planks and saw boards considerable 'by
    reason of the great expense of white servants'. Abbot
    Emerson Smith, op.cit., quoted in Davis, op.cit.
52 Alfred H.Conrad and John R.Meyer, 'The Economics of
    Slavery' (Chicago, 1964), p.82.
53 Judith Nagata, Adaptation and Integration of Greek
    Working Class Immigrants in the City of Toronto,
    Canada: a Situational Approach, 'International
    Migration Review', 1968.
54 'The Cambridge History of the British Empire', vol.
    VII, pt II: 'New Zealand' (Cambridge, 1933), p.4.

55 Joseph P.L.Jlang, The Chinese in Thailand: Past and
    Present, 'Journal of Southeast Asian History', 1966,
    vol.7, pp.48-9. Also G.W.Skinner, Chinese Assimila-
    tion and Thai Politics, 'Journal of Asian Studies',
    XVI (February 1957).
56 L.A.P.Gosling, Migration and Assimilation of Rural
    Chinese in Trengganu, in J.Bastin and R.Roolwink
    (eds), 'Malayan and Indonesian Studies' (Oxford,
    1964).
57 Lim Boon Keng, quoted in Song Ong Siang, One Hundred
    Years, History of the Chinese in Singapore: A Case of
    Local Identity and Socio-cultural Accommodation,
    'Journal of Southeast Asian History', vol.X, no.1
    (March 1967), p.97.
58 J.Edmonds, Religion, Intermarriage and Assimilation:
    The Chinese in Malaya, 'Race', vol.10, no.1 (July
    1968), p.61.
59 C.C.Wrigley, Kenya: The Patterns of Economic Life,
    1902-1905, in Vincent Harlow and F.M.Chilver (eds),
    'History of East Africa' (Oxford, 1965), p.213.
60 'The Wealth of Nations' (Everyman edn), vol.II, pp.
    120 ff, quoted in Dike, op.cit., p.10.
61 Wrigley, loc.cit.
62 Ibid., p.228. But as it turned out, active resistance
    to British rule came from the Kikuyu; the Masai,
    while showing a 'haughty indifference to European
    ways', remained quiescent partly because they were not
    seriously interfered with. G.H.Mungeam, Masai and
    Kikuyu Responses to the Establishment of British
    Administration in the East Africa Protectorate,
    'Journal of African History', vol.11, no.1(1970),
    p.128.
63 A.K.H.Weinrich (Sister Mary Aquina OP), 'Black and
    White Elites in Rural Rhodesia' (Manchester, 1973),
    p.9.
64 De Jong, loc.cit., p.22.
65 Augustine Bernard, Rural Colonization in North Africa
    (Algeria, Tunis and Morocco), in American Geographical
    Society, Special Publication, No.14, 'Pioneer Settle-
    ment' (New York, 1932), pp.226-7.
66 E.R.Wolf, 'Peasant Wars of the Twentieth Century' (New
    York, 1969), p.223.
67 Several relevant essays are in Michael Crowder (ed.),
    'West African Resistance' (New York, 1971), especially
    Obaro Ikime, Nigeria-Ijebu, ibid., p.205.
68 David Kimble, 'A Political History of Ghana 1850-1928'
    (Oxford, 1963), referred to by H.Hymer, Economic Forms
    in Pre-Colonial Ghana, 'Journal of Economic History',
    vol.30, no.1 (March 1970), p.48.

69 W.O.Henderson, Germany's Trade With Her Colonies,
    1884-1914, 'Economic History Review', vol.9, no.1
    (November 1938), pp.2,9 and 11. Also W.O.Henderson,
    German East Africa, in Vincent Harlow and F.M.Chilver
    (eds), 'History of East Africa' (Oxford, 1965), pp.
    137 ff.
70 Wrigley, loc.cit., p.220. E.A.Brett, 'Colonialism and
    Underdevelopment in Africa' (London, 1973), p.50.
71 De Jong, loc.cit., p.35.
72 Wrigley, loc.cit., p.220. The sons of leading Creole
    families in the Spanish Indies when travelling in
    Europe about the end of the eighteenth century were
    'shocked to see white men in Spain cheerfully perform-
    ing menial tasks which in the Indies were left to
    Indians' (J.H.Parry, 'The Spanish Seaborne Empire'
    (London, 1966), p.340).
73 Robequain, op.cit., pp.181-2. In works on economic
    development the scorn of labour has been given a dis-
    torted emphasis. But work by itself, or in the ab-
    stract, is neither inferior nor superior; its status
    derives from the treatment accorded by society to
    those who work. In the Roman empire a contempt for
    manual labour was engendered by slavery. Likewise in
    the Southern states of America, where the Whites con-
    sidered manual labour as 'menial and revolting', and
    to work hard was 'to work like a nigger'.
74 P.T.Drake is wide of the mark when he attributes the
    high payments made to Europeans in 'backward tropical
    countries', among other reasons, to 'the risks (his-
    torically high) of tropical illness, early death and
    the discomforts and limitations of life away from
    home' (Natural Resources Versus Foreign Borrowing in
    Economic Development), 'Economic Journal', vol.82,
    no.237 (September 1972), p.959). Thomas Eden, Deputy
    Secretary to the Government of Sri Lanka in 1829, ad-
    vocated generous salaries to British civil servants,
    among other grounds, to conform with 'the style of
    living they are obliged to adopt to support the Eng-
    lish character with credit' (evidence given by him on
    public service reforms, Colombo, 26 October-3 November
    1829, SLNA, 19/48).
75 'The Political Economy of Slavery' (London, 1966),
    p.18.
76 A.J.Meyer, 'Middle Eastern Capitalism' (Cambridge,
    Mass., 1954), p.157.
77 'When Indians come to London some of them became
    members of the most exclusive clubs, to which it was
    not possible for some of their English friends in
    India to belong, but when these same Indians went back

to India they were not allowed even to enter the doors of this or that English club - except perhaps as waiters' (Social Life in Bengal, Sir Satyendra Sinha, member of the Imperial War Council. His address to a meeting of the Union of the East and West, in London, in 1918 was preceded by Lord Islington remarking about 'the magnificent victories achieved during the past few days, in which Indian troops played a conspicuous part', 'Straits Times', 12 December 1918).

78 K.S.Sandhu, Sikh Immigration into Malaya during the Period of British Rule, in Jerome Ch'en and Nicholas Tarling, 'Studies in the Social History of China and South-East Asia' (Cambridge, 1970), p.339.

79 Op.cit., p.168.

80 Charles-Henri Favrod, 'La F.L.N. et L'Algérie' (Paris, 1962), p.137, quoted in Wolf, op.cit., p.22.

81 Op.cit., p.168.

82 Quoted in Elspeth Huxley, 'White Man's Country: Lord Delamere and the Making of Kenya' (London, 1968), vol.1, p.v.

83 'The East Africa Protectorate', quoted in Huxley, ibid.

84 'A History of Northern Rhodesia' (London, 1964), p. 216. Also L.H.Gann and P.Duignan, 'White Settlers in Tropical Africa' (Harmondsworth, 1962), pp.62-3. The contention was that the white farmers had to protect themselves from the ill-disciplined agricultural practices of Africans. The possibility of the Africans emulating the settlers was not considered. However, in the nonsettler colonies, the British tea and rubber planters in Sri Lanka and Malaysia and the Dutch tea planters in Indonesia produced plantation crops in the vicinity of indigenous smallholders and of peasant paddy cultivators.

CHAPTER 3 EXPORT STAPLES AND THEIR CONTRASTING IMPACT ON DEVELOPMENT - THE SETTLER AND THE NONSETTLER REGIONS

1 W.A.Peffer, 'The Farmer's Side, His Troubles, and their Remedy' (New York, 1891), part II, p.56, quoted by Rosa Luxemburg, 'The Accumulation of Capital' (London, 1951), pp.396-7.

2 Peffer, op.cit., pp.58 ff, quoted Luxemburg, op.cit., p.401.

3 Stanley B.Ryerson, 'Unequal Union' (New York, 1968), p.39.

4 'On the streams from New Hampshire to Georgia, mills were built to process grain and saw logs into various

types of lumber. Sometimes the two processes were
combined at a single mill, often they were separated.
In Pennsylvania enterprising flour millers barrelled
their flour for shipment and even erected shops for
baking bread and manufacturing the famous hardstick
biscuits served to sailors on naval and merchant
vessels' (Charles and Mary Beard, 'The Beards' New
History of the United States' (New York, 1960), p.49).

5   Colonial Socialism in Australia, 1860-1900, in H.G.J.
Aitken (ed.), 'The State and Economic Growth' (New
York, 1959), p.26; also p.32.

6   From data in Butlin, loc.cit., p.28, n.8.

7   W.A.Sinclair, Capital Formation, in C.Foster (ed.),
'Australian Economic Development in the Twentieth
Century' (London, 1970), p.40.

8   It was first propounded by H.A.Innis to explain the
growth of the Canadian economy, starting from the establishment of cod fisheries and the fur trade - the
earliest export staples. A further development of the
theory was by R.F.Baldwin and D.C.North.

9   Location Theory and Regional Economic Growth, 'Journal
of Political Economy', vol.63 (June 1955).

10 Charles and Mary Beard, op.cit., p.49.

11 'Unequal Exchange' (New York, 1972), p.156, n.25.

12 L.M.Hacker, 'The Triumph of American Capitalism' (New
York, 1965), p.63.

13 Merchants and Planters, 'Economic History Review'
Supplement (Cambridge, 1960), pp.4-5.

14 Charles and Mary Beard, op.cit., p.52.

15 J.W.McCarty, The Staples Approach in Australian
Economic History, 'Business Archives and History',
vol.IV, no.1 (February 1964), reprinted in N.T.Drohan
and J.H.Day (eds), 'Readings in Australian Economics'
(Melbourne, 1965), p.139.

16 H.W.Broude, The Role of the State in American Economic
Development 1820-1890, in Aitken (ed.), op.cit.

17 T.A.Coghlan, 'Labour and Industry in Australia'
(London, 1918), p.1411, quoted Butlin, loc.cit., p.75,
n.69.

18 International Investment Today in the Light of
Nineteenth Century Experience, 'Economic Journal',
vol.64 (December 1954), pp.746-7.

19 R.Nurkse, Comment on International Investment, in B.F.
Haley (ed.), 'A Survey of Contemporary Economics',
vol.II (Homewood, Ill., 1952), p.350. 'Why is it that
private business investment has tended in the past ...
to shy away from industries working for the domestic
market in underdeveloped areas? ... There is the obvious economic explnation: on the one hand, the

poverty of the local consumers; on the other, the
large and, in the nineteenth century, vigorously expanding markets for primary products in the world's
industrial centers' (R.Nurkse, Some International
Aspects of the Problem of Economic Development,
'American Economic Review', vol.42, no.2 (May 1952),
p.573). Also, H.Myint: 'A thickly populated country
with a small population base such as Ceylon seems to
be especially handicapped by the smallness of its
market' ('The Economics of Developing Countries'
(London, 1964), p.32).

20 Michael Barratt Brown, 'After Imperialism' (London,
1970), p.x; Harry Magdoff, 'The Age of Imperialism'
(New York, 1969), p.38.

21 Brown, op.cit.

22 A.K.Sen, The Pattern of British Enterprises in India,
1854-1914; A Causal Analysis, in Baljit Singh and V.B.
Singh (eds), 'Social and Economic Change' (Bombay,
1967).

23 Capital Formation and Economic Development, 'International Economic Papers', no.4 (London, 1954), p.126.
Cf. P.L.Rosenstein-Rodan: 'Indivisibilities of
inputs, processes, or outputs give rise to increasing
returns, that is economies of scale, and may require a
high optimum size of a firm. This is not a very important obstacle to development since with some exceptions (for instance in Central America) there is
usually sufficient demand, even in small, poor countries, for at least one optimum scale firm in many
industries' (Notes on the Theory of the 'Big Push',
in H.S.Ellis (ed.), 'Economic Development for Latin
America' (London, 1961), p.60).

24 'A Report on International Comparisons of Productivity', National Institute of Economic and Social
Research, UK, circa 1948.

25 Causes of the Superior Efficiency of U.S.A. Industry
compared with British Industry, 'Economic Journal'
(September), 1946, p.385.

26 I owe this idea to Dr Nam Joshi, formerly of the
Gokhale Institute of Politics and Economics, Poona.

27 D.H.Buchanan, 'The Development of Capitalistic
Enterprise in India' (New York, 1934).

28 J.S.Puthucheary, 'Ownership and Control in the Malayan
Economy' (Singapore, 1960), p.156.

29 E.L.Wheelwright, 'Industrialization in Malaya' (Melbourne, 1965), p.106.

30 Sjovald Cunyngham-Brown, 'The Traders' (London, 1971),
pp.173,192.

31 Buchanan, op.cit., pp.160,167.

32 Op.cit., p.36.
33 G.D.Babcock, 'History of the United States Rubber
    Company' (Indiana, 1966), p.6.
34 Charlotte Leubuscher, 'The Processing of Colonial Raw
    Materials' (London, HMSO, 1951), p.10.
35 D.C.North, Ocean Freight and Economic Development
    1750-1913, 'Journal of Economic History', vol.18,
    no.4(1958).
36 'Report of the Commission appointed by His Excellency
    the Governor of the Straits Settlements to enquire
    into and report on the Trade of the Colony 1933-34',
    vol.1 (Government Printing Press, 1934), p.149.
37 North, loc.cit. (1958).
38 Chiang Hai Ding, The Shipping Conference System,
    1897-1911, 'Journal of Southeast Asian History', vol.
    10, no.1(1969).
39 Leubuscher, op.cit., p.9.
40 H.G.Johnson, 'Economic Policies Towards Less Developed
    Countries' (London, 1969), pp.84 ff.
41 The heavy discrimination by the developed countries
    against the import of coconut oil, in favour of copra,
    is seen from the rates of general non-preferential
    duties as at 1 June 1969 (Table N1).

TABLE N1

	USA	UK	Japan	Canada	Denmark	EEC
	(Dollar cents)					
Copra	1.25 per lb	10%	O	O	O	O
Coconut oil	3 per lb	15%	15 yen per kg or 10%	10-17½%*	8-12½%*	5-15%*

Source: B.H.Davey and S.J.Rogers, 'The World Coconut
Markets', Department of Agricultural Economics,
University of Newcastle-upon-Tyne (May 1971), p.11.
* The lowest rate applied to the crudest material, and
  the highest rate to the most refined material.

42 Expenditure, in terms of the sums involved and the
    cost per pound of produce, is classified by production
    activities (cultivation, harvesting, manufacture,
    packing and dispatch) and by overheads or 'General
    Charges'. Similarly on-going work is summarized ac-

cording to the extents weeded, manured, replanted and
so on.

43   'James Finlay & Company Limited, 1750-1950' (Glasgow,
1951), p.102.

44   For example, in Gordon Frazer & Co.Ltd, one such firm
in Sri Lanka which was reconstituted, the Articles of
Association, gave the former partners 'the power to
appoint and remove any of the other Directors, and ...
from time to time to appoint, define, limit and restrict the powers and duties, and fix the qualification and remuneration of any other Directors, and ...
remove any other Director and ... at any time convene
a General Meeting of the Company.'

45   An example in Sri Lanka is Maddema Trading Co.Ltd, a
tea exporting firm registered in 1953. With a paid-up
capital of only Rs 1,000 it had a turnover of Rs 12.9
million in 1960, but showed a pre-tax profit of only
Rs 2,398. Lipton Ltd had provided its finance,
amounting to Rs 1.1 million in 1960, as well as its
directorate. Maddema Trading Co. had no office of its
own, was not listed in the telephone directory, and
outgoing correspondence was dealt with (and signed) by
the Accountant of Lipton Ltd. Linked with Lipton Ltd
were two other tea exporting firms, R.O.Mennel & Co.
(Ceylon) Ltd, and A.F.Jones & Co.Ltd. The former,
like Maddema Trading Co., was a legal fiction. It was
financially interlocked with A.F.Jones & Co.Ltd, which
in 1939 held one half of the share capital; both
firms had the same directors in 1949. One quarter of
the share capital of A.F.Jones & Co.Ltd in 1965 was
owned by Lipton (Overseas) Ltd, whose Chief Accountant
and Accountant were the only directors of A.F.Jones &
Co.Ltd. The rest of the capital of R.O.Mennel & Co.
(Ceylon) Ltd (i.e. 75 per cent) was jointly held by
two persons resident in the UK.

46   'The Metropolitan Organization of British Colonial
Trade' (London, 1951), p.162.

47   H.A. de S.Gunasekera, 'From Dependent Currency to
Central Banking' (London, 1963), p.192.

48   For example, Darley Butler & Co.Ltd, and E.B.Creasy &
Co.Ltd, formerly separate businesses (registered in
Sri Lanka as rupee companies), are both subsidiaries of
Steel Bros & Co.Ltd, London - an outstanding example
of horizontal integration and concentration. With
assets valued in 1939 at £4.8 million, Steel Bros
owned oil wells, refineries, mines, rice mills, tea
plantations, cotton mills, etc. in several countries.

49   'James Finlay & Company Limited, 1750-1950', op.cit.,
p.99. George Steuart & Co.Ltd in 1836 bought a

similar property in Colombo for £160. 'James Steuart,
Recollections Personal and Official of James Steuart,
1817-1866. With a short history of the firm of George
Steuart and Co.', (ed.) Thomas Villiers (Colombo,
circa 1935), p.58.

50 Cunyngham-Brown, op.cit., pp.102,146.

51 Donald and Joanna Moore, 'The First 150 Years of
Singapore' (Singapore, 1969), p.482.

52 The British Ceylon Corporation (the largest coconut
oil exporting firm in Sri Lanka) invested heavily on
internal transport facilities during 1959-63. A bulk
oil pipe line, more than a mile long from its storage
tanks to the wharf, did away with the need for oil
drums and motor vehicles. Based on the Company's
Annual Reports.

53 'James Finlay & Company Limited', op.cit., pp.92,100.
George Steuart & Co. commenced shipping and insurance
work only in 1957, upon amalgamation with J.M.
Robertson & Co. whose agencies it took over.

54 H.E.Raynes, 'A History of British Insurance' (London,
1954), p.267.

55 Steuart, op.cit., p.59.

56 Chairman of the Ceylon Tea Plantations Company, at the
4th Annual General Meeting of the Ceylon Association
in London. 'The Times of Ceylon', 6 June 1892.

57 Ibid., 15 March 1892.

58 Ibid. Representations by plantation owners both in
Sri Lanka and in London caused the Sun Fire Office
alone to lower its rates. Ibid., 30 June 1892. Also
'Report of the Ceylon Chamber of Commerce for Half-
year Ending 30 June 1892', p.4.

59 'James Finlay & Company Limited', op.cit., p.130.

60 H.A. de S.Gunasekera stated incorrectly that in Sri
Lanka 'the import of rice ... had all along been in
the hands of Chettiar and other Indian traders' (op.
cit., p.192). From about 1919 Whittall & Co. began
importing rice for directly supplying the estates
under its agency. Harrisons & Crosfield followed this
example as indenting agents for British rice exporters
in Rangoon.

61 J.S.Furnivall, 'Netherlands India' (Cambridge, 1944),
p.432.

62 'Report of the Commission appointed by His Excellency
the Governor of the Straits Settlements to enquire
into and report on the Trade of the Colony 1933-34',
vol.1, op.cit.

63 Natural Resources Versus Foreign Borrowing in Economic
Development, 'Economic Journal', vol.84, no.327 (September 1972), p.959.

64   Arthur Hazlewood, The Economics of Colonial Monetary
     Arrangements, 'Social and Economic Studies', vol.III,
     no.34 (December 1954).
65   'British Malaya' (London, 1948), pp.262-3.
66   Yip Yat Hoong, 'The Development of the Tin Mining
     Industry of Malaya' (Kuala Lumpur, 1969), p.95.
67   J.H.Drabble, 'Rubber in Malaya 1876-1922' (Kuala
     Lumpur, 1973), p.21.
68   In a letter to W.T.Dyer, 30 January 1889 ('Kew Gardens
     Correspondence', vol.166, quoted by Drabble, op.cit.,
     p.7. Related remarks by Drabble, ibid., pp.6,79).
69   'No competition arose between the numerous Europeans
     who were desirous of acquiring land. It became an es-
     tablished practice that at whatever upset price it was
     put up for that it was sold' (from Governor Campbell
     to Lord Stanley, Despatch 132, dated 8 August 1844.
     Colonial Office 53/277). 'There was no lack of forest
     land at the upset price of 5 shillings an acre; and
     any competition was considered such "bad form", that
     as soon as a pioneer made his selection, he cut the
     boundaries and began forming a nursery as if the land
     had already been knocked down to him and the Crown
     transfer made out' (A.M. & J.Ferguson, 'Pioneers of
     the Planting Enterprise in Ceylon (from 1830 onwards).
     Biographical notices and portraits' (Colombo, 1884)).
70   Drabble, op.cit., pp.24,72; J.C.Jackson, 'Planters
     and Speculators' (Kuala Lumpur, 1968), pp.232-3.
71   N.Ramachandran, 'Foreign Plantation Investment in
     Ceylon' (Colombo, 1963), p.16.
72   Op.cit., p.63.
73   Ibid.
74   Jackson, op.cit., pp.248-9. In the 1890s a leading
     firm of London stock brokers warned British investors
     against investing in India and Sri Lanka by quoting
     the 'immortal advice given by Punch to people who are
     about to get married: "Don't"', 'Stock Exchange
     Investments', 7th edn (London, 1899), p.79.
75   'An unusually large number of younger sons, and others
     with a certain amount of capital of their own, have
     settled in the higher and healthier districts - pos-
     sessing in fact one of the finest climates in the
     world - and have formed comparatively permanent
     houses, in the midst of their tea as well as coffee
     and cinchona fields. The number of resident proprie-
     tory and of married planters has largely increased
     within the past twenty years, notwithstanding depres-
     sion and difficulty' (John Ferguson, 'Ceylon in 1903'
     (Colombo, 1903), pp.84-5).
76   North, loc.cit. (June 1955), p.249.

77 The Kendawe Tea and Rubber Co., Chairman's statement
    for 1907. It was not unusual for plantation compa-
    nies, before sufficient profits were made, even to
    withhold the agents and secretaries' fees; these were
    shown in the balance sheet as 'sundry liabilities'.
    In 1913 the Kaluganga Valley Tea & Rubber Co.Ltd
    raised fresh capital in the form of secondary non-
    convertible debentures, but only to meet 'the cost of
    a rubber factory, interest on debentures, management
    expenses etc.'; it was expressly stated that 'none of
    the money subscribed is to be used for opening new
    land' (Chairman's report for 1913).
78 Loc.cit.
79 Cited in L.H.Jenks, 'The Migration of British Capital
    to 1875' (London, 1963), pp.221-2; also L.H.Jenks,
    British Experience with Foreign Investments, 'Journal
    of Economic History' Supplement (December 1944).
80 Peter Harnetty, 'Imperialism and Free Trade:
    Lancashire and India in the Mid-Nineteenth Century'
    (Manchester, 1972), pp.77-81.

CHAPTER 4   ECONOMIC DEVELOPMENT IN THE SETTLER AND THE
NONSETTLER COLONIES: DIFFERENCES IN SCOPE AND ORIENTATION

1 For instance, in Rhodesia in 1938, for eight of its
   products 71 per cent of the total output by value was
   marketed locally, and for thirteen others the proportion was 40 per cent. Based on data in S.H.Frankel,
   'Capital Investment in Africa' (London, 1938), p.20.
2 R.Hallett, 'Africa Since 1875' (Michigan, 1974),
   p.519.
3 W.J.Barber, 'The Economy of British Central Africa'
   (London, 1961), p.129.
4 Michael Barratt Brown, 'After Imperialism' (London,
   1970), p.168.
5 Lord Hailey, 'African Survey' (London, New York,
   Toronto, revised edn 1957), p.1270.
6 Barratt Brown, op.cit., p.170.
7 C.C.Wrigley, Kenya: The Patterns of Economic Life,
   1902-1905, in Vincent Harlow and F.M.Chilver (eds),
   'History of East Africa' (Oxford, 1965), p.225.
8 Ibid., p.218.
9 In Rhodesia the divergence between the settlers and
   the expatriate interests was expressed even in constitutional matters. The settlers wanted responsible
   government (which they finally achieved) whereas the
   expatriate interests favoured amalgamation with the
   Union of South Africa. Giovanni Arrighi, The

Political Economy of Rhodesia, in G.Arrighi and J.S.
Saul, 'Essays on the Political Economy of Africa' (New
York, 1973), p.344.   Though South Africa was also
settler dominated, the expatriate interests were unconcerned with questions of economic autonomy.

10 G.J.Ligthart and B.Abbai, Economic Development in
Africa: Aims and Possibilities, in E.A.G.Robinson
(ed.), 'Economic Development for Africa South of the
Sahara' (London, 1964), p.13.   Also A.M.Kamarack, 'The
Economics of African Development' (London, 1967),
p.140.

11 Ligthart and Abbai, op.cit., pp.18-19 and 20.

12 The corresponding figure for South Africa was 21 per
cent.   United Nations, 'World Economic Situation'.
Table given in Jack Woddis, 'Africa - The Roots of
Revolt' (London, 1961), p.118.

13 C.H.Thompson and H.W.Woodruff, 'Economic Development
in Rhodesia and Nyasaland' (London, 1954), tables on
pp.197 and 199.

14 Ibid., p.164.

15 Ibid., p.163.

16 Arrighi, op.cit., pp.353,354.

17 'Central African Territories: Geographical, Historical
and Economic Survey' (HMSO, London, 1951 Cmd 8234),
p.25.

18 Thompson and Woodruff, op.cit., p.167.

19 'Central African Territories: Geographical, Historical
and Economic Survey', op.cit.

20 Ibid., p.28.

21 The exclusions are RAF and NAAFI personnel, 'Immigrants seeking employment', and 'Other Immigrants
(usually dependants)'.   Based on figures in Thompson
and Woodruff, op.cit., p.63.

22 L.H.Gann and M.Gelfand, 'Huggins of Rhodesia' (London,
1964), p.212, quoted in Arrighi, loc.cit., p.351.

23 Based on data in Arrighi, ibid., p.64.

24 Barber, op.cit., p.131.

25 Ibid., p.130.

26 Arrighi, loc.cit., pp.218-19.

27 The sketch of Zambia's economic structure given in
this and the next paragraph is based on L.H.Gann, 'A
History of Northern Rhodesia' (London, 1964), pp.
389-91;   also Barber, op.cit., p.140;   Thompson and
Woodruff, op.cit., p.161 ff;   A.Hazlewood and P.H.
Henderson, 'Nyasaland, The Economics of Federation'
(Oxford, 1960).

28 Peter Worsley, 'The Third World' (London, 1971), pp.
154-61;   Aidan Southall, The Impact of Imperialism
upon Urban Development, in Victor Turner (ed.),
'Colonialism in Africa 1870-1960' (Cambridge, 1971),
vol.3, pp.243-5.

29   Wrigley, loc.cit., p.262.
30   Barber, op.cit., p.198. Arrighi gives an estimate of
     Africans in wage employment of 377,000 for 1946 and
     over 600,000 for 1956, loc.cit., p.351.
31   Barber, op.cit., p.198.
32   In Kenya Lord Delamere, who settled in the Njoro
     District in 1903, made outstanding agronomic progress,
     though the problems encountered were without precedent
     anywhere in the world. He developed several varieties
     of wheat that were resistant to every species and
     strain of rust, and evolved grain of good milling
     quality (Elspeth Huxley, 'White Man's Country: Lord
     Delamere and the Making of Kenya' (London, 1968),
     vol.1, p.174.
33   G.Arrighi, Labor Supplies in Historical Perspective:
     A Study of the Proletarianization of the African
     Peasantry in Rhodesia, op.cit., p.213.
34   L.H.Gann, 'A History of Southern Rhodesia' (London,
     1965), p.168.
35   R.Davies, The White Working-Class in South Africa,
     'New Left Review', no.82 (November-December 1973),
     pp.48-9. Also B.Banting, 'The Rise of the South
     African Reich' (London, 1969), p.382, quoted in
     Davies, ibid.
36   The Margolis Report of 1946 recommended fiscal as-
     sistance only if a market existed for at least 'two
     competing manufacturing concerns' ('Report of the
     Committee of Enquiry into the Protection of Secondary
     Industries in Southern Rhodesia', 1946, cited by
     Barber, op.cit., p.142).
37   R.L.Buell, 'The Native Problem in Africa', vol.1
     (London, 1965), p.405.
38   E.A.Brett, 'Colonialism and Underdevelopment in
     Africa' (London, 1973), pp.269-75.
39   Charlotte Leubuscher, The Policy Governing External
     Trade, in M.Perham (ed.), 'The Economics of a Tropical
     Dependency', vol.II, 'Mining, Commerce, and Finance in
     Nigeria' (London, 1948), p.158.
40   J.Mars, in Perham (ed.), op.cit., p.74. Also Carl
     Liedholm, The Influence of Colonial Policy on the
     Growth and Development of Nigeria's Industrial Sector,
     in C.K.Eicher and C.Liedholm, 'Growth and Development
     of the Nigerian Economy' (Michigan, 1970), p.57.
41   International Bank for Reconstruction and Development,
     'The Economic Development of Nigeria' (Baltimore,
     1955), p.387.
42   Overseas Economic Survey, 'Nigeria' (HMSO, London,
     1957), p.90.
43   E.L.Wheelwright, 'Industrialization in Malaya' (Mel-
     bourne, 1965), p.90.

44 Hailey, op.cit., p.1291.
45 Ibid., p.1290.
46 Sidney Dell, 'Trade Blocs and Common Markets' (London, 1963), pp.177-80. 'East Africa', Report of the Economic and Fiscal Commission, Cmd Paper 1279 (HMSO, London, 1961), p.8. Kenya's role in the East Africa economic union is also discussed in Brett, op.cit., pp.99-105.
47 Samir Amin, 'The Maghreb in the Modern World' (Harmondsworth, 1970), pp.72,73.
48 Ultimately, in 1954, in the French zone of Morocco, 23 per cent of the total private investment by the French was in urban real estate. James A.Paul, The Moroccan Crisis; Nationalism and Imperialism on Europe's Periphery, 'Monthly Review', vol.24, no.5 (October 1972), p.17.
49 J.M.Abun-Nasr, 'A History of the Maghreb' (Cambridge, 1971), p.293.
50 Ibid., p.313.
51 Op.cit., pp.28 and 56.
52 Hassan Awad, Morocco's Expanding Towns, 'Geographical Journal', vol.130, part 1 (March 1964), p.49.
53 J.I.Clark, North-West Africa since Mid-Century, in R.M.Prothers (ed.), 'A Geography of Africa' (London, 1969).
54 Amin, op.cit., p.43.
55 Nevill Barbour, 'A Survey of North West Africa' (London, 1959), p.178.
56 Estimated from data in an official report referred to by Barbour, ibid., p.249.
57 For Algeria, Amin, op.cit., p.62; for Tunisia, ibid., p.64.
58 Barbour, op.cit., p.246.
59 Ibid.
60 Amin, op.cit., p.44.
61 'Belgian Congo', vol.1, published by the Ruanda-Urundi Information and Public Relations Office (Brussels, 1959), p.392.
62 Crawford Young, 'Politics in the Congo' (Princeton University Press, 1965), p.11.
63 A.P.Merriam, 'Congo: Background to Conflict' (Evanston, Ill., 1961), p.34.
64 Loc.cit., p.13.
65 Ibid., p.73.
66 Catherine Hoskyns, 'The Congo Since Independence' (Oxford, 1965), p.14.
67 'Belgian Congo', vol.1, op.cit., p.310. The raw material for the first atomic bombs was supplied by the uranium mines of the Congo (Garry Fullerton,

'UNESCO in the Congo' (UN Education, Scientific and Cultural Organization, Geneva, 1964), p.27).

68 'Belgian Congo', vol.1, op.cit., p.308; also 'A Manual of the Congo' (compiled by the Geographical Section of the Naval Intelligence Division, Naval Staff, Admiralty, I.D. 1213 (HMSO, London, 1920), pp. 204-5.

69 Hoskyns, op.cit., p.14.

70 'Belgian Congo', vol.2, published by the Belgian Congo and Ruanda-Urundi Information and Public Relations Office (Brussels, 1960). Table on p.109. Also ibid., vol.1 (Brussels, 1959), p.331.

71 Buell, op.cit., p.509.

72 UN, 'Economic Bulletin for Africa', vol.2, no.2 (June 1962), p.74.

73 F.Bezy, Development of the Congo, in Robinson (ed.), op.cit., p.73.

74 Ibid., p.88.

75 Ligthart and Abbai, loc.cit., p.21.

76 In 1950 about 40 per cent of the mine workers had done ten years' continuous service (Hailey, op.cit., p.1392).

77 Young, op.cit., p.21.

78 Frankel, op.cit., p.292.

79 'Economic Bulletin for Africa', vol.2, no.2 (June 1962), p.69. Also 'Belgian Congo', vol.1, op.cit., pp.264-5.

80 UN, 'Economic Bulletin for Africa', vol.1, no.1 (January 1961), p.93.

81 Hailey, op.cit., p.1299.

82 Bezy, loc.cit., p.75. Building and building materials constituted 16 per cent of the total value of industrial output, and the processing of agricultural produce (mainly palm kernels) 12 per cent (ibid).

83 Hoskyns, op.cit., p.15. Based on UN, 'Economic Bulletin for Africa', June 1961, pp.79-81.

84 I owe to Dr Carlos Fortin much of the explanation given in this and the preceding paragraph of the different spread effects of copper mining in the Congo and in Zambia.

85 'Belgian Congo', vol.1, published by the Belgian Congo and Ruanda-Urundi Information and Public Relations Office (Brussels, 1959), pp.264-5; W.O.Jones, 'Manioc in Africa' (Stanford, 1959), p.139.

86 Buell, op.cit., p.508.

87 Young, op.cit., p.45.

88 Ibid., pp.516-17.

89 Frankel, op.cit., p.301.

90 Ibid., p.295.

91 Hoskyns, op.cit., p.19; also Merriam, op.cit., p.276.
92 Ibid., p.12.
93 Thomas Kanza, the first Congolese to register at a university (in 1952), needed high-level intervention from colonial personages before he could proceed to Belgium for his studies (Young, op.cit., p.94).
94 Le colour bar au Congo Belge, 'Zaire', vol.7, no.5 (May 1959), p.503.
95 Georges N.Nzongola, The Bourgeoisie and Revolution in the Congo, 'Journal of Modern African Studies', vol.8, no.4(1970).
96 Robequain seemed to underrate the industrialization that occurred: 'It has not been given to any colony to develop its industries freely; even the possibility of such development has always seemed paradoxical, almost inconceivable. Indochina has not escaped this law' (quoted in Jack Shepherd, 'Industry in Southeast Asia' (New York, 1941), p.13). A sense of perspective is also lacking in a comment by F.H. Golay et al., 'Underdevelopment and Economic Nationalism in Southeast Asia' (Ithaca, N.Y., 1969), p.408.
97 Data on industrial exports from Indochina during 1935-1938 are given in Shepherd, op.cit., p.33.
98 Ibid., p.134; Virginia Thompson, Indochina - France's Great Stake in the Far East, 'Far Eastern Survey', vol.4, no.2 (20 January 1937), p.18.
99 Robequain, op.cit., p.279.
100 Shepherd, op.cit., p.33.
101 Callis, op.cit., p.77.
102 Virginia Thompson, loc.cit., p.19.
103 All the same, in these (the nonsettler) colonies British exporters had a privileged market, independently of tariff preference. They were tied up with long-established importing firms, which until the depression of the 1930s, held a monopoly of imported consumer goods and throughout controlled the purchasing policies of plantation and mining enterprises.
104 Robequain, op.cit., p.328.
105 Ibid., p.340.
106 Geographical Handbook Series, B.R. 506 A, 'Algeria', vol.II (British Admiralty Naval Intelligence Division, October 1942), p.278.
107 The Tonkin Agricultural Chamber complained of 'French importers who pay 5 or 6 francs a kilogram for a product which they sell to the consumer for at least 50' (Robequain, op.cit., p.341).

108 Thompson, loc.cit., p.19.
109 Robequain, op.cit., p.289.
110 Dorothy Borg, French Considering Industrialization of Indochina, 'Far Eastern Survey', vol.8(1939), p.44.
111 'Foreign' firms were not given mining rights or land concessions. Three-fourths of the board members of a mining company were required to be French nationals, and in the case of an unincorporated mining enterprise, half the members of the managing body.

CHAPTER 5   SETTLER AUTONOMY AS A BASIS OF GROWTH IMPULSES

1 Michael Barratt Brown, 'After Imperialism' (London, 1970), p.168.
2 H.W.Arndt, Economic Development: Some Lessons of Australian Experience, a lecture delivered in 1954 to the Economic Development Secretariat of the United Nations. Published in 'Berichte Weltwirtschaftliches Archiv', Bd. 73, Heft 1, 1954, p.162.
3 Eamon MaCann, 'War and an Irish Town' (Harmondsworth, 1974), p.132.
4 E.J.Hobsbawm and George Rude, 'Captain Swing' (London, 1969), pp.24,36,243.
5 'The Invasion of New Zealand by People, Plants and Animals' (New Brunswick, 1949), pp.76-84,128.
6 L.H.Gann, 'A History of Southern Rhodesia' (London, 1965), p.163.
7 Robert Davies, The White Working-Class in South Africa, 'New Left Review', no.82 (November-December), 1973, p.46.
8 Commonwealth Parliamentary Papers 1907-8, vol.II, pp. 1887-9, cit. M.Clark, 'Sources of Australian History' (London, 1971), p.507.
9 Loc.cit., p.163.
10 Arndt's analogy may possibly apply to the French settler colonies, for example those in the Maghreb which we discussed elsewhere. These colonies had sizeable groups of European settlers and at the same time remained very much metropolitan in their orientation. Their metropolitan orientation was, however, an impediment on their development, compared to the British settler colonies (e.g. Rhodesia and Kenya) which politically and economically were far less tied to Britain.
11 A.K.H.Weinrich (Sister Mary Aquina OP), 'Black and White Elites in Rhodesia' (Manchester, 1973), pp.10 and 35. The term caste was used by Banton in multi-racial situations such as those discussed here.

These situations involved a large area of superior/
inferior relationships which are heritable and thus
independent of any changes that may occur in economic
or class positions. Michael Banton, 'Race Relations'
(London, 1967), pp.142-5.

12 'The lower the native wage, the greater the danger to
the white man not efficient enough to occupy a position at the top' (R.L.Buell, 'The Native Problem in
Africa', vol.1 (London, 1965), p.14).

13 Quoted in L.H.Gann, 'A History of Northern Rhodesia'
(London, 1964), p.146.

14 Buell, op.cit., vol.1, p.15, n.51.

15 P.Bower, The Mining Industry, in Margery Perham (ed.),
'The Economics of a Tropical Dependency', vol.II,
'Mining, Commerce, and Finance in Nigeria' (London,
1948), p.10.

16 The Adaptation of African Labour Systems to Social
Change, in M.J.Herskovits and M.Harwitz (eds),
'Economic Transition in Africa' (Evanston, Ill.,
1964), p.285.

17 'Ceylon Banking Commission' (1934), II, Memoranda and
Evidence, Ceylon Sessional Paper XIII - 1934, p.434.

18 'Colonial Office', 54/235, 21 April 1847.

19 T.F.Chipp, 'Report on Rubber Estates visited in Perak
and Selangor', dated 28 March 1911, enclosed in
Despatch from High Commissioner to the Colonial
Office, 3 May 1911. Colonial Office, 273/373. Quoted
in J.H.Drabble, 'Rubber in Malaya 1876-1922' (Kuala
Lumpur, 1973), p.119, n.2.

20 A Malayan Review, 'Straits Times', 8 February 1911.
'Many of them [Estate Managers] have at the present
moment less knowledge of practical agriculture than
the average squatter growing vegetables around our
town, and less administrative knowledge than the
average office clerk' (ibid., 16 February 1911).

21 Reinsch, 'Intellectual and Political Currents in the
Far East', p.45, quoted by Amaury de Reincourt, op.
cit., p.252.

22 Quoted, ibid.

23 Quoted, ibid., p.251.

24 An official report in Ghana stated: 'Nothing im-
pressed us more than the interest of the peoples of
the Gold Coast in education.... It does not spring
solely from any mercenary assessment of material benefits but from a genuine desire for learning itself'
('The Report of the Commission of Inquiry into the
Disturbance in the Gold Coast in 1948' (HMSO, London,
1948), ch.8, quoted by Adam Curle, 'Educational
Strategy for Developing Societies' (London, 1963),
p.92, n.4).

25 Boris Gussman, 'Out in the Midday Sun' (London, 1962),
    p.101, cited in Michael Banton, Urbanization and the
    Colour Line in Africa, in Victor Turner (ed.),
    'Colonialism in Africa 1870-1960', vol.3 (Cambridge,
    1971), p.261.
26 Curle, op.cit.; Economic Development in Africa: Aims
    and Possibilities, in E.A.G.Robinson (ed.), 'Economic
    Development for Africa South of the Sahara' (London,
    1964), p.28.
27 O.F.Raum, Changes in African Life under German
    Administration, 1892-1914, in Vincent Harlow and E.M.
    Chilver (eds), 'History of East Africa' (Oxford,
    1965), p.204. 'Missions were concerned about supply-
    ing Christian clerks to the Government, since they
    felt that the Muhammadan clerks helped to spread Islam
    in the interior' (ibid., p.205).
28 H.S.Scott, The Development of the Education of the
    African in Relation to Western Contact, 'The Year Book
    of Education', 1938 (London, 1937), p.737, quoted by
    Curle, op.cit., p.89. Penelope Bower, commenting on
    the complete absence of technical training facilities
    for Africans, noted that a large mining company in
    Nigeria employed twelve Eurasian engineers trained in
    India to operate its six draglines, ostensibly because
    'no African has yet been found equal to the job';
    yet, in the same company Africans were driving
    machines such as dredges and tractors under European
    supervision (loc.cit., p.10).
29 Lord Hailey, 'African Survey' (London, New York,
    Toronto, revised edn 1957), p.1933; also p.220.
30 J.Mars, Extra-Territorial Enterprises, in Perham
    (ed.), op.cit., vol.II, p.73.
31 British Parliamentary Papers, vol.XXXVI of 1849.
32 Colonial Office Papers, 55/98, 26 September 1853,
    quoted in I.H. Van den Driesen, Some Aspects of the
    Coffee Industry in Ceylon, PhD thesis submitted to
    the University of London.
33 Arghiri Emmanuel, White-Settler Colonialism and the
    Myth of Investment Imperialism, 'New Left Review',
    no.73 (May-June 1972), p.40. 'It should not be for-
    gotten that if England is a second class power today,
    this is due to her defeat in a conflict of this type
    and the subsequent founding of the United States'
    (ibid.).
34 L.H.Gann and P.Duignan, 'White Settlers in Tropical
    Africa' (Harmondsworth, 1962), p.30.
35 Elspeth Huxley, 'White Man's Country: Lord Delamere
    and the Making of Kenya' (London, 1968), vol.1, pp.
    180 ff.

36   M.R.Dilley, 'British Policy in Kenya Colony' (London, 1966), p.43.
37   Op.cit.
38   R.D.Wolff, 'The Economics of Colonisation' (Yale University Press, 1974), p.89.
39   E.A.Brett, 'Colonialism and Underdevelopment in Africa' (London, 1973), p.77.
40   Dilley, op.cit., p.43.
41   Kathleen Stahl, 'The Metropolitan Organisation of British Colonial Trade' (London, 1951), p.181.
42   Ibid.
43   Brett, op.cit., p.88.
44   Ibid., pp.393-5; L.H.Gann, 'A History of Southern Rhodesia' (London, 1965), pp.290-2.
45   Barratt Brown, op.cit., p.165. Based on A.Hazlewood and P.D.Henderson, Nyasaland, The Economics of Federation, 'Bulletin of the Oxford Institute of Statistics', February 1960, pp.43 and 45-6.
46   Samir Amin, 'The Maghreb in the Modern World' (Harmondsworth, 1970), pp.107-8.
47   Quoted in Nevill Barbour, 'A Survey of North West Africa' (London, 1959).
48   In expressing his hostility to any reforms, a powerful colon in 1947 threatened reprisals against metropolitan France: 'You appear only to fear the possibility of an Arab insurrection. Try to grasp the fact that there is another danger facing uncomprehending metropolitan Frenchmen, that of a colon uprising.... We want no more governors drenched in anachronistic sentimentality, but strong men who can ensure respect for our rights by showing force and, if necessary, by using it. In 1936 I sabotaged the Blum-Viollette project and the government capitulated before me. What business had General de Gaulle in meddling once again in this business? Believe me, I know how to bring them to heel' (quoted by W.B.Quandt, 'Revolution and Political Leadership: Algeria, 1954-1968' (Cambridge, Mass., 1969), p.6).
49   J.M. Van der Kroef, 'Indonesia in the Modern World' (Bandung, 1954), pp.14-15.
50   M.W.Meyer Ranneft, quoted in ibid., p.14. In the face of vigorous Japanese competition the foreign trade of Indonesia from the early 1930s was increasingly linked to Holland, through clearing agreements and restrictions on Japanese imports. This policy was defended, inter alia, on the principle of trade reciprocity and the need to correct an adverse balance of payments with Japan. The Java Bank, Annual Reports from 1933-4.

51 Gann and Duignan, op.cit., p.85.
52 G.Arrighi and J.S.Saul, Nationalism and Revolution in sub-Saharan Africa, 'The Socialist Register, 1967' (London, 1967), p.152.   Perry Anderson, Portugal and the End of Ultra Colonialism, 'New Left Review', nos 16,17,18(1962).
53 Amin, op.cit., pp.169,171.
54 James A.Paul, The Moroccan Crisis, Nationalism and Imperialism on Europe's Periphery, 'Monthly Review', vol.24, no.5 (October 1972), p.19.
55 Amin, op.cit., p.174. Ahmed El Kodsy, Nationalism and Class Struggles, 'Monthly Review', July-August 1970, pp.59-60.
56 Paul, loc.cit., p.29.
57 Amin, op.cit., p.177.
58 Ibid.
59 Loc.cit., p.39.
60 In Malaysia an official spokesman referred to the employment of Malays by business firms as 'Tokenism'. Tengku Razaleih Hamzah, Tokenism in Business, 'Straits Times' (Malaysian edition), 9 October 1973.
61 Within a few days of his appointment the (Trotskyist) Minister of Plantation Industries expressed the likelihood of action being taken against the foreign interests. He declaimed to newsmen: 'The international monopolies will not retreat without dealing counter-blows.' Three months later the Chairman of the British Exchange Banks Association in Sri Lanka cleared the air when after a meeting with the (Trotskyist) Finance Minister, he announced, 'We shall go on banking!'
        As indicated in the text, this failure to carry out the threat implied by the Minister of Plantation Industries soon after assuming power must be seen in the context of an abandonment of revolutionary politics by the traditional Left parties, including the Trotskyists.
62 In Malaysia, 15 years after Independence the compulsory paper in the Malay language for the Certificate of Education was still sent to Cambridge for grading. At the Universiti Sains Malaysia the graduands' gowns for the 1972 convocation were made in England and air-freighted to Penang; a gold medal for Physics was given for casting to a jeweller's firm in England; the university's coat of arms was designed in England and registered at the College of Arms (for a fee of 100 guineas); a Christmas party by the dons in 1973 included arrangements (notified in a staff circular) for an 'English pub atmosphere complete with an

English serving maid'. At a staff-student party after
an off-campus course Malaysian army officers performed
a Scottish dance, attired in kilts and playing bag-
pipes. The first prime minister of Malaysia throughout his tenure of office from 1958 to 1969 had a Press
Secretary who was British.

63 W.C.Johnstone, 'Burma's Foreign Policy' (Cambridge,
    Mass., 1963).

64 L.D.Stifel, Economics of the Burmese Way to Socialism,
    'Asian Survey', vol.11, no.8 (August, 1971); L.D.
    Stifel, Burmese Socialism; Economic Problems of the
    First Decade, 'Pacific Affairs', vol.45(1972); Ruth
    Pfanner, Burma, in Frank H.Golay et al. (eds),
    'Underdevelopment and Economic Nationalism in
    Southeast Asia' (Ithaca, N.Y., 1969).

65 'British Rule in Burma, 1824-1942' (London, 1946),
    p.30.

66 The Port of Akyab rose to prominence as a result of
    its trade with India, exporting rice and salt and im-
    porting textiles (J.Nisbet, 'Burma Under British Rule
    - and Before' (2 vols, Westminster, 1901), pp.417-18,
    cit. F.N.Trager, 'Burma: from Kingdom to Republic: a
    Historical and Political Analysis' (Praeger, 1966),
    p.144).

67 N.R.Chakravarti, 'The Indian Minority in Burma'
    (London, 1971), chs VI and VII.

68 Cheng Siok-Hwa, 'The Rice Industry of Burma' (Kuala
    Lumpur, 1968), p.224.

69 Ibid., p.83, Table IV.4; and p.85, Table IV.5. Based
    on official data.

70 J.H.Andrews, Foreign Investments in Burma, 'Pacific
    Affairs', vol.45, no.1 (March 1944), p.91.

71 Government of Burma, 'Report of the Land and Agricul-
    tural Committee', Part II, 'Land Alienation' (Rangoon,
    1949), p.58, quoted by J.Silverstein, 'The Struggle
    for National Unity in the Union of Burma' (Ann Arbor,
    1970), pp.65-6.

72 Everett Hagen, 'The Economic Development of Burma'
    (Washington, D.C., n.d. circa 1956), p.21.

73 'The Rice Economy of Monsoon Asia' (Stanford, 1941),
    p.216.

74 Op.cit. (1944), p.193. Also A.H.Fenichel and W.G.
    Huff, 'The Impact of Colonialism on Burmese Economic
    Development' (Centre for Developing Area Studies,
    McGill University, Montreal, August 1971), p.21. B.O.
    Binns, 'Agricultural Economy in Burma' (Rangoon,
    1948), pp.58-9.

75 J.S.Furnivall, 'Colonial Policy and Practice; a
    Comparative Study of Burma and Netherlands India'
    (Cambridge, 1948), p.116.

76 Richard Allen, 'An Introduction to the History and
    Politics of Southeast Asia' (New York, London,
    Toronto, 1970), p.97.
77 Harvey, op.cit., pp.40-2.
78 Op.cit., p.96.
79 Allen, op.cit., p.97.
80 Chakravarti, op.cit., p.96.
81 By, for example, Jack Woddis, 'Africa - The Roots of
    Revolt' (London, 1961), p.118.
82 Geographical Handbook Series, Naval Intelligence
    Division, 'Algeria', vol.II (May 1944), p.285.
83 Albert Waterston, 'Planning in Morocco' (Baltimore,
    1962), p.5.
84 'Algeria', vol.II (cited earlier), pp.197-8.
85 Amin, op.cit., pp.100-3.
86 Geographical Handbook Series, Naval Intelligence
    Division, 'Morocco', vol.II (October 1952), p.124.
87 Robin Hallett, 'Africa Since 1875' (Michigan, 1974),
    p.210; Paul, loc.cit., p.17.
88 Amin, op.cit., p.101; also pp.102-3.
89 Op.cit., pp.190-2.
90 Walter Elkan, Migrant Labour in Africa, an Economist's
    Approach, 'American Economic Review' (May 1959),
    reprinted in P.J.M.McEvan and R.B.Sutcliffe (eds),
    'The Study of Africa' (London, 1965).
91 Third Interim Report of the Industrial and Agricul-
    tural Requirements Commission, 'Fundamentals of
    Economic Policy in the Union', Union Government no.40,
    1941, para. 168, quoted in Hailey, op.cit., p.1288.
92 'South African manufactured goods have proved so much
    more expensive than imported articles that the
    [Durban] City Council ... is considering an approach
    to the Minister of Economic Affairs to have the issue
    of special import permits reviewed. The municipality
    has found that where tenders for South African goods
    have had to be accepted because no import permits were
    granted the city had to pay substantially more for
    local items' ('The Times Review of Trade and
    Industry', April 1954, quoted in Hailey, op.cit.,
    p.1289).
93 Ibid.

CHAPTER 6   SETTLER GROWTH AND THE REPRESSION OF INDIGENOUS
INTERESTS

1   R.M.Prothero (ed.), 'A Geography of Africa' (London,
    1966), p.16.
2   Quoted in Philip Mason, 'The Birth of a Dilemma: The

Conquest and Settlement of Rhodesia' (London, 1958),
p.214. Also quoted in Michael Banton, Urbanization
and the Colour Line in Africa, in Victor Turner (ed.),
'Colonialism in Africa 1870-1960', vol.3 (Cambridge,
1971), p.258.

3 'The Dual Mandate in British Tropical Africa' (London,
1922), p.397. Cited in J.F.Weeks, Wage Policy and the
Colonial Legacy - a Comparative Study, 'Journal of
Modern African Studies', vol.9, no.3(1971), p.363.

4 An Interpretation of Economic Backwardness, 'Oxford
Economic Papers', New Series, vol.6, no.2 (June 1954),
reprinted in A.N.Agarwala and S.P.Singh (eds), 'The
Economics of Underdevelopment' (London, Oxford, New
York, 1970), p.108.

5 Michael Banton, 'Race Relations' (London, 1967),
p.223.

6 Myint in Agarwala and Singh, op.cit., pp.125 ff. 'As
we have said before, the nature of economic backwardness cannot be fully appreciated until we go beyond
the distribution of incomes to the distribution of
economic activities: for it is to changes in the for
forms of efforts and activities that we must turn when
in search for the keynotes of the history of mankind'
(Alfred Marshall, 'Principles of Economics' (London,
1956), p.72, quoted by Myint in Agarwala and Singh
(eds), op.cit., p.123).

7 J.S.Hogendorn, The Origins of the Groundnut Trade in
Northern Nigeria, in C.K.Eicher and C.Liedholm,
'Growth and Development of the Nigerian Economy'
(Michigan, 1970), p.30.

8 Richenda Scott, Palm Products and Ground-nuts, in
M.Perham (ed.), 'The Economics of a Tropical
Dependency, vol.1: The Native Economics of Nigeria'
(London, 1946), p.245.

9 P.Kilby, 'Industrialization in an Open Economy:
Nigeria, 1945-1966' (Cambridge, 1969), pp.137,309;
J.Mars, Extra-Territorial Enterprises, in M.Perham
(ed.), 'The Economics of a Tropical Dependency', vol.
II, 'Mining, Commerce, and Finance in Nigeria'
(London, 1948), p.121.

10 Stephen Resnick, in his perceptive study of Filipino
capitalism, offers too general an observation on its
origin: 'Different types of colonial rule found in
various areas together with different crops and associated techniques of production can be expected to
produce several forms of results' (The Second Path to
Capitalism: A Model of International Development,
'Journal of Contemporary Asia', vol.3, no.2(1973),
p.136). An earlier observation by Peter F.Bell and

Stephen Resnick, that 'the economic surplus generated
was not expropriated by the Americans but was reinvested within the country', misses the point (ibid.,
vol.1 (Autumn 1970), p.40). The nub of the matter is
the non-involvement of American capital in the purely
agricultural side of the colonial export economy,
which left a portion of the surplus in the hands of
the indigenous interests.

11   Quoted in M.P.K.Sorenson, 'Origins of European
Settlement in East Africa' (London, 1968), p.59.

12   S.N.Kimani, The Structure of Land Ownership in
Nairobi, 'Journal of East African Research and
Development', vol.2, no.2(1972).

13   B.H.Hodder and D.W.Harris (eds), 'Africa in Transition' (London, 1967).

14   D.J.Reader, 'The Black Man's Portion' (Cape Town,
1961), pp.120-2, cit. Aidan Southall, The Impact of
Imperialism upon Urban Development in Africa, in
Turner (ed.), op.cit., p.249.

15   Nevill Barbour, 'A Survey of North West Africa'
(London, 1959), pp.237-8.

16   L.H.Palmier, 'Indonesia and the Dutch' (London, 1965),
p.27, based on J.S.Furnivall, 'Colonial Policy and
Practice; a Comparative Study of Burma and Netherlands India' (Cambridge, 1948), p.377.

17   J.M. Van der Kroef, 'Indonesia in the Modern World',
Part 1 (Bandung, 1954), p.16.

18   'Annual Report on Education for the Year 1967', p.27,
quoted in A.K.H.Weinrich (Sister Mary Aquina OP),
'Black and White Elites in Rural Rhodesia' (Manchester, 1973), p.27.

19   Ibid., p.29.

20   Palmier, op.cit., pp.13-14.

21   Weinrich, op.cit., p.29.

22   Banton, op.cit., p.223.

23   In Rhodesia the number of females per 1,000 males grew
from 407 in 1904 to 864 in 1936. Out of a total
European population of 55,408 in 1936, 34.1 per cent
of them had been born in Rhodesia (L.H.Gann, 'A
History of Southern Rhodesia' (London, 1965), p.198,
n.2.

24   Such liaisons had their value, according to P.L.
Beaufort, an English judge who was acting Administrator of North Eastern Rhodesia. He felt they were
beneficial to health, discouraged the influx of South
African prostitutes, and removed suspicion on the part
of Africans about unnatural practices among European
males (referred to in Gann, ibid., p.151).

25   Van der Kroef, op.cit., p.278.

26   Philip Mason, 'Patterns of Dominance' (Oxford, 1971),
     p.97.
27   E.P.Seda, 'Necora': The Subculture of Workers on a
     Government-Owned Sugar Plantation, in J.H.Steward
     (ed.), 'The People of Puerto Rico' (Evanston, Ill.,
     1966), p.274.
28   In colonial situations European women were far more
     race-prejudiced than men. In Madagascar this pre-
     judice, Mannoni observed, assumed 'preposterous pro-
     portions' ('Prospero and Caliban' (New York, 1965),
     pp.114-15, English trans. of 'Psychologie de la colo-
     nisation', Paris, 1950).
29   Banton, loc.cit., p.280.
30   Ibid., pp.155-8.
31   In 'The Grass is Singing', Mary Turner vehemently dis-
     liked the African women: 'She hated the exposed
     fleshiness of them, their soft brown bodies and soft
     bashful faces that were also insolent and inquisitive.
     ... She could not bear to see them sitting there on
     the grass, their legs tucked under them in that tra-
     ditional timeless pose, peaceful and uncaring....
     Above all, she hated the way they suckled their
     babies, with their breasts hanging down for everyone
     to see; there was something in their calm satisfied
     maternity that made her blood boil' (Paul Schlueter,
     'The Novels of Doris Lessing' (Evanston, Ill., 1973),
     p.17).
32   Banton, loc.cit., p.263, based on L.H.Gann, 'The Birth
     of a Plural Society: The Development of Northern
     Rhodesia Under the British South African Company
     1894-1914' (Manchester, 1958), p.153.
33   Lord Hailey, 'African Survey' (London, New York,
     Toronto, revised edn 1957), p.1288.
34   Quoted in Anthony H.Richmond, 'The Colour Problem'
     (rev.edn, Harmondsworth, 1961), pp.152-3, also in
     Banton, loc.cit., p.264.
35   'Fourth Report of the East India Company', Appendix
     47, pp.23-4, quoted in R.S.Rungta, 'The Rise of the
     Business Corporations in India' (Cambridge, 1970),
     p.292. The Europeans were most particularly sensitive
     to revealing themselves to educated or competing oc-
     cupational groups. In segregating themselves as an
     ethnic group in colonial societies they, however, felt
     that the reaction of the servants in European house-
     holds and in clubs did not really matter (Banton, loc.
     cit., pp.278-9).
36   Ibid., pp.263-4. Based on Boris Gussman, Industrial
     Efficiency and the Urban African, 'Africa', vol.23
     (1953), p.85.

37 Quoted in Rex Stevenson, Cinemas and Censorship in
    Colonial Malaya, 'Journal of Southeast Asian Studies',
    vol.5, no.2 (September 1974), p.210.
38 Ibid. As Michael Banton indicates, it was the Second
    World War which both in Europe and in Asia crumpled
    the image of white superiority. 'African soldiers ...
    saw Europeans defeated in battle and subordinated as
    prisoners-of-war. They visited other lands, sometimes
    lay with white prostitutes, and acquired a new image
    of the white man ... [that was different from] the
    pukkah-sahib conventions of the colonial civil
    servant' (loc.cit., p.277).
39 Quoted in Schlueter, op.cit., p.9.
40 Robin Hallett, 'Africa Since 1975' (Michigan, 1974),
    pp.215-16.
41 L.H.Gann and P.Duignan, 'White Settlers in Tropical
    Africa' (Harmondsworth, 1962), p.68.
42 Ibid. On New Zealand, A.L.McLeod (ed.), 'The Pattern
    of New Zealand Culture' (Ithaca, N.Y., 1968).
43 J.M.Abun-Nasr, 'A History of the Maghreb' (Cambridge,
    1971), p.256.
44 Hallett, op.cit., p.216. The return of the Maghrebin
    settlers to France 'posed difficulties of adjustment
    and absorption' (J.I.Clarke, North-West Africa Since
    Mid-Century, in Prothero (ed.), op.cit., p.36).
45 Kimani, loc.cit., p.105.
46 L.H.Gann, 'A History of Northern Rhodesia' (London,
    1964), p.215.
47 Amin, op.cit., pp.74-5. When the settlers left
    Algeria in 1963 90,000 jobs fell vacant (ibid., p.
    137).
48 Richard Allen in giving this example states erroneous-
    ly that the problem of the 'small whites' was 'pecul-
    iar to the French colonial system' ('An Introduction
    to the History and Politics of Southeast Asia' (New
    York, London, Toronto, 1970), p.121.
49 From a letter written by Delamere, dated August 1907.
    Quoted in Elspeth Huxley, 'White Man's Country: Lord
    Delamere and the Making of Kenya' (London, 1968),
    vol.1, pp.206-7.
50 In the case of Indonesia, Van der Kroef observed: 'It
    wasn't by any means only the barr or totok, the full
    blood, cheese-and-butter-fed Dutch immigrant (who
    stepped from the gang plank in Priok harbour ...) who
    was subject to this racially discriminative and dif-
    ferentiative temper. Perhaps more racially conscious
    still were the empire builders par excellence, the
    native born Dutch families with ancient ancestry (and
    carefully hidden native mésalliances)' (op.cit.,
    Part I, p.41).

51   Huxley, op.cit., p.204.
52   Warren S.Thompson, 'Danger Spots in World Population'
     (New York, 1930), p.169. In O.C.Cox, 'Caste, Class
     and Race' (New York, 1959), p.351, n.58.
53   Administration and Politics in Uganda, 1919-1945, in
     Vincent Harlow and E.M.Chilver (eds), 'History of East
     Africa', vol.II (Oxford, 1965), pp.512 ff.
54   Ibid., p.512.
55   Ibid., p.511.
56   C.C.Wrigley, Kenya: The Patterns of Economic Life,
     1902-1905, in Harlow and Chilver (eds), op.cit.,
     p.237.
57   Banton, loc.cit., p.258.
58   Op.cit., p.212.
59   Southall, loc.cit., p.238.
60   Gann, op.cit. (1964), p.103.
61   George Bennett, Settlers and Politics in Kenya, in
     Harlow and Chilver (eds), op.cit., p.270.
62   An interesting comment was that of Albuquerque when
     recommending the annexation of Malacca by Portugal at
     the beginning of the sixteenth century. He took care
     to mention that ample funds could be collected by
     taxation to defray the expenses of administering it
     (Furnivall, op.cit., p.5).
63   H.A.Will, Colonial Policy and Economic Development in
     the West Indies, 1895-1903, 'Economic History Review',
     vol.23 (1970), p.129.
64   Wrigley, loc.cit., p.51.
65   In Sri Lanka the British retained until 1832 a
     lucrative government monopoly over cinnamon; in that
     year the revenue from it was £90,000 (James Steuart,
     'Notes on Ceylon and its Affairs' (London, 1862),
     p.69).
66   In the Gold Coast popular resistance led to the
     abandonment of a poll tax. In Sierra Leone (also a
     nonsettler colony) indirect taxes were adopted after
     the 'Hut Tax War' of 1898 (Hallett, op.cit., p.309).
67   Banton, loc.cit., pp.258-9.
68   Legislative Council Debates, 14 July 1930, quoted in
     M.R.Dilley, 'British Policy in Kenya' (London, 1966),
     p.202. Emphasis added. Another member referred to
     'the express invitation of Sir Charles Eliot' at which
     many of the settlers came to Kenya and to 'the clear
     understanding that European interests were to be
     paramount'. The Chairman of the Colonists Association
     in Kenya asserted in 1930: 'We were invited here as
     colonists, and as colonists we intend to stay. Over
     one thousand white children in the schools of the
     country have no other home than Kenya, and their

birthright is in no wise secondary to that of any
other native of Africa' ('The Times', 7 July 1930,
quoted in Dilley, ibid., p.198).
69 Ibid., p.181.
70 There was also in the export sector of the plantation-
type economies a significant contribution to output by
smallholders (especially in Malaysia).
71 This 'irrationality' was largely due to the nature of
labour demand and supply. The timing of labour requirements in grain cultivation based on monsoonal
rains was both uneven and erratic, and the resulting
variations in the demand for labour were aggravated by
a maldistribution in the supply, intra-seasonally,
inter-regionally, and even between holdings in the
same district.
72 Michael Crowder, 'West Africa under Colonial Rule'
(London, 1970), p.347; also p.274.
73 Michael Adas, 'The Burma Delta: Economic Development
and Social Changes on an Asian Rice Frontier,
1852-1941' (Wisconsin, 1974).
74 The decisions of the English law courts, which alone
became legally binding, were seldom accessible to the
peasant without considerable delay and expense; and
when availed of he suffered from the total unacquaintance of the judges with the complicated details of
paddy cultivation.
75 The peasantry in Malaysia was less affected because
land was more plentiful and artificial irrigation was
not needed.
76 H.G.Ward, Second Minute on the Eastern Province, 1857,
'Speeches and Minutes of Sir Henry George Ward,
1855-1860' (Colombo, 1864).
77 In Sri Lanka the disruption of the peasant economy due
to the growth of the plantations was judiciously assessed by one writer: 'It is true that Ceylon had her
own version of the enclosure movement, and the effects
of such ordinances as the Crown Lands (Encroachments)
Ordinance of 1840 and the Waste Lands Ordinance No.1
of 1897 on the condition of the peasantry were disastrous. However, what appears to have taken place
was that the peasantry was deprived of the village
chena and forest land, thus causing impoverishment but
not reducing them to the level of landless paupers'
(N.S.G.Kuruppu, History of the Working Class Movement
in Ceylon, 'Ceylon Historical Journal', no.3 (July
1951), p.133).
78 J.A.Hobson, 'The Evolution of Modern Capitalism' (New
York, 1926), p.12.
79 Ioan Davies, 'African Trade Unions' (Harmondsworth,
1966), pp.16-17.

80 Hodder and Harris (eds), op.cit.; Barbour, op.cit., p.243; J.I.Clarke, North-West Africa Since Mid-Century, loc.cit.
81 Davies, op.cit., pp.16-17.
82 This rationalizing ideology is seen in the statement of Sir Edward Northey relating to his Circular of 1891. The Africans, by working for Europeans, he said, would 'learn to be proud of their proper place in the world and be ashamed of their idleness' (Dilley, op.cit., p.181).
83 The Northey Circular is discussed, among other sources, in Dilley, op.cit., pp.224 ff; Wrigley, loc. cit., pp.237 ff; and Davies, op.cit., pp.32-5.
84 'Kikuyu Annual Report', 1907-8. The development possibilities of the 'native reserves' and the financial benefits that could accrue to the Thika tramway and the Uganda railway by the carriage of produce were noted in the 'Kikuyu Annual Report', 1910-11. Based on Wrigley, loc.cit., pp.52-3, n.3.
85 Dilley, op.cit., p.181.
86 Quoted in Jack Woddis, 'Africa - The Roots of Revolt' (London, 1961), p.50.
87 M.A.Buxton, 'Kenya Days' (London, 1927), p.10, quoted in Wrigley, loc.cit.

CHAPTER 7 PLANTATIONS AND THEIR METROPOLITAN ORIENTATION

1 Robert Brenner, The Origins of Capitalist Development; a Critique of Neo-Smithian Marxism, 'New Left Review', no.104 (July-August 1977), pp.87-8.
2 Lilian M.Penson, The London West Indian Interest in the Eighteenth Century, in R.Mitchison (ed.), 'Essays in Eighteenth Century History' (London, 1966), p.1, originally in 'English Historical Review', vol.36 (July 1921).
3 Daniel J.Boorstin, 'The Americans 1: The Colonial Experience' (Harmondsworth, 1958), p.123.
4 S.H.Frankel, 'Capital Investment in Africa' (London, 1938), pp.307-12; R.M.Prothero, Recent Developments in Nigerian Export Crop Production, 'Geography', vol. 40(1955), pp.19,22,24; H.R.Jarrett, The Oil Palm and its Changing Place in the Economy of Sierra Leone, ibid., vol.42(1957), pp.55-6.
5 'Rubber in Malaya 1876-1922' (Kuala Lumpur, 1973), pp. 26,72. Also Lim Teck Chee, Perak: Aspects of British Land Policy 1874-97 (Master's thesis, University of Malaya, 1968).
6 W.K.Hancock, 'Survey of British Commonwealth Affairs', vol.II, part 2 (London, 1964), p.200.

7   Plantations in World Economy, 'Seminar on the
    Plantation Systems of the New World', San Juan, Puerto
    Rico, November 1957. Introduction by Vera Rubin. Pan
    American Union, Division of Science Development
    (Social Sciences), p.14.
8   Stuart Bruchey, 'The Roots of American Economic
    Growth' (London, 1965), p.44.
9   A Note on Labour Requirements in Plantation Agri-
    culture, 'Geography', vol.23(1935), p.156.
10 Towards an Understanding of Plantation Agriculture,
    'AREA' (London, Institute of British Geographers). An
    occasional publication of the Institute, undated
    (circa 1970).
11 Plantation Wares, 'Encyclopaedia of the Social
    Sciences' (New York, 1933), vol.XII, p.157.
12 'Plantation Agriculture' (London, 1969), p.4.
13 Loc.cit., p.14.
14 E.g. J.C.Jackson: 'Plantation Agriculture represents
    ... a commercial venture producing for export'
    ('Planters and Speculators' (Kuala Lumpur, 1968), p.
    xiv). Jackson defined plantations as 'a commercial
    [agricultural] activity producing for export', as dis-
    tinct from domestic food production. 'In the context
    of nineteenth-century Malaya the important distinction
    lies between export-oriented or plantation agriculture
    and domestic food-crop production or kampong agricul-
    ture' (ibid.).
15 Ruth C.Young, The Plantation Economy and Industrial
    Development in Latin America, 'Economic Development
    and Cultural Change', vol.18, no.3, p.356.
16 D.S.Landes, 'The Unbound Prometheus' (Cambridge,
    1969), p.37.
17 Richard Pares, The Economic Factors in the History of
    the Empire, in E.M.Carus-Wilson (ed.), 'Essays in
    Economic History' (London, 1966), p.442.
18 Hugh E.Egerton, Colonies and the Mercantile System, in
    G.H.Nadel and P.Curtis, 'Imperialism and Colonialism'
    (New York, 1964), p.64.
19 Charles P.Nettles, Imperial Problems and Revolution,
    'Journal of Economic History', vol.12 (Spring 1952),
    reprinted in Abraham Eisenstadt, 'American History',
    Book I: 'To 1887' (New York, 1962).
20 'The Economics of the Developing Countries' (London,
    1969), p.154.
21 Op.cit., p.60. Drabble (ibid., pp.65-6) when quoting
    a remark of J.A.Schumpeter, that British capital
    flowed into the Malayan rubber plantations 'because
    the hevea tree grows there and not in Norway', miscon-
    strued its context. It was not that Schumpeter was

'content to explain the convergence of capital for rubber in Malaya' in terms of environmental factors alone. He was merely rejecting the view that British capital exports during the rubber boom of 1910-11 were due to 'shrinking rates of surplus value in an old capitalist country ... [and to] new opportunities for the exploitation of labour elsewhere' ('Business Cycles' (New York, 1939), vol.1, p.432).

22 N.Bukharin, 'Imperialism and World Economy' (London, 1972), p.20.

23 Bruno Lasker, 'Human Bondage in Southeast Asia' (Chapel Hill, N.C., 1950), pp.200-11. Courtenay, by confusing the wage rate with the high proportion of wages in the cost of production of plantation crops, made the crass assertion that plantation labour is expensive. 'The idea that ... labour ... is cheap is based on a rather facile comparison with the cost of employing similar numbers of work-people in North America or Europe where, of course, wages are very much higher' (op.cit., p.54). 'It is not unusual for labour costs to represent 60% of a plantation's total operating costs' (ibid., pp.54-5).

24 Saw Swee Hock, The Structure of the Labour Force in Malaysia, 'International Labour Review', vol.98, no.1 (July 1968), p.60.

25 International Labour Office, 'Plantation Workers' (Geneva, 1966), pp.262-5. Likewise a Labour Investigation Committee stated in regard to tea plantation labour of Assam in 1946: '[The labourers] merely exist. They have hardly any belongings except a few clothes (mostly tattered) and a few pots (mostly earthen).... Their houses present a picture of stark poverty' ('Report of an Enquiry into Conditions of Labour in Plantations in India' (Delhi, 1946), p.368).

26 'The Wages and Cost of Living of Estate Labourers', Ceylon Sessional Paper - XXXI, 1923, p.9.

27 E.L.Wheelwright, 'Industrialization in Malaya' (Melbourne, 1965), p.97.

28 Lim Teck Ghee, op.cit., pp.222-3.

29 G.L.Beckford, 'Persistent Poverty: Underdevelopment in Plantation Economies of the Third World' (New York, 1972), p.162,n.8.

30 'The Processing of Colonial Raw Materials' (HMSO, London, 1951), p.47.

31 H.Hurstfield, The Control of British Raw Material Supplies 1919-1954, 'Economic History Review', vol.14 (1944-5), no.1. In a few special instances metropolitan governments were directly engaged in colonial export production, as in the Belgian Congo and under

the Culture System in Java. The colonial power in
these territories was both 'sovereign and merchant'.

32 Parliamentary Paper, 'Tea' (1837-9), p.7. Quoted by
S.K.Bose, 'Capital and Labour in the Indian Tea
Industry' (Bombay, 1954). Also H.H.Mann, Tea Industry
in N.E. India, 'Bengal Economic Journal', vol.1(1919),
reprinted in H.H.Mann, 'The Social Framework of
Agriculture' (Bombay, 1967), p.402.

33 Drabble, op.cit., p.134. Earlier discussed by him in
The Plantation Rubber Industry in Malaya up to 1922,
'Journal Malay Branch Royal Asiatic Society', vol.40,
part 1, 1967, pp.65-6.

34 Quoted in E.V.Francis, 'Britain's Economic Strategy'
(London, 1939), p.129, and in Hurstfield, loc.cit.

35 Loc.cit., pp.72-3.

36 US Department of Commerce, 'American Direct Investments in Foreign Countries' (Washington, D.C., 1929),
p.27, quoted in Callis, op.cit., p.31; Drabble, op.
cit., p.65.

37 Landes, op.cit., p.458; also pp.457,516.

38 The UK with her tropical colonies and control over
shipping, felt relatively secure and, with the income
from the several activities connected with the production and export of organic materials, she lagged
seriously behind in the development of synthetic substitutes.

39 Op.cit., p.154.

40 According to an estimate of Michael Barratt Brown a
few years back, the developed countries' imports of
primary products from the underdeveloped countries
were a little more than a third of their total im-o
ports, compared to over two-thirds earlier ('Imperialism and Working Class Interests in the Developed
Capitalist Countries' (Mimeo Sheffield, March 1970)).

41 The changing composition of primary product imports
into the USA and of American overseas investment, has
been referred to by F.Stirton Weaver, The Dynamics of
U.S. Investment in Latin America, 'Science and
Society', vol.33(1969); also Harry Magdoff, The Age
of Imperialism, Part I, 'Monthly Review', vol.20 (June
1968), cited by Weaver, op.cit.

CHAPTER 8 PROBLEMS OF LABOUR SUPPLY AND THE RECOURSE TO
MIGRANT LABOUR: I. LABOUR SHORTAGES AND THE NON-
AVAILABILITY OF INDIGENOUS LABOUR

1 John Capper, Coffee Planting in Olden Times, in 'Old
Ceylon' (London, 1878), p.41.

2   E.F.C.Ludowyk, 'The Modern History of Ceylon' (London, 1966), pp.68-9.
3   Ibid., p.71.
4   Received by the Duke of Newcastle on 22 February 1861. Ceylon no.1721, Colonial Office 54/377 - 1861.
5   'Times of Ceylon', 19 February 1892.
6   'The Economist', 6 July 1895.
7   Ibid., 7 February 1903.
8   Ibid., 6 July 1901.
9   'Labour Recruiting Agency', Papers laid before the Legislative Council of Ceylon (Colombo, 1909), Ceylon Sessional Paper, LXIX - 1908, p.731.
10 'The Economist', 9 April 1910.
11 'Times of Ceylon', 13 January 1910.
12 Ibid., 18 January 1910.
13 Ibid.
14 Ibid., 18 January 1910.
15 Ibid., 12 January 1910.
16 Ibid., 18 January 1910.
17 'Despatches relating to the Government Contribution Towards the Labour Recruiting Agency', Ceylon Sessional Paper, VIII - 1908, p.2.
18 'In Ceylon every estate is burdened with advances to coolies, which has [sic] grown in recent years, and now amounts, at least to Rs.50 per head, or even at worst to considerably over Rs.100' ('The Economist', 29 December 1915). 'On one estate the advances which are put down among the recoverable assets of every company amounted to Rs.75,000 on 1,100 coolies, a total of which though not very high for Ceylon, represents a yearly loss of interest of Rs. 6,600 to Rs. 8,000' (ibid.).
19 Ibid., 15 July 1911.
20 One of them plaintively described their plight: 'I had a kangany on this estate without command of labour. He started trying to crimp coolies from the other minor kanganies, here, being backed somewhere, as is usual in these cases, by a neighbouring head kangany or chetty. As he became a nuisance, I gave him his "tundu" [discharge ticket] and he went to another district ... which was all I wanted. After two months or so he again gets his "tundu" and returned with the few coolies he had to where his family had been living [on a neighbouring estate] ... and gets taken on against my wish. [Since] I have Mr. Thorpe's written promise not to take coolies from here [this] is a clear breach of [the] agreement.... Though in this case I suffered no loss I might have had to bid against his kangany to retain my own labour, the very

thing the Federation was started to put an end to'
(R.H.Maclean, 'Times of Ceylon', 13 January 1910).
21 16 May 1914. The high wages in Malaysia were partly
    due to the prevailing level of costs and prices, the
    unhealthy conditions in the pioneer tracts, and the
    longer distance from South India to Malaysia than to
    Sri Lanka.
22 Sir Percival Griffiths, 'The History of the Indian Tea
    Industry' (London, 1967), p.64.
23 'The Tea Commissioner's Report', 1868, p.20.
24 Amalendu Guha, Colonisation of Assam: Second Phase
    1840-1859, 'Indian Economic and Social History
    Review', vol.4, no.4 (December 1967), p.295.
25 'Of the many difficulties in the way of remunerative
    cultivation of tea in Assam, Cachar and Sylhet, the
    scanty supply and high price of labour are among the
    most formidable' (ibid.).
26 D.R.Snodgrass, 'Ceylon: An Export Economy in Transi-
    tion' (Homewood, Ill., 1966), p.24.
27 Ibid.
28 An Interpretation of Economic Backwardness, 'Oxford
    Economic Papers', vol.6, no.2 (June 1954), pp.148-9.
29 W.E.Moore, 'Industrialization and Labour' (Ithaca and
    New York, 1951), p.35.
30 D.A.Kotelawele, Agrarian Policies of the Dutch in
    South West Ceylon - 1743-1767, 'A.A.G. Bijdragen', 14
    Afdeling Agrarische Gesehiedenis, Landbouwhogeshool,
    Wageningen, 1967, p.16.
31 Diaries of Assistant Agent for Ratnapura, Sri Lanka
    National Archives (hereafter SLNA), Group 45.
32 'The use of money in trade may have been more recent
    than trade itself, but, however recent, it goes far
    beyond the beginnings of European civilization and is
    probably older than the oldest of the written records'
    (The Rise of a Money Economy, 'Economic History
    Review', vol.14, no.2(1944), p.125).
33 H.R.C.Wright, 'East-Indian Economic Problems' (London,
    1961), p.272.
34 'Journal of Malay Branch of Royal Asiatic Society'
    (1927), pp.134,146,179, quoted in Wright, op.cit.,
    p.214. '... the excessive indolence of the Malays,
    who can never be induced to work in warehouses, or in
    the loading or unloading of ships except when their
    necessities oblige them' (F.Jourdan, 19 February 1772.
    Sumatra Records at India Office, 15, cit. Wright,
    ibid., p.250).
35 'Report of the Administration of the Straits Settle-
    ments during the Year 1855-56', p.13.
36 'For such is the listless idleness of a Cingalese that

as long as he possesses a couple of coconut trees
whose shade protects him while its fruits support his
half-finished existence no hope of gain, no prospect
of independence can allure him to more active pursuits.' 'The Cingalese are a mistrustful as well as
indolent people.' (J.Deane's report upon the District
of Colombo, 1 May 1820, in the Circuit of Mr D'Oyly,
Collector of the District of Colombo 1808 and 1809.
Colonial Office 416/26.)

37 Reports of Messrs Eden, Orr and Granville for Matara
1809, 1812, 1813. Colonial Office 416/26.

38 Memorandum by Messrs Beaufort and Hensham, 25 July
1828. SLNA, 10/26.

39 'The Bungalow and the Tent' (London, 1854), p.48,
quoted in Ludowyk, op.cit., p.67.

40 Op.cit., p.24.

41 Two legal cases out of a large number whose proceedings are on record may be cited. For instance,
Damayagamme Mul Achariya vs. Kandoonuwatte Sattamby
and Wellegedera Sattamby, 1 February 1817; Batcho vs.
Phillippo Appoo for the recovery of debt of 60 RD.
9 March 1818. Board of Judicial Commissioners for the
Kandyan Provinces, SLNA Group 23.

42 Moir, Collector, Colombo, to J.Sutherland, 11 September 1815. SLNA, 9/250.

43 For instance, Adigar Maha Nillame Atapattoo Lekam
Weerasooriya Appoo vs. Beddiwellagey Apoo of Mahakahe-
welle in Four Korles. Alleged wrongful possession of
land and non-payment of debt. 5 May 1819. Board of
Judicial Commissioners for the Kandyan Provinces, SLNA
Group 23.

44 Madige Vidahn vs. Narayanan for the recovery of a loan
of 1400 RD. 10 December and 27 December 1815. Ibid.

45 W.Malcolm, Agent of Government to George Lusignan,
Secretary for the Kandyan Provinces. Dated Ratnapoore
[Ratnapura], 4 February 1818. SLNA, 6/551; W.Mal-
colm, Agent of Government to Capt. Ingham, Acting
General, Ratnapura, dated Agent's Office, February
1818. Ibid.

46 W.Malcolm, Agent of Government to George Lusignan,
4 February 1818. SLNA, 6/551.

47 General Description and History of the District [of
Mannar], SLNA, 31/44. Mannar, taken from the Raja of
Jaffna by the Portuguese in 1560, was fortified for
the protection of their trade. The Dutch seized it in
1658.

48 'Report of a Tour through Mannar District by H.R.
Sneyed', Collector, July 1810. Reports and diaries of
Messrs Tolfrey and Sneyed upon the District of Mannar.
Colonial Office 416/26.

49   Report of I.M.Codrington upon the District of Jaffna
     30 January 1816. Colonial Office 416/26.
50   Private Letters, No.15. Robert Arbuthnot to Ensign
     Pendergrasst, Colombo, 30 January 1804. 'The want of
     salt by adding to the distress of the Insurgents would
     probably hasten their submission.' From H.Wright to
     G.Lusignan. Ratnapore [Ratnapura], 2 July 1818. Also
     No.115, Arbuthnot to Montgomery Esq., Chilaw. Colom-
     bo, 20 June 1804.
51   From H.Wright to G.Lusignan, Ratnapore [Ratnapura],
     27 July 1818.
52   From Robert Brownrigg to the Rt. Hon. The Earl of
     Bathurst, Secretary of State. 'If you cannot protect
     all the salt in your district either by lodging it in
     godowns or by stationing guards to secure it ...' the
     Governor wrote, 'it would be better to destroy an
     article the want of which is so severely felt by the
     enemy than leave it exposed in places where they might
     have an opportunity of [obtaining] it.' Colombo, 30
     January 1804. Conveyed by Richard Plasket to John
     D'Oyly in Matara. Colombo, 2 June 1807.
53   Report of Messrs Eden, Orr and Granville for Matara,
     1809, 1812, 1813, p.380.
54   Letter from the Revenue Commissioners, Kandy, 20 April
     1818. SLNA, 6/321.
55   Letter to George Lusignan, Secretary, Kandyan Provin-
     ces. Dated Ratnapura, 29 January 1818. SLNA, 6/551.
56   No.99, Arbuthnot to John D'Oyly, Galle, Colombo, 7
     June 1804.
57   From W.Malcolm, Agent of Government to James Suther-
     land, Secretary, Kandyan Provinces, 22 January 1815.
     SLNA Group 6/551.
58   'Replies of the European Merchants in Ceylon to the
     Commissioners of Enquiry relative to the internal and
     external commerce of the Island.' SLNA Group 19/60.
59   Kotelawele, loc.cit., p.10.
60   Colombo, 25 July 1828. SLNA Group 10/206.
61   Agent's Court, Ratnapura, 20 January 1815. SLNA Group
     5/551.
62   The Sociological Consequences of Imperialism with
     Special Reference to Ceylon, PhD thesis, University of
     London, 1950, p.134. He repeats this assertion in
     'Sinhalese Social Organization' (Colombo, 1956), p.1.
63   In similar circumstances, and about the same period,
     the Chinese rulers shut their doors to Western mer-
     chants (Michael Greenberg, 'British Trade and the
     Opening of China 1800-42' (Cambridge, 1951), p.44).
64   'Ceylon' (London, 1859), I, p.608.
65   B.J.Perera, The Foreign Trade and Commerce of Ancient

Ceylon - II, 'Ceylon Historical Journal' (January 1952), p.198.

66   Enclosure to letter from R.Boyd to Secretary, Kandyan Provinces. Commissioner of Revenue's Office, Colombo, 27 April 1815. SLNA Group 6/520 B, p.125.

67   Ratnapoore [Ratnapura], Cutcherry, 30 May 1818. SLNA Group 6/551.

68   SLNA Group 6/551.

69   Kotelawele, loc.cit., p.18.

70   History of the Mahabedde and its establishment in the Island of Ceylon, Colonial Office 416/5.

71   'The delay and difficulty which frequently occurs in drying of it [the cinnamon] from heavy rains which sometimes prevent them from collecting any for days added to the sudden rise of the numerous rivulets in the interior (which I witnessed twice when at Batugedera) may totally prevent them from coming to the store or detain them several days on road' (J. Maitland to R.Boyd, dated the Cinnamon Department, Colombo, 8 August 1815).

72   Report of the Assistant Government Agent (hereafter AGA) on the District of Saffregam for 1864. SLNA Group 33/100, p.1.

73   Ratnapore [Ratnapura], 20 September 1815. SLNA Group 6/551.

74   From H.Wright to G.Lusignan, Ratnapore [Ratnapura], 6 October 1818. SLNA Group 6/551.

75   No.67, Arbuthnot to John D'Oyly, Matura [Matara] Colombo, 20 April 1804. SLNA Group 6.

76   No.70, Arbuthnot to John D'Oyly, Matura [Matara] Colombo, 5 May 1804. Ibid.

77   Reports of Messrs Eden, Orr and Granville for Matara 1809, 1812, 1813 (cited earlier).

78   From J.Maitland, included as annexure to a letter from Robert Boyd, Commissioner of Revenue, to the Chief Secretary to Government, Colombo. Commissioner of Revenue's Office, Colombo, 22 April 1815. SLNA Group 13.

79   Secret Letter from I.W.Falck to the Hon'ble the Chief of Galle Arnholders de Ly in charge of the management of the affairs at that place with the Council. Dated Colombo, 23 June 1766. Also Extract of a letter addressed to the Commander and the Council of Galle, dated 23 October 1767. SLNA, 6/321, Sabaragamuwa Diaries.

80   From Philip Mossellamany to James Sutherland, Secretary to Candian Provinces. (Proposition concerning the purchase of the Areka Rent of the Saffragam Korle.) Dated Colombo, 4 July 1815. SLNA, 6/520 B, p.315.

81   Dated Kandy, 23 September 1815. SLNA, 6/521.
82   From Robert Brownrigg to the Rt. Hon'ble the Earl of
     Bathurst, Secretary of State, no.103, 8 June 1815.
     SLNA Group 5.
83   Letter from J.Gay to Thomas Eden, Provincial Judge of
     Colombo, 17 October 1815. Ibid., p.625.
84   Statement of Dekum or Annual Tribute. SLNA, 9/520,
     p.819.
85   Ibid.
86   Copies of this statement were forwarded by the
     Collector of Colombo, W.H.Kerr, to J.Sutherland,
     Secretary for the Kandyan Provinces. Letter No.176,
     dated Colombo, 2 September 1815. SLNA, 9/250.
87   Sawers to Lusignan, Secretary, Kandyan Provinces,
     Badulla, 2 June 1818. SLNA, 6/548(1), p.94.
88   Diary of the Agent of Sabaragamuwa, 22 May 1818.
89   Sir John D'Oyly, Sabaragamuwa Diaries, 22 August
     1815. SLNA, 6/321.
90   Sabaragamuwa Diaries, 9 June 1815. SLNA, 6/321.
91   Ibid., 24 January 1815.
92   Letter from Capt. Coxon to H.E.Brownrigg. Dated
     Padukka, 19 August 1815. Ibid., p.545.
93   Translation of letter to H.E. The Governor and Maha
     Dissawe at the fort of Badulla. SLNA, 6/548/2, p.
     232.
94   In a letter to Lusignan, dated Badulla, 11 August
     1818. Ibid., p.226.
95   'Cooly Hire', Minute by the Governor, Letters
     received from the Collector of Districts respecting
     rates of 1825. SLNA, 10/122.
96   Letter No.228 from C.P.Layard to the Chief Secretary,
     dated Colombo Cutcherry, 5 November 1825. Ibid.
97   Letter from P.Anstruther, Collector to the Commis-
     sioners of Eastern Enquiry. Dated 9 February 1830.
     SLNA, 19/9.
98   Ibid.
99   Report of George Boyd for Galle 'to April 1820'.
     SLNA, 416/26, p.232.
100 Colonial Office 416/27.
101 Sabaragamuwa Diaries, 24 May 1815. SLNA, 6/322.
102 Sawers to Lusignan. Badulla, 30 September 1818.
     SLNA, 6/548/2, p.330. In the same year H.Wright in-
     formed G.Lusignan of his intention 'to raise 150 to
     200 men for the purpose of clearing the Idalgasheena
     Pass and sought authorisation to pay them 2 fanams
     and a seer of rice each a day and a seer of salt each
     for 30 days.' Ratnapore [Ratnapura], 22 July 1818.
103 Sawers to Lusignan. Badulla, 3 October 1818. Ibid.,
     p.339.

104 Letter from Capt. J.Hobbs to Capt. Prager [both of
     the Royal Engineers Department], dated Kandy, 10 May
     1815. SLNA, 520 B, p.173.
105 S.Sawers to G.Lusignan. Badulla, 13 June 1818.
     SLNA, 6/548, p.121.
106 Evidence of George Bird Esq. upon Agriculture in the
     Kandyan Province. Kandy, 23 September 1829. SLNA,
     33/300.
107 Ibid.
108 In the source given earlier.
109 'Diaries', 3 May 1889.
110 Ibid., 12 May 1889.
111 Ibid., 4 March 1890.
112 Ibid.
113 Ibid.
114 AGA for Kegalle, 'Diaries', 4 June 1894. SLNA Group
     30.
115 Ibid., 19 December 1892. The AGA for this district
     in 1854 had observed that during the 2nd quarter 1853
     there were 21,642 Tamils employed on 83 estates.
     'The Sinhalese employed represent probably 5,000
     more' (ibid.).
116 'Times of Ceylon', 19 February 1892. In a comment on
     tea production in Ceylon in 1901, this newspaper
     noted that the low-country tea pluckers were Sin-
     halese. Ibid., 2 January 1901.
117 'Diaries', 26 May 1898. SLNA, 47/4.
118 Ibid., 14 February 1889.
119 'Mercantile Lore' (Colombo, 1940), pp.39-40.
120 Government Agent for the Province of Uva. 'Diaries',
     23 May 1907. SLNA Group 57.
121 Ibid., 14 December 1907.
122 The Assistant Agent gave the source of this informa-
     tion. 'In connection with the employment of Sin-
     halese village labour on Estates Mr. John Rettie at
     my request has sent me figures relating to such
     labour on one newly opened estate in Wiyaluwa'
     (ibid.).
123 'In continuation of the subject of Sinhalese labour
     mentioned in my entry of 24th. Mr. Vicaresso writes
     that on his leased rubber land he had 25,000 days
     labour and paid out Rs.15,517 to Sinhalese during the
     year' (ibid., 30 December 1907).
124 Ibid., 7 May 1907.
125 Ibid., 14 July 1895.
126 'The repair of the Yodi Ela, in particular, has been
     almost at a standstill since the withdrawal of vil-
     lage labour last year, and the cost of supervising
     small gangs of imported labour is out of all propor-

tion to the expenditure on construction, and unless
the village labour is again requisitioned the earth-
work, besides being protracted over 3 or 4 years,
will cost a great deal more than is contemplated by
the estimate' (from C.A.Fisher, G.A. Anuradhapura to
Colonial Secretary. No.270, 15 June 1885. SLNA,
41/56).

127   AGA's 'Diaries', Kegalle, 8 May 1894.
128   GA's 'Diaries', North Western Province, 12 August
       1901. SLNA Group 42.
129   Ibid., 29 January 1902.
130   Ibid., 29 July 1901.
131   AGA's 'Diaries', Ratnapura, 1883, entry no.34. SLNA
       Group 45.
132   GA's 'Diaries', North Western Province, 26 July 1898.
       SLNA Group 42.
133   'Philanthropy! Conversed with some of the patients.
       Numbers of them are pit coolies. To my surprise they
       told me that the plumbago people had no dispensary at
       the pits. Till recently they said Mr. F.R.Senanayake
       had 800 odd coolies but some of them have bolted
       owing to the fever and now he had only about 400'
       ('Diary' of AGA Kurunegala, 16 February 1919. SLNA
       Group 38).
134   Ibid., 28 July 1896.
135   GA's 'Diaries', North Western Province, 28 July 1896.
       SLNA Group 42.
136   AGA's 'Diaries', Ratnapura, 1883, entry no.34;
       ibid., 23 February 1885. SLNA Group 45.
137   Ibid., 23 February 1885.
138   GA's 'Diaries', North Western Province, 28 July 1896.
       SLNA Group 42.
139   Ratnapura, 'Diaries', 13 October 1899. SLNA Group
       45.
140   GA's 'Diaries', North Western Province, 1 June 1901.
       SLNA Group 42.
141   An alternative possibility is shown by the experience
       of Japan, where underemployed rural labour was
       mobilized within the confines of the rural economy,
       without a transfer of such labour to the towns. The
       growth of rural industries, some of them producing
       component parts for urban based industries, enabled
       industrial by-employment to be built into the agri-
       cultural cycle.
142   P.Page Arnot, 'A History of the Scottish Miners from
       the Earliest Times' (London, 1955), p.7, quoted by
       J.Kuczynski, 'The Rise of the Working Class' (London,
       1967), p.25.
143   The nature of surplus labour in the peasant sector of

underdeveloped countries, and the somewhat broader
and more basic question of the growth of capitalism
in agriculture, are discussed, in terms of Marx's
distinction between production time and labour time,
by Susan A.Mann and James M.Dickinson, Obstacles to
the Development of a Capitalist Agriculture, 'Journal
of Peasant Studies', vol.5, no.4 (July 1978).

CHAPTER 9   PROBLEMS OF LABOUR SUPPLY AND THE RECOURSE TO
MIGRANT LABOUR: II.   THE RESPONSE OF INDIGENOUS LABOUR TO
THE PLANTATION SYSTEM

1   International Labour Office, 'Plantation Workers'
    (Geneva, 1966), p.52, n.1.
2   Bruno Lasker, 'Human Bondage in Southeast Asia'
    (Chapel Hill, 1950), p.214.
3   'Report of the Commission to Inquire into Abuses
    Alleged to Exist of Coolies to Mauritius and Dema-
    rara, October to December 1840', quoted by C.Kondapi,
    'Indians Overseas 1838-1949' (New Delhi, 1951).
4   Assam Labour Enquiry Report of 1926, p.26, cit. R.K.
    Das, 'Plantation Labour in India' (Calcutta, n.d.),
    p.65.
5   The Malaysian Commissioner of Labour, Madras,
    enumerated the 'principal irregularities' of recruit-
    ers: '(A) Getting the recruits passed by the munsif
    of a village other than that of the recruits.   (b)
    Forging the munsif's signature in the licence.   (c)
    Working upon petty domestic quarrels between son and
    father, husband and wife, etc. and inducing them to
    leave their home in the heat of the moment.   (d)
    Seducing young men with the promise of getting them
    married in the colony.   (e) Catching recruits at the
    weekly shandies.   (f) Matching strangers as brothers,
    father and son, brother and sister and husband and
    wife (mainly to avoid the restriction of Rule 22).
    (g) Misrepresenting the nature of the work and rates
    of wages on the estate' (Planters' Association of
    Malaya, Annual Report for 1925-6).
6   J.W.Edgar, 'Report on Tea Cultivation in Bengal',
    British Parliamentary Papers 1874, vol.XLVIII, Cd
    Paper 982, cit. D.H.Buchanan, 'The Development of
    Capitalistic Enterprise in India' (New York, 1934),
    p.61.
7   Ibid., pp.62-3.
8   'Papers Regarding Tea Trade', cit. Sanat Kumar Bose,
    'Capital and Labour in the Indian Tea Industry'
    (Bombay, 1954).

9   'The Tea Commissioner's Report', p.26.
10 Ibid.
11 D.Chaman Lal, 'The Cooly', vol.II, p.6.
12 K.S.Sandhu, 'Indians in Malaya' (Cambridge, 1969),
    p.81.
13 Planters' Association of Malaya, 'Annual Report for
    1923-4', p.144.
14 'The Proposals of the Labour Commission', Despatches
    relating to the Labour Commission, Ceylon Sessional
    Paper III - 1909.
15 'Times of Ceylon', 5 January 1910.
16 United Planters' Association, Report for 1904, p.3.
17 'Colonial Labour Policy and Administration' (New York,
    1964), p.254.
18 'Times of Ceylon', 24 February 1892.
19 'Report of the Ceylon Labour Commissioner, June 1 to
    December 31, 1904', in Despatches relating to the
    Government Contribution Towards the Labour Recruiting
    Agency, Ceylon Sessional Paper VIII - 1908, p.6.
20 'Times of Ceylon', 24 February 1892.
21 18 September 1848. Leases, payment of Rent in first
    year. Sri Lanka National Archives (SLNA), 10, nos
    170-4.
22 'Diaries', 27 September 1884.
23 'The great difficulty is, of course, the fact that the
    paddy crops have to be attended to.... Some of the
    interior villages are now in a state of unprecedented
    prosperity' ('Times of Ceylon', 20 January 1910).
24 Ibid.
25 D.J.Blake, Labour Shortage and Unemployment in
    Northeast Sumatra, 'Malayan Economic Review', vol.7,
    no.2, October 1962.
26 G.M.Meir, 'Leading Issues in Economic Development'
    (Oxford, 1971), p.147.
27 Dharma Kumar, Agricultural Wages in the 19th century
    in Madras, in Tapan Raychaudhuri (ed.), 'Contributions
    to Indian Economic History', vol.II (Calcutta, 1963).
28 'The Report of the Silver Currency Commission'
    (Colombo, 1894), p.viii.
29 Indian Currency Committee, Minutes of Evidence, p.165,
    quoted in H.A. de S.Gunasekera, 'From Dependent
    Currency to Central Banking in Ceylon' (London, 1962),
    p.103, n.28.
30 E.F.C.Ludowyk, 'The Modern History of Ceylon' (London,
    1966), p.67.
31 Swettenham Commission, quoted in Gunasekera, op.cit.,
    p.106.
32 Gunasekera, ibid., p.106.
33 'Diaries', 12 October 1897.

34   Ibid., 28 October 1897.
35   Ibid.
36   'Diaries', 16 August 1897.
37   Ibid., 14 December 1897.
38   The Assistant wrote in his Diary: 'Bribery of Police
     Inspector Moore. I caught this officer taking bribes
     today. He has come up to Nuwara Eliya, to test
     weights and measures in the bazaars, at least that is
     the reason he gave me a few days ago and two of the
     N.E. [Nuwara Eliya] boutique keepers came to me this
     morning and said he has seized their weights and
     measures with a number of others and would only
     release them on payment to him of Rs. 20 a piece.
     They brought me the money in notes and begging [me] to
     mark it and to verify their statements ... I took the
     men to the bank and there Mr. Ryan, the Agent, in my
     presence took down the numbers of the notes, and then
     sent the men away to do what they had been ordered to
     do by the Inspector. Meanwhile Mr. Ryan walked down
     the road and watched them enter the Police Station and
     from a friend's house opposite saw them shortly after-
     wards come out again with their weights and measures.
     They all then returned to the bank where I was waiting
     and then accompanied me to the Police Station. Then I
     entered the room where the Inspector was told of the
     complaint against him and searched him and his boxes,
     Mr. Ryan being present, and in one of his boxes which
     he opened himself, I found six out of the eight notes
     whose numbers we had taken down in the bank a few
     minutes before. There was a lot of money in the box,
     the proceeds I have no doubt of similar work'
     ('Diaries', 13 November 1890).
39   'Diaries', 3 May 1889.
40   From F.C.Fisher, Government Agent, Anuradhapura, to
     Colonial Secretary, No. 220, 5 June 1885, SLNA, 41/56.
41   'Diaries', 5 October 1900.
42   Ibid., 2 November 1884.
43   Ibid., 22 September 1884.
44   Ibid., 2 July 1901.
45   Ibid.
46   'Times of Ceylon', 20 June 1910.
47   GA's 'Diaries', 22 October 1889.
48   Ibid., 10 May 1886.
49   Ibid., 26 February 1886.
50   Ibid., 4 August 1884.
51   'Diaries', 1 July 1887.
52   Ibid., 9 October 1890.
53   Governor Sir H.E.McCallum to the Right Hon. The Earl
     of Crewe, dated Colombo, 12 November 1908. 'The

Proposals of the Labour Commission', Despatches
relating to the Labour Commission (cited earlier),
para. 21.

54 Ibid.

55 Island of Ceylon and its Produce, Colombo, 8 April
1846, 'The Economist', 25 July 1846.

56 Retrospect of Financial and General Policy since our
assumption of Government. Despatch No.46 from
Torrington to Earl Grey, 11 December 1848. British
Parliamentary Papers, vol.XXXVI, 1849.

57 'Diaries', 9 March 1884.

58 Letters to J.D'Oyly, dated Kandy, 28 August 1815.
SLNA, 6/521. On government projects the work involved
was 'laborious and labourers are sometimes necessarily
flogged'. 'Replies of the Principal Modeliars and
Native Landholders in Colombo the Adjoining districts
to the questions addressed to them by the Commissioner
of Enquiry relative to the agricultural resources of
the country' (Answer to question no.20), Colombo, 12
December 1829. SLNA, 193.

59 M.W.Roberts, Indian Estate Labour in Ceylon during the
Coffee Period 1830-1880, 'Indian Economic and Social
History Review', vol.3, no.1 (March 1966), p.1.

60 Quoted in E.F.C.Ludowyk, 'The Modern History of
Ceylon' (London, 1966), p.66.

61 Colonial Office, 54/235. Tennent's minute of 19 April
1847 to Grey. Ludowyk, op.cit., p.66.

62 Ibid.

63 Retrospect of Financial and Commercial Policy since
our assumption of Government, Despatch No.46 from
Torrington to Earl Grey, 11 December 1848. Cited
earlier.

64 'I am not reporting in this specially cases in which
wages are settled up to the end of 1883 or later',
'Diaries', 7 July 1884.

65 Ibid., 20 July 1886.

66 Ibid., 17 January 1885. 'Wrote again to G.A. on the
subject of the need for further clerical work in the
Kachcheris, showing ... [the] amount of new business
brought about by the Cooly Wages Ordinance and arrears
of wages which now require to be taken notice of and
enquired into' (ibid., 10 September 1885). When the
labourers of Brookside Estate received 3 months' wages
(some Rs 2,500) under the new Ordinance, 'the work of
paying them occupied 2 hours. The hearing of cases
occupied the rest of the day' (ibid., 16 December
1884).

67 Ibid., 17 June 1885.

68 Ibid., 8 April 1895.

69   Ibid.
70   Ibid., 24 July 1889.
71   Ibid., 9 March 1884.
72   'Mr. Anstruther did not keep his word, and no part of the proceeds of the bark has been sent to me. He now says he found out after the bark had gone that there was a lien over it, which he did not know of before. But this is not true - as I ascertained in Kandy on the 22nd from the people who had this lien. Mr. Anstruther was well aware all the time of this lien' (ibid., 24 July 1889).
73   Ibid. Referring to a 'case against Mr. Bagot in D.C. [District Court] for the value of the timber cut by him in Crown forests adjoining Morgherita [estate]', the Assistant Agent wrote, 'Mr. Bagot actually stated on oath that he did not know where the timber used in a large new factory on the estate lines and bungalow had come from although it was proved to have been cut in the forest within 1/4 to 1/2 mile of the estate bungalow. Comment is needless. Judgement reserved' (ibid., 15 February 1889).
74   'Diaries', 23 May 1885.
75   Ibid., 4 July 1885.
76   Ibid., 10 September 1885.
77   Ibid., 20 May 1887. 'The Head Kangany of Clarendon Estate attends the Kachcheri, having been sent for to give information required to enable the Attorney General to take legal steps in the matter of cooly wages. He is unable as might have been expected to furnish the particulars called for, viz. statement of wages due to each cooly and period each claims for' (ibid., 15 October 1884).
78   Ibid., 13 October 1887.
79   Ibid.
80   Ibid., 20 May 1887.
81   Ibid., 13 October 1887. 'It can hardly be expected that the G.A. of a Province or the A.G.A. of a District can dance attendance at the Police Court in such cases especially when on conviction Mr. Northmore usually fines the defaulter one rupee.'
82   Ibid.
83   Ibid.
84   'Diaries', 10 September 1886.
85   Ibid., 13 February 1887.
86   Ibid., 5 April 1889.
87   Op.cit., p.70.
88   Kondapi, op.cit. 'Correspondence relating to the Royal Commission of Enquiry into the Condition of Indian Immigrants in Mauritius' (1875), c. 1188 16, para. 3, quoted in Kondapi, op.cit.

89 5 June 1849. House of Commons Papers, vol.XLI. In
    1844 the Secretary of State wrote to the Governor,
    'I have received a letter in which it is incidentally
    mentioned that several officers of the Government are
    constantly absent from the Capital at their coffee
    plantations' (Despatch from Lord Stanley to Governor
    Sir Colin Campbell, 4 December 1844. House of
    Commons Papers, vol.XXI).

90 Despatch from Lord Stanley to Governor Sir Colin
    Campbell, 30 November 1844. Ibid.

91 Despatch from Governor Sir Colin Campbell to Lord
    Stanley, 12 February 1845. Ibid.

92 Ibid.

93 In 1745, according to Lilian Penson, 'we still find
    traces of antagonism between merchants and planters'
    (The London West Indian Interest in the Eighteenth
    Century, 'English Historical Review', vol.36, July
    1921, reprinted in 'Essays in Eighteenth Century
    History', arranged by R.Mitchison (London, 1966)).

94 The cordiality and informal nature of the relations
    among Britishers in Sri Lanka are apparent, for in-
    stance, from the following correspondence received
    by the Registrar of Companies in Colombo. In one
    letter dated 19 April 1883, the Managing Director of
    the Dimbulla Coffee Co. wanted exemption from the
    penalty for delay in furnishing the Company's balance
    sheet: 'My dear Thwaites, Grant forwarded to me your
    official letter. Please give the directors one more
    week as I have such difficulty in getting together a
    board meeting for a quorum. Sometimes there is only
    one director in the District. I have called a
    meeting for Monday and will be able to send you the
    Balance Sheet in the course of next week. Yours
    sincerely, G.H.D.Elphinstone.' Another revealing
    letter was from the Oriental Bank Corporation, dated
    13 May 1878: 'My dear Thwaites, the other night at
    the club you kindly promised to send me a copy of the
    Dimbulla Coffee Co.'s balance sheet for year 1878,
    and if not giving you too much trouble I shall be
    glad if you can let me have it, and will charge the
    Company with the cost. Yours very truly ... [signed
    illegibly].' File on the Dimbulla Coffee Co., at the
    Office of the Registrar of Companies, Colombo.

95 'Diaries', 17 January 1889.

96 Ibid., 16 April 1889.

97 Ibid., 20 February 1890: 'I have asked for an ex-
    planation and he is as successful in this explanation
    as he was in Mr. Tunbridge's case.'

98 'The Forest Department is trying to act very unfairly

to certain of its employees in this district. Mr.
Alexander [head of the Forest Department] wants to
replace the Nanu Oya depot keeper and the 2 Forest
Rangers' (ibid.).

99 Ibid., 31 January 1889.

100 'Mr. Armitage brought me for instructions a letter to
himself from Mr. Alexander, accusing him of having
given me incorrect information in a manner evidently
intended to intimidate him. I sent it on to the G.A.
[Government Agent], and asked him to take serious
note of it' (ibid., 6 March 1890).

101 'Diaries', 3 December 1897.

102 Ibid., 3 June 1889.

103 Ibid., 4 February 1889. Mr Bagot was to be tried in
the Police Court 'for cutting the trace of a channel
through the Crown forest near Morgherita estate and
thereby destroying about Rs.600 worth of trees....
It was clearly proved that the trace had been made
by Mr. Bagot's order' (ibid., 9 February 1889).

104 Ibid., 5 March 1888.

105 'Diaries', 5 April 1889.

106 Ibid., 13 March 1891. The background to this case as
described by the Assistant Agent explains his mis-
giving: 'Inspector Moore's Case. Went down to Kandy
for this case and gave evidence before the Supreme
Court. A great point was made for the defence that I
should not as Police Magistrate have laid a trap for
the man, in fact that a Magistrate should not be a
detective but I maintained that I acted rightly. I
received information that an Inspector of Police is
acting in a most unjust and oppressive manner in a
station in my charge, that he is taking bribes wholesale from the boutique keepers in the town and there-
upon take such measures that shall finally put a stop
to it, or if the information is false, as shall prove
it to be so, and enable me to punish the informants.
I am not only the Magistrate but I am the A.G.A. and
as such am supposed to look after the Police and to
suppress crime. If I was the P.M. [Police Magis-
trate] and the P.M. only had to act in a judicial
capacity only the point might have some force in it
but I am far more A.G.A. than P.M. and am expected to
protect as well as judge the people entrusted to my
care.'

107 'Assam Labour Report', 1900, p.23, quoted in Das, op.
cit., p.98.

108 Philip Woodruff, 'The Men Who Ruled India: the
Guardians' (London, 1954), p.55.

109 In a memorandum to the Secretary of the Government of

Bengal, Parliamentary Papers, 1867, Paper 124, pp. 6-7, quoted in Buchanan, op.cit., p.63.

110   Parliamentary Papers Relating to Coolie Trade in Assam, Parl. Reports, 1867, vol.I, p.359, quoted in Bose, op.cit.

111   Buchanan, op.cit., pp.37-8.

112   Mary Wilhelmine Williams, writing on Slavery in the 'Encyclopedia of the Social Sciences' (New York, 1934), vol.14, p.83, quoted in W.E.Burghardt Du Bois, 'The World and Africa' (New York, 1965), p.47. Also John W.Blake, 'European Beginnings in Africa' (New York, 1937).

113   Christopher Hill, 'Reformation to Industrial Capitalism' (Harmondsworth, 1969), p.229.

114   'Modern India and the West' (London, 1941), p.45.

115   'The Cambridge History of the British Empire', vol. III, part II, 'New Zealand' (Cambridge, 1933), p.55.

116   Ibid.

117   Jean Woolmington, 'Aborigines in Colonial Society' (Melbourne, 1973), p.154. In Sarawak, James Brook after a time lost patience with the missionaries. 'Personally, I think bishops are a bit of nuisance out here', he said (George Woodcock, 'The British in the Far East' (London, 1969), p.103).

118   August Meir and Elliott Rudwick, 'From Plantation to Ghetto' (New York, 1970).

119   A Direction for Choice of Servants for Maryland, 1635, in Oscar Handlin (ed.), 'Readings in American History' (New York, 1960), pp.28-9.

120   Maryland Act Concerning Negroes and Other Slaves, 1664, Maryland Archives, I, 533-4, reprinted in Handlin, op.cit.

121   Hacker, op.cit., p.103.

122   Donnan (ed.), 'Documents' II, pp.327-8, cit. D.B. Davis, 'The Problem of Slavery in Western Culture' (Harmondsworth, 1971), p.208.

123   The stamp of religion was even found in the bills of lading of the American slave ship Sierra Leone in the mid-eighteenth century. They bore the inscription: 'Shipped by the Grace of God in good order and well conditioned by William Joyson & Co., owners of the said schooner, whereof is master under God for this present voyage, David Lidsay, and now residing at Anchor in the harbour of Newport, and by God's grace bound for the coast of Africa ... and so God send the good schooner to the desired port in safety. Amen' (John R.Spears, 'The American Slave Trade', p. 40, quoted in A.C.Burns, 'History of Nigeria' (London, 1942), p.76).

124   Meir and Rudwick, op.cit., p.67.
125   Ibid.
126   'Origins and Distribution of Racism' (New York, 1967).
127   Ibid.
128   Ibid.
129   W.J.Clutterbuck, 'About Ceylon and Borneo' (London, 1891), p.41, quoted in Ludowyk, op.cit., pp.67-8.
130   Landes, op.cit., p.60.
131   O.C.Cox, 'Caste, Class and Race' (New York, 1959), p.339. Based on Edgar S.Furniss, 'The Position of the Labourer in a System of Nationalism' (Boston, 1922), pp.19-20; B.Mandeville, 'Brittania Languens', 1st edn, p.153, quoted in E.F.Hecksher, 'Mercantilism', vol.II (London, 1955), p.164; also by Cox, op.cit., p.339.
132   E.J.Hobsbawm, 'The Age of Revolution' (London and New York, 1964), p.70.
133   'Religion and the Rise of Capitalism' (New York, 1926), p.269, quoted in W.E.Moore, 'Industrialization and Labour' (Ithaca and New York, 1951), p.37.
134   Moore, ibid. A comparable change during the development of bourgeois civilization is in society's attitude towards mendicancy. The mendicant was stripped of the aura of sanctity that was attached to him throughout the Middle Ages, and he began to be regarded as a vagabond, a 'professional loafer'. Governments in Europe from the beginning of the sixteenth century passed legislation and established institutions to set the poor to work. This change in attitudes was most evident in regions where the development of capitalism and manufactures had proceeded farthest (Henri Pirenne, 'A History of Europe' (London, 1961), pp.529 ff).
135   Davis, op.cit.
136   J.F.Rees, Mercantilism and the Colonies, 'Cambridge History of the British Empire', vol.I (Cambridge, 1929), p.563.
137   'In the case of a few later writers, the employment argument gave rise to a new balance-of-trade concept, in which the amounts weighed against each other were not the values respectively of the exports and the imports, but the respective amounts of labour or employment they represented, i.e., the "balance of labour" or the "balance of employment"' (J.Viner, 'Studies in the Theory of International Trade' (London, 1955), p.52, quoted in Haroldur Johannsson, 'Mercantilist and Classical Theories of Foreign Trade' (Kuala Lumpur, 1968), p.29).

138 Rees, loc.cit., p.564.
139 Op.cit., p.163.
140 Edith Abbott, 'Women in Industry' (New York, 1910),
     pp.58 ff, quoted by J.Kuczynski, 'The Rise of the
     Working Class' (London, 1967), p.61.
141 J.T.Krause, Some Neglected Factors in the English
     Industrial Revolution, 'Journal of Economic History',
     vol.19, 1959, reprinted in M.Drake (ed.), 'Population
     in Industrialization' (London, 1969).
142 Celso Furtado, 'Development and Underdevelopment'
     (Berkeley and Los Angeles, 1967), p.105.
143 Op.cit., p.60.
144 Changing Attitudes to Labour in the Mid-Eighteenth
     Century, 'Economic History Review', 2nd Ser. XI
     (1958), pp.46-8, referred to by Landes, ibid.
145 Colonial Office 54/190. Stephen's Minute of 16
     October 1841 on Campbell's despatch of the Annual
     Blue Book, quoted by Ludowyk, op.cit., p.68.
146 'Modern Production Among Backward Peoples' (London,
     1935), p.196.
147 Op.cit., p.67.
148 Op.cit., p.63.
149 Edgar, 'Report on Tea Cultivation in Bengal', British
     Parliamentary Papers, 1874, vol.XLVIII, Cd Paper 982
     (cited earlier), p.22.
150 Op.cit., p.334.

CHAPTER 10   THE SCALE OF PLANTATION OPERATIONS AND
PRODUCTIVE EFFICIENCY - A DISTORTED IMAGE

  1 D.H.Penny and M.Zulkifli, Estates and Smallholdings:
     An Economic Comparison, 'Journal of Farm Economics',
     December 1963, p.1017.
  2 P.T.Bauer, 'The Rubber Industry' (London, 1947), p.4.
  3 Amalendu Guha, Colonization in Assam: Second phase
     1840-1859, 'Indian Economic and Social History
     Review', vol.4, no.4 (December 1967), based on H.A.
     Antrobus, 'A History of the Assam Company 1839-1953'
     (Edinburgh, 1957).
  4 K.E.Knorr, 'World Rubber and Its Regulation'
     (Stanford University Press, 1945), p.25.
  5 Chairman's report of the Strathmore Rubber Co.Ltd to
     the 2nd Annual Meeting held in Edinburgh, December
     1909.
  6 Op.cit., p.28.
  7 Some Thoughts on the Economic Development of Malaya
     under British Administration, 'Journal of Southeast
     Asian Studies', vol.5, no.2 (September 1974), p.206.

8 L.A.Harper, The Effect of the Navigation Acts on the Thirteen Colonies, in R.B.Morris (ed.), 'The Era of the American Revolution' (New York, 1939), reprinted in H.N.Scheiber (ed.), 'United States Economic History, Selected Readings' (New York, 1964). Also J.F.Rees, Mercantilism and the Colonies, 'The Cambridge History of the British Empire', vol.I (Cambridge, 1929).

9 Daniel Boorstin, 'The Americans', vol.1, 'The Colonial Experience' (London, 1958), pp.126-7.

10 Allan Nevins, 'Ordeal of the Union' (New York, London, 1947), vol.I, p.423; also Barrington Moore, Jnr, 'Social Origins of Dictatorship and Democracy' (Boston, 1967), p.119.

11 Nevins, op.cit. (1947), p.424.

12 Census data cited by V.I.Lenin, 'Capitalism in Agriculture. Collected Works' (Moscow, 1964), vol.IV, pp.131-2.

13 Allan Nevins, 'The Emergence of Modern America, 1865-1878' (New York, 1927), p.20.

14 'Estates changed hands freely, but the original acreage of an estate remained much the same from that day to this, though of course the cultivated areas rose year by year' (T.L.Villiers, 'Some Pioneers of the Tea Industry' (Colombo, 1951)).

15 'Coffee, Tea and Cocoa' (Stanford, 1951), p.466.

16 An example from Sri Lanka is the Weddemulle estate in Ramboda district planted with tea. Weddemulle is bordered by three other estates, viz. Labookellie upwards towards Nuwara Eliya; Rangbodde, down on the main road towards Ramboda; and Frotoft, across the saddle of the hill towards Pussellawa. Weddemulle estate comprises three divisions: Weddemulle (the lowest in elevation), Rambodde, and Camnethan. The Weddemulle division has one field on the far side of Labookellie estate, while certain fields of Labookellie estate can only be reached through the Weddemulle division, which is on the same contour. Though the divisions of each estate are fairly close to each other, one division is not easily accessible from another. Rambodde division of the Weddemulle estate, which is on the higher side of a whole division of the Rangbodde estate, cannot be reached from its estate factory (situated, as also is the Superintendent's bungalow, in the Weddemulle division) without traversing 2 miles across Rangbodde estate. To reach the Camnethan division of the Weddemulle estate from the Rambodde division one must travel 3 miles across a whole division of Frotoft estate.

17   In 1925 the Chairman's report for Apthorpe Estates Ltd
     stated: 'The Board regrets to announce that the Crown
     Land of 378 acres which it was originally hoped to
     acquire at Rs. 60 an acre was sold at nearly Rs. 480
     an acre, and the directors did not consider the pur-
     chase justified.'   The Theresia Estates Co.Ltd stated
     in 1927:   'Of the 70 acres Crown-land referred to in
     the last report, it has only been possible to purchase
     25 acres from government.'
18   Youngil Lim, Impact of the Tea Industry on the Growth
     of the Ceylonese Economy, 'Social and Economic
     Studies', vol.17, no.4 (December 1968), p.460.
19   D.M.Etherington, 'Smallholders Tea Production in
     Kenya' (Nairobi, 1973), p.4.
20   D.M.Etherington, Economies of Scale and Technological
     Efficiency: A Case Study in Tea Production, 'East
     African Journal of Rural Development', vol.4, no.1
     (1971), p.75.
21   Ibid., p.81.
22   Ibid., p.82.
23   Phin-Keong Voon, The Adoption of Technological
     Innovations in Rubber Processing: The Case of
     Malaysian Smallholders, 'Malayan Economic Review',
     vol.22, no.2 (October 1977), p.35.   Robert Ho, Labour
     Inputs of Rubber Producing Smallholders in Malaya,
     ibid., vol.12, no.1 (April 1967), p.80.   In Malawi the
     peak demand for labour in tea cultivation coincides
     with that in subsistence agriculture.
24   Martin Rudner, The State and Peasant Innovation in
     Rural Development: The Case of Malaysian Rubber,
     'Asian and African Studies', vol.6, 1970, p.76.
25   'Rubber News Letter', 30 September 1936, p.2, cit.
     Knorr, op.cit., p.111.
26   Loc.cit., p.124.
27   R.K.Udo, Sixty Years of Plantation Agriculture in
     Southern Nigeria: 1902-1962, 'Economic Geography',
     vol.41(1965), p.357.
28   S.H.Hymer, Economic Forms in Pre-Colonial Ghana,
     'Journal of Economic History', vol.30, no.1 (March
     1970), pp.47-8.
29   Op.cit., p.167.
30   H.Myint, An Interpretation of Economic Backwardness,
     'Oxford Economic Papers', June 1954, p.154.
31   Loc.cit., p.1020.
32   Elaine Gunewardena, 'External Trade and the Economic
     Structure of Ceylon 1900-1955' (Central Bank of
     Ceylon, Colombo, 1965), p.75.
33   D.R.Snodgrass, 'Ceylon: An Export Economy in
     Transition' (Homewood, Ill., 1966), p.37.

34   Ibid.
35   'Accumulation on a World Scale' (New York, 1974), vol.
     1, pp.23,40,42,60,62.
36   Ng Choong Soi, Colin Barlow and Chan Chee-Keong,
     Factors Affecting the Profitability of Rubber Produc-
     tion on West Malaysian Estates, Paper presented at the
     Natural Rubber Conference, Kuala Lumpur, 1968, Pre-
     print, pp.12,14.
37   Colin Barlow and Chan Chee-Keong, Towards an Optimum
     Size of Rubber Holdings, Paper presented at the
     Natural Rubber Conference, Kuala Lumpur, 1968, Pre-
     print, p.1.
38   Penny and Zulkifli, loc.cit., p.1017.
39   G.R.Chandrasiri et al., The Specification and Estima-
     tion of a Production Function for Smallholding Rubber
     in Sri Lanka, 'Journal of the Rubber Research
     Institute of Sri Lanka', vol.54 (part 1, no.2), 1977,
     p.414.
40   Knorr, op.cit., p.178.
41   J.G.Stigler explains by a theory of vertical integra-
     tion and disintegration the extent of division of
     labour and specialization of functions or processes.
     Initially an enterprise would include processes that
     are subject to increasing returns and others that are
     not. When the enterprise has grown sufficiently the
     processes subject to increasing returns are turned
     over to specialist firms, which at a further point of
     time will abandon some of its processes to be taken
     over by others. Conversely, when the industry is in
     decline, surviving enterprises will reappropriate
     functions which are no longer of a sufficient scale
     to support independent firms (The Division of Labour
     is limited by the Extent of the Market, 'Journal of
     Political Economy', vol.59, no.3 (June 1951), espe-
     cially pp.188,190).
42   Advertisement of W.H.Davies & Co., 'The Times of
     Ceylon', 20 April 1892.
43   Advertisement in R.J.Johnson, 'Notebook for Tea
     Planters' (4th edn, Colombo, 1961).
44   Chairman's Report, 'The Times of Ceylon', 23 February
     1910.
45   Ibid.
46   Wickizer, op.cit., p.468.
47   Manuel Moreno Fraginals, 'The Sugarmill' (New York,
     1976), p.21.
48   E.T.Thompson, Population Expansion and the Plantation
     System, 'American Journal of Sociology', vol.41 (July
     1935-May 1936).
49   Annual Report for the year ending 31 March 1911.

50   Out of about $(M) 20 advanced to each labourer, about
     $(M) 12 was taken by the recruiting agent as his com-
     mission (R.N.Jackson, 'Immigrant Labour and the
     Development of Malaya' (Kuala Lumpur, 1961)).
51   Report of the Standing Committee to be presented at
     the 9th Annual Meeting of the Association, to be held
     on 26 April 1916. In its report for the following
     year the Association complained that 'Local Recruiting
     still continues to a very large extent'.
52   E.F.C.Ludowyk, 'The Modern History of Ceylon' (London,
     1966), p.73.
53   However, in Kenya where tea cultivation is based on
     non-resident, indigenous labour, despite a large
     labour demand there is 'a distinct range of flexibili-
     ty in timing which minimises the competition between
     tea and other crops for labour services' (Etherington,
     op.cit., p.25).
54   Quoted in P.S.Taylor, Plantation Agriculture in the
     United States: Seventeenth to Twentieth Centuries,
     'Land Economics', vol.30 (May 1954), p.148. A second
     criterion used by Phillips in his classification of
     crops was the system of labour relations including
     patterns of management and supervision. Cereal grow-
     ing, truck farming and dairying require a versatile
     force participating in some degree or another in the
     management of the farm, but plantations a mass of
     routinized labour subjected to harsh methods of labour
     discipline and control.
55   E.R.Wolf, San Jose, Subcultures of a 'Traditional'
     Coffee Municipality, in J.H.Steward (ed.), 'The People
     of Puerto Rico' (Urbana, 1966), pp.181,195.
56   S.W.Mintz, Canemelar: The Subculture of a Rural Sugar
     Plantation Proletariat, in Steward (ed.), op.cit.,
     p.352. The material in this and the succeeding para-
     graph is based on Mintz.
57   Ibid., p.354.
58   In Sri Lanka (in 1968) labour employed in tea plucking
     accounted for 53 per cent of the total production
     costs; the corresponding figure for Kenya (in 1970)
     was 68 per cent. International Bank for Reconstruc-
     tion and Development, International Development
     Association, 'Report on the World Tea Economy' (30
     June 1971), p.42.
59   A.B.Richardson, The Field Stalk Clipper, 'Tea
     Quarterly', vol.24, Parts I and II (June 1953), p.48.
60   R.W.Palmer-Jones, 'Production and Marketing of Tea in
     Malawi', University of Reading, Dept of Agricultural
     Economics and Management, Development Study No.15
     (1974), p.11.

61 The statutory daily basic wage since 1966 has been
    Rs 1.40 for male workers compared with Rs 1.35 in tea;
    for female and child workers Rs 1.30 and Rs 1.45 re-
    spectively for rubber, and Rs 1.05 and Rs 0.90 respec-
    tively for tea.
62 John M.Brewster, The Machine Process in Agriculture
    and Industry, 'Journal of Farm Economics', August
    1950, pp.70 ff.
63 W.E.A.Stanner, 'Plantation Economy and Peasant
    Agriculture in India and Malaya' (Canberra, 1953),
    roneoed, prepared for the Cambridge Economic History,
    Library of the Australian National University.
64 Palmer-Jones, op.cit., p.5.
65 'Indians in Malaya' (Cambridge, 1969), p.52.
66 Quoted in 'Report of United Planters' Association of
    Malaya' to be presented to the 13th Annual General
    Meeting to be held on 28 April 1920.
67 'Report of the Standing Committee' to be presented at
    the 9th Annual Meeting of the Association, to be held
    on 26 April 1916, p.7.
68 Ibid., p.72.
69 'The Hevea tree apparently stands a lot of rough
    treatment and neglect' (Knorr, op.cit., p.34).
    Judgment and skill are however needed when the virgin
    bark of a tree is tapped. The angle at which the bark
    is cut should be carefully determined, but subsequent
    tapping follows the shape of the original excision.
70 D.H.Buchanan, 'The Development of Capitalistic
    Enterprise in India' (New York, 1934), p.65.
71 James McPherson, The Neilgherry Tea Planter, quoted in
    K.J.Tanna, 'Plantations in the Nilgiris - A Synoptic
    View' (Publisher and Date - 1967 ? not stated.
    Author's address is given as The Glen Morgan Tea
    Estates Co., Glen Morgan Estate, The Nilgiris).
72 Fraginals explained: 'Life was a chore, an endless
    task like that of the blacks who went to the forest
    to cut wood. Firewood was measured in "tasks".' The
    plantation kept careful count and punished those who
    did not fulfil the required amount of tasks just as
    Jesus Christ the omnipresent overseer condemned them
    for neglecting their religious duty (op.cit., p.54).
    The Indian Labour Code, which applied to plantation
    workers in Sri Lanka, asserted that the eviction of
    the entire family of any worker who was dismissed
    'preserved the sanctity of the family'.
73 Sayuti Hasibuan, The Palm-Oil Industry on the East
    Coast of Java, in D.S.Paauw (ed.), 'Prospects for East
    Sumatran Plantation Industries: A Symposium' (Mono-
    graph Series No.3, Yale University Southeast Asia

Studies, New Haven, Conn., 1962), pp.31-2. 'The
general conclusion is that a greater incentive component is needed in the traditionally paternalistic wage
structure. A final solution to the problem will
require labour's recognition of the relationship
between its return and its productivity' (ibid.,
p.32).

74 D.G.Blake, Labour Shortage and Unemployment in North
East Sumatra, 'Ekonomi Dan Keuangan Indonesia'
(Economics and Finance in Indonesia), vol.4, no.1. 12,
1962, p.30.

75 Weeding, transplanting and reaping are carried out by
women, whereas the initial preparation of the soil
(including the construction of field bunds), as well
as ploughing and threshing, are done by men. The
extent of mechanization and the amount of energy used
in the form of steam or electricity are also greater
for paddy milling than for the processing of tea and
rubber.

76 'Proceedings of the Royal Colonial Institute'
(London), vol.XXVII (1895-6), p.32. Clarence was a
former Chief Justice of Sri Lanka and had lived in the
country for over 25 years. Cf. H.Myint: 'There is
usually very little specialization beyond a natural
adaptability to the tropical climate, among the backward peoples in their roles of unskilled labourers'
(loc.cit., p.154).

77 Dr Etherington in his study of tea growing in Kenya
found no evidence of higher work efficiency on the
large estates employing permanent labour than on
smallholdings. A greater amount of tea was plucked
by an individual worker per hour on estates, but this
was partly due to the tea plants being more than 20
years old (at the time this comparison was made). As
a result, the closer concentration of shoots than on
the immature plants on smallholdings facilitated
plucking (op.cit., p.107).

CHAPTER 11   PLANTATIONS AND TECHNOLOGICAL STAGNATION

1 Changes of a similar nature occurred in the tobacco
plantations of Deli in Sumatra. Research into soil
conditions, fertilizer use and plant pathology, and
improvements made to the drying sheds where the leaf
was processed, led to a considerable improvement in
the quality of the manufactured tobacco (Lim Kim Liat,
The Deli Tobacco Industry: Its History and Outlook, in
D.S.Paauw (ed.), 'Prospects for East Sumatran Planta-

tion Industries: A Symposium' (Yale University Southeast Asia Studies, Monograph No.3, New Haven, Conn.,
1962), pp.11,13.

2 For example, on rubber plantations, the bicycle has
taken the place of the shoulder pole and two buckets
for conveying latex to a reception point, from where
it is taken by tractor-drawn trailers to the factory.
Only small quantities of latex could be carried at a
time by hand or on a bicycle. Traditional methods of
'crop lifting' persist, the latex being emptied by the
tapper from cups into buckets (T.Y.Pee, Economics of
Field Collection, Paper presented at the Rubber
Research Institute of Malaysia Planters' Conference,
July 1970, reprint, pp.G-1,G-2,G-7).

3 E.g. Howard F.Gregor: 'Certainly the plantation has
been anything but conservative in its record of
economic innovation and aggressiveness' (The Changing
Plantation, 'Annals of the Association of American
Geographers', vol.55(1965), p.226, n.2); J.C.Jackson
asserted that plantation agriculture was not 'an un-
differentiated, unchanging agricultural system. It is
indeed, both complex, and highly variable' (Towards an
Understanding of Plantation Agriculture, 'AREA'
(London, Institute of British Geographers), p.39).

4 Rudolf Sinaga and William Collier, Social and Regional
Implications of Agricultural Development Policy,
'Prisma' (November 1975), p.29.

5 Clifford Geertz, 'Agricultural Involution' (Berkeley,
1968), pp.132-3, based on K.Okhawa and H.Rossovsky,
The Role of Agriculture in Modern Japanese Economic
Development, 'Economic Development and Cultural
Change', vol.9, part II(1960).

6 Geertz, who used this expression with reference to
sugar production in Java, explained that while the
production of both coffee and sugar expanded rapidly
under the Culture System during the nineteenth
century, the dynamism of sugar was unmatched by any
tropical crop. Labour productivity rose substantially
and costs per unit of output declined (op.cit., pp.
65-8).

7 Manuel Moreno Fraginals, 'The Sugarmill' (New York,
1976), p.25.

8 A comparable situation is in the tea plantations of
Malawi, where sharp seasonal fluctuations in the crop
have necessitated much larger tea factories than in
other countries.

9 For example, in Puerto Rico the number of mills with
an investment of over $1 million increased from 3 (out
of a total of 108) in 1909 to 18 (out of a total of

55) in 1919 while those with an investment less than
$500,000 declined over the same period from 105 to 23
(S.W.Mintz, Canemelar: The Subculture of a Rural Sugar
Plantation Proletariat, in J.H.Steward (ed.), 'The
People of Puerto Rico' (Urbana, 1966), p.352). In
Mauritius, the number of sugar mills declined from 303
in 1863 to 21 in 1972, and the annual output per mill
rose from 450 to about 33,000 tonnes (N.Deerr, 'The
History of Sugar', 2 vols (London, 1949-50)).

10 Loc.cit., p.351.

11 Fraginals, op.cit., pp.20,112.

12 Ibid., p.148.

13 J.K.Eastham, Rationalisation in the Tin Industry, in
T.H.Silcock (ed.), 'Readings in Malayan Economics'
(Singapore, 1961), p.352. Also Ooi Jin Bee, Mining
Landscapes of Kinta, 'Malayan Journal of Tropical
Geography', vol.4, 1955, reprinted in Silcock (ed.),
op.cit.

14 E.W.Zimmerman, 'World Resources and Industries' (New
York, 1951), p.157.

15 'Capital', vol.I (Moscow, n.d.), pp.663-4, quoted in
Joseph M.Gillman, 'The Falling Rate of Profit'
(London, 1957), p.80. Also Celso Furtado, Comments on
Professor Rosenstein-Rodan's Paper (on 'Notes on the
Theory of the Big Push'), in H.S.Ellis (ed.),
'Economic Development for Latin America' (London,
1961), p.72.

16 The developmental significance of external economies
was propounded by Marx: 'The productivity of labour
in one branch of industry ... [becomes] a lever for
cheapening and improving the means of production in
another and thereby raising the rate of profit'
('Capital', vol.I, op.cit., p.85).

17 D.S.Landes, 'The Unbound Prometheus' (Cambridge,
1969), p.21.

18 Science and the Brewing Industry, 1850-1900, 'Economic
History Review', Second Series, vol.17(1964-5).

19 'The Agrarian Origins of Modern Japan' (Stanford,
1959), p.101.

20 The Gains from International Trade and the Backward
Countries, in his 'Economic Theory and the Underdeveloped Countries' (London, 1971), p.106, originally
published in 'Review of Economic Studies', vol.23(2),
no.48(1954-5). Another argument by him in this connection is somewhat obscure: 'The attempt to switch
over from a cheap labour policy to one of higher wages
and a more intensive use of labour usually involved
taking decisions about "lumpy" investments, both in
the form of plant and machinery and in the form of

camps and villages, where it was necessary to change
over from casual labour to a permanent labour force'
(ibid.).

21 Ibid., p.93.
22 V.D.Wickizer, 'Coffee, Tea and Cocoa' (Stanford,
    1951), p.161.
23 'The Economist', 14 January 1939, cit. Wickizer, op.
    cit., p.162.
24 Impact of the Tea Industry on the Growth of the
    Ceylonese Economy, 'Social and Economic Studies', vol.
    17, no.4 (December 1968), p.463, n.1.
25 S.J.Wright, Report on the Possibilities of Mechanizing
    Tea Cultivation in Ceylon, 'Tea Quarterly', 24 (Sep-
    tember 1953), p.64. The anti-technology bias of the
    plantation system is frequently rationalized in
    academic discussions in terms of employment creation.
    But employment creation was not what underlay the
    choice of technology by the planters. Also, the goal
    of employment creation must not be abstracted from
    questions of labour productivity and production costs
    which alone would determine the viability of the plan-
    tations.
26 'Capital' (Moscow, 1962), vol.III, p.741.
27 A.G.Barnes, 'The Sugar Cane' (New York, 1964), p.302.
28 Gregor, loc.cit.
29 J.Kuczynski, 'The Rise of the Working Class' (London,
    1967), p.44.
30 J.H.Street, Cotton Mechanization and Economic Develop-
    ment, 'American Economic Review', vol.45, no.4 (Sep-
    tember 1955), p.569.
31 Ibid., p.572.
32 US Government report on 'Technological Trends' (pub-
    lished in 1937), p.58, quoted in S.Lilley, 'Men,
    Machines and History' (New York, 1966), p.168.
33 J.H.Street, 'The New Revolution in the Cotton Economy'
    (Chapel Hill, 1957), p.34, quoted in Jay R.Mandle, The
    Plantation Economy and its Aftermath, 'Review of
    Radical Political Economics', vol.6, no.1 (Spring
    1974).
34 Under the traditional method of tea withering the
    spreading of leaf on the mats and its subsequent
    removal required a considerable number of workers
    using long bamboo-arms.
35 In the tea factories in Kenya all maintenance and
    repair work is done by their own engineering staff (as
    in the case of a sugarmill), whereas in Sri Lanka very
    few tea factories have even a welding plant.
36 Wage policy on plantations in this respect differed,
    for example, from that in the copperbelt of Zambia,

where after the Second World War large expenditures
were made on housing and welfare, with a view to
stabilizing the labour force. The expenditures in
kind were part of a sharp overall increase in wage
levels. By 1945, the average money wage in the mining
industry was 'substantially above the rates prevailing
in the rest of ... *[Zambia]*' (W.J.Barber, 'The Economy
of British Central Africa' (London, 1961), pp.232-3)

37   Op.cit., pp.327-8. The problem involved here is not
the same as what Fraginals (op.cit., p.144) calls a
'functional disequilibrium' between production phases,
arising from the uneven development of technology and
causing bottlenecks in the production line. (In the
early development of the English textile industry,
there was thus a continual disparity in productivity
between spinning and weaving.) The plantation system
only allows that degree of mechanization which is compatible with resident labour.

38   Richard Pares, Merchants and Planters, 'Economic
History Review', Supplement 4 (Cambridge, 1960), p.23.

39   P.S.Taylor, Plantation Agriculture in the United
States: Seventeenth to Twentieth Centuries, 'Land
Economics', vol.30 (May 1954), p.144.

40   Gillman, op.cit., p.71.

41   UN, FAO, Committee on Commodity Problems, Second Ad
Hoc Consultation on Tea, 'The Structure and Organisa-
tion of the Primary Market for Tea', by Board Richard
Stokke, Economic Affairs Officer GATT - International
Trade Centre, Mimeo, CCP: Tab.67/WP 2, 20 February
1967.

42   P.P.Courtenay, 'Plantation Agriculture' (London,
1969), p.54.

43   T.L.Haskell, Were Slaves More Efficient? Some Doubts
about 'Time on the Cross', 'New York Review', 19 September 1974, p.41.

44   Dutch entrepreneurs ousted from Indonesia were a
serious threat to the Deli tobacco plantations. They
tried to cultivate tobacco in Italy and the USA which
would match the quality of the Deli wrapper, and even
to produce a synthetic and shade-grown substitute for
Deli tobacco (Lim Kim Liat, loc.cit., p.17).

45   The reduction in plantation wages often took the form
of increasing work norms or 'task' sizes (The
Planters' Association of Malaysia, 'Annual Report',
1929-30).

46   'Economic experience has now dictated the desirability
of requiring tappers to do two hours' field work in
the afternoon ... and many company executives insisted
upon the arbitrary enforcement of the full day for

tappers. The Association recommended the principle that, as a permanent measure, labourers on estates should be employed for a full working day if they are to qualify for a day's pay at the prescribed standard rate' (The Planters' Association of Malaysia, 'The Year Book', 1931).

47   Martin Rudner, The State and Peasant Innovation in Rural Development: The Case of Malaysian Rubber, 'Asian and African Studies', vol.6, 1970. In Malaysia 'colonial rubber policy implicitly favoured high prices over efficient production' (ibid., pp.81-3).

48   V.I.Lenin, 'The Development of Capitalism in Russia' (Moscow, 1956), p.309.

49   Based mainly on Fraginals, op.cit., pp.109-10.

50   K.E.Knorr, 'World Rubber and its Regulation' (Stanford, 1945), pp.24-5.

51   'Foreign Plantation Investment in Ceylon 1889-1958' (Central Bank of Ceylon, Colombo, 1963), p.173.

52   'Persistent Poverty: Underdevelopment in Plantation Economies of the Third World' (New York, 1972), p.159.

53   Op.cit., p.25, based on P.T.Bauer, Notes on Cost, 'Economica', vol.12 (May 1945), p.95.

54   Pares, loc.cit., p.43. Emphasis added.

55   'The Export Economies' (Cambridge, Mass., 1969), p.68.

56   Ibid., p.72.

57   The Tea Research Institute of Sri Lanka in the mid-1960s established the possibility of replicating these attributes of quality by activating different enzymes in the leaf (as part of a process of 'upgrading' quality). However, a potential obstacle was the sectional interests of tea growers in the different districts which required maintaining the natural specificity in the quality of tea produced.

58   In Japan over a long period shears have been used for harvesting tea. 'Scissor picking' 'increases the daily output per worker about ten times over that by hand picking, but there is less control over quality [and therefore of the price of tea]' (Wickizer, op. cit., p.177).

59   Pee, loc.cit., pp.G-6,G-7.

60   Ethyrel had the effects of controlled slaughter tapping. Yields fell abruptly after the first year and in some instances were below the normal level, causing a dryness in the rubber trees. There was also a wastage factor - rainfall conditions in most plantation districts in Sri Lanka caused the chemical to be easily washed away. Further, the Rubber Research Institute found a 5 per cent concentrate of Ethyrel to be as effective as the 10 per cent one recommended by

the manufacturers (and the 5 per cent dosage was subsequently accepted by the Rubber Research Institute of
Malaysia as well).

61 At the meeting of the International Rubber Study Group
in Lagos in 1966 the delegates were subjected to a
sales promotion campaign by a team of executives sent
out by the manufacturers of Ethyrel.

62 Op.cit., p.21.

63 Pee, loc.cit., p.G-10.

64 Colin Barlow and O.S.Peries contend, on the ground
that plantation technology involves an increased use
of capital, that such technology is capital intensive
and biased against smallholders. As already explained, plantation technology is of a non-mechanical
nature and requires additional labour as a complementary input, so that the capital-labour ratio is
still small. The technology is not designed to save
labour but to maximize output. The smallholder's difficulties are of an institutional nature, viz. limitations of credit and marketing and a division of
effort between two or more products, and probably also
an inability to finance wage labour. (In paddy cultivation small peasants for the same reason neglect
labour intensive practices - transplanting and weeding.) Smallholders in rubber as well as in tea operate in a deprived social environment, which prevents
them from adopting what is agronomically best. The
article by Barlow and Peries referred to is On Some
Biases in the Generation of Technologies by Rubber
Research Institutes, 'Journal of the Rubber Research
Institute of Sri Lanka', vol.4(1977), part 1, no.2.

65 The marketing of sugar at the most advantageous price
required a timely supply of boxes and hogsheads, and
delays in supplying were a 'typical form of commercial
reprisal and coercion'. The merchant-moneylender
could also speculate and charge exorbitant rates for
warehouses. His extortion at the last stage of production took the form of appropriating the molasses
drained off during the storage of the brown sugar
(Fraginals, op.cit., p.121).

66 Ibid., p.49.

67 Ramiro Guerra, 'Sugar and Society in the Caribbean'
(New Haven, 1964), pp.188-90.

68 Fraginals, op.cit., pp.28-9.

CHAPTER 12 LABOUR RELATIONS IN PLANTATIONS

1 R.D.Lambert, The Modernisation of the Labour Force, in
   Myron Weiner (ed.), 'Modernisation' (New York, London,
   1966), p.282.
2 Karl Marx, 'Capital' (Moscow, n.d.), vol.1, p.714.
3 'Hawaii Planters' Monthly', I(1882), p.187, quoted by
   Edgar T.Thompson, Comparative Education in Colonial
   Areas, with Special Reference to Plantations and
   Mission Frontiers, 'American Journal of Sociology',
   vol.48 (May 1943), p.720.
4 Quoted by M.R.Stenson, 'Industrial Conflict in Malaya'
   (London, 1970). Also, The United Planters' Association of Malaya, 'Annual Report', 1936.
5 R.K.Jain, 'South Indians on the Plantation Frontier in
   Malaya' (Singapore, 1970), p.20.
6 Karl Marx, 'Capital: A Critique of Political Economy',
   in Lewis Feuer (ed.), 'Marx and Engels, Basic Writings
   on Politics and Philosophy' (New York, 1969), p.190.
7 'Straits Settlements Labour Commission Report' 1890,
   para.368, quoted in R.N.Jackson, 'Immigrant Labour and
   the Development of Malaya' (Kuala Lumpur, 1961),
   p.101.
8 Ibid.
9 'Indian Immigration Department Annual Report for
   1906', quoted in Jackson, op.cit., p.115. 'The Labour
   Department Annual Report for 1913' also noted a 'large
   number of desertions among labourers on contracts of
   service' (Jackson, ibid., p.130).
10 'Indian Immigration Department Annual Report for
   1904', Jackson, op.cit., p.114; 'Indian Immigration
   Department Annual Report for 1907', Jackson, op.cit.,
   p.138.
11 Charles Gamba, 'The National Union of Plantation
   Workers' (Singapore, 1962), p.6.
12 J.A.Barnes, foreword to Jain, op.cit., p.viii.
13 F.Oritz, 'Cuban Counterpoint', trans. Harriet de Ouis
   (New York, 1957), pp.52-64, quoted by S.W.Mintz, The
   Subculture of a Rural Sugar Plantation Proletariat, in
   J.N.Steward (ed.), 'The People of Puerto Rico'
   (Urbana, 1956), p.350.
14 Thompson, loc.cit., p.713.
15 Jain, op.cit., p.295.
16 Ibid., p.321.
17 Stenson, op.cit., p.209.
18 Planters' Association Malaya, 'Annual Report for
   1952-6'.
19 Federated Malay States, Johore, 'Annual Report for
   1910', p.7.

20 'Colonial Labour Policy and Administration' (New York, 1960), p.254.
21 Federated Malay States, Johore, 'Annual Report for 1921'. The same rates of pay were mentioned in 'Annual Report for 1910'.
22 'Report of the Standing Committee presented at the 8th Annual Meeting of the Planters' Association of Malaya', p.9.
23 'Indians in Malaya' (Cambridge, 1969), p.259, n.1, and p.261.
24 'Thus the disparity remained considerably larger than the [rubber] industry's estimate [in 1948] of 40 cents for housing and other services provided to Indians and probably continued to average between 80 cents and 81 cents a day' (Stenson, op.cit., p.187).
25 J.Thompson, 'The Straits of Malacca, Indochina and China' (London, 1875), ch.2, quoted by Jackson, op. cit., p.28.
26 Report of the Chairman presented to the first annual meeting, 'Straits Times', 4 January 1911.
27 Gedong (Perak) Rubber Estates Ltd, Chairman's report presented to the first annual meeting, 'Straits Times', 15 March 1911.
28 Malayan Union, Labour Department, 'Annual Report for 1948', p.20.
29 Parmer, op.cit., p.170, n.10.
30 Future of Plantation Rubber, 'Straits Times', 9 August 1906.
31 'Report of the Standing Committee to be presented at the 9th Annual Meeting of the Planters' Association of Malaya', 1916, p.7.
32 Jackson, op.cit., p.28.
33 Op.cit., p.271, Table 8.
34 G.G.Shrieke, The Rubber Industry in the Malay Peninsula, 'Rubber Growers' Association Bulletin', vol.4 (September 1922), p.440, quoted by Drabble, op.cit., p.186, n.4.
35 Federated Malay States, Johore, 'Annual Report for 1910', p.7.
36 'Intisari' (Published by Malaysian Sociological Research Institute Ltd), vol.3 (n.d., circa 1971), n.4; editorial by Shirle Gordon, p.10.
37 Some Preliminary Observations of the Origins and Characteristics of Indian Migration to Malaya 1788-1957, op.cit., p.25. The sentence quoted above also appears unchanged in his 'Indians in Malaya', cited earlier (p.55). In the latter source Dr Kernial Singh Sandhu rates the qualities of the different ethnic groups in Malaysia. The North Indians come out

best, followed by the Chinese; the Malays are placed
below the Chinese and the South Indians at the bottom.
    North Indians - The 'tall, sturdy' Sikhs were
'wholly reliable, fairly incorruptible, conscientious
and generally quick to learn.... [Their] stature,
bearing and martial traditions and reliability were
invaluable' for police and military duties (pp.69,72).
As a money lender, the Sikh provided loans 'usually at
usurious, though not unrealistic (given the social
context), [!] interest rates' (p.292).
    Chinese - 'The Chinese was an economic man par
excellence.... As such he was not prepared to remain
in any employment of low income any longer than absolutely necessary' (pp.54-5).
    Malays - They 'appeared quite happy with the cus-
tomary farms and fishing stakes and were not inclined
to work fixed hours of labour day in and day out'
(p.52). The Malays were 'unmotivated' (p.56).
    South Indians - The South Indian migrant 'was
generally not an "economic man" in the sense of, say,
his Chinese counterpart' (p.59). 'Political economy
[!] had virtually no meaning to him' (p.64). 'The
Madrasi ... was malleable, worked well under supervision and was easily manageable. He was not as am-
bitious as most of his Northern Indian compatriots and
certainly not like the Chinese.... He had little of
the self-reliance or the capacity of the Chinese, or
for that matter of many of his own countrymen from the
other parts of the subcontinent' (p.56). The South
Indians 'were a cringing social group ... [who] had
neither the skill nor the enterprise to rise above the
level of manual labour' (p.57).
38 'The Chinese in Malaya' (Kuala Lumpur, 1967), p.239.
39 'The Malayan Tin Industry to 1914' (Tucson, 1965),
    p.219. 'Chinese labourers ... generally would not
    exert themselves unless they had a personal interest
    in the mines [but the Indians would]' (ibid.).
40 The Structure of the Labour Force in Malaya,
    'International Labour Review', vol.98, no.1 (July
    1968), p.58.
41 A reference to contract labour in Sri Lanka is given
    in E.C.P.Hull, 'Coffee Planting in Southern India and
    Ceylon' (London, 1877), p.69.
42 Malay Union, 'Annual Reports of the Labour Department'
    for 1947, and 1948.
43 J.N.Parmer, Chinese Estate Workers' strikes in Malaya
    in March 1937, in C.D.Cowan (ed.), 'The Economic
    Development of Southeast Asia' (New York, London,
    1964), p.154.

44   Anthony Reid, Early Chinese Migration into North
     Sumatra, in Jerome Ch'en and Nicholas Tarling (eds),
     'Studies in the Social History of China and South-East
     Asia' (Cambridge, 1970), p.302.
45   Ibid.
46   W.F.Wertheim, 'Indonesian Society in Transition' (The
     Hague, 1969), p.251.
47   Based on the data on labour contracts made at the
     Straits Settlements, 1881-96, in Wong, op.cit., p.68.
48   A contemporary British planter with interests in both
     Province Wellesley and Sumatra, noted a 'perfect
     hatred of the name of "Deli" which operates not only
     inimically to that particular place but also as
     regards the whole island - so much that Chinese who
     will ship willingly to Langkat or Serdang, in ig-
     norance of the precise "locale" of those places will
     become perfectly mad if the word "Deli" be heard on
     board' (quoted by Reid, loc.cit., p.299).
49   Ibid., p.303.
50   Parmer, op.cit., p.221;   also p.169.
51   Ibid., p.101.
52   'Report of the Standing Committee to be presented at
     the 19th Annual Meeting of the Association', 1917.
53   Planters' Association of Malaya, 'Annual Report',
     1920-1.
54   Parmer, op.cit., p.98;   also p.98, n.1.
55   Planters' Association of Malaya, 'Annual Report',
     1935.
56   The Ghee Hin, composed of Cantonese, was, according to
     a press report in 1867, a sort of working-class guild:
     'a large society of the working class, working as
     pirates, fishermen and labourers' ('Penang Gazette',
     4 August 1867).
57   Khoo Kay Kim, 'The Western Malay States 1850-1873'
     (Kuala Lumpur, 1972), p.116. Also Blythe, Historical
     Sketch of Chinese Labour in Malaya, 'Journal Malay
     Branch of Royal Asiatic Society', vol.20, pt 1, p.107,
     quoted in Jackson, op.cit., p.47.
58   'Penang Gazette', 4 August 1867, contained an English
     translation of the Chief Kathi's exhortation to the
     Malays. A copy of this newspaper is exhibited in the
     State Museum in Penang.
59   Irving's memo on Perak, 24 July 1872, in correspond-
     ence relating to Malay Peninsula, quoted by Khoo, op.
     cit.
60   'Supplement to the F.M.S. Government Gazette', 22 June
     1928.
61   This policy in the sphere of labour relations was ex-
     pressed by a planter in 1894: 'To secure your inde-

pendence work with Javanese and Tamils, and if you
have sufficient experience, also with Malays and
Chinese; you can then always play the one against the
other' ('Selangor Journal', vol.4(1895), p.428, quoted
in Jackson, op.cit., p.104).

62 Governor Frederick Weld had written in 1887 to the
Secretary of State: 'I am also anxious for political
reasons that the great preponderance of the Chinese
over other races in these settlements and to a less
marked degree in some of the native states under our
administration shall be counterbalanced as much as
possible by the influx of Indian and other nationali-
ties' (Despatch No.397 from Frederick Weld to the
Secretary of State. 24 September 1887, quoted in
Parmer, op.cit., p.19).

63 Loc.cit.

64 Planters' Association of Malaya, 'Annual Report',
1936, p.47.

65 J.M.Gullick, 'Malaysia' (London, 1969), p.29.

66 Op.cit., p.427.

67 M.W.Roberts, Indian Estate Labour in Ceylon during the
Coffee Period, 1830-1880, Part I, 'Indian Economic and
Social History Review', vol.3, no.1 (March 1966), pp.
11-12.

68 P.D.Millie, 'Thirty Years Ago' (Colombo, 1878), ch.
III, cit. Roberts, op.cit.

69 A copy of this form is reproduced in the initial
report of the Ceylon Labour Commissioner, 1 June to
31 December 1904. 'Despatches relating to the
Government Contribution Towards the Labour Recruiting
Agency', Ceylon Sessional Paper, VIII-1908.

70 The scrupulous observance of caste distinctions was
noted in a plantation biography: 'The head-Kangani
who went to India returned. We were in hopes that he
could bring with him some additional coolies, and especially a few of the low-caste who could condescend
to carry our "beef-box" and occasionally fill gaps
about the bungalow. The dearth on Ranee tottam [the
estate] of Pariah coolies causes us continual per-
plexity for none but they will act as kitchen cooly.
The cooly who usually takes the "beef-box" has hurt
his leg, two other Pariahs were engaged on necessary
estate work.... So there was none left to undertake
this very necessary duty without breaking caste, a
thing not to be thought of for a moment' (Mary
Stewart, 'Everyday Life on a Ceylon Cocoa Estate'
(London, 1906), p.47, quoted in R.Jayaraman, Indian
Emigration to Ceylon: Some Aspects of the Historical
and Social Background of the Emigrants, 'Indian

Economic and Social History Review', vol.4, no.4 (December 1967)).

71 S.Arasaratnam, Aspects of Society and Cultural Life of Indians in Malaysia, in S.T.Alisjabhana et al. (eds), 'The Cultural Problems of Malaysia in the Context of Southeast Asia' (Kuala Lumpur, n.d. 1966 ?), p.104.

72 Chandra Jayawardena, Religious Belief and Social Change: Aspects of the Development of Hinduism in British Guiana, 'Comparative Studies in Society and History', vol.8(1965-6).

73 D.S.Landes, 'The Unbound Prometheus' (Cambridge, 1969), p.191.

74 Robert L.Brendfon, 'Cotton Kingdom of the New South' (Cambridge, Mass., 1967), pp.133-4.

75 'Politics in the Congo' (New Haven, 1965), p.59. Michael Roberts, in arguing that the social conditions of plantation labour in Sri Lanka from about the 1850s were 'satisfactory and certainly much improved', takes planter-paternalism at its face value (Indian Estate Labour in Ceylon during the Coffee Period, 1830-1880, pt II, 'Indian Economic and Social History Review', vol.3, no.2 (June 1966), p.117.

76 Planters' Association of Malaya, 'Report to be presented to the 13th Annual General Meeting to be held on April 28, 1930'.

77 Ibid.

78 Jain, op.cit., p.218. In a letter to the 'Straits Echo' in 1956 a planter said: 'Like many people in this country I had become attached to the South Indian labourer and his need for guidance in the most simple matters. Who is not acquainted with his plaintive cry, "You are my father and my mother!"' (Stenson, op. cit., p.152).

79 Jain, op.cit., p.292.

80 Ibid., p.218.

81 'During the first two decades of the century the head kangany is said to have wielded the authority to kill people for indulging in premarital sexual intercourse, without fear of legal proceedings being brought against him. While there is no conclusive evidence that he could shoot people, as some of my informants asserted, it is conceivable as one informant stated, that sometimes the wounds caused by excessive beating with a cane became septic, so that the victim was declared sick and sent to the hospital where he later died' (ibid., p.280).

82 J.A.Barnes, envisaging only two categories of labour, wrote somewhat confusingly that the plantation workers are 'proletarians, not peasants who have no fixed pro-

perty in land or houses and who sell their labour in
a very restricted market' (Foreword to Jain, op.cit.,
pp.vii,ix). Stenson's remark that the position of
plantation labour in its dealings with the manager was
'perhaps more akin to those of an industrial proletarian and his capitalist directors' is a misstatement
(op.cit., p.3).

83 Ibid., p.40.
84 R.K.Jain notes the disapproval by the office staff on
the rubber estate of his plan to reside on the labour
lines when carrying out his research (Preface to his
'Indians on the Plantation Frontier in Malaya', op.
cit.). A sterling plantation company in Sri Lanka
expressed the same attitude when Dr R.Jayaraman,
formerly of the Delhi School of Economics, tried to
interview plantation labour. The manager facetiously
replied that the labourers were happy as they were
without having to answer any sociological queries.
85 G.St J.Orde Browne, 'Labour Conditions in Ceylon,
Mauritius and Malaya' (HMSO, London, 1943).
86 Straits Settlements, 'Annual Report of the Labour
Department for 1953'.
87 'The Planter', vol.21, no.10 (October 1947), p.243,
quoted in Stenson, op.cit., p.162.
88 Ibid., p.96, n.3.
89 Ibid., p.29.
90 Michael Banton, 'Race Relations' (London, 1967), pp.
147-8.
91 One of them admitted to the Universiti Sains Malaysia
in 1971 was not infrequently derided on the campus
with an epithet suggestive of his origins as a plantation worker.
92 Malaya Union, 'Annual Report of the Labour Department'
for the year 1946, p.6.
93 Editorial by Shirle Gordon, 'Intisari', vol.3, no.4
(op.cit.), p.15.
94 Jayawardena, loc.cit. K.Hazareesingh, The Religion
and Culture of Indian Immigrants in Mauritius and the
Effect of Social Change, op.cit.
95 An interpretation by Dr Judith Nagata of the commercial success of the Indian Muslims in the port
towns of Malaysia, and of the relative failure of the
Malays, is also based largely on ethnic stereotypes
(Muslim Entrepreneurs and the Second Malaysian Plan:
Some Socio-Cultural Considerations, 'Asia Research
Bulletin', 1-31 August 1972, p.1140).
96 Henri Pirenne, 'A History of Europe' (London, 1961),
p.211. 'Landless men are men who have nothing to
lose, and men who have nothing to lose have everything

to gain. They are adventurers, relying only on themselves; they have given no hostages to fortune.
They are resourceful people, who know their way
about; they have seen many countries, can speak many
languages, are acquainted with many different customs
and their poverty makes them ingenious' (ibid.).

97 Syed Hussein Alatas, in Hans-Dieter Evers (ed.),
'Modernisation in South-East Asia' (Singapore, 1973),
p.161.

98 'There was no inherent theological reason for the
protestant emphasis on frugality, hard work, accumulation, but the emphasis was a natural consequence of the religion of the heart in a society
where industry was developing' (Protestantism and the
Rise of Capitalism, in David S.Landes (ed.), 'The
Rise of Capitalism' (New York, 1966), p.51). Also
Robert Ashton: 'The environment in which Puritanism
took root is crucial to any arguments about the
social role which it came to play. In nineteenth
century London its economic significance was profoundly different from that in New Zealand or Scotland' (Puritanism and Progress, 'Economic History
Review', vol.49).

99 Pirenne, op.cit., p.529.

100 J.Kuczynski, 'The Rise of the Working Class' (London,
1967), p.22.

101 Ingrid Palmer, 'Science and Agricultural Production'
(Geneva, 1972), p.93.

102 'The Indian in Burma, having hopefully migrated to a
country known for ages as Subarnabhumi ... suffered
silently from the long hours of hard work, scanty
wages, rotten food and wretched shelter.... [He was]
a beast of burden. His only pleasures or recreations
were crude opium, unrefined country liquors and other
harmful cheap drugs in which he indulged to find some
solace for his soul and to snatch some rest for his
tired frame' (N.R.Chakravarti, 'The Indian Minority
in Burma' (London, 1971).

103 In Foreword to Jain, op.cit., p.ix.

104 J.H.Drabble, 'Rubber in Malaya 1876-1922' (Kuala
Lumpur, 1973), p.187.

105 U.A.Aziz, Land Disintegration and Land Policy in
Malaya, 'Malayan Economic Review', vol.3, no.1
(April) 1958.

106 Jain, op.cit., p.438.

107 Supplement to the F.M.S. Government Gazette, 31
August 1928, p.4, in Federated Malay States, 'Annual
Report', for 1927.

108 'Annual Report of the Labour Department, Malaya
Union, for the year 1946', p.222.

109   Jain, op.cit., pp.327-8.
110   Ibid.

CHAPTER 13   THE FRAMEWORK AND MECHANISMS OF METROPOLITAN
CONTROL

1   Rubber Industry, editorial in 'Straits Times', 25
    November 1918.   Also H.Price, Growth of the Rubber
    Trade, in W.Makepeace et al., 'One Hundred Years of
    Singapore, 1819-1919' (Singapore, 1921);   J.H.
    Drabble, 'Rubber in Malaya 1876-1922' (Kuala Lumpur,
    1973), p.164, n.3.
2   'Straits Times', 25 March 1911.
3   J.Mars, Extra-Territorial Enterprises, in Margery
    Perham (ed.), 'The Economics of a Tropical Dependen-
    cy', II (London, 1948).   Also P.T.Bauer, 'West
    African Trade' (Cambridge, 1954), p.100.
4   'The Growth and Distribution of Tea', Memorandum sub-
    mitted by the Ceylon Association to the Monopolies
    and Restrictive Practices Committee in Britain, Feb-
    ruary 1956.
5   An advance of Rs 2.4 million by Brooke Bond Ltd
    (Ceylon) to its London Office in the late 1950s was
    shown in the latter's accounts as an 'investment'.
    The branch had also given a loan to Brooke Bond & Co.
    (South Africa) Pty Ltd.
6   Two such companies are Imperial Tea Co.Ltd (India),
    and Longai Valley Tea Co.Ltd.   From the 'Stock
    Exchange Year Book'.
7   Despatch No.537 from Secretary of State to Governor
    Ridgeway, 27 August 1909, Colonial Office Papers,
    54/27.
8   Despatch No.I, dated 1 January 1861, from Secretary
    of State to the Governor, with enclosure from Board
    of Trade.   (The Board of Trade could review colonial
    legislation and recommend to the Privy Council the
    disallowance of such enactments as might affect the
    home interests.)
9   Dated 13 May 1856.
10 In Burma imports of salt seriously undermined domes-
    tic production, to the detriment also of two other
    traditional trades, viz. salt fish and fish paste and
    pottery.   (J.S.Furnivall, 'Colonial Policy and
    Practice, a Comparative Study of Burma and Nether-
    lands India' (Cambridge, 1948).)
11 Despatch No.27 from Secretary of State to Governor
    Ward, 26 February 1856.
12 Quoted in Lady Betty Balfour, 'The History of Lord

Lytton's Indian Administration, 1876 to 1880' (London, 1899), p.477. Also in A.K.Sen, The Pattern of British Enterprises in India, in Baljit Singh and V.B.Singh (eds), 'Social and Economic Change' (Bombay, 1967).

13 'It may be accepted as proved that India possesses the means of supplying all her wants in respect of cast iron, wrought iron, and steel and that such supply could be produced remuneratively on a strictly commercial basis' ('Gazette of India, 5 August 1882, quoted in R.S.Rungta, 'Rise of the Business Corporations in India' (Cambridge, 1970), p.131).

14 11 November 1882, quoted in Rungta, op.cit., p.132; also pp.134,185.

15 'The Age of Imperialism' (New York, London, 1969), p.38.

16 'After Imperialism' (London, 1970), p.x.

17 D.H.Aldcroft (ed.), 'The Development of British Industry and Foreign Competition, 1875-1914' (London, 1968), pp.199-201.

18 N.Bukharin, 'Imperialism and World Economy' (London, 1972), p.99.

19 Quoted in E.A.Brett, 'Colonialism and Underdevelopment in Africa' (London, 1973), p.118.

20 Quoted in R.A.Bradshaw, 'Crisis in Britain' (Berkeley, 1950), pp.577-8.

21 'Final Reports of the Committee on Commercial and Industrial Policy after the War', Cmd 9053 of 1918, p.27, quoted in Brett, op.cit., p.121. The term 'Empire' by this period was taken to exclude the white dominions.

22 Ibid. Emphasis added.

23 Peter Ady, Britain and Overseas Development, in G.D.N. Worswick and P.H.Ady (eds), 'The British Economy 1945-1950' (Oxford, 1952).

24 E.J.Hobsbawm, 'The Age of Revolution 1789-1848' (New York, 1962), p.52.

25 'The Accumulation of Capital' (London, 1951), p.420.

26 Maurice Dobb, 'Studies in the Development of Capitalism' (London, 1963), p.297. Based on L.H. Jenks, 'The Migration of British Capital' (London, 1963), pp.207 ff. About a third of Great Britain's overseas investments before the First World War was estimated by Sir George Paish to have been in railway bonds (Great Britain's Investment in Other Lands, 'Journal of the Royal Statistical Society', vol.62 (1911), pp.168-72, cit. Trevor Lloyd, Africa and Hobson's Imperialism, 'Past and Present', no.55(1972), p.142, n.47.

27 Hobsbawm, op.cit., pp.62-3.

28 Michael Crowder (ed.), 'West African Resistance' (New York, 1971), p.11.
29 Aldcroft (ed.), op.cit., p.199.
30 Based on data in ibid.
31 Kenya, 'Railway Report', 1903, p.8, quoted in Brett, op.cit., p.82.
32 E-tu Zen Zen, 'Chinese Railways and British Interests 1898-1911' (New York, 1971).
33 'The Complete Works of Chang Chih-tung' (Peking, 1928), quoted in E-tu Zen Zen, op.cit., p.102.
34 The Origin and Functions of the Department of the Crown Agents for Colonies, Memorandum by Sir Penrose G.Julyan in British Parliamentary Papers 1881 (vol. LXIV), pp.593-6.
35 'Report of the Crown Agents Enquiry Committee', 10 December 1908. Included among enclosures to Despatch from the Secretary of State to the Governor of Ceylon, 18 February 1909. Also 'Times of Ceylon', 25 February 1910.
36 Vincent Ponko, Jr, Economic Management in a Free-Trade Empire: Work of the Crown Agents for the Colonies in the Nineteenth and Early Twentieth Centuries, 'Journal of Economic History', vol.36, no.3 (September 1966), p.364.
37 Ibid.
38 The cost, delay and inconvenience of having to purchase from the colonial stores was noted by a provincial administrator in Sri Lanka. 'Wrote to ask for a reconsideration of the rule that all materials for irrigation works are to be drawn from the colonial stores - in the case of votes of Rs. 100 and less.... If I indent each time I wanted a pound or two of powder - or a small quantity of cement, some jumpers or a few yards of fuse, the cost of transport and the trouble and the correspondence involved would be far more than the advantage to government from buying the things from the colonial store' (Assistant Government Agent for the Nuwara Eliya District, 'Diaries', Entry No.276, 29 October 1889. Sri Lanka National Archives, 47/23).
39 Despatch from Governor Ridgeway to the Secretary of State, 20 November 1908.
40 'Proceedings of the Federal Council of the Federated Malay States for the year 1932', B.129.
41 'Report of the Commission on the Trade of the Colony [of Singapore] 1933-34' (Singapore, 1934), p.221; also pp.219-21.
42 Letter dated 11 February 1910. Ceylon Chamber of Commerce, 'Report for Half Year ended June 1910'.

43 Quoted in a letter to the Ceylon Chamber of Commerce,
    dated 4 January 1909. Ceylon Chamber of Commerce,
    'Report for Half Year ended June 1909'.
44 Ibid. 'Report for Half Year ended June, 1903'.
45 Ibid. Significantly, the Municipal Commissioner of
    Singapore (who was not bound by the Colonial Regula-
    tions) called for tenders both locally and in Britain
    ('Report of the Commission on the Trade of the Colony
    - 1933-34' (cited earlier), p.221).
46 Letter dated 4 January 1909 to the Ceylon Chamber of
    Commerce, signed by Colombo Commercial Co.Ltd, and
    Darley Butler & Co. Ceylon Chamber of Commerce,
    'Report for Half Year ended June, 1909'.
47 W.K.Hancock, 'Survey of British Commonwealth Affairs',
    vol.II, Part I (Oxford, 1940).
48 British Parliamentary Debates (Commons), 17 July 1923,
    cit. Herbert Feis, 'Europe, the World's Banker
    1870-1914' (New Haven, 1930).
49 'Times of India', 12 May 1879, quoted in Rungta, op.
    cit., pp.129-30.
50 Lennox Mills, 'British Rule in Eastern Asia' (London,
    1942), p.153.
51 'Home and Foreign Investment 1870-1913' (Cambridge,
    1953), p.233.
52 Daniel Thorner, Great Britain and the Development of
    Indian Railways, 'Journal of Economic History', Fall
    1951, p.398.
53 Aldcroft, op.cit., p.80.
54 'Moral and Material Progress and Conditions of India
    in 1924-25', pp.178-9, quoted in Buchanan, op.cit.,
    pp.472-3. The stores policy of the colonial govern-
    ment in India is also referred to by Helen Lamb, in
    The State and Economic Development in India, in
    'Economic Growth: Brazil, India, Japan' (Durham, N.C.,
    1955), p.481.
55 'The Oxford History of India' (Oxford, 1958), p.710.
56 Marx/Engels to Nikolayon (St Petersburg, 1890), p.75,
    cited in Luxemburg, op.cit., p.288, n.1.
57 Loc.cit. In 1900 Mr Chamberlain, Secretary of State
    for the Colonies, was one of the largest shareholders
    of the Colombo Commercial Co., an engineering and
    estate agency firm. He was connected with this compa-
    ny from the inception in 1877 ('Times of Ceylon', 11
    December 1900).
58 'Straits Times', 4 August 1923.
59 Brett, op.cit., pp.128-9.
60 Dobb, op.cit., p.297, n.3.
61 Feis, op.cit., p.88.
62 G.C.Allen, The Industrialization of the Far East, in

'The Cambridge Economic History of Europe', vol.VI, part II, ed. by H.Habakkuk and M.Postan (Cambridge, 1965), p.910.

63   Barratt Brown, op.cit.; also his 'Imperialism and Working Class Interests in the Developed Countries' (Sheffield, March 1971, mimeograph).

64   'The wealth of rich lands, such as Britain's', he stated, was 'not a function of the poverty of poor lands, but ... followed rather from the steadily growing productivity over nearly two centuries' (Op.cit. (1970), p.xii).

65   30 October 1937, p.217, quoted in Jenks, op.cit.

66   Lord Hailey, 'African Survey' (London, New York, Toronto, revised edn 1957).

67   Feis, op.cit.

CHAPTER 14   THE DOMINATION OF PLANTATION INTERESTS BY MERCHANT CAPITAL: AGENCY HOUSE-PLANTATION RELATIONS

1   Kathleen M.Stahl, 'The Metropolitan Organization of British Colonial Trade' (London, 1951), p.105. 'In the case of some agency houses, it is laid down in writing that the [estate] manager is free to buy anywhere. In the case of others, this freedom is an understood convention. But there is reason to believe that in some cases, the manager is not so free and might be heavily penalised if he attempted to exercise this prerogative' (ibid.).

2   A.M. and J.Ferguson, 'The Ceylon Handbook and Directory for 1866-68' (Colombo, 1868), p.120.

3   Ibid., p.102.

4   Ibid., p.114.

5   A Malayan Review, by a Commercial Correspondent, 'Straits Times', 8 February 1911.

6   Ibid.

7   The Chairman of the Planters' Association of Sri Lanka, when opposing the price ceiling, made out at first that the expensive supplies from Britain were superior and that the use of any other brand would affect tea exports. However, after the Tea Research Institute rejected the quality of netting sold by Messrs Elastic Nets Ltd, an improved sample of netting (with a modified size of mesh) was submitted and gained approval.

8   The prices were for full chests of comparable quality made of birch wood; those for half-chests were as follows: Japanese birch 62.5 pence, Russian birch 51 pence, Japanese beech (72 pence full) and 56.5 pence (half).

9 'Whenever we look closely into the nature of British
   free trade', wrote Marx, 'monopoly is pretty generally
   found to lie at the bottom of its freedom' (The Opium
   Trade, 'New York Daily Tribune', 25 September 1858;
   reprinted in K.Marx and F.Engels, 'On Colonialism'
   (Moscow, n.d.), p.217).

10 According to Customs invoices that were traceable. In
   1964, Carson Cumberbatch & Co.Ltd, Bosanquet & Skrine
   Ltd, Colombo Commercial Co.Ltd, and Whittall Boustead
   imported battens to a value of £30,301 from Sweden,
   compared with £1,077 from Japan.

11 In a circular issued by this group on 12 November 1960
   to shareholders of the company.

12 Messrs F.V.Evans, P.R.Walton and A.I. de Montfort.

13 'Members usually have the names of members represented
   by proxy or attorney. They [the Managing Agents] also
   give the names of those voting for and against the
   Resolution.... In this case the Scrutineer was appointed by the agency votes; by that I mean agency
   men and their creatures, the Directors.'
        'The departure from the usual procedure and the non-
   compliance of my request asking that the names for and
   against the Resolution be given, make me feel that all
   is not above board especially as an offer of Rs.24
   lakhs was not intimated to the shareholders' (from the
   Registrar of Companies' file on The Opalgalla Tea &
   Rubber Co.Ltd).

14 (UK) Monopolies and Restrictive Practices Commission
   of 1956, cited earlier. The Commission was told that
   the agency houses 'do not control the policy of the
   companies which they represent, whether with regard to
   production, sale or otherwise. Policy in these
   matters is in fact controlled by the individual companies themselves and the Secretaries carrying out the
   instruction of the Boards of those companies' (ibid.).

15 J.A.Schumpeter, 'Capitalism, Socialism and Democracy'
   (London, 1957), p.141. Also F.J.Allen, 'The Big
   Change' (New York, 1952), pp.235-6.

16 'Times of Ceylon', 2 January 1910. The names of
   shareholders attending company meetings were given in
   press reports. At the Annual General Meetings of
   three plantation companies held in Colombo on 12 February 1910, only five shareholders were present including the directors. The meetings were held at the
   office of the managing agency, The Colombo Commercial
   Co.Ltd, and each meeting was scheduled to last five
   minutes ('Times of Ceylon', 12 February 1910).

17 The ease with which British companies, with their
   large number of small investors, could be dominated

led Siemens, a leading industrialist in Germany before the First World War, to regard 'the one-pound share as the basis of British Imperialism'. German company law, to his regret, disallowed the issue of shares of lower face value than 1,000 marks (V.I.Lenin, 'Imperialism', with New Data compiled by E.Varga and L.Mendelssohn (Bombay, 1944), p.110). The control of companies by the few largest owners, which fragmentation of ownership makes possible, is shown by Michael Barratt Brown, in The Controllers - II, 'Universities and Left Review' (London), Spring 1956.

18 Among those excluded were individuals whose only perceivable connection with an agency house was that they had given the agency address in the register of shareholders. Even in these cases the agency is likely to hold proxies or powers of attorney.

19 In Ceylon Financial Investments Ltd, 29,947 out of 30,000 shares were held by Tessy Eva Woodman, the widow of George Ernest Woodman, who along with Gordon Frazer was one of the founders of Gordon Frazer & Co. Ltd. In 1912, G.E.Woodman held 50 per cent of the share capital of the firm. In Darton Development Co. Ltd, 19,947 out of 20,000 shares were held by F.J. Hawkes, a former director of Gordon Frazer, and by his two daughters, and J.M.Hawkes; and the few remaining shares by the Directors of Gordon Frazer. F.J.Hawkes in 1921 held one-third of the capital of the firm, and G.E.Woodman two-thirds.

20 The names of directors of the London Agency houses included in this study were obtained from the agencies (mostly private firms) with the assistance of Sri Lanka's Commercial attaché in the UK at the time. The directors of sterling plantation companies were ascertained from the balance sheets. An alternative source is the 'Stock Exchange Official Year Book'.

21 Colombo Commercial Co.Ltd, James Finlay & Co.Ltd, and Harrisons & Crosfield Ltd.

22 Out of the 11 rupee companies in which there was no interlocking with the agency house, 6 were private companies.

23 On the penultimate rung, holding 15 plantation company directorships, yielding an income from directors' fees alone of Rs 18,533 a year, was Mr G.I. de Glanville - President of the Association for the Protection of British Interests in Ceylon.

24 The investments of non-agency directors are even greater if we exclude certain nominal directorships based on family connections. A few public companies, in fact, are virtually family concerns, in which the

governing director (who has complete financial and
managerial control) has allotted directorships to his
wife and children, with a nominal shareholding.

25 Directors' Report for 1964. The company in Sri Lanka
was therefore wound up and its business transferred to
Consolidated Commercial Agencies Ltd.

26 The staff of both companies were accommodated in the
offices of Lee Hedges & Co.Ltd, suitably extended and
altered; a portion of the storage capacity of Shaw
Wallace & Co.Ltd was given to Lee Hedges & Co.Ltd,
and some of the latter's original land and buildings
were disposed of and the proceeds used to redeem its
preference capital (Shaw Wallace & Hedges Ltd,
'Directors' Report' for 1962).

27 The agents are also entitled to a commission on estate
equipment and materials purchased by them for the
company.

28 The other charges are on account of freight, insurance, wharfage, selling brokers' fees, and the prompt
discount.

29 Articles of Association of the Indo-Malay Estates Ltd,
adopted in 1906, and of the Perak River Coconut Co.
Ltd, adopted in 1927.

30 Correspondence in the Registrar of Companies' files
in Colombo on the Kinnersley (Kalutara Rubber Co.Ltd,
the Biddescar Rubber Co.Ltd, and the Indo-Malay
Estates Ltd.

31 George B.Baldwin, 'Industrial Growth in South India'
(Illinois, 1958).

32 Agreements between the Rubber Estate Agency Ltd, and
the Kadienlena Tea Estate Ltd, and between Sharp,
Estall & Co.Ltd and the Kurunegala Rubber Co.Ltd.

33 Agreements between the Rubber Estates Agency Ltd and
the Kadienlena Tea Estates Ltd, and between the
Colombo Commercial Co.Ltd and Rosehaugh (Ceylon) Tea
Co.Ltd. 'If the company shall sell its estates to
any new company promoted by the company, the company
shall procure the agency to be appointed secretaries,
consignees and agents of such new company upon the
same terms as those contained in this Agreement as
far as possible and upon any sale to any company, the
company will use its best endeavour to procure the
agency to be appointed in the capacity and upon the
terms aforesaid.'

CHAPTER 15   MERCHANT CAPITALISM AND UNDERDEVELOPMENT

1 In a commentary on Violet Barbour, Characteristics of
   Amsterdam Capitalism, in G.Ranis, 'Searching for
   Modern Times', vol.II, '1650-1789' (New York, Toronto,
   1969), p.188.
2 'Indigenous Political Systems of Western Malaya'
   (London, 1969), p.131.
3 John Stuart Mill, 'Principles of Political Economy'
   (London, 1873), p.12. Cf. Marx: 'The bourgeoisie is
   too enlightened, it calculates too well, to share the
   prejudices of the feudal lord who makes a display by
   the brilliance of his retinue. The conditions of
   existence of the bourgeoisie compel it to calculate'
   ('Wage Labour and Capital' (Moscow, 1970), p.38). The
   extreme asceticism of the bourgeoisie in this period
   was eloquently referred to by Marx: 'Political
   economy, this science of wealth ... simultaneously the
   science of asceticism, and its true ideal is the
   ascetic but extortionate miser and the ascetic but
   productive slave ... self renunciation is its principal thesis. The less you eat, drink and buy books;
   the less you go to the theatre, the dance hall, the
   public house; the less you think, love, theorise,
   sing, paint, fence, etc. the more you save - the
   greater becomes your treasure which neither moths nor
   dust will devour, your capital' ('The Economic and
   Philosophical Manuscripts of 1844', edited, with an
   introduction by Dirk J.Struik (New York, 1964), p.
   149).
4 English Merchant Capitalism in the Late Seventeenth
   Century, 'Past and Present', no.46(1970), pp.87-8.
5 'Industrial Organization in the Sixteenth and Seventeenth Centuries' (London, 1963), p.75.
6 F.Engels, in Supplement to Marx, 'Capital' (Moscow,
   1959), vol.III, p.877. The origins of the merchant
   class and its convulsive effects on the society of the
   Middle Ages were depicted by Henri Pirenne: 'The merchants (mercatores) were "new men".... They were
   without roots in the soil. They did not produce anything; they were merely carriers ... offering jewellery for the women, ornaments for the altar, cloth of
   gold for the churches. With them came not only the
   spirit of gain and enterprise, but also the free
   labourer, the man of independent trade, detached alike
   from the soil and from the authority of the seigneur;
   and above all the circulation of money.... Compared
   with the noble and the peasant ... [the merchant] was
   a mobile and active element. He was not indispensable

to human existence; it was possible to live without
him. He was essentially an agent of social progress
and civilization' ('A History of Europe' (London,
1961), pp.210-22.

7 Grassby, loc.cit., p.106.
8 D.S.Landes, 'The Unbound Prometheus' (Cambridge,
   1969), p.65.
9 The small clothier unable to wait till his goods were
   sold accepted half their value as an advance from a
   trader who undertook to sell them on a consignment
   basis (G.Unwin, The Merchant Adventurers' Company in
   the Reign of Elizabeth, in N.E.F.Helleiner (ed.),
   'Readings in European Economic History' (Toronto,
   1946), pp.268-9,288).
10 Engels, in Supplement to 'Capital', vol.III (cited
   earlier), p.882.
11 Marx, ibid., p.295.
12 Ibid.
13 Engels, in Supplement to Marx, ibid., pp.900-1.
14 E.g. during the sixteenth century the Vintners controlled the French wine trade, the Spanish Company
   (1577) the import trade with Spain in wine, oil and
   fruit, and the Eastland Company (1578) had a hold over
   the Baltic trade. 'Very high prices' were charged for
   imported goods and the government threatened to fix a
   tariff of prices for the protection of the public
   (Unwin, loc.cit., p.260).
15 Grassby, loc.cit., p.98.
16 V.I.Lenin, 'The Development of Capitalism in Russia'
   (Moscow, 1956), p.158.
17 'The increases in population in the 13th century, the
   growth of the corn market and a steep rise in the
   price of corn caused an increase in demesne farming -
   a growth in labour services' (E.A.Kosminsky, 'Studies
   in the Agrarian History of England' (Oxford, 1956),
   p.178).
18 Karl Marx, 'Grundrisse' (Harmondsworth, 1973), p.510.
19 According to Sweezy, it was 'on the periphery of the
   exchange economy [where] the worker cannot run away
   because he has no place to go [that] for all practical
   purposes he is at the mercy of the lord' (in Rodney
   Hilton (ed.), 'The Transition from Feudalism to
   Capitalism' (New Left Books, 1976).
20 Marx, 'Capital', vol.III (cited earlier), p.322.
21 One merchant capitalist who in the 1890s organized the
   manufacture of nails paid the blacksmiths partly in
   money and partly in iron, and to make them 'more
   tractable' he always had them working in their homes
   (Lenin, op.cit., pp.483-4).

22 '1905' (Harmondsworth, 1971), pp.351-2. Andreyevich
    Chernykh, the Siberian merchant (for whom Trotsky
    worked briefly as a ledger clerk), had, by virtue of
    his long-distance trade, control over economic life in
    the Kerensk district. Yet, he 'was the most con-
    vincing expression of our economic backwardness, our
    barbarity and primitiveness, our illiteracy, the
    sparseness of our population, the dispersion of our
    peasant villages and our dirt roads which form block-
    ades of impassable bog for two months every spring and
    autumn' (ibid.).
23 Marx, 'Capital', quoted in Lenin, op.cit., p.478.
24 Marx, 'Capital', vol.II (Chicago, 1907), p.63, quoted
    in K.Takahashi, A Contribution to the Discussion, in
    Hilton (ed.), op.cit., p.72, n.13.
25 Marx, 'Capital', vol.III (cited earlier), p.333.
26 Lenin, op.cit., p.356.
27 Trotsky, op.cit. (1971), pp.351-2.
28 Grassby, loc.cit., p.106.
29 Unwin, op.cit., p.90.
30 Elizabeth Lamond, 'Discourse of the Common Weal',
    edited by W.S.Cambridge, 1893, p.12, cited by Unwin,
    op.cit., p.101.
31 Ibid.
32 Ibid., p.89.
33 Ibid., p.90.
34 Ibid.
35 Ibid., p.85. A craftsman was forbidden to import or
    export a cargo for himself and a shipper or merchant
    would not act as his agent (ibid., p.77).
36 'Capital', vol.III (cited earlier), p.331.
37 Ibid., pp.327-8.
38 'British Investments in Latin America' (Minnesota
    University Press, 1959), pp.22,32, quoted by Michael
    Barratt Brown, 'The Age of Imperialism' (New York and
    London, 1969), p.192. Significantly the shape of
    things was different in the white dominions and to
    some extent in the settler colonies where production
    capital from the metropolis was invested directly,
    without the mediation of merchant capital. Likewise
    in the current phase of world capitalism, when the
    internationalization process as carried out by the
    MNCs is one of production, not merely of markets, the
    role of merchant capital in the periphery has been
    reduced to a low key.
39 Ralph Davis, English Foreign Trade, 1660-1700,
    'Economic History Review', 2nd series, VII(1954),
    no.2, reprinted in F.M.Carus Wilson (ed.), 'Essays in
    Economic History', vol.2 (London, 1966), p.268. Also

A.H.John, Aspects of English Growth in the First Half of the Eighteenth Century, 'Economica' (1961), reprinted in Carus-Wilson (ed.), op.cit., p.363.

40   Davis, loc.cit., p.260.

41   Stuart Bruchey, 'The Roots of American Economic Growth' (London, 1965), p.46. The sale proceeds realized and the prices of plantation supplies were the source of frequent disputes between planters and merchants, and in Jamaica and Barbados there was open hostility between them till the formation of the West India Committee (Lilian M.Penson, The London West India Interest in the Eighteenth Century, 'English Historical Review', vol.36 (July 1921), reprinted in R.Mitchison (ed.), 'Essays in Eighteenth Century History' (London, 1966), p.5.

42   Klause E.Knorr, 'British Colonial Theories 1570-1850' (Toronto, 1968), pp.149-50.

43   J.F.Rees, Mercantilism and the Colonies, in 'The Cambridge History of the British Empire', vol.I (Cambridge, 1929), p.567.

44   Knorr, op.cit., p.56; also p.101.

45   L.M.Hacker, 'The Triumph of American Capitalism' (New York, 1965), pp.142-3.

46   Charles P.Nettles, Imperial Problems and Revolution, 'Journal of Economic History', vol.12 (Spring 1952).

47   'The Works of Thomas Jefferson', vol.XI, pp.90-1, quoted in Frederick Clairmonte, 'Economic Liberalism and Underdevelopment' (Bombay, 1960), p.30.

48   G.V.Taylor, Types of Capitalism in Eighteenth Century France, in Ranis, op.cit., p.240.

49   Ibid., pp.239-40.

50   In seventeenth-century Holland where merchant capitalism flourished the Amsterdam merchants were notoriously unpatriotic. They 'invested in Dunkirk privateers which preyed on Dutch shipping'. They traded with England during the Anglo-Dutch wars, selling cordage and sail cloth to be used by the English navy; one merchant was accused of selling munitions to England (Violet Barbour, Characteristics of Amsterdam Capitalism, ibid., pp.189-90).

51   Grassby, loc.cit., p.107.

52   An account of the evolution of the agency system in India was given by R.S.Rungta in 'Rise of Business Corporations in India 1851-1900' (Cambridge, 1970), pp.227-8. In the light of our discussion, Dr Rungta's exposition would appear to be imprecise and conceptually misleading.

53   A supercargo was an 'officer on a merchant ship who superintends the cargo and commercial transactions'

(Michael Greenberg, 'British Trade and the Opening of
China 1800-1842' (Cambridge, 1951), p.118).
54 The 'Block' was the entire assets of an estate: 'The
whole fixture, appurtenances and even the growing
crops' ('The Economist', 21 October 1843, p.116).
55 Ceylon Chamber of Commerce, 'Report' for half-year
ending June 1874, pp.31-2.
56 T.L.Villiers, 'Some Pioneers of the Tea Industry'
(Colombo, 1951), p.7.
57 John Capper, Coffee Planting, in 'Old Ceylon' (London,
1878), p.14. The transport charge from Kandy to
Colombo was eight or nine shillings per hundredweight,
or 'twice as much for conveying ... [produce] less
than a hundred miles as it costs for freight to England, about sixteen thousand miles (via the Cape)'
(ibid.).
58 Essay by Mr Millie on Estate Expenditure, submitted in
1868 for a prize ('The Ceylon Handbook and Directory
for 1866-68' (Colombo, 1868), p.114).
59 British Parliamentary Papers (Commons), 1847, vol.
XXXVII.
60 'The Economist', 21 October 1843, p.116 (cited
earlier).
61 Ibid., 1847, p.1334.
62 Ibid.
63 Ibid., 21 July 1846, p.961.
64 18th Report: 'Tea' (HMSO, 1931), p.24, cit. Wickizer,
op.cit., p.181. For example, in 1900 Alexander Philip
& Co., 'Estate Commission, Banking and General Agent',
advertised its banking functions as follows: 'Current
deposits opened and conducted, fixed deposits received
and interest allowed payable in England or Ceylon,
drafts issued at current rates of exchange, advances
made against produce for shipment' ('Times of Ceylon',
6 September 1900).
65 H.D.Andree, The Progress of Banking in Ceylon, in A.M.
and J.Ferguson, 'The Ceylon Handbook and Directory for
1865' (Colombo, circa 1866), p.82.
66 'James Finlay & Co. Limited, 1750-1950' (Glasgow,
1951), p.105.
67 Ibid.
68 James Steuart, 'Recollections Personal and Official of
James Steuart, 1817-1866. With a Short History of the
Firm of George Steuart and Co.', ed. Thomas Villiers
(Colombo, circa 1935), p.56.
69 'Tea' (HMSO, 1931), op.cit.
70 'The Ceylon Company Limited:- Advances Money to owners
of Coffee Estates on Mortgage of Block and on Coffee
crops, upon condition that the produce be consigned to

the Company for Curing and for sale' (advertisement of
The Ceylon Company Ltd (regd. 1863), in A.M.Ferguson,
'Ferguson's Ceylon Handbook and Directory for 1866-68'
(Colombo, n.d.), p.XXII.

71 For example, Bois Bros & Co., Ltd was from 1861 agent
for the Chartered Bank of India, Australia and China;
Darley Butler & Co. was allied with the financial
house of Matheson & Co., Ltd, London; Hudson,
Chandler & Co. was connected to Baring Bros 'in
lending money on the security of mortgages on coffee
estates, coffee crops and house property in Colombo'
(T.L.Villiers, 'Mercantile Lore' (Colombo, 1940), pp.
56,115-16, and 218). George Steuart & Co., another
estate agency, started out as a merchant banking business, as agent of Messrs Coutts & Co. (Steuart, op.
cit., p.59).

72 Millie, loc.cit., p.114. The critical dependence of
even the coffee companies on the agencies for credit
is seen from the few extant directors' reports. The
Oodoowerre Estate Company Ltd, with an issued capital
of Rs 108,500, had in 1898 borrowed Rs 17,426, practically the whole of this from Tarrant, Henderson & Co.
In the next year the agent intervened for the last
time - to settle the liquidator's fees. The Nyasaland
Coffee Co., Ltd raised money from Messrs Carson & Co.
- Rs 5,000 in 1898-9 and Rs 34,246 in 1900-1. Its
financial dependence on the agents was repeatedly expressed in the directors' reports. The Dimbulla
Coffee Co., Ltd had also borrowed heavily. With an
issued capital of Rs 285,000, its total debt (mainly
loans payable on demand, 'acceptances' and mortgages)
increased from Rs 98,346 in 1877 to Rs 1,233,000 in
1880.

73 The importance of the agent's assessment is seen from
the following comment in the report of the Sapumal-
kande Rubber Co., Ltd in 1920: 'Mr. Nicol Thomson,
who made the report and valuation upon which the
company was formed, stated it to be among the finest
he had seen in the low country of Ceylon.'

74 A.M. and J.Ferguson, The Coolie Labour Supply, in 'The
Ceylon Handbook and Directory for 1885-86' (Colombo,
n.d. circa 1886), p.29.

75 Prospectus of the Gedong (Perak) Rubber Estates Ltd,
formed in 1910 to acquire the Gedong Bidor Estate.
The Rini (Java) Rubber Estate Co. claimed that its
agents 'are distinctly representative and are associated with other well-known undertakings of this
class'. The Monerakelle Rubber Estates Ltd, which had
made a 6 per cent debenture issue in 1909, acknow-

ledged the 'great assistance given' by Mr Eustace
Wilding of Messrs Bendon & Co. He then 'accepted an
invitation to join the Board'. From an account of new
companies published in the 'London Daily Express'.
Reproduced in 'Times of Ceylon', 14 February 1910.

76 In Malaysia a similar pattern prevailed in tin mining
and in oil palm. Estates were opened up by Guthrie &
Co. from 1924 to be later sold to companies, of which
the firm became agents and secretaries (S.Cunyngham-
Brown, 'The Traders' (London, 1971), pp.207,252-3).

77 Ibid., p.77.

78 'Straits Settlements' was the collective name for the
unified administration of Penang, Singapore and
Malacca; it was created in 1826 and made a Crown
Colony in 1827.

79 'Any attempt at independent action not only forfeited
the rebate but also involved a danger of being refused
space by the Conference steamers' ('Report of the
Commission appointed by His Excellency the Governor
of the Straits Settlements to enquire and report on
the Trade of the colony', 1933-4).

80 Chiang Hai Ding, The Early Shipping Conference System
of Singapore 1879-1901, 'Journal of Malayan Branch of
the Royal Asiatic Society'.

81 'Studies in the Development of Capitalism' (London,
1963), p.377.

82 'Britain and the Onset of Modernization in Brazil
1850-1914' (Cambridge, 1968), pp.80,111,320.

83 J.Mars, Extra-Territorial Enterprises, in M.Perham
(ed.), 'Mining, Commerce, and Finance in Nigeria'
(London, 1948), p.69.

84 Jon Halliday, 'A Political History of Japanese
Capitalism' (New York, 1975), p.9.

85 E.S.Craucour, The Tokugawa Heritage, in W.W.Lockwood
(ed.), 'The State and Economic Enterprise', p.42, cit.
Halliday, ibid.

86 Yasukaza Takenaka, Endogenous Formation and Development of Capitalism in Japan, 'Journal of Economic
History', vol.29 (March 1969), no.1.

87 Halliday, op.cit., p.56.

88 Thomas C.Wilkinson, 'The Urbanisation of Japanese
Labour, 1868-1966' (Amherst, Mass., 1965), p.28, cit.
Halliday, op.cit., p.9. Also E.Kay Trimberger, State
Power and Modes of Production; Implications of the
Japanese Transition to Capitalism, 'Insurgent Soci-
ologist', vol.7, no.2 (Spring 1977), p.91.

89 Op.cit., p.160.

90 'Anglo-Dutch Commerce and Finance in the Eighteenth
Century', pp.200-1, quoted in Dobb, op.cit., p.195.

91   Ibid.
92   Trimberger, loc.cit., p.96.
93   P.Baran, 'The Political Economy of Growth' (New York
     and London, 1957), p.194.

CHAPTER 16   PLANTATIONS, ECONOMIC DUALISM AND THE COLONIAL
MODE OF PRODUCTION

1   D.M.Kannangara, Review article on D.R.Snodgrass,
    'Ceylon: An Export Economy in Transition' (Homewood,
    Ill., 1966), in 'Economic Record', December 1967,
    p.618.
2   B.Higgins, 'Economic Development' (New York, 1959),
    p.325.
3   'Asian Drama' (Harmondsworth, 1968), vol.1, p.445.
4   'Exports from the periphery do not arise from
    "traditional" sectors in which productivity is low:
    three-quarters of them come from *ultramodern* sectors
    where *productivity is high* (oil, mineral products, the
    produce of *modern capitalist plantations* ...) where
    productivity is equal to that of the centre' (p.23).
    'At least half of [the agricultural products of under-
    developed countries] come from *modern capitalist plan-
    tations*.... Thus, three-quarters of the exports of
    the periphery [including industrial raw materials]
    come from *highly productive modern* sectors which are
    the expression of capitalist development in the
    periphery' (p.42).   '75 per cent of the exports from
    the periphery come from *modern enterprises with high
    productivity*' (p.62).   'The exports of the underde-
    veloped world are made up ... [also] of raw materials
    and agricultural products originating from *modern,
    high-productivity sectors* - mines, plantations, oil
    wells whose productivity is comparable to that found
    in the advanced countries' (p.69).   Emphasis added.
    'Accumulation on a World Scale' (New York, 1974),
    vol.1.
5   H.Myint, 'The Economics of the Developing Countries'
    (London, 1964), p.40.
6   'The Manchester School of Economic and Social
    Studies', vol.22, no.2 (May 1954), p.147.
7   Op.cit., p.56.   'The effect of international trade was
    to create a dual economy, that is two broad sectors
    which differed radically from each other in patterns
    of resource use and technology' (ibid., p.4).
8   'Agricultural Involution' (Berkeley, 1968), p.138.
    Geertz in support of this view also quoted Higgins:
    'Development in [Southeast] Asia, centered as it was

on plantations, mines, oil fields and exports of raw
material, brought more *industrialisation* than *urbanisation*' (Western Enterprise and the Economic Development of Southeast Asia: A Review Article, 'Pacific
Affairs', vol.31, Geertz, op.cit., pp.138-9, n.34).

9   North-West Africa Since Mid-Century, in R.M.Prothero
(ed.), 'A Geography of Africa' (London, 1969), p.24.

10 Leon Trotsky, Prospects and Tasks in the East, in
'Leon Trotsky Speaks' (New York, 1972), p.198.

11 Capitalism 'compels all nations, on pain of extinction, to adopt the bourgeois mode of production ...
to become bourgeois themselves. In one word it creates a world after its own image.' Engels in 1847
had held out this prospect for both India and China;
the import of English manufactures would 'revolutionise' them 'from top to base' ('Selected Works', vol.1,
p.85, cit. Bipan Chandra, 'Karl Marx - His Theories of
Societies and Colonial Rule' (Mimeo, Centre for
Historical Studies, School of Social Sciences,
Jawarharlal Nehru University), p.31, n.2). Dr Bipan
Chandra has suggested that in the case of India Marx
was only 'seeing the potential and not the real'
(ibid., pp.36,40-1).

12 'A Contribution to the Critique of Political Economy'
(Moscow, 1977), pp.202-3.

13 Engels to Marx, 23 May 1856 (Marx and Engels, 'Selected Correspondence' (London, 1943), p.94).

14 'Capital', vol.I, quoted in Chandra, op.cit., p.117.
He referred to the interest of the English bourgeoisie
in 'transforming Ireland into a mere pasture land
which provides the English market with meat and wool
at the cheapest possible prices' (Marx to Meyer and
Vogt, 9 April 1870, Marx and Engels, op.cit. (1943),
p.289).

15 Ibid. 'The lever must be applied in Ireland. That is
why the Irish question is so important for the social
movement in general' (Marx to Engels, 10 December
1869, op.cit., p.281). Also Marx to Kugelmann, 29
November 1869 (ibid., pp.278-9).

16 Hélène Carrère d'Encausse and Stuart R.Schram,
'Marxism and Asia' (London, 1969); also John P.
Haithcox, The Roy-Lenin Debate on Colonial Policy: a
New Interpretation, 'Journal of Asian Studies', vol.
33, no.1 (November 1963).

17 Leon Trotsky, 'The Third International After Lenin'
(New York, 1970), p.19. 'The economic methods, social
powers and levels of development [become] more identical' (ibid., p.20).

18 Ibid., p.19.

19   Leon Trotsky, 'The History of the Russian Revolution'
     (London, 1934), pp.26-7.
20   Ibid., p.117.
21   Trotsky, op.cit. (1970), p.19.
22   Trotsky, op.cit. (1934), p.26.
23   Leon Trotsky, '1905' (London, 1971), p.334; Leon
     Trotsky, 'Permanent Revolution and Results and
     Prospects' (London, 1962), p.181.
24   N.Bukharin, 'Imperialism and World Economy' (London,
     1972), p.35.
25   'Economics of the Transformation Period' (New York,
     1971), p.12.
26   Ibid., p.213.
27   A.Toussaint, 'Archives of the Indian Ocean', trans.
     June Guicharand (London, 1966).
28   Yasukaza Takenaka, Endogenous Capital Formation and
     Development of Capitalism in Japan, 'Journal of
     Economic History', vol.29 (March 1969), no.1.
29   Henri Pirenne, 'A History of Europe' (London, 1961),
     p.382.
30   Habib Inalik, Capital Formation in the Ottoman Empire,
     'Journal of Economic History', vol.29 (March 1960),
     no.1.
31   The Slave South: An Interpretation, 'Science and
     Society'.
32   'Equilibrium and Growth in the World Economy' (Cam-
     bridge, Mass., 1962), p.251.
33   Op.cit., p.46.
34   V. Gordon Childe, 'New Light on the Most Ancient
     East', 4th edn (London, 1952), p.138; also pp.88-9,
     124,129.
35   R.C.Majmudar, H.C.Raychaudhuri and K.Datta, 'An
     Advanced History of India' (London, Melbourne,
     Toronto, 1967), p.559.
36   Michael Lowe, 'Imperial China' (New York, 1966),
     p.136.
37   W.H.Moreland, 'India at the Death of Akbar' (London,
     1920), pp.88-9, referred to in Barrington Moore, Jnr,
     'Social Origins of Dictatorship and Democracy'
     (Boston, 1967), pp.320-1.
38   'Employment Aspects of Planning in Underdeveloped
     Economies' (Cairo, 1957), p.24.
39   Scitz-Hettlesater Engineers, 'Economic and Engineering
     Feasibility Study, Storage, Handling and Marketing of
     Selected Crops in the Philippines' (Kansas City,
     Missouri, June 1968), p.140.
40   'The Present Agrarian Problem in China' (Shanghai,
     1933), p.18, quoted by Harold R.Isaacs, 'The Tragedy
     of the Chinese Revolution' (New York, 1966), p.31.

41 J.U.Nef, 'Economic History Review', vol.5, no.1, p.18.
   Also M.H.Dobb, 'Studies in the Development of
   Capitalism' (London, 1963), pp.140-1.
42 T.S.Ashton, 'Iron and Steel in the Industrial
   Revolution' (Manchester, 1951), p.227.
43 D.S.Landes, 'The Unbound Prometheus' (Cambridge,
   1969), p.57.
44 Daniel Defoe, 'Tour Thro' the Whole Island of Great
   Britain', ed. G.D.H.Cole, 2 vols (London, 1927),
   p.108, quoted by Landes, op.cit., p.120.
45 Economic Aspects of the Construction of Warships in
   Venice in the Sixteenth Century, 'Revistica Storica
   Italiana', vol.1, no.16 (1954), trans. and reprinted
   in Brian Pullman (ed.), 'Crisis and Change in the
   Venetian Economy' (London, 1968).
46 A.L.Basham, 'The Wonder That Was India' (Fontana,
   Collins, 1971), p.221.
47 Karl Marx, 'Capital', vol.I (Moscow, n.d.), p.335.
48 Ibid.
49 'Capital', vol.III (cited earlier), p.596. 'For the
   continued creation of surplus-value it by no means
   suffices for capital to take over the labour process
   in the form under which it has been historically
   handed down, and then simply to prolong the duration
   of that process. The technical and social conditions
   of that process, and consequently the very mode of
   production must be revolutionised, before the produc-
   tiveness of labour can be increased.'
50 Ibid.
51 Ibid., p.880.
52 Quoted by Marx, 'Capital', vol.I (cited earlier),
   p.770.
53 'Capital', vol.III (cited earlier), p.766.
54 'Capital', vol.I (cited earlier), p.769. It was to
   meet this problem that E.G.Wakefield propounded his
   policy of 'Systematic Colonization'. He cited the
   experience of a Mr Peel. This resourceful English
   capitalist had taken with him to Swan River, West
   Australia, £50,000 and the means of subsistence and
   of production as well as 3,000 working-class persons;
   but when he reached his destination he was 'left
   without a servant to make his bed or fetch him water
   from the river'. Marx commented: 'Unhappy Mr. Peel
   who provided for everything except the export of
   English modes of production to Swan River!' (ibid.,
   p.766).
55 Ibid., p.769.
56 Ibid., p.766.
57 Op.cit., p.121.

58   'Capital', vol.I (cited earlier), pp.714-15;   Marx,
     'Grundrisse' (Harmondsworth, 1974), p.508.
59   'Capital', vol.I (cited earlier), p.762.
60   'Capital', vol.III (cited earlier), p.594. 'Usury
     centralises money wealth where the means of production
     are dispersed. It does not alter the mode of produc-
     tion, but attaches itself to it like a parasite and
     makes it wretched' (ibid., p.596).
61   'Capital', vol.I (cited earlier), p.510.
62   Adam Smith, 'The Wealth of Nations', edited by Andrew
     Skinner (Harmondsworth, 1976), p.374.
63   According to the classicists a capitalist makes a
     profit on the plant and equipment used in the produc-
     tive process by retaining them in his possession and
     not by 'parting' with them, as he does with the raw
     materials he embodies in the commodity, or with wage
     payments, or the farmer with the maintenance expenses
     of his cattle. 'The whole value of the [farmer's]
     seed, too, is properly a fixed capital. Though it
     goes backwards and forwards between the ground and
     the granary, it never changes masters, and therefore
     does not properly circulate.' Circulating capital,
     consisting of wages and raw materials, 'changes
     masters [owners] i.e. it circulates via the commodity'
     (ibid., p.375).
64   Bukharin, op.cit. (1972), p.113.
65   L.A.Clarkson, 'The Pre-Industrial Economy in England
     1500-1750' (London, 1971);   Phyllis Deane, The Role of
     Capital in the Industrial Revolution, 'Explorations in
     Entrepreneurial History', vol.10, no.4 (Summer 1973);
     S.D.Chapman, Fixed Capital Formation in the British
     Cotton Industry 1770-1815, 'Economic History Review',
     vol.23 (1970);   T.S.Ashton, 'An Economic History of
     England: The Eighteenth Century' (Methuen, 1955), pp.
     90 ff;   Peter Mathias, Review of Seymour Shapiro,
     'Capital and the Cotton Industry in the Industrial
     Revolution' (Cornell, 1967), 'Journal of Economic
     History', vol.29 (1969);   Sidney Pollard, Fixed
     Capital in the Industrial Revolution in Britain,
     ibid., vol.24, no.37 (September 1964);   C.H.Fei and
     G.Ranis, Economic Development in Historical Perspec-
     tive, 'American Economic Review', vol.59, pt 2 (1969);
     and R.E.Baldwin, Discussion of the Paper by Fei and
     Ranis, ibid.
66   Marx, 'Capital', vol.III (Moscow, 1974), p.323.
67   Ibid., p.331.
68   Clarkson, op.cit., p.99.
69   Nef, op.cit., pp.140-1.
70   Landes, op.cit., p.42.

71 Ibid., p.43.
72 Deane, loc.cit., p.357.
73 Prelude to the Industrial Revolution, 'Science and Society', vol.28, no.1 (Winter 1964), pp.39-40.
74 'Problems of Capital Formation in Underdeveloped Countries' (Delhi, 1974), pp.11-14.
75 Industrial Revolution, in R.M.Hartwell, 'The Causes of the Industrial Revolution in England' (London, 1967), p.40.
76 The cotton industry in England was the outstanding case. 'The price of cotton yarn had fallen to perhaps more than one twentieth of what it had been', precluding competition from the cheapest Indian labour (Landes, op.cit., p.42). It is equally significant that when the scope for technical improvements lessened, the cotton industry lost ground to synthetics.
77 Marx, 'Capital', vol.II, quoted in V.I.Lenin, 'The Development of Capitalism in Russia' (Moscow, 1956), p.34.
78 Op.cit., p.3.
79 Ping-ti Ho, The Salt Merchants of Yang-Chou: A Study of Commercial Capitalism in Eighteenth-Century China, 'Harvard Journal of Asiatic Studies', 1954, vol.17.
80 Harry Johnson, 'Economic Policies Towards Less Developed Countries' (London, 1966), p.45.
81 Ibid., p.46.
82 A conception of industrialization merely in terms of 'manufacturing and other *secondary* production as compared with agriculture and other primary production', said Pei-Kang Chang, excludes 'the case where agriculture itself has become industrialised' ('Agriculture and Industrialization' (Harvard, 1949), p.69, n.3. Emphasis in original).
83 Op.cit. (1977), p.213.
84 Johanna Boer, Industrialization and Urbanization in the Province of Drenthe, the Netherlands, in John Higgs (ed.), 'People in the Countryside' (London, 1966), p.185.
85 V.I.Lenin, 'The Development of Capitalism in Russia' (Moscow, 1956), p.335.
86 Ibid., p.282.
87 The Gains from International Trade and the Backward Countries, 'Review of Economic Studies', vol.22 (1954-5), p.133.
88 Myint, op.cit., p.40.
89 Higgins, op.cit., p.325.
90 The production of tea and rubber fluctuates between seasons as well as during a season. Fluctuations during a season are more pronounced in the case of rubber, since bark tapping ceases during wet weather.

91 Ooi Jin Bee, Mining Landscapes in Kinta, in T.H.
    Silcock (ed.), 'Readings in Malayan Economics'
    (Singapore, 1961), pp.358-9.
92 'Capital', vol.III (cited earlier), p.809.
93 Ibid., p.810.
94 Ibid., p.809.
95 For instance on a 'typical tea estate' in Sri Lanka
    manufacturing costs, including the cost of tea
    chests, were estimated at 16 per cent of the total
    production costs; only 3.5 per cent of these costs
    represented the expenses of machinery, and 3 per cent
    fuel for the engine and the tea dryers. Youngil Lim,
    Impact of the Tea Industry on the Growth of the
    Ceylon Economy, 'Social and Economic Studies', vol.
    17, no.4 (December 1968), Appendix I.
96 A. Baron Homes, The Gold Coast and Nigeria, in W.A.
    Lewis (ed.), 'Tropical Development 1880-1913'
    (London, 1971), pp.164-5; also 'Trade and Politics
    in the Niger Delta' (Oxford, 1956), p.19.
97 Department of Agriculture, 'Burma', Markets Section
    Survey No.9, 'Rice' (Rangoon, 1958), p.51.
98 Loc.cit., p.323.
99 Marx, 'Capital', vol.III (cited earlier), chapter
    VIII: 'Different Compositions of Capital in Differ-
    ent Branches of Production and Resulting Differences
    in Rates of Profit.'
100 Ibid., pp.213-14.
101 K.S.Sandhu shares this popular belief: 'Allured by
    the almost fabulous fortunes promised by Raja [King]
    Rubber, millions of pounds worth of money [sic] was
    poured into the Malayan countryside.' He refers to
    one rubber company which in 1903 paid a dividend of
    325 per cent and another of 125 per cent for 1909-10
    ('Indians in Malaya' (Cambridge, 1969), p.50, and
    n.i). The fact is that as plantation enterprises,
    these companies individually had a relatively small
    amount of issued capital, so that the fortunes were
    'fabulous' only in that they were a very high return
    on a small investment.
102 'Unequal Exchange' (New York, 1972), p.89.
103 Op.cit., p.23.
104 L.M.Hacker, The American Revolution: Economic
    Aspects, in G. McWhiney and R.Wiebe (eds), 'Historic-
    al Vistas', vol.I: '1807-1877' (Boston, 1963), p.
    161.
105 'Capital', vol.III (cited earlier), p.787.
106 Ibid., p.804.
107 Historical Experience of Economic Development, in
    E.A.G.Robinson (ed.), 'Problems in Economic Develop-
    ment' (London and New York, 1965), p.122.

108 Kohachiro Takahashi, A Contribution to the Discus-
     sion, in Rodney Hilton (ed.), 'The Transition from
     Feudalism to Capitalism' (London, 1976), p.71.
109 'Uneven and Combined Development in History' (New
     York, August 1966), p.20.
110 Cf. C.G.F.Simkin, 'The Instability of a Dependent
     Economy: Economic Fluctuations in New Zealand,
     1840-1914' (London, 1931).
111 Jairus Banaji, Backward Capitalism, Primitive
     Accumulation and Modes of Production, 'Journal of
     Contemporary Asia', vol.3, no.4(1973), p.396. The
     term 'restructuring' was also used by Harry Magdoff,
     in Imperialism: A Historical Survey, 'Monthly
     Review', May 1972, p.8.
112 Hamza Alavi, India and the Colonial Mode of Produc-
     tion, 'Economic and Political Weekly', Special No.
     1975, p.1253.
113 'What is underdevelopment? A dwarf with an enormous
     head and a swollen chest is "underdeveloped" in the
     sense that his weak legs and short arms do not corre-
     spond to the rest of his anatomy; he is the mon-
     strous product of a malformation that distorted his
     development.... Ours are countries with distorted
     economies.... "Underdevelopment" or distorted
     development brings a dangerous specialisation in raw
     materials.... We are ... the countries of monocul-
     ture, of the single market' (Cuba, Exceptional Case?,
     'Monthly Review', July-August 1961, pp.61-2).
114 Samir Amin, 'Capitalism, Imperialism and Under-
     development' (Monthly Review Press, 1974).
115 'Capitalism and Underdevelopment in Latin America'
     (New York, 1967), pp.3 and 9. 'Indeed, it is this
     exploitative relation which in chain-like fashion
     extends the link between the capitalist world and
     national metropolises (part of whose surplus they
     appropriate), and from those to local centres, and
     so on to large landowners or merchants who expropri-
     ate surplus from small peasants or tenants, and some-
     times even from these latter to landless labourers
     exploited by them in turn' (ibid., p.7).
116 A frequent writer on the Malaysian economy called
     foreign capitalists 'welcome invaders'.
117 Loc.cit., pp.17-18.
118 Realities of Southeast Asian Development, 'Socialist
     Register, 1971' (London, 1971), p.273.
119 Leon Trotsky, 'The Chinese Revolution, Problems and
     Perspectives' (Pathfinder Press, New York, n.d.),
     p.4.
120 Economic Development in Historical Perspective,

'American Economic Review', vol.59, pt 2 (1969), p.397.

121 E.A.Kosminsky, 'Studies in the Agrarian History of England in the Thirteenth Century', trans. Ruth Kinch (Oxford, 1956).

122 T.H.Ashton, The English Manor (Review Article), 'Past and Present', November 1956, p.8. The contradictory effects of the advance of capitalism were also noted by Pirenne: 'In some countries [they] had the effect of enfranchising the peasant while in others it forced him back into a state of servitude far completer, above all, much harsher than that of the Middle Ages' (op.cit., p.532).

123 Barrington Moore, Jnr, op.cit., p.344. 'The agrarian system that emerged from this fusion of British administration and Indian rural society was enough to eliminate decisively the Japanese alternative' (ibid.).

124 'Capital', vol.III (cited earlier), p.238.

125 Bukharin, op.cit. (1972), p.165.

126 E. Kay Trimberger, State Power and Modes of Production; Implications of the Japanese Transition to Capitalism, 'Insurgent Sociologist', vol.7, no.2 (Spring 1977), p.92; also P.Baran, 'The Political Economy of Growth' (New York and London, 1957), p.156.

127 Mao Tse-tung, Problems of Strategy in China's Revolutionary War (December 1936), in 'Selected Works of Mao Tse-tung' (Peking, 1967), vol.1, p.197.

128 E.J.Hobsbawm, The Seventeenth Century in the Development of Capitalism, 'Science and Society', vol.24, no.2 (Spring 1960), p.108.

129 'Economic Theory and Underdeveloped Regions' (London, 1957), p.55.

130 Kenjiro Ichikawa, The Nineteenth Century Materials on Thailand in the Toyo Bunko, Tokyo, International Conference on Asian History, University of Malaya, 1968, mimeo, pp.8-9. The materials examined by Ichikawa were a 'large collection' of books, pamphlets, periodicals and manuscripts on Thailand which had belonged to George Ernest Morrison, a correspondent of 'The Times', London, in the late nineteenth century.

131 Op.cit., p.355.

CHAPTER 17   THE POLITICAL ECONOMY OF UNDERDEVELOPMENT

1   W.Davies, 'The Pharmaceutical Industry' (London,
    1967), p.184, quoted by L.E.N.Fernando, Multinational
    Enterprise in Manufacturing Industry with Special
    Reference to Ceylon, Central Bank of Ceylon, 'Staff
    Studies', vol.2, no.2 (September 1972), p.42, n.2.
2   Sanjay Lall and Senaka Bibile, The Political Economy
    of Controlling Transnationals: The Pharmaceutical
    Industry in Sri Lanka (1972-76), 'World Development'
    (1977), vol.5, no.8, p.686.
3   In Indonesia, the Lockheed Aircraft Corporation
    wanting to know which family groups to influence when
    Suharto seized power in 1965 consulted the CIA through
    the US Air Attaché in Djakarta ('Multinational Corpo-
    rations and United States Foreign Policy', Part 12,
    Hearings, Senate Foreign Relations Committee 1975,
    pp.945-61, quoted in Lenny Siegel, I am AURI-Fly Me
    (AURI was, until 1975, the acronym for the Indonesian
    Air Force), 'Pacific Research and World Empire
    Telegram', vol.7, no.5 (March-April), 1976, p.9).
4   'Fortune' (15 September 1968), p.105, data reproduced
    in Fred Cohen, Private Power and U.S. Foreign Policy,
    in 'Pacific Research and World Empire Telegram',
    vol.1, no.5 (June 1970), p.7.
5   Has America lost its Innovative Edge?, 'Newsweek',
    4 June 1979, pp.32 ff.
6   'Labour and Monopoly Capital' (New York and London,
    1974).
7   H.L.Wilensky, Work, Careers and Social Integration,
    'International Social Science Journal', vol.12 (1960),
    reprinted in Tom Burns (ed.), 'Industrial Man' (Har-
    mondsworth, 1969), p.111.
8   Peter Evans, Multinationals, State-owned Corporations,
    and the Transformation of Imperialism: A Brazilian
    Case Study, 'Economic Development and Cultural
    Change', vol.36, no.1 (October 1977), p.46.
9   Lester R.Brown, 'World Without Borders' (New York,
    August 1973), pp.194-6.
10 Pieree Jalee's comment that the oil and metalliferous
    ores of the Third World are an 'ace up its sleeve;
    [that] its hand is on the tap controlling an essential
    flow, and thus it enjoys a position of strength' is
    only potentially true ('The Pillage of the Third
    World' (New York, 1968), p.19).
11 Rockefeller-Brothers Fund, 'Foreign Economic Policy
    for the Twentieth Century' (New York, 1958), p.16.
12 Subcommittees on Foreign Economic Policy of the Joint
    Economic Committee, Congress of the United States,

84th Congress, December 10, 12 and 13, 1956, pp.127, 131. This and the preceding quote are from Harry Magdoff, 'The Age of Imperialism' (New York, 1969), pp.53,54.

13 Asia After Vietnam, 'Foreign Affairs', vol.46, no.1 (October 1967), p.111.

14 Malcolm Rutherford, Third World Warning, 'Financial Times' (London), 29 October 1977. Indeed a clue to the dogged tenacity with which America fought the Vietnam war lies in the rich and variegated mineral resources endowment of the Indochinese peninsula. The Tonkin incident and the offshore oil potential of the Gulf of Tonkin are hardly unrelated phenomena. Not unexpectedly, the conflict between 'Big' China and 'Small' Vietnam may have a resource dimension as its unstated premise.

15 In Hong Kong, according to a survey by the Christian Industrial Committee, 'almost all workers in the industry [girls between the ages of 16 and 25] suffer eyesight defects caused by the strain required for intricate work.... Every girl operator suffered a reduction in eyesight after an average of 3-7 years' (Paul Strauss, Electronics Industry Faces 'Eye Trouble', 'Straits Times' (Malaysia), 22 November 1971). In Singapore, out of 103 workers in six electronics factories 40 per cent suffered from eye complaints - such as migraine and conjunctivitis (Eyes and Electronics, editorial comment, ibid., 16 February 1972).

16 Steven Langdon, Multinational Corporations, Taste Transfer and Underdevelopment: A Case Study for Kenya, 'Review of African Political Economy', no.2 (January-April) 1975, p.23. Donald Rothschild, 'Racial Bargaining in Independent Kenya' (London, 1973), p. 181, cited in Martin Godfrey and Steven Langdon, Partners in Underdevelopment? The Transnationalization Thesis in Kenya Context, 'Journal of Commonwealth and Comparative Politics', vol.14, no.1 (March 1976), p.58.

17 Giovanni Arrighi, International Corporations, Labour Aristocracies and Economic Development in Tropical Africa, in G.Arrighi and S.Saul, 'Essays on the Political Economy of Africa' (New York, 1973), p.123.

18 Along the road from Butterworth to Alor Star in Malaysia the welcome board to the state of Kedah informs that one is entering the 'Rice Bowl' of Malaysia. The next billboard 200 yards away says 'Kubota Country'. Kubota refers to a Japanese two-wheeled tractor used in agriculture.

19 In Kenya in the late 1960s 'over half of the net
    private long-run capital inflow' was from various
    sources outside the Sterling Area. The East African
    Association, which had earlier been virtually British,
    drew one-third of its membership in 1971 from non-
    British companies (Godfrey and Langdon, loc.cit.,
    p.47).

20 Jean-Jacques Servan-Schriber, 'The American Challenge'
    (London, 1968), p.76.

21 Vera McCarthy, Philippine Copper, 'Pacific Research
    and World Empire Telegram', vol.3, no.3 (March-April-
    May 1972), p.20.

22 Lenny Siegel, Freeport Mines Indonesian Copper, ibid.,
    vol.7, no.2 (January-February 1976), pp.8-9.

23 Godfrey and Langdon, loc.cit., p.47.

24 Loc.cit., p.9.

25 Asked about the 'considerable economic pressure' the
    US had put on Japan and whether 'It wasn't time that
    Japan shouted back', Fukuda answered: 'I think the
    Americans have been simply saying things with candour
    to us. We don't mind hearing these things. But nowa-
    days when we talk with Americans we discuss matters of
    global interest rather than little bilateral matters'
    ('Newsweek', 8 May 1978, p.7).

26 Tracy Dahlby, Japan and U.S. Agree to Agree, 'Far
    Eastern Economic Review', 15 June 1979.

27 Hearings, Asian Development Bank Act, 89th Congress,
    2nd session, 16 February 1966, cited by Robert Coates,
    Indonesian Timber, 'Pacific Research and World Empire
    Telegram, vol.2, no.4 (May-June 1971), p.12.

28 'Late Capitalism' (London, 1976), pp.91-2. According
    to Mandel, capital exports were mostly cross-invest-
    ments among the developed countries; there was 'a
    relative decline in capital exports to underdeveloped
    regions', owing to 'constant revolutionary ferment
    even since the second world war' and the displacement
    of organic materials by inorganic ones (ibid., pp.
    319-20). In our view, while there was a decline in
    capital exports to the underdeveloped countries in the
    decolonization phase, this is certainly not true of
    the succeeding phase when there was a relinking of the
    periphery with the centre. The effects of the
    'constant revolutionary ferment' on capital exports
    referred to by Mandel seem to us to be exaggerated.
    In fact, large capital flows, with the MNCs as the
    main agency, have gone into infrastructure and mineral
    extracting industries located in the periphery.

29 'Meanwhile as the EEC dangles worm ridden carrots in
    front of some developing nations and makes political

pay offs in the Mediterranean and Eastern Europe, the
countries which will suffer are just those which over
the years proved most prepared to adjust themselves,
through bilateral arrangements under the MFA [Multi-
Fibre Arrangement] and its predecessor, to European
products' (Additional Weapon; Bargaining Power, 'Far
Eastern Economic Review', 7 October 1977; also ibid.,
12 August 1977).

30 André Farhi, 'Strategies of the North and Strategies
of the South: Some Assumptions for Africa', mimeo,
UN Africa Institute for Economic Development and
Planning (Dakar), n.d. (S. 3796-A), p.23.

31 The Colombo Bureau Meeting of the Non-Aligned
Countries, 'Tribune' (Sri Lanka), vol.23, no.48
(9 June 1979), p.34. 'In one way or another they
[the developed capitalist nations] have ensured that
resolutions emanating from the different conferences,
and even the Charter of Economic Rights and Duties of
States approved by the United Nations General Assembly
in December 1974 - shall remain dead letters.'

32 'Commercio Exterior de Mexico', Banco National de
Commercio Exterior, S.A., vol.24, no.11 (November
1978), p.453.

33 Raul Prebisch, the first Secretary-General of UNCTAD,
stated: 'We have seen the appeals of the developing
countries meet only with objections - negative attitudes and indifference, if not with hostility. A few
enlightened Northern countries have adopted positive
attitudes, but their economic influence is unfortunately much smaller than their moral and intellectual
weights' (UN, 'Trade and Development', an UNCTAD
Review, no.1 (Spring 1979), p.1).

34 Siegel, loc.cit., p.9.

35 Loc.cit., p.15, n.41.

36 Overseas Development Council, 'Annual Report 1971',
quoted in 'International Dependency in the 1970s',
published by Africa Research Group (ARG), Cambridge,
Mass., n.d., also quoted in Steve Weissman, Foreign
Aid, Who Needs It?, 'Pacific Research and World Empire
Telegram', June 1972, p.2.

37 One of the latest sallies with the self-same objective
is the Trilateral Commission, set up by Nelson
Rockefeller and a group of about 100 leading financial
and political figures, wanting, in their own style,
'democratization and liberalization' of the periphery
and its receptivity to foreign capital.

38 The following examples relate to the period preceding
the recent liberalization of the economy: a ban on
the import of automobile tyres of the sizes manufac-

tured by the State Tyre Corporation was circumvented
by importing tyres whose sizes were marked in metric
units whereas the restrictive order was expressed in
terms of the imperial unit. When the order was amended to include metric equivalents, the tyres imported
were embossed on the outside with the permissible
tyre-sizes while the actual size, for the guidance of
consumers, was marked inside. When the import of
razor blades was banned, large quantities of very
inferior plastic holders were imported, with one super
quality razor blade per holder. Upon clearance from
the Customs, the holders were discarded and the blades
were marketed. A ban on the import of sun glasses was
overcome by declaring them as goggles, a safety device
used by welding workers and whose import was permitted. Permission to import equipment for water-purify-
ing plants led to the import of aluminium filters for
domestic use, which were prohibited so as to encourage
local manufacture. A ban on the import of sand paper
was flouted by stamping different names on the prohibited articles such as 'abrasive paper', 'flint
paper', 'glass flint paper', etc.

39 ASEAN in Perspective and the Role of Singapore, in You
Poh Seng and Lim Chong Yah (eds), 'The Singapore
Economy' (Singapore, 1971), pp.377,380-1 and 382.

40 Larry E.Westphal, The Republic of Korea's Experience
with Export-led Industrial Growth, 'World Development', 1978, vol.6, no.3, p.375.

41 Sang-Woo Rhee, Land Reform in South Korea: A Macro-
level Policy Review, paper presented at the Asian-
Pacific Development Centre, Kuala Lumpur, August 1978,
mimeo, p.33.

42 Ibid., p.33.

43 'Hon. de Mel [Minister of Finance]: In other words,
up to date the only attraction in Sri Lanka is to
collar the quotas which are still available to Sri
Lanka. Korea has exhausted her quota. Hong Kong has
exhausted, Singapore is exhausting; so the only thing
[the foreign investors] find attractive in Sri Lanka
is to collar Sri Lanka's quota. Do you agree?
Mr Gnanam [a leading Sri Lankan industrialist]: I
agree.
Hon. de Mel: *Could Sri Lankan industrialists not have
got this quota and done this industry without any
foreign help?*
Mr Gnanam: If you had announced your offer of a five-
year tax holiday to industrialists in your last but
one Budget, then all the garment industries would have
done very much better than anyone else, because Sri

Lanka has got the best garment industries.... If they
were allowed to export [with a tax holiday] they would
have done without the Free Trade Zone.
Hon. de Mel: *In other words, the Free Trade Zone has
only deprived the Sri Lankan industrialists.'*
('Parliamentary Series No.17 of the First Parliament
of the Democratic Socialist Republic of Sri Lanka',
Second Report (22 February 1980), p.271. Emphasis
added.

44 Steven Langdon, The Invasion of the Kenya Soap
Industry, 'Review of African Political Economy', no.2
(January-April 1975), pp.14 and 22-6.

45 Ibid., Editorial, p.1.

46 K.Yoshihara, 'Foreign Investment and Domestic
Response' (Singapore, 1975).

47 Ibid., pp.25,148.

48 Muto Ichiyo, The Free Trade Zone and Mystique of
Export-Oriented Industrialization, 'AMPO: Japan-Asia
Quarterly Review', vol.8, no.4 and vol.9, nos 1 and 2
(1977), p.23.

49 In this connection, Singapore's Prime Minister
ruefully observed: 'Our products must be sold under
the label of the well established multinational company' ('Straits Times' (Singapore), 27 April 1976).

50 Evans, loc.cit., p.58.

51 C.P.Kindleberger, 'American Business Abroad' (New
Haven, 1969), p.146.

52 For instance in Sri Lanka, raw materials for
tetracyclene capsules were imported in 1974 by Pfizer
Ltd at US $99 per kg, compared with a price of US $20
per kg at which the State Pharmaceuticals Corporation
was importing the same materials from Hoechst
Aktiengesellschaft in Frankfurt. Despite a cholera
epidemic that was prevalent at the time, Pfizer Ltd
declined to accede to a request by the Minister of
Industries and Scientific Affairs that it should
produce capsules from the raw materials imported from
the cheaper source (Disclosure by the Minister of
Industries and Scientific Affairs in the 'Sunday
Observer' (Colombo), 7 May 1978). Glaxo Ltd was
importing chlorophenisamine from its parent firm at
US $411 per kg compared with a price of $53 from
Halewood, a smaller British firm (Lall and Bibile,
loc.cit., p.686).

53 Quoted in Nakano Kenji, Japan's Overseas Investment
Patterns and FTSs, in 'AMPO', loc.cit., p.44.

54 'Development and Underdevelopment: A Marxist Analysis'
(London, 1976), p.95.

55 'An Integrated Programme for Commodities: Trade

Measures to expand Processing of Primary Commodities
in Developing Countries', Report by the Secretary-
General of UNCTAD, TD/BC, 1/166/Supp. 5, 18 December
1974, p.5.
56   Brown, op.cit., p.223.

Index

Routledge Social Science Series

Routledge & Kegan Paul   London, Henley and Boston

39 Store Street,
London WC1E 7DD
Broadway House,
Newtown Road,
Henley-on-Thames,
Oxon RG9 1EN
9 Park Street,
Boston, Mass. 02108

Contents

*Authors wishing to submit manuscripts for any series
in this catalogue should send them to the Social Science Editor,
Routledge & Kegan Paul Ltd, 39 Store Street,
London WC1E 7DD.*
● *Books so marked are available in paperback.*
○ *Books so marked are available in paperback only.*
*All books are in metric Demy 8vo format (216 × 138mm approx.)
unless otherwise stated.*

International Library of Sociology
General Editor   John Rex

GENERAL SOCIOLOGY

Barnsley, J. H. The Social Reality of Ethics. *464 pp.*
Brown, Robert. Explanation in Social Science. *208 pp.*
●   Rules and Laws in Sociology. *192 pp.*
Bruford, W. H. Chekhov and His Russia. *A Sociological Study. 244 pp.*
Burton, F. and **Carlen, P.** Official Discourse. *On Discourse Analysis, Government Publications, Ideology. About 140 pp.*
Cain, Maureen E. Society and the Policeman's Role. *326 pp.*
● **Fletcher, Colin.** Beneath the Surface. *An Account of Three Styles of Sociological Research. 221 pp.*
Gibson, Quentin. The Logic of Social Enquiry. *240 pp.*
Glassner, B. Essential Interactionism. *208 pp.*
Glucksmann, M. Structuralist Analysis in Contemporary Social Thought. *212 pp.*
Gurvitch, Georges. Sociology of Law. *Foreword by Roscoe Pound. 264 pp.*
Hinkle, R. Founding Theory of American Sociology 1881–1913. *About 350 pp.*
Homans, George C. Sentiments and Activities. *336 pp.*
Johnson, Harry M. Sociology: *A Systematic Introduction. Foreword by Robert K. Merton. 710 pp.*
● **Keat, Russell** and **Urry, John.** Social Theory as Science. *278 pp.*
Mannheim, Karl. Essays on Sociology and Social Psychology. *Edited by Paul Keckskemeti. With Editorial Note by Adolph Lowe. 344 pp.*
Martindale, Don. The Nature and Types of Sociological Theory. *292 pp.*
● **Maus, Heinz.** A Short History of Sociology. *234 pp.*
Myrdal, Gunnar. Value in Social Theory: *A Collection of Essays on Methodology. Edited by Paul Streeten. 332 pp.*
Ogburn, William F. and **Nimkoff, Meyer F.** A Handbook of Sociology. *Preface by Karl Mannheim. 656 pp. 46 figures. 35 tables.*
Parsons, Talcott and **Smelser, Neil J.** Economy and Society: *A Study in the Integration of Economic and Social Theory. 362 pp.*
Payne, G., Dingwall, R., Payne, J. and **Carter, M.** Sociology and Social Research. *About 250 pp.*
Podgórecki, A. Practical Social Sciences. *About 200 pp.*
Podgórecki, A. and **Łos, M.** Multidimensional Sociology. *268 pp.*
Raffel, S. Matters of Fact. *A Sociological Inquiry. 152 pp.*
● **Rex, John.** Key Problems of Sociological Theory. *220 pp.*
   Sociology and the Demystification of the Modern World. *282 pp.*
● **Rex, John.** (Ed.) Approaches to Sociology. *Contributions by Peter Abell, Frank Bechhofer, Basil Bernstein, Ronald Fletcher, David Frisby, Miriam Glucksmann, Peter Lassman, Herminio Martins, John Rex, Roland Robertson, John Westergaard and Jock Young. 302 pp.*
Rigby, A. Alternative Realities. *352 pp.*
Roche, M. Phenomenology, Language and the Social Sciences. *374 pp.*
Sahay, A. Sociological Analysis. *220 pp.*
Strasser, Hermann. The Normative Structure of Sociology. *Conservative and Emancipatory Themes in Social Thought. About 340 pp.*
Strong, P. Ceremonial Order of the Clinic. *267 pp.*
Urry, John. Reference Groups and the Theory of Revolution. *244 pp.*
Weinberg, E. Development of Sociology in the Soviet Union. *173 pp.*

FOREIGN CLASSICS OF SOCIOLOGY

● **Gerth, H. H.** and **Mills, C. Wright.** From Max Weber: *Essays in Sociology. 502 pp.*

● **Tönnies, Ferdinand.** Community and Association *(Gemeinschaft und Gesell-schaft).|Translated and Supplemented by Charles P. Loomis. Foreword by Pitirim A. Sorokin. 334 pp.*

SOCIAL STRUCTURE

Andreski, Stanislav. Military Organization and Society. *Foreword by Professor A. R. Radcliffe-Brown. 226 pp. 1 folder.*

Broom, L., Lancaster Jones, F., McDonnell, P. and **Williams, T.** The Inheritance of Inequality. *About 180 pp.*

Carlton, Eric. Ideology and Social Order. *Foreword by Professor Philip Abrahams. About 320 pp.*

Clegg, S. and **Dunkerley, D.** Organization, Class and Control. *614 pp.*

Coontz, Sydney H. Population Theories and the Economic Interpretation. *202 pp.*

Coser, Lewis. The Functions of Social Conflict. *204 pp.*

Crook, I. and **D.** The First Years of the Yangyi Commune. *304 pp., illustrated.*

Dickie-Clark, H. F. Marginal Situation: *A Sociological Study of a Coloured Group. 240 pp. 11 tables.*

Giner, S. and **Archer, M. S.** (Eds) Contemporary Europe: *Social Structures and Cultural Patterns, 336 pp.*

● **Glaser, Barney** and **Strauss, Anselm L.** Status Passage: *A Formal Theory. 212 pp.*

Glass, D. V. (Ed.) Social Mobility in Britain. *Contributions by J. Berent, T. Bottomore, R. C. Chambers, J. Floud, D. V. Glass, J. R. Hall, H. T. Himmelweit, R. K. Kelsall, F. M. Martin, C. A. Moser, R. Mukherjee and W. Ziegel. 420 pp.*

Kelsall, R. K. Higher Civil Servants in Britain: *From 1870 to the Present Day. 268 pp. 31 tables.*

● **Lawton, Denis.** Social Class, Language and Education. *192 pp.*

McLeish, John. The Theory of Social Change: *Four Views Considered. 128 pp.*

● **Marsh, David C.** The Changing Social Structure of England and Wales, 1871–1961. *Revised edition. 288 pp.*

Menzies, Ken. Talcott Parsons and the Social Image of Man. *About 208 pp.*

● **Mouzelis, Nicos.** Organization and Bureaucracy. *An Analysis of Modern Theories. 240 pp.*

● **Ossowski, Stanislaw.** Class Structure in the Social Consciousness. *210 pp.*

● **Podgórecki, Adam.** Law and Society. *302 pp.*

Renner, Karl. Institutions of Private Law and Their Social Functions. *Edited, with an Introduction and Notes, by O. Kahn-Freud. Translated by Agnes Schwarzschild. 316 pp.*

Rex, J. and **Tomlinson, S.** Colonial Immigrants in a British City. *A Class Analysis. 368 pp.*

Smooha, S. Israel: Pluralism and Conflict. *472 pp.*

Wesolowski, W. Class, Strata and Power. *Trans. and with Introduction by G. Kolankiewicz. 160 pp.*

Zureik, E. Palestinians in Israel. *A Study in Internal Colonialism. 264 pp.*

SOCIOLOGY AND POLITICS

Acton, T. A. Gypsy Politics and Social Change. *316 pp.*

Burton, F. Politics of Legitimacy. *Struggles in a Belfast Community. 250 pp.*

Crook, I. and **D.** Revolution in a Chinese Village. *Ten Mile Inn. 216 pp., illustrated.*

Etzioni-Halevy, E. Political Manipulation and Administrative Power. *A Comparative Study. About 200 pp.*

Fielding, N. The National Front. *About 250 pp.*

● **Hechter, Michael.** Internal Colonialism. *The Celtic Fringe in British National Development, 1536–1966. 380 pp.*

Kornhauser, William. The Politics of Mass Society. *272 pp. 20 tables.*

4

Korpi, W. The Working Class in Welfare Capitalism. *Work, Unions and Politics in Sweden. 472 pp.*

Kroes, R. Soldiers and Students. *A Study of Right- and Left-wing Students. 174 pp.*

Martin, Roderick. Sociology of Power. *About 272 pp.*

Merquior, J. G. Rousseau and Weber. *A Study in the Theory of Legitimacy. About 288 pp.*

Myrdal, Gunnar. The Political Element in the Development of Economic Theory. *Translated from the German by Paul Streeten. 282 pp.*

Varma, B. N. The Sociology and Politics of Development. *A Theoretical Study. 236 pp.*

Wong, S.-L. Sociology and Socialism in Contemporary China. *160 pp.*

Wootton, Graham. Workers, Unions and the State. *188 pp.*

CRIMINOLOGY

Ancel, Marc. Social Defence: *A Modern Approach to Criminal Problems. Foreword by Leon Radzinowicz. 240 pp.*

Athens, L. Violent Criminal Acts and Actors. *104 pp.*

Cain, Maureen E. Society and the Policeman's Role. *326 pp.*

Cloward, Richard A. and Ohlin, Lloyd E. Delinquency and Opportunity: *A Theory of Delinquent Gangs. 248 pp.*

Downes, David M. The Delinquent Solution. *A Study in Subcultural Theory. 296 pp.*

Friedlander, Kate. The Psycho-Analytical Approach to Juvenile Delinquency: *Theory, Case Studies, Treatment. 320 pp.*

Gleuck, Sheldon and Eleanor. Family Environment and Delinquency. *With the statistical assistance of Rose W. Kneznek. 340 pp.*

Lopez-Rey, Manuel. Crime. *An Analytical Appraisal. 288 pp.*

Mannheim, Hermann. Comparative Criminology: *A Text Book. Two volumes. 442 pp. and 380 pp.*

Morris, Terence. The Criminal Area: *A Study in Social Ecology. Foreword by Hermann Mannheim. 232 pp. 25 tables. 4 maps.*

Rock, Paul. Making People Pay. *338 pp.*

● Taylor, Ian, Walton, Paul and Young, Jock. The New Criminology. *For a Social Theory of Deviance. 325 pp.*

● Taylor, Ian, Walton, Paul and Young, Jock. (Eds) Critical Criminology. *268 pp.*

SOCIAL PSYCHOLOGY

Bagley, Christopher. The Social Psychology of the Epileptic Child. *320 pp.*

Brittan, Arthur. Meanings and Situations. *224 pp.*

Carroll, J. Break-Out from the Crystal Palace. *200 pp.*

● Fleming, C. M. Adolescence: Its Social Psychology. *With an Introduction to recent findings from the fields of Anthropology, Physiology, Medicine, Psychometrics and Sociometry. 288 pp.*

● The Social Psychology of Education: *An Introduction and Guide to Its Study. 136 pp.*

Linton, Ralph. The Cultural Background of Personality. *132 pp.*

● Mayo, Elton. The Social Problems of an Industrial Civilization. *With an Appendix on the Political Problem. 180 pp.*

Ottaway, A. K. C. Learning Through Group Experience. *176 pp.*

Plummer, Ken. Sexual Stigma. *An Interactionist Account. 254 pp.*

● Rose, Arnold M. (Ed.) Human Behaviour and Social Processes: *an Interactionist Approach. Contributions by Arnold M. Rose, Ralph H. Turner, Anselm Strauss, Everett C. Hughes, E. Franklin Frazier, Howard S. Becker et al. 696 pp.*

Smelser, Neil J. Theory of Collective Behaviour. *448 pp.*

Stephenson, Geoffrey M. The Development of Conscience. *128 pp.*

Young, Kimball. Handbook of Social Psychology. *658 pp. 16 figures. 10 tables.*

5

SOCIOLOGY OF THE FAMILY

Bell, Colin R. Middle Class Families: *Social and Geographical Mobility. 224 pp.*
Burton, Lindy. Vulnerable Children. *272 pp.*
Gavron, Hannah. The Captive Wife: *Conflicts of Household Mothers. 190 pp.*
George, Victor and **Wilding, Paul.** Motherless Families. *248 pp.*
Klein, Josephine. Samples from English Cultures.
    1. Three Preliminary Studies and Aspects of Adult Life in England. *447 pp.*
    2. Child-Rearing Practices and Index. *247 pp.*
Klein, Viola. The Feminine Character. *History of an Ideology. 244 pp.*
McWhinnie, Alexina M. Adopted Children. *How They Grow Up. 304 pp.*
● **Morgan, D. H. J.** Social Theory and the Family. *About 320 pp.*
● **Myrdal, Alva** and **Klein, Viola.** Women's Two Roles: *Home and Work. 238 pp.*
    27 tables.
    Parsons, Talcott and **Bales, Robert F.** Family: Socialization and Interaction Process.
    In collaboration with James Olds, Morris Zelditch and Philip E. Slater. 456 pp.
    50 figures and tables.

SOCIAL SERVICES

Bastide, Roger. The Sociology of Mental Disorder. *Translated from the French by Jean McNeil. 260 pp.*
Carlebach, Julius. Caring For Children in Trouble. *266 pp.*
George, Victor. Foster Care. *Theory and Practice. 234 pp.*
    Social Security: *Beveridge and After. 258 pp.*
George, V. and **Wilding, P.** Motherless Families. *248 pp.*
● **Goetschius, George W.** Working with Community Groups. *256 pp.*
Goetschius, George W. and **Tash, Joan.** Working with Unattached Youth. *416 pp.*
Heywood, Jean S. Children in Care. *The Development of the Service for the Deprived Child. Third revised edition. 284 pp.*
King, Roy D., Ranes, Norma V. and **Tizard, Jack.** Patterns of Residential Care. *356 pp.*
Leigh, John. Young People and Leisure. *256 pp.*
● **Mays, John.** (Ed.) Penelope Hall's Social Services of England and Wales. *368 pp.*
Morris, Mary. Voluntary Work and the Welfare State. *300 pp.*
Nokes, P. L. The Professional Task in Welfare Practice. *152 pp.*
Timms, Noel. Psychiatric Social Work in Great Britain (1939–1962). *280 pp.*
●   Social Casework: *Principles and Practice. 256 pp.*

SOCIOLOGY OF EDUCATION

Banks, Olive. Parity and Prestige in English Secondary Education: a Study in Educational Sociology. *272 pp.*
● **Blyth, W. A. L.** English Primary Education. *A Sociological Description.*
    2. Background. *168 pp.*
Collier, K. G. The Social Purposes of Education: *Personal and Social Values in Education. 268 pp.*
Evans, K. M. Sociometry and Education. *158 pp.*
● **Ford, Julienne.** Social Class and the Comprehensive School. *192 pp.*
Foster, P. J. Education and Social Change in Ghana. *336 pp. 3 maps.*
Fraser, W. R. Education and Society in Modern France. *150 pp.*
Grace, Gerald R. Role Conflict and the Teacher. *150 pp.*
Hans, Nicholas. New Trends in Education in the Eighteenth Century. *278 pp. 19 tables.*
●   Comparative Education: *A Study of Educational Factors and Traditions. 360 pp.*
● **Hargreaves, David.** Interpersonal Relations and Education. *432 pp.*
●   Social Relations in a Secondary School. *240 pp.*
    School Organization and Pupil Involvement. *A Study of Secondary Schools.*

- **Mannheim, Karl** and **Stewart, W. A. C.** An Introduction to the Sociology of Education. *206 pp.*
- **Musgrove, F.** Youth and the Social Order. *176 pp.*
- **Ottaway, A. K. C.** Education and Society: An Introduction to the Sociology of Education. *With an Introduction by W. O. Lester Smith. 212 pp.*

Peers, Robert. Adult Education: *A Comparative Study. Revised edition. 398 pp.*

Stratta, Erica. The Education of Borstal Boys. *A Study of their Educational Experiences prior to, and during, Borstal Training. 256 pp.*

- **Taylor, P. H., Reid, W. A.** and **Holley, B. J.** The English Sixth Form. *A Case Study in Curriculum Research. 198 pp.*

SOCIOLOGY OF CULTURE

Eppel, E. M. and **M.** Adolescents and Morality: *A Study of some Moral Values and Dilemmas of Working Adolescents in the Context of a changing Climate of Opinion. Foreword by W. J. H. Sprott. 268 pp. 39 tables.*

- **Fromm, Erich.** The Fear of Freedom. *286 pp.*
- The Sane Society. *400 pp.*

Johnson, L. The Cultural Critics. *From Matthew Arnold to Raymond Williams. 233 pp.*

Mannheim, Karl. Essays on the Sociology of Culture. *Edited by Ernst Mannheim in co-operation with Paul Kecskemeti. Editorial Note by Adolph Lowe. 280 pp.*

Merquior, J. G. The Veil and the Mask. *Essays on Culture and Ideology. Foreword by Ernest Gellner. 140 pp.*

Zijderfeld, A. C. On Clichés. *The Supersedure of Meaning by Function in Modernity. 150 pp.*

SOCIOLOGY OF RELIGION

Argyle, Michael and **Beit-Hallahmi, Benjamin.** The Social Psychology of Religion. *256 pp.*

Glasner, Peter E. The Sociology of Secularisation. *A Critique of a Concept. 146 pp.*

Hall, J. R. The Ways Out. *Utopian Communal Groups in an Age of Babylon. 280 pp.*

Ranson, S., Hinings, B. and **Bryman, A.** Clergy, Ministers and Priests. *216 pp.*

Stark, Werner. The Sociology of Religion. *A Study of Christendom.*
  Volume II. *Sectarian Religion. 368 pp.*
  Volume III. *The Universal Church. 464 pp.*
  Volume IV. *Types of Religious Man. 352 pp.*
  Volume V. *Types of Religious Culture. 464 pp.*

Turner, B. S. Weber and Islam. *216 pp.*

Watt, W. Montgomery. Islam and the Integration of Society. *320 pp.*

SOCIOLOGY OF ART AND LITERATURE

Jarvie, Ian C. Towards a Sociology of the Cinema. *A Comparative Essay on the Structure and Functioning of a Major Entertainment Industry. 405 pp.*

Rust, Frances S. Dance in Society. *An Analysis of the Relationships between the Social Dance and Society in England from the Middle Ages to the Present Day. 256 pp. 8 pp. of plates.*

Schücking, L. L. The Sociology of Literary Taste. *112 pp.*

Wolff, Janet. Hermeneutic Philosophy and the Sociology of Art. *150 pp.*

SOCIOLOGY OF KNOWLEDGE

Diesing, P. Patterns of Discovery in the Social Sciences. *262 pp.*

● **Douglas, J. D.** (Ed.) Understanding Everyday Life. *370 pp.*
● **Hamilton, P.** Knowledge and Social Structure. *174 pp.*
Jarvie, I. C. Concepts and Society. *232 pp.*
Mannheim, Karl. Essays on the Sociology of Knowledge. *Edited by Paul Kecskemeti. Editorial Note by Adolph Lowe. 353 pp.*
Remmling, Gunter W. The Sociology of Karl Mannheim. *With a Bibliographical Guide to the Sociology of Knowledge, Ideological Analysis, and Social Planning. 255 pp.*
Remmling, Gunter W. (Ed.) Towards the Sociology of Knowledge. *Origin and Development of a Sociological Thought Style. 463 pp.*
Scheler, M. Problems of a Sociology of Knowledge. *Trans. by M. S. Frings. Edited and with an Introduction by K. Stikkers. 232 pp.*

URBAN SOCIOLOGY

Aldridge, M. The British New Towns. *A Programme Without a Policy. 232 pp.*
Ashworth, William. The Genesis of Modern British Town Planning: *A Study in Economic and Social History of the Nineteenth and Twentieth Centuries. 288 pp.*
Brittan, A. The Privatised World. *196 pp.*
Cullingworth, J. B. Housing Needs and Planning Policy: *A Restatement of the Problems of Housing Need and 'Overspill' in England and Wales. 232 pp. 44 tables. 8 maps.*
Dickinson, Robert E. City and Region: *A Geographical Interpretation. 608 pp. 125 figures.*
The West European City: *A Geographical Interpretation. 600 pp. 129 maps. 29 plates.*
Humphreys, Alexander J. New Dubliners: *Urbanization and the Irish Family. Foreword by George C. Homans. 304 pp.*
Jackson, Brian. Working Class Community: *Some General Notions raised by a Series of Studies in Northern England. 192 pp.*
● **Mann, P. H.** An Approach to Urban Sociology. *240 pp.*
Mellor, J. R. Urban Sociology in an Urbanized Society. *326 pp.*
Morris, R. N. and **Mogey, J.** The Sociology of Housing. *Studies at Berinsfield. 232 pp. 4 pp. plates.*
Mullan, R. Stevenage Ltd. *About 250 pp.*
Rex, J. and **Tomlinson, S.** Colonial Immigrants in a British City. *A Class Analysis. 368 pp.*
Rosser, C. and **Harris, C.** The Family and Social Change. *A Study of Family and Kinship in a South Wales Town. 352 pp. 8 maps.*
● **Stacey, Margaret, Batsone, Eric, Bell, Colin** and **Thurcott, Anne.** Power, Persistence and Change. *A Second Study of Banbury. 196 pp.*

RURAL SOCIOLOGY

Mayer, Adrian C. Peasants in the Pacific. *A Study of Fiji Indian Rural Society. 248 pp. 20 plates.*
Williams, W. M. The Sociology of an English Village: *Gosforth. 272 pp. 12 figures. 13 tables.*

SOCIOLOGY OF INDUSTRY AND DISTRIBUTION

Dunkerley, David. The Foreman. *Aspects of Task and Structure. 192 pp.*
Eldridge, J. E. T. Industrial Disputes. *Essays in the Sociology of Industrial Relations. 288 pp.*
Hollowell, Peter G. The Lorry Driver. *272 pp.*
● **Oxaal, I., Barnett, T.** and **Booth, D.** (Eds) Beyond the Sociology of Development.

Economy and Society in Latin America and Africa. 295 pp.

Smelser, Neil J. Social Change in the Industrial Revolution: *An Application of Theory to the Lancashire Cotton Industry, 1770–1840. 468 pp. 12 figures. 14 tables.*

Watson, T. J. The Personnel Managers. *A Study in the Sociology of Work and Employment, 262 pp.*

ANTHROPOLOGY

Brandel-Syrier, Mia. Reeftown Elite. *A Study of Social Mobility in a Modern African Community on the Reef. 376 pp.*

Dickie-Clark, H. F. The Marginal Situation. *A Sociological Study of a Coloured Group. 236 pp.*

Dube, S. C. Indian Village. *Foreword by Morris Edward Opler. 276 pp. 4 plates.*
India's Changing Villages: *Human Factors in Community Development. 260 pp. 8 plates. 1 map.*

Fei, H.-T. Peasant Life in China. *A Field Study of Country Life in the Yangtze Valley. With a foreword by Bronislaw Malinowski. 328 pp. 16 pp. plates.*

Firth, Raymond. Malay Fishermen. *Their Peasant Economy. 420 pp. 17 pp. plates.*

Gulliver, P. H. Social Control in an African Society: a Study of the Arusha, Agricultural Masai of Northern Tanganyika. *320 pp. 8 plates. 10 figures.*
Family Herds. *288 pp.*

Jarvie, Ian C. The Revolution in Anthropology. *268 pp.*

Little, Kenneth L. Mende of Sierra Leone. *308 pp. and folder.*
Negroes in Britain. *With a New Introduction and Contemporary Study by Leonard Bloom. 320 pp.*

Tambs-Lyche, H. London Patidars. *About 180 pp.*

Madan, G. R. Western Sociologists on Indian Society. *Marx, Spencer, Weber, Durkheim, Pareto. 384 pp.*

Mayer, A. C. Peasants in the Pacific. *A Study of Fiji Indian Rural Society. 248 pp.*

Meer, Fatima. Race and Suicide in South Africa. *325 pp.*

Smith, Raymond T. The Negro Family in British Guiana: *Family Structure and Social Status in the Villages. With a Foreword by Meyer Fortes. 314 pp. 8 plates. 1 figure. 4 maps.*

SOCIOLOGY AND PHILOSOPHY

Adriaansens, H. Talcott Parsons and the Conceptual Dilemma. *About 224 pp.*

Barnsley, John H. The Social Reality of Ethics. *A Comparative Analysis of Moral Codes. 448 pp.*

Diesing, Paul. Patterns of Discovery in the Social Sciences. *362 pp.*

● **Douglas, Jack D.** (Ed.) Understanding Everyday Life. *Toward the Reconstruction of Sociological Knowledge. Contributions by Alan F. Blum, Aaron W. Cicourel, Norman K. Denzin, Jack D. Douglas, John Heeren, Peter McHugh, Peter K. Manning, Melvin Power, Matthew Speier, Roy Turner, D. Lawrence Wieder, Thomas P. Wilson and Don H. Zimmerman. 370 pp.*

Gorman, Robert A. The Dual Vision. *Alfred Schutz and the Myth of Phenomenological Social Science. 240 pp.*

Jarvie, Ian C. Concepts and Society. *216 pp.*

Kilminster, R. Praxis and Method. *A Sociological Dialogue with Lukács, Gramsci and the Early Frankfurt School. 334 pp.*

● **Pelz, Werner.** The Scope of Understanding in Sociology. *Towards a More Radical Reorientation in the Social Humanistic Sciences. 283 pp.*

Roche, Maurice. Phenomenology, Language and the Social Sciences. *371 pp.*

Sahay, Arun. Sociological Analysis. *212 pp.*

● **Slater, P.** Origin and Significance of the Frankfurt School. *A Marxist Perspective. 185 pp.*

Spurling, L. Phenomenology and the Social World. *The Philosophy of Merleau-Ponty and its Relation to the Social Sciences. 222 pp.*

Wilson, H. T. The American Ideology. *Science, Technology and Organization as Modes of Rationality. 368 pp.*

International Library of Anthropology
General Editor Adam Kuper

● Ahmed, A. S. Millennium and Charisma Among Pathans. *A Critical Essay in Social Anthropology. 192 pp.*
  Pukhtun Economy and Society. *Traditional Structure and Economic Development. About 360 pp.*
Barth, F. Selected Essays. *Volume I. About 250 pp.* Selected Essays. *Volume II. About 250 pp.*
Brown, Paula. The Chimbu. *A Study of Change in the New Guinea Highlands. 151 pp.*
Foner, N. Jamaica Farewell. *200 pp.*
Gudeman, Stephen. Relationships, Residence and the Individual. *A Rural Panamanian Community. 288 pp. 11 plates, 5 figures, 2 maps, 10 tables.*
  The Demise of a Rural Economy. *From Subsistence to Capitalism in a Latin American Village. 160 pp.*
Hamnett, Ian. Chieftainship and Legitimacy. *An Anthropological Study of Executive Law in Lesotho. 163 pp.*
Hanson, F. Allan. Meaning in Culture. *127 pp.*
Hazan, H. The Limbo People. *A Study of the Constitution of the Time Universe Among the Aged. About 192 pp.*
Humphreys, S. C. Anthropology and the Greeks. *288 pp.*
Karp, I. Fields of Change Among the Iteso of Kenya. *140 pp.*
Lloyd, P. C. Power and Independence. *Urban Africans' Perception of Social Inequality. 264 pp.*
Parry, J. P. Caste and Kinship in Kangra. *352 pp. Illustrated.*
Pettigrew, Joyce. Robber Noblemen. *A Study of the Political System of the Sikh Jats. 284 pp.*
Street, Brian V. The Savage in Literature. *Representations of 'Primitive' Society in English Fiction, 1858–1920. 207 pp.*
Van Den Berghe, Pierre L. Power and Privilege at an African University. *278 pp.*

International Library of Phenomenology and Moral Sciences
General Editor John O'Neill

Apel, K.-O. Towards a Transformation of Philosophy. *308 pp.*
Bologh, R. W. Dialectical Phenomenology. *Marx's Method. 287 pp.*
Fekete, J. The Critical Twilight. *Explorations in the Ideology of Anglo-American Literary Theory from Eliot to McLuhan. 300 pp.*
Medina, A. Reflection, Time and the Novel. *Towards a Communicative Theory of Literature. 143 pp.*

International Library of Social Policy
General Editor Kathleen Jones

Bayley, M. Mental Handicap and Community Care. *426 pp.*
Bottoms, A. E. and McClean, J. D. Defendants in the Criminal Process. *284 pp.*
Bradshaw, J. The Family Fund. *An Initiative in Social Policy. About 224 pp.*

Butler, J. R. Family Doctors and Public Policy. *208 pp.*
Davies, Martin. Prisoners of Society. *Attitudes and Aftercare. 204 pp.*
Gittus, Elizabeth. Flats, Families and the Under-Fives. *285 pp.*
Holman, Robert. Trading in Children. *A Study of Private Fostering. 355 pp.*
Jeffs, A. Young People and the Youth Service. *160 pp.*
Jones, Howard and Cornes, Paul. Open Prisons. *288 pp.*
Jones, Kathleen. History of the Mental Health Service. *428 pp.*
Jones, Kathleen with **Brown, John, Cunningham, W. J., Roberts, Julian** and **Williams, Peter.** Opening the Door. *A Study of New Policies for the Mentally Handicapped. 278 pp.*
Karn, Valerie. Retiring to the Seaside. *400 pp. 2 maps. Numerous tables.*
King, R. D. and **Elliot, K. W.** Albany: Birth of a Prison—End of an Era. *394 pp.*
Thomas, J. E. The English Prison Officer since 1850: *A Study in Conflict. 258 pp.*
Walton, R. G. Women in Social Work. *303 pp.*
● **Woodward, J.** To Do the Sick No Harm. *A Study of the British Voluntary Hospital System to 1875. 234 pp.*

International Library of Welfare and Philosophy
General Editors Noel Timms and David Watson

● **McDermott, F. E.** (Ed.) Self-Determination in Social Work. *A Collection of Essays on Self-determination and Related Concepts by Philosophers and Social Work Theorists. Contributors: F. P. Biestek, S. Bernstein, A. Keith-Lucas, D. Sayer, H. H. Perelman, C. Whittington, R. F. Stalley, F. E. McDermott, I. Berlin, H. J. McCloskey, H. L. A. Hart, J. Wilson, A. I. Melden, S. I. Benn. 254 pp.*
● **Plant, Raymond.** Community and Ideology. *104 pp.*
Ragg, Nicholas M. People Not Cases. *A Philosophical Approach to Social Work. 168 pp.*
● **Timms, Noel** and **Watson, David.** (Eds) Talking About Welfare. *Readings in Philosophy and Social Policy. Contributors: T. H. Marshall, R. B. Brandt, G. H. von Wright, K. Nielsen, M. Cranston, R. M. Titmuss, R. S. Downie, E. Telfer, D. Donnison, J. Benson, P. Leonard, A. Keith-Lucas, D. Walsh, I. T. Ramsey. 320 pp.*
● Philosophy in Social Work. *250 pp.*
● **Weale, A.** Equality and Social Policy. *164 pp.*

Library of Social Work
General Editor Noel Timms

● **Baldock, Peter.** Community Work and Social Work. *140 pp.*
○ **Beedell, Christopher.** Residential Life with Children. *210 pp. Crown 8vo.*
● **Berry, Juliet.** Daily Experience in Residential Life. *A Study of Children and their Care-givers. 202 pp.*
○ Social Work with Children. *190 pp. Crown 8vo.*
● **Brearley, C. Paul.** Residential Work with the Elderly. *116 pp.*
● Social Work, Ageing and Society. *126 pp.*
● **Cheetham, Juliet.** Social Work with Immigrants. *240 pp. Crown 8vo.*
● **Cross, Crispin P.** (Ed.) Interviewing and Communication in Social Work. *Contributions by C. P. Cross, D. Laurenson, B. Strutt, S. Raven. 192 pp. Crown 8vo.*

- **Curnock, Kathleen** and **Hardiker, Pauline.** Towards Practice Theory. *Skills and Methods in Social Assessments. 208 pp.*
- **Davies, Bernard.** The Use of Groups in Social Work Practice. *158 pp.*
- **Davies, Martin.** Support Systems in Social Work. *144 pp.*
  Ellis, June. (Ed.) West African Families in Britain. *A Meeting of Two Cultures. Contributions by Pat Stapleton, Vivien Biggs. 150 pp. 1 Map.*
- **Hart, John.** Social Work and Sexual Conduct. *230 pp.*
- **Hutten, Joan M.** Short-Term Contracts in Social Work. *Contributions by Stella M. Hall, Elsie Osborne, Mannie Sher, Eva Sternberg, Elizabeth Tuters. 134 pp.*
  Jackson, Michael P. and **Valencia, B. Michael.** Financial Aid Through Social Work. *140 pp.*
- **Jones, Howard.** The Residential Community. *A Setting for Social Work. 150 pp.*
- (Ed.) Towards a New Social Work. *Contributions by Howard Jones, D. A. Fowler, J. R. Cypher, R. G. Walton, Geoffrey Mungham, Philip Priestley, Ian Shaw, M. Bartley, R. Deacon, Irwin Epstein, Geoffrey Pearson. 184 pp.*
  Jones, Ray and **Pritchard, Colin.** (Eds) Social Work With Adolescents. *Contributions by Ray Jones, Colin Pritchard, Jack Dunham, Florence Rossetti, Andrew Kerslake, John Burns, William Gregory, Graham Templeman, Kenneth E. Reid, Audrey Taylor. About 170 pp.*
- ○ **Jordon, William.** The Social Worker in Family Situations. *160 pp. Crown 8vo.*
- **Laycock, A. L.** Adolescents and Social Work. *128 pp. Crown 8vo.*
- **Lees, Ray.** Politics and Social Work. *128 pp. Crown 8vo.*
- Research Strategies for Social Welfare. *112 pp. Tables.*
- ○ **McCullough, M. K.** and **Ely, Peter J.** Social Work with Groups. *127 pp. Crown 8vo.*
- **Moffett, Jonathan.** Concepts in Casework Treatment. *128 pp. Crown 8vo.*
  Parsloe, Phyllida. Juvenile Justice in Britain and the United States. *The Balance of Needs and Rights. 336 pp.*
- **Plant, Raymond.** Social and Moral Theory in Casework. *112 pp. Crown 8vo.*
  Priestley, Philip, Fears, Denise and **Fuller, Roger.** Justice for Juveniles. *The 1969 Children and Young Persons Act: A Case for Reform? 128 pp.*
- **Pritchard, Colin** and **Taylor, Richard.** Social Work: Reform or Revolution? *170 pp.*
- ○ **Pugh, Elisabeth.** Social Work in Child Care. *128 pp. Crown 8vo.*
- **Robinson, Margaret.** Schools and Social Work. *282 pp.*
- ○ **Ruddock, Ralph.** Roles and Relationships. *128 pp. Crown 8vo.*
- **Sainsbury, Eric.** Social Diagnosis in Casework. *118 pp. Crown 8vo.*
- Social Work with Families. *Perceptions of Social Casework among Clients of a Family Service. 188 pp.*
  Seed, Philip. The Expansion of Social Work in Britain. *128 pp. Crown 8vo.*
- **Shaw, John.** The Self in Social Work. *124 pp.*
  Smale, Gerald G. Prophecy, Behaviour and Change. *An Examination of Self-fulfilling Prophecies in Helping Relationships. 116 pp. Crown 8vo.*
  Smith, Gilbert. Social Need. *Policy, Practice and Research. 155 pp.*
- Social Work and the Sociology of Organisations. *124 pp. Revised edition.*
- **Sutton, Carole.** Psychology for Social Workers and Counsellors. *An Introduction. 248 pp.*
- **Timms, Noel.** Language of Social Casework. *122 pp. Crown 8vo.*
- Recording in Social Work. *124 pp. Crown 8vo.*
- **Todd, F. Joan.** Social Work with the Mentally Subnormal. *96 pp. Crown 8vo.*
- **Walrond-Skinner, Sue.** Family Therapy. *The Treatment of Natural Systems. 172 pp.*
- **Warham, Joyce.** An Introduction to Administration for Social Workers. *Revised edition. 112 pp.*
- An Open Case. *The Organisational Context of Social Work. 172 pp.*
- ○ **Wittenberg, Isca Salzberger.** Psycho-Analytic Insight and Relationships. *A Kleinian Approach. 196 pp. Crown 8vo.*

Primary Socialization, Language and Education
General Editor Basil Bernstein

Adlam, Diana S., *with the assistance of Geoffrey Turner and Lesley Lineker.* Code in Context. *272 pp.*

Bernstein, Basil. Class, Codes and Control. *3 volumes.*
- 1. *Theoretical Studies Towards a Sociology of Language. 254 pp.*
   2. *Applied Studies Towards a Sociology of Language. 377 pp.*
- 3. *Towards a Theory of Educational Transmission. 167 pp.*

Brandis, W. and **Bernstein, B.** Selection and Control. *176 pp.*

Brandis, Walter and **Henderson, Dorothy.** Social Class, Language and Communication. *288 pp.*

Cook-Gumperz, Jenny. Social Control and Socialization. *A Study of Class Differences in the Language of Maternal Control. 290 pp.*

- **Gahagan, D. M.** and **G. A.** Talk Reform. *Exploration in Language for Infant School Children. 160 pp.*

Hawkins, P. R. Social Class, the Nominal Group and Verbal Strategies. *About 220 pp.*

Robinson, W. P. and **Rackstraw, Susan D. A.** A Question of Answers. *2 volumes. 192 pp. and 180 pp.*

Turner, Geoffrey J. and **Mohan, Bernard A.** A Linguistic Description and Computer Programme for Children's Speech. *208 pp.*

Reports of the Institute of Community Studies

Baker, J. The Neighbourhood Advice Centre. A Community Project in Camden. *320 pp.*

- **Cartwright, Ann.** Patients and their Doctors. *A Study of General Practice. 304 pp.*

Dench, Geoff. Maltese in London. *A Case-study in the Erosion of Ethnic Consciousness. 302 pp.*

Jackson, Brian and **Marsden, Dennis.** Education and the Working Class: *Some General Themes Raised by a Study of 88 Working-class Children in a Northern Industrial City. 268 pp. 2 folders.*

Marris, Peter. The Experience of Higher Education. *232 pp. 27 tables.*
- Loss and Change. *192 pp.*

Marris, Peter and **Rein, Martin.** Dilemmas of Social Reform. *Poverty and Community Action in the United States. 256 pp.*

Marris, Peter and **Somerset, Anthony.** African Businessmen. *A Study of Entrepreneurship and Development in Kenya. 256 pp.*

Mills, Richard. Young Outsiders: *a Study in Alternative Communities. 216 pp.*

Runciman, W. G. Relative Deprivation and Social Justice. *A Study of Attitudes to Social Inequality in Twentieth-Century England. 352 pp.*

Willmott, Peter. Adolescent Boys in East London. *230 pp.*

Willmott, Peter and **Young, Michael.** Family and Class in a London Suburb. *202 pp. 47 tables.*

Young, Michael and **McGeeney, Patrick.** Learning Begins at Home. *A Study of a Junior School and its Parents. 128 pp.*

Young, Michael and **Willmott, Peter.** Family and Kinship in East London. *Foreword by Richard M. Titmuss. 252 pp. 39 tables.*
The Symmetrical Family. *410 pp.*

Reports of the Institute for Social Studies in Medical Care

Cartwright, Ann, Hockey, Lisbeth and **Anderson, John J.** Life Before Death. *310 pp.*
Dunnell, Karen and **Cartwright, Ann.** Medicine Takers, Prescribers and Hoarders. *190 pp.*
Farrell, C. My Mother Said. . . *A Study of the Way Young People Learned About Sex and Birth Control. 288 pp.*

Medicine, Illness and Society
General Editor   W. M. Williams

Hall, David J. Social Relations & Innovation. *Changing the State of Play in Hospitals. 232 pp.*
Hall, David J. and **Stacey, M.** (Eds) Beyond Separation. *234 pp.*
Robinson, David. The Process of Becoming Ill. *142 pp.*
Stacey, Margaret *et al.* Hospitals, Children and Their Families. *The Report of a Pilot Study. 202 pp.*
Stimson, G. V. and **Webb, B.** Going to See the Doctor. *The Consultation Process in General Practice. 155 pp.*

Monographs in Social Theory
General Editor   Arthur Brittan

● **Barnes, B.** Scientific Knowledge and Sociological Theory. *192 pp.*
  Bauman, Zygmunt. Culture as Praxis. *204 pp.*
● **Dixon, Keith.** Sociological Theory. *Pretence and Possibility. 142 pp.*
  The Sociology of Belief. *Fallacy and Foundation. About 160 pp.*
  Goff, T. W. Marx and Mead. *Contributions to a Sociology of Knowledge. 176 pp.*
  Meltzer, B. N., Petras, J. W. and **Reynolds, L. T.** Symbolic Interactionism. *Genesis, Varieties and Criticisms. 144 pp.*
● **Smith, Anthony D.** The Concept of Social Change. *A Critique of the Functionalist Theory of Social Change. 208 pp.*

Routledge Social Science Journals

The British Journal of Sociology. *Editor – Angus Stewart; Associate Editor – Leslie Sklair. Vol. 1, No. 1 – March 1950 and Quarterly. Roy. 8vo. All back issues available. An international journal publishing original papers in the field of sociology and related areas.*
Community Work. *Edited by David Jones and Marjorie Mayo. 1973. Published annually.*
Economy and Society. *Vol. 1, No. 1. February 1972 and Quarterly. Metric Roy. 8vo. A journal for all social scientists covering sociology, philosophy, anthropology, economics and history. All back numbers available.*

Ethnic and Racial Studies. *Editor – John Stone. Vol. 1 – 1978. Published quarterly.*

Religion. Journal of Religion and Religions. *Chairman of Editorial Board, Ninian Smart. Vol. 1, No. 1, Spring 1971. A journal with an inter-disciplinary approach to the study of the phenomena of religion. All back numbers available.*

Sociology of Health and Illness. *A Journal of Medical Sociology. Editor – Alan Davies; Associate Editor – Ray Jobling. Vol. 1, Spring 1979. Published 3 times per annum.*

Year Book of Social Policy in Britain. *Edited by Kathleen Jones. 1971. Published annually.*

Social and Psychological Aspects of Medical Practice
Editor   Trevor Silverstone

Lader, Malcolm. Psychophysiology of Mental Illness. *280 pp.*

● **Silverstone, Trevor** and **Turner, Paul.** Drug Treatment in Psychiatry. *Revised edition. 256 pp.*

Whiteley, J. S. and **Gordon, J.** Group Approaches in Psychiatry. *240 pp.*

Printed and bound in Great Britain by
Redwood Burn Limited, Trowbridge & Esher